THE CIVIL PROCEDURE RULES IN ACTION

Second Edition

THE CIVIL PROCEDURE RULES IN ACTION

Second Edition

Ian Grainger and Michael Fealy

of

One Essex Court, Temple, London

with chapters on Personal Injuries by

Martin Spencer

of

4 Paper Buildings, Temple, London

Cavendish
Publishing
Limited

London • Sydney

First published in 2000 by Cavendish Publishing Limited, The Glass House, Wharton Street, London WC1X 9PX, United Kingdom

Telephone: +44 (0)20 7278 8000   Facsimile: +44 (0)20 7278 8080

E-mail: info@cavendishpublishing.com

Website: http://www.cavendishpublishing.com

© Grainger, I and Fealy, M   2000

First edition   1999

Second edition   2000

British Library Catalogue in Publication Data

Grainger, Ian

The civil procedure rules in action – 2nd edn

1 Civil procedure – England 2 Civil procedure – Wales

I Title II Fealy, Michael III Spencer, Martin

347.4'2'05

ISBN 1 85941 589 X

Printed and bound in Great Britain

The old order changeth, yielding place to new,
And God fulfils Himself in many ways,
Lest one good custom should corrupt the world.

Tennyson, *Morte d'Arthur*

It is not good to look too long upon these turning wheels of vicissitude, lest we become giddy.

Sir Francis Bacon, *Of Vicissitude of Things*

FOREWORD TO THE SECOND EDITION

The overriding objective of the Civil Procedure Rules, now just over a year in operation, is to enable those who have the misfortune to litigate to do so economically and without delay, so that the system may produce for them a just result. Intrinsically you do not need a large body of rules to achieve this. Indeed a complicated structure, hidebound by precedent, is likely to be an expensive and time consuming obstacle course. You undertake (and someone has to pay for) the next procedural step, not because it is necessary or worth doing in itself, but because inflexible rules or precedent say that you have to. The main aim of the CPR is to eliminate obstacles and, by simple procedures, simply expressed, to make civil justice accessible. A concern often overlooked is that most disputes are eventually compromised. The structure of the rules should promote earlier and less expensive settlement. The judges who now manage cases should do so assuming that they are managing settlement negotiations, not an eventual trial.

It was clear to me when this book was first published last year that the authors embraced the essential purpose of the new rules, and were intent on promoting it. The result is well organised, easily accessible and simply expressed. They rightly cut loose from the past, abandoned obstructive clutter and presented the rules in their proper simplicity. This is carried forward in this updated and timely second edition, which brings into account developments since the rules were introduced with the further rules and practice directions which have come along meanwhile. I am delighted to commend it to everyone concerned with civil litigation at all levels.

Anthony May

Royal Courts of Justice, London

12 May 2000

FOREWORD TO THE FIRST EDITION

On 26 April 1999, as I write, just over two months away, the new Civil Procedure Rules will come into force. They will affect all lawyers and their clients. They involve a complete change of culture.

The change we face is therefore huge, particularly because of the 'big bang' approach that has necessarily been adopted for the implementation of the Rules. From 26 April, we can throw away our White and Green Books (until the new editions arrive!). But the Civil Procedure Rules will not bring about the change in culture that the civil justice system so badly needs by themselves. It will be the effective and efficient operation of the Rules by practitioners and judges that will result in the quicker, cheaper and fairer disposal of disputes. It is therefore of the greatest importance that the judiciary, the professions and litigants are properly prepared for 26 April.

The publication of *An Introduction to the New Civil Procedure Rules* will therefore be a valuable source of reference to assist with the task of preparing for what lies ahead. In simple and clear terms, it introduces us to the new landscape. I congratulate One Essex Court, and Ian Grainger and Michael Fealy, in a job well done.

The Right Honourable

The Lord Woolf

Master of the Rolls

February 1999

CONTENTS

PART B

Contents

Contents

PART C

THE CORE RULES OF THE CPR, WITH RELEVANT PRACTICE DIRECTIONS INTERLEAVED

Contents

Contents

Contents

TABLE OF CASES

Note: Most cases referred to as 'unreported' are available, in full or in an abbreviated form, on the New Law website (www.newlawonline.com).

ABBREVIATIONS

References to the **Woolf Reports** are shown thus:

IR chap ..., para ...   the Interim Report on *Access to Justice*, July 1995.

FR chap ..., para ...   the Final Report on *Access to Justice*, July 1996.

References to the **core Rules** are shown thus:

Part 32.1(1)   the court's power to control evidence.

Part 32   referring to the whole of Part 32.

References to the **practice directions** are shown thus:

PD7, para 2.1   being paragraph 2.1 of the practice direction corresponding to Part 7 of the core Rules (How to start proceedings – the claim form).

RSC   refers to the **Rules of the Supreme Court** 1965.

CCR   refers to the **County Court Rules** 1981.

INTRODUCTION

In February 1999, when we published *An Introduction to the New Civil Procedure Rules*, we predicted that a further work would soon be needed 'as the courts pronounce on the scope and interpretation of the new Rules, as new practice directions are introduced and as the Rules themselves are varied'. However, if we can thereby claim to have had some degree of prescience, we doubt if we are alone in not having expected either the sheer volume of new material that has since emerged, nor the speed with which it has done so.

In addition to the various weighty practice directions on costs (which had not been published at the date of our *Introduction*), there have been two substantial sets of amendments to the CPR themselves and seemingly endless – but in fact only monthly – variations to the practice directions. There is indeed some truth in the observation that one of the more difficult tasks in preparing for an interlocutory application after 26 April 1999 has been ensuring that one is actually looking at the right version of the applicable rules and practice directions! Equally striking and daunting has been the ever-increasing quantity of judicial pronouncements on the new regime – most of them as yet still unreported.

26 April 2000 is the first birthday of the CPR. It therefore seems to us an appropriate moment at which to pause and take stock. That is particularly the case when the second set of substantial amendments to the Rules (those contained in SI 2000/221) come fully into force only a few days after the birthday party – on 2 May 2000. What, then, have we tried to do in this, our second, overview of the CPR?

Like its predecessor, this book has strictly limited intellectual pretensions. In his Foreword to our earlier work, Lord Woolf was good enough to describe it as introducing practitioners to the new landscape in simple and clear terms. In the face of a tidal wave of material, simplicity and clarity are certainly virtues that we have striven hard to retain. However, our view of the landscape has inevitably altered and it is worth saying a few words on how and why that is so.

In February 1999, untrammelled by judicial pronouncement of any kind, one could take a fairly Olympian view of the new world – soaring eagle-like, as it were, over the mountain tops. Now, however, the common law system has set to work in all its haphazard magnificence, throwing up problems for judicial decision in no order whatever, so that points of detail can fall to be examined and resolved early on, while points of more fundamental significance remain unconsidered. In order to deal with the case law developments, the eagle has had, if you like, to leave the mountain tops and swoop down a little into the valleys of the new world – without, we would hope, entangling itself in the thickets that undoubtedly abound in the lowest reaches! We certainly hope that this loss of height has not entailed a loss of focus, but some variations in the pace and smoothness of exposition are, we fear, inevitable. All that we can say by way of apology is that the common law system is none of our doing and that readers must not be surprised if the vagaries of that system require certain topics to be addressed at greater length than others which, in the abstract, might seem to be of greater significance.

Even so and despite the wealth of new material, this book has much in common with its forerunner. It seeks to be an essentially brief account of the general structure and nature of the CPR. We have deliberately sought to retain a fairly generalised approach, since at this stage in the life of the new regime, we firmly believe that that is what most practitioners will find useful. To our general structure, we have added references to case law, or indulged in reflections of our own, whenever it has seemed appropriate. (It is fair to say that we have indulged in rather more criticism than we felt appropriate in our *Introduction*.) Despite the increasing welter of detail, we would hope that it is yet possible to read our commentary from beginning to end, so as to acquire a general overview of the new regime. Equally, it is possible to dip into specific sections in search of a quick reminder, or (who knows?) food for thought.

Nevertheless, two general words of caution on the scope of the book are in order.

First, it is a book on the CPR and is not a general book on all aspects of civil procedure. A work with ambitions of that kind would have required a great deal of detailed exposition of earlier learning and case law, of a kind that we have simply not had time to consider. To take but one example, since April 1999, there have been a number of cases on wasted costs orders and on costs against non-parties. We have dealt with some of these cases in Chapter 24, but in neither area have we attempted an exhaustive statement of the law applicable to such applications as laid down in the earlier authorities. In short, both in this area and generally, we have assumed the existing law as at 26 April 1999 to be a 'given' with which practitioners are already broadly familiar.

Secondly, our commentary is not and cannot be a substitute for the CPR themselves. The Rules (in their latest form and with all relevant and up to date practice directions) will have to be carefully studied whenever any practical problem falls to be resolved.

Having thus indicated what our book does not seek to be, we should perhaps say what is in it! As before, Part A describes the overall structure of the new Rules, including case management in general and the tracking system in particular. Not surprisingly, many of the courts' pronouncements since the introduction of the new regime throw light, either through illustration or discussion, on the 'overriding objective'. In particular, therefore, the chapter on that all important concept has been hugely expanded.

Part B deals with particular aspects of the conduct of a case, taken chronologically from the issue of proceedings through to judgment, decisions on costs and appeals. Some of the less digestible Parts of the core rules (from which we confess that we shied away last time!) have now been considered in detail. We should perhaps also explain that we have deliberately not dispensed with all examination of the genesis of the new Rules in Lord Woolf's two reports on *Access to Justice*. From time to time, it has seemed to us that a knowledge of these roots may be useful. However, the simple but crucial point here is that those two reports can in no sense be regarded as a commentary on the Rules themselves, so great and manifold were the alterations that crept in during the initial drafting process and as a result of subsequent amendments. The reports, therefore, remain useful background knowledge but must be approached with considerable caution whenever it comes to matters of detail.

Part C contains the core Rules themselves (printed as they are as at 2 May 2000), with the related practice directions interleaved. So that the reader can rapidly tell whether he is looking at a rule or a practice direction, the practice directions are printed in a shaded form. These practice directions are printed as they are after the 13th and 14th sets of amendments, both of which came into force on 2 May 2000. Part C also contains the practice direction on pre-action protocols and the protocols applying to personal injury and clinical negligence actions.

Part C does not, however, contain the text of the various scheduled rules. Some commentators felt this to be a failing in our earlier work and, for all we can tell, may take the same view this time. However, after considerable reflection, we have decided to print only the core rules. This is partly in the interests of economy and partly because the scheduled rules are now readily available from any number of other sources. The main reason, however, is that this book is simply not intended as a compendious work of reference on all aspects of the new regime, but rather as a useful working handbook and guide, which practitioners will, for example, be able to slip into their briefcases for use at home or on the train. It is certainly useful, when reading a text that expounds the new Rules and related judicial decisions, to have the core rules to hand. Those rules contain the heart of the new system and any matters of real importance in the scheduled rules will, little by little, be brought within their scope. Despite their obvious practical importance within their scope, we do not feel that the same is true of the scheduled rules. In fact, the only scheduled rules that either of us have looked at since 26 April 1999 – those on security for costs, service out of the jurisdiction and appeals – have already, in the latest amendments, been redrafted and brought within the fold of the core rules.

We should also say a word or two about references to authorities. By glancing at the Table of Cases at the front of this book, the reader will see that many of the cases referred to are described simply as 'unreported'. In the vast majority of cases, our own knowledge of such cases derives from the New Law site on the Internet, where they can for the most part be found, either in full or in an abridged form[1] (www.newlawonline.com). Obviously, if a case is reported elsewhere – whether in the official or unofficial reports, or in *The Times* or *The Independent* – we have endeavoured to give that reference instead. As to the required methods of citing authority in court, practitioners will of course be familiar with the practice directions at [1995] 1 WLR 1096; [1996] 1 WLR 854; and [1998] 1 WLR 825. We would not pretend that we have always followed the precepts contained in those practice directions here!

One very significant gap in our earlier work has been filled. Our own ignorance of personal injury and clinical negligence work previously led us to avoid discussion of the specific rules that apply to such actions and of the particular problems that can arise in relation to them. With characteristic generosity, Martin Spencer (of 4 Paper Buildings) has now splendidly remedied our earlier failings. We are both hugely grateful to him for writing the two chapters on such actions and for keeping an eye on anything else that we may have said about such matters in other parts of the book.

Other regions still remain untravelled. We say repeatedly throughout the book – but it is a point worth setting out clearly here at the beginning – that the various 'specialist jurisdictions' apply the CPR and their general philosophy with a rather different emphasis in the light of the particular problems of litigation in those fields. Given our own interests, Chapter 27 attempts a brief resumé of some of the principal differences of practice and emphasis that apply in the Commercial Court. However, both there and in the Chancery Division, in the Technology and Construction Court and in any other proceedings which are subject to a specialist practice direction, practitioners will have to consider the precise terms of the various specialist guides and practice directions as well as the generality of the CPR.

We finish by assuring our readers that it has not been easy trying to keep on top of the various developments considered in this book and to run our respective practices at the same time. However, it will be a source of considerable satisfaction if our own efforts enable friends and colleagues to do precisely that, and with rather less blood and sweat!

Ian Grainger

Michael Fealy

One Essex Court, Temple

12 May 2000

---

1   The use of such summaries in court is rarely likely to be appropriate – see *Hamblin v Field* (2000) *The Times*, 26 April.

PART A

CHAPTER 1

THE SCOPE AND STRUCTURE OF THE CPR

We begin by considering the scope of the CPR – first, in terms of the proceedings to which they apply and, secondly, in point of time. We then consider their structure.

THE SCOPE OF THE CPR – IN TERMS OF THE PROCEEDINGS COVERED

With certain exceptions (for example, insolvency proceedings, non-contentious probate proceedings and family and adoption proceedings), the CPR apply to all proceedings in the county court, the High Court and the Civil Division of the Court of Appeal (Part 2.1).

However, in the case of *'specialist proceedings'*, which are listed in Part 49, the CPR only apply 'subject to the provisions of the relevant practice direction which applies to those proceedings'. (These specialist proceedings are admiralty proceedings, arbitration proceedings, commercial actions, Patents Court business, Technology and Construction Court business, proceedings under the Companies Acts and contentious probate proceedings.) In the case of all such proceedings, therefore, the CPR may apply, or may not apply, or may apply in some varied form, as set out in the particular practice direction.

THE SCOPE OF THE CPR – IN POINT OF TIME

Subject to the matters set out above, the CPR apply to all proceedings commenced on or after 26 April 1999.

As to proceedings issued before 26 April 1999 ('existing proceedings'), there are complicated transitional arrangements set out in PD51. Those arrangements will already have been applied to the vast majority of existing proceedings, so that the reader needing further information can be safely referred to the detail of the practice direction itself. However, in general terms, the scheme was that:

(a) undefended cases continued to be subject to the previous rules (of the RSC or CCR), so that they could progress to a rapid conclusion; but that

(b) the CPR were to be applied to defended cases 'so far as ... practicable'.

The overriding objective set out in Part 1 applied to all existing proceedings from 26 April 1999 onwards (PD51, para 12). Furthermore, the general principle was that any new step to be taken in any existing proceedings on or after that date was to be taken under the CPR (PD51, para 11). On the first occasion after 26 April 1999 that a case came before a judge, whether at a hearing or on paper, the judge could make directions as to the extent to which the CPR should apply (PD51, para 15(1)). The general presumption – which experience of actual orders has amply justified – was that the CPR would apply to the proceedings from then onwards (PD51, para 15(2)).

If a case does *not* come before a judge before 25 April 2000, then (with minor exceptions) it will be automatically stayed – though the parties will have the right to apply for such stay to be lifted (PD51, para 19).

The transitional provisions did not deal expressly with the question of appeals against orders made prior to 26 April 1999. However, that question arose for consideration in *McPhilemy v Times Newspapers Ltd* [1999] 3 All ER 775. Lord Woolf said that the general approach should be obvious:

> In reviewing a decision made prior to 26 April 1999, this court will not interfere after that date, if it would not have done so if the appeal had been heard prior to that date ... However, if the decision is one with which this court would have interfered prior to 26 April 1999, in deciding what order should be made for the future, this court will take into account, in particular, Part 1 of the rules. [p 792f]

THE STRUCTURE OF THE CPR – THE 'CORE' RULES AND THE 'SCHEDULED' RULES

It is important to appreciate that, although the RSC and the CCR were revoked with effect from 26 April 1999, large parts of them have effectively been preserved in a different guise and for a limited period of uncertain duration. Only the most important rules of general application (often referred to as the 'core' rules) have so far been redrafted from scratch and these are now in the main body of the CPR. Other, usually more specialist, rules of the RSC or CCR were preserved – albeit they have been amended in certain respects, usually to fit in with the language and philosophy of the new regime. These preserved rules are to be found in Schedules 1 and 2 to the CPR (containing respectively the preserved parts of the RSC and the CCR) – whence they are usually referred to as the 'scheduled' rules, or (less commonly) the 'interlocking' rules.

Many of the scheduled rules relate to some special statutory jurisdiction of the court and deal with such matters as the particular court (or Division) to be used and the precise procedure to be followed in order to invoke the jurisdiction in question. Others, however, are of more general application and importance. In due course, it is proposed entirely to redraft the scheduled rules in the same way as the core rules have been. Indeed, this process has already begun. Purely by way of example, after 26 April 1999 service *within* the jurisdiction was governed by Part 6 of the core rules but service *outside* the jurisdiction continued to be governed by the scheduled and redrafted RSC Ord 11. Likewise, applications for security for costs continued to be governed by RSC Ord 23. Now, however, with the amendments to the CPR contained in SI 2000/221 (L1), both of these matters are (with effect from 2 May 2000) brought within the scope of the core rules – being governed by Section III of Part 6 and Section II of Part 25 respectively.

Part 50 deals with the scheduled rules. Part 50(2) says, rather obscurely, 'These Rules apply in relation to the proceedings to which the Schedules apply subject to the provisions in the Schedules and the relevant practice directions'. The most obvious effect of this is that the scheduled rules, just like the core rules, fall to be interpreted and applied in the light of the overriding objective set out in Part 1.1.

THE STRUCTURE OF THE CPR – PARTS, RULES, DEFINITIONS

The core Rules are divided into 51 '*Parts*'. Each Part is sub-divided into rules and each rule into sub-rules.

In the original published version of the CPR, there were *no notes* of the kind with which we had grown familiar in the White and Green Books. Authors and publishers are of course rapidly undoing that situation. However, the original purity was deliberate. The opening words of rule 1.1(1) are 'These Rules are a *new* procedural code ...'. These words are said to have been inserted at the personal behest of the Lord Chancellor, to bring home to litigants and to the courts the fact that references to old authorities on the corresponding old rules are to be strongly discouraged. Certainly the courts have been seeking to interpret the CPR in the light of their own underlying 'philosophy' – a topic to which we return in Chapter 2 below.

Certain expressions in the CPR bear *general definitions* (Part 2.3(1)). There is also a glossary of certain legal words and phrases that are used. Most expressions appearing in the glossary are identified in the Rules by the appearance of the letters '(GL)' immediately after the words in question. A glossary definition is not to be taken as giving the relevant expression a meaning in the Rules which it does not have in the law generally (Part 2.2(1)).

Quite apart from these defined expressions, the CPR contain a great deal of new vocabulary, to which we should all by now have grown accustomed! For the benefit of any who still tend to think in terms of the old vocabulary, Appendix 1 contains a list of the words and phrases most commonly encountered and of the old expressions that roughly corresponded to them. Latin expressions have, of course, been almost totally abolished from the CPR – though the odd remaining dodo can still be spotted, for example 'affidavit' and 'in rem'. Indeed, recent authority evidences a more general attack on the use of Latin by lawyers – see *Fryer v Pearson* (2000) *The Times*, 4 April, in relation to the maxim '*res ipsa loquitur*'.

THE STRUCTURE OF THE CPR –
PRACTICE DIRECTIONS AND FORMS

The substance of a Part is usually supplemented by a *practice direction*. For example, Part 7 ('How to start proceedings: the claim form') is supplemented by a similarly headed practice direction. Anyone using the CPR has to be familiar not only with the terms of the relevant Part but also with the contents of any corresponding practice direction. Though the distinction is not always clearly drawn, a Part generally contains the 'bare bones' of the rules, while the corresponding practice direction contains practical guidance on how the rules are to be implemented. Some, but by no means all, practice directions are divided up into helpful 'glosses' on the particular rules contained in a particular Part. Others, however, are more generally discursive.

Some practice directions are not linked to a particular Part at all but are wholly general in their application – the most obvious example being that on pre-action protocols. Others, though linked to a particular Part, far exceed that Part in terms of the topics covered and the detail employed – for example, the various lengthy specialist practice directions, which all stem from the one-page Part 49.

The practice directions themselves contain a number of *standard forms*. Such forms may be varied by the court or a party if the circumstances of a particular case require it – see generally in this regard Part 4.

THE STRUCTURE OF THE CPR – PRE-ACTION PROTOCOLS

The reader of the Rules will also come across frequent references to '*pre-action protocols*'. The glossary defines these as:

> Statements of understanding between legal practitioners and others about pre-action practice and which are approved by a relevant practice direction.

The protocols are, in short, 'codes' of responsible pre-action behaviour, drafted by the profession. Their provisions are designed to encourage a sensible exchange of views and a pooling of information between the parties even before a dispute develops into litigation – all with a view to the promotion of early settlements or at least the minimisation of expense through greater 'focussing' on the real issues.

Whether the parties have complied with a relevant pre-action protocol will be taken into account by the court when making case management decisions (Part 3.1(4)), particularly decisions on costs (Part 44.3(4) and (5)). By giving the protocols 'teeth' in this way, the court is able to extend its encouragement of reasonable litigious behaviour well into the pre-action sphere.

Pre-action protocols have so far been produced for personal injury claims, for clinical disputes and (on a pilot basis) for road traffic accidents. The personal injury and clinical negligence protocols are printed in Part C and are considered in detail in Chapters 25 and 26 below. Furthermore – and very importantly – paragraph 4.1 of the general practice direction on protocols provides that:

> In cases not covered by any approved protocol, the court will expect the parties, in accordance with the overriding objective and the matters referred to in CPR 1.1(2)(a), (b) and (c), to act reasonably in exchanging information and documents relevant to the claim and generally in trying to avoid the necessity for the start of proceedings.

The general aim of encouraging reasonable pre-action behaviour is thus effectively extended to actions of all types. (As to the question of pre-action behaviour in the context of costs, see the judgments of the Court of Appeal in *Ford v GKR Construction* [2000] 1 All ER 802 – especially of Lord Woolf at p 810 – and in *London Borough of Brent v Aniedobe* (1999) unreported, 23 November.)

CHAPTER 2

THE OVERRIDING OBJECTIVE

INTRODUCTORY

Not the least revolutionary aspect of the CPR is the way in which they begin with a statement of intent – a manifesto, as it were, of their aims and purpose. This follows a very early proposal of Lord Woolf's. In FR chap 20, Lord Woolf decried the tendency of the old rules to provide for every eventuality, with resultant technicality and complexity. His own early version of the draft rules (the 'Brown Book') was 'deliberately not designed expressly to answer every question which could arise'. As he put it: 'Although the rules can offer detailed directions for the technical steps to be taken, the effectiveness of those steps depends upon the spirit in which they are carried out.' He therefore proposed a statement of objective as 'a compass to guide courts and litigants and legal advisers as to their general course'. The precise wording of this statement altered in the course of the drafting process but the overriding objective as set out in Part 1.1 of the rules – and its practical manifestation in the court's duty actively to manage cases – remain the cornerstone of the CPR, or, to vary Lord Woolf's metaphor, their 'polar star'.

Rule 1.1 reads as follows:

1.1. (1) These Rules are a new procedural code with the overriding objective of enabling the court to deal with cases justly.

(2) Dealing with a case justly includes, so far as is practicable

    (a) ensuring that the parties are on an equal footing;

    (b) saving expense;

    (c) dealing with the case in ways which are proportionate –

        (i) to the amount of money involved;

        (ii) to the importance of the case;

        (iii) to the complexity of the issues; and

        (iv) to the financial position of each party;

    (d) ensuring that it is dealt with expeditiously and fairly; and

    (e) allotting to it an appropriate share of the court's resources, while taking into account the need to allot resources to other cases.

Various elements in this definition warrant detailed examination – for example, the phrases 'new procedural code', 'dealing with a case justly' and 'proportionate'. However, before considering the precise implications of the constituent elements of the overriding objective, one should mention the means by which the rules seek to give it practical effect. The central provision here is Part 1.4, which requires the court to 'further the overriding objective by actively managing cases'. What precisely that can involve will be considered in detail in Chapter 3 below. At this stage, however, it is vital to appreciate that the court is not expected to perform its case-management functions in some kind of splendid isolation. True it is that when interpreting the CPR or when exercising any power under them, the court is obliged to seek to give effect to the overriding objective (Part 1.2) – and that obligation extends to the interpretation and application of the scheduled rules as well as of the core rules. But (and this is a vital aspect of the new regime), the burden of the court's obligation is to be shared with the parties – they also are expressly required to help the court to further the overriding objective (Part 1.3).[1]

The general structure of the remainder of this chapter is as follows:

A The 'new procedural code' provision (Part 1.1(1)):

    (i)   'A new procedural code': what the courts have decided. (This section considers in particular the various problems that have arisen in relation to what used to be called striking out for want of prosecution.)

    (ii) 'A new procedural code': some unanswered questions.

    (iii) The overriding objective and methods of interpretation.

    (iv) The overriding objective and the doctrine of precedent.

B 'Dealing with a case justly' – Part 1.1(2):

    (i)   'Ensuring that the parties are on an equal footing' – Part 1.1(2)(a).

    (ii) 'Saving expense' – Part 1.1(2)(b).

    (iii) Proportionality – Part 1.1(2)(c).

    (iv)' Ensuring that the case is dealt with expeditiously and fairly' – Part 1.1(2)(d).

    (v) Appropriate allotment of resources – Part 1.1(2)(e).

A   THE 'NEW PROCEDURAL CODE' PROVISION (PART 1.1(1))

The general legislative intent behind the provision that the CPR are 'a new procedural code' seems tolerably clear. At a fairly abstract level, it was designed to emphasise the radical nature of the reforms. More practically, it was intended to discourage practitioners from citing old authorities decided under the old rules. However, while some of the effects of this provision have been clarified in decisions of the courts after 26 April 1999, its full implications remain emphatically to be determined.

We begin by considering what has been determined by the courts and then turn to some unanswered questions.

---

1   One specific, if minor, application of this requirement is the obligation on the parties, where judgment has been reserved, to tell the court immediately when there is a possibility of agreement, so that the court's resources can be properly and efficiently deployed: *HFC Bank plc v Midland Bank* (2000) *The Times*, 26 April, CA.

A(i) 'A new procedural code' – what the courts have decided (including striking out for want of prosecution)

The courts have already received and acted upon the message about not referring to old authorities when seeking to apply or interpret the CPR. There have been some interesting consequences and indeed 'casualties'.

One early casualty was the old rule that a defendant in a civil matter cannot make a submission of no case without being 'put to his election' – that is, the rule that if a defendant wanted to submit that there was no case to answer, then before making his submission, he had to elect not to call any evidence himself. Given the risks, such submissions were pretty rare in civil matters. However, in *Mullan v Birmingham City Council* (1999) *The Times*, 29 July, David Foskett QC (sitting as a Deputy High Court Judge) held that, under the CPR, a judge deciding whether to hear a submission of no case had complete flexibility as to whether or not to put a defendant to his election. He said that he had looked at the old cases but had not heard submissions upon them and given Part 1.1(1), that 'might not have been appropriate in any event'. Under Part 3.1(2)(m), the court had a general power to make any order 'for the purpose of furthering the overriding objective' and this wording was broad enough to allow the court to hear a submission of no case without putting the defendant to his election – though the course to be adopted in any particular case would depend entirely on its facts.[2]

Another and more important piece of deadwood may be the old learning on *striking out for want of prosecution*.

It is fair to say that, even before the CPR came into force, the authority of the House of Lords' decision in *Birkett v James* [1978] AC 297 was being subtly – some might say not so subtly – eroded. The test laid down in that case was that a case should not be struck out for want of prosecution except:

(1) where the plaintiff's default had been intentional and contumelious; or

(2) where there had been (a) inordinate and inexcusable delay on the part of the plaintiff or his lawyers which (b) gave rise to a substantial risk that it was not possible to have a fair trial or was such as to have caused serious prejudice to the defendant.

As the House of Lords itself recognised in *Grovitt v Doctor* [1997] 2 All ER 417, part 2(b) of this test was preserving all too many cases of outrageous delay by plaintiffs – it often being extremely difficult, even after years of inactivity, to say that a fair trial was impossible or that prejudice had been suffered. The consequence was the recognition in *Grovitt v Doctor* and in subsequent Court

---

2 The Court of Appeal has since dealt with the question of submissions of no case in *Blinkhorn v Hall* (2000) unreported, 13 April – a judge still had a discretion to put a defendant making such a submission to his election and could not be criticised for doing so.

of Appeal decisions (particularly *Arbuthnot Latham v Trafalgar Holdings* [1998] 2 All ER 181) of a separate 'abuse of process' basis for striking out, whereby a wholesale disregard of procedural requirements could be held to constitute an abuse of process itself justifying a striking out order, even without prejudice being shown.

The question of the effect of the introduction of the CPR on all these cases arose in *Biguzzi v Rank Leisure* [1999] 4 All ER 934. In that case, a District Judge had struck out a claim on abuse grounds before 26 April 1999 but an appeal (by way of re-hearing) came before Judge Kennedy QC after that date. On the particular facts, the judge did not strike out. However, dealing with the relevance of the old cases, he said:

> I very much doubt whether any of the authorities can assist, although it is perfectly true, as counsel both pointed out to me, that in some of the later striking out cases ... there were foreshadowings and expressions of view as to how things might be under the new order. I have to say that this court's view, after extensive training and a good deal of discussion and thought, is that the new order will look after itself and develop its own ethos and ... references to old decisions and old rules are a distraction. [p 938a]

On appeal to the Court of Appeal, this approach was commended by Lord Woolf. There was, he said, no need for judges to look 'over their shoulders' at the old authorities. In short:

> [The judge] took the right course as to the previous authorities. The whole purpose of making the CPR a self-contained code was to send the message which now generally applies. Earlier authorities are no longer generally of any relevance once the CPR applies. [p 941h]

Biguzzi was, of course, a transitional case and Lord Woolf stressed that in such a case the judge 'could not, and should not, ignore the fact that the parties previously had been acting under a different regime' (p 939e). However, that did not mean that the judge was constrained to make the same sort of decision as would have been made under the old regime. In future, given its case management powers, the court would itself be more involved in the establishment and policing of vigorous procedural timetables than it had in the past. Furthermore, it now has a wider array of weapons at its disposal. The court is no longer confined to the draconian striking-out power but can make orders for summary assessment of costs, for the payment of indemnity costs, for payments into court, for reduced or increased rates of interest and so forth.[3] Such measures can be invoked to discourage or punish delay as an action proceeds and should lead to far fewer expensive interlocutory appeals about striking out.

---

3   Though obviously available generally, these other '*Biguzzi* options' will be particularly useful in a case of delay by a claimant where liability is not in issue – see the remarks of Stuart Smith LJ in *Walsh v Misseldine* (2000) unreported, 29 February, CA (at para 100 *et seq*).

Given the breadth of Lord Woolf's remarks on the general irrelevance of earlier authorities under the CPR, one might have thought that all the old case law on striking out for want of prosecution was now mere history and that we were indeed starting again with a completely clean slate.[4] In reality, of course, life is rarely that simple.

The general effect of *Biguzzi* would appear to be that while *Birkett v James* remains of relevance in transitional cases as part of the factual background against which such cases were conducted prior to the CPR, it is no longer determinative on strike out applications once the CPR are held to apply. Prejudice to the defendant is no longer a separate requirement but only one of several factors going to discretion.[5] However, if that aspect of *Birkett v James* is gradually fading into legal history, the same is not so obviously true of those immediately pre-CPR authorities which sought to ameliorate the failings of *Birkett v James*, namely, the *Arbuthnot Latham* line of cases.

In *UCB Bank plc v Halifax (SW) Ltd* (1999) *The Times*, 23 December, a claim was struck out on *Arbuthnot Latham* abuse grounds. On appeal, it was argued that following the introduction of the CPR and Lord Woolf's remarks in *Biguzzi* about the irrelevance of earlier authorities, it was no longer correct to apply *Arbuthnot Latham*, or at any rate dangerous to apply it in isolation. Ward LJ rejected the submission, saying:

> [Counsel] suggests that *Biguzzi* is some landmark decision which throws all of the previous law on its head, though he does not put it as inelegantly as that. That, however, is not how I read that judgment. When the Master of the Rolls said ... 'Earlier authorities are no longer generally of any relevance once the CPR applies', he was not saying that the underlying thought processes that informed those judgments, especially those such as *Arbuthnot*, which were written mindful of the way the new wind was blowing, should be completely thrown overboard ... His Lordship was therefore not saying that it would no longer be a proper approach to a question of strike out to treat abuse of the court's process as sufficient to justify the extreme remedy. That is how Judge Prosser QC approached it, and I can see no error in that approach.

Arbuthnot Latham and 'abuse of process' logic were also expressly invoked by the Court of Appeal in *Shikari v Malik* (1999) *The Times*, 20 May and in *Co-operative Retail Services Ltd v Guardian Assurance plc* (1999) unreported, 28 July. However, in both of these cases (as distinct from *UCB Bank v Halifax*), the judgments appealed from were *before* 26 April 1999 and therefore pre-CPR authorities were properly applicable. What was different about *UCB Bank* was the apparent application of *Arbuthnot Latham* in a case where the judgment

---

4   So much might have seemed likely when in *Biguzzi*, nine authorities had been mentioned in the skeleton arguments but only one (*Birkett v Jones*) was cited in the judgments.

5   For an example of a case where a post-CPR judgment applying only *Birkett v James* principles was overruled, see *Axa Insurance Co Ltd v Swire Fraser Ltd* (2000) *The Times*, 19 January, CA.

appealed from was post-26 April 1999 and where, therefore, pre-CPR authorities were *prima facie* irrelevant.

Some of these problems undoubtedly arose from the transitional difficulties which the courts had to tackle in relation to striking out cases over this period. They were recently accurately described by Brooke LJ, in the case of *Walsh v Misseldine* (2000) unreported, 29 February, CA, as follows:

> Transitional difficulties are always bound to arise when a procedural revolution takes place on this scale. For the first year or two (and, perhaps, sadly, for longer), the courts will be confronted with cases left over from the former regime, in which the absence of any effective court control gave rise to all the difficulties that have arisen. There was also during 1999 a period when the lower courts had to decide whether to apply the pre-CPR rules or the post-CPR rules to the appeals and applications which came before them after 26th April 1999. Further difficulties arose when some judges and practitioners interpreted post-April decisions of this court as if they were made under the new CPR regime when all that the court was doing was to review the exercise of discretion by a judge under the pre-CPR regime. Still further difficulties arose when pre-CPR decisions of the courts started creeping back into the case-law, despite a number of authoritative dicta in this court to the effect that recourse should not be had to them for the purposes of interpreting a quite new procedural regime.

As His Lordship recognised, this situation was very confusing for practitioners. Fortunately, matters appear to have been put back on track by the decision in *Purdy v Cambran* (1999) unreported, 17 December, CA. The judgment of May LJ in that case was described, in *Walsh v Misseldine*, as clearly setting out the ground rules under which the courts are now required to operate. May LJ said:

> When the court is considering, in a case to be decided under the CPR, whether or not it is just in accordance with the overriding objective to strike out a claim, it is not necessary or appropriate to analyse that question by reference to the rigid and overloaded structure which a large body of decisions under the former rules had constructed.

In a transitional case, he repeated what Lord Woolf had said in *Biguzzi*, namely, that 'You do not ignore the fact that the parties were previously operating under a different regime. But the decision has to be made applying the principles under the CPR, not those under the previous regime'. Then, having referred to the *Biguzzi* range of options that is available to the court, His Lordship continued:

> The effect of this is that, under the new procedural code of the CPR, the court takes into account all relevant circumstances and, in deciding what order to make, makes a broad judgment after considering the available possibilities. There are no hard and fast theoretical circumstances in which the court will strike out a claim or decline to do so. The decision depends on the justice in all the circumstances of the individual case. As I read the judgments of Lord Lloyd of Berwick and Ward LJ in *UCB Corporate Services Ltd v Halifax*, they are saying nothing different from this. As Ward LJ said in the *UCB* case, Lord Woolf MR in *Biguzzi* was not saying that the underlying thought processes of

previous decisions should be completely thrown overboard. It is clear, in my view, that what Lord Woolf was saying was that reference to authorities under the former rules is generally no longer relevant. Rather is it necessary to concentrate on the intrinsic justice of a particular case in the light of the overriding objective.

It is this formulation, in all its beguiling simplicity and clarity, which presently seems to hold sway.

However, one other point remains open for consideration. It still remains to be seen what approach the courts will adopt towards the more basic aspect of *Birkett v James* learning on striking out, namely the general rule that in the case of non-contumelious delay, a case would not be struck out for want of prosecution prior to the expiration of the limitation period – the logic being that the court would not get rid of properly constituted litigation at a time when a plaintiff could simply start proceedings all over again. Our own view is that, in an appropriate case, the court is most unlikely to allow the former practice to prevent it from exercising its striking out powers even before the expiration of the limitation period. This is particularly the case when the pre-CPR cases were already heading towards a more flexible attitude in relation to expiry of the limitation period. Thus, in *Arbuthnot Latham* [1998] 2 All ER 181, when speaking of the abuse of process ground for striking out, Lord Woolf himself said, at page 191j:

> The more ready recognition that wholesale failure, as such, to comply with the rules justifies an action being struck out, as long as it is just to do so, will avoid much time and expense being incurred in investigating questions of prejudice, and allow the striking out of actions *whether or not the limitation period has expired*. The question whether a fresh action can be commenced will then be a matter for the discretion of the court when considering any application to strike out that action, and any excuse given for the misconduct of the previous action (see *Janov v Morris* [1981] 3 All ER 780; [1981] 1 WLR 1389). The position is the same as it is under the first limb of *Birkett v James*. In exercising its discretion as to whether to strike out the second action, that court should start with the assumption that if a party has had one action struck out for abuse of process some special reason has to be identified to justify a second action being allowed to proceed. [Our emphasis]

The question of the relevance of non-expiry of the limitation period was adverted to in the judgment of Ian Hunter QC, sitting as a Deputy Judge of the Chancery Division, in *Securum Finance Ltd v Ashton Ltd* [1999] 2 All ER (Comm) 331. (The judgment has gone to appeal and at the time of writing the judgments of the Court of Appeal are awaited.) The *Securum* case is in fact the second stage of the *Arbuthnot Latham* litigation and is complicated by the fact that the claimant had two separate causes of action – a simple contractual debt (already struck out in *Arbuthnot Latham*) and a specialty mortgage claim (at issue in the present application). The continuing validity of the rule that actions will not be struck out before the expiry of the limitation period seems effectively to have been left unchallenged, both by counsel and the judge. However, the learned deputy judge did have this to say:

[*Birkett v James*] proceeded, of course, against the practice and culture of the period under which it was the parties who by and large set the pace of the proceedings and the role of the court in that respect was limited to occasional whistle-blowing. But all has now changed with the court's duty under CPR Rule 1.4 to ensure active case management. Once that system has been fully implemented there should in theory be no place or need for the procedure of striking out for want of prosecution as we have known it in the past. But perfection is rarely achievable and it is perfectly possible that cases (albeit a reduced number) may come before the courts where the defendant applies to strike out for abuse of process based on want of prosecution.

If that proves to be the case it does seem to me that there may be good reason to revisit *Birkett v James*. The fact that the legislature has determined that a claimant is entitled to a particular period of time within which to commence proceedings does not seem to me necessarily to mean that if he chooses to commence an action well within that period and then conducts the action in such a dilatory fashion that the claim is ultimately struck out for want of prosecution he should be able to conduct himself in that way safe in the knowledge that, provided he issues fresh proceedings within the limitation period, those proceedings cannot be struck out as an abuse of process. Court time is precious and there is an important public interest in its proper use. [p 341a]

One final point worthy of mention is that, as before, the duty of a claimant to pursue an action expeditiously and in accordance with the rules is all the more important when he has already obtained a significant benefit at the expense of the defendant from the action, such as a search order or a continuing interim injunction – see *Annodeus Entertainment v Gibson* (2000) *The Times*, 3 March, Neuberger J. The judgment in that case contains a useful summary of relevant and irrelevant considerations in relation to strike-out applications under the CPR. It also provides an interesting example of other '*Biguzzi* options' being preferred to a strike out order.

So much for what has been decided since 26 April 1999 about the new code provision. Other questions remain up for debate and to them we now turn.

A(ii)   'A new procedural code' – some unanswered questions

What if the CPR say nothing about a particular procedural topic? – does the old law then 'fill the gap' or, since we are starting afresh, is one to assume that there is no law on that topic? In strict theory, the latter may be correct. However, the practical outcome in any such situation is likely to be that the old practice will be applied, if only for want of anything better – unless, of course, it conflicts with the overriding objective. One early example of this happening may be *Harrison v Bloom Camillin* (1999) *The Independent*, 28 June, where Neuberger J had to decide whether to vary or set aside a witness summons under Part 34.3(4). The CPR provided no express guidance on the approach to be adopted. In those circumstances, the judge said that, despite the dangers of referring to old authorities on the old rules, it was 'at least helpful' for the court to have regard to the statement of the old law contained in the dissenting judgment of Ralph Gibson LJ in *Re State of Norway's Application (No 1)* [1988] 3 WLR 603. (*Harrison v Bloom Camillin* is further considered in section F of Chapter 18 below.)

Again, what if the CPR effectively reproduce the wording of the old rules or encapsulate the old test for some particular problem? In such a case, are references to old authorities possible, if not as binding, then at least as helpful guidance to a court seeking a solution? One assumes that many such references will be attempted, though it goes without saying that any guidance they afford could not be followed if it conflicted with the overriding objective. So much is clear from the decision of Hart J in *NatWest Lombard Factors Ltd v Arbis* (1999) *The Times*, 10 December. On an appeal from the county court in a bankruptcy matter, the question arose whether new evidence could be adduced and the status of *Ladd v Marshall* [1954] 1 WLR 1484 therefore fell to be considered. The relevant provision of the old rules (RSC Ord 59 r 10(2)) was in precisely the same terms as the relevant provision of the new rules (Rule 59.10 in Schedule 1 to the CPR). Hart J said that, because of the imperative contained in Part 1.2 of the CPR, the principles of interpretation by which the new rules were to be interpreted were not the same as those applied by the Court of Appeal in *Ladd v Marshall*. Accordingly, even though the rules were identically worded, authorities on the old rules could not necessarily be followed in interpreting the new. Nevertheless, both counsel took the view that in appropriate cases *Ladd v Marshall* remained applicable today and the judge therefore dealt with the case on that basis.[6]

Yet further questions – theoretically, perhaps, even more fundamental – still remain unconsidered. For example, it has been suggested that the overriding objective of the CPR may herald a completely new and different approach to the permissible methods of judicial interpretation. Again, it has been suggested that there could be a tension between the overriding objective and traditional learning on the doctrine of precedent. Without wishing to get embroiled in academic debate on either of these topics, we hazard the following brief statement of our own views.

A(iii)   The overriding objective and methods of interpretation

Many lawyers' first reaction to the CPR was one of bemusement at the relatively open and (dare one say it?) imprecise drafting style that had been

---

6   *Ladd v Marshall* also fell to be considered by Sir Richard Scott VC in *Re Club Europe Trade Mark* (1999) *The Times*, 2 August, a case about the High Court's powers to hear new evidence on an appeal from a tribunal or person under RSC Ord 55. The Vice Chancellor followed earlier authority to the effect that *Ladd v Marshall* did not apply to the power to hear new evidence under Ord 55 r 7(2) in the way that it applied to Court of Appeal hearings but, in any event, stressed that the power now fell to be exercised in accordance with the overriding objective and with the concept of proportionality. Fresh evidence was admitted because of the parties' earlier failure to identify the real issues.

adopted. However, given the views of Lord Woolf quoted in the opening paragraph of this chapter and the requirement that the Rules are to be interpreted and applied so as to achieve the overriding objective, such lack of precision is neither particularly surprising nor (at least from the court's point of view) much to be lamented. It is perhaps self-evident – but is nevertheless worth stating expressly – that one effect of the overriding objective will be a more purposive approach to the interpretation of the new rules. Questions of construction of the CPR will, or should be, approached with the overriding objective in mind, rather than as a matter of narrow and detailed syntactical analysis. 'For the letter killeth, but the spirit giveth life.'

On the other hand, while one obviously cannot exclude the possibility of some long term 'knock-on' effect on methods of judicial interpretation generally, the terms of the CPR and of rule 1.2 in particular could not justify the adoption of a more purposive approach to the interpretation of any legislation other than the CPR themselves. In particular, the terms of the CPR cannot justify any different or more generous approach being adopted in relation to the interpretation of statutes or of other subordinate legislation.

Of course, with the coming into force of the Human Rights Act 1998, the CPR (like all primary and subordinate legislation) must, so far as possible, be read and given effect in a way which is compatible with rights under the European Human Rights Convention – see section 3(1) of the 1998 Act.

A(iv)   The overriding objective and the doctrine of precedent

The argument has been advanced[7] that there is a tension between the overriding objective and the doctrine of precedent. The argument is as follows. The court must interpret and apply the CPR so as to further the overriding objective. This implies that the rules must be used so as to achieve a just result in the particular circumstances of the case before the court. But doing justice in a particular case may involve an interpretation or application of the rules which is in conflict with earlier binding decisions on how the rules should be interpreted and applied.

Our own view is that this argument is based on a fallacious reading of Part 1.1(1). That rule does not say that the overriding objective is to enable the court to do 'justice' in a particular case. (And even if it did, that would have to mean justice according to law as laid down in, amongst other sources, binding case law.) What the rule does say is that the objective is to enable the court 'to deal with cases justly'. The emphasis is thus emphatically on procedural fairness in the court's management of cases, rather than on any concept of substantive justice. Furthermore, it is apparent – if not from the reference to 'cases' (in the plural) in Part 1.1(1), then at least from the terms of Part 1.1(2)(e)

---

7   For example, in *Blackstone's Guide to the CPR*, 2nd edn, p 19.

– that procedural fairness in one case will have to be balanced against procedural fairness in others, in particular through an appropriate allotment of the court's resources. In making general pronouncements on the meaning and application of the CPR, the appellate courts will have to have this exhortation to 'managerial juggling' and indeed all the other limbs of the overriding objective well in mind.

It is certainly true that the CPR afford huge and on occasions open-ended discretions to a judge of first instance, particularly when exercising case management powers; and it is quite likely that the Court of Appeal will be even less prepared than previously to interfere with the exercise of such discretions. But to go from these propositions to arguing that the overriding objective is somehow at odds with the doctrine of precedent, or that case law on the CPR will in future operate merely as guidance rather than as binding authority, seems to us to go much too far.

Certainly – and this is probably an appropriate note on which to finish this section – any idea that we can all stop reading our law reports is emphatically to be dispelled. On the contrary, the judgments of the Court of Appeal in *Copeland v Smith* [2000] 1 All ER 457 contain strongly worded reminders of an advocate's duty to bring all relevant authority (helpful and unhelpful) to the attention of the court. Brooke LJ said:

> It is going to be increasingly important with the regime under the new Civil Procedure Rules that judges dealing with interlocutory issues are afforded up-to-date assistance on the law by advocates appearing in front of them. The whole thrust of the CPR is antagonistic to the endless appeals in interlocutory matters which characterised the pre-26 April 1999 regime. If proposals which are at present out for consultation are accepted, the regime for appeals from district judges to circuit judges is going to be changed, so that the decision of a district judge in an interlocutory matter is going to be of greater significance than it was under the old regime.[8]
>
> In these circumstances, it is quite essential for advocates who hold themselves out as competent to practise in a particular field to bring and keep themselves up to date with recent authority in their field. By 'recent authority' I am not necessarily referring to authority which is only to be found in specialist reports, but authority which has been reported in the general law reports. [p 462e]

B   'DEALING WITH A CASE JUSTLY' (PART 1.1(2))

This concept has already been discussed in section A(iv) above. There are two other points to highlight. First, like most of the central definitions in the CPR, the definition in rule 1.1(2) is not exhaustive – 'Dealing with a case justly

---

8   Authors' note: the changes here foreshadowed are those dealt with in Chapter 28 below, particularly the transformation of appeals from Masters to High Court Judges (and from District Judges to Circuit Judges) from appeals by way of rehearing to appeals by way of review.

includes ...'. Accordingly, other judicial concerns not expressly mentioned in rule 1.1(2) will be perfectly permissible, provided that they can fairly be subsumed under the general heading of 'dealing with a case justly'. Secondly and telling in the opposite direction, even the listed aims may properly be qualified or set aside by a court where circumstances demand – the proviso 'so far as is practicable' is emphatically not to be overlooked.

We turn to consider the particular elements of Part 1.1(2).

B(i)   'Ensuring that the parties are on an equal footing' – Part 1.1(2)(a)

One of the boldest attempts to say that the brave new world of the CPR had strange creatures in it came in a copyright case on only the second day of the new regime. This was *Maltez v Lewis*, 27 April 1999, reported in (1999) *The Times*, 4 May.

Both sides were legally aided, the claimant being represented by junior counsel and the defendant by a silk without a junior. About two weeks before trial, the claimant sought an order barring the defendant from using a silk. Relying on rule 1.1(2)(a), she argued that there should be a level playing field between the parties, which there could not be if one was represented by a silk when the other was not. She further contended that using a silk was disproportionate (that is, that there was a breach of rule 1.1(2)(c)) and that silks cost too much money (that is, that there was a breach of rule 1.1(2)(b)). Indeed, she went so far as to allege a breach of rule 1.1(2)(d). This last argument was presumably on the footing that silks are slow, rather than that they are inherently unfair – though it is difficult to be entirely sure since this claimant was clearly a bold spirit!

In any event, Neuberger J would have none of it. He said he had no jurisdiction to make the order sought and that even if he had, he would not exercise it.

He acknowledged that the court now had much wider case management powers than previously and that the circumstances in which those powers would be exercised were also much wider. However, it was a citizen's fundamental right to be represented by the advocate and/or solicitors of his choice. That right was obviously not absolute. (For example, a litigant cannot, as of right, demand that a hearing be adjourned because his lawyer is ill or unavailable. Again, the Legal Aid Board might refuse to fund a particular lawyer on costs grounds.) But, in general terms, a litigant can choose to use whomsoever he likes. The judge pointed out that the court was not powerless to achieve compliance with the overriding objective in other ways – for example, by refusing the costs of senior counsel, if instructing a silk was in truth unnecessary, or by ordering the big City firm to do the bundling and copying rather than leaving it with the High Street firm, or whatever.

In passing, we point out another feature of interest in *Maltez v Lewis*, namely the court's evident aversion to the possibility that the CPR might be used tactically in the way that the old rules so often were. Nobody hearing this particular application two weeks before trial could have been blind to its essentially 'spoiling' nature. As Neuberger J said:

> It seems to me that if a claim such as that made by the claimant here could be made, it would lead to undesirable uncertainty and inappropriate waste of costs and court time. Parties and their legal advisers would not be sure what view the court would take of the appropriate level of legal representation in a particular case. Thus, they might always feel at risk of being required to change legal representatives. The court might be bombarded by applicants, *quite often acting tactically*, seeking to remove their opponents' established legal advisers. [Emphasis added]

It is worth adding to any consideration of *Maltez v Lewis* that there are other more basic limits on a poorer litigant's ability to rely on his own lack of means as an argument for 'equality' in relation to case management decisions. In particular, while the court has power to deal with issues in whatever order seems most appropriate, it obviously cannot seek to redefine the true issues between the parties purely in order to save costs. Nor is it likely to exclude evidence that is clearly of relevance to those issues on purely cost-saving grounds. *Dicta* of May LJ in *McPhilemy v Times Newspapers Ltd* [1999] 3 All ER 775, at p 791b, well illustrate the kind of balancing exercise that is involved:

> The court will ... strive to manage the case so as to minimise the burden on litigants of slender means. This includes excluding all peripheral material which is not essential to the just determination of the real issues between the parties, and whose examination would be disproportionate to its importance to those issues. It does not, in my judgment, extend in this case to excluding potentially important evidence, which is central to a legitimate substantial defence.

It is also worth pointing out – albeit fairly self-evident – that if a litigant is to advance his own want of means as a reason why a case should be managed in some particular way, he is less likely to be listened to if his own handling of the case has not been calculated to save costs generally. As Lord Woolf put it in *McPhilemy*, at p 793h:

> ... if a party, because of his or her personal circumstances, wishes the court to restrain the activities of another party with the object of achieving greater equality, then that party must behave in a way which makes it clear that he or she is conducting the proceedings in a manner which demonstrates a desire to limit the expense as far as practical. In this case this is not the way that proceedings have been conducted on behalf of [the claimant].

B(ii) 'Saving expense' – Part 1.1(2)(b)

This is self-explanatory. As a matter of construction, it probably refers to saving the parties expense – and perhaps witnesses and other immediately interested third parties. However, the question is academic since the public purse and the interests of other litigants are well catered for by Part 1.1(2)(e).

B(iii)   Proportionality – Part 1.1(2)(c)

This is, of course, the central concept of the entire new regime. By now, busy litigators up and down the country will be accustomed to making an appropriate (proportionate) use of it as 'buzz-word' or 'sound-bite' in all their case management submissions. So much is it used in all argument and discussion about the new regime that we feel it is worth pausing simply to remind ourselves of what it actually means.

The factors against which proportionality is to be measured are, of course, expressly listed in Part 1.1(2)(c) – the amount of money involved, the importance of the case, the complexity of the issues and the financial position of the parties. More generally, however, it may be worth quoting a passage from IR chap 5, para 5, which well exemplifies the entire philosophy behind the CPR. Lord Woolf began by quoting with approval certain words of Lord Devlin:

> Is it right to cling to a system that offers perfection for the few and nothing at all for the many? Perhaps; if we could really be sure that our existing system was perfect. But of course it is not. We delude ourselves if we think that it always produces the right judgment. Every system contains a percentage of error; and if by slightly increasing the percentage of error, we can substantially reduce the percentage of cost, it is only the idealist who will revolt.

Lord Woolf went on:

> If 'time and money are no object' was the right approach in the past, then it certainly is not today. The achievement of the right result needs to be balanced against the expenditure of the time and money needed to achieve that result. I believe that both the profession and the judiciary, in making decisions as to the conduct of litigation, must take into account, more than they do at present, questions of cost and time and the means of the parties.

These thoughts have now crystallised into hard reality. The concept of proportionality underlies the very structure of entire sections of the new system – most obviously, the tracking system. Furthermore, whatever track a case is on, the court and the parties are obliged to perform their duties of co-operative case management in the light of the concept of proportionality as codified in Part 1.1(2)(c).

Such is the courts' enthusiasm for the idea of proportionality that they have occasionally come close to using it, not as a reason for giving scaled-down directions for a particular claim, but rather for rejecting a claim altogether, as being quite simply too silly. Thus, in *Flynn v Robin Thompson & Partners (a firm)* (2000) *The Times*, 14 March, CA, one issue in dispute was an alleged assault by a solicitor on a litigant's lay representative during the course of a hearing before a District Judge. There was alleged to have been some sort of scuffle during the handing over of certain papers and the claimant now sought to put responsibility for it on the solicitor's firm. Regardless of the exciting questions that arose under the Partnership Act and the question of any lack of damage caused by the incident, the Court of Appeal was prepared to invoke proportionality as a reason for striking out this claim as against the partnership. Thorpe LJ said that 'on any worldly application of the principles of proportionality' this particular issue should not go to trial. Mance LJ said that it would be totally disproportionate to allow the matter to proceed to trial against the partnership, as distinct from the individual solicitor, 'simply to establish a technical trespass'.

B(iv) 'Ensuring that (a case) is dealt with expeditiously and fairly' – Part 1.1(2)(d)

In certain circumstances, the concepts of expedition and of fairness can conflict. The tension between them is perhaps most acute when an application is made to strike out a claim altogether on the basis of delay. Largely for historical reasons (i.e. a backlog of cases of extreme delay hanging over from the old regime and a continuing debate over the present status of *Birkett v James* and its sister authorities), the topic of striking out for delay has been extensively considered in the case law since 26 April 1999. It has been examined at length in section A(i) of this chapter. However, the same tension will occur in a less acute form every time that directions are set by a court; or every time counsel takes too long in cross-examination. For example, in an undisclosed county court, after only the third question on a particular topic: 'Mr Grainger, there is such a thing as proportionality, you know.'

B(v) Appropriate allotment of resources – Part 1.1(2)(e)

The court is not only concerned to ensure that there should be a level playing field between the parties to a particular piece of litigation (rule 1.1(2)(a)). It is also concerned to provide a level playing field as between all court users. Furthermore, it is concerned not only with saving expense as between the parties (this being probably what is intended by rule 1.1(2)(b)), but also with not wasting the court's own resources of time and manpower. In short, dealing with a case justly also includes (so far as practicable):

> (e) allotting to [a case] an appropriate share of the court's resources, while taking into account the need to allot resources to other cases.

This provision has had a particularly vigorous airing in the decisions of the courts since 26 April 1999. We give two examples.

Stephenson (SBJ) Limited v Mandy (1999) *The Times*, 12 July, dealt with a common situation in employment cases. The defendant employee's contract contained post-employment restrictive covenants prohibiting the use of confidential information and the solicitation of staff and clients. The defendant's employment ceased in January 1999 and, in March, injunctions were granted in support of the covenants, with the claimant giving the usual cross-undertaking in damages. There was also an order for a speedy trial. The defendant appealed against the interim injunctions but by the time his appeal came on, the trial had been fixed to float only three weeks away. The claimant employer took the preliminary point that, under the CPR, the Court of Appeal should dismiss the appeal without even examining its merits.

It was held that, in the circumstances, it would not be a good use of the court's resources to go into the merits of the appeal, which should be dismissed at once. It was too near trial. Expenses should be saved and resources appropriately allotted. Clearly important in the court's reasoning was the fact that the defendant was adequately protected by the cross-undertaking in damages – there being no evidence of any additional damage which would occur in the short time before trial.[9]

The Court of Appeal took a similarly tough line in *Adoko v Jemal* (1999) *The Times*, 8 July. This concerned a defamation action arising out of the defendant's complaint to the Professional Conduct Committee of the General Council of the Bar that the claimant was holding himself out as a solicitor. The master struck the action out on the basis that it related to an occasion of absolute privilege. The claimant applied to the judge for an extension of time to appeal but this was refused. Leave to appeal against the judge's decision was granted. However, by the time the case got to the Court of Appeal, it was clearly in considerable disarray. It is worth quoting a few words of May LJ, as reported in *The Times*:

> The court must as far as practicable allot an appropriate share of the court's resources to each case. The notice of appeal before the court purported to be a notice of appeal from the decision of Master Eyre when it should have been an appeal from Mr Justice Curtis.
>
> The matter had come before the court in complete disarray. The claimant had completely failed to supply a bundle of the relevant material in chronological order as had been specifically required when leave to appeal was granted.
>
> The time of three lord justices had been wasted for an hour and a quarter to sort out the mess. That was not a proper use of the court's time.
>
> It was neither appropriate nor just that any further share of the court's resources should be allocated to a [case] conducted in that way.

Laws LJ went so far as to say that an appropriate proportional use of the court's resources was now to be considered a part of substantial justice.

---

9 Compare, on the subject of the overriding objective and academic appeals, the remarks of Peter Gibson LJ in *AG Holder & Co v Bodytonic Products Ltd* (1999) unreported, 12 November, CA.

CHAPTER 3

CASE MANAGEMENT

The concept of case management was at the heart of Lord Woolf's Reports and not surprisingly, therefore, underpins the entire structure of the CPR. The fundamental idea is that the 'ultimate responsibility for the control of litigation must move from the litigants and their legal advisors to the court' (FR chap 1, para 1). Linked to this is the idea that the court's time should be used at an early stage 'in order to save more time' (FR chap 1, para 6). The traditional adversarial concept of litigation is not abandoned but lawyers will now perform their adversarial roles 'in a managed environment governed by the courts and by the rules which will focus effort on the key issues rather than allowing every issue to be pursued regardless of time and expense, as at present' (FR chap 1, para 3).

Given the fluidity (and to some extent the novelty) of these ideas, it is hardly surprising that the concept of case management is not exhaustively defined by the new Rules. We are given instead two open-ended lists. The first, in Part 1.4(2), contains various legitimate judicial aims or concerns in relation to any given action. The second, in Part 3.1(2), details the general powers that the court has at its command when seeking to realise these aims or concerns. Both these lists repay careful study. Furthermore, it is worth repeating that both are expressly not exhaustive. There is self-evidently huge scope for judicial flexibility and inventiveness in the battle to achieve the overriding objective.

We consider each list in turn, first quoting its terms and then considering some of its more important elements. We will then consider some of the more important ancillary provisions upon which the court will rely in its management of cases.

The list of judicial 'aims' in Part 1.4(2) reads as follows:

Active case management includes –

(a) encouraging the parties to co-operate with each other in the conduct of the proceedings;

(b) identifying the issues at an early stage;

(c) deciding promptly which issues need full investigation and trial and accordingly disposing summarily of the others;

(d) deciding the order in which issues are to be resolved;

(e) encouraging the parties to use an alternative dispute resolution procedure if the court considers that appropriate and facilitating the use of such procedure;

(f) helping the parties to settle the whole or part of the case;

(g) fixing timetables or otherwise controlling the progress of the case;

(h) considering whether the likely benefits of taking a particular step justify the cost of taking it;

(i) dealing with as many aspects of the case as it can on the same occasion;

(j) dealing with the case without the parties needing to attend at court;

(k) making use of technology;

(l) giving directions to ensure that the trial of a case proceeds quickly and efficiently.

Some of these aims are more revolutionary than others. Thus, (b), (c), (d), (g) and (l) contain nothing particularly surprising – though the stress on the court's, rather than the parties', role in the early identification of the issues is new, as also is the court's more 'pro-active' role in itself deciding which issues can be dealt with summarily.

However, some of the other aims listed are, at least by the standards of the old regime, pretty stunning. Not least, in this regard, is the opening exhortation to *co-operation between the parties*. The notion that parties should be open with one another and that they should sensibly co-operate towards the early and cost-efficient resolution of their dispute would, in past years, have seemed extraordinary. However, these ideas underlie much of the CPR, not least perhaps the pre-action protocols and the court's new preparedness to encourage alternative dispute resolution, or 'ADR' (see below).

References to the new culture of co-operation are liberally scattered through the cases decided since 26 April 1999. Purely by way of example, one might mention *Cadogan Properties v Mount Eden* (1999) unreported, 30 June, CA. This was a complicated case to do with highly technical points on service out of the jurisdiction and extensions of time for the service of proceedings. It was also extremely hard-fought. We mention it not for any of the intricacies of the arguments advanced, but for the simple fact that even the victor was criticised (by Waller LJ) for 'pursuing a technical course', and for 'having pursued an appeal without any real purpose other than to teach (the other side) or their advisors a lesson' – all of which was said to be 'contrary to the spirit of the new rules, and to be discouraged'.[1]

It is worth pointing out that the rules contain not only a general exhortation to co-operation between the parties (Part 1.4(2)(a)) but also a positive duty to co-operate with the court in achieving the overriding objective (Part 1.3). Co-operation between the parties cannot exclude the court's role. For example, the court will not regard itself as bound by agreed

---

[1] Another good example is *Burt v Montague Wells* (1999) unreported, 26 July, CA, especially the judgment of May LJ – 'Those who conduct litigation really must embrace the new culture so as to avoid by co-operation the sort of useless and wasteful gladiatorial contest which has occurred here.'

case management directions which are inappropriate – see, for example, *Re Debtors (No 13-MISC 2000 and No 14-MISC 2000)* (2000) *The Times*, 10 April, Neuberger J (whether a question should be dealt with in the county court or High Court).

The court's case management responsibilities also now enable it – or rather require it – to encourage and to facilitate the use of *alternative dispute resolution* whenever that is felt appropriate (Part 1.4(2)(e)). Even more generally – and to old-fashioned eyes, strangely – it must help the parties to settle the case, either in whole or in part (Part 1.4(2)(f)).

As far as the court is concerned, the question of alternative dispute resolution, or 'ADR', will most commonly crop up at the stage when a case is allocated to a particular management track. At that stage, the parties are asked (in the allocation questionnaires) whether they would like the action to be stayed for a month to allow an attempt at settlement, either by ADR or otherwise. In most cases, ADR will mean mediation. That the matter is raised expressly on allocation should not, of course, discourage the parties from considering, or indeed trying, ADR even before that stage. Furthermore, paragraphs (e) and (f) of Part 1.4(2) will justify the court's returning to the possibility of a stay for mediation – even a second mediation – at any later stage in the history of an action. The power to order a stay for mediation can be exercised – and apparently on occasions is being exercised – even where one party objects.

For many practitioners, mediation will, of course, still be a new experience. However, it is one that few of us seem likely to avoid. ADR organisations have already reported a major increase in the number of court-referred mediations since 26 April 1999, a trend which seems likely to continue. CEDR (The Centre for Dispute Resolution) has even produced a 'Guide for the Judiciary' as to the facilitation of the process. There is already a well established mediation scheme at the Central London County Court – which may, funding permitting, be extended to other county courts. There is also a scheme in the Court of Appeal. Finally, the Lord Chancellor's Department have put out an extensive consultation paper on ADR and on how it might be used more extensively in the administration of justice generally. In short, watch this space!

Before leaving the question of the court's interest in promoting settlements, one might briefly mention *Unilever plc v Proctor and Gamble Co* (1999) *The Times*, 4 November, CA, a case on the scope of the 'without prejudice' privilege in the rather esoteric context of patents litigation. Robert Walker LJ said that 'The expansion of exceptions [to the scope of the privilege] should not be encouraged when an important ingredient of Lord Woolf's reforms of civil justice is to encourage those who are in dispute to engage in frank discussions before they resort to litigation'. The underlying culture of the new regime is beginning to inform the courts' decisions on the substantive law of evidence, as well as their purely procedural pronouncements.[2]

The second list (of the court's general powers) is in Part 3.1(2). That reads as follows:

> Except where these Rules provide otherwise, the court may –
>
> (a) extend or shorten the time for compliance with any rule, practice direction or court order (even if an application for extension is made after the time for compliance has expired);
>
> (b) adjourn or bring forward a hearing;
>
> (c) require a party or a party's legal representative to attend the court;
>
> (d) hold a hearing and receive evidence by telephone or by using any other method of direct oral communication;
>
> (e) direct that part of any proceedings (such as a counterclaim) be dealt with as separate proceedings;
>
> (f) stay the whole or part of any proceedings either generally or until a specific date or event;
>
> (g) consolidate proceedings;
>
> (h) try two or more claims on the same occasion;
>
> (i) direct a separate trial of any issue;
>
> (j) decide the order in which issues are to be tried;
>
> (k) exclude an issue from consideration;
>
> (l) dismiss or give judgment on a claim after a decision on a preliminary issue;
>
> (m) take any other step or make any other order for the purpose of managing the case and furthering the overriding objective.

The powers listed here are expressly additional to any others the court may have (Part 3.1(1)). Their breadth is self-evident but nowhere more than in paragraph (m). The wide terms of this open-ended paragraph have already been used as the justification for abandoning the strict pre-CPR rules on making a submission of no case to answer in a civil matter – see *Mullan v Birmingham City Council*, discussed in section A(i) of Chapter 2 above.

In addition to the above, the court has power to make *conditional orders* – including orders subject to conditions as to payments into court (Part 3.1(3)). This generally worded power as to conditional orders will be of great practical significance, especially in the context of applications for summary judgment. As before, it is likely to be subject to the rule in *Yorke Motors v Edwards* [1982] 1 WLR 444 that the condition must not be one incapable of fulfilment (compare *Sweetman v Shepherd* (2000) *The Times*, 29 March, CA. There is also a quite

---

2   *Unilever* was cited with approval in *Instance v Denny Bros Printing Ltd* (2000) *The Times*, 28 February, Lloyd J – in the context of the privilege's extending so as to prevent use of 'without prejudice' communications in subsequent litigation.

distinct *power to require a party to pay money into court* 'if that party has, without good reason, failed to comply with a rule, practice direction or pre-action protocol' (Part 3.1(5)). This latter power can be used as a general sanction for non-compliance. However, when exercising it, the court must have regard to the amount in dispute and to the costs that have been or may be incurred (Part 3.1(6)).

It is also important to realise that all of these broad-ranging powers can in most cases be exercised by the court, not only on application by a party but also of its own initiative (Part 3.3(1)). Indeed, before making an order of its own initiative, the court need not necessarily call a hearing or give the parties an opportunity to make representations (Part 3.3(4)) – though this will, no doubt, be an exceptional course in practice.[3] Certainly, if the court does make an order in this robust fashion, the parties will be able to apply to have it set aside, varied or stayed (Part 3.3(5)).

It seems likely that one of the most effective means of case management will continue to be *striking out a pleading/statement of case* (Part 3.4(2)). Indeed, this power seems likely to acquire a new vigour. It can be exercised not only on substantive grounds (where a pleading discloses 'no reasonable grounds for bringing or defending the claim' – paragraph (a)); and on grounds of abuse (where a pleading is 'an abuse of the court's process or is otherwise likely to obstruct the just disposal of the proceedings' – paragraph (b)); but also for simple failure to comply with a rule, practice direction or court order – paragraph (c).

As to the scope of paragraphs (a) or (b), the related practice direction 3.4 provides useful practical examples of the kind of situation in which the striking out power may be used, either by the court of its own initiative or on application. Within range of the striking out power are cases where the particulars of claim 'are incoherent and make no sense', as well as those where they contain a coherent set of facts but where 'those facts, even if true, do not disclose any legally recognisable claim' (PD3.4, para 1.4). Likewise, a defence 'consisting of a bare denial or otherwise (setting out) no coherent statement of facts' may be struck out, as well as one where the pleaded facts are coherent but do not, even if true, afford a defence in law (PD3.4, para 1.6). The court may even refuse to serve an offending claim form or defence. The practice direction makes for a breezy read and evidences the considerable overlap that will exist between the striking out power and the court's powers of summary determination under Part 24.

Quite apart from substantive defects in a claim, mention should be made of two other situations in which the striking out power in Part 3.4 might be used. Firstly, it is, of course, under Part 3.4(2)(c) that most applications to

---

3   Compare the approach of Neuberger J in *Benning & Peltz (a firm) v Deutsch* (2000) unreported, 8 February, Chancery Division.

strike out for prolonged delay are presently being made. We have already considered at length (in section A(i) of Chapter 2 above) the present state of the authorities (old and new) on what used to be called striking out for want of prosecution. Suffice to say that as judicial case management takes hold, there ought, at least in theory, to be much less scope for procedural delays and therefore far fewer applications to strike out on this basis than previously. Furthermore, as Lord Woolf emphasised in *Biguzzi v Rank Leisure* [1999] 4 All ER 934, the court now has many other sanctions, short of the draconian striking out power, which will in practice often be invoked first in order to discourage or punish delay.

Secondly, one ought to mention the question of striking out a claim where there has been a contumacious breach of the rules. In this area, the law seems to be in a state of change, as is apparent from the first instance decisions of Laddie J in *Re Swaptronics Ltd* (1998) *The Times*, 17 August, and of Evans-Lombe J in *Arrow Nominees Inc v Blackledge* (1999) *The Times*, 8 December. In the latter case, after a detailed review of the authorities, the learned judge said:

> I conclude that it is not a proper exercise of the Court's power under the rules or its inherent power to strike out a claimant's case where the claimant has been found to be in contumacious breach of the rules or an order of the Court or even is guilty of conduct amounting to a fraud on the Court and so a gross contempt, if it can be shown that notwithstanding the claimant's conduct there is no substantial risk that a fair trial of his claim cannot follow ... I agree with the conclusion of Mr Justice Laddie in the *Swaptronics* case that to conclude that a contemnor should have his case struck out by reason of his contempt notwithstanding that the Court takes the view that a fair trial can follow is likely to be a breach of Article 6.1 of the European Convention on Human Rights as being a breach of the contemnor's right to 'the determination of his civil rights and obligations' at 'a fair and public hearing within a reasonable time by an independent and impartial tribunal established by the law'. Plainly to strike out a contemnor's case where the Court takes the view that the acts constituting a contempt lead to a real risk that a fair trial cannot happen would not constitute a breach of the article.

One possibility short of an immediate order for striking out is, of course, an *'unless order'* – that a claim should be struck out unless a step is taken by a certain date. Part 3.5 contains the procedure for obtaining judgment where a statement of case has been struck out, in whole or in part, pursuant to non-compliance with such an order. As to the continuing need for precision in relation to such orders, see *Morgans (a firm) v Needham* (1999) *The Times*, 5 November, CA.

Rule 3.8(1) contains a new provision of general effect that where a rule, practice direction or court order imposes a sanction for non-compliance, that sanction has effect *unless* the defaulting party applies for and obtains relief. Furthermore, where something is required to be done within a specified time and the rule, practice direction or court order specifies the consequence of failure to comply, time may not be extended by agreement between the parties (Part 3.8(3)). Any application for relief must be supported by evidence and the matters that the court will take into account in deciding whether to grant it are set out in Part 3.9.

On a less draconian note, there is (reassuringly) a general power to rectify errors of procedure 'such as a failure to comply with a rule or practice direction' (Part 3.10).

The precise way in which the court will exercise its broad-ranging management powers in a particular case depends, above all, on the tracking system. That system provides for the allocation of a case to one of three different 'management tracks' depending on, *inter alia*, its nature, value and complexity. The three tracks are:

- the small claims track;
- the fast track; and
- the multi-track.

The next chapter briefly describes the allocation system and the scope of each track (all matters dealt with in Part 26 of the Rules). There then follow three chapters dealing with the chief distinguishing features of the procedure under each track (dealt with in Parts 27, 28 and 29 of the Rules). Throughout, the assumption is made that none of the specialist practice directions or Guides apply.

CHAPTER 4

THE ALLOCATION OF CASES TO 'MANAGEMENT TRACKS'

The allocation of a case to a particular management track has important consequences for the conduct of that litigation. In the most general terms, the pace at which a case must progress to trial and the degree to which it will be subjected to 'hands on' judicial management increases as one moves from the small claims to the fast track and from the fast to the multi-track. Purely by way of example, fast track trials will not ordinarily exceed one day in length and the extent to which expert evidence can be adduced is strictly controlled. Again, the extent to which costs can be recovered from an opponent depends on the track to which a case is allocated – broadly, costs are scarcely awarded at all on the small claims track and are (generally) fixed on the fast track.

SCOPE OF THE TRACKS

In definitional terms, the divisions between the different tracks are essentially (though not wholly) financial. Thus, the small claims track is the normal track for most claims with a financial value not exceeding £5,000. The fast track is the normal track for most claims between £5,000 and £15,000. The multi-track is the normal track for any claim for which the others are not normal, that is, generally for claims in excess of £15,000. However, this over-simplifies the relevant definitions, which are set out in Part 26.6 and which should be studied in detail. Purely by way of example, a personal injury claim may be worth less than £5,000 but if the element of damages claimed in respect of pain, suffering and loss of amenity exceeds £1,000, the small claims track is not the normal track. Again, the fast track is only the normal track for a claim between £5,000 and £15,000 where the trial is likely to last for no more than one day and where oral expert evidence will be limited to one expert per party in any field of expertise and where no more than two fields are to be covered.

Moreover, the financial value of a claim is far from being the only matter to be taken into account when deciding on allocation. We consider the process of allocation, first in terms of its mechanics, and secondly in terms of the test to be applied by the court.

ALLOCATION QUESTIONNAIRES AND STAYS FOR SETTLEMENT

Consistent with the new culture of court-managed litigation, the allocation of a defended claim to a particular track is a matter for the court (Part 26.5). However, the choice of track is made by the court on the basis of information provided by the parties in 'allocation questionnaires'. Where a defendant files a defence, the court will serve a questionnaire on each party (Part 26.3(1)) and they must be completed and filed by the specified date (Part 26.3(6)).[1]

Before allocating the case, the court may seek further information from a party or, if it thinks it necessary, hold an allocation hearing. Failure to return a questionnaire on time will be a highly dangerous thing to do. It could invite an unless order. Alternatively, it might cause the court to hold an allocation hearing and the party in default is likely to be ordered to pay the costs on an indemnity basis (see PD26, para 6.6). Alternatively, the court may proceed without an allocation hearing and give such directions as it sees fit. The parties are expected to consult one another and to co-operate in filling in their questionnaires and in returning them to the court (PD26, para 2.3). Indeed, the court will not usually take information into account unless it has been agreed or at least exchanged (PD26, para 2.2).

One important feature is that the very first question in an allocation questionnaire is whether the party wishes the action to be stayed for a month in order to allow an attempt at settlement. Such attempt may be by alternative dispute resolution or by other means (Part 26.4(1)). Such a stay will be granted by the court if all parties request it, or if the court of its own initiative considers that it would be appropriate (Part 26.4(2)). It is the claimant's job to inform the court of any settlement reached, but if he does not do that and the stay period expires, the court will make directions for the further management of the case (Part 26.4(5)). There is power to extend the stay for longer periods if thought appropriate but clear reasons will have to be given to justify an extension of more than four weeks (PD26 para 3.1(2)). In general terms, court-imposed mediations seem much more likely in future.

Amongst other things, the allocation questionnaire asks a party to state whether he has complied with any applicable pre-action protocol (and if not, why not); which management track he considers most suitable; and (if he has not already done so) whether he intends to apply for summary judgment or to issue a claim against a third party. He must identify his witnesses of fact and the facts to which they are witness and he must give details of his proposed expert evidence. A trial time estimate and desired trial locations must also be specified. An estimate of overall costs, together with details of costs actually incurred to date, must also be provided.

---

1   If there is more than one defendant and a defence has been filed by at least one of them, the court's service of the questionnaires is delayed until such time as all defendants have filed a defence or until the time for their doing so has expired, whichever is the sooner (Part 26.3(2)).

THE COURT'S DECISION ON ALLOCATION

In deciding whether to allocate a claim to its normal track, the court is required to have regard to a variety of specified matters. These are listed in Part 26.8(1) and include the financial value of the claim (as assessed by the court); the nature of the remedy sought; the likely complexity of the facts, law or evidence; the number of parties; the value and complexity of any counterclaim; the likely amount of oral evidence; the importance of the case to persons not party to it; and the views and circumstances of the parties.

It should be stressed that the assessment of a claim's financial value is a matter for the court and not the parties. In making its assessment, the court is to ignore any sums not in dispute, any claims for interest or costs and any questions of contributory negligence (Part 26.8(2)). Taking all the listed matters into account, the court is entitled to allocate a claim to a track of a higher financial value. However, the court will not allocate a claim to a track of a lower financial value without the consent of all parties (Part 26.7(3)). Claims with no financial value, for example for injunctions or declarations, will be allocated to the track which the court considers most suitable in the light of the listed matters (Part 26.7(2)).

The parties will be informed of the court's decision by way of a 'notice of allocation'. Unless the parties were agreed, brief reasons will usually be given for the choice of track.

Finally, there is provision for the re-allocation of a claim to a different track (Part 26.10). Whilst one can imagine situations where this might be appropriate (for example, a case raising totally straightforward questions on liability but complicated questions of law and fact on quantum), it seems likely that this power will only be used in exceptional circumstances.

CHAPTER 5

THE SMALL CLAIMS TRACK

The system of small claims arbitration in the county court was one of the few features of the old rules that Lord Woolf regarded as meeting his objectives of resolving disputes in a proportionate, cost-effective and fair manner (IR chap 16, para 1). Accordingly, it is not surprising that the old system was essentially preserved in the form of the new small claims track. Indeed, the principal change was an expansion in the number of claims which can be litigated in this manner – through an increase in the relevant limit from £3,000 to £5,000. The rather inappropriate word 'arbitration' has been dropped.

The new rules applicable to the small claims track are in Part 27. They aim at the resolution of disputes in a relatively informal manner with strictly limited possibilities of appeal. The rules are designed with the interests of litigants in person in mind and in what is effectively a codified application of the overriding objective, many of the standard features of litigation are excluded (Part 27.2(1)). For example, the rules on disclosure, on requests for further information and on offers to settle do not apply to small claims. Furthermore, the use of lawyers is discouraged by the general rule that only the fixed costs of issuing proceedings will be awarded to a successful party (Part 27.14(2)). In the vast majority of cases, it will only be where the other party has behaved unreasonably that the costs of legal representation will be recoverable by a successful party. In any event, on the small claims track using a lawyer or doing it yourself are not the only options. In most situations, a party may use a lay representative to present his case – see PD27, para 3 and the Lay Representatives (Rights of Audience) Order 1999 (SI 1999/1225).[1]

On allocation to the small claims track, a date for the final hearing of the claim will be fixed by the court and directions given (Part 27.4). The practice direction contains standard form directions for various common types of claim. The parties will be given at least 21 days' notice of the final hearing.

The court also has the option of directing that a preliminary hearing be held. However, this will normally only occur where the small claim requires special directions or where the court proposes to dispose of a claim summarily or to strike out a statement of case (Part 27.6). When considering whether or not to hold a preliminary hearing, the court is expressly directed to have regard to the desirability of limiting expense. With the consent of all

---

1   As to difficulties that can arise with unruly lay representatives, see *Bache v Essex County Council* (2000) *The Times*, 2 February, CA (dealing in fact with lay representation before the Employment Tribunal).

parties, the court can decide to deal with a case without any kind of hearing (Part 27.4(e) and 27.10).

As before, procedure at the final hearing is extremely flexible. Such hearings will, however, now generally be in public (PD27, para 4.1(1)). The court may adopt any method of proceeding that it considers to be fair. Hearings are informal and the strict rules of evidence do not apply. Evidence is not generally given on oath and the court may limit cross-examination (Part 27.8(5)). The court must, however, give reasons for its decision (Part 27.8(6)).

It is perhaps worth highlighting one particular feature of small claims hearings, namely, that expert evidence, written or oral, may not be given without permission (Part 27.5). In *Bandegani v Norwich Union Fire Insurance Society Ltd* (1999) unreported, 20 May, CA, Henry LJ had this to say about how that provision should operate in the context of a dispute about the value of a car:

> I would say nothing to encourage the grant of such a permission in a case such as this for reasons of proportionality. There are published guides available in newsagents and used in the trade that give some indication as to the market price of second-hand cars which judges may find helpful. I suggest that, in the ordinary case, such guides would give better evidential value for money than the expensive calling of two live experts.

Bad news, then, for experts in the motor trade and for publishers of textbooks on the law of evidence but good news for the corner shop!

The CPR even permit a party to bring or defend a small claim without actually attending the final hearing. Provided that a party gives the court seven days' written notice of his intention not to attend and requests that a decision be made in his absence, the court will take into account that party's statement of case and any other documents filed by him (Part 27.9(1)). In the event that a party simply fails to attend (that is, without giving prior notice), the court has – depending on the particular circumstances – a number of options open to it, including striking out the claim or deciding the claim in the party's absence (see generally, in this regard, Part 27.9). Such a non-attending party may subsequently apply to set aside any judgment given in his absence (Part 27.11(1)). However, such an application must be made within 14 days and good reason will have to be shown for the earlier failure to attend or to give written notice. The applicant will also have to show that he has a reasonable prospect of success at any rehearing.

The right of appeal is severely restricted on the small claims track. The only possible grounds of appeal are a serious irregularity affecting the proceedings or a mistake of law by the court (Part 27.12(1)).

CHAPTER 6

THE FAST TRACK

INTRODUCTORY

As already explained in Chapter 5, the fast track is the normal track for most defended claims worth between £5,000 and £15,000. Lord Woolf envisaged the fast track as a means of rapidly resolving disputes of relatively low value in a manner proportionate to the amount claimed (IR chap 7, para 1). He viewed the uncertain and potentially disproportionate costs of such litigation under the old rules as impeding access to justice. His recommendation of a 'no frills' form of litigation – subject to fixed costs, and a timetable of not more than 30 weeks leading to a trial not exceeding one day – was, broadly speaking, implemented by the CPR.

Given that, of the three tracks, the fast track is the least like pre-existing procedures, the new rules in Part 28 seem, at first sight, surprisingly thin. However, the related practice direction contains much vital further reading matter.

Directions for the management of cases on the fast track will be given at two principal stages – on initial allocation to that track and on the filing of listing questionnaires. As far as possible, the court will attempt to restrict the giving of directions to those two occasions and, even then, will attempt to dispense with a hearing (PD28, para 2.2). Parties are encouraged to 'concentrate' their applications to these two points in the action and to attempt to agree directions in standard form. In the event that further applications do prove necessary (for example, in relation to amendments), they must be made as soon as possible in order to minimise the need to change the original directions timetable (PD28, para 2.8).

ALLOCATION DIRECTIONS

On allocation to the fast track, directions will be given which must cover disclosure, service of witness statements and expert evidence (Part 28.3(1)). The court's first concern will be to ensure 'that the issues between the parties be identified and that the necessary evidence is prepared and disclosed' (PD28, para 3.3). Agreed directions are possible and guidance is provided as to what must be covered (PD28, para 3.6). The court need not approve such agreed directions but must take them into account. It can also, if need be, direct an allocation hearing.

PD28, para 3.12 contains a typical timetable as follows (all periods running from the date of the notice of allocation):

Disclosure	4 weeks
Exchange of witness statements	10 weeks
Exchange of experts' reports	14 weeks
Sending of listing questionnaires by the court	20 weeks
Filing of completed listing questionnaires	22 weeks
Hearing	30 weeks

One vital new feature is that in the notice of allocation, the court will at once fix a trial date or else specify a period not exceeding three weeks ('a trial window') within which the trial will take place (Part 28.2(2)). The concept of leaving the parties to set a case down for trial is abolished. The standard period between the giving of directions and the trial will not be more than 30 weeks (Part 28.2(4)).

It is a defining feature of the fast track that the trial date or period which is fixed on allocation must be adhered to. There are elaborate provisions designed to ensure that directions are followed and that the timetable is not allowed to 'slide'. Thus, though paragraph 4 of the practice direction contains provisions dealing with variations to directions, the bottom line of those provisions is that any party who is dissatisfied with a direction must take steps to vary it as soon as possible – either by appealing (if he attended or had notice of the hearing at which the direction was given) or by asking the court to reconsider the matter (if he did not). If a party does neither of these things within 14 days of service of the relevant order, the court will assume that he 'was content that (the directions) were correct in the circumstances then existing' (PD28, para 4.2(2)).

Even agreed variations will not always be possible. In particular, there are three dates which cannot be altered merely by agreement. These are the dates for the return of a listing questionnaire and the trial date or the trial period. Indeed, the ban on consensual variations without an order is even broader than this. Part 28.4(2) provides:

> Any date set by the court or these Rules for doing any act may not be varied by the parties if the variation would make it necessary to vary any of [the three dates mentioned above].

PD 28, para 5 deals with breaches of the directions timetable. The reader will not be surprised to learn that sanctions can be imposed – such as a party's losing the right to raise or contest an issue or to lead particular types of evidence. However, the point that really requires to be emphasised is, once again, the centrality of the idea of holding the trial date. The practice direction states that the court will not allow a failure to comply with directions to lead to the postponement of the trial 'unless the circumstances of the case are exceptional' (PD28, para 5.4(1)). In order to hold a trial date, the court can order a revised (and accelerated) timetable with appropriate sanctions for non-compliance. Alternatively, if there are *some* issues which are (or can be made) ready for trial by the trial date, the court may direct that those issues be tried <u>at once</u> and that there be a later trial of all remaining issues. The court may order that <u>no costs</u> should be allowed in respect of the later trial or that such costs should <u>be paid by the party in default</u> (PD28, para 5.4(4)).

In the unlikely event that an adjournment is allowed, it will be for the 'shortest possible time' and will be accompanied by directions for all remaining steps to be taken 'as rapidly as possible' in the meantime. Furthermore, such brief respite may only be obtained at the cost of monumental embarrassment, in front of the most exacting critic of all. PD28, para 5.4(6) reads as follows:

> Litigants and lawyers must be in no doubt that the court will regard the postponement of a trial as an order of last resort. *The court may exercise its power to require a party as well as his legal representative to attend court at a hearing where such an order is to be sought.* [Emphasis added]

Two other aspects of the vigour of these procedural timetables ought perhaps to be emphasised. First, one major assumption behind the brisk interlocutory timetable for fast track cases is that, where they are applicable, the pre-action protocols will already have been fully complied with. In particular, a large proportion of fast track cases are personal injury actions governed by the protocol for such claims. If both sides have done a good deal of preparation even before proceedings start, it is not felt to be unreasonable thereafter to subject them to a vigorous timetable. Secondly, one important aim behind the requirement that procedural directions be promptly challenged during the interlocutory stage is to ensure that the trial itself is not cluttered up with unnecessary procedural arguments, say about disclosure. The basic presumption is that the trial will proceed 'in accordance with any order previously made' (Part 28.7). Interlocutory arguments should therefore be resolved promptly as and when they arise and not deliberately stored up to be sorted out by the trial judge, as was often done in the past. If unsatisfactory directions are not promptly challenged, then the opportunity to do anything about them may be lost altogether.

LISTING QUESTIONNAIRES AND DIRECTIONS

The second principal stage at which case management directions will be given on the fast track is on the filing of listing questionnaires. The date specified for return of such questionnaires must be no more than eight weeks before the trial date (Part 28.5(2)). If a questionnaire is not completed or is completed inadequately, the court may call a listing hearing, no doubt with predictable consequences in costs for whoever is in default. Alternatively, it may give listing directions without a hearing. If neither party files a listing questionnaire, the court will usually order that both claim and counterclaim be struck out if questionnaires are not filed within three days (PD28, para 6.5).

The listing questionnaire covers a wide range of topics – as to whether the existing directions have been complied with (and if not, why not); and as to the identity and availability of witnesses, experts and lawyers. As soon as practicable after the return date for listing questionnaires, the court will make further directions. These must include confirming or fixing the trial date, specifying the place of trial and giving a time estimate. The parties are encouraged to agree other listing directions – which should include directions on the evidence to be given, on the preparation of a trial bundle and on a trial timetable (for example, a quarter of an hour for cross-examination of witness A, half an hour for cross-examination of witness B, a quarter of an hour for each closing speech and so forth). The court may or may not endorse such agreed directions. In particular, any direction giving permission for expert evidence must say whether oral evidence is to be allowed. The court will not allow oral expert evidence on this track 'unless it believes it is necessary in the interests of justice to do so' (PD28, para 7.2(4)(b)).

FAST TRACK TRIALS

As explained above, unless the trial judge orders otherwise, the trial will be conducted in accordance with any order previously made (Part 28.7). As far as possible, therefore, procedural arguments of all kinds should be resolved before rather than at trial.

The maximum duration of the trial is, of course, one day, though the last paragraph of the practice direction reluctantly acknowledges that a trial may have to go over to the next day! Trials are likely to focus on what are viewed as the key issues. Liability and quantum are increasingly likely to be tried separately – not only because liability can often be dealt with without experts, but also because a decision on liability often either concludes matters altogether or else makes a settlement on quantum more likely. The normal procedure will be for costs to be assessed summarily and the parties are under a duty to provide the judge with the relevant information to allow that to take place (PD28, para 8.5).

FAST TRACK COSTS (PART 46)

Lord Woolf's original intention was that on the fast track there should be strict limits on the costs that could be recovered from another party, both at the pre-trial stage and at trial. To date, however, the CPR have only fixed costs at the trial stage, the relevant rules being in Part 46. In due course, the fixed costs regime may be extended to the whole course of an action.

Part 46 fixes an upper limit on the amount of costs awardable to a successful party in respect of 'the costs of an advocate for preparing for and appearing at (a fast track) trial' (Part 46.1(1)). The amounts specified vary according to the value of the award (or rejected claim) but are in all cases surprisingly low. The assumption is that the advocate will be the only lawyer present at trial. However, Part 46.3 lists a number of situations in which higher costs can be awarded – including an additional £250 if the court considers that another legal representative's attendance at the trial was necessary. (It is perhaps noteworthy that the test for recovering this extra sum is not merely one of reasonableness but of necessity.)

In relation to interlocutory costs (not presently covered by the fixed costs regime), the costs of the (relatively few) interlocutory hearings on the fast track will no doubt be assessed and paid summarily in accordance with the general policy of 'pay as you go' – see Chapter 24 below. In all likelihood, the tendency of such awards will also be towards austerity rather than generosity.

CHAPTER 7

THE MULTI-TRACK

The significance of the multi-track is somewhat obscured by its definition as 'the normal track for any claim for which the small claims track or the fast track is not the normal track' (Part 26.6(6)). It is, in truth, the track to which claims in excess of £15,000 will normally be allocated and it will therefore be the track along which most substantial High Court actions will proceed.[1]

The hallmarks of the multi-track are the court's ability to deal with cases of widely differing values and complexity; and the flexibility given to the court in the way it will manage cases according to their particular needs (PD29, para 3.2). As Lord Woolf put it, 'The central principle is that the court will manage every case, but the type of management will vary according to the needs of the case' (FR chap 5, para. 2).

As with the fast track, the rules themselves (set out in Part 29) are fairly 'thin'. Reference should also be made to the substantive practice direction.

As with the other tracks, directions for the management of a case will be given on allocation and a trial date or period will be fixed then or as soon as practicable thereafter. However, the flexibility of the court's approach to each case makes it difficult to generalise about what course will be adopted thereafter. The practice direction (inevitably) seems rather 'multi-targeted'. Thus, some straightforward cases over £15,000 may well proceed with standard directions without the need for a case management conference. The court's general approach when giving such directions is set out in PD29, para 4.10.[2] In more complicated cases, a more elaborate structure of directions hearings is envisaged. The likely pattern in most multi-track actions will be as follows:

Case management conference

Listing questionnaires

Pre-trial review

Trial

The dates set for these 'milestones' in the progress of an action cannot be varied without the court's permission (Part 29.5(1)). Nor can the parties agree any variation to any date set by the court or the Rules, if such variation would make it necessary to vary any of the milestone dates (Part 29.5(2)).

---

1   Most claims begun in the High Court for less than £50,000 are likely to be transferred to the county court – see, generally, PD29, para 2.2.
2   Of course, if a claim is *particularly* straightforward, the court can itself invoke its powers of summary determination – see Chapter 15 below.

Whatever the precise mechanics by which directions are given, the court's general approach is clear. It will strive from an early stage to ensure that the issues are identified and that the necessary evidence is prepared and disclosed (PD29, para 4.3). Furthermore, it will at all stages have one eye on the possibility of settlement. Assuming that alternative dispute resolution has not already been tried pursuant to the stay procedure described in Chapter 4 above, the question may surface again at a case management conference. Both in that context and more generally, one apparently innocuous provision of the Rules is worth highlighting. Part 29.3(2) reads as follows:

> If a party has a legal representative, a representative –
>
> (a) familiar with the case; and
>
> (b) with sufficient authority to deal with any issues that are likely to arise,
>
> must attend case management conferences and pre-trial reviews.

This provision is expanded upon in the practice direction and warning is given that 'Where the inadequacy of the person attending or of his instructions leads to the adjournment of a hearing, the court will expect to make a wasted costs order' (PD29, para 5.2(3)). Beware the use of generalised last-minute instructions to local agents or to anyone who happens to be free tomorrow! One aim of this provision is, of course, to ensure that the court is given the best possible assistance when exercising its case management powers. Equally importantly, however, case management conferences and pre-trial reviews provide excellent opportunities for settlement and the court will therefore often invoke its power to order clients as well as lawyers to attend on such occasions – Part 3.1(2)(c). The settlement opportunity may well be wasted if the legal representatives in attendance are ill-briefed, or if the clients fail to attend.

The dangers of neglecting these provisions were spelt out by Brooke LJ in *Baron v Lovell* (1999) *The Times*, 14 September, CA:

> If a defendant's lawyers choose not to send a representative with appropriate authority to attend a pre-trial review and choose not to ensure that the client (who in this case should be equated with the defendant's insurer) attends the review, the judge, who is likely to be the trial judge, is likely to note their absence. If he considers that that party has acted unreasonably in this way in connection with the litigation in breach of a direction of the court, there may come a time when he decides that it is appropriate to make an order for indemnity costs against that party, or to exercise his power to award interest on damages at a much higher rate than what is usual, if those powers are available to him.

The extremely broad-ranging topics that the court will review at a case management conference are set out at length in the practice direction, as also are the preparations that the parties attending such a conference must make. Apart from assembling all relevant documents and preparing draft orders, practitioners are exhorted to consider whether the parties should attend and whether a 'case summary' would be useful. This new document is defined as follows:

A case summary:

(a) should be designed to assist the court to understand and deal with the questions before it,

(b) should set out a brief chronology of the claim, the issues of fact which are agreed or in dispute and the evidence needed to decide them,

(c) should not normally exceed 500 words in length, and

(d) should be prepared by the claimant and agreed with the other parties if possible. [PD29, para 5.7]

There are provisions dealing with challenges and variations to directions, and with failure to comply with directions, which are broadly similar (and equally robust) to those already considered in relation to the fast track (see Chapter 6 above for the general aims of those provisions). Once again, the extreme difficulty of shifting a trial date is stressed. It is worth repeating that where a case is not fully ready for trial, a trial can still take place on those issues that are ready, with a later trial being directed on those that are not. The party in default can expect to be ordered to pay the costs of such later trial (PD29, para 7.4(4)).

As on the fast track, there are provisions for listing questionnaires and listing hearings. In many cases, a pre-trial review may also be ordered, usually about eight weeks before trial. The expectation is that such reviews would be attended, wherever practicable, by the trial judge, the advocates and the parties (or someone authorised to settle). The aim is to provide an opportunity for settlement, even at the eleventh hour, and if that is not possible, to give directions for the trial – including the preparation of a bundle, the giving of time estimates, the making of arrangements for skeleton arguments and reading lists, and the setting of a trial timetable. The judge will obviously be concerned to explore the extent to which the issues and/or the evidence can be agreed.

As on the fast track, the general approach is that unless the trial judge orders otherwise, the trial will be conducted in accordance with any order previously made (Part 29.9). The judge will generally have read the papers in advance and may dispense with an opening address (PD29, para 10.2).

PART B

CHAPTER 8

SERVICE OF DOCUMENTS

Originally, CPR Part 6 (and the related practice direction) dealt only with service of documents within the jurisdiction – service outside the jurisdiction being governed by a revised version of RSC Ord 11 and by a related practice direction. However, following the amendments introduced by SI 2000/221, service outside the jurisdiction will, as from 2 May 2000, also fall within Part 6. As revised, Part 6 is divided into three sections – the first setting out the general rules on the service of documents; the second containing certain special rules on the service of claim forms; and the third governing service outside the jurisdiction. Certain other specialised rules on service will still be dealt with elsewhere, notably those dealing with service on the Crown (RSC Ord 77 r 4).

LORD WOOLF'S PROPOSALS ON SERVICE

In his Final Report (page 120), Lord Woolf recognised that the 'machinery for the service of documents relating to court proceedings is of fundamental importance'. It is the means by which parties are informed of claims against them and it puts them in a position to respond. As a result, the old regime had been essentially restrictive of the permissible methods of service, only gradually developing from a position where personal service was the norm. In contrast, Lord Woolf proposed that there ought, in principle, to be no restriction on the methods by which a document could be served, provided that the court was satisfied that the method used had put the recipient in a position to ascertain the document's contents. The new rules on service set out in Part 6 do *not* adopt Lord Woolf's radical approach.

CPR PART 6 – SERVICE WITHIN THE JURISDICTION

The new rules set out five methods by which documents may generally[1] be served (Part 6.2(1)). These are:

(a) by personal service;

(b) by first class post;

(c) by leaving the document at an address given for service;

---

[1] The general rule is expressly made subject to contrary provision, whether by statute, by another rule or practice direction, or by court order. The most obvious continuing exception will be injunctions or other orders containing a penal notice, where personal service will continue to be necessary.

(d) by sending the document through a document exchange; or

(e) (in certain limited circumstances) by fax or other means of electronic communication.

(In the case of service on companies, these methods are in addition to the special Companies Act methods – Part 6.2(2).) The precise circumstances in which a document may be served through a document exchange, by fax or electronically are detailed in the practice direction accompanying Part 6 – as also are the required mechanics of such service.[2] The rules also contain 'deeming provisions' as to when precisely a document sent by one of the five methods will be deemed to have been served (Part 6.7).

Other methods of service may be authorised by the court where there is good reason to do so (Part 6.8(1)). However, an application for service by any such alternative method must be supported by evidence explaining why an order for such service is sought and what steps have already been taken to serve by the usual methods (PD6, para 9.1). There is also a general new power to dispense with service of a document altogether if it is appropriate to do so (Part 6.9). Taken together, these provisions will no doubt deal with all those problems previously catered for by substituted service.

However, the most significant practical change made by the CPR is that any document 'issued or prepared' by the court will, in general, be served by the court itself, rather than by the relevant party (Part 6.3(1)). For example, the claim form commencing proceedings in the High Court or county court will now often be served by that court (Part 6.13).[3] This had previously been the practice in the county court but now applies to all proceedings. Any party preparing a document to be served by the court must provide a file copy and a copy for each party to be served (Part 6.3(3)). The precise method of service to be adopted is then a matter for the court (Part 6.3(2)) but will usually be by first class pre-paid post (PD6, para 8.1).

Despite this change in practice, there remains a general option for a party himself to serve a document issued or prepared by the court – though he will have to notify the court of his desire to take that course (Part 6.3(1)(b)). Furthermore, in the event that service through the court proves unsuccessful, the party seeking service will be notified of that fact and of the unsuccessful

---

2   On service by fax, see *Molins plc v GD SpA* (2000) *The Times*, 23 March. For service by fax to be valid, the receiving party or his legal representative must previously have indicated in writing that he is willing to accept service by that means and have provided the fax number to be used. The mere fact that a party has included a fax number on its notepaper will not be sufficient consent for these purposes. (It would seem that the position may be different in relation to a fax number included on a legal representative's notepaper – see PD6, para 3.1(3)(b) and the *dictum* of Aldous LJ in this regard.)

3   In the Commercial Court, service of the claim form continues to be by the parties – see para 8.3 of the Commercial Court Practice Direction and para B5.1 of the Commercial Court Guide.

methods used (Part 6.11). He will then be left to himself to effect service 'as the court is under no further duty' to do so (PD6, para 8.2).

Service of a document may be proved by a 'certificate of service' – which is required to detail the method of service adopted, certain (listed) details as to the date on which that method was effected and a statement that the document has not been returned undelivered (Part 6.10). Where the *court* serves a claim form, it will itself issue a notice of service (Part 6.14(1)). Where the *claimant* serves a claim form, he will be unable to obtain judgment in default until he has filed a certificate of service (Part 6.14(2)).

The second section of Part 6 also contains specific provisions dealing with the service of claim forms in certain contract actions – covering service by a contractually agreed method of service (Part 6.15), or, in the case where the contract was entered into within the jurisdiction through the defendant's agent, allowing service (with leave) on that agent (Part 6.16).

CPR PART 6 – SERVICE OUT OF THE JURISDICTION

From 2 May 2000, service out of the jurisdiction is dealt with in Section III of Part 6. The language of the relevant provisions has been very considerably simplified but in other respects, there is much that seems familiar. Certainly that is the case with the basic distinction between circumstances where service may be effected outside the jurisdiction *without* permission (Part 6.19) and circumstances where permission is required (Part 6.20).

The situations where permission is not required broadly correspond to those dealt with in the old RSC Ord 11 r 1(2) and as before, any claim form that is to be served out without permission must contain a statement of the grounds on which the claimant is entitled to serve out (Part 6.19(3)). The relevant forms of words to be used are set out in paragraph 1 of PD6B.

The long list of situations where the court can give permission to serve out (previously in RSC Ord 11 r 1(1)) has now been much simplified. Furthermore, the available grounds have been grouped into 'topics', namely:

General grounds

Claims for interim remedies

Claims in relation to contracts

Claims in tort

Enforcement

Claims about property within the jurisdiction

Claims about trusts, etc

Claims by the Inland Revenue

Claim for costs order in favour of or against third parties

Claims under various enactments

A little more should be said about two of these. First, the contract grounds include certain familiar grounds, namely, where:

    (5) a claim is made in respect of a contract where the contract –

        (a) was made within the jurisdiction;

        (b) was made by or through an agent trading or residing within the jurisdiction;

        (c) is governed by English law; or

        (d) contains a term to the effect that the court shall have jurisdiction to determine any claim in respect of the contract;

    (6) a claim is made in respect of a breach of contract committed within the jurisdiction.

However, there is also a new (effectively negative) contract ground, namely, where:

    (7) a claim is made for a declaration that no contract exists where, if the contract was found to exist, it would comply with the conditions set out in paragraph (5).

Secondly, the penultimate of the specified grounds is also new:

    (17) a claim is made by a party to proceedings for an order that the court exercise its power under section 51 of the Supreme Court Act 1981 to make a costs order in favour of or against a person who is not a party to those proceedings.

This provision appears to fill the potential lacuna identified and discussed in *National Justice Compania Naviera SA v Prudential Assurance (The Ikarian Reefer No 2)* [2000] 1 All ER 37, CA.

The mechanics of applications for permission to serve a claim form outside the jurisdiction are dealt with in Part 6.21 and are broadly familiar. Any order giving permission to serve a claim form out of the jurisdiction must specify periods within which the defendant may file an acknowledgment of service, file or serve an admission and serve a defence (Part 6.21(4)). In those circumstances where service is effected without permission, these periods are prescribed by rule – see Parts 6.22 and 6.23.

The rules obviously also deal with the various methods of service out of the jurisdiction. The provisions (in Parts 6.24 to 6.29) are extremely complicated and should be considered in detail, as also should the corresponding provisions of the new PD6B.

Part 6.30 deals with service outside the jurisdiction of documents other than the claim form.

CHAPTER 9

STARTING A CLAIM

THE USUAL PROCEDURE (PART 7)

The usual way of starting an action is the claim form (Part 7) procedure, which roughly corresponds to the old writ of summons procedure. (The alternative Part 8 procedure is to be used where the claimant seeks the court's decision 'on a question which is unlikely to involve a substantial dispute of fact' or where a practice direction permits or requires it. It roughly corresponds to the old originating summons procedure and is dealt with below.)

Proceedings are started when the court issues a claim form at the request of the claimant (Part 7.2(1)).[1] The claim form must then be served on the defendant, the general rule being that it must be served within four months of the date of issue (six months where service is to be out of the jurisdiction) – Part 7.5.

The time for service may be extended by the court in the circumstances set out in Part 7.6.[2] The general rule is that an application for such an extension must be made within the basic period for serving the claim form, or within the period of any current extension. If those deadlines are missed, then the position is governed by Part 7.6(3):

> If the claimant applies for an order to extend the time for service of the claim form after the end of the period specified by rule 7.5 or by an order made under this rule, the court may make such an order only if –
>
> (a) the court has been unable to serve the claim form;
>
> (b) the claimant has taken all reasonable steps to serve the claim form but has been unable to do so; and
>
> (c) in either case, the claimant has acted promptly in making the application.

---

1 The concept that proceedings exist as from issue (and not merely from service) has been held to apply equally to arbitration applications – *Cleveland Structural Engineering (Hong Kong) Ltd v Advanced Specialist Treatment Engineering Ltd* (2000) *The Times*, 7 February, Colman J.

2 In *Jones v Telford & Wrekin Council* (1999) *The Times*, 29 September, the Court of Appeal held that both under the CPR and the old county court rules, a failure to get medical evidence in order could not be a good justification for failing to serve proceedings in time. Lord Woolf said that the object of serving proceedings was to allow defendants to take the appropriate action to defend the case and, if they were not served, they were deprived of that opportunity.

It is not possible to circumvent the requirements of this rule by making an application to remedy an error of procedure under Part 3.10 – see the judgment of Colman J in *Amerada Hess v Rome* (2000) *The Times*, 15 March.

Particulars of claim (roughly speaking the old Statement of Claim) may be contained in or served with the claim form. If they are not, then the claim form must state that particulars of claim will follow (Part 16.2(2)) and must itself contain a concise statement of the nature of the claim, specify the remedy sought and (in a claim for money) contain a statement of value (Part 16.2(1)). A statement of value is a particularisation of the amount claimed and a statement *either* that the claimant expects to recover:

- not more than £5,000;
- more than £5,000 but not more than £15,000; or
- more than £15,000,

or that he cannot say how much he expects to recover (Part 16.3(2)). Any figure specified should disregard any possible award for interest or costs and any possible deductions for, *inter alia*, contributory negligence or any set-off or counter claim (Part 16.3(6)). The statement of value is essentially for the purposes of allocation between the different tracks and does not limit the court's power to give judgment for more than is specified (Part 16.3(7)).

The claim form itself falls within the definition of a 'statement of case' and it must therefore be verified by a statement of truth (Part 22 and PD7, para 7.1). Though it is not entirely clear, this requirement probably applies even where the claim form does not contain the particulars of claim – even then, there will be statements of fact in the claim form (for example, the statement of value) which the party can and should verify.

Also of interest is Part 7.7, whereby, after the issue but before the service of a claim form, the defendant may serve notice on the claimant requiring him either to serve the claim form, or to discontinue within a specified period of not less than 14 days. If the claimant persists in not serving, the court may, on the defendant's application, dismiss the claim altogether. This power could be used to discourage, or at least to limit, the improper and unjustified 'advertising' of claims by claimants who in truth are not prepared to go so far as actually serving proceedings.

THE ALTERNATIVE PROCEDURE UNDER PART 8

Part 8 provides an alternative procedure for use where the claimant seeks the court's decision 'on a question which is unlikely to involve a substantial dispute of fact' or where a practice direction permits or requires it (Part 8.1(2) and (6)). The procedure is therefore broadly similar to the old originating summons procedure and is suitable for claims turning purely on the construction of a document or on a point of law. The court may at any stage order that the claim should not proceed by the Part 8 procedure and allocate it to a track in the ordinary way (Part 8.1(3)).

The claimant must still issue a claim form but it must state that Part 8 applies and must provide the particulars set out in Part 8.2(b) – most importantly, it must state the question to be decided, or the remedy sought and the legal basis for it, and whether the claim is made under an Act.

If he wishes to be heard, a defendant must file an acknowledgment of service in response to a Part 8 claim (Part 8.3(1) and 8.4). However, a defence is not required and default judgment is not possible (Part 8.1(5)). Any written evidence on which a claimant relies is to be filed with the claim form (Part 8.5(1)). The defendant will either file his evidence in reply with his acknowledgment (Part 8.5(3)), or else will state in his acknowledgment why he considers the Part 8 procedure to be inappropriate (Part 8.8(1)).

All Part 8 claims are deemed to be allocated to the multi-track and Part 26 (allocation) does not therefore apply. Part 8.9 lists various other provisions of the Rules which do not apply to the alternative procedure.

There are two practice directions relating to Part 8. One is fairly short and is of general application to Part 8 claims. The other (which is much longer and of considerable intricacy) deals with a large number of different kinds of claims which will now proceed under Part 8. It details, in three Sections A, B and C, various matters including the particular claim form to be used, how the rules applicable to these proceedings may vary from the standard Part 8 model and so forth. Most of the proceedings in question are applications and appeals under the scheduled rules and it follows that a huge and disparate range of legal activity is covered. Frankly, the best one can do in a work of this sort is to exhort any reader who is about to commence Part 8 proceedings to read both practice directions with extreme care.

CHAPTER 10

RESPONDING TO A CLAIM
(PARTS 9, 10 AND 11)

Until a defendant receives particulars of claim, he need not do anything (Part 9.1(2)). However, once he is served with particulars of claim, he may do one of three things (Part 9.2):

(a) file a defence;

(b) file or serve an admission[1] (He may, of course, do both (a) and (b) if he admits only part of the claim); or

(c) file an acknowledgment of service.

If a defendant does *none* of these things within the relevant period, then a default judgment may be possible (Part 10.2).

It will be noted that these options are open to a defendant following service of particulars of claim. It follows that in most cases a defendant does not have to file an acknowledgment of service within a set period after the commencement of proceedings as he had to under the old regime. Indeed, a defendant does not have to file an acknowledgment of service at all. He will only do that if he is unable to file a defence within the appointed period, or if he wishes to dispute the court's jurisdiction (Part 10.1(3)).

Filing an acknowledgment does not involve losing any right to dispute the court's jurisdiction (Part 11.1(3)). On the contrary, in order to dispute jurisdiction, it is necessary, first, to file an acknowledgment and then to make an application within the period for filing a defence (Part 11.1(2) and (4)). Failure to make an application within that period will be treated as a submission to the jurisdiction (Part 11.1(5)).

It will be noted from the above account that one disadvantage of the new procedure is that, even in a case where a challenge to the jurisdiction is quite likely, a claimant cannot ordinarily avoid the expense of producing particulars of claim before learning for sure whether a challenge will be mounted. The

---

1   We do not consider Part 14, which deals with admissions. However, the reader should be aware that that Part deals not only with 'open-ended' judgment on admissions (Part 14.3) – where judgment will be such as 'it appears to the court that the applicant is entitled to on the admission' – but also contains an elaborate scheme for the obtaining of judgment on admissions in monetary claims. There are rules dealing with admissions of the whole of a claim for a specified amount of money (Part 14.4); with admissions of part of a claim for a specified amount (Part 14.5); with admissions of liability to pay the whole of a claim for an unspecified amount (Part 14.6); and with admissions of liability to pay a claim for an unspecified amount, where the defendant offers a sum in satisfaction (Part 14.7). Part 14 also deals with the resolution of arguments over time to pay.

position in the Commercial Court is totally different. Since challenges to the jurisdiction are there very common and since the preparation of complicated particulars of claim can be extremely expensive, the Commercial Court Guide provides that the defendant has to file an acknowledgment of service in all commercial cases – para B7.3 of the Commercial Court Guide.

CHAPTER 11

STATEMENTS OF CASE, AMENDMENTS AND FURTHER INFORMATION

LORD WOOLF'S PROPOSALS AND THE CPR

Lord Woolf said that the role of pleadings is 'to set out the facts relied upon so that the court and the parties can ascertain what the dispute is about and the court can take appropriate decisions about its management' (IR Chap 20, para 1). He felt that this basic function had been lost sight of. He therefore recommended a simplification both of the underlying rules and of the language used in pleadings. He also stressed the court's own role (as part of its case management responsibilities) in ensuring that the parties have plainly stated the factual ingredients of their case. He recommended that the procedural judge should scrutinise pleadings with that end in view and that the parties should produce a statement of the issues in dispute at any case management conference.

Though some of the details of Lord Woolf's proposals have been altered, these basic aims still underlie the new rules on pleadings as finally drafted.

The first point is that we no longer have 'pleadings'. The old word was felt to have 'acquired an unfortunate flavour of obfuscation rather than clarity' and the formal documents setting out the parties' respective cases are now known as 'statements of case'. However, the noun 'pleading' and the verb 'to plead' are both dying a slow death. In *McPhilemy v Times Newspapers* [1999] 3 All ER 775 – admittedly a transitional case – the Court of Appeal itself repeatedly referred to 'pleadings'. Certainly, nobody has yet found a satisfactory substitute for the verb.

The most common statements of case will now be the claim form, particulars of claim, defence (and counterclaim) and reply (and defence to counterclaim).[1] As before, no further statement of case will be possible without leave (Part 15.9).

We begin this chapter by considering some of the particular rules applicable to each of these common statements of case. We will then examine some more general features of the new rules on statements of case and various problems related to them. Finally, we will consider amendments and requests for further information. Accordingly, the structure of the chapter is as follows:

---

1   Part 20 claims (and defences) also fall within the definition of 'statement of case' – as also does any further information provided under Part 18 (Part 2.3(1)).

A Particular rules applicable to the common statements of case:

(i)   Claim form/particulars of claim.

(ii) Defence.

(iii) Reply.

B More general features of the new pleadings regime:

(i)   The system of verification by statements of truth.

(ii) The impact of the changes on pleading a defence.

(iii) The effect of the CPR on the art of pleading.

C Amendments.

D Further information.

We take each topic in turn.

A   PARTICULAR RULES APPLICABLE TO THE COMMON STATEMENTS OF CASE

A(i) Claim form/particulars of claim

Particulars of claim may either be contained in the claim form itself, or served with it, or served separately (Part 7.4(1)), but where practicable, the first course is to be adopted (PD16, para 3.1). If particulars of claim are served separately, that must be done within 14 days after service of the claim form and in any event, no later than the latest time for serving a claim form (Part 7.4(2)). (The position will not, therefore, be as it was under the old regime, when one could serve a writ just before it ceased to be valid and then wait a yet further period before serving a Statement of Claim. In the ordinary case, both the claim form and the particulars of claim will now have to be served within four months of the commencement of proceedings.)

The *particulars of claim* must:

(a) include a concise statement of the facts relied upon;

(b) state whether interest is claimed, and if so, the basis for and details of that claim;

(c) state whether aggravated or exemplary damages are claimed and if so, the grounds for such claim;

(d) state whether provisional damages are sought and if so, the grounds for such claim; and

(e) include such other matters as are set out in a practice direction. (Part 16.4(1).)

There are, of course, further detailed requirements in certain specific classes of case – for example, personal injury and fatal accident claims (see Chapter 26 below), actions for the recovery of land, mortgage and hire purchase claims.

Such requirements are set out in the practice direction.

Certain matters are required to be specifically pleaded by a claimant.[2] (PD16, para 9.2). These are:

(1) any allegation of fraud;

(2) the fact of any illegality;

(3) details of any misrepresentation;

(4) details of all breaches of trust;

(5) notice or knowledge of a fact;

(6) details of unsoundness of mind or undue influence;

(7) details of wilful default; and

(8) any facts relating to mitigation of loss or damage.

It is also worth setting out in full certain paragraphs of the practice direction that deal with the particulars to be provided of contractual claims:

8.3 Where a claim is based upon a written agreement:

(1) a copy of the contract or documents constituting the agreement should be attached to or served with the particulars of claim and the original(s) should be available at the hearing, and

(2) any general conditions of sale incorporated in the contract should also be attached (but where the contract is or the documents constituting the agreement are bulky this practice direction is complied with by attaching or serving only the relevant part of the contract or documents).

8.4 Where a claim is based upon an oral agreement, the particulars of claim should set out the contractual words used and state by whom, to whom, when and where they were spoken.

8.5 Where a claim is based upon an agreement by conduct, the particulars of claim must specify the conduct relied on and state by whom, when and where the acts constituting the conduct were done.

A(ii)   Defence

Unless the defendant files an acknowledgment of service (on which see Chapter 10), the usual period for filing a defence is 14 days after service of the

---

2   Surprisingly, despite the amendments to PD16, there are still no equivalent provisions relating to the pleading of these matters in a defence. This seems to us a continuing oversight. Furthermore, though a claimant is required by the practice direction specifically to set out any allegation of fraud, it does not expressly require him to give particulars of all facts and matters relied upon in support of that allegation. This clearly must, somehow or other, be required. By way of contrast, the Commercial Court Guide (para C1.2(d)) requires the pleading of 'full and specific details ... of any allegation of fraud, dishonesty, malice or illegality', including 'where an inference of fraud or dishonesty is alleged, the facts on the basis of which the inference is alleged'. Despite the non-specific terms of PD16, it is our view that such an approach will be followed generally, that is, outside as well as in the Commercial Court.

particulars of claim (Part 15.4(1)). The parties can agree to extend that period for up to 28 days but if so, the defendant must notify the court in writing (Part 15.5). As under the old rules, the period is also automatically extended in the case of an application for summary judgment.

A defence must say:

(a) which allegations in the particulars of claim the defendant denies – stating his reasons for doing so and giving any different version of events from the claimant's;

(b) which he admits; and

(c) which he is unable to admit or deny, but which he requires the claimant to prove. (Part 16.5(1) and (2).)

These, particularly the first, are important provisions and are considered in further detail in section B(ii) of this chapter. In addition, if the defendant disputes the claimant's statement of value, he must say so, giving his reasons and any competing estimate of the claim's worth (Part 16.5(6)).

The pleader of a defence is encouraged to deal specifically with each and every allegation in the particulars of claim through the basic preservation of the old rule that if a defendant does not deal with an allegation he is taken to admit it – Part 16.5(5). However, the severity of that rule is mitigated by Part 16.5(4), in relation to points of quantum in money claims, and by Part 16.5(3), in the case of the pleader who has, putting it broadly, 'tried hard'! Those rules read as follows:

(3) A defendant who –

(a) fails to deal with an allegation; but

(b) has set out in his defence the nature of his case in relation to the issue to which that allegation is relevant,

shall be taken to require that allegation to be proved.

(4) Where the claim includes a money claim, a defendant shall be taken to require that any allegation relating to the amount of money claimed be proved unless he expressly admits the allegation.

As before, any *counterclaim* will usually be contained in the same document as the defence, following on immediately after it. (Detailed provisions relating to counterclaims and third party proceedings are in Part 20 – see Chapter 12 below.)

A(iii) Reply

As under the old rules, a reply is not obligatory. Not to serve a reply is not an implied admission of matters in the defence – Part 16.7(1). Any defence to counterclaim will again follow on directly from the reply.

B   GENERAL FEATURES

We now turn to consider three more general features of the new regime on pleadings, namely:

(i)   the system of verification of statements of case by statements of truth;

(ii)   the impact of the changes on how to plead a defence; and

(iii) the effect of the CPR on certain of the old tenets of the art of pleading, in particular the apparent attrition of the old rule that one must plead facts but not the evidence by which those facts will be proved.

B(i)   Statements of truth

All statements of case now have to be verified by the party putting them forward or by his legal representative.

The aims of this vital provision are at least threefold.

First, it is desired that the pleading process and the attendant clarification of issues should be taken much more seriously than it often was under the old regime. One potent means of ensuring that pleadings are taken more seriously – and therefore that the issues are more accurately identified – is to require the parties themselves to approve the factual elements of the cases being advanced on their behalf, at an early stage and under pain of serious consequences if they lie. In short, statements of case will be the *parties'* documents, approved by them as affidavits always were and will not just be the lawyers' documents, as pleadings so often seemed to be under the old regime.

Linked to this is a second aim – that statements of case should be expressed in simpler terms than under the old regime and should concentrate on the facts, rather than on the making of elaborate technical pleas. After all, if a pleading is to be the client's document verified by him, it should (in terms both of language and substance) be in such a form that he *can* sensibly verify it.

Finally, in certain circumstances, the CPR allow a verified statement of case itself to be used as *evidence* of the matters it contains – that is to say, without the need for any separate verifying affidavit as used to be necessary under the old regime.

The statement of truth in relation to a statement of case must be signed by the party or his legal representative (Part 22.1(6)). The form of the statement of truth is '(I believe/The claimant or the defendant (or as appropriate) believes) that the facts stated in (these particulars of claim/this defence/ this whatever) are true'. To sign such a statement without an honest belief in the truth of the matters verified is a contempt of court, though proceedings for contempt may only be brought by the Attorney General or with the court's permission. (As to when such permission will be granted, see *Malgar Ltd v RE Leach Engineering Ltd* (2000) *The Times*, 17 February, Scott VC).

Where a lawyer signs, the statement of truth refers to his client's belief and not to his own (PD 22, para 3.7). It follows that (except in the rare case of the lawyer who involves himself in his client's dishonesty), it is the client – and not the lawyer who signs the certificate – who exposes himself to the risk of contempt proceedings if the client does not honestly believe in the truth of what is verified. Furthermore, where a lawyer signs, his signature is taken to mean not only that he is authorised to do so but also that he has explained to his client the significance of the statement of truth and the consequences of its being signed without an honest belief in the truth of the facts being verified (PD22, para 3.8).

There are detailed provisions dealing with the question of who may sign statements of truth on behalf of companies and corporations (PD22, paras 3.4 and 3.5); partnerships (PD22, para 3.6); and where insurers (or the Motor Insurers Bureau) are involved (PD22, para 3.6A). There are also non-binding examples of the possible application of these provisions in the case of managing agents, trusts, insurers, companies and in-house legal representatives (PD22, para 3.11).

If any statement of case is not verified in this way, then it remains effective unless struck out but it may not be relied upon as evidence (Part 22.1). Any party may apply to strike out an unverified statement of case (Part 22.2(2)).

The new rules on statements of truth may have an interesting side-effect. At least in the context of a single action, there has not in the past been anything strictly wrong with a litigant's running inconsistent cases. As Laddie J put it in the recent case of *Anderton v Hume* (1999) unreported, 12 November, Chancery Division):

> [Counsel submits that] there is nothing wrong in running inconsistent defences. Of course that is so. The difficulty with inconsistent defences is that they may put the defendant in an embarrassing position before the court in trying to reconcile them. But in theory there is nothing wrong with running inconsistent defences. There is, however, it appears to me, an enormous difference between running inconsistent defences in one court where one judge will have to decide which, if any, of those defences are right and running inconsistent claims or defences in two entirely different sets of actions before different courts.

However, the new system of verification should render it impossible for a litigant to run cases that are truly inconsistent even before one court. It will not, of course, prevent a litigant from advancing different legal analyses of a given factual situation – that will obviously continue – but it will prevent him from putting forward, even in the alternative, mutually inconsistent versions of events. There is no way that a party can, in one and the same breath, swear to the truth of two factually inconsistent versions of events.

B(ii) Pleading a defence under the CPR

Among the more ingenious provisions of the CPR are the new rules on how to plead a defence, or to be precise on the vexed business of admitting, denying and not admitting. The new provisions are contained, in narrow compass, in Part 16.5 but, if vigorously applied, they should – particularly when combined with the system of verification by a statement of truth – have far-reaching effects. In particular, they should, through the abolition of unparticularised 'bare denials', make the so called 'holding defence' a thing of the past and indeed serve to do away with unhelpful and ineloquent defences generally.

A party should *admit* an allegation in the same circumstances as before – that is to say when he knows it to be true. Once the defendant has admitted an allegation, then the claimant will not need to prove it.

In relation to *denials*, however, there are substantial changes. Under the CPR, if a party denies an allegation, he has to state his reasons for doing so and if he intends to put forward a different version of events from the claimant, must state his own version. Such a requirement could be very embarrassing for that kind of defendant who previously took every opportunity to string matters out, serving a defence full of bare denials in the hope that some advantageous opportunity for settlement might present itself before he actually had to commit himself to a positive case. Now, the need to give reasons for a denial – and the related need to verify those reasons – will bring forward the moment of truth.

Nor can such a defendant properly take refuge in merely *'not admitting'* an allegation. Whatever that formula may have meant under the old rules – and one suspects that in practice it was often abused – its meaning under the CPR is quite clear. If a party now says that he does 'not admit' an allegation, he is effectively saying (in the words of Part 16.5(1)(b)), that he is *'unable* to admit or deny [it]' and that he requires the claimant to prove it. The statement, express or implied, that he is *unable* – as distinct from unwilling – to admit or deny the particular allegation will, like all other statements of fact in the defence, have to be verified by a statement of truth. If it should subsequently emerge that the party was in truth perfectly able to deal with the allegation in question but was seeking for tactical reasons to avoid committing himself to a positive case, then in theory at least there would be a possibility of contempt proceedings against the verifying party.[3] In practice, however, especially since many such breaches will only become apparent at trial, it remains open to doubt how likely such contempt proceedings will be. Rather than spinning out a concluded action with contempt proceedings about the state of the pleadings,

---

3   In this regard, see also the Guidance from the Professional Standards Committee of the Bar Council on Part 16.5 and the 'tactical' use of non-admissions – Bar News No 121, March 2000.

a court indignant at a party's persisting with unjustified denials or non-admissions is, in most cases, more likely to have recourse to costs sanctions.[4]

B(iii) The effect of the CPR on the art of pleading

It remains presently unclear to what extent the CPR will alter some of the basic practices of the art of pleading. In the past, the most fundamental principle of pleading – deriving from the old RSC Ord 18 r 7(1) – was that one pleaded the material facts on which a party relied for his claim or defence but *not* the evidence by which those facts were to be proved. Furthermore, whilst the old rules did allow the pleading of law, in practice that was usually only done where not to plead the law in question might take the other side by surprise. To what extent do these basic tenets of the old approach to pleading still hold good?

On the face of it, both of these principles are now under attack. While (by Part 16.4) a claimant must still plead 'a concise statement of *the facts* on which (he relies)', there is no doubt that the CPR do *not* adhere to the strict demarcation line between facts and evidence that was embodied in the old rules and they also appear to adopt a rather more relaxed attitude to the pleading of law. Thus, PD16, para 14.3 contains a number of 'pleading options', which were originally expressed to apply only to claimants but which amendments to the practice direction have now made clear are available to pleaders generally. They read as follows:

A party may:
(1) refer in his statement of case to any point of law on which his claim or defence, as the case may be, is based,
(2) give in his statement of case the name of any witness he proposes to call, and
(3) attach to or serve with his statement of case a copy of any document which he considers is necessary to his claim or defence, as the case may be (including any expert's report to be filed in accordance with Part 35).

Apparently, therefore, a party can now refer to 'any point of law' on which his case is based. One can only ponder (doubtfully) whether this is to be taken as allowing references to authorities as well as to relevant statutory provisions. Certainly, one is clearly now entitled to plead (indeed, actually to attach) documentary evidence – para 14.3(3) – and to plead references to oral evidence – para 14.3(3). There is no express reference in the rules to the attaching of a summary of a witness's evidence (as there was in the original 'Brown Book' Woolf proposals) and it may be that the absence of any such

---

4   In this regard, see *Malgar Ltd v RE Leach Engineering Ltd* (2000) *The Times*, 17 February, Sir Richard Scott VC – confirming that the overriding objective applies to contempt proceedings under Part 32.14 as much as to any other proceedings.

reference was designed to discourage the development of any such practice. However, there is nothing in the rules to prevent a party's serving such a summary by separate letter and given the reference in para 14.3(3) to experts' reports, it might even be possible to read the practice direction as blessing the attachment of a particularly crucial witness summary or statement as being 'a document considered necessary to the claim or defence'.[5]

On the other hand, it is vital to appreciate that the provisions in PD16, para 14.3 are only permissive – they are, as we have said, options. The CPR do not require the pleading of law or evidence and in most situations, in our view, it will remain good practice to plead only those material allegations of fact which found the cause of action or defence and to give material particulars thereof, rather than to overload the pleading with references to relevant law or to the evidence, whether documentary or oral. Indeed, the principal authority so far to emerge on the post-CPR pleading regime seems, if anything, to tell in favour of sparser rather than fuller pleadings. Far from encouraging the inclusion of evidence in pleadings, certain observations in *McPhilemy v Times Newspapers Ltd* [1999] 3 All ER 775[6] could be said to favour a simplification of pleadings by 'trimming back' on what might previously have been regarded as material particulars and goes some way to suggesting that such particulars can be left until the witness statement stage. In that case, having lamented the cost and complexity of the pleadings in a particularly involved libel action, Lord Woolf said, at page 792j:

> The need for extensive pleadings including particulars should be reduced by the requirement that witness statements are now exchanged. In the majority of proceedings identification of the documents upon which a party relies, together with copies of that party's witness statements, will make the detail of the nature of the case the other side has to meet obvious. This reduces the need for particulars in order to avoid being taken by surprise. This does not mean that pleadings are now superfluous. Pleadings are still required to mark out the parameters of the case that is being advanced by each party. In particular they are still critical to identify the issues and the extent of the dispute between the parties. What is important is that the pleadings should make clear the general nature of the case of the pleader.

His Lordship went on to observe that excessive particulars could serve to obscure, rather than to clarify the issues, and could lead to fruitless but expensive tactical applications.

With these last observations, nobody could possibly quarrel. However, in our view, it is important to realise that Lord Woolf is not putting forward any invariable rule that particulars can now be relegated to the witness statements.

---

5   In passing, another possible qualification to the facts/evidence divide can be seen in PD 16, para 8.4 – pleading oral contracts – the text of which is set out above. This certainly infringes the facts/evidence divide if the reference to pleading 'the contractual words used' is taken as requiring any more than the pleading of the gist of the words used.

6   *McPhilemy* was applied by the Court of Appeal in *Tancic v Times Newspapers Ltd* (2000) *The Times*, 12 January.

Any such general rule could be a recipe for imprecision, procedural confusion and expense. It would be all too easy for the lazy or dishonest pleader to have recourse to the formula 'Full particulars will be provided in witness statements to be served later'. The purpose of pleadings is not simply to define the scope of the dispute for the judge's benefit at trial – they also define, for the benefit of the parties and their lawyers and (now) the case management judge, the scope of the necessary disclosure and the matters to be addressed in the witness statements. Obviously, at the end of the day, each case will involve a balancing exercise and the degree of particularisation required in a pleading will depend on the facts of the particular case. For example, in a simple running-down action, an account in a witness statement of what the witness actually saw and of how he viewed the defendant's driving is certainly likely to be more useful to all concerned than a lawyer's arcanely-expressed analysis of the quality of that driving in the particulars of claim. But in other contexts – say, an action for various breaches of warranty in a complex agreement for the sale of a company – full and precise particulars will be needed at a much earlier stage than the witness statements. One warranty may have been breached in 20 or 30 different ways, each breach leading to different heads of damage and requiring different evidential enquiries. Each of those breaches would have to be particularised in at least general terms, before disclosure could sensibly take place or the defendant's witness statements be prepared.[7]

Finally on this topic, it should be pointed out that the Commercial Court Guide takes a rather more traditional approach. Paragraph 12 of Appendix 4 to the Guide says baldly 'Evidence should not be included'; and paragraph C1.2(i) of the Guide emphasises that the permission to attach documents to pleadings is only that and should be regarded 'in the Commercial Court as applying only to obviously critical documents referred to in the particulars of claim and which are necessary for a proper understanding of the particulars of claim'. It is said to be 'possibly unlikely that an expert's report will be served with particulars of claim in the Commercial Court'. In short, anyone pleading in a Commercial Court action would be well advised to read the various variations to the basic CPR model that are contained in the Guide and its Appendices.

---

7   Though decided under the old rules, the judgment of the Court of Appeal in *Morris v Bank of America National Trust* [2000] 1 All ER 954 contains a number of important observations on pleadings under the new regime. It emphasises that 'the prolixity of the old pleading practices is to be a thing of the past' and certainly does not evidence any major sea change in relation to the pleading of evidence. On the contrary, dealing with allegations of dishonesty, it points out that while full particulars are required (including the facts on which any inference of dishonesty is alleged), 'this does not require or permit the recycling of pages and pages of evidence' (p 971j).

C AMENDMENTS TO STATEMENTS OF CASE (PART 17)

Amendments to any statement of case can be made without leave at any time before it has been served (Part 17.1(1)). After service, amendments can only be made with the written consent of all other parties or with the court's permission. Substantial amendments will, of course, have to be verified by a statement of truth (PD17, para 1.4). The practice as to whether and how to highlight amendments has been somewhat altered – see PD17, para 2.2 for the details.

In theory, there should be less need for amendments under the new regime – given, for example, increased pre-action preparation and the system of verification of the pleadings. Furthermore, at least in general terms, a court with an eye on robust case management should be much less likely to accede to last minute amendments, even where the amending party offers to bear the costs. Nevertheless, the jurisdiction to allow amendment is a flexible one and in appropriate circumstances can even be invoked after judgment – see *Charlesworth v Relay Roads Ltd* [2000] 1 WLR 230. The judgment of Neuberger J in that case contains a learned analysis of the competing arguments of principle that can arise on all applications to amend, as well as of the particular problems to do with applications after judgment.[8]

There are special rules governing amendments that add or substitute parties (Part 19), or that add or substitute new claims after the end of a relevant limitation period (Part 17.4).

D FURTHER INFORMATION (PART 18)

Requests for Further and Better Particulars and the Particulars themselves no longer exist as such. However, the court has power under Part 18 to order a party to 'clarify any matter in dispute' or to 'give additional information in relation to any such matter'. This power obviously covers what were previously Requests for Further and Better Particulars. However, it is important to note that it is expressly not restricted to the clarification of matters referred to in a statement of case, so that it seems likely also to be used for what were previously Interrogatories. Any response to a request for further information has to be verified by a statement of truth (PD18, para 3).

The related practice direction contains important observations on both the substance and form of Part 18 requests for further information. As to substance, they are to be 'concise and strictly confined to matters which are reasonably necessary and proportionate to enable the (requesting) party to

---

8   See, also, *Re Blenheim Leisure (Restaurants) Ltd (No 3)* (1999) *The Times*, 9 November, Neuberger J.

prepare his own case or to understand the case he has to meet' (PD 18, para 1.2). If vigorously implemented, this requirement may be the death-knell of lengthy and 'opponent-baiting' requests for particulars. The remarks of Lord Woolf in *McPhilemy* (set out above, in section B(iii) of this chapter) already evidence the courts' likely approach to the implementation of these provisions.

As to form, Part 18 requests are, as far as possible, to be in 'a single comprehensive document and not piecemeal' (PD18, para 1.3). They can be by letter or by separate document but there are specific provisions as to what must go in each. Responses can be either in the old Further and Better Particulars form (Request, Answer) or in a form that appears to be based on pre-contract enquiries (Question on the left hand side, Answer in box on right hand side).

If a party objects to complying with a request or part of it – or if he is unable to do so either timeously or at all – he must inform the requesting party promptly and certainly within the time appointed for a reply (PD18, para 4.1(1)). Reasons for the objection or inability to answer must be given – PD18, para 4.1(2). If a party simply fails to respond to a Part 18 request, he runs the risk that an application for an order will be made in his absence – PD18, para 5.5(1).

CHAPTER 12

PARTIES (PARTS 19 AND 20)

In their original form, Parts 19 and 20 both made provision for the involvement in a claim of persons other than the original parties to that claim. Part 19 dealt with the addition or substitution of parties, while Part 20 provided for counterclaims, third party proceedings and the like. However, with effect from 2 May 2000, the scope of Part 19 has been widened. Section I of that Part still deals with the addition and substitution of parties; but Section II now covers a number of topics, previously dealt with in RSC Ord 15 r 12 *et seq*, to do with representative parties and the like; and Section III contains new and important provisions concerning group litigation.

PART 19 (ADDITION AND SUBSTITUTION OF PARTIES; REPRESENTATIVE PARTIES; GROUP LITIGATION)

In general terms, the provisions of Part 19 are based on the policy that justice will be best achieved and the court's resources most efficiently applied where all the parties to a dispute are before the court and the court's decision is thereby binding upon them all. Thus, in Section I, broad provision is made for a party to be added to a claim where this is 'desirable' so as to resolve all matters in dispute in the proceedings, or to resolve a connected issue between an existing party and the new party (Part 19.2(2)). An obvious example would be where the dispute involves a contract binding more than two parties – either the claimant or the defendant might wish to add the other contractual parties to the action so as to bind them by the court's decision. The court also has a broad jurisdiction to remove an existing party (Part 19.2(3)). Substitution of a new party for an existing one is possible where the existing party's interest or liability has passed to the new party, or where such substitution is desirable so that the court can resolve the matters in dispute (Part 19.2(4)).

Part 19.3 deals with joint entitlement to a remedy. It requires a claimant who seeks a remedy to which some other person is jointly entitled with him to join all such other persons as parties. If any such person does not agree to be a claimant, then (unless the court orders otherwise) he must be joined as a defendant. This requirement protects the 'real' defendant to such an action, since it ensures that any judgment will bind all those who might be jointly entitled against him. The classic example is where two or more persons are jointly entitled to the payment of a debt but only one has sued.

Save where the claim form has not yet been served, the court's permission is required for the removal, addition or substitution of a party (Part 19.4(1)). Such permission can be sought either by an existing party or by the proposed new party. However, nobody may be joined as a claimant without his written consent being filed in court (Part 19.4(4)).

Part 19.5 gives effect to section 35 of the Limitation Act 1980, by permitting the addition or substitution of a party at a time when a relevant limitation period has expired. It permits such addition or substitution only if the limitation period was current when the proceedings were started and where addition or substitution is 'necessary'. The court can only be satisfied of such necessity in three situations, namely (1) where a new party is to be substituted for one who was named in the claim form by mistake for the new party;[1] (2) where the claim cannot be properly carried on by or against the existing party without the addition or substitution of the new party; and (3) where the original party has died or become bankrupt and his interest or liability has passed to the new party.

With effect from 2 May 2000, Section II of Part 19 contains the rules on *representative parties* – covering both the standard case of the representation of identified but numerous persons with the same interest (Part 19.6) and the more complicated situation of unborn or unascertainable persons with the same interest (Part 19.7). It also deals with the effect of the death of a party (Part 19.8) and with derivative claims brought by shareholders on behalf of a company. (All these matters were previously governed by the old rules in RSC Ord 15.)

Also with effect from 2 May 2000, Section III of Part 19 contains new provisions dealing with *Group Litigation*. The court can make a Group Litigation Order (known as a 'GLO') 'for the case management of claims which give rise to common or related issues of fact or law' (Part 19.10). Such issues, inevitably, are called the 'GLO issues'.

A GLO must contain directions about the establishment of a register on which the claims to be managed will be entered, must identify the GLO issues and must specify the court ('the management court') which will manage the claims. As can be imagined in a context where the rules are expressly catering for the running of an entire category of litigation, the managing court's powers of case management are extensive. It may, for example, vary the GLO issues; it may specify a date after which no new claim may be added to the

---

1   In *International Distillers & Vintners t/a Percy Fox & Co v JF Hillebrand (UK) Ltd* (1999) unreported, 17 December, David Foskett QC (sitting as a Deputy High Court Judge) rejected the suggestion that there was any conflict in this regard between the precise wording in relation to mistake of Part 17.4(3) and what is now Part 19.5(3)(a). He held further that the court's approach to determining an application under either provision had not changed materially since the introduction of the CPR, so that one might, in this context, have to look at old authorities. 'Doubtless only those authorities which truly illumine the court's path will be regarded as of importance. The odd glance in the rear-view mirror may, however, be necessary.' In section 9 of his judgment, he went on to refer to some of the old authorities dealing with mistake – especially *Ramsay and Maclain v Leonard Curtis (a firm)* (1999) unreported, 28 July, CA and *International Bulk Shipping & Services v Minerals & Metals Trading Corp of India* [1996] 1 All ER 1017, CA.

register without permission; it may appoint one firm of solicitors as 'lead solicitors'; and it may direct that one or more claims proceed to trial as test cases while all others are stayed (Part 19.13). This last provision is important since the judgment in a test claim will, *prima facie*, be binding on the parties to all other claims entered on the Group Register at the time of judgment – the court also having power to give directions as to the extent to which it will bind the parties to subsequently entered claims (Part 19.12).

The practice direction supplementing Section III of Part 19 contains important practical guidance as to when and how a GLO will be ordered; and as to how such litigation will proceed. It should be emphasised that they are not to be attempted lightly – for example, in the Queen's Bench Division the application is to be made to the Senior Master and no order can be made without the consent of the Lord Chief Justice.

PART 20 (COUNTERCLAIMS AND OTHER ADDITIONAL CLAIMS)

Part 20 seeks to promote the just and rapid resolution of related disputes – and incidentally to make the most efficient use of the court's own resources – by permitting the determination, in one action, of all issues arising between the original parties, as well as of those related issues which involve a third party. The awkward term 'Part 20 claim' is employed to describe all those claims which are parasitic to the Claimant's original claim and which are to be determined with it in the same action. A Part 20 claim is thus 'any claim other than a claim against a defendant' (Part 20.2). It therefore includes:

(a) a counterclaim by a defendant against the claimant or against the claimant and some other person;

(b) a claim by a defendant against any person (whether or not already a party) for contribution or indemnity or some other remedy; and

(c) where a Part 20 claim has been made against a person who is not already a party, any claim made by that person against any other person (whether or not already a party). [Part 20.2]

For most, though not all, purposes under the CPR, a Part 20 claim is treated as if it were a separate claim (see Part 20.3 as amended for full details).

The provisions of Part 20 make a distinction between counterclaims against the claimant (Part 20.4), counterclaims against persons other than the claimant (Part 20.5), a defendant's claim for contribution or indemnity against a co-defendant (Part 20.6) and any other Part 20 claim (Part 20.7). The provisions are complex and should be studied carefully. However, their general effect may be stated as follows.

A defendant may make a counterclaim against the claimant without permission of the court if he files it with his defence[2] (Part 20.4(2)(a)). Thereafter, permission will be required.

If the counterclaim is against a person other than the claimant, permission of the court is required (Part 20.5).

A defendant may make a Part 20 claim for contribution or indemnity against another defendant without permission and, it would seem, at any stage (Part 20.6). The procedure is simply to file a notice containing a statement of the nature and grounds of the claim and to serve a copy on the other defendant. Such claims can, of course, be made under the Civil Liability (Contribution) Act 1978, or pursuant to specific contractual provision.

As for all other Part 20 claims – most obviously, the traditional 'Third Party Notice' – they can be made without permission if issued before or at the same time as the defence is filed, but will otherwise require permission (Part 20.7). Particulars of the Part 20 claim must be contained in or served with the Part 20 claim.

Part 20.9 contains a list of the matters to which the court may have regard when deciding whether to give permission for a Part 20 claim, or whether to dismiss one, or whether to require it to be dealt with separately from the main claim. Unsurprisingly, the extent of any factual or legal overlap will be a significant factor. (PD20, para.2 contains further procedural guidance as to the making of applications for permission.)

Failure to file a defence to a counterclaim will render a claimant vulnerable to a default judgment – see Part 12.3(2).[3] Default judgments are also possible in relation to certain other types of Part 20 claim – see Part 20.11 for precise details.

The case management of Part 20 claims is dealt with in Part 20.13 and in PD20, para 5.

---

2   PD20, para 6 endorses the traditional practice of including Defence and Counterclaim in the one pleading. Similarly, the Defence to a Counterclaim is normally to be made in the same document as the Reply.

3   The same, it would seem, is intended to apply to counterclaims against persons other than the claimant – though Part 12.3(2), as amended, only refers to counterclaims made under Part 20.4, not to those made under Part 20.5.

CHAPTER 13

DEFAULT JUDGMENTS AND SETTING THEM ASIDE OR VARYING THEM

Default judgments are dealt with in Part 12 and the procedure for setting them aside or varying them in Part 13.

DEFAULT JUDGMENTS

In general terms under the new rules, a claimant may obtain a default judgment against a defendant who has failed to file an acknowledgment of service or a defence within the time allowed for doing so (Part 12.3(1) and (2)). Such a judgment may not be obtained in a claim for delivery of goods subject to an agreement regulated by the Consumer Credit Act, nor in any claim where the alternative Part 8 procedure is used, nor in certain other situations listed in the practice direction (Part 12.2). There are also other (less immediately apparent) exceptions of a 'procedural' kind set out in Part 12.3(3) – including the impossibility of a claimant's obtaining judgment in default where the defendant is applying to strike out or is exercising his newly-acquired right to apply for summary judgment under Part 24.

In some cases, default judgment may be obtained on the claimant's merely filing a request in the appropriate practice form (Part 12.4(1)). That is the case in money claims (either for a specified amount[1] or for an amount to be decided by the court) and in claims for delivery of goods where the defendant is given the alternative of paying their value. In other cases, however, an application to the court will be required. That is the case, for example, in relation to claims for declarations or injunctions; and in relation to claims for delivery of goods 'simpliciter'. An application is also required in certain other listed situations – including where the defendant has been served without leave outside the jurisdiction pursuant to the provisions of the 1982 Civil Jurisdiction and Judgments Act (Part 12.10). In mixed claims, the simple request procedure can still be pursued, provided that any claim that would require a hearing is abandoned (Part 12.4(3)).

A default judgment for a fixed sum of money may include any amount of interest which has been properly claimed in the particulars of claim (Part 12.6(1)). Otherwise, the court will award such interest as it sees fit (Part 12.6(2)). When entering a default judgment for an amount of money to be

---

1   The phrase 'a specified amount of money' in Part 12.4(1) seems wide enough to cover not only debts of a certain amount but also claims for damages where the claimant has put a fixed amount of damages in his claim form. In that latter situation, therefore, judgment in default for a fixed (effectively self-assessed) sum is now a possibility, just as it is in a debt claim.

decided by the court, the court can make directions, including directions for a 'disposal hearing' (as later assessment hearings are now known) – see PD26, para 12, especially 12.7 and 12.8, for the procedure.

A default judgment for money or the delivery of goods may be obtained on request against one of a group of multiple defendants and the claimant can then proceed against the others (Part 12.8(1)). However, in those cases where an application is required, default judgment will only be given against one of a number of defendants if the relevant claim can be dealt with separately from the claim against the other defendants. If it cannot, the application for a default judgment will have to be dealt with at the same time as the claim against the other defendants (Part 12.8(2)).

The CPR also contain a new procedure (in Part 12.9) for obtaining a default judgment for costs only. This usefully covers the situation where a recalcitrant debtor pays as soon as proceedings are issued but refuses, for some spurious reason, to pay the claimant's costs.

THE SETTING ASIDE OF DEFAULT JUDGMENTS

Part 13 draws a distinction between circumstances in which a default judgment must be set aside and circumstances in which the court has a discretion whether to set aside or vary.

The court is obliged to set a default judgment aside where it has been wrongly obtained, that is to say in circumstances where any of the preconditions to the obtaining of such a judgment have not been satisfied (Part 13.2). For example, a judgment in default of defence will have to be set aside where it has been obtained before the expiry of the time for service of a defence, or where the claimant had applied for summary judgment and so effectively extended the time for service.

Assuming, however, that a default judgment has been regularly obtained, the court may still choose to set it aside or vary it if, in the words of Part 13.3(1):

    (a) the defendant has a real prospect of successfully defending the claim; or

    (b) it appears to the court that there is some other good reason why –

        (i) the judgment should be set aside or varied; or

        (ii) the defendant should be allowed to defend the claim.

Whatever the position may have been under the old authorities, the words 'real prospect of successfully defending the claim' seem to put it beyond doubt that the relevant test for setting aside a regular default judgment is now the same as on an application for summary judgment (compare the wording in Part 24.2). The alternative ground, (b), which is clearly intended to be exceptional, again broadly corresponds to the wording of the summary judgment provisions and would cover, for example, any case where despite the weakness of the defence, there is some broader public interest justifying a trial.

It is worth highlighting the express provision (Part 13.3(2)) that the court must have regard to the promptness of any application to set aside. Given this provision, the defendant's evidence in support of an application to set aside should clearly attempt to explain any relevant delay. On the other hand, it is important to stress that delay is only one factor going to the exercise of the court's discretion. It may be worth citing certain *obiter dicta* of Brooke LJ in *McDonald v Thorn plc* (1999) *The Times*, 15 October, CA:[2]

> This court, in my judgment, would be doing nobody any service in seeking to reintroduce into the interpretation of these rules judgments of courts which were given under the old regime, insofar as the new regime has taken over from the old regime. I can see nothing in rule 13.3 or in the overriding objective in Part 1 to suggest that, if a defendant does not give a reason for the delay, that is somehow or other a knockout blow, on which a claimant is entitled to rely in support of an irresistible submission that there is no material on which the court can exercise its discretion in the defendants' favour.

> The fact that the defendants have given no reason for a delay is, of course, one of those matters which the court may wish to take into account if there is a long, unexplained delay, and if the claimants would be prejudiced if a judgment were set aside. This court should, however, in my judgment refrain from being prescriptive about the way Circuit Judges and District Judges in the exercise of their discretion should apply rule 13.3.

In *Rahman v Rahman* (1999) unreported, 24 November, His Honour Judge Boggis QC, sitting as a Deputy Judge of the Chancery Division, appears to have regarded four factors as relevant on applications to set aside, namely: the nature and strength of the defence; the period of and reason for any delay in applying to set aside; the prejudice that the claimant would suffer if judgment was set aside; and the overriding objective.

As with summary judgment, conditions may be attached when a judgment is set aside or varied (Part 3.1(3)).

One other practical point should be mentioned. It concerns the claimant who has purported to serve particulars of claim and who has subsequently entered a default judgment. If he 'subsequently has good reason to believe that the particulars of claim did not reach the defendant before (he) entered judgment', he *must* either file a request that the judgment be set aside or seek directions (Part 13.5). Furthermore, he is prohibited from taking any further step in the proceedings for the enforcement of the judgment until either the judgment has been set aside or the court has considered the directions application.

---

2   *McDonald v Thorn plc* was actually decided under the old rules. The *ratio* is that a defendant's pre-action, as opposed to post-judgment, delay is irrelevant on his application to set aside a default judgment.

CHAPTER 14

GENERAL RULES ABOUT APPLICATIONS FOR COURT ORDERS

Part 23 and the related practice direction will by now be bread and butter reading for all litigants. They contain the general rules about applications for court orders – dealing, for example, with such matters as the court to which an application should be made, the exceptional circumstances when an application can be made ex parte and so forth. Certain general points about the scope of Part 23 should perhaps be stressed:

(i)   Part 23 only contains the general rules for applications. Those rules are subject to any express provisions made elsewhere in relation to applications for particular orders.

(ii) Applications under Part 23 are not necessarily 'interlocutory' in the sense of being made in the course of an existing action. Applications to the court before proceedings are started can be made under Part 23 – for example, urgent applications for injunctions, or applications for pre-action disclosure under section 33 of the 1981 Supreme Court Act. Applications after judgment also fall under this Part.

(iii) Nor is Part 23 restricted to applications at first instance. Part 23 is also the basic method of making applications to the Court of Appeal, or to a single judge or the registrar thereof.

(iv) It should also be borne in mind that in general terms, the court is able to exercise its powers not only on application, but also of its own initiative (Part 3.3(1)). Furthermore, in certain situations, applications can and will continue to be made orally without service of any application notice – see PD23, paras 2.10 and 3.

(v)   Finally, it is also important to remember that the specialist practice directions and related Guides (Chancery Division,[1] Commercial Court, etc) can (and do) contain important variations on the basic Part 23 model. In those jurisdictions, therefore, an eye has to be kept firmly on the possibility of 'local variations'.

In these circumstances, one can do no more than generalise. Accordingly, we simply record that applications must usually be made by the filing and service of an 'application notice', the equivalent of the old summons (Parts 23.3 and 23.4). An application notice must state both the order the applicant is seeking and, briefly, why he is seeking it (Part 23.6). The general rule is that a copy of

---

1   See, also, *Practice Note (Chancery Division: Civil Procedure Rules)* (1999) *The Times*, 4 May, Neuberger J.

the application notice must be served as soon as practicable after it is filed (issued?) and, in any event, at least three days before the court is due to deal with the matter – compare, in this regard, the apparently divergent terms of Part 23.7(1) and PD23, para 4.1. The notice must be accompanied by a copy of any written evidence in support and by a copy of any draft order sought by the applicant (Part 23.7(3)).

An application will not necessarily result in a hearing, even if one is requested (Part 23.8). After all, dealing with a case without the parties needing to attend court is expressly part of 'active case management' (Part 1.4(2)(j)). In particular, applications may now be dealt with by telephone conference and PD23 sets out the obligations of the parties in relation to such conferences and the recording thereof.

The general rules on the filing and serving of evidence for applications to the court are also contained in the practice direction. The evidence relied upon (but not the exhibits) must now be filed with the court as well as being served on the parties (PD23, para 9.6). One important new feature to note is that an application can itself be used as evidence in support, provided that its contents have been verified by a statement of truth (PD23, para 9.7). The aim is to cut out the pointless expense of additional formal affidavits.

Part 23.10 deals with applications to set aside or vary orders made without notice (that is, orders made *ex parte*). Such applications normally have to be made within seven days of service of the order. However, in *Bua International Ltd v Hai Hing Shipping Co Ltd (The Hai Hing)* (2000) unreported, 14 January, Rix J held that on applications to discharge *ex parte* orders granting permission to serve out of the jurisdiction or to extend the time for service, the general seven days requirement in Part 23.10 was overridden by the specific provisions of Parts 10 and 11 which (if properly followed) effectively extend the time for making an application to dispute the jurisdiction to that allowed for filing a defence.

The court's power to proceed with an application when one party fails to attend is dealt with in Part 23.11. If an order results, the court has power, either on its own initiative or on application, to re-list the application and to hear it again (Part 23.11(2)). In *Riverpath Properties Ltd v Brammell* (2000) *The Times*, 16 February, Neuberger J held that this very flexible power could even be used to set aside an order which had been fulfilled.

More generally in relation to the 'revisiting' of interlocutory decisions before they are drawn up, one should mention the decision of Neuberger J in *Re Blenheim Leisure (Restaurants) Ltd (No 3)* (1999) *The Times*, 9 November. His Lordship said that the general principle was that it was undesirable to ask a court to reconsider an earlier decision unless there were strong reasons to do so. A non-exhaustive list of possible strong reasons was then given – including a party's failure to draw to the court's attention a fact or point of law that was plainly relevant or the discovery of new facts subsequent to judgment being given.

Finally, three other points in PD23 call for particular attention. First, paragraph 2.9 is an important element in the case management regime. It reads:

> The parties must anticipate that at any hearing the court may wish to review the conduct of the case as a whole and give any necessary case management directions. They should be ready to assist the court in doing so and to answer questions the court may ask for this purpose.

Secondly, paragraph 13 of the practice direction reminds us of the likely increased use of the court's powers to make a summary assessment of costs on interlocutory applications (see Chapter 24 below). Finally, we are also reminded that under the new rules, if an order makes no mention of costs, none will be payable in respect of the proceedings to which it relates. In other words, silence will *not* make costs 'in the cause' – each side will have to bear their own.

CHAPTER 15

SUMMARY JUDGMENT

LORD WOOLF'S PROPOSALS

Case management involves stopping a weak case from dragging on, and reducing complexity and cost by the gradual elimination of issues. Not surprisingly, therefore, Lord Woolf took the view that the court should exercise its powers of summary disposal on a wider basis than at present. He made proposals of both a structural and a substantive kind.

On the structural side, he recommended an enlarged and unified procedure for summary disposal, which would have replaced not only summary judgment and summary determination of points of law, but also the former rules on setting aside a default judgment and on striking out pleadings that showed no reasonable cause of action or defence. These structural proposals have *not* survived into the new rules, since there remain separate provisions on setting aside a default judgment (Part 13) and on striking out pleadings that disclose no reasonable grounds for bringing or defending a claim (Part 3.4).[1]

Lord Woolf's substantive proposals have survived rather better. He recommended:

(i)   That 'reverse Order 14s' should be possible – that is, that a defendant should be able to knock out an unmeritorious claim at an early stage without undue expense;

(ii) That the test for summary determination should be the same, whether it was raised at the behest of a claimant or a defendant, namely, that the opposing party had 'no realistic prospect of success' on all or part of his claim; and

(iii) That the court should be able to raise the question of summary determination of its own initiative.

---

1   There is obviously considerable overlap between the court's powers to give summary judgment under Part 24 and its powers to strike out statements of case under Part 3.4, particularly now that summary judgment is available to defendants as well as claimants. For a robust and interesting critique of this overlap, see Issue 10/99 of 'Civil Procedure News', where the CPR are in this regard characterised as being 'an unhappy mixture of old and new'.

THE NEW RULES ON SUMMARY JUDGMENT

Summary judgment is now covered by Part 24. It is defined as 'a procedure by which the court may decide a claim or a particular issue without a trial' (Part 24.1). It thus covers both points of fact and points of law such as might previously have been dealt with under RSC Ord 14A.

Summary judgment can be given against a claimant in any type of proceedings; and against a defendant in any type of proceedings except:

(a) proceedings for possession of residential premises against –

(i) a mortgagor; or

(ii) a tenant or a person holding over after the end of his tenancy whose occupancy is protected within the meaning of the Rent Act 1977 or the Housing Act 1988; and

(b) proceedings for an admiralty claim in rem; and

(c) contentious probate proceedings. [Part 24.3(2)]

It will be noted that even in these excluded cases there is nothing to stop the defendant from seeking summary judgment against the claimant.

There is no specific exclusion of claims in defamation, malicious prosecution or false imprisonment, as used to be the case under the old rules – though the possibility of a jury trial will doubtless often constitute a reason why summary judgment should not be given.[2] Nor is there any separate provision dealing with the seeking of a summary account, as used to be the case – such orders now fall within the general provisions of Part 24.

The question of summary judgment can, of course, be raised by the court as well as by a party, though the court will give the parties an opportunity to be heard before entering judgment. Unless the court gives permission, a claimant cannot apply for summary judgment until a defendant has responded to the claim by filing either an acknowledgment of service or a defence (Part 24.4(1)). (If the defendant does neither of these, then default judgment is the obvious route to adopt.) If a claimant applies for summary judgment before service of a defence, then time for service of that pleading is automatically extended (Part 24.4(2)). On the other hand, there is nothing to stop a *defendant* seeking summary judgment on the claimant's claim against him even before filing an acknowledgment of service or a defence. A defendant's so applying effectively stays the action until the hearing of his application, since default judgment is not possible when such an application has been made – see Part 12.3(3)(a).

---

2 In defamation proceedings, the appropriate course will presumably often be an application for summary disposal under sections 8 and 9 of the 1996 Defamation Act – on which see, now, Part 53.2 and PD53, para 5.

Part 24 applications will ordinarily have to be supported by evidence. Under the new system, that will usually be by witness statements (rather than by affidavits) and/or by a verified statement of case. The precise timetable for the service and filing of evidence is set out in Parts 23 and 24.5. The new 'formal' requirements for the claimant's evidence (that is, the equivalent of the old 'verily believe that there is no defence to this action') are in PD24, para 2(3).

As to the test to be applied by the court, it is now intended 'that the test for summary judgment should be easier for applicants to satisfy than the current test under the (old) rules' (IR chap 6, para 21). A case that is merely 'arguable' will not suffice to resist judgment. Summary judgment can now be given if:

(a) [the court] considers that –

    (i) that claimant has no real prospect of succeeding on the claim or issue; or

    (ii) that defendant has no real prospect of successfully defending the claim or issue; and

(b) there is no other reason why the case or issue should be disposed of at a trial. [Part 24.2]

The second limb of this test, that is, (b), reproduces the old position under Ord 14 and might apply, for example, to cases where, whatever the merits, there is some general public interest in a full trial. However, it is clearly intended to be exceptional and in general terms, summary judgment is now a possibility in any situation where a party has 'no real prospect of succeeding' on a claim or issue. It is probably wiser not to attempt to gloss these words. A previous attempt to do so – indeed one as authoritative as that contained in the original paragraphs 4.1 and 4.2 of PD24 itself – led to considerable confusion and an apparent conflict with the terms of Part 24.2 itself. The consequence was that the offending paragraphs of the practice direction were deleted, the Court of Appeal taking the opportunity to advertise their disappearance in the personal injuries case of *Swain v Hillman* (1999) *The Times*, 4 November. Lord Woolf there said that Part 24.2 gave the court a very salutary power to dispose summarily of claims or defences which had 'no real prospect of succeeding'. Those words did not need any amplification, since they spoke for themselves. The word 'real' directed the court to see whether there was a realistic, as opposed to a fanciful, prospect of success. As before, of course, an application for summary judgment will be inappropriate where there are vital disputes of fact.

The options open to the court on the hearing of an application for summary judgment are orders for:

(a) judgment on the claim;

(b) the striking out or dismissal of the claim;

(c) the dismissal of the application;

(d) a conditional order. [PD24, para 5.1]

A conditional order is one requiring a party to pay a sum of money into court (or to take some other step in relation to his claim or defence) and providing that his claim will be dismissed or his statement of case struck out if he does not comply. The practice direction expressly states that orders for 'unconditional (or conditional) leave to defend' will no longer be made – the equivalent orders would now presumably be (c) and (d) above. Following the determination of a summary judgment application, the court is once again given a general power to 'give further directions about the management of the case' (Part 24.6(b)).

Despite a general probability that the court will in future be more willing to grant summary judgment than hitherto, it seems to us that trigger-happy and over-enthusiastic applications are, if anything, likely to be even more dangerous than previously. First, given the new system of verifying statements of case, any application under Part 24 after defence will effectively have to challenge the defendant's statement of truth. Secondly, the court's rejecting an application under the new test of 'no real prospect of success' may well only serve to fuel an opponent's enthusiasm for his own case. Thirdly, an unduly aggressive claimant may not only fail to obtain summary judgment or the imposition of a conditional order, but – given the possibility of 'reverse Order 14s' – may even end up having to pay money into court as a condition of continuing with his own claim! Even where a claimant is successful, the recoverable costs in money claims are *prima facie* fixed and are extremely low (see in this regard Part 45).

CHAPTER 16

INTERIM REMEDIES AND SECURITY FOR COSTS

All interim (farewell 'interlocutory'!) remedies are now dealt with in Part 25. With effect from 2 May 2000, applications for security for costs also fall within this Part but are dealt with in a separate Section II.

INTERIM REMEDIES

In general terms, Part 25 is of interest not so much because the remedies mentioned are particularly new, whether in terms of substance or procedure, but because they are all now drawn together and dealt with comprehensively in one place. It constitutes an excellent example of the move towards simplification that underlies much of the CPR.[1]

The most familiar of the old interim remedies are listed in Part 25.1(1). So also are some newcomers. Thus, interim injunctions, orders for the custody or inspection of property, for the taking of samples, for delivery up of goods, freezing injunctions (farewell 'Marevas'!) and related disclosure orders, search orders (farewell 'Anton Piller's'!), interim accounts and many other long-used remedies are all here listed. So too are interim declarations, hitherto regarded as a legal impossibility. Furthermore, this list of remedies is not necessarily exhaustive. It is expressly provided that the fact that a particular kind of interim remedy is not listed does not affect any power that the court may have to grant it (Part 25.1(3)). New manifestations of the court's inherent jurisdiction and any other statutory powers (old or new) are thus preserved.

Applications for interim remedies may be made at any time, including before proceedings are started and after judgment has been given (Part 25.2(1)). However, interim relief will only be granted before a claim has been made, if the matter is urgent or if it is otherwise necessary to do so in the interests of justice. Without leave, a defendant is not able to apply for any of the listed remedies before he has filed an acknowledgment of service or a defence (Part 25.2(2)).[2]

---

1   In Chapter 14 above, we examined the general rules on applications for court orders as set out in Part 23. Part 25 (Interim remedies) deals with a major category of such orders, covering both the court's jurisdiction to grant particular remedies and the relevant procedure for applying for them. As far as procedure is concerned, the 'Part 23 application' remains the basic model but Part 25 also details specific procedural requirements in respect of certain particular interim remedies. Furthermore, in the Chancery Division, Commercial Court or other specialist jurisdictions, care must be taken (as always) to establish whether some particular local variation applies.

2   Contrast the position in relation to a defendant's application for summary judgment on the claimant's claim against him – which can be made at any point after proceedings have been started (see Chapter 15 above).

Interim remedies in aid of foreign proceedings are also covered by this Part (Part 25.4(1)).

Part 25 also contains elaborate, though not startlingly different, provisions on interim payments. As before, it is expressly provided (Part 25.7(4)) that the court must not order an interim payment of 'more than a reasonable proportion of the likely amount of the final judgment', taking account of contributory negligence and of any relevant set-off or counterclaim. As to interim payments in cases of multiple defendants and the problem previously identified in *Breeze v McKennon (R) & Sons* [1985] Build LR 41, see the section on interim payments in Chapter 26 below.

There are specific practice directions dealing with interim payments, with interim accounts and inquiries, and with interim injunctions. The last of these contains detailed provisions on applications for freezing and search orders – and examples of such orders.

SECURITY FOR COSTS

Security for costs was originally dealt with in RSC Ord 23, a scheduled rule. However with effect from 2 May 2000 and, as a result of SI 2000/221, it will be dealt with in Section II of Part 25.

The relevant provisions have been much simplified. They are drafted in terms of a defendant seeking security for his costs but they will, by virtue of Part 20.3, apply equally to a claimant who seeks security for the costs of resisting a counterclaim. (Nor will it be forgotten that the court has broader powers to order a party to make a payment into court under Part 3.3 and 3.5.)

The central jurisdictional provision in relation to security is Part 20.3. It says that the court may require security if 'it is satisfied having regard to all the circumstances of the case that it is just to make such an order' and when either an enactment permits the court to require security or one or more of certain specified conditions are satisfied. These conditions, or grounds, are listed in Part 25.13(2) and call for careful consideration.

Certain of these grounds are easily recognisable from the old RSC Ord 23 – such as the claimant whose address is not given, or not given correctly, in the claim form (condition (e));[3] the claimant who changes his address in the course of the litigation with a view to evading its consequences (condition (d)); and the nominal claimant who seems unlikely to be able to pay the defendant's costs (condition (f)).

---

3   There is no express exclusion, as there used to be, for innocent mistakes, but the reasons for the omission or misstatement of the claimant's address will, of course, constitute part of the overall circumstances to which the court must have regard.

Condition (g) is wholly new but is clearly influenced by Mareva-type thinking. It is that the claimant has 'taken steps in relation to his assets that would make it difficult to enforce an order for costs against him'.

However, the conditions calling for most comment are the first three, which deal with what one could loosely term foreign claimants and companies. It is not impossible to understand these provisions without reference to earlier case law and the courts will no doubt hold that as a matter of principle such reference is unnecessary and inappropriate. Nevertheless, these three conditions have clearly been drafted with earlier authorities in mind and it therefore seems appropriate briefly to provide some pointers, if only to assist anyone who finds them confusing.

Condition (a) is that:

> the claimant is an individual –
>
> (i)   who is ordinarily resident out of the jurisdiction; and
>
> (ii) is not a person against whom a claim can be enforced under the Brussels Conventions or the Lugano Convention, as defined by section 1(1) of the Civil Jurisdiction and Judgments Act 1982.

This condition appears to codify, in the words of the rule itself, the effect of the Court of Appeal's decision in *Fitzgerald v Williams* [1996] 2 All ER 171. In that case – and following the effect of the decision of the European Court of Justice in *Mund & Fester v Hatrex International Transport* [1994] ECR I-467 (Case C398/92) – Lord Bingham MR held that the English court should never exercise its discretion (under RSC Ord 23 r 1(1)(a)) to order security to be given by an individual plaintiff who is a national of and resident in another member state party to the Brussels Convention. Given the terms of the new rule, we will no longer have to read an apparently unfettered discretion in the light of complicated case law dealing with how that discretion should be exercised in the light of European law dealing with discrimination on the grounds of nationality. The second limb of condition (a) itself 'incorporates' the effect of that previous learning, so that (with any luck) we will not have to go beyond the words of the rule itself.[4]

In the past, in relation to an individual English plaintiff, mere impecuniosity was never in itself a ground for ordering security, for the simple reason that poverty should bar no one from access to the courts. The practical effect of *Fitzgerald* was, in most cases, to apply that logic equally to individual claimants from Brussels/Lugano Convention countries – it making no difference to the logic of the *Fitzgerald* decision whether an Irish or French

---

4   More generally, as to the present practice on ordering security for costs against a claimant ordinarily resident abroad, see *Leyvand v Barasch* (2000) *The Times*, 23 March, Lightman J (a decision, obviously, under the old Ord 23). His Lordship said that the old 19th century authorities were 'a distraction and should not be cited'.

claimant was rich or poor. We say 'in most cases' because Lord Bingham did add a proviso to the general effect of his judgment. He said:

> ... the English court should never exercise its discretion under [RSC Ord 23 r 1(1)(a)] to order security to be given by an individual plaintiff who is a national of and resident in another member state party to the Convention, *at any rate in the absence of very cogent evidence of substantial difficulty in enforcing a judgment in that other member state.* [Our emphasis]

His Lordship recognised that this qualification might or might not be sound in Community law. In the event, the terms of the new rules on security do not appear to give any room for the operation of such a qualification – save perhaps in circumstances where it might be justifiable under the new asset-manipulation ground (ground (g)), already mentioned above. There should be no question of discrimination in such circumstances since ground (g) applies equally to all claimants.

Condition (b) is the logical equivalent of (a) in relation to companies:

> the claimant is a company or other incorporated body –
>
> (i)   which is ordinarily resident out of the jurisdiction; and
>
> (ii) is not a body against whom a claim can be enforced under the Brussels Conventions or the Lugano Convention.

It follows that foreign residence can, in itself, be used as a ground for ordering security to be provided by, say, an Afghan company, but not by a French company. Even in the former case, of course, the decision whether to order security in any particular case will depend on all the circumstances.

Before the CPR, the position of the insolvent English corporate plaintiff was different from that of the insolvent English individual plaintiff – insolvent English companies could be ordered to provide security under section 726(1) of the 1985 Companies Act. It was the existence of this statutory jurisdiction as against English companies which led the Court of Appeal to hold, in *Chequepoint SARL v McClelland* [1997] 2 All ER 384, that it could not be discriminatory for security to be ordered against an impecunious foreign company ordinarily resident in a member state of the European Community. Such equality of treatment is now preserved in condition (c) of the new rules. It applies to all companies, wherever incorporated,[5] and reads as follows:

> the claimant is a company or other body (whether incorporated inside or outside the United Kingdom) and there is reason to believe that it will be unable to pay the defendant's costs if so ordered.

Security for the costs of appeals is dealt with in Part 25.15. The grounds are, at least broadly, the same as those already considered. We confess ourselves

---

5   Presumably, as against an insolvent English company, a defendant can now apply both under section 726 and on ground (c). However, the point seems academic. The wording of the new condition appears also to resolve the two anomalies referred to by Lord Bingham MR in *Chequepoint SARL v McClelland* [1997] 2 All ER 384, at p 390a–b.

unclear as to what is achieved by Part 25.15(2), since it is not obviously any broader than condition (c) in Part 25.13(2). It *may* be that it is intended to refer to the appellant's inability to pay not merely the applicant's costs but also the costs of other parties to the appeal. (As to the Court of Appeal's likely approach to security for the costs of appeals post-CPR, see *Federal Bank of the Middle East Ltd v Hadkinson* (1999) *The Times*, 7 December.)

Finally, there is provision in Part 25.14 for a defendant to seek *security for costs from persons other than the claimant*. One's initial instinct is that an application under this rule would be a preparatory step towards an application under Part 48.2 – that is, under section 51(3) of the Supreme Court Act 1981 and the *Symphony Group plc v Hodgson* jurisdiction (see Chapter 24 below). Indeed, the explanatory note following Part 25.14 cross-refers to Part 48.2. However, it should be noted that there are important distinctions. First, the Part 48.2 power to order a non-party to pay costs can (regardless of any complications to do with counterclaims) be invoked by either claimant or defendant – whereas the Part 25.14 power to order security to be provided by a non-party can only be invoked by a defendant (or by a claimant seeking security in respect of the costs of resisting a counterclaim). Secondly, and importantly, the circumstances in which security can be ordered under Part 25.14 are limited, so that the power only covers certain of the situations in which the court might, in due course, be persuaded to exercise its jurisdiction under Part 48.2. In addition to a general requirement that an order should be just in all the circumstances of the case, one or more of certain specified conditions has to be satisfied. They are that the person against whom security is sought:

(a) has assigned the right to the claim to the claimant with a view to avoiding the possibility of a costs order being made against him; or

(b) has contributed or agreed to contribute to the claimant's costs in return for a share of any money or property which the claimant may recover in the proceedings, and

is a person against whom a costs order may be made. [Part 25.14(2)]

CHAPTER 17

DISCLOSURE AND INSPECTION OF DOCUMENTS

THE BACKGROUND – LORD WOOLF'S PROPOSALS ON DISCOVERY AND THE EXTENT TO WHICH THEY WERE ADOPTED

Lord Woolf accepted the basic desirability of discovery, 'because of its contribution to the just resolution of disputes'. However, he was scathing about the cost and ineffectiveness of the existing system. He felt that two factors had combined to transform discovery into a hugely complicated and expensive exercise, often producing little of real evidential utility. The first factor was the sheer weight of paper in modern life – much of it the pointless progeny of a continuing love affair between lawyers and the photocopier. The second factor was the extended meaning of 'relevance', as laid down in the case of *Compagnie Financière du Pacifique v Peruvian Guano Co* (1882) 11 QBD 55. As the old White Book note put it:

> [Relevant documents] are not limited to documents which would be admissible in evidence ... nor to those which would prove or disprove any matter in question: any document which, it is reasonable to suppose, contains information which may enable the party applying for discovery either to advance his own case or to damage that of his adversary, or if it is a document which may fairly lead him to a train of inquiry which may have either of these two consequences must be disclosed.

The result was a discovery process that was 'monumentally inefficient', especially in the larger cases. And, as Lord Woolf put it, 'The more conscientiously it is carried out, the more inefficient it is'. He concluded that the benefit of discovery would only outweigh the disadvantages 'if substantially greater control over the scale of discovery is exercised than at present'. The solution was to find a satisfactory form of control and then to ensure that it was enforced.

Lord Woolf's own proposals hinged on the distinctions between four different categories of documents:

(1) A party's own documents, on which he relied in support of his contentions;

(2) Adverse documents, being documents of which a party was aware and which to a material extent adversely affected his own case or supported another party's case;

(3) The relevant documents, being documents which did not fall into category (1) or (2), because they did not obviously support or undermine

either side's case, but which were nevertheless part of the 'story' or background;

(4) Train of enquiry, or *Peruvian Guano*, documents.

Lord Woolf termed disclosure of documents in categories (1) and (2) 'standard discovery' and of documents in (3) and (4) as 'extra discovery'. He proposed that on the fast track only standard discovery should usually be allowed. On the multi-track, the breadth of discovery should vary according to the circumstances of a particular case. Only extremely rarely – say in dishonesty cases – would *Peruvian Guano* discovery be ordered. Furthermore, just as a judge might have a rolling programme for resolving issues, so Lord Woolf envisaged that he might order a rolling programme for discovery, possibly with different standards of discovery applying to different issues. What was to be avoided 'at all costs' was uncontrolled discovery of the sort that previously took place.

Some of the vocabulary of Lord Woolf's proposals survived into the CPR. So also did the overall spirit of attempting substantially to reduce the quantity of documents with which the parties and the court are required to deal. However, in one important respect, Lord Woolf's proposals did *not* survive and it is as well to highlight it at once. This concerned the test for limiting discovery. Lord Woolf was himself aware of the problem. In IR chap 21, paras 33–34, he said:

> It is essential to the controlled approach which I am recommending to be able to make a functional distinction between documents which are adverse (category 2) and those which are merely 'relevant' (category 3). The core of the problem is that conscientious lawyers and their clients might feel obliged to trawl through all category 3 documents in order to eliminate the possibility of overlooking category 2 documents. To do so would defeat the aims of controlled discovery. It is therefore necessary to find a practical test by which to limit the search for category 2 documents. The Bar in its submission suggested that initial disclosure should be confined to documents which are 'capable of being located without undue difficulty and expense'. I support the sense of this but would formulate the test in a slightly different way by saying that initial disclosure should apply to documents of which a party is aware at the time when the obligation to disclose arises.

In the event, the CPR do *not* link their definition of 'standard disclosure' to the disclosing party's actual knowledge in the way suggested by Lord Woolf. Rather, in their concept of a 'duty of reasonable search', the CPR return to the general spirit of the Bar's submission referred to in the above quotation.

DISCLOSURE BETWEEN PARTIES TO EXISTING PROCEEDINGS

The disclosure (new-speak for 'discovery') and inspection of documents are now dealt with in Part 31. That Part does not apply to the small claims track.

In the computer age, the definitions of 'document' and of 'copy' merit immediate emphasis:

In this Part –

'document' means anything in which information of any description is recorded; and

'copy', in relation to a document, means anything onto which information recorded in the document has been copied, by whatever means and whether directly or indirectly. [Part 31.4]

A party 'discloses' a document by stating that it exists or has existed (Part 31.2). However, unless the court orders otherwise, an order to give disclosure is an order to give *standard disclosure* (Part 31.5(1)). Even standard disclosure can be limited or dispensed with altogether, either by written agreement between the parties or by order. Standard disclosure is defined by Part 31.6 as follows:

Standard disclosure requires a party to disclose only –

(a) the documents on which he relies; and

(b) the documents which –

(i) adversely affect his own case;

(ii) adversely affect another party's case; or

(iii) support another party's case; and

(c) the documents which he is required to disclose by a relevant practice direction.

The duty to disclose is limited to documents which are or have been in a party's 'control', which is a defined expression (Part 31.8(2)). Only one copy of any document need be disclosed – though copies bearing significant modifications, marks or the like will count as separate documents (see Part 31.9). Disclosure may also be in stages (Part 31.13), a power which will doubtless be invoked when the court orders separate trials of different issues.

The definition of standard disclosure is supplemented by a party's duty 'to make a *reasonable search* for documents falling within rule 31.6(b) or (c)' (Part 31.7). Put at its simplest, this means that a party not only remains obliged to disclose unhelpful documents but that he may be obliged to search them out. The factors relevant in deciding the reasonableness of a search include the number of documents involved, the nature and complexity of the proceedings, the ease and expense of retrieval and the significance of any document likely to be found (Part 31.7(2)). The practice direction on disclosure and inspection exhorts the parties to bear in mind the overriding principle of proportionality and states by way of example, that it may be reasonable to decide not to search for documents coming into existence before a particular date, or to limit the search to documents in some particular place, or to documents in a particular category (PD31, para 2).

The procedure for disclosure by lists (Part 31.10) is basically familiar. A party is still required to list documents no longer in his control and to state what has become of them. However, there is one important new feature which should be highlighted, namely, the requirement that a list should include a *'disclosure statement'*. This is a statement made by the disclosing party setting out the extent of the search that has been made and certifying that he understands his duty of disclosure and that to the best of his knowledge he has carried out that duty (Part 31.10(6)). In the case of a statement given by a company, firm or other organisation, there must also be an identification of the person making the statement and an explanation of why he is an appropriate person to give it (Part 31.10(7)). The disclosure statement must expressly state that the disclosing party believes the extent of the search to have been reasonable in all the circumstances. In the event that he has not searched for a particular category of document because he takes the view that it would be unreasonable to do so, his disclosure statement will have to explain that fact and identify the category of document (see Part 31.7(3)). The same is true of any other limitations adopted for reasons of proportionality (PD31, para 4.2). Legal representatives are required to endeavour to ensure that the person signing the disclosure statement understands the duty of disclosure (PD31, para 4.4). Contempt proceedings can be brought against a person who makes a false disclosure statement without an honest belief in its truth, though only by the Attorney General or with permission of the court (Part 31.23).

Any duty of standard disclosure continues until the proceedings are concluded (Part 31.11). Supplemental lists of documents are therefore likely to continue to be commonplace (PD31, para 3.3). Furthermore, since the duty to make a reasonable search is one aspect of the duty of standard disclosure, it follows that more than one search may be required in the course of proceedings, perhaps even at a very late date. Nor (obviously) can there be any sitting on the fruits of any search. Apart from the relevant professional obligations, it is expressly provided that 'If documents to which (the duty of disclosure) extends come to a party's notice at any time during the proceedings, he must immediately notify every other party' (Part 31.11(2)).

The limited system of 'standard disclosure' is likely to be the norm even on the multi-track. However, Part 31.12 gives the court power to order *specific disclosure*. This is not necessarily an order for the disclosure of specific documents or classes of documents. The court may also direct the carrying out of a specified search and the disclosure of any documents located as a result. In theory, the power to order specific disclosure could be used to order full-scale old-fashioned discovery. In practice, however, that will be very unlikely in most cases.[1] If the new system functions well, the court and the parties

---

1   The position is rather different under the new Commercial Court Guide. Commercial cases may often call for more 'old-fashioned' disclosure orders. Both there and generally, however, the most obvious candidates for *Peruvian Guano*-style orders will be fraud cases and other cases involving issues of knowledge, misrepresentation or non-disclosure.

should co-operate at case management conferences to limit disclosure to a sensible scale proportionate to the value of the case, the parties' means and so forth. So much is, of course, implicit in the overriding objective.

What the new Rules essentially seek to achieve in relation to discovery is, of course, a change in attitude. One no longer needs to disclose every piece of paper which might just conceivably have some tangential relevance to some minor aspect of the case. Nor should time and money necessarily have to be spent in the search for aged files of doubtful relevance. On the other hand, a party does still have to disclose documents adverse to his own claim and is required to carry out a reasonable search for such documents. As the new regime beds down, the courts are increasingly likely to take the view that a well-prepared litigant will have done precisely that before even threatening proceedings in the first place.

In theory at least, disclosure under the new rules needs to be a far more reflective procedure than previously. It should no longer be possible to delegate the task of disclosure to some fresh-faced paralegal who has little or no understanding of the underlying issues in the case. Indeed, anyone who adopts such an approach and gives unnecessarily generous disclosure as a result is quite likely not to recover the costs of doing so.

The old Ord 24 r 10 (inspection of documents referred to in pleadings and affidavits) is effectively reproduced in the new Part 31.14. It also extends to documents referred to in witness statements, witness summaries and (to some extent) experts' reports.

Part 31.20 provides that:

> Where a party inadvertently allows a privileged document to be inspected, the party who has inspected the document may use it or its contents only with the permission of the court.

This is a slightly strange provision. The old rules on the mistaken disclosure of privileged documents were set out in the judgment of Aldous J in *IBM Corp v Phoenix International (Computers) Ltd* [1995] 1 All ER 413. The gist of that decision (and of earlier higher authority) was that while generally a litigant ought to be able to rely on the discovery of his adversary, the court had an equitable jurisdiction to grant an injunction restraining the recipient from making use of privileged material that had been disclosed. That jurisdiction would be exercised in cases of fraud and of 'obvious mistake'. A mistake was 'obvious' if it was in fact apparent to the recipient or if it would have been evident to the ordinary reasonable solicitor. The continuing authority of these principles was recently recognised by the Court of Appeal in B*reeze v John Stacey & Sons Ltd* (1999) unreported, 21 June. All three Lords Justices expressly said that the principles had not been affected by the recent introduction of the CPR.

Part 31.20 was not referred to in *Breeze v Stacey* – perhaps because it was not a case on inadvertent disclosure and inspection but on the inadvertent exhibiting of privileged material to an affidavit. However, Part 31.20 would appear, at least within its particular sphere, to have made one procedural change. In the past, if there was debate over whether a mistake was 'obvious', the procedural initiative lay with the sender of the document in question – unless he sought and obtained an injunction, the receiving party would be free to use the document as he saw fit. Now, however, the mere assertion of a mistake would seem to put the initiative on the receiving party – unless he obtains the leave of the court under Part 31.20, he may not use the document. Nevertheless, it is difficult to imagine that that question of leave will be decided by any criteria other than those that were approved and applied in *Breeze v Stacey* and *IBM v Phoenix*.

The new rules contain express provisions about the use of undisclosed and disclosed documents. Unsurprisingly, if a party has not disclosed or allowed inspection of a document, then he may not rely upon it without the court's permission (Part 31.21). As to the use by the receiving party of documents which have been disclosed, Part 31.22 now contains a 'mini-code', effectively covering the same ground as the old implied undertaking that disclosed documents would not be used other than for the purposes of the instant litigation, save by consent or with leave of the court. Part 31.22(1) now reads:

> A party to whom a document has been disclosed may use the document only for the purpose of the proceedings in which it is disclosed, except where –
>
> (a) the document has been read to or by the court, or referred to, at a hearing which has been held in public;
>
> (b) the court gives permission; or
>
> (c) the party who disclosed the document and the person to whom the document belongs agree.

(As to the first limb of this rule and the growing practice of judicial 'pre-reading' of documents to which only compendious or economical reference is made in open court, see the judgment of Lord Bingham LCJ in *SmithKline Beecham Biologicals SA v Connaught Laboratories Inc* [1999] 4 All ER 498.)

Just as disclosure can be limited on the grounds of proportionality (provided that the disclosure statement advertises what limitations have been adopted), so a party can withhold inspection on the grounds of proportionality – Part 31.3(2). Again, the disclosure statement must advertise the fact that inspection will not be allowed on this ground. Other bases for refusing inspection include the obvious ones that the document is no longer in the control of the disclosing party, or that that party has a right or duty to withhold inspection (Part 31.3(1)). The latter basis will cover refusals to allow inspection on the grounds of legal professional privilege or public interest immunity. The relevant right or duty must be asserted in writing (usually, of course, in the list of documents itself). As to the procedure for challenging such asserted rights or duties, see Part 31.19(5).[2] Part 31.19 also contains the procedure for *ex parte* applications to withhold disclosure on the grounds of damage to the public interest.

OTHER KINDS OF DISCLOSURE

So far, this chapter has considered disclosure between parties to existing proceedings. Parts 31.16 to 31.18 deal with certain other kinds of disclosure, namely:

(i)   The statutory power to order disclosure before proceedings start (Part 31.16);

(ii)   The statutory power to order disclosure against non-parties (Part 31.17);

(iii) The court's residual powers to order disclosure before proceedings start or against non-parties (Part 31.18).

The first of these powers covers applications for *pre-action disclosure* under section 33(2)of the Supreme Court Act 1981 (and under section 52(2) of the County Courts Act 1984). The previous restriction of those sections to actions for personal injuries or death was removed by amendment pursuant to the Civil Procedure (Modification of Enactments) Order 1998 (SI 1998/2940).[3] The court can only make an order for pre-action disclosure where both applicant and respondent are likely to be party to subsequent proceedings; where, if proceedings had started, the respondent's duty of standard disclosure would extend to the documents in question; and where early disclosure is desirable either to dispose fairly of the anticipated proceedings, to assist resolution of the dispute without proceedings or to save costs (Part 31.16(3)). Such applications should be supported by evidence and are made under Part 23 (see Part 25.4).

The second power covers applications for *disclosure against a non-party* under section 34(2) of the Supreme Court Act 1981 (and under section 53(2) of the County Courts Act 1984). These sections have also been amended by the statutory instrument referred to above, so that they too no longer apply only to actions for personal injuries or death. There must, however, be existing proceedings before an application for disclosure can be made under these sections. Furthermore, the court may not make an order unless the documents of which disclosure is sought are likely to support the applicant's case or

---

2   See, also, *Morris v Banque Arabe et Internationale d'Investissement SA* (1999) *The Times*, 23 December, Neuberger J, for a consideration of the discretionary power to withhold inspection, there in the context of an asserted inability to give inspection because of the alleged effect of foreign law. (Compare *Surzur Overseas Ltd v Koros* (1999) unreported, 20 July, Toulson J.)

3   In *Burrells Wharf Freeholders Ltd v Gulliard Homes* (1999) unreported, 1 July), an attempt to challenge this statutory instrument as '*ultra vires*' failed. (Dyson J, sitting in the Technology and Construction Court.)

adversely affect the case of some other party, and unless disclosure is necessary in order to dispose fairly of the action or to save costs (Part 31.17 (3)). These applications should be supported by evidence and are also made under Part 23.

(As to the costs of applications for pre-action disclosure or for disclosure by a non-party, see Part 48.1. The person against whom the order is made will normally be allowed his costs of the application and of complying with any order made on the application. However, the court may make a different order, particularly if that person unreasonably opposed the application, or if he had failed to comply with a relevant pre-action protocol.)

Part 31.18 expressly provides that rules 31.16 and 31.17 'do not limit any other power which the court may have' to order pre-action disclosure or disclosure against non-parties. The court's inherent powers under the *Norwich Pharmacal* jurisdiction ([1974] AC 133, HL) are thus preserved, as also are the extensions of that jurisdiction recognised in *Bankers Trust v Shapira* [1980] 3 All ER 353 and *Arab Monetary Fund v Hashim (No 5)* [1992] 2 All ER 911.

CHAPTER 18

EVIDENCE

In this section, we consider a variety of topics, including:

A The court's general power to control the evidence given to it.

B Evidence given at trial, and in particular the continuing system of exchanging witness statements and summaries.

C Evidence at hearings other than trial.

D The permissible uses of served witness statements.

E Hearsay.

F Depositions and court attendance by witnesses.

A THE COURT'S POWER TO CONTROL THE EVIDENCE

We have already stressed how broad and flexible are the court's case management powers. One potentially very significant aspect of those powers is the new provision giving the court the ability to control the evidence that is put before it. Such a provision was only possible because the enabling legislation – to be precise, paragraph 4 of Schedule 1 to the Civil Procedure Act 1997 – provided that the CPR might 'modify the rules of evidence as they apply to proceedings within the scope of the rules'. Part 32.1 reads as follows:

> (1) The court may control the evidence by giving directions as to –
>
>> (a) the issues on which it requires evidence;
>>
>> (b) the nature of the evidence which it requires to decide those issues; and
>>
>> (c) the way in which the evidence is to be placed before the court.
>
> (2) The court may use its power under this rule to exclude evidence that would otherwise be admissible.
>
> (3) The court may limit cross-examination.

These are novel and far-reaching provisions. They apply to the small claims track – even though the other provisions of Part 32 do not (Part 27.2(1)(c)). In relation to the fast and multi-tracks, the other more specific provisions of Part 32 must all be read with the new controlling powers of Part 32.1 well in mind.

In one sense, the new powers contained in Part 32.1 are merely an aspect, albeit an essential one, of the court's case management powers. In the past, the preponderant academic view was that a civil judge had no general power to refuse to hear evidence that was both relevant and admissible in relation to an issue in the matter before him. In strict theory, therefore, counsel could require a judge to listen to evidence however unhelpful the judge felt that evidence to be on a particular issue. Under the new regime, however, given the court's case management responsibilities itself to identify the issues, to direct trials of separate issues and (above all) to exclude issues from consideration, some general power to control the evidence before the court and more especially to exclude otherwise admissible evidence was essential. Given Part 32.1, it certainly cannot now be argued that a civil court has no jurisdiction to exclude relevant evidence – as the Court of Appeal has already made plain in *Grobelaar v Sun Newspapers Ltd* (1999) *The Times*, 12 August. Potter LJ said that there were no express limitations as to the manner and extent of exercise of the power to exclude evidence under Part 32.1 – 'although clearly it must be exercised in support of dealing justly with the case.'[1]

At the same time, the powers in Part 32.1 may have other more specific consequences.

Some such specific effects were clearly intended. For example, taken together, Part 32.1(1)(a) and Part 32.1(3) will allow a judge to limit cross-examination, either by the imposition of a time limit or by reference to particular topics. Part 32.1(1)(b) will allow the court to say that it does not need oral or expert evidence on a topic but is content to rely on the documents or on printed sources – for a robust example, see the Court of Appeal discussion in *Bandegani v Norwich Union Fire Insurance Society Ltd* (1999) unreported, 20 May, referred to in Chapter 5 above. Part 32.1(1)(c) will allow the court to say whether it requires a particular witness to give evidence 'viva voce' or whether evidence in writing will be sufficient.

Some other less clear (and perhaps unintended) consequences can also be imagined. For example, in the past, it was for the parties and for the parties alone to choose which witnesses should be called – a civil judge could not himself call a witness without the parties' consent. Part 32.1(1) might be argued to have altered these basic assumptions of our adversarial system. Though the wording of the rule is very broad – enabling the court to give 'directions as to ... the nature of the evidence which it requires ... and ... the way in which the evidence is to be placed before the court' – it is perhaps fanciful to imagine any judge accepting the argument that he now has power to *order* a party to call a witness who has relevant evidence to give, whether or not that party wants to see that witness in the box. Less fanciful in a world of judicial case-management, is the argument that Part 32.1(1) has empowered a judge himself to call a highly relevant witness even without the consent of the parties.[2] Doubtless, Part 3.1(2)(m) could also be prayed in aid to justify the

---

1   See also in this connection two Court of Appeal decisions on the control of evidence in libel cases – *Tancic v Times Newspapers Ltd* (2000) *The Times*, 12 January and *GKR Karate UK Ltd v Yorkshire Post Newspapers Ltd* (2000) *The Times*, 9 February.

2   But see *Phipson on Evidence*, 15th edn, para 10-14, for the view that there has been no change in this regard.

adoption of such a course in appropriate circumstances. Both parties would be able to cross-examine any witness called by the judge in that way.

B   EVIDENCE AT TRIAL – EXCHANGE OF WITNESS STATEMENTS AND SUMMARIES

The primary means of proving a fact at trial remains, as before, by oral evidence given in public (Part 32.2(1)). Even in the closing years of the old regime, that time-honoured system was, of course, significantly affected by the system of exchanging witness statements before trial and the attendant 'telescoping' of examination in chief. Chapter 22 of Lord Woolf's Interim Report contained an exhaustive analysis of the history and philosophy of the system of exchanging witness statements – namely, that a 'cards on the table' approach, allowing each party to see the evidentiary strengths and weaknesses of the other, is more likely to promote a just result, whether through settlement or an abbreviated trial. However, he acknowledged that, in larger cases in particular, the system had had 'a devastating effect on costs', with a 'new industry' devoted to the over-elaborate drafting of witness statements.

Though firmly endorsing the practice of exchanging witness statements, Lord Woolf exhorted lawyers drafting them not to 'gild the lily' and, in particular, not to include inappropriate matters such as purported legal argument or lengthy analysis of documents. He urged a concomitant relaxation of judicial attitudes towards the reasonable supplementation of a witness statement by the witness once he was in the box – whether leave to supplement should be given in any particular circumstances being likely to depend on whether the matter in question was wholly new, the disadvantage to the other party and so forth.

As far as evidence at trial is concerned, the CPR basically adopted the old witness statement system but altered it in certain particular respects with these aims of Lord Woolf in view. The CPR also introduced a number of changes in relation to the use of witness statements at hearings *other* than trial – those changes and their implications are considered below in Section C of this chapter.

A witness statement is now defined as 'a written statement signed by a person which contains the evidence, and only that evidence, which that person would be allowed to give orally' (Part 32.4(1)). The court *will* order the exchange of any witness statements (Part 32.4(2)), though it has power to direct the order in which they are to be served and whether they should be filed.

A witness's statement will ordinarily stand as his evidence in chief (Part 32.5(2)) and the basic emphasis of the rules is, as before, on not allowing him to give evidence on other matters not contained within it. Thus, while under

Part 32.5(3), it is possible, with the court's permission, to 'amplify' a witness statement and to give evidence in relation to new matters which have arisen since the statement was served, such permission will only be given if the court 'considers that there is good reason not to confine the evidence of the witness to the contents of his witness statement' (Part 32.5(4)). It follows that while, perhaps, witness statements need not now be as perfectly 'honed' as in the days of the old witness statement industry, they must certainly still cover the substance of all essential points. (There presumably still remains a general discretion to allow a witness to give evidence on matters that are not covered by his witness statement – even though they should have been – either because the word 'amplified' in Part 32.5(3) is broad enough to cover that situation or under Part 32.1.)

To date, there is no reported post-CPR authority dealing with the question of the amplification of a witness statement. However, in *Mealey Horgan plc v Horgan* (1999) *The Times*, 6 July, the court did deal with the more general problem of the late service of witness statements. A claimant's attempts to persuade Buckley J to impose draconian sanctions in this regard effectively came to nought. The defendant was two weeks late in serving his statements but they still reached the claimant company six weeks before trial and the claimant was said not to be not prejudiced in its pre-trial preparations. Granting the defendant's application for an extension of time, Buckley J said that it would be unjust to exclude a party from adducing evidence at trial save in very extreme circumstances – for example, where there had been deliberate flouting of court orders, or inexcusable delay such that the only way the court could fairly entertain the late evidence would be by adjourning the trial. Nor would the judge accept the claimant's suggestion that leave should only be granted on condition of a payment into court. That course might be appropriate in the event of repeated breaches of timetables, or where there was something about the applicant's conduct which suggested that it was not 'bona fide' and the court felt that the other side needed protection. Here, however, there was nothing of that kind and the trial had not been prejudiced.

The practice direction supplementing Part 32 contains detailed provisions on the *form of witness statements*. From the drafting point of view, the most important requirements are that a statement must be in the first person and in the witness's own words (PD32, para 18.1). In most cases, it should also deal with events in chronological order (PD32, para 19.2). Finally, a statement should indicate whether the witness speaks from his own knowledge, or on information or belief (and if the latter, it should identify his sources) – PD32, para 18.2). These last provisions tie in with certain changes in relation to hearsay notices, which are discussed below in Section E of this chapter. They also remove the principal difference between the drafting of witness statements and of affidavits under the old regime. Affidavits and witness statements will, in terms of the substance of their drafting, now be largely indistinguishable, a fact which is hardly surprising in view of the changes in relation to pre-trial evidence discussed in section C below.

A witness statement must also now contain a statement of truth – 'I believe that the facts stated in this witness statement are true' (PD32, para 20.1 and 2). To make such a statement without an honest belief in its truth is a contempt of court.

While dealing with questions of drafting in relation to witness statements, it is worth mentioning one post-CPR decision of the Court of Appeal which stresses the dangers of a lawyer's drafting written evidence and putting words – sometimes very sophisticated words – into his client's mouth. In *Alex Lawrie Factors Ltd v Morgan* (1999) *The Times*, 17 August, a wife was seeking to avoid liability on an indemnity in respect of her husband's indebtedness to a bank. She had sworn an affidavit in which she not only said that she had read the House of Lords' decision in *Barclays Bank v O'Brien* [1994] 1 AC 180 but also made a number of arguments based upon it. The judge concluded that she was clearly a lady of intelligence and partly, no doubt, in the light of that, disbelieved her evidence about the circumstances in which she had come to sign the indemnity. On appeal, however, an attempt was made to lead further evidence to show that the wife was not quite as bright as the judge had concluded from the affidavit drafted by her lawyer! Further evidence was allowed, Brooke LJ stressing that affidavits were for witnesses to say, in their own words, what the relevant evidence was. An affidavit should deal only with matters on which the witness could sensibly be cross-examined and not, for example, with legal argument. He added that though the case dealt with affidavits, the court's observations applied equally to any documents verified by a statement of truth under the CPR.

Given the court's power to limit the issues on which it requires evidence in any case, a witness statement will not in future necessarily have to deal with all aspects of the dispute between the parties. Subject to that point – and, of course, to the usual practice of not dealing with matters to be covered in cross-examination – a witness statement under the new rules should be like a full proof. However, the CPR also deal with another kind of document altogether, namely a '*witness summary*'. This will be much briefer. Even the old rules made provision for the service of such a shorter document in the situation (Ord 38 r 2A(5)) where a party was unable to obtain a witness statement from an intended witness – most obviously where he or she would only give evidence under subpoena and was refusing to co-operate before trial. That situation is now covered by Part 32.9(1), which allows a party to seek leave to serve a witness summary instead of a witness statement. The definition of a witness summary (Part 32.9(2)) is:

> ... a summary of –
>
> (a) the evidence, if known, which would otherwise be included in a witness statement; or
>
> (b) if the evidence is not known, the matters about which the party serving the witness summary proposes to question the witness.

C EVIDENCE AT HEARINGS OTHER THAN TRIAL

At any hearing other than the trial, any fact which needs to be proved by the evidence of a witness is to be proved by his or her evidence in writing (Part 32.2(1)). Under the old rules, written evidence at such interlocutory hearings was usually by affidavit but the CPR have made an important change in this regard. Now, unless the court, a practice direction or any other enactment requires otherwise, evidence at all hearings other than the trial will be by witness statement (Part 32.6(1)). This applies to evidence at any hearings after as well as before the trial.

There are certain exceptions to this change and various applications still *requiring* affidavit evidence are listed in PD32, para 1.4. Most importantly, applications for freezing orders (Marevas), for search orders (Anton Pillers) and for injunctions requiring access to land all still require affidavit evidence. Furthermore, there is still a general option to use affidavit evidence (rather than a witness statement) on all interlocutory applications – Part 32.15(2). In most situations, however, a party who exercises that option is unlikely to recover the extra cost of doing so. Indeed, where one can, there may be other good reasons for using a witness statement rather than an affidavit – the undertaking on collateral use in Part 32.12 (discussed in the next section of this chapter) applies to witness statements, but not to affidavits.[3]

Another interesting feature of the CPR, which flows from the new system of verifying pleadings, is that a party is now able to rely on his verified statement of case as *itself* constituting evidence of the matters stated in it (Part 32.6(2)). There is no need, as there used to be under the old regime, for a separate verifying affidavit (or now witness statement). In practice, of course, a party will often decide that he wants the evidence on an application to go much further than mere verification of the matters set out in his statement of case, but in a simple case (say a claim for debt), the verified statement of case may suffice. Provided that any statements of fact contained in it are verified by a statement of truth, an application notice can equally be used as evidence. In short, 'evidence in writing' under the CPR may include any or all of the following – affidavits, verified witness statements, verified statements of case and verified applications.

D THE PERMISSIBLE USES OF SERVED WITNESS STATEMENTS

Part 32.12(1) – roughly corresponding to the old RSC Ord 38 r 2A(11) – provides that a witness statement 'may be used only for the purpose of the

---

3   Under the old rules, there was a similar distinction in relation to the undertaking not to use for collateral purposes. Save in the case of affidavits sworn under compulsion (say pursuant to a Mareva), the undertaking applied to served witness statements but not to served affidavits. See, generally, *Phipson on Evidence*, 15th edn, paras 22.07-08 and 23.02-04.

proceedings in which it is served'. There are certain exceptions to this ban which are listed in Part 32.12(2):

> Paragraph 1 does not apply if and to the extent that –
>
> (a) the witness gives consent in writing to some other use of it;
>
> (b) the court gives permission for some other use; or
>
> (c) the witness statement has been put in evidence at a hearing held in public.

It is worth highlighting that the wording of the first of these exceptions has changed. Under RSC Ord 38 r 2A(11), the consent required was that of 'the party serving the statement'. Now, the consent in question must be given by the witness whose statement it is.

More generally, the wording of Part 32.12(2) ('some other use') makes it plain that it is concerned with defining the circumstances in which a served witness statement may be used other than in the current proceedings, that is, for some collateral purpose such as use of the witness statement in other, perhaps wholly unconnected, legal proceedings. What is less clear, however, is the precise use that can be made of a served witness statement even within the confines of the existing action. Use at trial is not so difficult – the receiving party may put the statement in cross-examination of the witness (if he is called); or, if the witness is not called, the receiving party may himself put it in as hearsay evidence (Part 32.5(5)).[4] What is unaddressed and unresolved is the extent to which the receiving party may use a statement for his own ends in the interlocutory stages of the action – say by relying on it in support of an application for discovery, for security for costs, for summary judgment or whatever.

In the past, difficulties of this kind had arisen in relation to RSC Ord 38 r 2A(11) and no satisfactory general test was laid down by the authorities.[5]

---

4   Though as to the impossibility of 'picking and choosing' between parts of a witness statement put in in this way, see *McPhilemy v Times Newspapers* (2000) unreported, 10 March, CA.

5   This is a complicated topic not suitable for development at length here. However, for an examination of some of the problems that can arise and a review of how they were dealt with under the old rules, see Ian Grainger's article on 'Witness statements – a new privilege?' (1995) 145 NLJ 961, 1000 and 1062. Under the old rules, the receiving party could certainly use a served witness statement to found an application for specific discovery of documents referred to therein – see *Black & Decker v Flymo* [1991] 1 WLR 753. The position in relation to an application for security for costs was, so far as we know, unresolved. The old case law certainly laid down no compendious test to distinguish between those interlocutory circumstances in which a served but unused witness statement could be put in evidence by the receiving party and those in which it could not. As a matter of principle, any such test seemed likely to have to take account of the confidential or 'quasi-without prejudice' nature of the handing over of a witness statement, the special status of the document only being lost (on the traditional view) by actually calling the witness and putting the statement in evidence as his evidence in chief.

Though the new rule does not expressly tackle the question of interlocutory use any more than the old one did, it *may* be that the scope for problems has in practice been reduced. In particular, exception (c) in Part 32.12(2) is likely to be of greater effect than the (roughly) equivalent exception under the old rules. Interlocutory hearings will now usually be held in public and evidence at them will also usually be given by witness statements. It follows that if a witness statement is not only served under Part 32.4(2) but is also put in evidence by the serving party at any public interlocutory hearing, the receiving party should be uninhibited in the use to which he can thereafter put it, either outside or (one would think) within the confines of the action.

Problems could still arise in relation to any witness statement that is served under Part 32.4 but *not* put in evidence at any public interlocutory hearing. Certainly, it would, in our view, be premature to imagine that just because you have been served with a witness statement under Part 32.4, you are free to use it (even within the confines of the action) in any way you choose, as if it were a witness statement that had already been used at an interlocutory hearing. Rule 32.12 would seem to make it clear that this was *not* intended. In short, there may yet be differences between the permissible interlocutory uses of a witness statement served under Part 32.4 but not yet used (that is, a trial witness statement of which early disclosure has been given but which the serving party has not yet committed himself to ever putting in evidence); and the permissible uses of a witness statement served for use at an interlocutory hearing, *a fortiori* of one already put in evidence by a party at a public interlocutory hearing.

E   **HEARSAY**

Part 33 deals with Miscellaneous Rules about Evidence. It does not apply to cases on the small claims track – Part 27.2(1)(d). The principal matter covered is hearsay evidence (and various related applications).

The 1995 Civil Evidence Act effected a fundamental change in the civil law of evidence by providing for the general admissibility of hearsay evidence. Though a party proposing to adduce hearsay evidence is required by the Act to give the other parties notice of that fact, any failure to do so does not affect the admissibility of the evidence in question but can be taken into account by the court 'in considering the exercise of its powers with respect to the course of the proceedings and costs, and as a matter adversely affecting the weight to be given to the evidence' (section 2(4)). In short, evidence is no longer to be *excluded* on the ground that it is hearsay but the court's attention will instead be closely focussed on the weight to be given to any particular item of hearsay evidence.

The provisions of the 1995 Act[6] were incorporated into the old RSC by Ord 38 rr 20–23, provisions which have now been replaced by Part 33.1–5 of the CPR. There is one significant practical difference between the CPR and the provisions in the amended RSC. Under the latter, Ord 38 r 21(5) contemplated the service of a witness statement and at the same time of a *separate* hearsay notice, identifying for the benefit of the recipient those passages of hearsay evidence in the witness statement on which the serving party proposed to rely at trial. The new rules much simplify this cumbersome process. Thus, Part 33.2(1) provides as follows:

> Where a party intends to rely on hearsay evidence at trial and either –
>
> (a) that evidence is to be given by a witness giving oral evidence; or
>
> (b) that evidence is contained in a witness statement of a person who is not being called to give oral evidence,
>
> that party complies with section 2(1)(a) of the Civil Evidence Act 1995 *by serving a witness statement* on the other parties in accordance with the court's order. [Emphasis added]

In other words, service of a witness statement will *itself* constitute compliance with the statutory obligation to serve a hearsay notice in respect of any hearsay evidence contained in the witness statement. Service of the witness statement should, in theory, be sufficient because as stated above, any well drafted witness statement will identify which of its contents are within the witness's own knowledge and which are hearsay.[7]

In this way, the CPR have removed yet another procedural technicality in relation to hearsay evidence. Of course, it remains emphatically the case that the weight to be given to any item of hearsay evidence is entirely a matter for the court's judgment in the specific circumstances of the case and in the light, in particular, of the various 'guidelines' as to weight set out in section 4(2) of the 1995 Act.

Under the CPR, there is no duty to give notice of intention to rely on hearsay evidence at hearings other than trials (Part 33.3).

In our earlier work on the CPR, we cast doubt on whether the new regime on hearsay evidence applied to actions commenced before 31 January 1997. This was essentially because of the Court of Appeal's decision in *Bairstow v*

---

6   This is not the place to attempt a more detailed analysis of the complicated provisions of the 1995 Act. Anyone who wants to know more about them can read Ian Grainger's articles in [1996] 140 SJ 536 (on the Act) and [1997] 141 SJ 112 (on the amendments to RSC Ord 38). In relation to actions commenced before 31 January 1997, both articles must be read subject to the later decision in *Bairstow v Queens Moat Houses plc* [1998] 1 All ER 343 and, now, to The Civil Procedure (Modification of Enactments) Order 1999, SI 1999/1217 and to the amended Practice Direction 33 made pursuant thereto.

7   We mention in passing that if it is proposed not to call the maker of the witness statement (that is, if Part 33.2(1)(b) applies), then the other parties must be informed of that fact and of the reasons why he will not be called (Part 33.2(2)).

Queen's Moat Houses plc [1998] 1 All ER 343 and the tangled confusion of statutory drafting that was dealt with in that case. However, events have moved on yet again. The relevant provision of the 1995 Act that was considered in *Bairstow* has now been amended by the Civil Procedure (Modification of Enactments) Order 1999, SI 1999/1217 and PD33 has been made (and itself amended) pursuant thereto. The ultimate result is that the 1995 Act does not apply to actions begun before 31 January 1997 if:

> before 26 April 1999 –
>
> (a) directions were given, or orders were made, as to the evidence to be given at the trial or hearing; or
>
> (b) the trial or hearing had begun. [PD33, para 3]

In practical terms, one imagines that this exclusion will by now have little continuing effect.

F   DEPOSITIONS AND COURT ATTENDANCE BY WITNESSES

These matters are dealt with in Part 34.

Part 34.2 deals with *witness summonses*. Though, of course, the Latin is not used, practitioners will recognise the reappearance in the CPR of the old distinction between subpoenas 'ad testificandum' (to give evidence) and 'duces tecum' (to produce documents to the court). Both kinds of summons can be issued in respect of the trial or in respect of hearings other than the trial. Furthermore, they can require attendance either on the date fixed for a hearing or on some other, that is, earlier, date (Part 34.2(4)). The practice of requiring a third party who is in possession of relevant documents to produce them at some earlier date well in advance of the trial will therefore be able to continue – see *Khanna v Lovell White Durrant* [1994] 4 All ER 267. Having said that, witness summonses in respect of hearings other than the trial cannot be issued without leave – nor can a summons to give evidence or to produce documents on any date other than the trial date (Part 34.3(2)).

As with other documents issued by the court, a witness summons will be served by the court itself, unless the party seeking the summons informs the court in writing that he wishes to serve it himself (Part 34.6). A witness summons no longer has to be served personally on the proposed witness – indeed, if the court is to effect service, the normal method will be by first class post (PD6, para 8.1). In some circumstances, no doubt, postal service should be sufficient but in others, a party may well take the view that personal service by a process server will remain the means most likely to secure the witness's attendance. If the court is to serve, the relevant attendance moneys will have to be lodged in advance (Part 34.6(2)): otherwise, they will have to be offered or paid to the witness at the time of service (Part 34.7).

A person served with a witness summons may, of course, apply to set it aside or to vary it – Part 34.3(4). The Rules give no express guidance on the approach that the court should adopt on such an application. However, in *Harrison v Bloom Camillin* (1999) *The Independent*, 28 June, Neuberger J, while recognising the need for care when referring to old authorities, said that it was at least helpful to note the summary of the old law put forward (albeit in a dissenting judgment) by Ralph Gibson LJ in *Re State of Norway's Application (No 1)* [1987] 1 QB 433, at 496E–H. The principles there set out would exclude summonses that were 'irrelevant or fishing, or speculative or oppressive'. Furthermore, even if a witness has relevant evidence to give, a summons may be set aside 'if, on balancing the value of the evidence to the applicant against the burden upon the witness, and the degree of intrusiveness of the proposed questioning and all the other circumstances, it seems to the court that the request is oppressive.' Having referred to other authority, Neuberger J accepted that the interests of a witness were not to be ignored under the CPR any more than under the old regime. However, he said that the interest of a witness 'normally comes second to the interests of the parties to the litigation, and, of course, to the overriding concern of the Court, namely the interests of justice'.

The provisions for *taking evidence on deposition* (whether in front of a judge or an examiner) that were previously in RSC Ord 39 are also now contained in Part 34. They include the rules for the conduct of such examinations and, where the examination is to take place outside the jurisdiction, the rules for the issuing of letters of request by the High Court. One suspects that these provisions may be used relatively infrequently in future, particularly given the possibility of the court's taking evidence by video link under Part 32.3.

The procedure to be followed for the taking of evidence by an examiner in aid of foreign proceedings, that is, under the Evidence (Proceedings in Other Jurisdictions) Act 1975, will continue to be governed by RSC Ord 70, one of the scheduled rules. However, paragraph 6 of PD34 (on Depositions and Court Attendance by Witnesses) also contains material of relevance to such examinations.

CHAPTER 19

EXPERTS AND ASSESSORS

THE BACKGROUND – LORD WOOLF'S PROPOSALS ON EXPERT EVIDENCE

In his Interim Report, Lord Woolf found much to lament about the old system of expert evidence, or more precisely about the way it functioned in practice. He pointed to the central tension that many experts felt between their roles as an agent of one party and as an independent witness giving expert opinion evidence to the court. He found that without remedial measures, there was a danger that experts could be wholly transformed into 'additional advocates of the parties', a phenomenon already well known in the USA. Furthermore, he explained that experts were often used in cases where their evidence was not really needed at all; or else on a scale way beyond the true demands of the case. As he said:

> The inappropriate use of experts to bolster cases leads to additional cost and delay. It arises and is allowed to continue because parties at present have complete control over the scope and management and presentation of their case. There is no pressure to narrow issues or to eliminate peripheral issues, and the current arrangements for costs provide insufficient or ineffectual sanctions against such excessive or inappropriate tactics. [IR chap 23, para 17]

Amongst other proposals, Lord Woolf therefore:

(i)   recommended that the calling of expert evidence should be under the complete control of the court;

(ii) argued for the wider use of 'single' (or neutral) experts, either jointly selected and instructed by the parties or else appointed by the court; and

(iii) made various proposals to bring home to experts and to the parties the fact that the expert's primary duty when preparing or giving evidence is to the court and not to the party instructing him.

The suggested abandonment of the parties' control over expert evidence caused widespread objection and Lord Woolf's proposals (or at least their wording) were considerably toned down in his Final Report. In particular, he there stressed that he did not suggest a uniform solution, such as a court-appointed expert, for all cases. The key to the court's approach to expert evidence would be flexibility and at least above the fast track, there would be no single answer applying to all cases.

PART 35 AND THE DEFINITION OF 'EXPERT'

The new rules on expert evidence are contained in Part 35. We will consider the provisions of that Part under the following headings:

A   The court's control over expert evidence.

B   Single joint experts

C   Impartiality and related matters.

D   Discussions between experts.

E   Assessors.

However, before turning to these topics, two general observations should be made.

First, experts have featured in quite a number of the courts' pronouncements on the new regime generally. For example, the duty of the parties to co-operate and to provide a court making timetabling decisions with full and up to date information on the commitments of proposed expert witnesses was considered by the Court of Appeal in *Matthews v Tarmac Brick* (1999) *The Times*, 1 July, and in *Rollinson v Kimberley Clark* (1999) *The Times*, 15 June. Again, in *Baron v Lovell* (1999) *The Times*, 14 September, delaying the service of an expert's report for tactical reasons (so as to coincide with a Part 36 offer) was said not to be 'in the spirit of Woolf'.

Secondly, it should be stressed that any reference to an 'expert' in Part 35 is 'a reference to an expert who has been instructed to give or prepare evidence for the purpose of court proceedings' (Part 35.2). In short, it is a party's instructing an expert 'to give or prepare evidence' that triggers the application of the various provisions set out in Part 35. If an expert is used for some other purpose, for example to provide purely internal advice, then on the face of it he will not be subject to the rules set out in Part 35. This distinction and its potential ramifications are returned to in Section C of this chapter.

A   THE COURT'S CONTROL OVER EXPERT EVIDENCE

We have already seen that under the case management system, the court has complete control over the evidence to be put before it (Part 32.1). This general principle is restated in more particular terms in relation to expert evidence. Thus, no expert can be called, nor his report put in evidence, without the court's permission (Part 35.4(1)). A party seeking permission will have to identify the relevant field of evidence and, where practicable, the name of the expert on whose evidence he wishes to rely. Any permission granted will be in relation only to that named expert or field. Furthermore, there is some discouragement against using unnecessarily 'grand' experts in the provision that the court may limit the amount of an expert's fees that may be recovered from any other party (Part 35.4(4)). Expert evidence is normally to be given in the form of a written report (Part 35.5(1)) and on the fast track, an expert's attendance at a hearing will be exceptional, his report in most cases merely being read.

Most important of all, however, is the general limiting principle enshrined in Part 35.1:

> Expert evidence shall be restricted to that which is reasonably required to resolve the proceedings.

It will be noted not only that this rule is headed 'Duty to restrict expert evidence' but also that it is worded neutrally, so as to be directed at the parties as well as at the court – wholly consistently with the general duty of co-operation contained in Part 1.3.

B   SINGLE JOINT EXPERTS

In his Final Report, Lord Woolf said that the court's discretionary control of expert evidence could lead to the adoption of various different solutions, depending on the circumstances of any individual case. For example, the court might:

- order that there should be no expert evidence at all, or only in relation to certain issues;
- limit the number or type of witness;
- order the use of a single joint expert (or experts);
- order that expert evidence should be given only in writing.

He acknowledged that 'it would not be realistic to expect a significant shift towards single experts in the short term'. Nevertheless, he felt that a single joint expert should always be considered by the court as a possibility. The court's powers in that regard are now contained in Part 35.7 and 35.8. There is certainly no presumption in favour of single joint experts. The most obvious use of such experts will be in circumstances where the case relates to a substantially established field of knowledge, or where there is no need for the court to sample a range of views.[1] Where a single joint expert is used, then in default of agreed instructions, each party will have the right to give him instructions (Part 35.8(1)), though a copy will have to be sent to other instructing parties. Furthermore, each party will have the right to cross-examine a single joint expert.

---

1   There are *obiter dicta* about the desirability of single experts in – *North Holdings Ltd v Southern Tropics Ltd* (1999) unreported, 17 June, CA (petition for relief under section 461(2)(d) of the 1985 Companies Act) and in *Field v Leeds City Council* (2000) *The Times*, 18 January (housing disrepair claim).

The situation where the parties agree to instruct a single joint expert, but one party is then dissatisfied with the ensuing report, has been considered by the Court of Appeal (Lord Woolf MR and Latham LJ) in *Daniels v Walker* (2000) *The Times*, 17 May: see Chapter 25 below where this case is considered in detail.

C   IMPARTIALITY AND RELATED MATTERS

It follows from what we have said above that the court has control over the nature and amount of expert evidence that is to be given to it and over the means by which it is to be presented. However, that is not the end of the matter. The court is also concerned to control the quality of the expert evidence that it receives, to ensure in short that that evidence is objective and not subject to improper pressures from those who have commissioned it. With that in mind, the CPR make it plain that the court is the person to whom the expert is addressing himself and to whom he owes his ultimate responsibility. That is not, of course, to say that he does not owe legal duties to the party instructing him – in most cases, he certainly will. However, there is no doubt where the balance lies. Part 35.3 reads as follows:

(1) It is the duty of an expert to help the court on the matters within his expertise.

(2) This duty overrides any obligation to the person from whom he has received instructions or by whom he is paid.

The relationship to which the CPR give primary emphasis is therefore that between the expert and the court. It is not inconceivable that in the preparation of his evidence an expert may find himself in a situation where his professional duties, his duties to the court and his duties to his client conflict or are not immediately reconcilable. In that or other situations of difficulty, the CPR make provision for an expert to file a written *request for directions* to assist him in carrying out his function (Part 35.14(1)). Indeed, this can be done without giving notice to any party. In giving directions to assist, the court may (or presumably may not) order that such directions (and the expert's request) be served on one or more of the parties (Part 35.14(3)).

The expert's essential impartiality is also bolstered by certain requirements of the new rules and practice direction in relation to the *contents of an expert's report*. These important requirements should be studied in detail but they include the fact that the report is 'to be addressed to the court and not to (the instructing party)' (PD35, para 1.1). If there is a range of opinion on an issue, that range must be summarised and reasons given for the expert's own opinion (PD35, para 1.2(5)). Perhaps most importantly, every expert's report must contain a statement of truth (in an appropriately modified form – PD35, para 1.3), and must conclude with a statement that:

(a) the expert understands his duty to the court; and

(b) he has complied with that duty. [Part 35.10(2)]

The practice direction also provides (in para 1.6) that an expert's report should comply with the requirements of any approved expert's protocol. At the time of writing, no such protocol has been published, though a Draft Code of Guidance for Experts was put out for consultation in the autumn of 1999.

Lord Woolf's original proposals to ensure the impartiality of expert witnesses had been even more radical. He had proposed that all *instructions given to experts* should be fully 'transparent' and indeed annexed to the expert's report. However, these proposals met with much opposition and the rules on instructions that ultimately appeared in Part 35.10(3) and (4) are more restrained.

An expert's report must now state 'the substance of all material instructions, whether written or oral, on the basis of which (it) was written' (Part 35.10(3)). The practice direction expands on this by saying that 'the statement should summarise the facts and instructions given to the expert which are material to the opinions expressed in the report or upon which those opinions are based' (PD35, para 1.2(8)). The expert's instructions are not privileged against disclosure but the court will not order any particular document to be disclosed, nor allow any questioning in court by another party, without being satisfied that there are 'reasonable grounds' to consider that the expert's summary of his instructions is inaccurate or incomplete (Part 35.10(4)).

The discretion afforded by Part 35.10(4) will allow the court to prevent experts being unnecessarily cross-examined about their instructions when they are clearly trying impartially to help the court. It should also arm the court with a means of dealing with any problems arising out of the simple fact of life that professionals who have initially been recruited for some broader (perhaps privileged) purpose often end up giving expert evidence to the court. The general intention would appear to be to preserve the distinction between an expert's being used 'internally' for fact-finding or general advisory purposes (where his instructions may or may not, depending on the circumstances, be privileged) and an expert's being instructed to go further and to prepare evidence for ultimate use in court (where his instructions will not be privileged but are potentially the subject of disclosure and cross examination).

As already mentioned above, this distinction seems to be inherent in the general definition of 'expert' in Part 35.2. It may be worth breaking off to give an example of how the distinction could work in practice.

Suppose that a landlord instructs a surveyor to inspect and report on the interior condition of certain demised premises. The likely outcome of the inspection is unknown and no litigation is at that stage in contemplation. Whatever other constraints he may be under in the preparation of his report, the surveyor will not be subject to the regime of Part 35, since he has not been instructed 'to prepare evidence for the purpose of court proceedings'. Nor, in all probability, will his report be privileged against disclosure in any proceedings that do subsequently take place in relation to the premises.

Suppose, however, that the landlord does not instruct surveyors at all before serving the relevant notices and issuing proceedings for forfeiture. If at that stage the landlord's solicitors instruct a surveyor to prepare a report on the premises, whether that surveyor is subject to the requirements of Part 35 will depend on the purpose of his being asked to prepare a report. If it is proposed to use the surveyor as a witness at trial and his report is merely the first stage in that process, then he will be subject to Part 35 – and (subject to what has been said above about Part 35.10) instructions to him will not be privileged. If, on the other hand, it is proposed to use the surveyor's report only for internal purposes within the landlord's legal team (perhaps for 'policing' the views of another surveyor who is to give evidence for the landlord in court, or for cross examining a single joint expert), then the preparation of his report will not be subject to Part 35 and will continue to be privileged.[2]

The distinction discussed above also underlies the Draft Code of Guidance for Experts, which speaks of experts who are instructed to act solely in an advisory capacity (the fruit of their labours being referred to in the Draft Code as 'advice') and experts who are asked to give or prepare evidence for the purpose of court proceedings (their labours leading to a 'report'). The Draft Code provides, in paragraph 11, that 'As and when experts' *advice* becomes a *report*, an opportunity must be afforded to the experts to amend their advice'. The oddity of the Draft Code, however, is that (unlike Part 35) it affords guidance not only to experts writing 'reports' but also to experts providing 'advice' – see, for example, paragraph 6. Presumably, this is just an example of the court endeavouring to ensure that sensible and reasonable behaviour is adopted on all fronts even outside the strict confines of proceedings governed by the CPR. Furthermore, of course, if common standards fall to be applied by experts drafting 'advice' and experts drafting 'reports', the opportunity to amend that is required by the Draft Code at the point of metamorphosis from one stage to another should (at least in theory) rarely need to be used.

---

2   It is perhaps worth stressing that laying aside questions of proportionality and the recoverability of costs, there is in principle no reason at all why a party should not instruct two experts – one purely internal to the litigation team, with whom communications will *prima facie* be privileged, and another 'true' expert witness, whose primary duty will be to the court and with whom communications are not privileged. Indeed, the possibility that parties might indeed recruit such 'shadow' experts was one of the principal arguments advanced against Lord Woolf's proposals on single joint experts, the fear being that three experts could end up being involved rather than the traditional two.

Just how seriously the courts view the new provisions on the impartiality of experts has already become apparent. In *Stevens v Gullis* [2000] 1 All ER 527,[3] a judge had debarred a witness from giving expert evidence on the basis that his report did not comply (despite an earlier order that it should) with the requirements of PD35. Most notably, the report lacked a statement that the witness understood and had complied with his duty to the court. Nor did it contain a summary of the substance of his instructions. The judge at first instance was severe:

> In my view it is in the interests of the administration of justice that Mr (X) should not give his evidence in the circumstances which I have outlined. It is essential in a complicated case such as this that the court should have a competent expert dealing with the matters which are in issue ... Mr (X), not having apparently understood his duty to the court and not having set out in his report that he understands it, is in my view a person whose evidence I should not encourage in the administration of justice. [p 532a]

The judge took this view even though he regarded the evidence in question as likely to be crucial.

On appeal, Lord Woolf was similarly robust. He refuted any suggestion that the CPR provisions on the impartiality of experts contained anything particularly novel:

> [PD35] did no more than reflect the position as it had been well enunciated in the authorities prior to the CPR coming into force. The position was made clear in numerous authorities but, in particular, in the decision of Cresswell J in *The Ikarian Reefer* [1993] 2 Lloyds Rep 68. In different words Cresswell J summarised the duties of an expert ... Those requirements are underlined by the CPR. It is now clear from the rules that, in addition to the duty which an expert owes to a party, he is also under a duty to the court. [p 533a]

And again:

> The requirements of the practice direction that an expert understands his responsibilities, and is required to give details of his qualifications and the other matters set out in paragraph 1 of the practice direction, are intended to focus the mind of the expert on his responsibilities in order that the litigation may progress in accordance with the overriding principles contained in Part 1 of the CPR. Mr (X) had demonstrated that he had no conception of those requirements and I am quite satisfied that the judge had no alternative but to take the action which he did notwithstanding the fact that the CPR had only recently come into force and that the consequences to the defendant of the course which was taken were draconian and could deprive him of a claim which he might otherwise have ... [p 533e]

On the other hand, the question of objectivity is to be addressed as one of substance and not merely of form. *Field v Leeds City Council* (2000) *The Times*, 18 January, is a case in point. The judge in a housing disrepair claim had

---

3   Applied by HH Judge Toulmin QC in *Anglo Group plc v Winther Brown & Co Ltd* (2000) unreported, 1 March, Technology and Construction Court.

refused to admit the evidence of a surveyor on the basis that he was employed by the defendant council. The Court of Appeal, led by Lord Woolf, held that the mere fact of employment by a party did not necessarily bar a witness from giving expert evidence – provided that he was otherwise properly qualified to give evidence and that he understood his duties to the court. In such a situation, the court should examine the witness's report and form a view on his suitability to give expert evidence. The case also contains observations on means of avoiding similar problems in future, including the possible use of a single joint expert in such cases.

There are yet further features of the new rules which depart from the historical tendency to regard experts as 'hired guns' for each side. Thus, a party is now able, before trial, to put *written questions to another party's expert* (Part 35.6). The answers are to be treated as 'part of the expert's report'. Unless the court or the other side agrees, such questions may only be put once (within 28 days of service of the original report) and must be 'for the purpose only of clarification' of the existing report. Nevertheless, this procedure (which also applies to the reports of single joint experts) could, if invoked with discretion, have telling tactical effects – particularly since, if a question is not answered by an expert, the court has power to forbid any reliance on that expert's evidence and/or the recovery of his costs from any other party (Part 35.6(4)).

The court effectively also has *power to direct a party to provide an expert report,* or at least something remarkably similar thereto. Part 35.9 reads:

> Where a party has access to information which is not reasonably available to the other party, the court may direct the party who has access to the information to –
>
> (a) prepare and file a document recording the information; and
>
> (b) serve a copy of that document on the other party.

The original intended purpose of this power (and the controversy that it provoked) is described in the Final Report, chapter 13, paragraphs 38–41. One notes the extraordinarily broad drafting of the final provision, being, on the face of it, a power to direct the preparation of 'a document recording information' because one party has better 'access to (that) information'. One can only assume that the appearance of the power in Part 35, dealing with expert evidence, will lead to the wording being construed within the context of expert evidence, rather than as giving any broader power. However, that frankly remains to be seen. Nor is it entirely clear whether this power can only be exercised after proceedings have been commenced – or whether, as Lord Woolf proposed, it could be exercised even before the start of proceedings, so as to compel a possible defendant with access to technical information to provide a potential claimant with that information. The aim, presumably, would be to 'nip in the bud' hopeless claims that are being put forward simply because of a lack of relevant information.

D   DISCUSSIONS BETWEEN EXPERTS

The stress on narrowing the issues in a case and on co-operation between parties and court also underlies the new provisions on discussions between experts. The new rules are expressly in terms of 'discussions' – not 'meetings' as in the old RSC – so that telephone communications should suffice. However, it seems unlikely that 'discussions' would cover E-mail or other written communications. Voice to voice (if not face to face) contact is apparently desired.

Not only may the court direct a discussion between experts so that issues can be identified and agreed; it may, in addition, itself specify the issues which the experts are to discuss (Part 35.12(2)). The court may direct the experts, following their discussions, to produce a statement for the court, showing the issues on which they agree and those on which they disagree, together with a summary of their reasons for disagreeing (Part 35.12(3)). Subject (presumably) to any such direction, the content of the experts' discussions is not to be referred to at trial without the parties' consent. Furthermore, no agreement that is in fact reached by the experts on an issue is formally binding on the parties without their express agreement (Part 35.12(5)). However, the evidentiary hurdle represented by any such agreement between experts is self-evident, especially if the agreement is communicated to the court in a statement prepared under rule Part 35.12(3).

E   ASSESSORS

Lord Woolf recommended that particularly in more complex cases, greater use should be made of existing powers to appoint expert assessors to assist the court itself. These powers are now in Part 35.15. Lord Woolf envisaged such assessors presiding over meetings between experts and 'helping them to reach agreement'. On the face of it, since the role of an assessor is to 'educate' the judge and to assist him in reaching his decision, there would appear to be difficulties in the way of an assessor's attending meetings that are effectively to be 'without prejudice'. Nor do the new rules expressly mention any such role for assessors. However, the Draft Code of Guidance for Experts certainly does contemplate them playing such a role.

CHAPTER 20

OFFERS TO SETTLE
AND PAYMENTS INTO COURT

On a first reading, Part 36 is far and away one of the least digestible parts of the new Rules. That is partly because of the technical matters with which it deals and partly because its structure does not entirely reflect what was proposed by Lord Woolf, whether in his Interim or Final Reports. Despite that fact, it seems easiest to begin with the Interim Report.

LORD WOOLF'S PROPOSALS

Lord Woolf began Chapter 24 of his Interim Report by saying:

> It is part of the policy of this report to develop measures which will encourage reasonable and early settlement of proceedings. It is a curious feature of our present procedure, as reflected in the rules of court, that, although the majority of disputes end in a settlement, the rules are mainly directed towards preparation for trial. My aim is to increase the emphasis on resolution otherwise than by trial.

He went on to discuss the two honourable exceptions to the trial-based flavour of the old rules, namely payments into court, and Calderbank (or Ord 22 r 14) offers made 'without prejudice save as to costs'. Under the old rules, a payment into court was suitable for a debt or damages claim and a Calderbank offer for other matters such as an offer on an issue, say the percentage of damages to be deducted for contributory negligence. The authorities suggested that the Calderbank procedure might not be used whenever a payment in could be made.

In his Interim Report, Lord Woolf recommended, *inter alia*:

(i)   That the system of actual payments into court should be abolished, so that a Calderbank offer would suffice in a debt or damages claim as well as more generally.

(ii) That cost-effective offers to settle should be able to be made by a plaintiff as well as by a defendant.

(iii) That such offers should be able to relate to the whole case or to individual issues or claims.

(iv) That such offers should be able to be made even before the commencement of proceedings.

(v)   That there should be financial incentives to encourage parties, particularly claimants, to make offers to settle.

In his Final Report, following pressure from the profession, Lord Woolf retreated from the proposed abolition of payments in. He recommended instead that:

> the making of an offer, in accordance with rules of court, should be the primary requirement, with payments in being a secondary and optional means of backing an offer. The absence of a payment in should not normally influence the court's view of whether an offer was reasonable. [FR chap 11]

THE NEW RULES

In general terms, the new Rules display a much greater attachment to the merits of the system of payments into court than Lord Woolf's proposals, even in their revised form. To those Rules we now turn. Given their complexity – and anyone seeking to use them should certainly study them in detail – we think it sensible if, for the purposes of exposition, we concentrate more on their overall structure than on the details of the relevant time limits and the like. That is not, of course, to say that the time limits will not in practice be vital.

Part 36 does *not* apply to the small claims track.[1] It contains, as its opening words state, rules about offers to settle and payments into court and 'the consequences *where an offer to settle or payment into court is made in accordance with this Part*' (emphasis added). So much is obviously not to say that a party is only able to settle a case through the Part 36 rules. However, if he does not follow those rules, he will not achieve the (relative) security in relation to costs that they afford. Part 36.1(2) puts it thus:

> Nothing in this Part prevents a party making an offer to settle in whatever way he chooses, but if that offer is not made in accordance with this Part, it will only have the consequences specified in this Part if the court so orders.

It follows from that that other attempts to settle are not irrelevant in relation to costs. Both defective attempts at following the Part 36 rules and offers that do not even make the attempt *may* be taken into account. The court will give them such weight as it thinks appropriate (PD36, para 1.3).

Definitions and general matters

Most of the rules are in Part 36 itself. However, the related practice direction also has to be considered, as also do Part 37 and the practice direction related to that.[2]

---

1 Part 27.2(1)(g) – though compare Part 36.2(5).
2 Part 37 contains various miscellaneous rules concerning payments into court, including in particular the payment out of monies in court, and payments in where a defendant is relying on the defence of tender before action.

Part 36.2(1) provides that:

> An offer made in accordance with the requirements of this Part is called –
>
> (a) if made by way of a payment into court, 'a Part 36 payment';
>
> (b) otherwise, 'a Part 36 offer'.

There remains a general ban on mentioning a payment in to the trial judge until after judgment on all questions of liability and quantum. The same result is achieved in relation to Part 36 offers by treating them as 'without prejudice save as to costs' (Part 36.19).

It is, of course, possible to make a Part 36 payment or offer in respect of a counterclaim (or other Part 20 claim) as well as in respect of a straightforward claim.

The making of Part 36 offers and payments

Part 36 offers can be made or improved (and Part 36 payments made or increased) at any time after proceedings have started. They can be made in relation to appeal proceedings as well as proceedings at first instance.

Under the CPR (and whatever Lord Woolf may have hoped for), a defendant seeking to settle a 'money claim' cannot generally achieve the costs protection of Part 36 except by way of payment in (Part 36.3(1)). As under the old rules, any money paid into court as a condition of defending an action can be appropriated so as to constitute a Part 36 payment (Part 37.2(1)). If a claim includes both a money and a non-money claim, then a defendant seeking to settle the whole claim with costs protection must make a Part 36 payment in relation to the money claim and a Part 36 offer in relation to the rest. The notice of payment in must identify the document that sets out the terms of the Part 36 offer and state that acceptance of the payment in will be treated as acceptance of the Part 36 offer (Part 36.4).

Part 36 offers must be in writing. They may, as suggested by Lord Woolf, relate to particular parts of (or issues in) proceedings as well as to the claim as a whole. The offer must identify whether it relates to the whole claim or only to part of it and must state whether any counterclaim is taken into account (Part 36.5(3)). If it is expressed not to be inclusive of interest, certain details as to interest must be provided. There are similar provisions relating to the details to be provided in Part 36 payment notices.

Clarification and withdrawal

There are also provisions allowing a party to seek clarification of another party's Part 36 offer or payment – initially in writing and, if need be, by court order (Part 36.9).

Part 36 payments may only be withdrawn with leave of the court (Part 36.6(5)). A Part 36 offer can, of course, be withdrawn without leave but if it is, it will not have Part 36 costs consequences (Part 36.5(8)).

Offers before proceedings are brought

The CPR also adopt Lord Woolf's proposal that offers with 'protective' consequences in costs should be possible even before the commencement of proceedings. The relevant provisions (Part 36.10) are complicated and should be studied in detail. However, they too demonstrate the draftsman's attachment to the system of payments in, since, in the case of a money claim, a defendant offeror seeking costs protection must within 14 days of service of proceedings make a payment in which is not less than the sum he had offered before proceedings were brought.

In *Ford v GKR Construction* [2000] 1 All ER 802, Lord Woolf stressed that the principle that parties should conduct litigation by making full, prompt and proper disclosure was even more important now that the CPR were in force. In particular, if the system of making pre-litigation Part 36 offers was to work in the way the rules intended, parties had to be provided with the information they required in order to assess whether to make or accept an offer. A failure to disclose material matters, which led to another party's being unable to assess properly whether to make or accept an offer (or to his reaching a decision different from that which he would have reached with proper disclosure), were material matters for the court to take into account in considering the eventual incidence of costs.

The consequences of acceptance

If a defendant's Part 36 offer or payment is accepted within the relevant period without the need for the court's permission, the claimant will be entitled to his costs on the standard basis up to the date of serving notice of acceptance (Part 36.13(1) and (4)).[3] Likewise, where a claimant's Part 36 offer is accepted within the relevant time without the need for the court's permission, the claimant will be entitled to his costs up to the date the defendant serves notice of acceptance (Part 36.14).

In technical terms, acceptance of a Part 36 offer or payment relating to the whole of a claim leads to the claim being stayed on the terms of the accepted offer. The aim of this provision is that the court should have the power to deal with questions of enforcement without any need for a fresh action (Part 36.15(2)).

In certain circumstances, of course, Part 36 offers and payments may only be accepted with leave of the court – most importantly, perhaps, where children or patients are involved, or where offers or payments are made just before trial or where the prescribed time for acceptance has expired (Parts 36.11(2) and 36.12(2)).

---

3   Unless the court orders otherwise, the same also applies where the offer or payment related to only part of the claim and the claimant abandons the balance of his claim (Part 36.13(2)).

The effect of unaccepted offers

If at trial a claimant fails to better a Part 36 payment or to obtain a judgment which is more advantageous than the defendant's Part 36 offer, the usual rule is that the court will order the claimant to bear the defendant's costs incurred after expiry of the time for acceptance (Part 36.20(2)). However, this is subject to the proviso 'unless (the court) considers it unjust (so to order)'.

Conversely, if at trial a defendant is held liable for more (or the judgment against him is more advantageous to the claimant) than the proposals contained in a claimant's Part 36 offer, the court may order interest at a higher rate than usual on all or part of any sum awarded to the claimant from the latest date upon which the defendant could have accepted the offer (Part 36.21). The court may also order that the claimant should have his costs for that period on an indemnity basis, together with interest thereon at a higher rate than usual. These provisions are also subject to the proviso 'unless (the court) considers it unjust (so to order)' (Part 36.21(4)).

Various factors are listed that must be taken into account when deciding on the justice or otherwise of the usual order. They include the terms of any Part 36 offer; the stage when any offer or payment in was made; the information available to the parties at the time it was made; and the conduct of the parties with regard to providing or refusing information for the purposes of enabling an offer or payment in to be made or evaluated (Part 36.21(5)).

A challenge to the *vires* of Part 36.21 recently failed – see *All-in-One Design & Build Ltd v Motcomb Estates Ltd* (2000) *The Times*, 4 April (Mr Michael Black QC, sitting as a Deputy High Court Judge), in which the analysis of David Foskett QC in *Little v George Little Sebire & Co* (1999) *The Times*, 17 November was approved.

For a consideration of how the principles considered above might work in practice, see the Court of Appeal decision in *Ford v GKR Construction* [2000] 1 All ER 802, referred to above. There, even though a claimant had failed to beat a payment in, a judge had ordered the defendant to pay all the costs. This was partly on the basis that relevant steps (surveillance to produce video evidence in support of an allegation of malingering) had not been taken by the defendant until a late stage, indeed during the trial itself. Though the damages were reduced as a result of the resulting film, the claimant was acquitted of any suggestion of dishonesty. She had attempted to settle for the payment in plus costs as soon as she saw the video. The Court of Appeal upheld the judge's decision, stressing that the question was for the judge's discretion. Judge LJ said:

> Civil litigation is now developing into a system designed to enable the parties involved to know where they stand in reality at the earliest possible stage, and at the lowest practicable cost, so that they may make informed decisions about their prospects and the sensible conduct of their cases. Among other factors,

the judge exercising his discretion about costs should consider is whether one side or the other has, or has not, conducted litigation with those principles in mind. That is what Judge Gaskell did here and he was right to do so. [p 807e]

All costs decisions turn on their particular facts but for another case concerning malingering and a claimant who failed to beat a payment in, this time with a rather different outcome, see *Burgess v British Steel* (2000) *The Times*, 29 February, CA.

Interest

If nothing is said about interest in a claimant's Part 36 offer or in a Part 36 payment notice, the offer or payment will be treated as being inclusive of all interest until the last date on which it could be accepted (Part 36.22(1)). However, if the offer is expressed not to be inclusive of interest, certain particulars have to be provided as to what interest (if any) is offered, and for what period (Part 36.22(2)).

CHAPTER 21

DISCONTINUANCE (PART 38)

On one view, the new regime of active case management could well lead to an increased use of the procedure of discontinuance. At least in theory, allowing a claim to become dormant is simply not an option that is any longer available to a claimant who has thought better of his proceedings. A case will now be pushed forward to trial by the court, unless it is settled or the claimant formally discontinues pursuant to Part 38.[1]

A claimant may discontinue all or part of his claim at any time (Part 38.2(1)). He does so by filing a notice to that effect and serving a copy of it upon all other parties to the proceedings (Part 38.3(1)). A claimant may discontinue all or part of his claim against one or more defendants but proceed with it against the remaining defendants (Part 38.3(4)). However, where a claimant claims a number of remedies, merely to abandon a claim to one particular remedy is not to be regarded as discontinuance (Part 38.1(2)).

Discontinuance takes effect against a defendant on the date of service of the notice of discontinuance and as against him, the proceedings are at an end from that date (Part 38.5). This will not affect any proceedings to do with costs.

A defendant does not usually require the court's permission to discontinue.[2] However, there are three specified exceptions – (1) where an interim injunction has been granted or an undertaking given to the court; (2) where the claimant has received an interim payment, whether voluntary or under Part 25, and the paying defendant has not consented in writing to discontinuance; and (3) where there are other claimants and they have not consented in writing (Part 38.2).

Furthermore, a defendant may apply to the court to set aside a notice of discontinuance. Such an application must be made within 28 days of the service of the notice (Part 38.4).

---

1   A competing view is that, under the CPR, all claimants will be so well prepared even before issuing proceedings that there will be far fewer cases where a claimant is driven into discontinuing.

2   This is an adoption of the old county court practice, rather than the old High Court procedure. The general need for leave to discontinue under the old RSC was, of course, designed to prevent a plaintiff discontinuing in a way that unfairly prejudiced the defendant. Now, however, the defendant will generally be protected in costs (see Part 38.6) and will, in any event, have a right to apply to set aside the notice of discontinuance (for example, where he seeks terms as to costs that are more generous than the usual ones).

Service of a notice of discontinuance is, in most cases, a recognition by a claimant that his case is bound to fail at trial. In consequence, the general rule is that the claimant is liable for the defendant's cost incurred on or before the date of discontinuance (Part 38.6(1)). An order for costs on the standard basis is deemed to have been made against the claimant – see Part 44.12(2)(d). However, if there are special circumstances, it is open to a claimant to apply to the court to seek an order that he should not be liable for the costs in the usual way.

A claimant who discontinues a claim needs the permission of the court to make another claim against the same defendant, if discontinuance was after the service of a defence and if the second claim arises out of facts which are the same or substantially the same as those relating to the discontinued claim (Part 38.7). The requirement for permission does not bite if the second set of proceedings is commenced before the earlier claim has been discontinued and further pursuit of the second action in that situation will not necessarily be an abuse – see *Stanway v Attorney General* (1999) *The Times*, 25 November (Lloyd J), for an example.

CHAPTER 22

MISCELLANEOUS PROVISIONS RELATING TO HEARINGS (PART 39)

PUBLIC/PRIVATE HEARINGS?

It has long been recognised that there is the strongest possible public interest in ensuring public access to the courts. Publicity, in the words of Bentham, 'keeps the judge himself while trying under trial'.[1] Quite apart from all earlier judicial pronouncements and statutory provisions, this public interest will shortly be enshrined in English law through Article 6 of the European Convention on Human Rights. Given these factors – and indeed the origins of the CPR in two reports entitled 'Access to Justice' – it is perhaps slightly ironic that the new rules deal with the issue of public access to the court only as a 'miscellaneous provision relating to hearings', which is buried away in Part 39.

Nevertheless, the general principle there set out is that a hearing is to be in public (Part 39.2(1)). Only where justified on one of various specified grounds, or 'where necessary in the interests of justice', may a hearing be held in private (Part 39.2(3)). The grounds specified for holding a hearing in private appear, broadly speaking, to be modelled on the exceptions in Article 6 of the Convention. One particularly broad one is where the hearing 'involves confidential information (including information relating to personal financial matters) and publicity would damage that confidentiality'. This exception provides the peg on which a whole range of hearings are in the first instance to be listed in private (PD39, para 1.5) – including, for example, a mortgagee's claim for possession of land, and a landlord's claim for possession of a dwelling house based on non-payment of rent.

However, it must be stressed that there is no exception in principle for interlocutory hearings in chambers before a master or a district judge. In consequence, the general rule now is that such hearings are open to the public just as much as a trial is. (Even before the CPR, such an approach had been foreshadowed by the Court of Appeal's decision in *Hodgson v Imperial Tobacco Ltd* [1998] 2 All ER 673.) Nevertheless, the realities of court accommodation across the country are reflected in the caveat that there is no requirement for the court 'to make special arrangements for accommodating members of the public' (Part 39.2(2)). In principle, it is difficult to understand how the public can enjoy an effective right of access to the courts where the courts are

---

1   As approved by Lord Shaw of Dunfermline in *Scott v Scott* [1913] AC 417, 477 and quoted by Potter LJ in *GIO Services Ltd v Liverpool and London Ltd* [1999] 1 WLR 984, 994.

specifically relieved of the burden of making 'special arrangements' for such access. Certainly considerations of cost and administrative convenience are not grounds of exception to the general rule contained in Article 6 of the European Convention and it may well be that in an appropriate case, the absence of reasonable facilities for accommodation of the public could lead to a challenge on human rights grounds.[2]

Whether a hearing is held in public or in private may have particular importance for a litigant in person who is seeking to use the services of a McKenzie friend. In public proceedings, such services should be allowed unless the judge is satisfied that fairness and the interests of justice require otherwise and the same applies to chambers proceedings that are not in private. But where proceedings are in private, then the nature of the proceedings making it appropriate for them to be in private may make a McKenzie friend undesirable. (See generally, in this regard, the judgment of Lord Woolf in *R v Bow County Court ex parte Pelling* [1999] 4 All ER 751.)

ACCESS TO JUDGMENTS, WITNESS STATEMENTS, ETC

When the court sits in public, a member of the public may obtain a copy of any order made or a transcript of any judgment given on payment of the appropriate fee. However, where the order is made or judgment given in private, such documents cannot be obtained by a third party without the permission of the court (PD39, paras 1.11 and 1.12). The transcript of a public hearing itself may also be obtained from the court upon the payment of a fee (PD39, para 6.3).

As to the right of members of the public to inspect witness statements tendered in evidence, see Part 32.13 and Part 5.4. However, despite the remarks of Potter LJ in *GIO Services Ltd v Liverpool and London Ltd* [1999] 1 WLR 984, at p 997B, there is not yet any specific provision governing access by members of the public to skeleton arguments and written submissions. The question of access to such documents will therefore continue to be governed by the court's inherent jurisdiction. In *GIO Services*, the Court of Appeal held that it was within the court's inherent jurisdiction to permit third parties to have access to copies of written openings that had been used in lieu of oral openings. Potter LJ held that a person with legitimate reasons for seeking a written opening or skeleton argument used in lieu of oral opening was *prima facie* entitled to obtain copies of them. The fact that in that case the third party

---

2   For a recent (and clear) example of proceedings being held to be invalid because, despite the best of intentions, they were not heard in public, see *Storer v British Gas plc* (2000) *The Times*, 1 March (employment tribunal sitting, due to pressure of business, in Regional Chairman's office behind door marked 'Private' and with a coded lock – held not in public).

had litigation with one of the parties, in which he wished to use the information as a springboard for making a specific discovery application, did not render his interest illegitimate.[3]

REPRESENTATION OF COMPANIES AND OTHER MISCELLANEOUS PROVISIONS

There is another important innovation in Part 39(6). This follows the recommendations of Lord Woolf (FR chap 12, p 131 *et seq*) by permitting a company or other corporation to be represented at trial by one of its employees. An employee may represent a company where he is authorised to do so and where the court has given permission. PD39, para 5.3 provides that such permission should be granted unless there is some particular reason why it should be withheld. The complexity of the issues in question and the experience and position of the proposed representative are expressly matters to be taken into account when deciding whether to grant permission. It will not normally be given in jury trials or in contempt proceedings. Effectively, a company represented by an employee in this way is a new class of litigant in person. This is equally true for costs purposes – see Part 48.6(6)(a). Similarly, a company commencing proceedings does not need to act by a solicitor – the old RSC Ord 5 r 6(2) having been repealed.

The other 'miscellaneous matters' dealt with in Part 39 include the consequences of a party's failure to attend the trial (Part 39.3), trial bundles (Part 39.5) and the release of documents impounded by the court (Part 39.7).

---

3 More generally as to an increasing tension between open and efficient justice, see the judgment of Lord Bingham CJ in *SmithKline Beecham Biologicals SA v Connaught Laboratories Inc* [1999] 4 All ER 498 (dealing with judicial pre-reading of documents and how such documents can be said to enter the public domain if never actually read or referred to in court).

CHAPTER 23

JUDGMENTS AND ORDERS (PART 40)

A judgment or order of the court must comply with the formal requirements contained in Part 40.2. In most cases, a judgment must bear the name and judicial title of the person who made it. It must also state the date on which the order was made and be sealed by the court.

In broad terms, the court itself will draw up a judgment or order, unless it orders a party to draw it up or accepts a party's offer to do so (Part 40.3(1)). It can order that the parties file an agreed statement of the terms of the order, before it is checked and sealed by the court (Part 40.3(2)). A party with responsibility for drawing up an order has, in the usual course, seven days within which to draw it up and file it. If he fails to do so within that period, then the other party may do so (Part 40.3(3)).

Under the new rules, orders will usually be served on the parties by the court (Part 40.4) – and indeed can be served on other persons, or on a party personally as well as on his solicitor (Part 40.5).

It is important to appreciate that a judgment or order takes effect from the moment that it is pronounced by the judge. Its effectiveness is not postponed to the completion of the formality of drawing it up as a sealed judgment (Part 40.7).[1]

As a general rule, a party ordered to pay a sum of money (including costs) must do so within 14 days of the date of the judgment. The court may specify a different date for payment or it may permit payment to be made by instalments (Part 40.11). Again, unless the court orders otherwise, interest under the Judgments Act 1838 or the County Courts Act 1984 runs from the date judgment is pronounced (Part 40.8).[2]

Part 40.6 contains a procedure whereby a consent order between legally-represented parties can, in certain specified situations, be entered by a court officer without the need to refer to a judge. Even where one of the parties is a litigant in person, the court may deal with the matter without a hearing (Part 40.6(5) and (6)). One of the most important practical applications of these provisions will be the making of Tomlin Orders – see Part 40.6(3)(b)(ii) and PD40, para 3.

---

1   Presumably the same will apply, in the absence of contrary order, to the periods for appealing under the new provisions on appeals.

2   As to rates of interest in commercial cases, even in the county court, see *Adcock v Co-operative Insurance Society Ltd* (2000) *The Times*, 26 April, CA.

Part 40.12 is the new 'slip rule', providing a convenient means of correcting any accidental slip or omission in a judgment or order. An application may be made informally by letter and may be considered without a hearing, if the other party consents or where the court does not consider that a hearing would be appropriate (PD40, para 4).

The practice direction contains important provisions about the wording of orders requiring acts to be done (PD40, para 8). Not only must the act itself be clearly identified but also the time within which it is to be done and, where appropriate, the consequences of failure to do it within that time. Standard examples of unless orders are given. Penal notices are dealt with at PD40, para 9.1.

CHAPTER 24

COSTS

INTRODUCTORY

Apart from the rules on payments into court and Part 36 offers (see Chapter 20 above), the new rules on costs are, for the most part, set out in Parts 43 to 48. The scope of these Parts is as follows:

Part 43	Scope of costs rules and definitions
Part 44	General rules about costs
Part 45	Fixed costs
Part 46	Fast track trial costs
Part 47	Procedure for detailed assessment and default provisions
Part 48	Costs – special cases

There is, of course, an enormous amount of detail in these provisions and only certain of the most prominent features can be highlighted here. In broad terms, we restrict our observations in this chapter to the multi-track, having already considered the general nature of the court's approach to costs on the other two tracks in Chapters 5 and 6 above. Furthermore, we do not tackle any complications arising out of Legal Aid but assume that both parties are privately funded.

To begin with, here as elsewhere, there is a considerable amount of *new vocabulary* to be learnt. For example, a taxing master is now a 'costs judge'. A party entitled to be paid costs is called the 'receiving party' and the party liable to pay the 'paying party'. The amount of costs is now fixed by 'assessment', which can be either 'summary' or 'detailed'. 'Summary assessment' is defined as the procedure whereby the court orders the payment of a sum of money, instead of 'fixed costs' or 'detailed assessment' (Part 43.3). 'Detailed assessment' is the old taxation.

It is also worth mentioning the *three different kinds of costs breakdowns* that are repeatedly referred to in the Rules. These are:

Statement of Costs (for use on a summary assessment)

Bill of Costs (for use on a detailed assessment)

Estimate of costs

Model forms of a Statement of Costs and of a Bill of Costs are provided – being Forms 1 and 2 respectively in the Schedule of Costs Forms. The first must be followed 'as closely as possible' (PD44, para 4.5(3)) and use of the second, though not compulsory, is encouraged. An Estimate of Costs is defined as 'an estimate of those costs already incurred and, if appropriate, to be incurred by the party who gives it which he intends, if he is successful in the case, to seek to recover from any other party under an order for costs' (para 4.2 of Section 4 of the Directions relating to Part 43). Such estimates form an important part of the new case management system. They should be substantially in the form of the model form for a Statement of Costs and the court can order them to be filed and served at any stage. In particular, estimates must be served with the allocation questionnaires. The court can also order them to be prepared 'in such a way as to demonstrate the likely effects of giving or not giving a particular case management direction which the court is considering, for example a direction for a split trial or for the trial of a preliminary issue'.

Perhaps, at this early stage, one should also add a word about the *transitional arrangements in relation to costs*. PD51, para 18 provides that any assessment of costs taking place after 26 April 1999 will be governed by Parts 43 to 48 but that the general presumption is that no costs for work done before that date will be disallowed if those costs would have been allowed on taxation before 26 April 1999. The decision whether to allow costs for work done on or after 26 April 1999 will generally be taken in accordance with Parts 43 to 48. There are also further detailed transitional arrangements in Section III of PD48.

THE COURT'S DISCRETION AS TO COSTS

The court's discretion over costs covers:
- whether they are payable by one party to another;
- the amount of those costs; and
- when they are to be paid. (Part 44.3(1))

We take each of these aspects in turn.

Who should pay?

The general rule is that the unsuccessful party will be ordered to pay the costs of the successful party (Part 44.3(2)). However, the court may make a different order and in deciding what order (if any) to make, it must have regard to all the circumstances including:

(a) the conduct of all the parties;

(b) whether a party has succeeded on part of his case, even if he has not been wholly successful; and

(c) any payment into court or admissible offer to settle made by a party which is drawn to the court's attention (whether or not made in accordance with Part 36). [Part 44.3(4)]

The conduct of the parties has, of course, always constituted one of the matters that a court could take into account when making a costs order. Now, it will be noted, conduct *must* be taken into account. It is broadly (but non-exhaustively) defined as including:

(a) conduct before, as well as during, the proceedings, and in particular the extent to which the parties followed any relevant pre-action protocol;

(b) whether it was reasonable for a party to raise, pursue or contest a particular allegation or issue;

(c) the manner in which a party has pursued or defended his case or a particular allegation or issue; and

(d) whether a claimant who has succeeded in his claim, in whole or in part, exaggerated his claim. [Part 44.3(5)]

It is worth stressing that the basic rule that 'costs follow the event' may well be applied rather differently after 26 April 1999 than before.

In order to explain this, it is perhaps best to begin with a recent statement of the court's general approach to costs under the old rules. In *Re Elgindata Ltd (No 2)* [1992] 1 WLR 1207, Nourse LJ set out the following general principles derived from the authorities:

> The principles are these. (i) Costs are in the discretion of the court. (ii) They should follow the event, except when it appears to the court that in the circumstances of the case some other order should be made. (iii) The general rule does not cease to apply simply because the successful party raises issues or make allegations on which he fails, but where that has caused a significant increase in the length or cost of the proceedings he may be deprived of the whole or a part of his costs. (iv) Where the successful party raises issues or makes allegations improperly or unreasonably, the court may not only deprive him of his costs but may order him to pay the whole or a part of the unsuccessful party's costs. [p 1214]

However, under a case management regime designed to identify the real issues and to confine the parties to them, the unnecessary pursuit of hopeless or peripheral issues (even by the eventual winner) may be more severely punished than previously. It is possible, in short, that there may be a more refined application of the general principle of 'costs follow the event', with costs being allowed on one issue but not on another. Lord Woolf himself explained the point in *AEI Rediffusion Music Ltd v Phonographic Performance Ltd* [1999] 1 WLR 1507. This was a pre-CPR case dealing with the slightly different costs regime in the Copyright Tribunal. However, looking forward to the CPR regime and having cited Part 44.3(2), (4) and (5), Lord Woolf said:

> I draw attention to the new Rules because, while they make clear that the general rule remains, that the successful party will normally be entitled to costs, they at the same time indicate the wide range of considerations which will result in the court making different orders as to costs. From 26 April 1999 the 'follow the event principle' will still play a significant role, but it will be a

starting point from which a court can readily depart. This is also the position prior to the new rules coming into force. The most significant change of emphasis of the new rules is to require courts to be more ready to make separate orders which reflect the outcome of different issues. In doing this the new Rules are reflecting a change of practice which has already started. It is now clear that too robust an application of the 'follow the event principle' encourages litigants to increase the costs of litigation, since it discourages litigants from being selective as to the points they take. If you recover all your costs as long as you win, you are encouraged to leave no stone unturned in your effort to do so. [p 1522H]

Similarly, in *Bank of Credit & Commerce International SA v Ali (No 4)* (2000) *The Times*, 2 March, Lightman J, having said that 'much of the learning developed prior to the adoption of [the CPR] on the court's approach to the award of costs is likely to prove today to be a mere distraction to a judge', went on to say:

Looking at the CPR as a whole, it is apparent that the overriding concern of the court must be to make the order which justice requires; that an order in favour of the successful party is generally to be adopted as calculated to achieve this end; but the court in any particular case may make a different order if on the facts of that case justice so requires; and the court should have regard to the success of the parties on parts only of their cases. The straight jacket imposed on the Court by the decision of the Court of Appeal in *Re Elgindata Ltd (No 2)* [1992] 1 WLR 1207, relaxed to a degree in cases of group litigation by the decision of Mrs Justice Smith in *Ochwat v Watson Burton* (18 February 1998), is gone, and the search for justice is untrammelled by constraints beyond those laid down by the new code itself. I may add that for the purposes of the CPR success is not in my view a technical term but a result in real life, and the question as to who succeeded is a matter for the exercise of common sense.

However, in *Burgess v British Steel* (2000) *The Times*, 29 February, the Court of Appeal seemed to apply the principles in *Re Elgindata (No 2)* without question and without reference to the remarks of Lord Woolf or Lightman J referred to above. An equally guarded approach to the CPR, apparently doubting or denying that they are 'issue based' in relation to costs, seems to have been adopted by Rimer J in *Deg-Deutsche Investitions und Entwicklungsgesellschaft mbH v Koshy* (2000) *The Times*, 30 March. His Lordship appears to have said that it was difficult to detect Lord Woolf's 'change of emphasis' in Part 44.3 and that *Re Elgindata* as interpreted in *Phonographic Performance* continued to provide at least a general working guide to the just approach for the disposal of a costs issue. However, at the time of writing, we have been unable to obtain access to the full judgment.

Toulson J reviewed most of these authorities in *Sinochem v Fortune Oil* (2000) unreported, 11 February. Although attracted by the approach of Lightman J in the *BCCI* case, Toulson J felt bound by the Court of Appeal's decision in *Burgess v British Steel* to apply the principles of the *Elgindata* case. Toulson J indicated that, had he considered it open to him, he would have disallowed the successful party a third of its costs, on the basis that two of its witnesses had given untruthful evidence to the court. Permission to appeal was given and it is understood that the Court of Appeal will consider the matter at the end of this year. Hopefully, definitive guidance will be given on whether the CPR actually involve any (and, if so, what) change of emphasis in relation to costs following the event.

Before leaving the topic of who is to pay, it is important to point out that if in future an order is silent as to costs, then no party will be entitled to costs in relation to that order (Part 44.13(1)). The costs in question will not be costs in the case.

The amount of costs

The rules retain the familiar distinction between assessment on a 'standard' or 'indemnity' basis. However, the definition of these expressions has altered. In neither case, will the court allow costs that have been unreasonably incurred or that are unreasonable in amount (Part 44.4(1)). On the indemnity basis, any doubt as to reasonableness will be resolved in favour of the receiving party (Part 44.4(3)). On the standard basis, on the other hand, the court will only allow costs which are 'proportionate to the matters in issue' and any doubt as to reasonableness will be resolved in favour of the paying party (Part 44.4(2)).

In deciding the amount of costs, the court is again to have regard to all the circumstances, including:

    (a) the conduct of all the parties, including in particular –

        (i) conduct before, as well as during, the proceedings; and

        (ii) the efforts made, if any, before and during the proceedings in order to try to resolve the dispute;

    (b) the amount or value of any money or property involved;

    (c) the importance of the matter to all the parties;

    (d) the particular complexity of the matter or the difficulty or novelty of the questions raised;

    (e) the skill, effort, specialised knowledge and responsibility involved;

    (f) the time spent on the case; and

    (g) the place where and the circumstances in which work or any part of it was done. [Part 44.5(3)]

One way or another, these provisions give ample weaponry to a judge determined to penalise a party who has not conducted himself in accordance with the spirit of the new regime, say by failing to comply with a pre-action protocol, by unreasonably refusing to agree to ADR or by producing chaotic and ill-focussed statements of case.

When must costs be paid?

If a judgment or order stipulates the amount of the costs payable, they are payable within 14 days. However, if detailed assessment is required, the costs are payable within 14 days of certification of the amount payable (Part 44.8) – though the court has a general power to order a payment on account pending assessment (Part 44.3(8)).

This brings us to the important new changes in relation to the method of assessment.

SUMMARY ASSESSMENT

When the court makes an order for costs (other than for fixed costs), assessment of the amount payable can be either summary or detailed (Part 44.7). However, as a matter of principle, whenever the court makes a costs order of this kind, it should consider whether to make a summary assessment (PD44, para 4.3). The general rule is that there should be a summary assessment at the conclusion of a fast-track trial, and at the conclusion of any other hearing which has not lasted more than one day. The general rule can be departed from if there is good reason not to have a summary assessment – for example, 'where the paying party shows substantial grounds for disputing the sum claimed for costs that cannot be dealt with summarily or there is insufficient time to carry out a summary assessment' (PD44, para 4.4(1)). In most cases, however, the court will make a summary assessment – the new policy being one of 'Pay as you go'![1]

In order to facilitate the new practice in relation to summary assessment, each party is under a duty to assist the court by preparing a written statement of the costs he intends to claim, broken down by hours worked, rates charged, disbursements incurred and so forth. (Full details of what is required are in PD44.) The statements should be filed and served no later than 24 hours before the hearing. A party's failure without reasonable excuse to follow these provisions will be taken into account by the court in relation to the costs of the hearing in question and indeed of any necessary further hearing (PD44, para 4.6).

If there still exist any old-fashioned judges disinclined to embroil themselves in the tedious business of costs, then they too may find these provisions difficult to side-step. It is not possible to order a summary assessment by a costs officer. If summary assessment is appropriate but cannot be done on the day, then the court must give directions for a further

---

1   The new practice in favour of summary assessment in fact slightly pre-dated the CPR – see the *Lord Chief Justice's and Vice Chancellor's Practice Direction* of 3 February 1999, in force from 1 March 1999 [1999] 1 All ER 670.

hearing to deal with the matter itself (PD44, para 4.8). In short, there is effectively a choice between summary assessment by the judge who heard the matter or a detailed assessment.[2]

One purpose behind the new summary assessment provisions is, of course, to bring home to litigants at as early a stage as possible the real cost of litigation – in the hope and expectation that such knowledge will lead to more settlements, or will at least reduce the number of fully-contested interlocutory applications. Another vital provision in this regard is Part 44.2. It provides that:

> Where –
>
> (a) the court makes a costs order against a legally represented party; and
>
> (b) the party is not present when the order is made,
>
> the party's solicitor must notify his client in writing of the costs order no later than 7 days after the solicitor receives notice of the order.

To add to the potential embarrassment, the practice direction also requires the solicitor to give an explanation of *why* the costs order came to be made (PD44, para 1.2).

Even where the court takes the view that detailed assessment is necessary, it should consider whether to order a payment on account under Part 44.3(8) – see PD44, para 4.11. Neither the rule nor the practice direction offer any guidance as to how the court should exercise this power. However, at least in relation to the position after a full trial, the matter was considered from the point of view of general principle by Jacob J in *Mars UK Ltd v Teknowledge Ltd* (1999) *The Times*, 8 July. His Lordship held that the court's general approach should be to order a payment on account, though it obviously has a discretion to be exercised in the light of the circumstances of the particular case. This approach commended itself for two reasons. One was fairness to the receiving party. As Jacob J put it:

> It does not seem to me to be a good reason for keeping him out of some of his costs that you need time to work out the total amount. A payment of some lesser amount which he will almost certainly collect is a closer approximation to justice. So I hold that where a party is successful the court should on a rough and ready basis also normally order an amount to be paid on account, the amount being a lesser sum than the likely full amount.

Case management considerations also told in favour of this approach. Appropriate payments on account are likely to reduce the number of fully-fought detailed assessments, thereby saving the court's and the parties' resources.

---

2   The manner in which the summary assessment provisions will work in the Court of Appeal is dealt with in a *Practice Note* at [1999] 2 All ER 638. Basically, the parties need not serve Statements of Costs unless the Court of Appeal has indicated that the case may be suitable for summary assessment of costs.

DETAILED ASSESSMENT

For us, as for most barristers, taxation has always been 'another country' – over the hills and far away. Given our own ignorance of the historical intricacies and the wealth of detail that still exists even under the new system, we confine ourselves to making certain points of general principle about detailed assessment.

Detailed assessment will not normally take place until the conclusion of the proceedings but the court can order otherwise (Part 47.1).[3] On the other hand, there is no stay on detailed assessment pending an appeal, unless the court orders otherwise (Part 47.2).

There is a new means of commencing detailed assessment (by serving notice of commencement and a copy bill of costs). Full details of what is required are set out in Part 47.6 and the practice direction. There are strict time limits for commencement[4] – basically of three months from the order or other event giving rise to the detailed assessment (Part 47.7).

If detailed assessment is not commenced within the relevant time, the receiving party can put pressure on the paying party by seeking an order that assessment proceedings be commenced within a specified time (Part 47.8(1)). On such applications, the court will have the power to make an unless order to the effect that if proceedings are not commenced within a specified time, the receiving party will be disallowed all or part of the costs to which he would otherwise be entitled. Alternatively, if detailed assessment proceedings are started late (which can be done without permission) but before the receiving party has applied under Part 47.8(1) as described above, then the court will be able to disallow all or part of the interest that would otherwise be payable under section 17 of the Judgments Act 1838.

The paying party can respond by serving points of dispute. If he does not do so, a default costs certificate can be obtained against him (Parts 47.9 and 47.10). Points of reply are optional (Part 47.13).

If points of dispute are served, it is for the receiving party to request a detailed assessment hearing and there is a strict timetable for doing that. If that timetable is not met, there is again provision for the imposition of unless orders (with adverse consequences as to the basic amount of costs recoverable) and for possible sanctions in interest, all roughly corresponding to the machinery described above in relation to late commencement (see generally Part 47.14).

---

3   As to when proceedings are concluded, see PD47, para 1.1.
4   These limits are, however, capable of alteration, either by consent or with permission of the court – see PD47, paras 2.7 and 2.8.

Both in relation to detailed assessment hearings and generally, it is important to realise that the overriding objective applies to costs proceedings as much as to any other kind of proceedings and that the court will therefore have all the general case management powers listed in Part 3. The powers of authorised court officers (who presently conduct certain detailed assessments in the Supreme Court Costs Office) are only slightly less extensive than those of a costs judge or district judge – see Part 47.3.

In addition to the Part 44.3(8) power to order a payment on account pending detailed assessment – which we have already considered above – there is a completely discretionary power to issue an interim costs certificate at any stage *after* the filing of the request for a detailed assessment hearing (Part 47.15).

What about the costs of detailed assessment proceedings? Here, the general rule is that the receiving party is entitled to his costs of the detailed assessment proceedings but the court may order otherwise (Part 47.18). It will by now come as no surprise that in deciding whether to make a different order, the court must have regard to all the circumstances, including:

(a) the conduct of all the parties;

(b) the amount, if any, by which the bill of costs has been reduced; and

(c) whether it was reasonable for a party to claim the costs of a particular item or to dispute that item. [Part 47.18(2)]

One particular matter that the court will certainly take into account when deciding on the costs of detailed assessment proceedings is the existence of any offer to settle without prejudice save as to the costs of those proceedings. Such 'Calderbank' offers are specifically provided for in Part 47.19. (As to the timing and required contents of such offers, see PD47, paras 7.4 and 7.5.)

As a general rule, the court will assess the receiving party's costs of the detailed assessment and add them to the bill of costs. If, exceptionally, the costs are awarded to the paying party, then assessment of those costs can itself be either summary or by detailed assessment (PD47, paras 7.1 and 7.2). As to the costs of any such further detailed assessment, the rules are thankfully silent and (in any case) we expect that your spirit has flagged!

Appeals against decisions in detailed assessment proceedings are dealt with in Section VIII of Part 47.

PARTS 45 AND 46

Part 45 deals with Fixed Costs. It sets out fixed commencement costs and the strictly limited amounts that can be recovered in respect of solicitors' charges in certain other specified situations. The most important examples are proceedings where the only claim is for a specified sum of money and which come to an early end through judgment in default, judgment on admissions, summary judgment or through various other specified means. The court does, of course, retain a discretion to alow larger amounts and in a case of sufficient moment will doubtless exercise it. Part 46 deals with *Fast Track trial costs* and has already been considered in Chapter 6 above.

SPECIAL CASES – PART 48

Part 48 brings together a variety of disparate topics to do with costs. Section I is headed 'Costs payable by or to particular persons' and Section II 'Costs relating to solicitors and other legal representatives'.

The matters covered by Section I include costs orders in respect of applications for pre-action disclosure, or for disclosure by a non-party (Part 48.1, already covered in Chapter 17 above); the assessment of costs payable pursuant to a contract (Part 48.3); the assessment of costs payable to trustees or personal representatives (Part 48.4); and the assessment of costs payable to litigants in person (Part 48.6).[5] They also include *costs orders in favour of or against non-parties*, that is, the jurisdiction under section 51(3) of the Supreme Court Act 1981, considered in *Symphony Group plc v Hodgson* [1993] 4 All ER 143 and later authorities.

Where the court is considering a section 51 application to order costs in favour of or against a non-party, that person must be added as a party to the proceedings for the purposes of costs only and must be given a reasonable opportunity to attend the hearing (Part 48.2(1)). As to the jurisdiction to make orders for costs against non-parties domiciled outside the jurisdiction (in particular in a Brussels Convention country), see *National Justice Compania Naviera SA v Prudential Assurance (The Ikarian Reefer) (No 2)* [2000] 1 All ER 37, CA.[6] That case referred to a possible lacuna in the CPR as to the mechanics of making a Part 48.2 application against a non-party outside the jurisdiction. However, any such lacuna would seem to have been filled, with effect from 2 May 2000, by Part 6.20(17), introduced by SI 2000/221.

It is worth mentioning one other important and learned post-CPR judgment in relation to section 51(3) applications. In *Robertson Research International Ltd v ABG Exploration BV* (1999) *The Times*, 3 November, the Queen's Bench Master had declined to hear a section 51(3) application (for which two to three days had been estimated), on the basis that the procedure was appropriate only for plain and straightforward cases taking hours not

---

5   Considered in *Mealing-McLeod v Common Professional Examination Board* (2000) unreported, 30 March, Buckley J.

6   Referred to in *Locabail (UK) Ltd v Bayfield Properties Ltd (No 3)*, Lawrence Collins QC sitting as a Deputy High Court Judge (2000) *The Times*, 29 February. The case (involving a non-party resident in Florida) considers the conditions to be satisfied for costs orders against non-parties generally, including the relevance of such a party's funding an action in the knowledge that the actual party will be unable to pay the costs. As to non-party costs orders against insurers, see *Cormack v Washbourne* (2000) *The Independent*, 31 March, CA.

days. On appeal to Laddie J (sitting unusually in the Queen's Bench Division), it was argued that this approach was correct because procedure in section 51(3) cases should be the same as in the wasted costs procedure, where some Court of Appeal authority suggests that the application must be capable of being dealt with in 'summary proceedings'. It was further argued that the guidelines in PD48, para 2.5 (dealing with wasted costs applications) should apply equally to section 51(3) applications:

> The court will give directions about the procedure that will be followed in each case in order to ensure that the issues are dealt with in a way which is fair and as simple and summary as the circumstances permit.

Laddie J rejected these arguments. To begin with, if the proceedings had to be 'summary', that word had to take some colour from the nature of the particular case and a 'summary' procedure could have been devised here, had the court exercised its case management powers appropriately. However, the judge went on to explore more fundamental questions. He accepted (for the purpose of this application) that there did exist a rule in relation to wasted costs applications that 'unless they can be dealt with summarily they will be dismissed without regard to the merits'. However, he raised the question (though leaving it to the Court of Appeal for decision) whether any such rule could survive the more flexible terms of the practice direction quoted above. Most fundamentally of all, Laddie J considered *in extenso* the nature and purpose of the wasted costs and section 51(3) jurisdictions and examined the distinctions between them. The first, he held, was partly compensatory and partly disciplinary; the latter 'truly and only compensatory', being 'simply designed to ensure that the whole or part of the costs burden of the winning party is borne by the person who is responsible for it, whether a party or not'. Given these distinctions, he did not accept that any 'summary rule' curtailing applications without regard to the merits should apply to section 51(3) applications.

As to how section 51(3) applications should themselves be handled, he said:

> All that is required is that the court should exercise its considerable administrative powers to ensure that the application should be dealt with as speedily and inexpensively as possible consistent with fairness to both sides. For example in many cases cross-examination will not be permitted, although sometimes it will [see *Nordstern v Internav* (1999) unreported, 25 May, CA].

> This does not mean that parties have a free hand to add applications under section 51(3) to the end of any trial. As the Court of Appeal stated in *Symphony Group plc v Hodgson*, an order for the payment of costs by a non-party will always be exceptional and the judge should treat any application for such costs with considerable caution. The simple rule that costs follow the event does not apply when it is sought to obtain costs against a non-party. The hurdle is much higher. If the judge can see that the claimant is almost bound to fail to negotiate that hurdle or that, as in *Bristol & West v Bhadresa*, the claim is merely speculative, he should dismiss it summarily. But if there is a good arguable case, he should allow the claimant to proceed with it, at risk as to costs.

We turn now to Section II of Part 48. *Wasted costs orders* are dealt with in Part 48.7.[7] The jurisdiction in question is, of course, that in section 51(6) of the 1981 Supreme Court Act (as substituted by section 4(1) of the Courts and Legal Services Act 1990) and as developed in *Ridehalgh v Horsefield* [1994] Ch 205 and subsequent authorities.

The substantive law on what must be shown in order to justify an order for wasted costs has not altered and is effectively set out in the practice direction. Nevertheless, the general view before implementation of the CPR was that wasted costs orders were likely to increase in importance under the new regime. Some limited support for that view can be derived from obiter dicta of Judge LJ in *Burt v Montague Wells* (1999) unreported, 26 July, CA:

> ... whatever the position may have been before 26th April 1999, since then wasted costs orders may be made with every justification when legal advisors on one side unreasonably insist that the processes of the court should be deployed to decide minor interlocutory issues which cry out for and are easily capable of sensible resolution between reasonable parties. Wasting court time in these sorts of circumstances depletes limited resources and in turn interferes with and delays the hearing of other cases, as well as adding to the complications and costs of the individual case. If it is eventually demonstrated that the entire process could and should have been avoided by a simple letter, that may potentially provide strong evidence that the decision to force the issue to a hearing was unreasonable and wholly disproportionate. Certainly it would be a sufficient basis for the court to consider whether it would be appropriate for a wasted costs order to be made, and would also provide ample justification for more frequent use than in the past of orders that would formerly have been regarded as unusual.

On the other hand, proportionality applies to wasted costs applications as much as to any other kind of proceedings – see Lindsay J in *Re Merc Property Ltd* (1999) *The Times*, 19 May. Furthermore, there is support, both in that case and in certain Court of Appeal decisions, for the view that wasted costs applications must necessarily be capable of being resolved 'summarily'. For a detailed examination of the cases in question, together with a discussion of whether any such requirement can survive the apparently more flexible terms of PD48, para 2.5, see the judgment of Laddie J in *Robertson Research International Ltd v ABG Exploration BV* (1999) *The Times*, 3 November, already discussed above in connection with orders for costs against non-parties.

One cannot leave Part 48.7 without recording one of the more dramatic upsets in the process of introducing the CPR. The original version of the rules purported, in Part 48.7(3), to give the court dealing with a wasted costs application power to direct that privileged documents should be disclosed,

---

7   There is a separate power under Part 44.14 to disallow costs or to order a party or his legal representatives to pay costs which he has caused another party to incur. This power applies where 'it appears to the court that the conduct of a party or his legal representative, before or during the proceedings ... was unreasonable or improper'.

both to the court and (if the court directed) to the other party to the application. However, this provision was held to be *ultra vires* in the extremely learned judgment of Toulson J in *General Mediterranean Holdings Ltd v Patel* [1999] 3 All ER 673. Paragraph 4 of Schedule 1 to the 1997 Civil Procedure Act provides that the CPR may 'modify the rules of evidence as they apply to proceedings in any court within the scope of the rules'. However, after a detailed consideration of the English, European Community and Human Rights Convention authorities, Toulson J held that legal professional privilege was founded on the right to legal confidentiality, which was not merely a rule of evidence but a substantive legal right. Such a fundamental right could not be overridden by general or ambiguous statutory words, especially words merely delegating a legislative power. Furthermore, there was nothing to suggest that Parliament had intended to abolish or limit the right to legal confidentiality. Following this decision, reminders of the existence of the supposed power were rapidly removed from the practice direction but, as yet, the offending rule 48.7(3) still remains (confusingly) in the published version of the CPR.

The basis of detailed assessment of *solicitor and client costs* is covered in Part 48.8 and the assessment of *conditional fees* in Part 48.9. The assessment of costs payable to a solicitor following an order under *Part III of the 1974 Solicitors Act* is dealt with in Part 48.10.

CHAPTER 25

PERSONAL INJURY AND CLINICAL NEGLIGENCE – THE PRE-ACTION PROTOCOLS

In this and the following chapter, we turn to consider personal injury and clinical negligence actions and how the matters dealt with in previous chapters impinge on them. Such actions are at present unique within the CPR in that they are the only ones where pre-action protocols have been approved by the Head of Civil Justice.[1] These protocols have the equivalent of statutory authority and, for actions within their scope,[2] form an essential part of compliance with the CPR. Accordingly, this chapter considers the protocols at length. Both protocols are printed in Part C. Chapter 26 will go on to consider certain other special features of personal injury actions under the CPR.

This chapter is structured as follows:

A   The aims of the pre-action protocols.

B   The Personal Injury Pre-action Protocol (PIPAP).

C   The Clinical Negligence Pre-action Protocol (CNPAP).

D   An assessment of the protocols.

E   Potential consequences of non-compliance with the protocols.

We take each topic in turn.

A   THE AIMS OF THE PRE-ACTION PROTOCOLS

The aims of the pre-action protocols are stated in the practice direction applying to them as follows:

(1) To encourage the exchange of early and full information about the prospective legal claim.

(2) To enable parties to avoid litigation by agreeing a settlement of the claim before the commencement of proceedings.

(3) To support the efficient management of proceedings where litigation cannot be avoided.

---

1   Although there is also in existence a pre-action protocol for road traffic cases, this is stated in para 1.2 thereof to be intended only to be run initially under a pilot scheme. Furthermore, the consent of both clients must first be obtained before it applies. No information seems to be available as to the status of the Road Traffic Accidents protocol – it does not even appear on the LCD's website – and in the circumstances, we shall confine ourselves to the two protocols which are fully in force.

2   In relation to any kind of action not within their scope, sight must not, of course, be lost of para 4.1 of the practice direction on protocols – requiring the parties 'to act reasonably in exchanging information and documents relevant to the claim and generally in trying to avoid the necessity for the start of proceedings' (see Chapter 1 above).

Without question, in the year since the CPR came into force, these aims have become reality. Before the CPR came into force, claimants' solicitors were able to exploit an in-built procedural bias by taking full advantage of the three year limitation period, investigating the claim fully and preparing the evidence, before launching proceedings and thereby often taking defendants and their solicitors by surprise. Many of the delays previously experienced were, at least in part, the result of the need then to give defendants time to catch up, by investigating the claim and gathering their own evidence. Nor were those representing defendants without sin: often, holding defences were served which gave away a minimal amount of information and which failed to inform the claimant or the court as to the true nature of the defence which would form the basis of the defendant's case in due course. Even worse, defences were served which indicated an intention to defend, when it turned out in due course that it was appropriate to admit liability, and had been from the start. No one could blame claimants' solicitors for exploiting the system to the greatest possible benefit of their clients, nor defendants' solicitors for wanting to give away as little as possible: but clearly, protocols to address the pre-action imbalance were necessary. It can fairly be claimed that the pre-action protocols for personal injury and clinical negligence actions have been one of the Woolf reforms' greatest successes, and have been acknowledged as such by claimants' solicitors and defendants' solicitors alike.

B   THE PERSONAL INJURY PRE-ACTION PROTOCOL (PIPAP)

Where a claimant's solicitor is instructed in a claim which includes an element of personal injury, his conduct of the claim will immediately be subject to the PIPAP. The PIPAP is primarily designed for fast track cases involving road traffic accidents, tripping and slipping accidents, and accidents at work with a value of less than £15,000. It is for such cases that its benefits are most felt because, when proceedings are issued, costs can very quickly become disproportionate to the damages at stake. However, the 'cards on the table' approach applies equally to cases involving serious accidents where, if proceedings are issued, the case is likely to be allocated to the multi-track. The parties' compliance with the PIPAP will be scrutinised by the court when proceedings are issued and the parties will fail to comply at their peril.

The letter of claim

The first step in the PIPAP is the sending of the letter of claim, and the protocol provides a specimen letter which can be suitably adapted to most personal injury actions. However, the guidance notes to the PIPAP encourage early notification that a claim is likely to be made even where insufficient information is available for sending a full letter of claim: for example, in a tripping claim against a local highway authority, the defendant may be wholly unaware even that an accident has been sustained. Early notification in such a case will not start the timetable for responding. Two copies of the letter of claim (one for the defendant, one for his insurer) are sent immediately that the claimant has sufficient information to substantiate a claim and before issues of quantum are addressed in detail. The PIPAP provides that the letter shall contain the following:

(i)   a clear summary of the facts on which the claim is based;

(ii) an indication of the nature of any[3] injuries suffered;

(iii) an indication of any financial loss incurred.

The letter should also ask for details of the defendant's insurer and inform the defendant of the need to send one copy to that insurer. Where the insurer is already known, one copy should be sent to the insurer direct. The protocol envisages that proceedings will not be issued within three months of the letter of claim to allow the defendant to investigate and respond. Although the PIPAP, unlike the clinical negligence pre-action protocol, does not specifically exclude from its scope the situation where the claimant's position needs to be protected (for example, because of the imminent expiry of a limitation period), such an exception clearly needs to be implied. The fundamental point is that if a claimant's solicitor issues proceedings before the defendant has had a chance to investigate and respond and within three months of the letter of claim, he may have to justify his actions to the court. The consequences of non-compliance are dealt with below.

The acknowledgment

After receiving a letter of claim, the defendant has 21 days to reply (42 days if the accident took place outside England and Wales or where the defendant is outside the jurisdiction), acknowledging the letter of claim and identifying the insurer. The claimant then sends to the insurer details of his National Insurance Number and date of birth. If no letter of acknowledgment is received within 21 days, the claimant is entitled to issue proceedings.

The response

After acknowledging the letter of claim, the defendant then has a maximum of three months from the date of the letter of claim (six months if the accident took place outside England and Wales or where the defendant is outside the jurisdiction) to investigate the claim and he must, before the end of that period, reply to the letter of claim stating whether liability is denied and, if it is, the reasons for the denial.

Where liability is *admitted*, then it is presumed that this admission will bind the defendant for all claims up to a total value of £15,000.

---

3   The use of the word 'any' in (ii) is slightly puzzling as there are bound to be injuries of some sort, or it would not be a personal injury action subject to the PIPAP at all!

Where liability is *denied*, the defendant must send with his letter of reply copies of the documents in his possession (which he will have gathered in the course of investigating the claim over the previous three months) which are material to the issues between the parties. Where he admits liability but alleges contributory negligence, the documents to be disclosed are those material to that issue. Annex B to the PIPAP provides lists of the documents likely to be material, but the basic test is whether the documents are of a kind which would be likely to be ordered to be disclosed by the court, either on an application for pre-action disclosure or during the proceedings.

The next stage is for the claimant to send to the defendant as soon as practicable a schedule of damages with supporting documents.

Experts

Clearly, in many such claims, one party or the other (but typically the claimant) will wish to instruct an expert, for example, an orthopaedic surgeon, to report on the injuries sustained, the claimant's present condition and the prognosis. Before doing so, the party should first give the other party a list containing the name of one or more experts whom he considers suitable, and the other party should then indicate within 14 days whether he objects to any expert on the list. The first party should then instruct a mutually acceptable expert (the claimant's solicitor first organising access to the relevant medical records) who thereby becomes a joint expert. If all the experts are objected to, then either party may instruct the expert of his choice and the court will later decide whether either of them has acted unreasonably. Where an expert has been instructed on an agreed basis, then the other party will not be entitled to rely on his own expert evidence within that speciality unless:

- the first party agrees; or
- the court so directs; or
- the first party's expert report has been amended and the first party is not prepared to disclose the original report.

The PIPAP also makes provision for either party to send to an agreed expert written questions relevant to the issues, and for the payment of the costs of the report and of answering such questions.

The final paragraph of the PIPAP deals with the situation where liability is admitted and a medical report is obtained from an agreed source: that report should then be disclosed and the claimant should delay issuing proceedings for 21 days from the date of disclosure to enable the parties to consider settlement. Either party can make a pre-action offer of settlement under Part 36.

Thus, the pre-action procedural timetable under the PIPAP is broadly as follows:

Steps to be Taken	By Whom	Time	Protocol Para
1 Early notification that a claim is likely to be made	Claimant		2.6
2 Letter of Claim	Claimant		3.2
3 Acknowledgment confirming identity of insurer	Defendant	21 days from letter of claim	3.6
4 Letter informing defendant of claimant's date of birth and National Insurance Number	Claimant	Upon receipt of Acknowledgment	3.4
4 Investigation of claim	Defendant	3 months from letter of claim	3.7
5(a) Response admitting liability	Defendant	3 months from letter of claim	3.9
5(b) Response denying liability and enclosing material documents	Defendant	3 months from letter of claim	3.10
6 Service of schedule of special damages with supporting documents	Claimant	As soon as practicable after receipt of Response	3.13
7 Proposal of 1 or more experts for approval	Claimant/ Defendant	Upon taking decision to instruct	3.14
8 Where expert proposed is medical, organisation of access to medical records	Claimant	Upon deciding to instruct, or upon receipt of proposal under 7	3.15
9 Objection to experts proposed	Claimant/ Defendant	14 days from proposal under 7	3.16
10 Instruction of agreed expert	Claimant/ Defendant	Upon receipt of objection under 8, or expiry of 14 days from proposal under 7	
11 Written questions of agreed expert	Defendant/ Claimant	Upon receipt of report	3.19

C	**THE CLINICAL NEGLIGENCE PRE-ACTION PROTOCOL (CNPAP)**

For cases involving allegations of clinical negligence, there is a separate protocol which has been compiled by a multi-disciplinary body known as the Clinical Disputes Forum. The CNPAP is similar to the PIPAP, but has the following differences:

(1) It is not expressed to be intended primarily for fast track cases, and it is considered that it will be followed in *all* cases of clinical negligence.

(2) Its aims are much more ambitious than those of the PIPAP: it actually seeks to change the relationship between patients and healthcare providers, and to dispel the mistrust that is perceived to exist in healthcare disputes by encouraging the development of a more co-operative culture.

(3) It addresses situations at a much earlier stage, and in particular before the involvement of lawyers, when the relationship is still one of patient and healthcare provider rather than of claimant and defendant.

The general aims of the CNPAP are expressed to be, first, to maintain/restore the patient/healthcare provider relationship and, second, to resolve as many disputes as possible without litigation. It specifically aims to encourage *openness* through early communication and exchange of information; *timeliness*, so that so that information should be obtained at an early stage and not just through the ultimate and blunt weapon of litigation; and *awareness of options*, so that litigation becomes the last resort, not the first. A detailed appraisal of the pre-litigation stages addressed by the CNPAP is beyond the scope of this book, and the reader is referred to the CNPAP itself. Suffice to say that it remains to be seen whether the ambitions of the CNPAP in reducing mistrust and encouraging co-operation between patients and healthcare providers will come to fruition and, if they do, whether the CNPAP as such will have played any significant part. We pick matters up at the stage when lawyers are likely to become involved.

Obtaining the health records

The first stage for a claimant's solicitor will often be the obtaining of the health records. Standard form letters have been approved in discussions between the Law Society and the Department of Health and are set out in Annex B to the CNPAP. The letter requesting the records also needs to give sufficient information to alert the particular healthcare provider where the adverse outcome has been serious or has had serious consequences. ('Adverse outcome' is the expression which the CNPAP uses, but it is not defined.) It is then the duty of the healthcare provider to supply the records within 40 days: if it is going to take longer, the problem should be explained quickly. Failure to comply on the part of the healthcare provider will justify the claimant in applying for an order for pre-action disclosure under Part 31.16.

Experts

As the CNPAP recognises, in cases of clinical negligence expert opinions are more likely to be needed in relation to breach of duty and causation than in ordinary personal injury actions, and such opinions may well be required before a decision can even be made as to whether there are grounds for a claim. In this regard, it may often be simply unrealistic to adopt a co-operative approach in relation to the instruction of experts and the sharing of their reports. (This is implicitly recognised in paragraph 4 of the CNPAP, as well as explicitly in paragraph 3.15.) However, even in high value cases such as cerebral palsy claims, it may be possible to agree joint experts on the more peripheral aspects, such as speech therapy or computer equipment.

In *Daniels v Walker* (2000) *The Times*, 17 May, the Court of Appeal considered the situation where a party agrees to the instruction of a joint expert and is then dissatisfied with the report. The case concerned a young claimant seriously brain-injured as a result of a road traffic accident. The parties agreed to instruct a joint expert in relation to his care needs, but the defendant's insurers were dissatisfied with the recommendations in respect of future care, which went well beyond their (fairly considerable) experience in similar cases. They therefore sought facilities for the claimant to be examined by their own expert with a view to obtaining their own report, but this was refused and the judge upheld such refusal. The Court of Appeal allowed the defendant's appeal and stated that the application should have been allowed.

It was stated by Lord Woolf MR (with whom Latham LJ agreed) that as long as the issue is a substantial one, so that the obtaining of a further report is not disproportionate, and as long as the dispute over the report of the joint expert is not merely fanciful, then the situation which ensues is the price to be paid for encouraging parties to agree to the instruction of joint experts whose reports will be, in the vast majority of cases, not merely the first but also the last. The 'quid pro quo' for this overall saving in time and costs is that, in cases such as this one, there may end up actually having to be three reports, that is, the initial joint report and then independently commissioned ones for each side. To have ruled otherwise would have been to discourage parties from agreeing the instruction of a joint expert in the first place. The court added that it would be premature to seek permission to call the further expert to give evidence: first, it would be necessary to see whether the defendant's expert disagreed with the joint expert, and, if so, whether the disagreement could be resolved, for example, by a meeting of the experts. If, however, the differences were incapable of resolution and were substantial in relation to the issues between the parties, then permission should be given for the party dissatisfied with the joint expert's report to call his own expert to give evidence.

As a result of this ruling, it is suggested that parties need not feel inhibited in agreeing to instruct a joint expert, even in relation to a relatively substantial matter, as they will not thereby be depriving themselves of the ability effectively to challenge that expert's report if dissatisfied with it on grounds that are not merely fanciful. Although we have discussed this case in the context of clinical negligence claims, it is important for all cases where the suggestion of a joint expert is raised and will have general application.

Finally, in relation to experts, the CNPAP encourages patients and healthcare providers to consider carefully how best to obtain any necessary expert help both quickly and cost-effectively – pointing out that the obtaining of expert evidence will often be an expensive step which may take time, especially in specialised areas of medicine where there are limited numbers of suitable experts. Thus, it may be obvious that causation is a particularly important and difficult issue which may be determinative of a claim: an example that often arises is whether, in a cerebral palsy claim, the claimant's condition was in fact the result of perinatal asphyxia. Rather than spend time and money instructing expert obstetricians, midwives and paediatricians on the question of whether the management of the claimant's birth was negligent, the quickest and most cost-efficient way to proceed may be to instruct – even jointly – a paediatric neurologist to advise on causation. If the report is negative, time and expense investigating negligence is avoided; if it is positive, this may induce the healthcare provider to settle the case rather than contest it.

The letter of claim

The CNPAP provides that the letter of claim should be sent 'as soon as practicable' once it has been decided that there are grounds for a claim. The purpose of the letter of claim is to give the healthcare provider sufficient information to enable it to commence investigations and to put an initial valuation on the claim. The letter should contain the following:

(i)   a clear summary of the facts on which the claim is based including the alleged adverse outcome;

(ii) the main allegations of negligence;

(iii) a description of the patient's injuries, present condition and prognosis;

(iv) an outline of the financial loss incurred, with an indication of the heads of damage to be claimed and the scale of loss, if practicable;

(v)   a chronology of the relevant events;

(vi) reference to (and, if possible, copies of) any relevant documents including health records not already in the healthcare provider's possession.

Although the CNPAP makes clear that the letter of claim is not intended to have the same formal status as a pleading, it nevertheless seems a significant and regrettable omission that it does not provide that the claimant should set out at least a summary of the nature of his case in relation to causation. As seen above, in clinical negligence actions, causation will often be one of the most significant matters to be investigated – and may well come to be the only live issue at a trial on liability – and the arguments for an early exchange of information seem to apply just as much to the question of causation as they do to the allegations of negligence. Indeed, this omission is even more bizarre when the CNPAP provides for the healthcare provider to specify in the response 'which issues of breach of duty *and/or causation* are admitted and which are denied' (para 3.25).

As with the PIPAP, the CNPAP provides for a three month moratorium on the issue of proceedings after the letter of claim. However, the CNPAP specifically excludes the situation where there is a limitation problem and/or the patient's position needs to be protected by early issue.

Offer to settle

At this point, the CNPAP includes an additional stage (which is not in the PIPAP), namely, an optional offer to settle. It is envisaged that in some cases – presumably in order to avoid further delay and the need to issue proceedings – the claimant may wish to put forward a sum which he would be prepared to accept, possibly including any costs incurred to date. When the CNPAP was drafted, the CPR were not yet in force and the protocol therefore states 'The Civil Procedure Rules are expected to set out the legal and procedural requirements for making offers to settle'. This expectation has been borne out by Part 36.10 (see Chapter 20 above). The protocol recommends that such an offer should be supported by a medical report on injuries, condition and prognosis, and by a schedule of loss with supporting documentation, although whether these are necessary will depend on the circumstances.

The acknowledgment

The CNPAP provides for acknowledgment of the letter of claim within 14 days (a week less than the PIPAP's 21 days) and additionally provides that the defendant should identify who will be dealing with the matter. On the other hand, the CNPAP does not provide for the claimant to provide the defendant with details of his National Insurance Number and date of birth. Though the latter will be readily ascertainable from the claimant's medical records, the former is just as relevant in clinical negligence claims as in personal injury claims and it is suggested that this omission is an oversight. So too is the failure to specify that the claimant will be entitled to issue proceedings if no acknowledgment is received within 14 days.

The response

Like the PIPAP, the CNPAP then gives the healthcare provider three months from the date of the letter of claim to investigate the claim and provide a response, during which time the claimant should not issue proceedings. The response should provide a reasoned answer to the letter of claim, saying (in clear terms) whether the claim is admitted, partly admitted or denied. Thus, the response should contain the following:

(i)   If the claim is admitted, a clear statement to that effect;

(ii) If only part of the claim is admitted, a clear statement as to which issues of breach of duty and/or causation are admitted and which are denied, and why;

(iii) If the claim is denied, specific comments on the allegations of negligence and the healthcare provider's version of any events alleged by the claimant which are in dispute;

(iv) Copies of any additional documents relied on, such as internal protocols;

(v) If the patient has made an offer to settle, the healthcare provider's response to that offer, preferably with reasons, together with any counter-offer, supported by any evidence relied upon in support in the healthcare provider's possession;

(vi) If the patient has not made an offer to settle, any such offer which the healthcare provider wishes to make together with supporting evidence, if any.

A template for the suggested contents of the response is contained at Annex C2 to the CNPAP.

It is not clear why the CNPAP provides specifically that, if the patient has made an offer to settle, the healthcare provider should respond to that offer *in the response letter*. If the case does not settle, then the court will want to see the letter of claim and the response at various later stages and in particular at trial – and offers to settle are clearly made without prejudice and so should not in principle be seen by the court. It would seem preferable for the CNPAP to require any offers to settle (and responses to such offers) to be made in separate letters marked 'without prejudice' – of which the court would be unaware were the matter to proceed, unless and until it is appropriate for it to be made aware of those offers.

Where, as a result of the letter of claim and response, liability is agreed but time is needed to resolve quantum, the protocol states (para 3.27) that the parties should seek to agree a reasonable period for such resolution.

Alternative dispute resolution

Finally, the CNPAP makes the point that the court increasingly expects parties to try to settle their differences by agreement before the issue of proceedings. Thus, it suggests that, before proceedings are issued, consideration should be given to using alternative means for resolving disputes such as:

• The NHS Complaints Procedure, which is designed to provide patients with an explanation of what happened and an apology if appropriate. (One situation where one can envisage this as being appropriate is the case of the death of a young adult, where the parents seek an explanation but there is no claim of value under the Fatal Accidents Act due to lack of dependency.)

- Mediation.
- Arbitration, determination by an expert and early neutral evaluation by a medical or legal expert.

Thus, the pre-action procedural timetable under the CNPAP looks as follows (a healthcare provider being referred to as 'HCP'):

Steps to be Taken	By Whom	Time	Protocol Para
1 Patient dissatisfied and seeks written explanation	Patient	As soon as possible after suffering adverse outcome	Annex A
2 Professional involved reports adverse outcome to clinical director	HCP	As soon as possible after learning of adverse outcome	Annex A
3 Medical director or complaints team investigates adverse outcome, obtains records and interviews staff	HCP	As soon as possible after receipt of complaint from patient or report from professional	Annex A
4 Explanation provided to patient	HCP	As soon as possible after conclusion of investigation	Annex A
5 Patient consults solicitor	Patient	Upon receipt of explanation, if dissatisfied	Annex A
6 Solicitor discusses options for pursuit and resolution of the dispute and what each might involve	Patient	Upon instruction of Solicitor	2.3
7 Request for health records	Patient	After discussion of options and decision on strategy	3.7
8(a) Supply of records	HCP	40 days from Request under 7	3.9

Steps to be Taken	By Whom	Time	Protocol Para
8(b) Explanation if HCP unable to supply records within 40 days	HCP	As soon as possible after HCP becomes aware of difficulty	3.10
8(c) Application for pre-action disclosure, if records not supplied within 40 days	Patient	After 40 days from Request for records under 7	3.12
9 Instruction of experts needed before advice can be given on whether there are grounds for a claim	Patient	Upon receipt of records under 8	4.1
10 Letter of claim	Claimant	As soon as practicable after deciding that there are grounds for a claim	3.14–3.20
11 (Optional) Offer to Settle	Claimant	At same time as Letter of Claim	3.22
12 Acknowledgment	Defendant	Within 14 days of Letter of Claim	3.24
13 Response	Defendant	Within 3 months of Letter of Claim	3.25
14 (Optional) Offer to settle	Defendant	At same time as Response	3.26
15 (Where there is agreement on liability) Agreement of reasonable time to resolve quantum	Claimant and Defendant	Upon agreement on liability	3.27

D   AN ASSESSMENT OF THE PROTOCOLS

The PIPAP and CNPAP clearly represent a major advance in the regulation of pre-action procedures and have avoided many unnecessary proceedings, with a consequent saving in costs and alleviation of the court's workload. The three month moratorium on proceedings, giving the defendant an opportunity to investigate and respond to the claim is, in particular, a hugely important provision. It tempers the enthusiasm of claimants and their solicitors for crossing the Rubicon of issuing proceedings, and enables the parties to make genuine efforts to settle the claim before the entrenchment of positions which litigation usually entails. However, as mentioned above, there are irritating differences between the protocols, such as the different time limits for the acknowledgment of the letter of claim. Efforts will hopefully be made to integrate and reconcile the two protocols, so that they are more harmonious, both internally and with each other.

E   POTENTIAL CONSEQUENCES OF NON-COMPLIANCE WITH THE PROTOCOLS

Whether a party has complied with the pre-action protocols may have consequences for him when the case comes before the court under the CPR. We mention some of the more important provisions.

- Part 3.1(4) provides that where the court gives directions, it may take into account whether or not a party has complied with a relevant pre-action protocol.

- Under Part 3.1(5), the court may order a party to pay a sum of money into court if that party has, without good reason, failed to comply with a relevant pre-action protocol. The court must have regard to the amount in dispute and the costs incurred or which may be incurred (Part 3.1(6)).

- Under Part 3.9, on an application for relief from any sanction imposed for failure to comply with any rule, practice direction or court order, the court will consider, among other things, the extent to which the party in default has complied with a relevant pre-action protocol.

- The practice directions dealing with the fast track and multi-track both provide that, in making directions on allocation, the court will have particular regard to the extent to which any pre-action protocol has or has not been complied with (PD28, para 3.2 and PD29, para 4.2).

- The multi-track practice direction provides that a party who obtains expert evidence before obtaining a direction about it does so at his own risk as to costs 'except where he obtained the evidence in compliance with a pre-action protocol' (PD29, para 5.5).

- In exercising its discretion as to costs, the court must have regard to all the circumstances including the conduct of the parties – which includes conduct before, as well as during, proceedings, 'and in particular the extent to which the parties followed any relevant pre-action protocol' (Part 44.3(5)(a)).

- Compliance or non-compliance with a relevant pre-action protocol is also relevant to questions of costs on applications for pre-action disclosure and for disclosure against a non-party (see, generally, Part 48.1).

The contrast between the wording of Parts 3.1(5) and 3.4(2)(c) should be noted and appears to be deliberate. The rules appear *not* to give the court the power to strike out a claim where there has been a failure to comply with a pre-action protocol, but it will take such a failure into account in deciding whether to grant relief from any sanction imposed for failure to comply with any rule, practice direction or court order. The main sanction for non-compliance is, of course, in relation to costs and the successful claimant is liable to find that in circumstances where he would otherwise have expected to be awarded all his costs, all or some of them will be disallowed where there has been a failure to comply with a relevant pre-action protocol.

In addition to the sanctions contained within the Rules, sanctions for non-compliance are also provided for in the practice direction which accompanies the pre-action protocols. The practice direction gives examples of the ways in which both claimants and defendants may be found not to have complied. Thus, *claimants* may be found not to have complied by:

- not having provided sufficient information; or
- not having followed the procedure laid down in the protocol, for example in relation to the instruction of an expert.

So far as *defendants* are concerned, they may have failed to comply by:

- not acknowledging the letter of claim in time;
- not making the response in time;
- not disclosing the required documents.

If any such default has led to unnecessary proceedings or the incurring of unnecessary costs, the practice direction suggests that the court may make an order:

(1) that the party at fault pay all or part of the costs of the proceedings, even on an indemnity basis;

(2) awarding the claimant interest for a shorter period, or at a lower rate, than it would otherwise have done;

(3) ordering the defendant to pay interest on damages at a higher rate than it would otherwise have done, though not exceeding 10% above base rate.

CHAPTER 26

OTHER FEATURES OF PERSONAL INJURY ACTIONS UNDER THE CPR

Once a decision has been made to issue a claim in a personal injury (or clinical negligence) case, the fact that it is such a case has certain consequences under the CPR. Under Part 2.3, a claim for personal injuries is defined as meaning 'proceedings in which there is a claim for damages in respect of personal injuries to the claimant or any other person or in respect of a person's death, and "personal injuries" includes any disease and any impairment of a person's physical or mental condition'.

CLAIM FORM

Various specific provisions are made for the claim form in personal injury actions. In Part 16.3(3), it is provided that in a claim for personal injuries, the claimant must state in the claim form whether the amount that he expects to recover as general damages for pain, suffering and loss of amenity is not more than £1,000 or more than £1,000. This provision ties in with the provisions on allocation to the small or fast track (see Chapter 4 above). Additionally, under Part 16.3(5), if a claim for personal injuries is to be issued in the High Court, the claim form must state that the claimant expects to recover £50,000 or more.

PROVISIONAL DAMAGES

Part 16.4 provides that, where a claimant is seeking provisional damages, the Particulars of Claim must include a statement to that effect and the grounds for claiming them and '(e) such other matters as may be set out in a practice direction'. This provision is effectively a re-enactment of the old RSC Ord 18 r 8, which provided that a claim for provisional damages must be specifically pleaded 'together with the facts on which the party pleading relies'. It is suggested that there is no important difference between pleading 'the facts relied upon' and the 'grounds for claiming provisional damages'. Such damages are claimable under section 32A of the Supreme Court Act 1981 where there is proved or admitted to be 'a chance that at some definite time in the future the injured person will, as a result of the act or omission which gave rise to the cause of action, develop some serious disease or suffer some serious deterioration in his physical or mental condition'. PD 16, para 4.4 specifies the matters that the claimant must set out in his particulars of claim, namely:

(1) the fact that he is seeking provisional damages;

(2) the fact that there is a chance that at some future time the claimant will develop some serious disease or suffer some serious deterioration in his physical or mental condition; and

(3) details of the disease or type of deterioration in respect of which an application may be made at a future date.

(Part 36, dealing with offers to settle and payments into court, contains specific provisions in relation to defendants who wish to make Part 36 payments in respect of claims for, or who are offering to make an award of, provisional damages: see Part 36.7.)

STATEMENTS OF CASE IN PERSONAL INJURY ACTIONS

PD16 also makes specific provision in relation to personal injury actions generally, in paragraphs 4.1–4.3. The Particulars of Claim must contain:

(1) the claimant's date of birth; and

(2) brief details of the personal injuries sustained.

Furthermore:

(3) a schedule containing details of past and future expenses and losses claimed must be attached; and

(4) a medical report must be attached or served with the Particulars of Claim where the claimant relies on such evidence.

Paragraph 5 of the practice direction makes provision for the matters which must be stated in the Particulars of Claim in a fatal accidents claim, namely:

(1) the fact that the claim is brought under the Fatal Accidents Act 1976;

(2) the dependants on whose behalf the claim is made;

(3) the date of birth of each dependant; and

(4) details of the nature of the dependency claim.

(Part 37.4 makes provision for apportionment between the different dependants and their claims where money paid into court in satisfaction of a claim under the Fatal Accidents Act and/or Law Reform (Miscellaneous Provisions) Act 1934 is accepted.)

Equally, PD16, para 13 contains specific provisions in relation to the Defence in personal injury actions where (as will almost invariably be the case) the claimant has attached a medical report in respect of his alleged injuries. The defendant should state in the defence whether he agrees, disputes, or neither agrees nor disputes but has no knowledge of, the matters contained in the medical report. If he disputes any part of the medical report, the defendant must say why, and where he has obtained his own medical report and intends to rely on it, must attach a copy to the defence. Where the claimant has attached a schedule of loss, then again the defendant should attach a counter-schedule indicating the items agreed, or disputed, or of which the defendant has no knowledge, and supplying alternative figures to the disputed items.

INTERIM PAYMENTS

The court's powers to grant interim remedies are contained in Part 25. The power to award an interim payment has long been an important one in personal injury and clinical negligence actions – an injured claimant may well be in urgent need of funds to alleviate the burden on relatives and others who have to care for him, often without adequate assistance or equipment and in wholly unsuitable premises. The usual conditions for the ordering of an interim payment under Part 25.7(1) are extended in the case of claims for personal injuries in that the defendant must be insured (or have his liability covered by an insurer under the Road Traffic Act 1988 or through the Motor Insurers Bureau) or the defendant must be a public body (Part 25.7(2)). Part 25.7(3) attempts to address a problem that arose in *Breeze v McKennon (R) & Son* [1985] Build LR 41. There it was clear that the claimant would succeed against one or other of two defendants, but not which one. The court held that, under the old rule, the claimant had to show that he could satisfy the requirements against the particular defendant against whom the order for an interim payment was sought. Part 29.7(3) now provides:

> In a claim for personal injuries where there are two or more defendants, the court may make an order for the interim payment of damages against any defendant if –
>
> (a) it is satisfied that, if the claim went to trial, the claimant would obtain judgment for substantial damages against at least one of the defendants (even if the court has not yet determined which of them is liable); and
>
> (b) paragraph (2) is satisfied in relation to each of the defendants.

Unfortunately, the drafting of this Rule is imprecise. It is clearly intended to widen the circumstances in which an interim payment can be obtained, but in one instance it would appear to narrow those circumstances. Thus, if there were two defendants, one of whom was insured and the other of whom was not, the wording of the rule would seem to exclude the obtaining of an interim payment against the insured defendant, even if it would have been possible to obtain one had he been the only defendant. However, such a situation is perhaps unlikely to arise too often – *ex hypothesi*, in this situation, the case would have to be relatively strong against the insured defendant, and in such circumstances there would be little point in also joining a second defendant who is uninsured.

Part 25.7 contains two further provisions. The court must not order an interim payment of more than 'a reasonable proportion of the likely amount of the final judgment' and it must take into account contributory negligence and any relevant set-off or counterclaim. These provisions attempt to address the very real problems that can occur if an over-payment is made and the claimant has used the money, for example on accommodation needs, and therefore may be in real difficulty in re-paying the amount of the overpayment. The powers of the court to make adjustments to interim payments (either on judgment or earlier) are contained in Part 25.8.

Finally, problems specific to personal injury actions are created by the rules in relation to the payment of recoverable benefits under the Social Security (Recovery of Benefits) Act 1997. In general, an interim payment counts as a 'compensation payment' for the purposes of the Act and so the defendant will have to obtain a Certificate of Recoverable Benefit and pay the amount due to the Compensation Recovery Unit before making the interim payment to the claimant. Where the application for an interim payment is other than by consent, specific provisions are contained in paragraph 4 of the Interim Payments practice direction for the obtaining and filing of the Certificate of Recoverable Benefit and for the court to set out in the order the amount by which the payment to be made to the claimant has been reduced pursuant to the set-off provisions contained in section 8 and Schedule 2 of the 1997 Act.

CASE MANAGEMENT AND ALLOCATION

As mentioned in Chapter 4 above, the fact that a claim is for personal injuries has consequences for the track to which a case is allocated. Whilst the small claims track is the normal track for claims for no more than £5,000, this is not the case where the damages claimed for pain, suffering and loss of amenity have a financial value of more than £1,000, even if the overall claim is still under £5,000 (Part 26.6). Thus, a claim comprising £1,500 for pain and suffering and £2,000 for loss of earnings will be allocated to the fast track, but a claim for £750 for pain and suffering and £4,000 for loss of earnings will be allocated to the small claims track. Part 26.8(2) provides that it is for the court to assess the financial value of a claim, disregarding any amount not in dispute, any claim for interest, any costs and any contributory negligence. The Small Claims Practice Direction supplementing Part 27 contains, at Form B, standard directions for use in claims arising out of road traffic accidents. Claims under the Fatal Accidents Act 1976 and claims which involve an allegation of professional negligence (which will include most clinical negligence claims) are considered suitable for trial at the Royal Courts of Justice in London and will thus be allocated to the multi-track (PD29, para 2.6).

PART 36 PAYMENTS AND OFFERS TO SETTLE

These have already been considered in detail in Chapter 20 above, but certain provisions are specific to actions for personal injuries. These are the provisions relating to offers to settle claims for provisional damages (already mentioned above) and those relating to the deduction of benefits. In relation to the latter, Part 36.23 makes provision for a defendant who wishes to make a Part 36 offer/payment and who has applied for but not yet received a Certificate of Recoverable Benefit. Under Part 36.23(2), such a defendant may make an offer to settle without making a payment in – and, so long as he follows up his offer with a Part 36 payment within seven days of receiving the certificate, it will have all the consequences of a Part 36 payment. Generally, Part 36 payments now have to specify in the payment notice:

(a) the amount of the gross compensation;

(b) the name and amount of any benefit by which that gross amount is reduced in accordance with section 8 and Schedule 2 of the 1997 Act; and

(c) that the sum paid in is the net amount after deduction of the amount of benefit (Part 36.23(3)).

(See also, in this regard, PD36, para 10.)

Part 36.23(4) provides that, for the purposes of Part 36.20, a claimant fails to better a Part 36 payment if he fails to obtain judgment for more than the gross sum specified in the Part 36 payment notice. It would seem to follow from this that the CPR anticipate that when judgment is given in a personal injuries action, this will be for the gross amount of damages before any set-off of benefits. However, this will not always be the case. For example, a claimant who has been in receipt of relevant benefits whilst off work by reason of personal injury and whose relevant benefits clearly exceed any claimable loss of earnings (so that this head of compensation would be reduced to nil) may simply not bother to claim loss of earnings.[1] However, when deciding whether a Part 36 payment has been bettered, the court will obviously follow a common-sense approach in ensuring that it is comparing like with like. (See also the provision for adjustment of the final judgment figure in respect of compensation recovery payments in paragraph 5.1 of the Judgments and Orders Practice Direction supplementing Part 40.)

PD36, para 11.2 provides that a defendant to a claim arising out of a road traffic accident must, where the damages claimed include a sum for hospital expenses and that sum has been paid to the hospital under section 157 of the Road Traffic Act 1988, give notice of that payment to the court and all other parties.

---

1   This is unlikely, though, on the law as it presently stands as he would thereby lose out on the interest to which he would be entitled on the notional loss of earnings – *Wadey v Surrey County Council* (2000) *The Times*, 7 April, HL.

AUTOMATIC STAY OF PROCEEDINGS

The automatic stay of proceedings which have not come before a judge between 26 April 1999 and 25 April 2000 does not apply to personal injury cases where there is no issue on liability and the proceedings have been adjourned by court order to determine the prognosis (PD51, para 19(3)).

CHILDREN AND PATIENTS

Very often, in personal injury and clinical negligence actions, the claimant will be a child or patient, and there are various provisions particular to such claimants – see, generally, Part 21. The practice direction supplementing that Part contains a specific provision governing settlements by or on behalf of a child or patient in personal injury actions. In addition to the usual information required for the court to approve such a settlement, the court will also require the following information:

(a) the circumstances of the accident;

(b) any medical reports;

(c) a schedule of loss, where appropriate; and

(d) where considerations of liability are raised, any evidence or police reports in any criminal proceedings or in an inquest and details of any prosecution brought (PD21, para 6.2).

Paragraph 7 of the same practice direction contains provisions on apportionment on judgment or settlement of claims under the Fatal Accidents Act 1976, specifying further information which the court will require for the purposes of approving an apportionment.

PD21, para 1.8 provides that 'A hearing of an application under Part 21 will take place in private unless the court directs otherwise.' However, in *Beatham v Carlisle Hospitals NHS Trust* (1999) *The Times*, 20 May, Buckley J held that approval for a proposed damages settlement involving a child or patient should be given in open court once the judge was satisfied that approval should be given – there being a public interest in the nature of such cases and their outcome which was not affected by paragraph 1.8.

Part 21.11, as supplemented by PD21, para 8, makes provision for the control of money recovered by or on behalf of a child or patient.

By PD36, para 11.4, it is provided that any money paid into court (either as a Part 36 payment which is not accepted or under a court order) and which is in respect of a child or patient will be placed in an special investment account rather than in a basic account.

challenge the jurisdiction) – and, even then, an acknowledgment will come after rather than before the Particulars of Claim.

This system does *not* apply to commercial cases, for two reasons:

(i) The preparation of Particulars of Claim in the Commercial Court can frequently be complex and expensive. There is no point in preparing them if the case is not in fact going to be defended.

(ii) There are many challenges to the jurisdiction in the Commercial Court. Again, there is no point preparing Particulars of Claim if the English court is never in fact going to have jurisdiction over the dispute.

For both these reasons and in the interests of uniformity of procedure within the Commercial Court, the old practice will continue to apply in the Commercial Court and a defendant will have to file an acknowledgment of service in every case, just as in the past – usually within 14 days of service of the claim form (B7.3). Particulars of claim will not generally have to be served until 28 days after acknowledgment (C2.4).

Statements of case

The Commercial Court rules on statements of case correct some of the more obvious drafting shortcomings of the general Part 16 practice direction. For example, the rules on attaching contracts (or parts thereof) apply to defendants as well as to claimants. Again, a pleader is required not only expressly to allege fraud or dishonesty but to provide full particulars of that allegation – which, surprisingly, the CPR do not expressly require. The Guide slightly discourages use of the option to exhibit documents 'considered necessary' to a party's case – C1.2(i).

There is also a separate 'mini-code' on statements of case in the Commercial Court (Appendix 4 to the Guide). It is in some respects fuller and more familiar than the general CPR rules. For example, it is expressly stated that evidence should not be included and that a party should plead any matter 'which if not stated might take the other party by surprise'. The pleading is 'to be signed by the individual person or persons who drafted it'.

There are provisions for the parties to provide 'summaries' of statements of case where the actual documents exceed 25 pages. In the Commercial Court, there are also longer periods for the service of pleadings (and the permissible periods of extension by agreement are also longer).

The provisions on amendments are also different, in that the original text normally has to be shown (C5).

Disclosure

The level of disclosure ordered will be tailored to the needs of the particular case. Anything wider than standard disclosure always needs to be justified.

Indeed, the parties are exhorted to think about the feasibility of limiting discovery, for example by the use of sampling methods.

Nevertheless, documents being self-evidently of particular importance in commercial cases, commercial court litigants are reminded that they 'can expect that disclosure beyond standard disclosure may be required either in a case as a whole, or on particular issues in a case' (E1.2). This is hardly surprising given the scale of much litigation in the Commercial Court – and the need to be proportionate to value, to the importance of the case, to the complexity of the issues and to the financial position of the parties. However, any impression that old-fashioned disclosure will be automatic has to be dispelled – flexibility is the name of the game.

The scope of disclosure will be addressed head-on at case management conferences. Should the scope of disclosure be standard, be reduced beneath standard disclosure or expanded beyond it? Are lists really necessary? Should disclosure be in stages? A party who proposes not to search in a particular place, because he thinks it unreasonable, will be asked to state that fact in advance in his case management information sheet (E3.3). The converse of limiting discovery – namely applications for specific disclosure – may also be raised as early as the case management conference (E4.2).

The Court will, in particular, decide whether to make a 'special disclosure' order – that is, one that a party should carry out a specified search for documents, perhaps including *Peruvian Guano* 'train of enquiry' documentation. Examples are given of when such an order is likely to be appropriate: where fraud, dishonesty or misrepresentation is alleged and in cases where knowledge/lack of knowledge or disclosure/non-disclosure is in issue (E5.4). A draft special disclosure order forms Appendix 9 to the Guide.

The 'disclosure statement' to go in a party's list of documents is also more exacting than in the CPR. A party will not only have to identify 'any respects in which the search has been limited' but will also have to 'set out in detail the facts considered in arriving at the decision that it was reasonable to limit the search in these respects'. He must also identify who conducted the search (E3.6).

Experts

There is no presumption in the Commercial Court in favour of single joint experts. If the parties want separate experts and the case is appropriate for separate experts, a direction for a single joint expert 'may possibly be infrequently made' (H2.4). The Guide also envisages the use of single experts, not as a substitute for separate experts (indeed not as somebody reporting or giving evidence at all) but as somebody chairing and facilitating meetings of separate experts (H2.6).

The Guide is clearly wary of any oppressive use of two new provisions in the CPR. First, it deals with the *right to put questions to another party's expert* 'for purposes of clarification' of that expert's report. The Guide says the court will pay close attention to the way that that right is used (especially where there are separate experts), to ensure that it remains an instrument 'for the helpful exchange of information' (H2.28). If questions are oppressive, either in number or content, or if they are put (without permission) for any purpose other than clarification, they will be disallowed and appropriate orders in costs made. Secondly, a similar wariness is evident in relation to improper use of the power to require *inspection of documents referred to in an expert's report* (H2.29).

There are other subtle differences from the provisions of the CPR on experts – for example, about what an expert has to disclose about his instructions (H2.12); in the procedure to be followed where an expert proposes to seek directions from the court (H2.16); in the defined purpose of experts' meetings (H2.20); and in the inclusion of an *automatic* requirement that experts prepare a joint memorandum for the court following a meeting (H2.24). There is also a new 'mini-code' on the nature of an expert's duty (Appendix 12). An expert will have to certify that he has read and understood that Appendix, that he has complied with it and that he will continue to do so at all stages of the case (H2.14).

Case management

As stated above, all Commercial Court cases will be multi-track, so the allocation procedure in Part 26 does not apply.

Furthermore, both the nomenclature and the precise details of the Court's case management system differ from the general system as set out in the CPR. For example, at an early point in the case, the solicitors and counsel for each party will have to liaise to produce a *'case memorandum'* (being a short and uncontroversial description of what the case is about, together with a short procedural history excluding such things as interim payments and Part 36 offers or payments). They will also have to produce an agreed *'list of issues'*, both factual and legal. These documents will have to be kept up to date. Furthermore, a *'case management bundle'* will have to be prepared by the claimant, and will likewise have to be regularly updated.

There will be a mandatory *case management conference* in commercial cases. It is viewed as an occasion of great importance and is emphatically not just a substitute for the old summons for directions. For each party, at least one of the advocates retained in the case is to attend. Case management information sheets will have to be provided a week in advance. These resemble the allocation questionnaire under the CPR but contain many more searching questions. Most actions will also have a *'progress monitoring date'* (D8) – when further information must be provided and when the case management conference may be reconvened. There will also be a *pre-trial review* (D13).

There is provision for a *two judge management team* in larger cases (D3).

ADR and early neutral evaluation

There has always been considerable enthusiasm for ADR in the Commercial Court. Some of the problems previously encountered with orders for ADR (confused practitioners going out into the corridor and asking each other 'What on earth do we do now?') are likely to be eased – both by the introduction of a new system whereby the Clerk to the Commercial Court will keep lists of information on ADR bodies and by the more precise terms of the draft ADR order which is attached to the Guide (Appendix 7). However, the court will not recommend any particular ADR body. That is felt to be inappropriate (G1.9).

The Guide also reminds us of the existing provisions for *'early neutral evaluation'* (G2). This is a 'without prejudice, non-binding, early neutral evaluation of the dispute or particular issues in it', undertaken by a Commercial Judge. If the procedure is used and no agreement results, the judge concerned will not, of course, be further involved in the case unless the parties agree otherwise.

Costs

One interesting different feature in the Commercial Court is a process called 'abridged assessment of costs' (I13.3). This process (the details of which are in Appendix 16 to the Guide) is to be used, not during the interlocutory stages of a case like summary assessment, but at the end, as an alternative to detailed assessment. It is a simpler and quicker assessment process, using summary bills of costs. Solicitors are told to warn their clients that it is deliberately more 'broad brush'. However, the process will require the consent of both parties. They would normally be expected to agree to it in advance of the trial at the case management conference.

The abridged assessment procedure operates by way of an exchange of schedules and the consequent narrowing of issues. There is provision for a hearing – usually limited to half a day – but no appeals are allowed. Calderbank offers are possible in relation to the abridged assessment procedure.

D   SOME OVERALL REFLECTIONS

We cannot leave this section without two general reflections, which are respectively the 'heads' and 'tails' of the same coin.

First, it may be suggested that there is some danger of fragmentation in the development of specialist rules that are markedly different from the generality of the CPR. We refrain from debating whether in the case of the Commercial Court, it is the Commercial Court rules or the general core rules that are, in any abstract sense, 'better'. The simple and inescapable fact of the matter is that in the Commercial Court one is dealing with bigger, more valuable and (very often) more complicated litigation. It is hardly surprising if, as a result, the Commercial Court rules are themselves 'fuller' and more detailed. Fears of fragmentation seem to us only likely to be realised in the unlikely event that the Queen's Bench judges and masters fail to make similarly proportionate case management directions in relation to those business disputes which end up before them rather than in the Commercial Court.

Secondly, the fact that there are procedural differences could be said to create opportunities for tactical thinking about which jurisdiction a claimant should opt for in the first place. The most usual choice will be between the Queen's Bench and the Commercial Court, the boundary between the two being – in a big enough case – a somewhat porous one. Having said that, there are obviously distinct limits to the kind of tactical thinking that one can indulge in. For example, while as a matter of first impression it could be said that disclosure is likely to be less extensive in the Queen's Bench Division than in the Commercial Court, it is obviously the case that any documents known to be unhelpful will have to be disclosed wherever one is! And again, if the Queen's Bench judges and masters have their wits about them (which they usually seem to have!), appropriate case management directions should iron out any difficulties stemming from the different wording of the rules, both in relation to discovery and more generally.

CHAPTER 28

APPEALS

SCOPE OF THE CHANGES TO THE APPEALS SYSTEM

The rules relating to all categories of appeals are to be consolidated and substantially changed, with effect from 2 May 2000. The relevant provisions are in Part 52 and its companion practice direction. These provisions apply to all appeals in the High Court and the county court (with the exception of appeals against orders made on the small claims track and appeals from the decisions of authorised court officers in detailed assessment proceedings)[1]. The provisions of Part 52 also apply to appeals to the Court of Appeal – though Section II of that Part contains a number of further provisions which apply only and specifically to appeals to the Court of Appeal.

As a matter of terminology, it is important to realise that Part 52 and the practice direction both distinguish the Court of Appeal from the 'appeal court'. The latter is a generic term used for all courts to which an appeal may be made and thus includes a Circuit Judge and a High Court Judge as well as the Court of Appeal. The court from which an appeal is brought is referred to, equally generically, as the 'lower court'.

Part 52.1(4) further provides that Part 52 is subject to the terms of any rule, practice direction or enactment 'with regard to any particular category of appeal'. The practice direction does indeed make specific provision for various special categories of appeal – such as statutory appeals and appeals by way of case stated (which are dealt with in Section II of the practice direction) and certain other specific categories of appeal, including contempt appeals to the Court of Appeal (dealt with in Section III of the practice direction). These special categories of appeal are not considered here.

As usual, the practice direction puts flesh on the bare bones of the new provisions, dealing in great detail with the mechanical minutiae of the appeal procedure. For example, it deals with the nature and content of the documents which must be lodged with an appeal court, the contents of skeleton arguments, notes of judgments and the like.

DESTINATION OF AN APPEAL

SI 2000/221 entirely revokes the old Ords 55, 56 and 58 to 61 of the RSC and Ord 13 and Ord 37 r 6 of the CCR. However, both Part 52 and the practice

---

1   Separate provision is made in Parts 27 and 47 in respect of such appeals.

direction (made pursuant to that statutory instrument) are silent as to the destination of any given appeal. The destination of appeals after 2 May 2000 is dealt with in a different statutory instrument altogether, namely, the Access to Justice Act 1999 (Destination of Appeals) Order 2000, SI 2000/1071 (L 10). It is printed as Appendix 4 to this book.

The broad effect of the statutory instrument is that appeals from decisions of Masters and District Judges of the High Court will continue to be to a High Court Judge (para 2). Similarly, in the county court, most appeals from a District Judge will be to a Circuit Judge (para 3(2)). However, there are other important changes. Appeals against final decisions[2] on multi-track cases and in specialist proceedings will be to the Court of Appeal (para 4). Otherwise, however – and forgetting family matters – appeals from the County Court will be to the High Court, not the Court of Appeal (para 3(1)). Finally, any appeal from a decision which is itself made on appeal will lie to the Court of Appeal and not to any other court (para 5).

In short, the proper route of appeal against a decision after 2 May 2000 will depend on a number of matters – whose decision it is, whether the case is fast or multi-track and whether the order appealed is or is not a 'final decision'. Subject to the crucial question of permission to appeal (on which, see below), we suppose that the new provisions will work as follows.

In *fast track* cases, appeals against the interim or final decisions of a District Judge will be to a Circuit Judge, whereas appeals against the interim or final decisions of a Circuit Judge will be to a High Court Judge.

In *multi-track cases in the county court*, appeals against the interim decisions of a District Judge will be to a Circuit Judge and appeals against the interim decisions of a Circuit Judge will be to a High Court Judge. In *multi-track cases in the High Court*, appeals against the interim decisions of a Master will be to a High Court Judge and appeals against the interim decisions of a High Court Judge will be to the Court of Appeal. All appeals against *final decisions in multi-track cases* will go direct to the Court of Appeal, regardless of the court of first instance.

In *all cases*, regardless of track, any second appeal is to the Court of Appeal.

On the scope and general significance of the new appeal provisions, see *Tanfern Ltd v Cameron-McDonald* (2000) *The Times*, 17 May, CA.

---

2   'Final decision' means 'a decision of a court that would finally determine (subject to any possible appeal or detailed assessment of costs) the entire proceedings whichever way the court decided the issues before it' (para 1(2)(c)) – including, obviously, such a decision made on the conclusive first part of a split trial (para 1(3)).

PERMISSION TO APPEAL

In broad terms, the effect of Part 52.3 would seem to be that permission is required to bring an appeal in almost all cases[3] – regardless of the person making the order or the destination of the appeal. We say 'would seem to be' because Part 52.3 says that permission is required 'where the appeal is from a decision *of a judge* in a county court or the High Court, except ...'. Ordinarily in the CPR, unless the context otherwise requires, the word 'judge' is to be read broadly, so as to include Masters and District Judges – see Part 2.3(1). It is not on the face of it obvious why the context should otherwise require in Part 52.3, so that leave will now be required to appeal from a Master to a High Court Judge, or from a District Judge to a Circuit Judge.

Permission to appeal can be sought either from the lower court making the decision to be appealed, or from the appeal court in an appeal notice (Part 52.3(2)). However, the lower court should ordinarily be asked for permission at the time of making its order (PD52, para 4.6). Where no such application is made to the lower court or where it refuses permission, an application for permission may be made to the appeal court (PD52, para 4.7). The appeal court may in the first instance decide such applications on paper. However, if the appeal court refuses permission, the applicant is entitled to have the matter reconsidered at a hearing (Part 52.3(4)). (The procedure in relation to applications for permission is fairly complicated and we refer the reader to the PD at para 4.11 *et seq* for full details.)

Crucially, Part 52.3(6) provides that :

Permission to appeal will only be given where –

(a) the court considers that the appeal would have a real prospect of success; or

(b) there is some other compelling reason why the appeal should be heard.

Appeals against case management decisions are particularly discouraged. In deciding whether to give permission to appeal from such a decision, the court may take various specified matters into account, all broadly falling under the heading of proportionality. The court may consider whether the significance of the issue in question justifies the costs of an appeal, the procedural consequences (for example, loss of a trial date) and whether the matter can be better dealt with at or after trial (PD52, paras 4.4 and 4.5).

Permission can also be given on particular issues or subject to conditions (Part 52.3(7) and PD52, para 4.18). There is, of course, separate provision for security for costs in respect of an appeal in the new Part 25.15.

---

3   There are three specified exceptions, all to do with liberty of the subject – Part 52.3(1)(a).

Permission to appeal is also required by any respondent who wishes to appeal from the decision of the lower court, or who wishes the appeal court to vary that decision in any way (PD52, para 7.1). Any respondent who appeals (or who wishes to uphold a decision for reasons different from or additional to those given by the lower court) will have to file a respondent's notice – see Part 52.5 and PD52, para 7 generally).

In most cases, an appeal does not operate as a stay of the order appealed against without specific order to the contrary (Part 52.7).

Full details must be sought in the practice direction but the timetable for appealing is in most respects quite tight. For example, an appeal notice (including, if needed, an application for permission to appeal) must usually be filed within 14 days of the judgment appealed from (Part 52.4(2)(b)). Given the terms of Part 40.7, this may well mean from the actual date of judgment, rather than from the date of sealing of the order as used to be the rule in relation to appeals to the Court of Appeal. Again, a request for an oral hearing to reconsider an appeal court's refusal of permission to appeal must be made within seven days of that refusal (PD52, para 4.14).

NATURE OF APPEALS

Another major change is in Part 52.11(1), which reads as follows:

> Every appeal will be limited to a review of the decision of the lower court unless –
>
> (a) a practice direction makes different provision for a particular category of appeal; or
>
> (b) the court considers that in the circumstances of an individual appeal it would be in the interests of justice to hold a re-hearing.

The most important practical effect of this provision is that appeals from a Master or District Judge will in future usually be by way of review, rather than by way of re-hearing as previously. Consequently, there are also now restrictions on the admission of fresh evidence in such appeals (Part 52.11(2)). Get your evidence right before the Master – you will no longer be able to rely on sorting it all out in front of the Judge!

The grounds for reviewing a decision on appeal are set out in Part 52.11(3). They are that the decision below was 'wrong', or that it was 'unjust because of a serious procedural or other irregularity in the proceedings'. The grounds of appeal in the appeal notice will have to set out clearly why these grounds are said to apply (PD52, para 3.2).

While the function of the appeal court is limited to a review of the decision of the lower court, it enjoys all of that court's powers in respect of the case (Part 52.10(1)). Thus, the appeal court may affirm, set aside or vary any order or judgment of the lower court, or direct that there be a new trial or hearing of any particular issue (Part 52.10(2)). An appeal court will not ordinarily receive oral evidence or evidence which was not before the lower court (Part 52.11(2)).

THE COURT OF APPEAL

The permission of the Court of Appeal is required for any appeal to that court from a decision of a county court or of the High Court which was itself made on appeal. Permission for such second appeals will not be given unless an important point of principle or practice is involved, or unless there is some other compelling reason (Part 52.13).

In cases that satisfy these tests of importance, there is also provision for a form of 'leapfrog' appeal direct to the Court of Appeal. A Master or District Judge (or a Circuit or High Court Judge to whom an appeal is made or from whom permission to appeal is sought) may order an appeal to be transferred to the Court of Appeal. However the Court of Appeal has the final say in relation to such leapfrogging, enjoying the power to remit the appeal to the court which would ordinarily hear it (Part 52.14). (The Master of the Rolls also has a similar power to direct that an appeal be transferred from an appeal court to the Court of Appeal – section 57(1)(a) of the Access to Justice Act 1999.)

Part 52.16 effectively creates a new kind of Master, known as a Master in the Court of Appeal (PD52, para 15.2). With the consent of the Master of the Rolls, legally-qualified court officers assigned to the Court of Appeals Office may exercise the jurisdiction of that court in relation to matters that are incidental to Court of Appeal proceedings. Such incidental matters include matters where there is no substantial dispute between the parties, and the dismissal of appeals or applications where there has been a failure to comply with an order, rule or practice direction. One imagines that the precise functions of such Masters will be outlined in a future practice direction.

COSTS

An appeal court will often have to deal with questions of costs, both of a substantive appeal and of various subsidiary applications. Costs are likely to be summarily assessed at the hearings listed in PD52, para 14.1. They include the hearing of appeals listed for a day or less; appeals from case management decisions; contested directions hearings and applications for permission to appeal at which the respondent is present. Parties to such hearings should presumably serve costs summaries in the usual way. It remains to be seen how practice in this regard will be varied in the Court of Appeal – for the present position, see the *Practice Note* at [1999] 2 All ER 638.

CHAPTER 29

CONCLUSION

We are not legal sociologists, nor statisticians, and anyone who wants an accurate analysis with supporting figures of the extent to which the anticipated effects of the CPR have become reality will have to look elsewhere than in this chapter. The ideas and conclusions here contained are entirely our own and are entirely impressionistic. Nevertheless, we feel that, at the end of our labours, it is worth pausing for a little reflection.

In the final chapter of our earlier work, we rashly attempted to summarise the aims and likely effects of the new Rules in four short paragraphs. It seems to us that those paragraphs have, broadly speaking, stood the test of the first year of the CPR's existence and we therefore set them out again here, adding the odd further comment.

(i) Consistently with Lord Woolf's aim of passing 'ultimate responsibility for the control of litigation ... from the litigants and their legal advisers to the court', there are now at least three parties to any litigation and never only two. The 'new' or 'extra' party is the court itself. Through active case management and all the multi-faceted powers that that involves, the court is also the party who is in control – a control that will be firmly exercised, particularly in relation to adherence to the various directions timetables.

(ii) A profound change of culture is called for on the part of everybody involved in the litigation process. Judges will have to learn to be 'pro-active', rather than merely reactive and at least in relation to case management matters, litigators will have to lay aside some of their natural aggression and adapt to being co-operative, both with one another and with the court. Let anyone who doubts these suggestions look again at the first of the many limbs of the definition of active case management in Part 1.4(2).

These almost psychological changes are obviously proving easier for some lawyers than for others – and are more easily applied in some types of litigation than in others, and at some stages of the litigious process than at others. Not surprisingly, lawyers and their clients seem to have adapted to them most easily when there is a structure that effectively requires it – for example, the pre-action protocols, or the one month stay for mediation.

(iii) One widely expected practical consequence of the CPR was a significant increase in the 'front loading' of work. So much seemed inevitable given that parties are now expected to comply with pre-action protocols, to produce fuller pleadings and to come to case management conferences armed with case summaries and details of the principal items of likely evidence. Such front loading was entirely expected by the authors of the Rules. Their aim was to kill the practice of 'bash out a writ and see what happens'. The Rules are firmly based on the conviction that a little more time and money spent in advance will save huge and pointless expense later on – or, to adapt an old proverb, the idea that 'A pound in time ...'.

However, old habits die hard and even if the philosophy of identifying issues in advance and of attempting settlement before issuing proceedings is understood, the realities of practice are often more demanding. The phenomenon of the issues in a case only becoming apparent when that case is pleaded is a very familiar one to many lawyers. A useful expedient, at least for claimants, may be to attempt a draft pleading of one's case, even at the pre-action stage.

(iv) Another significant practical consequence has almost certainly been greater client involvement in the interlocutory mechanics of litigation: in dealing with pre-action work, in the approval and verification of pleadings, in making disclosure statements and in attending case management conferences. Once again, this development will not distress the authors of the Rules. The view is clearly taken that the more clients are involved in their cases (and the less litigation is left at one remove, to acquire a monstrous life of its own in the hands of the lawyers), the more likely those cases are to settle, or at the very least to proceed with reasonable expedition and minimum expense.

More broadly, how do we think that the reforms are going?

There have, of course, been difficulties. Given the speed with which the CPR were introduced and the fundamental nature of the changes they seek to effect, that is hardly surprising. Such difficulties seem to have been encountered by practitioners and judges alike.

For practitioners, the most widely-heard lament is one of sheer incredulity at the phenomenon of monthly amendments to the practice directions by which they are expected to regulate their practices and their clients' affairs. Such amendments are only readily available to those who are prepared to scour the Lord Chancellor's website or to pay the Government's somewhat exorbitant charge for the Blue Book. 'Civil Procedure' (the equivalent of the old White Book, by which most courts and practitioners undoubtedly still regulate their business) was, until very recently, six monthly amendments out of date, with no supplement being available. For this state of affairs, one can hardly blame the publishers. One has frankly to wonder whether the advantages of monthly amendments (whatever they are) are not far outweighed by the debilitating confusion – and, if one is speaking frankly, irritation with the new system as a whole – that such amendments unquestionably engender.

Difficulties for the judiciary seem to have been greatest with the question of old authorities and the 'new procedural code' provision. We have considered this problem at length in Chapter 2. There has, not surprisingly, been something of a patchy reaction to the idea that old procedural authorities are now 'irrelevant'. In part, difficulty with that idea has been caused by the simple fact that procedural and substantive law are not always easily separable. Another more immediate difficulty is that we are still in a transitional stage – there are still many cases around where the old procedural law remains factually relevant to the exercise of judicial discretion, even though it does not ultimately form the test which must decide the fate or future conduct of those actions. Nowhere have these difficulties been more apparent than in cases for striking out for want of prosecution – see, in particular, the remarks of Brooke LJ in *Walsh v Misseldine* (2000) unreported, 29 February, quoted in Chapter 2 above. There also seems to be some variety of judicial approach in relation to the 'costs follow the event' principle and whether the CPR are in this regard more 'issue based' than the old rules (see Chapter 24 above).

Equally, of course, there have been successes. Mediation has certainly been one of them. The one month's stay provision in Part 26.4 has undoubtedly saved mediation institutions years of marketing expenditure. Lawyers who were previously (ridiculously and unjustifiably) ignorant and scared of mediation have been given a rapid education course in its merits. In ever increasing numbers, lawyers seem to be coming to understand the advantages that mediation can offer to their clients. Clients themselves never seem to need to have those advantages explained twice.

Another success, which has bedded fairly easily into existing habits, has been the process of summarily assessing costs. Now that lawyers have got into the habit of preparing and exchanging summaries of costs, and that they have accustomed themselves to the necessarily unscientific and 'broad brush' approach that is adopted on such occasions, the summary assessment system seems to be working well. Initially, there were anecdotal horror stories of huge and savage reductions to large bills of costs imposed by judges keen to teach the profession a thing or two about the proper scale of professional fees. These stories certainly caused some concern – after all, though the proportions are the same, there is all the difference in the world between reducing a bill of £15,000 to £10,000 and reducing a bill of £150,000 to £100,000! The amount of judicial time and effort that is devoted to the 'broad brush' approach may be the same in each case but in one, a litigant is left having to find £5,000 out of his own pocket and in the other £45,000. But then 'Such is the breath of kings'.[1] Even where detailed assessment is required, the provision for

---

1   *Richard II*, Act 1, scene 3.

payments on account (Part 44.3(8)) and Jacob J's interpretation of that provision in *Mars UK Limited v Teknowledge* (1999) *The Times*, 8 July – both discussed in Chapter 24 above – have fitted in well with the general new approach to assessment, namely that litigants should be brought to realise at an early stage that litigation costs.

It remains to be seen how other features of the new landscape will develop. One surprise, perhaps, has been in relation to sanctions. It was commonly expected by practitioners that the effect of the CPR would be to lead to more cases being struck out for delay and for failure to comply with strict timetables. However, this expectation may really only have been the product of old-fashioned 'all or nothing' ways of thinking in relation to case management. Though outrageously old cases from the *ancien régime* are being struck out under the CPR, the lesson for the future is rather that the court will (at least in the first instance) seek to take a more creative approach to sanctions – reducing in advance the rates of interest on any judgment, or whatever it may be (see Chapter 2 above). It remains to be seen how precisely these *'Biguzzi* options' will develop in practice.

Contrary to dire predictions of large numbers of appeals on procedural problems – and however it may appear to authors who have been scouring the Internet for anything vaguely relevant! – there have in truth been surprisingly few reported cases on the CPR in the first year of their existence. The impending changes to the appeals system and the in-built bias against appeals on case management decisions seem only likely to reinforce this phenomenon (see Chapter 28 above). Some areas have been surprisingly free of any kind of judicial pronouncement at all – most obviously, perhaps, the new disclosure regime.

At the end of the day, however, the baby is only one year old. Far from being over, the learning process has only just begun. Judges and practitioners seem set to be bombarded with further developments for many years to come. All that we can suggest by way of conclusion is that if there does not seem to be an answer in the Rules, the practice directions, the case law or this (or any other) book, stick to your instincts for common sense. You should not go too far wrong if you are seen to be trying to be reasonable rather than opportunistic, constructive and even-handed rather than technical or tactical. And, of course, *ab ovo usque ad mala,* say it in English, rather than in the tongue of Tacitus and the Cæsars!

NEW TERMINOLOGY

The Civil Procedure Rules attempt to modernise the language of the law by removing 'expressions which are meaningless or confusing to non-lawyers' or by using different expressions which 'would more adequately convey what is involved' (FR chap 20, para 13). The following list is put forward as a working tool for practitioners as they learn the new language. However, considerable care must be exercised because the new terms shown below are not exact synonyms for the old terms associated with them. For example, while disclosure replaces 'discovery', there are very significant differences between the new and old substantive rules.

NEW TERMINOLOGY	OLD TERMINOLOGY
Application notice	Summons in the High Court Notice of application in the county court
Claimant	Plaintiff
Costs judge	Taxing master
Disclosure	Discovery
Detailed assessment	Taxation of costs
Freezing injunction	Mareva injunction
Further information	Further and Better Particulars; Interrogatories
In private	In camera
Interim remedies	Interlocutory relief
Part 20 claim	Third party proceedings (also includes counterclaims and claims for contribution or indemnity – see Part 20.2 for full details)

Particulars of Claim	Statement of Claim in the High Court
Search order	Anton Piller order
Service by an alternative method (see Part 6.8)	Substituted service
Statements of case (See Part 2.3 for full definition)	Pleadings
Summary judgment (Part 24)	'Order 14'
Witness summons	'Subpoena ad testificandum' and 'subpoena duces tecum' in the High Court

RULES OF THE RSC (1965)
WHICH REMAIN 'SCHEDULED'

As at 2 May 2000, the following rules of the RSC (1965) remain scheduled in whole **OR IN PART**. (For full details, refer to Schedule 1 to the core rules, as amended by SI 2000/221.)

Ord 10   Service of claim form in certain actions for possession of land.

Ord 15   Causes of action, counterclaims and parties.

Ord 17   Interpleader.

Ord 30   Receivers.

Ord 44   Proceedings under judgments and orders: Chancery Division.

Ord 45   Enforcement of judgments and orders: General.

Ord 46   Writs of Execution: General.

Ord 47   Writs of Fieri Facias.

Ord 48   Examination of judgment debtor, etc.

Ord 49   Garnishee proceedings.

Ord 50   Charging Orders, Stop Orders, etc.

Ord 51   Receivers: equitable execution.

Ord 52   Committal.

Ord 53   Judicial Review.

Ord 54   Habeas Corpus.

Ord 57   Divisional Court proceedings: Supplementary provisions.

Ord 62   Costs (only part).

Ord 64   Sittings, vacations and office hours.

Ord 69   Service of foreign process.

Ord 70   Obtaining evidence for foreign courts.

Ord 71   Reciprocal enforcement of judgments and enforcement of EC Judgments and Recommendations under the Merchant Shipping (Liner Conferences) Act 1982.

Ord 74   Applications and Appeals under the Merchant Shipping Act 1995.

Ord 77   Proceedings by and against the Crown.

Ord 79	Criminal proceedings.
Ord 81	Partners.
Ord 85	Administration and similar actions.
Ord 87	Debenture Holders' claims: Receiver's Register.
Ord 88	Mortgage claims.
Ord 91	Revenue proceedings.
Ord 92	Lodgement, investment etc. of funds in Court: Chancery Division.
Ord 93	Applications and appeals to High Court under various Acts: Chancery Division.
Ord 94	Applications and appeals to High Court under various Acts: Queen's Bench Division.
Ord 95	Bills of Sale Acts 1878 and 1882 and The Industrial and Provident Societies Act 1967.
Ord 96	The Mines (Working Facilities and Support) Act 1966.
Ord 97	The Landlord and Tenant Acts 1927, 1954 and 1987.
Ord 98	Local Government Finance Act 1982, Part III.
Ord 99	Inheritance (Provision for Family and Dependants) Act 1975.
Ord 106	Proceedings Relating to Solicitors: The Solicitors Act, 1974.
Ord 108	Proceedings Relating to Charities: The Charities Act 1993.
Ord 109	The Administration of Justice Act 1960.
Ord 110	Environmental Control Proceedings.
Ord 112	Applications for Use of Blood Tests in Determining Paternity.
Ord 113	Summary Proceedings for Possession of Land.
Ord 114	References to the European Court.
Ord 115	Confiscation and Forfeiture in connection with criminal proceedings.
Ord 116	The Criminal Procedure & Investigations Act 1996

RULES OF THE CCR (1981)
WHICH REMAIN 'SCHEDULED'

As at 2 May 2000, the following rules of the CCR (1981) remain scheduled in whole **OR IN PART**. (For full details, refer to Schedule 2 to the core rules as amended by SI 2000/221.)

Ord 1   (Application of RSC to county court proceedings).

Ord 4   Venue for bringing proceedings.

Ord 5   Causes of action and parties.

Ord 6   Particulars of Claim.

Ord 7   Service of documents.

Ord 16   Transfer of Proceedings.

Ord 19   Reference to European Court.

Ord 22   Judgments and Orders.

Ord 24   Summary proceedings for the recovery of land.

Ord 25   Enforcement of Judgments and Orders: General.

Ord 26   Warrants of Execution, Delivery and Possession.

Ord 27   Attachment of Earnings.

Ord 28   Judgment Summonses.

Ord 29   Committal for breach of order or undertaking.

Ord 30   Garnishee proceedings.

Ord 31   Charging Orders.

Ord 33   Interpleader proceedings.

Ord 34   Penal and disciplinary provisions.

Ord 35   Enforcement of County Court judgments outside England and Wales.

Ord 37   Rehearing, setting aside and appeal from District Judge.

Ord 38   Costs (only part).

Ord 39   Administration Orders.

Ord 42   Proceedings by and against the Crown.

Ord 43   The Landlord and Tenant Acts 1927, 1954, 1985 and 1987.

Ord 44   The Agricultural Holdings Act 1986.

Ord 45   The Representation of the People Act 1983.

Ord 46   The Legitimacy Act 1976.

Ord 47   Domestic and Matrimonial Proceedings.

Ord 48B   Enforcement of Parking Penalties under the Road Traffic Act 1991.

Ord 48D   Enforcement of Fixed Penalties under the Road Traffic (Vehicle Emissions) (Fixed Penalty) Regulations 1997

Ord 49   Miscellaneous Statutes.

THE ACCESS TO JUSTICE ACT 1999 (DESTINATION OF APPEALS) ORDER 2000

STATUTORY INSTRUMENTS

2000 NO 1071 (L 10)

SUPREME COURT OF ENGLAND AND WALES

COUNTY COURTS, ENGLAND AND WALES

THE ACCESS TO JUSTICE ACT 1999 (DESTINATION OF APPEALS)

ORDER 2000

Made — — — — — — — — — — —   *15th April 2000*

Coming into force — — — — — —   *2nd May 2000*

The Lord Chancellor, in exercise of the powers conferred on him by section 56(1) and (3) of the Access to Justice Act 1999**(a)**, having consulted as required by section 56(4), makes the following Order of which a draft has, in accordance with section 56(6), been laid before and approved by resolution of each House of Parliament:

Citation, commencement and interpretation

1.—(1) This Order may be cited as the Access to Justice Act 1999 (Destination of Appeals) Order 2000 and shall come into force on 2nd May 2000.

(2) In this Order—

    (a) 'decision' includes any judgment, order or direction of the High Court or a county court;

    (b) 'family proceedings' means proceedings which are business of any description which in the High Court is for the time being assigned to the Family Division and to no other Division by or under section 61 of (and Schedule 1 to) the Supreme Court Act 1981**(b)**; and

    (c) 'final decision' means a decision of a court that would finally determine (subject to any possible appeal or detailed assessment of costs) the entire proceedings whichever way the court decided the issues before it.

(3) A decision of a court shall be treated as a final decision where it—

    (a) is made at the conclusion of part of a hearing or trial which has been split into parts; and

    (b would, if made at the conclusion of that hearing or trial, be a final decision under paragraph (2)(c).

(4) Articles 2 to 6—

    (a) do not apply to an appeal in family proceedings; and

(a) 1999 c. 22.

(b) 1981 c. 54.

(b) are subject to—
  (i) any enactment that provides a different route of appeal (other than section 16(1) of the Supreme Court Act 1981 or section 77(1) of the County Courts Act 1984**(a)**); and
  (ii) any requirement to obtain permission to appeal.

Appeals from the High Court

2. Subject to articles 4 and 5, an appeal shall lie to a judge of the High Court where the decision to be appealed is made by—
  (a) a person holding an office referred to in Part II of Schedule 2 to the Supreme Court Act 1981**(b)**;
  (b) a district judge of the High Court; or
  (c) a person appointed to act as a deputy for any person holding such an office as is referred to in sub-paragraphs (a) and (b) or to act as a temporary additional officer in any such office.

Appeals from a county court

3.—(1) Subject to articles 4 and 5 and to paragraph (2), an appeal shall lie from a decision of a county court to the High Court.

(2) Subject to articles 4 and 5, where the decision to be appealed is made by a district judge or deputy district judge of a county court, an appeal shall lie to a judge of a county court.

Appeals in a claim allocated to the multi-track or in specialist proceedings

4. An appeal shall lie to the Court of Appeal where the decision to be appealed is a final decision—
  (a) in a claim allocated by a court to the multi-track under rules 12.7, 14.8 or 26.5 of the Civil Procedure Rules 1998**(c)**; or
  (b) made in proceedings to which rule 49(2) of the Civil Procedure Rules 1998 refers.

Appeals where decision was itself made on appeal

5. Where—
  (a) an appeal is made to a county court or the High Court (other than from the decision of an officer of the court authorised to assess costs by the Lord Chancellor); and
  (b) on hearing the appeal the court makes a decision,
  an appeal shall lie from that decision to the Court of Appeal and not to any other court.

Transitional provisions

6. Where a person has filed a notice of appeal or applied for permission to appeal before 2nd May 2000—
  (a) this Order shall not apply to the appeal to which that notice or application relates; and
  (b) that appeal shall lie to the court to which it would have lain before 2nd May 2000.

(a) 1984 c. 28. Section 77(1) was amended by the Civil Procedure Act 1997 (c.12), section 10, Schedule 2, paragraphs 2(1) and (7).

(b) 1981 c. 54. Schedule 2 was substituted by the Courts and Legal Services Act 1990 (c. 41), section 71(2), Schedule 10, paragraph 49 and amended by the Access to Justice Act 1999 (c. 22), section 106, Schedule 15, Pt III.

(c) SI 1998/3132; there are no relevant amendments.

Consequential amendments

7. In section 16(1) of the Supreme Court Act 1981, before 'the Court of Appeal' the second time it appears, insert 'or as provided by any order made by the Lord Chancellor under section 56(1) of the Access to Justice Act 1999,'.
8. In section 77(1) of the County Courts Act 1984, after 'Act' insert 'and to any order made by the Lord Chancellor under section 56(1) of the Access to Justice Act 1999'.

Irvine of Lairg, C.

Dated 15th April 2000

EXPLANATORY NOTE

(This note is not part of the Order)

The primary purpose of this Order is to provide that from 2nd May 2000 appeals from the county courts other than in family proceedings will, in most cases, lie to the High Court rather than to the Court of Appeal (article 3(1)).

Appeals from decisions of masters, registrars and district judges of the High Court will continue to lie to a judge of the High Court (article 2). Similarly appeals from district judges in county courts will continue to lie to a judge of a county court (article 3(2)). These routes of appeal arc currently set out in RSC Order 58 (Schedule I to the Civil Procedure Rules 1998) and CCR Order 13, rule 1 and Order 37, rule 6 (Schedule 2 to the Civil Procedure Rules 1998). Because these Orders will be revoked from 2nd May by the Civil Procedure (Amendment) Rules 2000 (S.I. 2000/221), it is necessary to provide for the routes of appeal in this Order.

If the decision to be appealed is a final decision in a claim allocated to the multi-track or made in specialist proceedings or was itself made on appeal, the appeal will lie to the Court of Appeal irrespective of the court of first instance (articles 4 and 5).

PART C

THE CORE RULES OF THE CPR, WITH RELEVANT PRACTICE DIRECTIONS INTERLEAVED

PART 1
OVERRIDING OBJECTIVE

Contents of this Part

The overriding objective

1.1 (1) These Rules are a new procedural code with the overriding objective of enabling the court to deal with cases justly.

 (2) Dealing with a case justly includes, so far as is practicable –

  (a) ensuring that the parties are on an equal footing;

  (b) saving expense;

  (c) dealing with the case in ways which are proportionate –

   (i) to the amount of money involved;

   (ii) to the importance of the case;

   (iii) to the complexity of the issues; and

   (iv) to the financial position of each party;

  (d) ensuring that it is dealt with expeditiously and fairly; and

  (e) allotting to it an appropriate share of the court's resources, while taking into account the need to allot resources to other cases.

Application by the court of the overriding objective

1.2 The court must seek to give effect to the overriding objective when it –

 (a) exercises any power given to it by the Rules; or

 (b) interprets any rule.

Duty of the parties

1.3 The parties are required to help the court to further the overriding objective.

Court's duty to manage cases

1.4 (1) The court must further the overriding objective by actively managing cases.

 (2) Active case management includes –

  (a) encouraging the parties to co-operate with each other in the conduct of the proceedings;

  (b) identifying the issues at an early stage;

  (c) deciding promptly which issues need full investigation and trial and accordingly disposing summarily of the others;

  (d) deciding the order in which issues are to be resolved;

  (e) encouraging the parties to use an alternative dispute resolution(GL) procedure if the court considers that appropriate and facilitating the use of such procedure;

    (f) helping the parties to settle the whole or part of the case;

    (g) fixing timetables or otherwise controlling the progress of the case;

    (h) considering whether the likely benefits of taking a particular step justify the cost of taking it;

    (i) dealing with as many aspects of the case as it can on the same occasion;

    (j) dealing with the case without the parties needing to attend at court;

    (k) making use of technology; and

    (l) giving directions to ensure that the trial of a case proceeds quickly and efficiently.

PART 2

APPLICATION AND INTERPRETATION OF THE RULES

Contents of this Part

Application of the Rules

2.1 (1) Subject to paragraph (2), these Rules apply to all proceedings in –

    (a) county courts;

    (b) the High Court; and

    (c) the Civil Division of the Court of Appeal.

  (2) These Rules do not apply to proceedings of the kinds specified in the first column of the following table (proceedings for which rules may be made under the enactments specified in the second column) except to the extent that they are applied to those proceedings by another enactment –

Proceedings	Enactments
1 Insolvency proceedings	Insolvency Act 1986[1], ss 411 and 412
2 Non-contentious or common form probate proceedings	Supreme Court Act 1981[2], s 127
3 Proceedings in the High Court when acting as a Prize Court	Prize Courts Act 1894[3], s 3
4 Proceedings before the judge within the meaning of Part VII of the Mental Health Act 1983[4]	Mental Health Act 1983, s 106
5 Family proceedings	Matrimonial and Family Proceedings Act 1984[5], s 40
6 Adoption proceedings	Adoption Act 1976[6], s 66

The glossary

2.2 (1) The glossary at the end of these Rules is a guide to the meaning of certain legal expressions used in the Rules, but is not to be taken as giving those expressions any meaning in the Rules which they do not have in the law generally.

(2) Subject to paragraph (3), words in these Rules which are included in the glossary are followed by '(GL)'.

(3) The words 'counterclaim', 'damages', 'practice form' and 'service', which appear frequently in the Rules, are included in the glossary but are not followed by '(GL)'.

Interpretation

2.3 (1) In these Rules –

'child' has the meaning given by rule 21.1(2);

'claim for personal injuries' means proceedings in which there is a claim for damages in respect of personal injuries to the claimant or any other person or in respect of a person's death, and "personal injuries" includes any disease and any impairment of a person's physical or mental condition;

'claimant' means a person who makes a claim;

'CCR' is to be interpreted in accordance with Part 50;

'court officer' means a member of the court staff;

'defendant' means a person against whom a claim is made;

'defendant's home court' means –

(a) if the claim is proceeding in a county court, the county court for the district in which the defendant's address for service, as shown on the defence, is situated; and

---

(1) 1986 c.45.

(2) 1981 c.54.

(3) 1894 c.39.

(4) 1983 c.20.

(5) 1984 c.42. Section 40 was amended by the Courts and Legal Services Act 1990 (c.41), Sched 18, para 50.

(6) 1976 c.36.

(b) if the claim is proceeding in the High Court, the district registry for the district in which the defendant's address for service, as shown on the defence, is situated or, if there is no such district registry, the Royal Courts of Justice;

(Rule 6.5 provides for a party to give an address for service)

'filing', in relation to a document, means delivering it, by post or otherwise, to the court office;

'judge' means, unless the context otherwise requires, a judge, Master or district judge or a person authorised to act as such;

'jurisdiction' means, unless the context requires otherwise, England and Wales and any part of the territorial waters of the United Kingdom adjoining England and Wales;

'legal representative' means a barrister or a solicitor, solicitor's employee or other authorised litigator (as defined in the Courts and Legal Services Act 1990[7]) who has been instructed to act for a party in relation to a claim.

'litigation friend' has the meaning given by Part 21;

'patient' has the meaning given by rule 21.1(2);

'RSC' is to be interpreted in accordance with Part 50;

'statement of case' –

(a) means a claim form, particulars of claim where these are not included in a claim form, defence, Part 20 claim, or reply to defence; and

(b) includes any further information given in relation to them voluntarily or by court order under rule 18.1;

'statement of value' is to be interpreted in accordance with rule 16.3;

'summary judgment' is to be interpreted in accordance with Part 24.

(2) A reference to a 'specialist list' is a reference to a list[GL] that has been designated as such by a relevant practice direction.

(3) Where the context requires, a reference to 'the court' means a reference to a particular county court, a district registry, or the Royal Courts of Justice.

Power of Judge Master or District Judge to perform functions of the court

2.4 Where these Rules provide for the court to perform any act then, except where an enactment, rule or practice direction provides otherwise, that act may be performed –

(a) in relation to proceedings in the High Court, by any judge, Master or district judge of that Court; and

(b) in relation to proceedings in a county court, by any judge or district judge.

Court staff

2.5 (1) Where these Rules require or permit the court to perform an act of a formal or administrative character, that act may be performed by a court officer.

(2) A requirement that a court officer carry out any act at the request of a party is subject to the payment of any fee required by a fees order for the carrying out of that act.

(Rule 3.2 allows a court officer to refer to a judge before taking any step.)

---

(7) 1990 c.41.

Court documents to be sealed

2.6 (1) The court must seal$^{(GL)}$ the following documents on issue –

(a) the claim form; and

(b) any other document which a rule or practice direction requires it to seal.

(2) The court may place the seal$^{(GL)}$ on the document –

(a) by hand; or

(b) by printing a facsimile of the seal on the document whether electronically or otherwise.

(3) A document purporting to bear the court's seal$^{(GL)}$ shall be admissible in evidence without further proof.

Court's discretion as to where it deals with cases

2.7 The court may deal with a case at any place that it considers appropriate.

Time

2.8 (1) This rule shows how to calculate any period of time for doing any act which is specified –

(a) by these Rules;

(b) by a practice direction; or

(c) by a judgment or order of the court.

(2) A period of time expressed as a number of days shall be computed as clear days.

(3) In this rule 'clear days' means that in computing the number of days –

(a) the day on which the period begins; and

(b) if the end of the period is defined by reference to an event, the day on which that event occurs

are not included.

Examples

(i) Notice of an application must be served at least 3 days before the hearing. An application is to be heard on Friday 20 October. The last date for service is Monday 16 October.

(ii) The court is to fix a date for a hearing. The hearing must be at least 28 days after the date of notice. If the court gives notice of the date of the hearing on 1 October, the earliest date for the hearing is 30 October.

(iii) Particulars of claim must be served within 14 days of service of the claim form. The claim form is served on 2 October. The last day for service of the particulars of claim is 16 October.

(4) Where the specified period –

(a) is 5 days or less; and

(b) includes –

(i) a Saturday or Sunday; or

(ii) a Bank Holiday, Christmas Day or Good Friday,

that day does not count.

Example

Notice of an application must be served at least 3 days before the hearing. An application is to be heard on Monday 20 October. The last date for service is Tuesday 14 October.

(5) When the period specified –

(a) by these Rules or a practice direction; or

(b) by any judgment or court order,

for doing any act at the court office ends on a day on which the office is closed, that act shall be in time if done on the next day on which the court office is open.

Dates for compliance to be calendar dates and to include time of day

2.9 (1) Where the court gives a judgment, order or direction which imposes a time limit for doing any act, the last date for compliance must, wherever practicable –

(a) be expressed as a calendar date; and

(b) include the time of day by which the act must be done.

(2) Where the date by which an act must be done is inserted in any document, the date must, wherever practicable, be expressed as a calendar date.

Meaning of 'month' in judgments, etc

2.10 Where 'month' occurs in any judgment, order, direction or other document, it means a calendar month.

Time limits may be varied by parties

2.11 Unless these Rules or a practice direction provide otherwise or the court orders otherwise, the time specified by a rule or by the court for a person to do any act may be varied by the written agreement of the parties.

(Rules 3.8 (sanctions have effect unless defaulting party obtains relief), 28.4 (variation of case management timetable – fast track); 29.5 (variation of case management timetable – multi-track) and RSC O.59 r.2C (appeals to the Court of Appeal) in Schedule 1, provide for time limits that cannot be varied by agreement between the parties.)

PRACTICE DIRECTION – COURT OFFICES
THIS PRACTICE DIRECTION SUPPLEMENTS CPR PART 2

Central Office of the High Court at the Royal Courts of Justice

1 The Central Office shall be divided into such departments, and the business performed in the Central Office shall be distributed among the departments in such manner, as is set out in the Queen's Bench Division Guide.

Business in the Offices of the Supreme Court

2.1 (1) The offices of the Supreme Court shall be open on every day of the year except

(a) Saturdays and Sundays,

(b) Good Friday and the day after Easter Monday,

(c) Christmas Day and, if that day is a Friday or Saturday, then 28th December,

(d) Bank Holidays in England and Wales under the Banking and Financial Dealings Act 1971, and

(e) such other days as the Lord Chancellor, with the concurrence of the Lord Chief Justice, the Master of the Rolls, the President of the Family Division and the Vice-Chancellor ("the Heads of Division") may direct.

(2) The hours during which the offices of the Supreme Court shall be open to the public shall be as follows:

(a) at the Principal Probate Registry at First Avenue House, 42–49 High Holborn, London WC1V 6HA, from 10 a.m. to 4.30 p.m.,

(b) at the Supreme Court offices at the Royal Courts of Justice (including the Construction and Technology Court Registry in St. Dunstan's House, 133–137 Fetter Lane, London EC4A 1HD), from 10 a.m. to 4.30 p.m., except during the month of August in every year, when the hours shall be from 10 a.m. to 2.30 p.m.,

> (c) such other hours as the Lord Chancellor, with the concurrence of the Heads of Division, may from time to time direct.
>
> (3) Every District Registry shall be open on the days and during the hours that the Lord Chancellor from time to time directs and, in the absence of any such directions, shall be open on the same days and during the same hours as the county court offices of which it forms part are open.

2.2 One of the Masters of the Queen's Bench Division (the "Practice Master") shall be present at the Central Office on every day on which the office is open for the purpose of superintending the business performed there and giving any directions which may be required on questions of practice and procedure.

County Courts

3.1 Every County Court shall have an office or, if the Lord Chancellor so directs, two or more offices, situated at such place or places as he may direct, for the transaction of the business of the court.

3.2 (1) Every County Court office, or if a court has two or more offices at least one of those offices, shall be open on every day of the year except-

    (a) Saturdays and Sundays,

    (b) the day before Good Friday from noon onwards and Good Friday,

    (c) the Tuesday after the Spring bank holiday,

    (d) Christmas Day and, if that day is a Friday or Saturday, then the 28th December,

    (e) bank holidays and

    (f) such other days as the Lord Chancellor may direct.

  (2) In this paragraph "bank holiday" means a bank holiday in England and Wales under the Banking and Financial Dealings Act 1971 and "Spring holiday" means the bank holiday on the last Monday in May or any day appointed instead of that day under section 1(2) of that Act.

3.3 Subject to paragraph 3.2(1)(b), the hours during which any court office is open to the public shall be from 10 a.m. to 4 p.m. or such other hours as the Lord Chancellor may from time to time direct.

PRACTICE DIRECTION
ALLOCATION of CASES to LEVELS of JUDICIARY

1.1 Rule 2.4 provides that Judges, Masters and District Judges may exercise any function of the court except where an enactment, rule or practice direction provides otherwise. This Practice Direction sets out the matters over which Masters and District Judges do not have jurisdiction or which they may deal with only on certain conditions. It does not affect jurisdiction conferred by other enactments. Reference should also be made to other relevant Practice Directions (eg Part 24, paragraph 3 and Part 26, paragraphs 12.1–10). References to Circuit Judges include Recorders and Assistant Recorders and references to Masters and District Judges include Deputies.

1.2 Wherever a Master or District Judge has jurisdiction, he may refer the matter to a Judge instead of dealing with it himself.

THE HIGH COURT

Injunctions

2.1 Search orders (rule 25.1(1)(h)), freezing orders (rule 25.1(1)(f)), an ancillary order under rule 25.1(1)(g) and orders authorising a person to enter land to recover, inspect or sample property (rule 25.1 (1)(d)) may only be made by a Judge.

2.2 Except where paragraphs 2.3 and 2.4 apply, injunctions and orders relating to injunctions, including orders for specific performance where these involve an injunction, must be made by a Judge.

2.3 A Master or a District Judge may only make an injunction

    (a) in terms agreed by the parties;

    (b) in connection with or ancillary to a charging order;

    (c) in connection with or ancillary to an order appointing a receiver by way of equitable execution; or

    (d) in proceedings under RSC Order 77 rule 16 (order restraining person from receiving sum due from the Crown).

2.4 A Master or District Judge may make an order varying or discharging an injunction or undertaking given to the court if all parties to the proceedings have consented to the variation or discharge.

Other pre-trial Orders and Interim Remedies

3.1 A Master or District Judge may not make orders or grant interim remedies:

    (a) relating to the liberty of the subject;

    (b) relating to criminal proceedings or matters except procedural applications in appeals to the High Court (including appeals by case stated) under any enactment;

    (c) relating to proceedings for judicial review, except applications under RSC Order 53 rule 8 (interlocutory applications);

    (d) relating to appeals from Masters or District Judges;

    (e) in appeals against a costs assessment under Parts 43–48, except –

        (i) on an appeal under rule 47.22 against the decision of an authorised court officer; or

        (ii) on an application for the grant of permission where rule 47.24 requires this.

    (f) in applications under section 42 of the Supreme Court Act 1981 by a person subject to a Civil or a Criminal or an All Proceedings Order (vexatious litigant) for permission to start or continue proceedings.

3.2 This Practice Direction is not concerned with family proceedings. It is also not concerned with proceedings in the Family Division except to the extent that such proceedings can be dealt with in the Chancery Division or the Family Division eg proceedings under the Inheritance (Provision for Family and Dependants) Act 1975 or under section 14 of the Trusts of Land and Appointment of Trustees Act 1996. District Judges (including District Judges of the Principal Registry of the Family Division) have jurisdiction to hear such proceedings, subject to any Direction given by the President of the Family Division.

Trials and Assessments of damages

4.1 A Master or District Judge may, subject to any Practice Direction, try a case which is treated as being allocated to the multi-track because it is proceeding under Part 8 (see rule 8.9(c)). He may try a case which has been allocated to the multi-track under Part 26 only with the consent of the parties. Restrictions on the trial jurisdiction of Masters and District Judges do not prevent them from hearing applications for summary judgment or, if the parties consent, for the determination of a preliminary issue.

4.2 A Master or a District Judge may assess the damages or sum due to a party under a judgment without limit as to the amount.

Chancery Proceedings

5.1 In proceedings in the Chancery Division, a Master or a District Judge may not deal with the following without the consent of the Vice-Chancellor:–

    (a) approving compromises (other than applications under the Inheritance (Provision for Family and Dependants) Act 1975) (i) on behalf of a person under disability where that person's interest in a fund, or if there is no fund, the maximum amount of the claim, exceeds £100,000 and (ii) on behalf of absent, unborn and unascertained persons;

    (b) making declarations, except in plain cases;

    (c) making final orders under section 1(1) of the Variation of Trusts Act 1958, except for the removal of protective trusts where the interest of the principal beneficiary has not failed or determined;

    (d) where the proceedings are brought by a Part 8 claim form in accordance with paragraph A.1(2) or (3) of the Part 8B Practice Direction (statutory or other requirement to use originating summons), determining any question of law or as to the construction of a document which is raised by the claim form;

    (e) giving permission to executors, administrators and trustees to bring or defend proceedings or to continue the prosecution or defence of proceedings, and granting an indemnity for costs out of the trust estate, except in plain cases;

    (f) granting an indemnity for costs out of the assets of a company on the application of minority shareholders bringing a derivative action, except in plain cases;

    (g) making an order for rectification, except for rectification of the register under the Land Registration Act 1925 in plain cases;

    (h) making orders to vacate entries in the register under the Land Charges Act 1972, except in plain cases;

    (i) making final orders on applications under section 19 of the Leasehold Reform Act 1967, section 48 of the Administration of Justice Act 1985 and sections 21 and 25 of the Law of Property Act 1969;

    (j) making final orders under the Landlord and Tenant Acts 1927 and 1954, except (i) by consent, (ii) orders for interim rents under section 24A of the 1954 Act and (iii) on applications to authorise agreements under section 38(4) of the 1954 Act;

    (k) making orders in proceedings in the Patents Court except (i) by consent, (ii) to extend time, (iii) on applications for permission to serve out of the jurisdiction and (iv) on applications for security for costs.

5.2 A Master or District Judge may only give directions for early trial after consulting the Judge in charge of the relevant list.

5.3 Where a winding-up order has been made against a company, any proceedings against the company by or on behalf of debenture holders may be dealt with, at the Royal Courts of Justice, by a Registrar and, in a District Registry with insolvency jurisdiction, by a District Judge.

Assignment of Claims to Masters and Transfer between Masters

6.1 The Senior Master, and the Chief Master will make arrangements for proceedings to be assigned to individual Masters. They may vary such arrangements generally or in particular cases, for example, by transferring a case from a Master to whom it had been assigned to another Master.

6.2 The fact that a case has been assigned to a particular Master does not prevent another Master from dealing with that case if circumstances require, whether at the request of the assigned Master or otherwise.

Freezing Orders: Cross Examination of Deponents about Assets

7 Where the court has made a freezing order under rule 25.1(f) and has ordered a person to make a witness statement or affidavit about his assets and to be cross-examined on its contents, unless the Judge directs otherwise, the cross-examination will take place before a Master or a District Judge, or if the Master or District Judge directs, before an examiner of the Court.

COUNTY COURTS

Injunctions and Committal

8.1 Injunctions which a county court has jurisdiction to make may only be made by a Circuit Judge, except:-

    (a) where the injunction is to be made in proceedings which a District Judge otherwise has jurisdiction to hear (see paragraph 11.1 below);

    (b) where the injunction is sought in a money claim which has not yet been allocated to a track, where the amount claimed does not exceed the fast track financial limit;

    (c) in the circumstances provided by paragraph 2.3.

8.2 A District Judge may make orders varying or discharging injunctions in the circumstances provided by paragraph 2.4.

8.3 A District Judge may not make an order committing a person to prison except where an enactment authorises this: see section 23 of the Attachment of Earnings Act 1971, sections 14 and 18 of the County Courts Act 1984, sections 152-157 of the Housing Act 1996, section 3 of the Protection from Harassment Act 1997, and the relevant rules.

Homelessness Appeals

9 A District Judge may not hear appeals under section 204 of the Housing Act 1996.

Other pre-trial Orders and Interim Remedies

10.1 In addition to the restrictions on jurisdiction mentioned at paragraphs 9.1-3, paragraph 3.1(d) and (e) above applies.

Trials and Assessments of Damages

11.1 A District Judge has jurisdiction to hear the following:–

    (a) any claim which has been allocated to the small claims track or fast track or which is treated as being allocated to the multi-track under rule 8.9(c) and Table 2 of the Practice Direction to Part 8, except proceedings under:–

        (i) CCR Order 43 rules 4, 6 and 18 (certain applications under the Landlord and Tenant Acts 1927 and 1954);

        (ii) CCR Order 43, rule 20 (Landlord and Tenant Act 1987);

        (iii) CCR Order 44, (Agricultural Holdings Act 1986);

        (iv) CCR Order 46, rule 1 (Legitimacy Act 1976);

        (v) CCR Order 49, rule 5 (Fair Trading Act 1973);

        (vi) CCR Order 49, rule 10 (Local Government and Finance Act 1982);

        (vii) CCR Order 49, rule 12 (Mental Health Act 1983);

    (b) proceedings for the recovery of land;

    (c) the assessment of damages or other sum due to a party under a judgment without any financial limit;

    (d) with the consent of the parties and the permission of the Designated Civil Judge in respect of that case, any other proceedings.

11.2 A case allocated to the small claims track may only be assigned to a Circuit Judge to hear with his consent.

Freezing Orders: Cross Examination of Deponents about Assets

12 To the extent that a county court has power to make a freezing order, paragraph 8 applies as appropriate.

Distribution of Business between Circuit Judge and District Judge

13 Where both the Circuit Judge and the District Judge have jurisdiction in respect of any proceedings, the exercise of jurisdiction by the District Judge is subject to any arrangements made by the Designated Civil Judge for the proper distribution of business between Circuit Judges and District Judges.

14.1 In District Registries of the High Court and in the county court, the Designated Civil Judge may make arrangements for proceedings to be assigned to individual District Judges. He may vary such arrangements generally or in particular cases.

14.2 The fact that a case has been assigned to a particular District Judge does not prevent another District Judge from dealing with the case if the circumstances require.

PART 3

THE COURT'S CASE MANAGEMENT POWERS

Contents of this Part

The court's general powers of management

3.1 (1) The list of powers in this rule is in addition to any powers given to the court by any other rule or practice direction or by any other enactment or any powers it may otherwise have.

(2) Except where these Rules provide otherwise, the court may –

  (a) extend or shorten the time for compliance with any rule, practice direction or court order (even if an application for extension is made after the time for compliance has expired);

  (b) adjourn or bring forward a hearing;

  (c) require a party or a party's legal representative to attend the court;

  (d) hold a hearing and receive evidence by telephone or by using any other method of direct oral communication;

  (e) direct that part of any proceedings (such as a counterclaim) be dealt with as separate proceedings;

  (f) stay$^{(GL)}$ the whole or part of any proceedings or judgment either generally or until a specified date or event;

  (g) consolidate proceedings;

  (h) try two or more claims on the same occasion;

  (i) direct a separate trial of any issue;

  (j) decide the order in which issues are to be tried;

  (k) exclude an issue from consideration;

  (l) dismiss or give judgment on a claim after a decision on a preliminary issue;

  (m) take any other step or make any other order for the purpose of managing the case and furthering the overriding objective.

(3) When the court makes an order, it may –

  (a) make it subject to conditions, including a condition to pay a sum of money into court; and

  (b) specify the consequence of failure to comply with the order or a condition.

(4) Where the court gives directions it may take into account whether or not a party has complied with any relevant pre-action protocol$^{(GL)}$.

(5) The court may order a party to pay a sum of money into court if that party has, without good reason, failed to comply with a rule, practice direction or a relevant pre-action protocol.

(6) When exercising its power under paragraph (5) the court must have regard to –

    (a) the amount in dispute; and

    (b) the costs which the parties have incurred or which they may incur.

(6A) Where a party pays money into court following an order under paragraph (3) or (5), the money shall be security for any sum payable by that party to any other party in the proceedings, subject to the right of a defendant under rule 37.2 to treat all or part of any money paid into court as a Part 36 payment.

(Rule 36.2 explains what is meant by a Part 36 payment)

(7) A power of the court under these Rules to make an order includes a power to vary or revoke the order.

Court officer's power to refer to a judge

3.2 Where a step is to be taken by a court officer –

    (a) the court officer may consult a judge before taking that step;

    (b) the step may be taken by a judge instead of the court officer.

Court's power to make order of its own initiative

3.3 (1) Except where a rule or some other enactment provides otherwise, the court may exercise its powers on an application or of its own initiative.

(Part 23 sets out the procedure for making an application)

(2) Where the court proposes to make an order of its own initiative –

    (a) it may give any person likely to be affected by the order an opportunity to make representations; and

    (b) where it does so it must specify the time by and the manner in which the representations must be made.

(3) Where the court proposes –

    (a) to make an order of its own initiative; and

    (b) to hold a hearing to decide whether to make the order,

it must give each party likely to be affected by the order at least 3 days' notice of the hearing.

(4) The court may make an order of its own initiative, without hearing the parties or giving them an opportunity to make representations.

(5) Where the court has made an order under paragraph (4) –

    (a) a party affected by the order may apply to have it set aside[(GL)], varied or stayed[(GL)]; and

    (b) the order must contain a statement of the right to make such an application.

(6) An application under paragraph (5)(a) must be made –

    (a) within such period as may be specified by the court; or

    (b) if the court does not specify a period, not more than 7 days after the date on which the order was served on the party making the application.

(CCR O.42, in Schedule 2, sets out the circumstances when the court may not make an order of its own initiative against the Crown.)

Power to strike out a statement of case

3.4 (1) In this rule and rule 3.5, reference to a statement of case includes reference to part of a statement of case.

(2) The court may strike out[(GL)] a statement of case if it appears to the court –

(a) that the statement of case discloses no reasonable grounds for bringing or defending the claim;

(b) that the statement of case is an abuse of the court's process or is otherwise likely to obstruct the just disposal of the proceedings; or

(c) that there has been a failure to comply with a rule, practice direction or court order.

(3) When the court strikes out a statement of case it may make any consequential order it considers appropriate.

(4) Where –

(a) the court has struck out a claimant's statement of case;

(b) the claimant has been ordered to pay costs to the defendant; and

(c) before the claimant pays those costs, he starts another claim against the same defendant, arising out of facts which are the same or substantially the same as those relating to the claim in which the statement of case was struck out,

the court may, on the application of the defendant, stay$^{(GL)}$ that other claim until the costs of the first claim have been paid.

(5) Paragraph (2) does not limit any other power of the court to strike out $^{(GL)}$ a statement of case.

Judgment without trial after striking out

3.5 (1) This rule applies where –

(a) the court makes an order which includes a term that the statement of case of a party shall be struck out if the party does not comply with the order; and

(b) the party against whom the order was made does not comply with it.

(2) A party may obtain judgment with costs by filing a request for judgment if –

(a) the order referred to in paragraph (1)(a) relates to the whole of a statement of case; and

(b) where the party wishing to obtain judgment is the claimant, the claim is for –

(i) a specified amount of money;

(ii) an amount of money to be decided by the court;

(iii) delivery of goods where the claim form gives the defendant the alternative of paying their value; or

(iv) any combination of these remedies.

(3) Where judgment is obtained under this rule in a case which paragraph (2) (b) (iii) applies, it will be judgment requiring the defendant to deliver goods, or (if he does not do so) pay the value of the goods as decided by the court (less any payments made).

(4) The request must state that the right to enter judgment has arisen because the court's order has not been complied with.

(5) A party must make an application in accordance with Part 23 if he wishes to obtain judgment under this rule in a case to which paragraph (2) does not apply.

Setting aside judgment entered after striking out

3.6 (1) A party against whom the court has entered judgment under rule 3.5 may apply to the court to set the judgment aside.

(2) An application under paragraph (1) must be made not more than 14 days after the judgment has been served on the party making the application.

(3) If the right to enter judgment had not arisen at the time when judgment was entered, the court must set aside$^{(GL)}$ the judgment.

(4) If the application to set aside$^{(GL)}$ is made for any other reason, rule 3.9 (relief from sanctions) shall apply.

Sanctions for non-payment of certain fees

3.7 (1) This rule applies where –

    (a) an allocation questionnaire or a listing questionnaire is filed without payment of the fee specified by the relevant Fees Order; or

    (b) the court dispenses with the need for an allocation questionnaire or a listing questionnaire or both; or

    (c) these Rules do not require an allocation questionnaire or a listing questionnaire to be filed in relation to the claim in question.

(Rule 26.3 provides for the court to dispense with the need for an allocation questionnaire and rules 28.5 and 29.6 provide for the court to dispense with the need for a listing questionnaire)

(2) The court will serve a notice on the claimant requiring payment of the fee which the relevant Fees Order specifies as being due –

    (a) on the filing of the allocation questionnaire or the listing questionnaire; or

    (b) in the circumstances where the claimant is not required to file an allocation questionnaire or a listing questionnaire,

if, at the time the fee is due, the claimant has not paid the fee or made an application for exemption from or remission of the fee.

(3) The notice will specify the date by which the claimant must pay the fee.

(4) If the claimant does not –

    (a) pay the fee; or

    (b) make an application for an exemption from or remission of the fee,

by the date specified in the notice –

    (i) the claim shall be struck out; and

    (ii) the claimant shall be liable for the costs which the defendant has incurred unless the court orders otherwise.

(Rule 44.12 provides for the basis of assessment where a right to costs arises under this rule)

(5) Where an application for exemption from or remission of a fee is refused, the court will serve notice on the claimant requiring payment of the fee by the date specified in the notice.

(6) If the claimant does not pay the fee by the date specified in the notice –

    (a) the claim shall be struck out; and

    (b) the claimant shall be liable for the costs which the defendant has incurred unless the court orders otherwise.

(7) If –

    (a) a claimant applies under rule 3.9 (relief from sanctions) to have the claim reinstated; and

    (b) the court grants relief under that rule,

the relief shall be conditional on the claimant –

    (i) paying the fee; or

    (ii) filing evidence of exemption from payment or remission of the fee, within 2 days of the date of the order.

(Rule 25.11 provides for when an interim injunction shall cease to have effect when a claim is struck out under this rule.)

Sanctions have effect unless defaulting party obtains relief

3.8 (1) Where a party has failed to comply with a rule, practice direction or court order, any sanction for failure to comply imposed by the rule, practice direction or court order has effect unless the party in default applies for and obtains relief from the sanction.

(Rule 3.9 sets out the circumstances which the court may consider on an application to grant relief from a sanction)

(2) Where the sanction is the payment of costs, the party in default may only obtain relief by appealing against the order for costs.

(3) Where a rule, practice direction or court order –

(a) requires a party to do something within a specified time, and

(b) specifies the consequence of failure to comply,

the time for doing the act in question may not be extended by agreement between the parties.

Relief from sanctions

3.9 (1) On an application for relief from any sanction imposed for a failure to comply with any rule, practice direction or court order the court will consider all the circumstances including –

(a) the interests of the administration of justice;

(b) whether the application for relief has been made promptly;

(c) whether the failure to comply was intentional;

(d) whether there is a good explanation for the failure;

(e) the extent to which the party in default has complied with other rules, practice directions, court orders and any relevant preaction protocol[(GL)] ;

(f) whether the failure to comply was caused by the party or his legal representative;

(g) whether the trial date or the likely trial date can still be met if relief is granted;

(h) the effect which the failure to comply had on each party; and

(i) the effect which the granting of relief would have on each party.

(2) An application for relief must be supported by evidence.

General power of the court to rectify matters where there has been an error of procedure

3.10 Where there has been an error of procedure such as a failure to comply with a rule or practice direction –

(a) the error does not invalidate any step taken in the proceedings unless the court so orders; and

(b) the court may make an order to remedy the error.

PRACTICE DIRECTION – STRIKING OUT A STATEMENT OF CASE
THIS PRACTICE DIRECTION SUPPLEMENTS CPR RULE 3.4

INTRODUCTORY

1.1 Rule 1.4(2)(c) includes as an example of active case management the summary disposal of issues which do not need full investigation at trial.

1.2 The rules give the court two distinct powers which may be used to achieve this. Rule 3.4 enables the court to strike out the whole or part of a statement of case which discloses no reasonable grounds for bringing or defending a claim (rule 3.4(2)(a)), or which is an abuse of the process of the court or otherwise likely to obstruct the just disposal of the proceedings (rule 3.4(2)(b)) Rule 24.2 enables the court to give summary judgment against a claimant or defendant where that party has no real prospect of succeeding on his claim or defence. Both those powers may be exercised on an application by a party or on the court's own initiative.

1.3 This practice direction sets out the procedure a party should follow if he wishes to make an application for an order under rule 3.4.

1.4 The following are examples of cases where the court may conclude that particulars of claim (whether contained in a claim form or filed separately) fall within rule 3.4(2)(a):

  (1) those which set out no facts indicating what the claim is about, for example 'Money owed £5,000',

  (2) those which are incoherent and make no sense,

  (3) those which contain a coherent set of facts but those facts, even if true, do not disclose any legally recognisable claim against the defendant.

1.5 A claim may fall within rule 3.4(2)(b) where it is vexatious, scurrilous or obviously ill-founded.

1.6 A defence may fall within rule 3.4(2)(a) where:

  (1) it consists of a bare denial or otherwise sets out no coherent statement of facts, or

  (2) the facts it sets out, while coherent, would not even if true amount in law to a defence to the claim.

1.7 A party may believe he can show without a trial that an opponent's case has no real prospect of success on the facts, or that the case is bound to succeed or fail, as the case may be, because of a point of law (including the construction of a document). In such a case the party concerned may make an application under rule 3.4 or Part 24 (or both) as he thinks appropriate.

1.8 The examples set out above are intended only as illustrations.

CLAIMS WHICH APPEAR TO FALL WITHIN RULE 3.4(2)(a) OR (b)

2.1 If a court officer is asked to issue a claim form which he believes may fall within rule 3.4(2)(a) or (b) he should issue it, but may then consult a judge (under rule 3.2) before returning the claim form to the claimant or taking any other step to serve the defendant. The judge may on his own initiative make an immediate order designed to ensure that the claim is disposed of or (as the case may be) proceeds in a way that accords with the rules.

2.3 The judge may allow the claimant a hearing before deciding whether to make such an order.

2.4 Orders the judge may make include:

  (1) an order that the claim be stayed until further order,

  (2) an order that the claim form be retained by the court and not served until the stay is lifted,

  (3) an order that no application by the claimant to lift the stay be heard unless he files such further documents (for example a witness statement or an amended claim form or particulars of claim) as may be specified in the order.

2.5 Where the judge makes any such order or, subsequently, an order lifting the stay he may give directions about the service on the defendant of the order and any other documents on the court file.

2.6 The fact that a judge allows a claim referred to him by a court officer to proceed does not prejudice the right of any party to apply for any order against the claimant.

DEFENCES WHICH APPEAR TO FALL WITHIN RULE 3.4(2)(a) OR (b).

3.1 A court officer may similarly consult a judge about any document filed which purports to be a defence and which he believes may fall within rule 3.4(2)(a) or (b).

3.2 If the judge decides that the document falls within rule 3.4(2)(a) or (b) he may on his own initiative make an order striking it out. Where he does so he may extend the time for the defendant to file a proper defence.

3.3 The judge may allow the defendant a hearing before deciding whether to make such an order.

3.4 Alternatively the judge may make an order under rule 18.1 requiring the defendant within a stated time to clarify his defence or to give additional information about it. The order may provide that the defence will be struck out if the defendant does not comply.

3.5 The fact that a judge does not strike out a defence on his own initiative does not prejudice the right of the claimant to apply for any order against the defendant.

GENERAL PROVISIONS

4.1 The court may exercise its powers under rule 3.4(2)(a) or (b) on application or on its own initiative at any time.

4.2 Where a judge at a hearing strikes out all or part of a party's statement of case he may enter such judgment for the other party as that party appears entitled to.

APPLICATIONS FOR ORDERS UNDER RULE 3.4(2)

5.1 Attention is drawn to Part 23 (General Rules about Applications) and to the practice direction that supplements it. The practice direction requires all applications to be made as soon as possible and before allocation if possible.

5.2 While many applications under rule 3.4(2) can be made without evidence in support, the applicant should consider whether facts need to be proved and, if so, whether evidence in support should be filed and served.

APPLICATIONS FOR SUMMARY JUDGMENT

6.1 Applications for summary judgment may be made under Part 24. Attention is drawn to that Part and to the practice direction that supplements it.

VEXATIOUS LITIGANTS

7.1 This Practice Direction applies where a "civil proceedings order" or an "all proceedings order" (as respectively defined under section 42(1A) of the Supreme Court Act, 1981) is in force against a person ("the litigant").

7.2 An application by the litigant for permission to begin or continue, or to make any application in, any civil proceedings shall be made by application notice issued in the High Court and signed by the litigant.

7.3 The application notice must state:

    (1) the title and reference number of the proceedings in which the civil proceedings order or the all proceedings order, as the case may be, was made,

    (2) the full name of the litigant and his address,

    (3) the order the applicant is seeking, and

    (4) briefly, why the applicant is seeking the order.

7.4 The application notice must be filed together with any written evidence on which the litigant relies in support of his application.

7.5 Either in the application notice or in written evidence filed in support of the application, the previous occasions on which the litigant made an application for permission under section 42(1A) of the said Act must be listed.

7.6 The application notice, together with any written evidence, will be placed before a High Court judge who may:

    (1) without the attendance of the applicant make an order giving the permission sought;

    (2) give directions for further written evidence to be supplied by the litigant before an order is made on the application;

(3) where the remedy sought, or the grounds advanced, substantially repeat those submitted in support of a previous application which has been refused, make an order dismissing the application without a hearing; or

(4) in any case where (3) does not apply, give directions for the hearing of the application.

7.7 Directions given under paragraph 6(3) may include an order that the application notice be served on the Attorney General and on any person against whom the litigant desires to bring the proceedings for which permission is being sought.

7.8 Any order made under paragraphs 6 or 7 will be served on the litigant at the address given in the application notice. CPR Part 6 will apply.

7.9 A person may apply to set aside the grant of permission if:

(1) the permission allowed the litigant to bring or continue proceedings against that person or to make any application against him, and

(2) the permission was granted other than at a hearing of which that person was given notice under paragraph 7.

7.10 Any application under paragraph 9 must be made in accordance with CPR Part 23.

PRACTICE DIRECTION – SANCTIONS FOR NON-PAYMENT OF FEES

THIS PRACTICE DIRECTION SUPPLEMENTS CPR RULE 3.7

1. If a claim is struck out under rule 3.7, the court will send notice that it has been struck out to the defendant.

2. The notice will also explain the effect of rule 25.11. This provides that any interim injunction will cease to have effect 14 days after the date the claim is struck out under rule 3.7. Paragraph (2) provides that if the claimant applies to reinstate the claim before the interim injunction ceases to have effect, the injunction will continue until the hearing of the application unless the court orders otherwise. If the claimant makes such an application, the defendant will be given notice in the ordinary way under rule 23.4.

PART 4

FORMS

4 (1) The forms set out in a practice direction shall be used in the cases to which they apply.

(2) A form may be varied by the court or a party if the variation is required by the circumstances of a particular case.

(3) A form must not be varied so as to leave out any information or guidance which the form gives to the recipient.

(4) Where these Rules require a form to be sent by the court or by a party for another party to use, it must be sent without any variation except such as is required by the circumstances of the particular case.

(5) Where the court or a party produces a form shown in a practice direction with the words 'Royal Arms', the form must include a replica of the Royal Arms at the head of the first page.

PRACTICE DIRECTION – FORMS
THIS PRACTICE DIRECTION SUPPLEMENTS CPR PART 4

Scope of this practice direction:

1.1 This practice directions lists the forms to be used in civil proceedings on or after 26th April 1999, when the Civil Procedure Rules (CPR) come into force.

1.2 The forms may be modified as the circumstances require, provided that all essential information, especially information or guidance which the form gives to the recipient, is included.

1.3 This practice direction contains 3 tables –

- Table 1 lists forms required by CPR Parts 1–48 and therefore applicable in both the High Court and county court

- Table 2 lists High Court forms in use before 26th April 1999 that will remain in use on or after that date (see paragraph 4 below)

- Table 3 lists county court forms in use before 26th April 1999 that will remain in use on or after that date (see paragraph 5 below)

Other forms:

2.1 Other forms may be authorised by practice directions supplementing Part 49 (specialist proceedings). For example the forms relating to Admiralty proceedings are authorised by, and annexed to, the Admiralty practice direction.

Table 1

"N" Forms

Contents:

3.1 This table lists the "N" forms that are referred to and required to be used by Practice Directions supplementing particular Parts of the CPR. A Practice Direction and its paragraphs are abbreviated by reference to the Part of the CPR which it supplements and the relevant paragraph of the Practice Direction, for example; PD 34 1.2.

No.	Title
N1	Part 7 (general) claim form (Pt 7 PD 3.1)
N1 CPC	Claim Production Centre ("CPC") claim form – rule 7.10)
N1A	Notes for claimant
N1C	Notes for defendant
N1(FD)	Notes for defendant (Consumer Credit Act cases)
N9	Acknowledgment of service/response pack (Pt 10 PD 2)
N9 CPC	CPC acknowledgment of service/response pack (Pt 10 PD 2)
N9A	Admission and statement of means (specified amount) (Pt 14 PD 2.1)
N9B	Defence and counterclaim (specified amount) (Pt 15 PD 1.3)
N9C	Admission and statement of means (unspecified amount and non money claims) (Pt 14 PD 2.1)
N9D	Defence and counterclaim (unspecified amount and non money claims) (Pt 15 PD 1.3)
N10	Notice that acknowledgment of service has been filed – rule 10.4
N17	Judgment for claimant (amount to be decided by court) – rules 12.5(3), 14.6(7) and 14.7(10)
N20	Witness summons (Pt 34 PD 1.2)
N21	Order for Examination of Deponent before the hearing (Pt 34 PD 4.1)
N24	Blank form of order or judgment

N30	Judgment for claimant (default HC) – rule 12.5(2)
N30	Judgment for claimant (default CC) – rule 12.5(2)
N30(1)	Judgment for claimant (acceptance HC) (Pt 14 PD 4.2)
N30(1)	Judgment for claimant (acceptance CC) (Pt 14 PD 4.2)
N30(2)	Judgment for claimant (after determination HC) (Pt 14 PD 10 (4))
N30(2)	Judgment for claimant (after determination CC) (Pt 14 PD 10 (4))
N30(3)	Judgment for claimant (after re-determination HC) – rule 14.13
N30 (3)	Judgment for claimant (after re-determination CC) – rule 14.13
N32	Judgment for return of goods
N32 (1) HP/CCA	Judgment for delivery of goods
N32 (2) HP/CCA	Judgment for delivery of goods (suspended)
N32 (3) HP/CCA	Judgment for delivery of goods
N32 (4)	Variation order (return of goods)
N32 (5) HP/CCA	Order for balance of purchase price
N33	Judgment for delivery of goods
N34	Judgment for claimant (after amount decided by court HC)
N34	Judgment for claimant (after amount decided by court CC)
N150	Allocation Questionnaire (Pt 26 PD 2.1)
N150A	Master/DJ's directions on allocation
N151	Allocation Questionnaire (amount to be decided by court)
N151A	Master/DJ's directions on allocation
N152	Notice that [defence][counterclaim] has been filed (Pt 26 PD 2.5)
N153	Notice of allocation or listing hearing (Pt 26 PD 6.2)
N154	Notice of allocation to fast track (Pt 26 PD 4.2 and 9)
N155	Notice of allocation to multi track (Pt 26 PD 4.2 and 10)
N156	Order for further information (for allocation) (Pt 26 PD 4.2(2))
N157	Notice of allocation to small claims track (Pt 26 PD 4.2 and 8)
N158	Notice of allocation to small claims track (preliminary hearing) (Pt 26 PD 4.2 and 8)
N159	Notice of allocation to small claims track (no hearing) (Pt 26 PD 4.2 and 8)
N160	Notice of allocation to small claims track (with parties consent) (Pt 26 PD 4.2 and 8)
N161	Appellant's Notice
N161A	Guidance notes on completing the appellant's notice
N161B	Important notes for respondents
N162	Respondent's Notice
N162A	Guidance notes for completing the respondent's notice
N170	Listing questionnaire (Pt 26 PD 6.1 and Pt 28 PD 8.1)
N171	Notice of date for return of listing questionnaire (Pt 26 PD 6.1 and Pt 28 PD 8.1)
N172	Notice of trial date
N173	Notice of non-payment of fee – rule 3.7
N205A	Notice of issue (specified amount)
N205B	Notice of issue (unspecified amount)
N205C	Notice of issue (non-money claim)
N208	Part 8 claim form (Pt 8 PD 2.2)
N208A	Part 8 notes for claimant
N208C	Part 8 notes for defendant
N209	Part 8 notice of issue
N210	Part 8 acknowledgment of service (Pt 8 PD 3.2)

N211	Part 20 claim form – rule 20.7
N211A	Part 20 notes for claimant
N211C	Part 20 notes for defendant
N212	Part 20 notice of issue
N213	Part 20 acknowledgment of service – rule 20.12
N215	Certificate of service – rule 6.10
N216	Notice of non-service – rule 6.11
N217	Order for substituted service – rule 6.8
N218	Notice of service on a partner (Pt 6 PD 4.2)
N225	Request for judgment and reply to admission (specified amount) (Pt 12 PD 3)
N225A	Notice of part admission (specified amount) – rule 14.5
N226	Notice of admission (unspecified amount) – rule 14.7
N227	Request for judgment by default (amount to be decided by the court) –rule 12.5
N228	Notice of admission (return of goods) (Pt 7 PD Consumer Credit Act 8.5)
N235	Certificate of suitability of litigation friend (Pt 21 PD 2.3)
N236	Notice of defence that amount claimed has been paid – rule 15.10
N242A	Notice of payment into court (in settlement) – rule 36.6(2)
N243	Notice of acceptance of payment into court (Pt 36 PD 7.7)
N244	Application notice (Pt 23 PD 2.1)
N244A	Notice of hearing of application (Pt 23 PD 2.2)
N252	Notice of commencement of assessment (Pt 47 PD 2.3)
N253	Notice of amount allowed on provisional assessment (Pt 47 PD 6.5)
N254	Request for default costs certificate (Pt 47 PD 3.1)
N255	Default costs certificate HC (Pt 47 PD 3.3)
N255	Default costs certificate CC (Pt 47 PD 3.3)
N256	Final costs certificate HC (Pt 47 PD 5.11)
N256	Final costs certificate CC (Pt 47 PD 5.11)
N257	Interim costs certificate (Pt 47 PD 5.11)
N258	Request for assessment hearing (Pt 47 PD 4.3)
N259	Notice of appeal against a detailed assessment (Pt 47 PD 8.16)
N265	List of documents (Pt 31 PD 3.1)
N266	Notice to admit facts/admission of facts – rule 32.18
N268	Notice to prove documents at trial – rule 32.19
N271	Notice of transfer of proceedings – rule 30
N279	Notice of discontinuance – rule 38.3
N292	Order on settlement on behalf of child or patient (Pt 21 PD 11.3)
N294	Claimants application for a variation order
N367	Notice of hearing to consider why fine should not be imposed – rule 34.10
N434	Notice of change of solicitor – rule 42.2

Table 2

Practice Forms

Contents:

4.1 This table lists the Practice Forms that may be used under this Practice Direction. It contains forms that were previously-

- Prescribed Forms contained in Appendix A to the Rules of the Supreme Court 1965
- Queen's Bench Masters' Practice Forms
- Chancery Masters' Practice Forms

4.2 The former prescribed forms are shown as "No 00". The former practice forms where they are appropriate for use in either the Chancery or Queen's Bench Division (or where no specific form is available for use in the county court, in that court also) are prefixed "PF" followed by the number. Where the form is used mainly in the Chancery or Queen's Bench Division, the suffix CH or QB follows the form number.

4.3 Where a rule permits, a party intending to use a witness statement as an alternative to an affidavit should amend any form in this Table to be used in connection with that rule so that "witness statement" replaces "affidavit" wherever it appears in the form.

4.4 The forms in this list are reproduced in an Appendix to the Chancery and Queen's Bench Guides, and in practitioners' text books.

No.	Title
No 8A	Arbitration application/claim form
No 15	Acknowledgment of service on non-party
No 15A	Acknowledgment of service of Arbitration application
No 32	Order for examination within jurisdiction of witness before trial (rule 34.8)
No 33	Application for issue of letter of request to judicial authority out of jurisdiction (Pt 34 PD 5.2)
No 34	Order for issue of letter of request to judicial authority out of jurisdiction (Pt 34 PD 5.1)
No 35	Letter of request for examination of witness out of jurisdiction (Pt 34 PD 5.3(1))
No 37	Order for appointment of examiner to take evidence of witness out of jurisdiction (rule 34.13(4))
No 41	Default judgment in claim relating to detention of goods
No 42	Default judgment in claim for possession of land
No 42A	Order for possession (sched. 1 – RSC O.113)
No 44	Judgment under Part 24
No 45	Judgment after trial before judge without jury (Pt 40 PD 14)
No 46	Judgment after trial before judge with jury (Pt 40 PD 14)
No 47	Judgment after trial before a master/technology and construction court judge (Pt 40 PD 14)
No 48	Judgment after decision of preliminary issue
No 49	Judgment against personal representatives (Pt 40 PD 14)
No 50	Judgment for defendant's costs on discontinuance
No 51	Judgment for costs after acceptance of money paid into court
No 52	Notice of [claim][proceedings]
No 52A	Notice of judgment or order to an interested party
No 53	Writ of fieri facias (sched. 1 – RSC O.46 and 47)
No 54	Writ of fieri facias on order for costs (sched. 1 – RSC O.46 and 47)
No 55	Notice of seizure (sched. 1 – RSC O.45)
No 56	Writ of fieri facias after levy of part (sched. 1 – RSC O.45)
No 57	Writ of fieri facias against personal representatives (sched. 1 – RSC O.45)
No 58	Writ of fieri facias de bonis ecclesiasticis (sched. 1 – RSC O.45)
No 59	Writ of sequestrari de bonis ecclesiasticis (sched. 1 – RSC O.45)
No 62	Writ of fieri facias to enforce Northern Irish or Scottish judgment (sched. 1 – RSC O.45)
No 63	Writ of fieri facias to enforce foreign registered judgment (sched. 1 – RSC O.45)
No 64	Writ of delivery: delivery of goods, damages and costs (sched. 1 – RSC O.45)
No 65	Writ of delivery: delivery of goods or value, damages and costs (sched.1 – RSC O.45)

No 66	Writ of possession (sched. 1 – RSC O.45)
No 66A	Writ of possession (sched. 1 – RSC O.113)
No 67	Writ of sequestration (sched. 1 – RSC 45)
No 68	Writ of restitution (sched. 1 – RSC 46)
No 69	Writ of assistance (sched. 1 – RSC 46)
No 71	Notice of renewal of writ of execution (sched. 1 – RSC 46)
No 72	Garnishee order to show cause (sched. 1 – RSC 49 r.1)
No 73	Garnishee order absolute: garnishee owes more than judgment debt (sched. 1 – RSC 49 r.1)
No 74	Garnishee order absolute: garnishee owes less than judgment debt (sched. 1 – RSC 49 r.1)
No 75	Charging order: notice to show cause (sched. 1 – RSC 50 r.1)
No 76	Charging order absolute (sched. 1 – RSC 50 r.3)
No 79	Stop order on capital and income of funds in court (sched. 1 – RSC 50 r.10)
No 80	Affidavit and notice under RSC 0.50, scheduled to Part 50 CPR
No 81	Order on claim to restrain transfer of stock (sched. 1 – RSC 50)
No 82	Application for appointment of a receiver (sched. 1 – RSC 51 r.3)
No 83	Order directing application for appointment of receiver and granting injunction meanwhile (sched. 1 – RSC 51 r.3)
No 84	Order for appointment of receiver by way of equitable execution (S37 of Supreme Court Act and sched. 1 – RSC 51)
No 85	Order of committal (sched. 1 – RSC 52)
No 86	Claim form for judicial review (sched. 1 – RSC 53 r. 5(2A))
No 86A	Application for permission to apply for judicial review (sched. 1 – RSC 53 r.3)
No 86B	Renewal application for permission to apply for judicial review (sched. 1 – RSC 53 r.3)
No 87	Claim form for writ of habeas corpus ad subjiciendum
No 88	Notice of adjourned application for writ of habeas corpus
No 89	Writ of habeas corpus ad subjiciendum
No 90	Notice to be served with writ of habeas corpus ad subjiciendum
No 91	Writ of habeas corpus ad testificandum
No 92	Writ of habeas corpus ad respondendum
No 93	Order under the Evidence (Proceedings in Other Jurisdictions) Act 1975
No 94	Order for production of documents in marine insurance action (Pt 49 PD 49D.7.1)
No 95	Certificate of order against the Crown (sched. 1 – RSC 0.77 r.15)
No 96	Certificate of order for costs against the Crown (sched. 1 – RSC 0.77 r.15)
No 97	Claim form to grant bail (criminal proceedings) (sched. 1 – RSC 0.79 r.9)
No 97A	Claim form to vary arrangements for bail (criminal proceedings) (sched. 1 – RSC 0.79 r.9)
No 98	Order to release prisoner on bail (sched. 1 – RSC 0.79 r.9)
No 98A	Order varying arrangements for bail (sched. 1 – RSC 0.79 r.9)
No 99	Order of Court of Appeal to admit prisoner to bail (sched. 1 – RSC 0.59 r.20)
No 100	Notice of sureties for bail
No 101	Witness summons– Crown Court
No 103	Witness summons– Crown Court
No 104	Attachment of earnings order (Attachment of Earnings Act 1971)
No 105	Notice under s.10(2) of the Attachment of Earnings Act 1971
No 108	Application for reference to the European Court (sched. 1 - RSC 0.114 r.2(2))

No 109	Order for reference to the European Court (sched. 1 – RSC 0.114 r.2)
No 110	Certificate under s.12 of the Civil Jurisdiction and Judgments Act 1982 (sched. 1 – RSC 0.71 r.36(3))
No 111	Certificate of money provisions contained in a judgment for registration under Schedule 6 to the Civil Jurisdiction and Judgments Act 1982 (sched. 1 – RSC 0.71 r.37(3))
No112	Certificate of non-money provisions contained in a judgment under Schedule 7 to the Civil Jurisdiction and Judgments Act 1982 (sched. 1 – RSC 0.71 r.38(2))
PF 1	Application for time (rule 3.1(2)(a))
PF 2	Order for time (rule 3.1(2)(a))
PF 3	Application for an extension of time for serving a claim form (rule 7.6(1))
PF 4	Order for an extension of time for serving a claim form (rule 7.6(1))
PF 5	Order as to service in claim for possession where premises empty (sched. 1 – RSC O.10 r.4)
PF 6	Order for service out of the jurisdiction (rule 6A.4)
PF 7 QB	Request for service of document abroad (rule 6A.11)
PF 8	Application for judgment for possession
PF 9	Order for possession
PF 11	Application for Part 24 judgment (whole claim)
PF 12	Application for Part 24 judgment (one or some of several claims)
PF 13	Order under Part 14 (No 1)
PF 14	Order under Part 14 (No 2)
PF 15	Order under Part 14 (for assessment of solicitor's bill of costs) (Part 48)
PF20	Application for Part 20 directions
PF21	Order for Part 20 directions
PF23 QB	Notice of claim to goods taken in execution (sched. 1 – RSC O.17)
PF24 QB	Notice by claimant of admission or dispute of title of interpleaderclaimant (sched. 1 – RSC O.17)
PF25 QB	Interpleader application by defendant (sched. 1 – RSC O.17)
PF26 QB	Interpleader application by sheriff (sched. 1 – RSC O.17)
PF27 QB	Evidence in support of interpleader application (sched. 1 – RSC O.17)
PF28 QB	Interpleader order (1) claim barred where Sheriff interpleads (sched. 1 – RSC O.17)
PF29 QB	Interpleader order (1a) Sheriff to withdraw (sched. 1 – RSC O.17)
PF30 QB	Interpleader order (2) interclaimant substituted as defendant (sched. 1 – RSC O.17)
PF31 QB	Interpleader order (3) trial of issue (sched. 1 – RSC O.17)
PF32 QB	Interpleader order (4) conditional order for Sheriff to withdraw and trial of issue (sched.1- RSC O.17)
PF34 QB	Interpleader order (6) summary disposal (sched. 1 – RSC O.17)
PF43	Application for security for costs
PF44	Order for security for costs
PF48	Court record available for use before and at hearing
PF49	Request to parties to state convenient dates for hearing
PF50	Application for directions (Part 29)
PF52	Order for directions following an application or otherwise (Part 29)
PF53	Order for trial of an issue
PF 56	Request for further information or clarification with provision for response (Pt 18 PD 1.6(2))
PF 57	Application for further information or clarification (Pt 18 PD 5)
PF 58	Order for further information or clarification (rule 18.1)

PF63	Interim order for receiver in pending claim (sched. 1 – RSC O.30)
PF67	Evidence in support of application to make order of House of Lords an order of the High Court (Pt 40B PD 13.2)
PF68	Order making an order of the House of Lords an order of the High Court (Pt 40B PD 13.3)
PF72	List of exhibits
PF74	Order for trial by Master
PF78 QB	Solicitor's undertaking as to expenses (re letter of request) (rule 6A.11 and Pt 34 PD 5.3.(5))
PF79	Default judgment for possession of land, damages and costs (Part 12)
PF83	Judgment (non attendance of party) (rule 39.3)
PF84	Judgment as a consequence of failure to comply with an order or condition (rules 3.1(3) and 3.5)
PF86	Praecipe for writ of fieri facias (sched. 1 – RSC O.46 and 47)
PF87	Praecipe for writ of sequestration (sched. 1 – RSC O.46)
PF88	Praecipe for writ of possession (sched. 1 – RSC O.45)
PF89	Praecipe for writ of possession and fieri facias combined (sched. 1 – RSC O.45)
PF90	Praecipe for writ of delivery (sched. 1 – RSC O.45)
PF91	Evidence in support of application to enforce judgment for possession (sched. 1 – RSC O.45)
PF97 QB	Order for sale by Sheriff by private contract (sched. 1 – RSC O.47)
PF98	Evidence in support of application for order for examination of judgment debtor or officer (sched. 1 – RSC O.48)
PF99	Order for oral examination of judgment debtor or officer (sched. 1 – RSC O.48)
PF100	Evidence in support of garnishee order (sched. 1 – RSC O.49)
PF101	Evidence in support of charging order (sched. 1 – RSC O.49)
PF103	Warrant of committal (general) (sched. 1 – RSC O.52)
PF104	Warrant of committal (in face of court) (sched. 1 – RSC O.52)
PF105	Warrant of committal (failure of witness to attend) (sched. 1 – RSC O.52)
PF110	Notice of appeal to judge from Master or district judge (sched. 1 – RSC O.58)
PF113	Evidence in support of application for service by an alternative method (Pt 6 PD 9.1)
PF114	Order for service by an alternative method (rule 6.8)
PF130	Form of advertisement
PF141	Evidence of personal service
PF147	Application for order declaring solicitor ceased to act (death etc) (rule 42.4)
PF148	Order declaring solicitor has ceased to act (rule 42.4)
PF149	Application by solicitor that he has ceased to act (rule 42.3)
PF150	Order that solicitor has ceased to act (rule 42.3)
PF152QB	Evidence in support of application for examination of witness under the Evidence (Proceedings in Other Jurisdictions) Act 1975
PF153QB	Certificate witness under the Evidence (Proceedings in Other Jurisdictions) Act 1975 (sched. 1 – RSC O.70)
PF154QB	Order for registration of foreign judgment under the Foreign Judgments (Reciprocal Enforcement) Act 1933 (sched. 1 – RSC O.71)
PF155QB	Certificates under s.10 of the Foreign Judgments (Reciprocal Enforcement) Act 1933 (sched. 1 – RSC O.71)
PF156QB	Evidence in support of application for registration of a Community judgment (sched. 1 – RSC O.71)
PF157QB	Order for registration of a Community judgment (sched.1- RSC O.71)

PF158QB	Notice of registration of a Community judgment (sched. 1 – RSC O.71)
PF159QB	Evidence in support of application for registration of a judgment of another Contracting State (sched. 1 – RSC O.71)
PF160QB	Order for registration of a judgment of another Contracting State under s.4 of the Civil Jurisdiction and Judgments Act 1982 (sched. 1 – RSC O.71)
PF161QB	Notice of registration of a judgment of another Contracting State (sched. 1 – RSC O.71)
PF163QB	Evidence in support of application for certified copy of a judgment for enforcement in another Contracting State (sched. 1 – RSC O.71)
PF164QB	Evidence in support of application for certificate as to money provisions of a judgment of the High Court for registration elsewhere in the United Kingdom (sched. 1 – RSC O.71)
PF165QB	Evidence in support of application for registration of a judgment of a court in another part of the United Kingdom containing non-money provisions (sched. 1 – RSC O.71)
PF166QB	Certificate as to finality etc. of Arbitration Award for enforcement abroad (Arbitration Act 1996, s.58)
PF167QB	Order to stay proceedings under s. 9 of the Arbitration Act 1996
PF168	Order to transfer claim to county court (County Courts Act 1984)
PF170	Application for child or patient's settlement in personal injury or fatal accident claims (Pt 21 PD 6 and 7)
PF172QB	Application in respect of funds in court or to be brought into court (Pt 21 PD 8)
PF177	Order for written statement as to partners in firm (sched. 1 – RSC O.81 r.2)
PF179QB	Evidence in support of an application for registration of a Bill of Sale (sched. 1 – RSC O.95)
PF180QB	Evidence in support of an application for registration of an Absolute Bill of Sale, Settlement and Deed of Gift (sched. 1 – RSC O.95)
PF181QB	Evidence in support of an application for re-registration of a Bill of Sale (sched. 1 – RSC O.95)
PF182QB	Order for extension of time to register or re-register a Bill of Sale (sched.1-RSC O.95)
PF183QB	Evidence in support of an application for permission to enter a memorandum of Satisfaction on a Bill of Sale (sched. 1 – RSC O.95)
PF184QB	Claim form for entry of satisfaction on a registered Bill of Sale (sched. 1 – RSC O.95)
PF185QB	Order for entry of Satisfaction on a registered Bill of Sale (sched. 1 – RSC O.95)
PF186QB	Evidence in support of application for registration of Assignment of Book Debts (sched. 1 – RSC O.95)
PF187	Application for Solicitor's Charging order (sched.1- RSC O.106 r.2)
PF188	Charging order: Solicitor's costs (sched. 1- RSC O.106 r.2)
PF197	Application for order for transfer from the Royal Courts of Justice to a district registry or vice-versa or from one district registry to another (rule 30.2(4))
PF198	Order under PF197
PF200	Notice of proposed order to transfer to county court or strike out (s.40(1) and (8) of the County Courts Act 1984)
PF201	Notice of hearing to decide whether to order transfer to county court or strike out
PF202	Notice of proposed order to transfer to county court (s.40(2) of the County Courts Act 1984)
PF203	Notice of objection to proposed transfer to county court (s.40(2) of the County Courts Act 1984)

PF205	Evidence in support of application for permission to execute for earlier costs of enforcement under s.15(3) and (4) of the Courts and Legal Services Act 1990
PF5CH	Order for possession on mortgaged property
PF6CH	Certificate on application for leave to issue execution on suspended order for possession where defendant in default of acknowledgment of service
PF7CH	Inquiry for persons entitled to the property of an intestate dying on or after 1st January 1926
PF8CH	Summons after masters findings on kin enquiry for re Benjamin order giving leave to distribute estate upon footing
PF9CH	re Benjamin order giving leave to distribute estate upon footing
PF10CH	Judgment in beneficiaries administration action where deceased died on or after 1st January 1926
PF11CH	Judgment in creditors administration action where deceased died on or after 1st january 1926
PF12CH	Advertisement for creditors
PF13CH	Advertisement for claimants other than creditors
PF14CH	Affidavit verifying list of creditors claims
PF15CH	List of claims sent in pursuant to advertisement by persons claiming to be creditors.
PF16CH	List of claims by persons claiming to be creditors other than those sent in pursuant to advertisement
PF17CH	List of sums of money which may be due in respect of which no claim has been received
PF18CH	Notice to creditor to prove claim
PF19CH	Notice to creditor or other claimant to produce documents
PF20CH	Notice to creditor of allowance of claim
PF21CH	Notice to creditor of disallowance of claim
PF22CH	Order for administration: beneficiaries action reconstituted as creditors claims
PF23CH	Affidavit verifying list of claims other than creditors claims
PF24CH	List of claims not being creditors' claims sent in pursuant to advertisement
PF25CH	List of claims not being creditors' claims other than those sent in pursuant to advertisement
PF26CH	Notice to claimant other than a creditor to prove claim
PF27CH	Affidavit verifying accounts and answering usual enquiries in administration action
PF28CH	Executors (or administrators account)
PF29CH	Masters order stating the results of proceedings before him on the usual accounts and inquiries in an administration action
PF30CH	Security of receiver or administrator
PF31CH	Consent to act as trustee
PF32CH	Affidavit in support of application for appointment of new next friend of minor plaintiff
PF33CH	Order for cross examination of deponents on their affidavits
PF34CH	Order in inquiry as to title in proceedings to enforce charging order where the defendants title is not disclosed
PF35CH	Subpoena to bring in a script
PF36CH	Order appointing administrator
PF37CH	Affidavit of testamentary scripts
PF38CH	Order approving compromise in probate action

Table 3

Contents

5.1 This table lists county court forms in use before 26 April 1999 that will continue to be used on or after that date.

5.2 Where a rule permits, a party intending to use a witness statement as an alternative to an affidavit should amend any form in this Table to be used in connection with that rule so that "witness statement" replaces "affidavit" wherever it appears in the form.

No.	Title
N5	Summons for possession of property
N5A	Application for accelerated possession (assured tenancies) s. 8 HA 1988
N5B	Application for accelerated possession (assured tenancies) s. 21 HA 1988
N6	Possession Summons (forfeiture and right of re-entry)
N8	Notice to Respondent when a matter will be heard
N8(1)	Notice to Respondent when a matter will be heard under Order 24
N8(2)	Notice to Respondent in application under section 53
N8(4)	Notice to respondent in application under section 17–18 of the Leasehold Reform Act
N11	Form of Reply – Possession Summons
N11A	Form of Reply to application for accelerated possession (assured tenancies) s. 8 HA 1988
N11(B)	Acknowledgment of Service Business List Actions
N11B	Form of reply to application for accelerated possession (assured tenancies) s. 21 HA 1988
N11M	Form of Reply (mortgaged property)
N11R	Form of Reply (rented property)
N16	General form of injunction
N16(1)	General form of injunction (formal parts only)
N16A	General form of application for injunction
N26	Order for possession (Rented property)
N26A	Order that claimant have possession (assured tenancies)
N27	Judgment for claimant in Action of Forfeiture for non payment of rent
N27(1)	Judgment for claimant – Forfeiture for Non Payment of Rent where order refused under Rent Acts
N27(2)	Judgment for claimant – for Non Payment of Rent where Order suspended under Rent Acts
N28	Order for Possession (possession suspended) (rented property)
N29	Order for possession (mortgaged property)
N31	Order for Possession of mortgaged property suspended under s 36 of the Administration of Justice Act 1970
N35	Variation Order
N35A	Variation Order (determination)
N36	Order for Possession under Order 24
N37	Oral Examination of Judgment Debtor
N38	Oral Examination (person other than Judgment Debtor)
N39	Order for Defendants Attendance at an adjourned hearing of an Oral Examination
N40	Warrant of Committal (Oral Examination)
N41	Order suspending judgment or Order, and/or Warrant of Execution/Committal
N41A	Order suspending warrant (determination)

N42	Warrant of Execution
N46	Warrant of Delivery and Execution for damages and Costs
N48	Warrant of Delivery, where, if goods are not returned, Levy is to be made for their value
N49	Warrant for Possession of Land
N50	Warrant of Restitution (Order 26, rule 17)
N51	Warrant of Restitution (Order 24, rule 6(1))
N52	Warrant of Possession under Order 24
N53	Warrant of Execution or Committal to District Judge of Foreign Court
N55	Notice of Application for Attachment of Earnings Order
N55A	Notice of application for attachment of earnings order (maintenance)
N56	Form for replying to an attachment of Earnings application (statement of means)
N58	Order for Defendants attendance at an adjourned Hearing of an Attachment of Earnings Application (maintenance)
N59	Warrant of Committal under section 23(1) of the Attachment of Earnings Act 1971
N60	Attachment of Earnings Order (Judgment Debt)
N61	Order for production of Statement of Means
N61A	Order to employer for production of statement of earnings
N62	Summons for Offence under Attachment of Earnings
N63	Notice to show Cause section 23 of the Attachment of Earnings Act 1971
N64	Suspended Attachment of Earnings Order
N64A	Suspended Attachment of Earnings Order (maintenance)
N65A	Attachment of Earnings Arrears Order
N65	Attachment of Earnings Order (Priority Maintenance)
N66	Consolidated Attachment of Earnings Order
N66A	Notice of Application for Consolidated Attachment of Earnings Order
N67	Judgment Summons under the Debtors Act 1869
N68	Certificate of Service (Judgment Summons)
N69	Order for Debtors Attendance at an Adjourned Hearing of Judgment Summons
N70	Order of Commitment under section 110 of the County Court Act 1984
N71	Order revoking an Order of Commitment under section 110 of the County Courts Act 1984
N72	Notice to Defendant where a Committal Order made but directed to be suspended under Debtors Act
N73	New Order on Judgment Summons
N74	Warrant of Committal Judgment Summons under the Debtors Act 1869
N75	Indorsement on a warrant of Committal sent to a Foreign Court
N76	Certificate to be indorsed on duplicate Warrant of Committal issued for re-arrest of Debtor
N77	Notice as to consequences of disobedience to Court Order
N78	Notice to show good reason why an order for your committal to prison should not be made (Family proceedings only)
N79	Committal of other Order upon proof of disobedience of a court order or breach of undertaking
N80	Warrant for Committal to Prison
N81	Notice to solicitor to show cause why an undertaking should not be enforced by committal to prison
N82	Order for committal for failure by solicitor to carry out undertaking
N83	Order for discharge from custody under warrant of committal

N84	Garnishee order to show cause
N85	Garnishee Order Absolute
N86	Charging Order nisi
N87	Charging Order absolute
N88	Interpleader Summons to Execution Creditor
N88(1)	Interpleader Summons to Claimant claiming goods or rent under an execution
N89	Interpleader summons to persons making adverse claims to debt
N90	Summons for assaulting an officer of the court or rescuing goods
N91	Order of Commitment and or Imposing a fine for assaulting an officer of the court or rescuing goods
N92	Request for Administration Order
N93	List of Creditors furnished under the Act of 1971
N94	Administration Order
N95	Order revoking an administration order
N95A	Order suspending or varying an administration order
N110	Power of arrest attached to injunction under section 2 Domestic Violence and Matrimonial Proceedings Act 1976
N110A	Anti social behaviour injunction – power of arrest s. 152–153 HA 1996
N112	Order for Arrest under section 110 of County Courts Act 1984
N112A	Power of arrest, section 23 Attachment of Earnings Act 1971
N117	General form of undertaking
N118	Notice to Defendant where committal order made but directed to be suspended
N119	Particulars of claim for possession (rented property)
N120	Particulars of claim for possession (mortgaged property)
N130	Application for possession including application for interim possession order
N131	Notice of application for interim possession order
N132	Affidavit of Service of notice of application for interim possession order
N133	Affidavit to occupier to oppose the making of an interim possession order
N134	Interim possession order
N135	Affidavit of Service of interim possession order
N136	Order for possession
N138	Injunction order
N139	Application for warrant of arrest
N140	Warrant of arrest
N206	Notice of Issue of fixed date claim
N206A	Notice of Issue of application (assured tenancies)
N207	Plaint note (Adoption freeing for Adoption)
N200	Petition – Note old number was N208
N201	Request for entry of appeal – Note old number was N209
N202	Order for party to sue or defend on behalf of others having the same interest – Note old number was N210
N203	Notice to persons on whose behalf party has obtained leave to sue or defend – Note old number was N211
N204	Notice to person against whom party has obtained leave to sue or defend on behalf of others – Note old number was N212
N220	Request for service of Possession Summons on Defendants Representative
N220(1)	Notice to Representative of Defendant in Action for recovery of land
N224	Request for Service out of England and Wales through the Court
N229	Notice of Admission in Possession Action

N245	Application for suspension of a warrant and/or variation of an instalment order
N246	Claimant's Reply to Defendant's application to vary instalment order
N246A	Claimant's reply to Defendant's application to suspend warrant of execution
N270	Notes for guidance (application for administration order)
N276	Notice of Hearing of Interpleader Proceedings transferred from High Court
N277	Notice of Pre Trial Review of Interpleader proceedings transferred from the High Court
N280	Order of reference of proceedings or questions for inquiry and report
N285	General form of affidavit
N288	Order to produce prisoner
N289	Judgment for Defendant
N291	Judgment for Defendant in action for recovery of land
N293	Certificate or judgment or order
N293A	Combined certificate of judgment and request for writ of fi fa
N295	Order for sale of land
N296	Notice of Judgment or order to party directed to be served with notice
N297	Order for accounts and Inquiries in Creditors Administration Action
N298	Order for Administration
N299	Order for foreclosure nisi of legal mortgage of land
N300	Order for sale in action by equitable mortgagee
N302	Judgment in action for specific performance (vendors action title accepted)
N303	Order for dissolution of partnership
N304	Notice to parties to attend upon taking accounts
N305	Notice to creditor to prove his claim
N306	Notice to creditor of determination of claim
N307	District Judges order (accounts and inquiries)
N309	Order for foreclosure absolute
N310	Partnership order on further consideration
N311	Administrative action order on further consideration
N312	Claim form for possession under Order 24
N313	Indorsement on certificate of judgment (transfer)
N316	Request for oral examination
N317	Bailiffs report
N317A	Bailiff's report to the claimant
N319	Notice of execution of warrant of committal
N320	Request for return of, or to, warrant
N322	Order for recovery of money awarded by tribunal
N322A	Application for an order to recover money awarded to a tribunal or other body
N322H	Request to register a High Court Judgment or order for enforcement
N323	Request for warrant of execution
N324	Request for warrant of goods
N325	Request for warrant for possession of land
N326	notice of issue of warrant of execution
N327	notice of issue of warrant of execution to enforce a judgment or order
N328	notice of transfer of proceedings to the high court
N329	notes for guidance on completion of N 79
N330	Notice of sale or payment under execution in respect of a judgment for a sum exceeding £500

N331	Notice of withdrawal from possession or payment of moneys on notice of receiving or winding up order
N332	Inventory of goods removed
N333	Notice of time when and where goods will be sold
N334	Request to hold walking possession and authority to re-enter
N336	Request and result of search in the attachment of earnings index
N337	Request for attachment of earnings order
N338	Request for statement of earnings
N339	Discharge of attachment of earnings order
N340	Notice as to payment under attachment of earnings order made by the High Court
N341	Notice of intention to vary attachment of earnings order under section 10(2) of AE Act 1971
N342	Request for judgment summons
N343	Notice of result of hearing of a judgment summons issued on a judgment or order of the High Court
N344	Request for warrant of committal on judgment summons
N345	Certificate of payment under the debtors act 1869
N349	Affidavit in support of application for Garnishee order
N353	Order appointing receive of real and personal property
N354	Order appointing receiver of partnership
N355	Interim order for appointment of receiver
N356	Order for appointment of receiver by way of equitable execution
N358	Notice of claim to goods taken in execution
N359	Notice to claimant to goods taken in execution to make deposit or give security
N360	Affidavit in support of interpleader summons other than an execution
N361	Notice of application for relief in pending action
N362	Order on interpleader summons under an execution where the claim is not established
N363	Order on interpleader summons under an execution where the claim is established
N364	Order on interpleader summons (other than execution) where there is an action
N365	Order on interpleader summons (other than execution) where there is no action
N366	Summons for neglect to levy execution
N368	Order fining a witness for non-attendance
N370	Order of commitment or imposing a fine for insult or misbehaviour
N372	Order for rehearing
N373	Notice of application for an administration order
N374	Notice of intention to review an administration order
N374A	Notice of intention to revoke an administration order
N375	Notice of further creditors claim
N376	Notice of hearing administration order (by direction of the court)
N377	Notice of dividend
N388	Notice to probate registry to produce documents
N390	Notice that a claim has been entered against the Crown
N391	Crown Proceedings Act affidavit in support of application directing payment by Crown to judgment creditor
N392	Crown Proceedings Act notice of application for order directing payment by the Crown to the judgment creditor

N394	Claim form for determining the right to compensation for improvement (Landlord and Tenant Act 1927)
N395	Claim form for certificate or determination of question other than compensation (Landlord and Tenant Act 1927)
N396	Claim form for statutory tenancy under part I of the Landlord and Tenant Act 1954
N397	Claim form for new tenancy under part II of the Landlord and Tenant Act 1954
N398	Order on application for certificate as to improvement (Landlord and Tenant Act 1927)
N399	Final order (Landlord and Tenant Act 1927)
N400	Answer to claim form for new tenancy under Part II of the Landlord and Tenant Act 1954
N401	Order on application for a new tenancy under Part II of the Landlord and Tenant Act 1954
N402	Order substituting date in Landlord's notice or tenant's request
N403	Application for certificate of ground for refusing new tenancy
N404	Certificate of ground for refusing new tenancy
N404(1)	Order authorising agreement excluding act
N405	Notice of proceedings
N425	Notice to repair
N426	Notice of proceedings
N432	Affidavit on payment into court under section 63 of the Trustee Act 1925
N436	Order for sale of land under charging order
N437	District Judges report
N438	Notice to charge holder under Matrimonial Homes Act 1983
N440	Notice of application for time order by debtor or hirer – CC Act 1974
N441	Notification of request for certificate of satisfaction or cancellation
N441A	Certificate of satisfaction or cancellation of judgment debt
N444	Details of sale under a warrant of execution
N445	Request for re-issue of warrant
N446	Request for re-issue of post-judgment process (other than warrant)
N447	Notice to claimant of date fixed for adjourned hearing
N448	Request to defendant for employment details, attachment of earnings
N449	Notice to employer, failure to make deductions under attachment of earnings order

PART 5

COURT DOCUMENTS

Contents of this Part

Scope of this Part

5.1 This part contains general provisions about –

(a) documents used in court proceedings; and

(b) the obligations of a court officer in relation to those documents.

Preparation of documents

5.2 (1) Where under these Rules, a document is to be prepared by the court, the document may be prepared by the party whose document it is, unless –

(a) a court officer otherwise directs; or

(b) it is a document to which –

(i) CCR Order 25, rule 5(3) (reissue of enforcement proceedings);

(ii) CCR Order 25, rule 8(9) (reissue of warrant where condition upon which warrant was suspended has not been complied with); or

(iii) CCR Order 28, rule 11(1) (issue of warrant of committal), applies.

(2) Nothing in this rule shall require a court officer to accept a document which is illegible, has not been duly authorised, or is unsatisfactory for some other similar reason.

Signature of documents by mechanical means

5.3 Where any of these Rules or any practice direction requires a document to be signed, that requirement shall be satisfied if the signature is printed by computer or other mechanical means.

Supply of documents from court records

5.4 (1) Any party to proceedings may be supplied from the records of the court with a copy of any document relating to those proceedings (including documents filed before the claim was commenced), provided that the party seeking the document –

(a) pays any prescribed fee; and

(b) files a written request for the document.

(2) Any other person who pays the prescribed fee may, during office hours, search for, inspect and take a copy of the following documents, namely –

(a) a claim form which has been served;

(b) any judgment or order given or made in public;

(c) any other document if the court gives permission.

(3) An application for permission under paragraph (2)(c) may be made without notice.

(4) This rule does not apply in relation to any proceedings in respect of which a practice direction makes different provision.

PRACTICE DIRECTION – COURT DOCUMENTS
THIS PRACTICE DIRECTION SUPPLEMENTS CPR PART 5

Signature of documents by mechanical means

1   Where, under rule 5.3, a replica signature is printed electronically or by other mechanical means on any document, the name of the person whose signature is printed must also be printed so that the person may be identified. This paragraph does not apply to claim forms issued through the Claims Production Centre.

Form of documents

2.1 Statements of case and other documents drafted by a legal representative should bear his/her signature and if they are drafted by a legal representative as a member or employee of a firm they should be signed in the name of the firm.

2.2 Every document prepared by a party for filing or use at the Court must

(1) Unless the nature of the document renders it impracticable, be on A4 paper of durable quality having a margin, not less than 3.5 centimetres wide,

(2) be fully legible and should normally be typed,

(3) where possible be bound securely in a manner which would not hamper filing or otherwise each page should be endorsed with the case number,

(4) have the pages numbered consecutively,

(5) be divided into numbered paragraphs,

(6) have all numbers, including dates, expressed as figures, and

(7) give in the margin the reference of every document mentioned that has already been filed.

2.3 A document which is a copy produced by a colour photostat machine or other similar device may be filed at the court office provided that the coloured date seal of the Court is not reproduced on the copy.

Supply of documents to new parties

3.1 Where a party is joined to existing proceedings, the party joined shall be entitled to require the party joining him to supply, without charge, copies of all statements of case, written evidence and any documents appended or exhibited to them which have been served in the proceedings by or upon the joining party which relate to any issues between the joining party and the party joined, and copies of all orders made in those proceedings. The documents must be supplied within 48 hours after a written request for them is received.

3.2 If the party joined is not supplied with copies of the documents requested under paragraph 3.1 within 48 hours, he may apply under Part 23 for an order that they be supplied.

3.3 The party by whom a copy is supplied under paragraph 3.1 or, if he is acting by a solicitor, his solicitor, shall be responsible for it being a true copy.

Supply of documents from court records

4.1 Where a person makes a search for the documents mentioned in CPR rule 5.4(2), that search may be conducted by means of a computer, if the court office has a computer with the appropriate search facility.

4.2 When the document searched for under CPR rule 5.4(2) is identified and upon payment of the prescribed fee, the document will be produced for inspection by a member of the Court staff.

4.3 If, in the course of a computer search, the computer identifies documents held on the Court file, other than those which the person searching is entitled to inspect, that person may not, without the Court's permission, inspect, take a copy or make any note of, or relating to, those documents.

4.4 An application for inspection of a document under CPR rule 5.4(2)(c), even if made without notice, must be made under CPR Part 23 and the application notice must identify the document in respect of which permission is sought and the grounds relied upon.

4.5 CPR rules 5.4(2) and 5.4(3) do not apply to proceedings in a county court. (It is intended that these rules will be applied to county courts once the facilities for a computer search have been installed.)

Documents for filing at court

5.1 The date on which a document was filed at court must be recorded on the document. This may be done by a seal or a receipt stamp.

5.2 Particulars of the date of delivery at a court office of any document for filing and the title of the proceedings in which the document is filed shall be entered in court records, on the court file or on a computer kept in the court office for the purpose. Except where a document has been delivered at the court office through the post, the time of delivery should also be recorded.

5.3 Filing by Facsimile

(1) Subject to paragraph (6) below, a party may file a document at court by sending it by facsimile ("fax").

(2) Where a document is filed by fax, the party filing it is not required in addition to send the court a copy by post or document exchange.

(3) A party filing a document by fax should be aware that the document is not filed at court until it is delivered by the court's fax machine, whatever time it is shown to have been transmitted from the party's machine.

(4) The time of delivery of the faxed document will be recorded on it in accordance with paragraph 5.2.

(5) It remains the responsibility of the party to ensure that the document is delivered to the court in time.

(6) If a fax is delivered after 4p.m. it will be treated as filed on the next day the court office is open.

(7) If a fax relates to a hearing, the date and time of the hearing should be prominently displayed.

(8) Fax should not be used to send letters or documents of a routine or non-urgent nature.

(9) Fax should not be used, except in an unavoidable emergency, to deliver:

   (a) a document which attracts a fee

   (b) a Part 36 payment notice

   (c) a document relating to a hearing less than two hours ahead

   (d) trial bundles or skeleton arguments

(10) Where (9)(a) or (b) applies, the fax should give an explanation for the emergency and include an undertaking that the fee or money has been dispatched that day by post or will be paid at the court office counter the following business day.

(11) Where courts have several fax machines, each allocated to an individual section, fax messages should only be sent to the machine of the section for which the message is intended.

5.4 Where the Court orders any document to be lodged in Court, the document must, unless otherwise directed, be deposited in the office of that Court.

5.5 A document filed, lodged or held in any court office shall not be taken out of that office without the permission of the Court unless the document is to be sent to the office of another court (for example under CPR Part 30 (Transfer)), except in accordance with CPR rule 39.7 (impounded documents) or in accordance with paragraph 5.5 below.

5.6 (1) Where a document filed, lodged or held in a court office is required to be produced to any Court, Tribunal or arbitrator, the document may be produced by sending it by registered post (together with a Certificate as in paragraph 5.6(8)(b)) to the Court, Tribunal or arbitrator in accordance with the provisions of this paragraph.

   (2) Any Court, Tribunal or arbitrator or any party requiring any document filed, lodged or held in any court office to be produced must apply to that court office by sending a completed request (as in paragraph 5.5(8)(a)), stamped with the prescribed fee.

   (3) On receipt of the request the court officer will submit the same to a Master in the Royal Courts of Justice or to a District Judge elsewhere, who may direct that the request be complied with. Before giving a direction the Master or District Judge may require to be satisfied that the request is made in good faith and that the document is required to be produced for the reasons stated. The Master or District Judge giving the direction may also direct that, before the document is sent, an official copy of it is made and filed in the court office at the expense of the party requiring the document to be produced.

   (4) On the direction of the Master or District Judge the court officer shall send the document by registered post addressed to the Court, Tribunal or arbitrator, with:

      (a) an envelope stamped and addressed for use in returning the document to the court office from which it was sent;

      (b) a Certificate as in paragraph 5.6(8)(b);

      (c) a covering letter describing the document, stating at whose request and for what purpose it is sent, referring to this paragraph of the Practice Direction and containing a request that the document be returned to the court office from which it was sent in the enclosed envelope as soon as the Court or Tribunal no longer requires it.

(5) It shall be the duty of the Court, Tribunal or arbitrator to whom the document was sent to keep it in safe custody, and to return it by registered post to the court office from which it was sent, as soon as the Court, Tribunal or arbitrator no longer requires it.

(6) In each court office a record shall be kept of each document sent and the date on which it was sent and the Court, Tribunal or arbitrator to whom it was sent and the date of its return. It shall be the duty of the court officer who has signed the certificate referred to in para 5.6(8)(b) below to ensure that the document is returned within a reasonable time and to make inquiries and report to the Master or District Judge who has given the direction under paragraph (3) above if the document is not returned, so that steps may be taken to secure its return.

(7) Notwithstanding the preceding paragraphs, the Master or District Judge may direct a court officer to attend the Court, Tribunal or arbitrator for the purpose of producing the document.

(8) (a) I,   of   , an officer of the   Court/Tribunal at   /an arbitrator of /the Claimant /Defendant /Solicitor for the Claimant/ Defendant [describing the Applicant so as to show that he is a proper person to make the request] in the case of   v.   [19 No.]

   REQUEST that the following document [or documents] be produced to the Court /Tribunal/arbitrator on the day of 19 [and following days] and I request that the said document [or documents] be sent by registered post to the proper officer of the Court/Tribunal/arbitrator for production to that Court/ Tribunal/arbitrator on that day.

   (Signed).

   Dated the day of 1999/2   .

   (b) I, A.B., an officer of the   Court of certify that the document sent herewith for production to the Court/Tribunal/arbitrator on the day of 1999/2 in the case of   v.   and marked "A.B." is the document requested on the day of 1999/2 and I FURTHER CERTIFY that the said document has been filed in and is produced from the custody of the Court.

   (Signed)

   Dated the day of 1999/2   .

Enrolment of Deeds and other Documents

6.1 (1) Any deed or document which by virtue of any enactment is required or authorised to be enrolled in the Supreme Court may be enrolled in the Central Office of the High Court.

   (2) Attention is drawn to the Enrolment of Deeds (Change of Name) Regulations 1994 which are reproduced in the Appendix to this Practice Direction .

6.2 The following paragraph of the Practice Direction describes the practice to be followed in any case in which a child's name is to be changed and to which the 1994 Regulations apply.

6.3 (1) Where a person has by any order of the High Court, County Court or Family Proceedings Court been given parental responsibility for a child and applies to the Central Office, Filing Department, for the enrolment of a Deed Poll to change the surname (family name) of a child who is under the age of 18 years (unless a child who is or has been married), the application must be supported by the production of the consent in writing of every other person having parental responsibility.

   (2) In the absence of that consent, the application will be adjourned generally unless and until permission is given in the proceedings, in which the said order was made, to change the surname of the child and the permission is produced to the Central Office.

   (3) Where an application is made to the Central Office by a person who has not been given parental responsibility for a child by any order of the High Court, County Court or Family Proceedings Court for the enrolment of a Deed Poll to change the surname of the child who is under the age of 18 years (unless the child is or has been married), permission of the Court to enrol the Deed will be granted if the consent in writing of every person having parental responsibility is produced or if the person (or, if more than one, persons) having parental responsibility is dead or overseas or despite the exercise of reasonable diligence it has not been possible to find him or her for other good reason.

(4) In cases of doubt the Senior Master or, in his absence, the Practice Master will refer the matter to the Master of the Rolls.

(5) In the absence of any of the conditions specified above the Senior Master or the Master of the Rolls, as the case may be, may refer the matter to the Official Solicitor for investigation and report.

APPENDIX

Regulations made by the Master of the Rolls, Sir Thomas Bingham M.R. on 3 March 1994 (S.I. 1994 No.604) under s.133(1) of the Supreme Court Act 1981.

1   (1) These regulations may be cited as the Enrolment of Deeds (Change of Name) Regulations 1994 and shall come into force on April 1, 1994.

(2) These Regulations shall govern the enrolment in the Central Office of the Supreme Court of deeds evidencing change of name (referred to in these Regulations as "deeds poll").

2   (1) A person seeking to enrol a deed poll ("the applicant") must be a Commonwealth citizen as defined by section 37(1) of the British Nationality Act 1981.

(2) If the applicant is a British citizen, a British Dependent Territories citizen or a British Overseas citizen, he must be described as such in the deed poll, which must also specify the section of the British Nationality Act under which the relevant citizenship was acquired.

(3) In any other case, the applicant must be described as a Commonwealth citizen.

(4) The applicant must be described in the deed poll as single, married, widowed or divorced.

3   (1) As proof of the citizenship named in the deed poll, the applicant must produce

(a) a certificate of birth; or

(b) a certificate of citizenship by registration or naturalisation or otherwise; or

(c) some other document evidencing such citizenship.

(2) In addition to the documents set out in paragraph (1), an applicant who is married must

(a) produce his certificate of marriage; and

(b) show that the notice of his intention to apply for the enrolment of the deed poll had been given to his spouse by delivery or by post to his spouse's last known address; and

(c) show that he has obtained the consent of his spouse to the proposed change of name or that there is good reason why such consent should be dispensed with.

4   (1) The deed poll and the documents referred to in regulation 3 must be exhibited to a statutory declaration by a Commonwealth citizen who is a householder in the United Kingdom and who must declare that he is such in the statutory declaration.

(2) The statutory declaration must state the period, which should ordinarily not be less than 10 years, during which the householder has known the applicant and must identify the applicant as the person referred to in the documents exhibited to the statutory declaration.

(3) Where the period mentioned in paragraph (2) is stated to be less than 10 years, the Master of the Rolls may in his absolute discretion decide whether to permit the deed poll to be enrolled and may require the applicant to provide more information before so deciding.

5   If the applicant is resident outside the United Kingdom, he must provide evidence that such residence is not intended to be permanent and the applicant may be required to produce a certificate by a solicitor as to the nature and probable duration of such residence.

6   The applicant must sign the deed poll in both his old and new names.

7   Upon enrolment the deed poll shall be advertised in the London Gazette by the clerk in charge for the time being of the Filing and Record Department at the Central Office of the Supreme Court.

8   (1) Subject to the following provisions of this regulation, these Regulations shall apply in relation to a deed poll evidencing the change of name of a child as if the child were the applicant.

(2) Paragraphs (3) to (8) shall not apply to a child who has attained the age of 16, is female and is married.

(3) If the child is under the age of 16, the deed poll must be executed by a person having parental responsibility for him.

(4) If the child has attained the age of 16, the deed poll must, except in the case of a person mentioned in paragraph (2), be executed by a person having parental responsibility for the child and be endorsed with the child's consent signed in both his old and new names and duly witnessed.

(5) The application for enrolment must be supported

    (a) by an affidavit showing that the change of name is for the benefit of the child, and

        (i) that the application is submitted by all persons having parental responsibility for the child; or

        (ii) that it is submitted by one person having parental responsibility for the child with the consent of every other person; or

        (iii) that it is submitted by one person having parental responsibility for the child without the consent of every other such person, or by some other person whose name and capacity are given, for reasons set out in the affidavit; and

    (b) by such other evidence, if any, as the Master of the Rolls may require in the particular circumstances of the case.

(6) Regulation 4(2) shall not apply but the statutory declaration mentioned in regulation 4(1) shall state how long the householder has known the deponent under paragraph (5)(a) and the child respectively.

(7) Regulation 6 shall not apply to a child who has not attained the age of 16.

(8) In this regulation "parental responsibility" has the meaning given in section 3 of the Children Act 1989.

9   The Enrolment of Deeds (Change of Name) Regulations 1983 and the Enrolment of Deeds (Change of Name) (Amendment) Regulations 1990 are hereby revoked.

PART 6

SERVICE OF DOCUMENTS

Contents of this Part

III Special provisions about service out of the jurisdiction

I General rules about service

Part 6 Rules about service apply generally

6.1 The rules in this Part apply to the service of documents, except where –
  (a) any other enactment, a rule in another Part, or a practice direction makes a different provision; or
  (b) the court orders otherwise.
  (Other rules which deal with service include the following –
  (a) service on the Crown – see RSC Order 77 r.4 and CCR Order 42 r.7;
  (b) service in proceedings for the recovery of land and mortgage possession actions – see RSC Order 10 r.4 and CCR Order 7 rr.15 and 15A.)

Methods of service – general

6.2 (1) A document may be served by any of the following methods –
  (a) personal service, in accordance with rule 6.4;
  (b) first class post;
  (c) leaving the document at a place specified in rule 6.5;
  (d) through a document exchange in accordance with the relevant practice direction; or
  (e) by fax or other means of electronic communication in accordance with the relevant practice direction.

(Rule 6.8 provides for the court to permit service by an alternative method)

  (2) A company may be served by any method permitted under this Part as an alternative to the methods of service set out in –
  (a) section 725 of the Companies Act 1985[8] (service by leaving a document at or posting it to an authorised place);

_____

(8) 1985 c.6.

(b) section 695 of that Act (service on overseas companies); and

(c) section 694A of that Act (service of documents on companies incorporated outside the UK and Gibraltar and having a branch in Great Britain).

Who is to serve

6.3 (1) The court will serve a document which it has issued or prepared except where –

(a) a rule provides that a party must serve the document in question;

(b) the party on whose behalf the document is to be served notifies the court that he wishes to serve it himself;

(c) a practice direction provides otherwise;

(d) the court orders otherwise; or

(e) the court has failed to serve and has sent a notice of non-service to the party on whose behalf the document is to be served in accordance with rule 6.11.

(2) Where the court is to serve a document, it is for the court to decide which of the methods of service specified in rule 6.2 is to be used.

(3) Where a party prepares a document which is to be served by the court, that party must file a copy for the court, and for each party to be served.

Personal service

6.4 (1) A document to be served may be served personally, except as provided in paragraph (2).

(2) Where a solicitor –

(a) is authorised to accept service on behalf of a party; and

(b) has notified the party serving the document in writing that he is so authorised,

a document must be served on the solicitor, unless personal service is required by an enactment, rule, practice direction or court order.

(3) A document is served personally on an individual by leaving it with that individual.

(4) A document is served personally on a company or other corporation by leaving it with a person holding a senior position within the company or corporation.

(The service practice direction sets out the meaning of 'senior position')

(5) A document is served personally on a partnership where partners are being sued in the name of their firm by leaving it with –

(a) a partner; or

(b) a person who, at the time of service, has the control or management of the partnership business at its principal place of business.

Address for service

6.5 (1) Except as provided by Section III of this Part (service out of the jurisdiction) a document must be served within the jurisdiction.

('Jurisdiction' is defined in rule 2.3)

(2) A party must give an address for service within the jurisdiction.

(3) Where a party –

(a) does not give the business address of his solicitor as his address for service; and

(b) resides or carries on business within the jurisdiction,

he must give his residence or place of business as his address for service.

(4) Any document to be served –

    (a) by first class post;

    (b) by leaving it at the place of service;

    (c) through a document exchange; or

    (d) by fax or by other means of electronic communication,

must be sent or transmitted to, or left at, the address for service given by the party to be served.

(5) Where –

    (a) a solicitor is acting for the party to be served; and

    (b) the document to be served is not the claim form;

the party's address for service is the business address of his solicitor.

(Rule 6.13 specifies when the business address of a defendant's solicitor may be the defendant's address for service in relation to the claim form)

(6) Where –

    (a) no solicitor is acting for the party to be served; and

    (b) the party has not given an address for service,

the document must be sent or transmitted to, or left at, the place shown in the following table.

(Rule 6.2(2) sets out the statutory methods of service on a company)

Nature of party to be served	Place of service
Individual	• Usual or last known residence.
Proprietor of a business	• Usual or last known residence; or • Place of business or last known place of business.
Individual who is suing or being sued in the name of a firm	• Usual or last known residence; or • Principal or last known place of business of the firm.
Corporation incorporated in England and Wales other than a company	• Principal office of the corporation; or • Any place within the jurisdiction where the corporation carries on its activities and which has a real connection with the claim.
Company registered in England and Wales	• Principal office of the company; or • Any place of business of the company within the jurisdiction which has a real connection with the claim.
Any other company or corporation	• Any place within the jurisdiction where the corporation carries on its activities; or • Any place of business of the company within the jurisdiction

(7) This rule does not apply where an order made by the court under rule 6.8 (service by an alternative method) specifies where the document in question may be served.

Service of documents on children and patients

6.6 (1) The following table shows the person on whom a document must be served if it is a document which would otherwise be served on a child or a patient –

Type of document	Nature of party	Person to be served
Claim form	Child who is not also a patient	• One of the child's parents or guardians; or • If there is no parent or guardian, the person with whom the child resides or in whose care the child is.
Claim form	Patient	• The person authorised under Part VII of the Mental Health Act 1983[9] to conduct the proceedings in the name of the patient or on his behalf; or • If there is no person so authorised, the person with whom the patient resides or in whose care the patient is.
Application for an order appointing a litigation friend, where a child or patient has no litigation friend	Child or patient	See rule 21.8.
Any other document	Child or patient	The litigation friend who is conducting proceedings on behalf of the child or patient.

(2) The court may make an order permitting a document to be served on the child or patient, or on some person other than the person specified in the table in this rule.

(3) An application for an order under paragraph (2) may be made without notice.

(4) The court may order that, although a document has been served on someone other than the person specified in the table, the document is to be treated as if it had been properly served.

(5) This rule does not apply where the court has made an order under rule 21.2(3) allowing a child to conduct proceedings without a litigation friend.

(Part 21 contains rules about the appointment of a litigation friend)

(9) 1983 c.20.

Deemed service

6.7 (1) A document which is served in accordance with these rules or any relevant practice direction shall be deemed to be served on the day shown in the following table –

(Rule 2.8 excludes a Saturday, Sunday, a Bank Holiday, Christmas Day or Good Friday from calculations of periods of 5 days or less.)

Method of service	Deemed day of service
First class post	The second day after it was posted.
Document exchange	The second day after it was left at the document exchange.
Delivering the document to or leaving it at a permitted address	The day after it was delivered to or left at the permitted address.
Fax	If it is transmitted on a business day before 4pm, on that day; or In any other case, on the business day after the day on which it is transmitted.
Other electronic method	The second day after the day on which it is transmitted.

(2) If a document is served personally –
   (a) After 5 pm, on a business day; or
   (b) At any time on a Saturday, Sunday or a Bank Holiday,
   it will be treated as being served on the next business day.

(3) In this rule –
   'business day' means any day except Saturday, Sunday or a Bank Holiday; and 'Bank Holiday' includes Christmas Day and Good Friday.

Service by an alternative method

6.8 (1) Where it appears to the court that there is a good reason to authorise service by a method not permitted by these Rules, the court may make an order permitting service by an alternative method.

(2) An application for an order permitting service by an alternative method –
   (a) must be supported by evidence; and
   (b) may be made without notice.

(3) An order permitting service by an alternative method must specify –
   (a) the method of service; and
   (b) the date when the document will be deemed to be served.

Power of court to dispense with service

6.9 (1) The court may dispense with service of a document.

(2) An application for an order to dispense with service may be made without notice.

Certificate of service

6.10 Where a rule, practice direction or court order requires a certificate of service, the certificate must state –

(a) that the document has not been returned undelivered; and

(b) the details set out in the following table –

Method of service	Details to be certified
Post	Date of posting
Personal	Date of personal service
Document exchange	Date of delivery to the document exchange
Delivery of document to or leaving it at a permitted place	Date when the document was delivered to or left at the permitted place
Fax	Date and time of transmission
Other electronic means	Date of transmission and the means used
Alternative method permitted by the court	As required by the court

Notice of non-service

6.11   Where –

(a) a document is to be served by the court; and

(b) the court is unable to serve it,

the court must send a notice of non-service stating the method attempted to the party who requested service.

II   Special provisions about service of the claim form

General rules about service subject to special rules about service of claim form

6.12   The general rules about service are subject to the special rules about service contained in rules 6.13 to 6.16.

Service of claim form by the court – defendant's address for service

6.13(1) Where a claim form is to be served by the court, the claim form must include the defendant's address for service.

(2) For the purposes of paragraph (1), the defendant's address for service may be the business address of the defendant's solicitor if he is authorised to accept service on the defendant's behalf but not otherwise.

(Rule 6.5 contains general provisions about the address for service)

Certificate of service relating to the claim form

6.14(1) Where a claim form is served by the court, the court must send the claimant a notice which will include the date when the claim form is deemed to be served under rule 6.7.

(2) Where the claim form is served by the claimant –

(a) he must file a certificate of service within 7 days of service of the claim form; and

(b) he may not obtain judgment in default under Part 12 unless he has filed the certificate of service.

(Rule 6.10 specifies what a certificate of service must show)

Service of claim form by contractually agreed method

6.15(1) Where –

    (a) a contract contains a term providing that, in the event of a claim being issued in relation to the contract, the claim form may be served by a method specified in the contract; and

    (b) a claim form containing only a claim in respect of that contract is issued,

the claim form shall, subject to paragraph (2), be deemed to be served on the defendant if it is served by a method specified in the contract.

  (2) Where the claim form is served out of the jurisdiction in accordance with the contract, it shall not be deemed to be served on the defendant unless –

    (a) permission to serve it out of the jurisdiction has been granted under rule 6.20; or

    (b) it may be served without permission under rule 6.19.

Service of claim form on agent of principal who is overseas

6.16(1) Where –

    (a) the defendant is overseas; and

    (b) the conditions specified in paragraph (2) are satisfied,

the court may, on an application only, permit a claim form relating to a contract to be served on a defendant's agent.

  (2) The court may not make an order under this rule unless it is satisfied that –

    (a) the contract to which the claim relates was entered into within the jurisdiction with or through the defendant's agent; and

    (b) at the time of the application either the agent's authority has not been terminated or he is still in business relations with his principal.

  (3) An application under this rule –

    (a) must be supported by evidence; and

    (b) may be made without notice.

  (4) An order under this rule must state a period within which the defendant must respond to the particulars of claim.

(Rule 9.2 sets out how a defendant may respond to particulars of claim)

  (5) The power conferred by this rule is additional to the power conferred by rule 6.8 (service by an alternative method).

  (6) Where the court makes an order under this rule, the claimant must send to the defendant copies of –

    (a) the order; and

    (b) the claim form.

(Other rules about service can be found –

    (a) in Schedule 1, in the following RSC – O.10 (certain actions for the possession of land); O.11 (service out of the jurisdiction); O.30 (receivers); O.52 (application for committal order); O.54 (writ of habeas corpus); O.69 (foreign process); O.77 (service on the Crown); O.97 (Landlord and Tenant Acts); O.106 (Solicitors Act 1974); O.113 (summary proceedings for possession of land);

    (b) in Schedule 2, in the following CCR – O.3 (appeal to the county court); O.7 (recovery of land and mortgage possession claims); O.24 (summary proceedings for recovery of land and interim possession orders); O.33 (interpleader); O.42 (service on the Crown); O.43 (Landlord and Tenant Acts); O.45 (application for detailed assessment of returning officer's account); O.47 (application for direction for use of blood tests); O.48B (order for enforcement of parking penalties); O.49 (notice to repair under Chancel Repairs Act 1932; applications under various statutes); and

(c) in relation to certain enforcement proceedings, in the provisions in the Schedules dealing with those proceedings.)

III Special provisions about service out of the jurisdiction

Scope of this section

6.17   This Section contains rules about –

(a) service out of the jurisdiction;

(b) how to obtain the permission of the court to serve out of the jurisdiction; and

(c) the procedure for serving out of the jurisdiction.

(Rule 2.3 defines 'jurisdiction')

Definitions

6.18   For the purposes of this Part –

(a) 'the 1982 Act' means the Civil Jurisdiction and Judgments Act 1982[10];

(b) 'the Hague Convention' means the Convention on the service abroad of judicial and extra-judicial documents in civil or commercial matters signed at the Hague on November 15, 1965[11];

(c) 'Contracting State' has the meaning given by section 1(3) of the 1982 Act;

(d) 'Convention territory' means the territory or territories of any Contracting State to which the Brussels or Lugano Conventions (as defined in section 1(1) of the 1982 Act) apply;

(e) 'Civil Procedure Convention' means the Brussels and Lugano Conventions and any other Convention entered into by the United Kingdom regarding service outside the jurisdiction;

(f) 'United Kingdom Overseas Territory' means those territories as set out in the relevant practice direction.

(g) 'domicile' is to be determined in accordance with sections 41 to 46 of the 1982 Act;

(h) 'claim form' includes petition and application notice; and

(i) 'claim' includes petition and application.

(Rule 6.30 provides that where an application notice is to be served out of the jurisdiction under this Part, Rules 6.21(4), 6.22 and 6.23 do not apply)

Service out of the jurisdiction where the permission of the court is not required

6.19(1) A claim form may be served on a defendant out of the jurisdiction where each claim included in the claim form made against the defendant to be served is a claim which the court has power to determine under the 1982 Act and –

(a) no proceedings between the parties concerning the same claim are pending in the courts of any part of the United Kingdom or any other Convention territory; and

(b) (i) the defendant is domiciled in the United Kingdom or in any Convention territory;

---

(10) 1982 c.27, as amended by the Civil Jurisdiction and Judgments Act 1991 (c.12).

(11) Cmnd 3986.

       (ii) Article 16 of Schedule 1, 3c or 4 to the 1982 Act refers to the proceedings; or

       (iii) the defendant is a party to an agreement conferring jurisdiction to which Article 17 of Schedule 1, 3C or 4 to the 1982 Act refers.

(2) A claim form may be served on a defendant out of the jurisdiction where each claim included in the claim form made against the defendant to be served is a claim which, under any other enactment, the court has power to determine, although –

    (a) the person against whom the claim is made is not within the jurisdiction; or

    (b) the facts giving rise to the claim did not occur within the jurisdiction.

(3) Where a claim form is to be served out of the jurisdiction under this rule, it must contain a statement of the grounds on which the claimant is entitled to serve it out of the jurisdiction.

Service out of the jurisdiction where the permission of the court is required

6.20   In any proceedings to which Rule 6.19 does not apply, a claim form may be served out of the jurisdiction with the permission of the court if –

General grounds

(1) a claim is made for a remedy against a person domiciled within the jurisdiction.

(2) a claim is made for an injunction ordering$^{(GL)}$ the defendant to do or refrain from doing an act within the jurisdiction.

(3) a claim is made against someone on whom the claim form has been or will be served and –

    (a) there is between the claimant and that person a real issue which it is reasonable for the court to try; and

    (b) the claimant wishes to serve the claim form on another person who is a necessary or proper party to that claim.

Claims for interim remedies

(4) a claim is made for an interim remedy under section 25(1) of the 1982 Act[12]

Claims in relation to contracts

(5) a claim is made in respect of a contract where the contract –

    (a) was made within the jurisdiction;

    (b) was made by or through an agent trading or residing within the jurisdiction;

    (c) is governed by English law; or

    (d) contains a term to the effect that the court shall have jurisdiction to determine any claim in respect of the contract.

(6) a claim is made in respect of a breach of contract committed within the jurisdiction.

(7) a claim is made for a declaration that no contract exists where, if the contract was found to exist, it would comply with the conditions set out in paragraph (5).

Claims in tort

(8) a claim is made in tort where –

---

(12) 1982 c.27. Section 25 has been amended by the Civil Jurisdiction and Judgments Act 1991 (c.12), Schedule 2, paragraph 12, and extended by SI 1997/302.

(a) damage was sustained within the jurisdiction; or

(b) the damage sustained resulted from an act committed within the jurisdiction.

Enforcement

(9) a claim is made to enforce any judgment or arbitral award.

Claims about property within the jurisdiction

(10) the whole subject matter of a claim relates to property located within the jurisdiction.

Claims about trusts etc

(11) a claim is made for any remedy which might be obtained in proceedings to execute the trusts of a written instrument where –

(a) the trusts ought to be executed according to English law; and

(b) the person on whom the claim form is to be served is a trustee of the trusts.

(12) a claim is made for any remedy which might be obtained in proceedings for the administration of the estate of a person who died domiciled within the jurisdiction.

(13) a claim is made in probate proceedings which includes a claim for the rectification of a will.

(14) a claim is made for a remedy against the defendant as constructive trustee where the defendant's alleged liability arises out of acts committed within the jurisdiction.

(15) a claim is made for restitution where the defendant's alleged liability arises out of acts committed within the jurisdiction.

(Probate proceedings are defined in the Contentious Probate Proceedings practice direction supplementing Part 49)

Claims by the Inland Revenue

(16) a claim is made by the Commissioners of the Inland Revenue relating to duties or taxes against a defendant not domiciled in Scotland or Northern Ireland.

Claim for costs order in favour of or against third parties

(17) a claim is made by a party to proceedings for an order that the court exercise its power under section 51 of the Supreme Court Act 1981[13] to make a costs order in favour of or against a person who is not a party to those proceedings.

(Rule 48.2 sets out the procedure where the court is considering whether to exercise its discretion to make a costs order in favour of or against a non-party.)

Claims under various enactments

(18) a claim made under an enactment specified in the relevant practice direction.

Application for permission to serve claim form out of the jurisdiction

6.21(1) An application for permission under rule 6.20 must be supported by written evidence stating –

(a) the grounds on which the application is made and the paragraph or paragraphs of rule 6.20 relied on;

(b) that the claimant believes that his claim has a reasonable prospect of success; and

(c) the defendant's address or, if not known, in what place or country the defendant is, or is likely, to be found.

---

(13) 1981 c.54. Section 51 was substituted by section 4 of the Courts and Legal Services Act 1990 (c.41), and is amended prospectively by section 31 of the Access to Justice Act 1999 (c.22).

(2) Where the application is made in respect of a claim referred to in rule 6.20(3), the written evidence must also state the grounds on which the witness believes that there is between the claimant and the person on whom the claim form has been, or will be served, a real issue which it is reasonable for the court to try.

(2A)The court will not give permission unless satisfied that England and Wales is the proper place in which to bring the claim.

(3) Where –

    (a) the application is for permission to serve a claim form in Scotland or Northern Ireland; and

    (b) it appears to the court that the claimant may also be entitled to a remedy there, the court, in deciding whether to give permission, shall –

        (i) compare the cost and convenience of proceeding there or in the jurisdiction; and

        (ii) (where relevant) have regard to the powers and jurisdiction of the Sheriff court in Scotland or the county courts or courts of summary jurisdiction in Northern Ireland.

(4) An order giving permission to serve a claim form out of the jurisdiction must specify the periods within which the defendant may –

    (a) file an acknowledgment of service;

    (b) file or serve an admission; and

    (c) file a defence.

(Part 11 sets out the procedure by which a defendant may dispute the court's jurisdiction)

Period for acknowledging service or admitting the claim where the claim form is served out of the jurisdiction under rule 6.19

6.22(1) This rule sets out the period for filing an acknowledgment of service or filing or serving an admission where a claim form has been served out of the jurisdiction under rule 6.19.

(Part 10 contains rules about the acknowledgment of service and Part 14 contains rules about admissions)

(2) If the claim form is to be served under rule 6.19(1) in Scotland, Northern Ireland or in the European territory of another Contracting State the period is –

    (a) where the defendant is served with a claim form which states that particulars of claim are to follow, 21 days after the service of the particulars of claim; and

    (b) in any other case, 21 days after service of the claim form.

(3) If the claim form is to be served under rule 6.19(1) in any other territory of a Contracting State the period is –

    (a) where the defendant is served with a claim form which states that particulars of claim are to follow, 31 days after the service of the particulars of claim; and

    (b) in any other case, 31 days after service of the claim form.

(4) If the claim form is to be served under –

    (a) rule 6.19(1) in a country not referred to in paragraphs (2) or (3); or

    (b) rule 6.19(2), the period is set out in the relevant practice direction.

Period for filing a defence where the claim form is served out of the jurisdiction under rule 6.19

6.23(1) This rule sets out the period for filing a defence where a claim form has been served out of the jurisdiction under rule 6.19.

(Part 15 contains rules about the defence)

(2) If the claim form is to be served under rule 6.19(1) in Scotland, Northern Ireland or in the European territory of another Contracting State the period is –
  (a) 21 days after service of the particulars of claim; or
  (b) if the defendant files an acknowledgment of service, 35 days after service of the particulars of claim.

(3) If the claim form is to be served under rule 6.19(1) in any other territory of a Contracting State the period is –
  (a) 31 days after service of the particulars of claim; or
  (b) if the defendant files an acknowledgment of service, 45 days after service of the particulars of claim.

(4) If the claim form is to be served under –
  (a) rule 6.19(1) in a country not referred to in paragraphs (2) or (3); or
  (b) rule 6.19(2),
  the period is set out in the relevant practice direction.

Method of service – general provisions

6.24(1) Where a claim form is to be served out of the jurisdiction, it may be served by any method –
  (a) permitted by the law of the country in which it is to be served;
  (b) provided for by –
    (i) rule 6.25 (service through foreign governments, judicial authorities and British Consular authorities); or
    (ii) rule 6.26 (service on a State); or
  (c) permitted by a Civil Procedure Convention.

(2) Nothing in this rule or in any court order shall authorise or require any person to do anything in the country where the claim form is to be served which is against the law of that country.

Service through foreign governments, judicial authorities and British consular authorities

6.25(1) Where a claim form is to be served on a defendant in any country which is a party to the Hague Convention, the claim form may be served –
  (a) through the authority designated under the Hague Convention in respect of that country; or
  (b) if the law of that country permits –
    (i) through the judicial authorities of that country, or
    (ii) through a British Consular authority in that country.

(2) Where –
  (a) paragraph (4) (service in Scotland etc., other than under the Hague Convention) does not apply; and
  (b) a claim form is to be served on a defendant in any country which is a party to a Civil Procedure Convention (other than the Hague Convention) providing for service in that country,
  the claim form may be served, if the law of that country permits –
    (i) through the judicial authorities of that country; or
    (ii) through a British Consular authority in that country (subject to any provisions of the applicable convention about the nationality of persons who may be served by such a method).

(3) Where –
  (a) paragraph (4) (service in Scotland etc., other than under the Hague Convention) does not apply; and
  (b) a claim form is to be served on a defendant in any country with respect to which there is no Civil Procedure Convention providing for service in that country,

  the claim form may be served, if the law of that country so permits –
    (i) through the government of that country, where that government is willing to serve it; or
    (ii) through a British Consular authority in that country.

(4) Except where a claim form is to be served in accordance with paragraph (1) (service under the Hague Convention), the methods of service permitted by this rule are not available where the claim form is to be served in –
  (a) Scotland, Northern Ireland, the Isle of Man or the Channel Islands;
  (b) any Commonwealth State;
  (c) any United Kingdom Overseas Territory; or
  (d) the Republic of Ireland.

Procedure where service is to be through foreign governments, judicial authorities and British consular authorities

6.26(1) This rule applies where the claimant wishes to serve the claim form through –
  (a) the judicial authorities of the country where the claim form is to be served;
  (b) a British Consular authority in that country;
  (c) the authority designated under the Hague Convention in respect of that country; or
  (d) the government of that country.

(2) Where this rule applies, the claimant must file –
  (a) a request for service of the claim form by the method in paragraph (1) that he has chosen;
  (b) a copy of the claim form;
  (c) any translation required under rule 6.28; and
  (d) any other documents, copies of documents or translations required by the relevant practice direction.

(3) When the claimant files the documents specified in paragraph (2), the court officer will –
  (a) seal$^{(GL)}$ the copy of the claim form; and
  (b) forward the documents to the Senior Master.

(4) The Senior Master will send documents forwarded under this rule –
  (a) where the claim form is being served through the authority designated under the Hague Convention, to that authority; or
  (b) in any other case, to the Foreign and Commonwealth Office with a request that it arranges for the claim to be served by the method indicated in the request for service filed under paragraph (2) or, where that request indicates alternative methods, by the most convenient method.

(5) An official certificate which –
  (a) states that the claim form has been served in accordance with this rule either personally, or in accordance with the law of the country in which service was effected;
  (b) specifies the date on which the claim form was served; and

(c) is made by –
  (i) a British Consular authority in the country where the claim form was served;
  (ii) the government or judicial authorities in that country; or
  (iii) any other authority designated in respect of that country under the Hague Convention,
shall be evidence of the facts stated in the certificate.

(6) A document purporting to be an official certificate under paragraph (5) shall be treated as such a certificate, unless it is proved not to be.

Service of claim form on State where court permits service out of the jurisdiction

6.27(1) This rule applies where a claimant wishes to serve the claim form on a State.

(2) The claimant must file in the Central Office of the Royal Courts of Justice –
  (a) a request for service to be arranged by the Foreign and Commonwealth Office;
  (b) a copy of the claim form; and
  (c) any translation required under rule 6.28.

(3) The Senior Master will send documents filed under this rule to the Foreign and Commonwealth Office with a request that it arranges for the claim form to be served.

(4) An official certificate by the Foreign and Commonwealth Office stating that a claim form has been duly served on a specified date in accordance with a request made under this rule shall be evidence of that fact.

(5) A document purporting to be such a certificate shall be treated as such a certificate, unless it is proved not to be.

(6) Where –
  (a) section 12(6) of the State Immunity Act 1978[14] applies; and
  (b) the State has agreed to a method of service other than through the Foreign and Commonwealth Office,
the claim may be served either by the method agreed or in accordance with this rule.

(Section 12(6) of the State Immunity Act 1978 provides that section 12(1) of that Act, which prescribes a method for serving documents on a State, does not prevent the service of a claim form or other document in a manner to which the State has agreed)

(7) In this rule 'State' has the meaning given by section 14 of the State Immunity Act 1978.

Translation of claim form

6.28(1) Except where paragraph (4) or (5) applies, every copy of the claim form filed under rule 6.26 (service through judicial authorities, foreign governments etc.) or 6.27 (service on State) must be accompanied by a translation of the claim form.

(2) The translation must be –
  (a) in the official language of the country in which it is to be served; or
  (b) if there is more than one official language of that country, in any official language which is appropriate to the place in the country where the claim form is to be served.

(14) 1978 c.33.

(3) Every translation filed under this rule must be accompanied by a statement by the person making it that it is a correct translation, and the statement must include –

    (a) the name of the person making the translation;

    (b) his address; and

    (c) his qualifications for making a translation.

(4) The claimant is not required to file a translation of a claim form filed under rule 6.26 (service through judicial authorities, foreign governments, etc.) where the claim form is to be served-

    (a) in a country of which English is an official language; or

    (b) on a British subject, unless a Civil Procedure Convention expressly requires a translation.

(5) The claimant is not required to file a translation of a claim form filed under rule 6.27 (service on State) where English is an official language of the State where the claim form is to be served.

Undertaking to be responsible for expenses of the Foreign and Commonwealth Office

6.29   Every request for service filed under rule 6.26 (service through judicial authorities, foreign governments, etc.) or rule 6.27 (service on State) must contain an undertaking by the person making the request-

    (a) to be responsible for all expenses incurred by the Foreign and Commonwealth Office or foreign judicial authority; and

    (b) to pay those expenses to the Foreign and Commonwealth Office or foreign judicial authority on being informed of the amount.

Service of documents other than the claim form

6.30(1) Where an application notice is to be served out of the jurisdiction under this Section of this Part –

    (a) rules 6.21(4), 6.22 and 6.23 do not apply; and

    (b) where the person on whom the application notice has been served is not a party to proceedings in the jurisdiction in which the application is made, that person may make an application to the court under rule 11(1) as if he were a defendant and rule 11(2) does not apply.

(Rule 6.21(4) provides that an order giving permission to serve a claim form out of the jurisdiction must specify the periods within which the defendant may (a) file an acknowledgment of service, (b) file or serve an admission, and (c) file a defence.)

(Rule 6.22 provides rules for the period for acknowledging service or admitting the claim where the claim form is served out of the jurisdiction under rule 6.19.)

(Rule 6.23 provides rules for the period for filing a defence where the claim form is served out of the jurisdiction under rule 6.19.)

(The practice direction supplementing this Section of this Part provides that where an application notice is to be served out of the jurisdiction in accordance with this Section of this Part, the court must have regard to the country in which the application notice is to be served in setting the date for the hearing of the application and giving any direction about service of the respondent's evidence.)

(Rule 11(1) provides that a defendant may make an application to the court to dispute the court's jurisdiction to try the claim or argue that the court should not exercise its jurisdiction. Rule 11(2) provides that a defendant who wishes to make such an application must first file an acknowledgment of service in accordance with Part 10.)

(2) Unless paragraph (3) applies, where the permission of the court is required for a claim form to be served out of the jurisdiction the permission of the court must also be obtained for service out of the jurisdiction of any other document to be served in the proceedings.

(3) Where –

  (a) the court gives permission for a claim form to be served out of the jurisdiction; and

  (b) the claim form states that particulars of claim are to follow,

  the permission of the court is not required to serve the particulars of claim out of the jurisdiction.

Proof of service

6.31   Where –

  (a) a hearing is fixed when the claim is issued;

  (b) the claim form is served on a defendant out of the jurisdiction; and

  (c) that defendant does not appear at the hearing,

  the claimant may take no further steps against that defendant until the claimant files written evidence showing that the claim form has been duly served.

PRACTICE DIRECTION – SERVICE
THIS PRACTICE DIRECTION SUPPLEMENTS CPR PART 6

Methods of service

1.1 The various methods of service are set out in rule 6.2.

1.2 The following provisions apply to the specific methods of service referred to.

Service by non-electronic means

Service by Document Exchange

2.1 Service by document exchange (DX) may take place only where:

  (1) the party's address for service[1] includes a numbered box at a DX, or

  (2) the writing paper of the party who is to be served or of his legal representative[2] sets out the DX box number, and

  (3) the party or his legal representative has not indicated in writing that they are unwilling to accept service by DX.

2.2 Service by DX is effected, unless the contrary is proved, by leaving the document addressed to the numbered box:

  (1) at the DX of the party who is to be served, or

  (2) at a DX which sends documents to that party's DX every business day.

Service by electronic means

Service by facsimile

3.1 Subject to the provisions of paragraph 3.2 below, where a document is to be served by facsimile (fax):

---

1   See rule 6.5.

2   See rule 2.3 for the definition of legal representative.

(1) the party who is to be served or his legal representative must previously have indicated in writing to the party serving –

   (a) that he is willing to accept service by fax, and

   (b) the fax number to which it should be sent.

(2) if the party on whom the document is to be served is acting by a legal representative, the fax must be sent to the legal representative's business address, and

(3) a fax number

   (a) provided in writing expressly for the purpose of accepting service where the party to be served is acting in person, or

   (b) set out on the writing paper of the legal representative of the party who is to be served, or

   (c) set out on a statement of case or a response to a claim filed with the court,

shall be taken as sufficient written indication for the purposes of paragraph 3.1(1).

3.2 A legal representative's business address must be within the jurisdiction and is the physical location of his office. Where an electronic address or identification is given in conjuction with the business address, the electronic address will be deemed to be at the business address.

3.3 Service by other electronic means may take place only where:

(1) the party serving the document and the party on whom it is to be served are both acting by legal representative,

(2) the document is served at the legal representative's business address, and

(3) the legal representative who is to be served has previously expressly indicated in writing to the party serving his willingness to accept service by this means and has provided

   (a) his e-mail address, or

   (b) other electronic identification such as an ISDN or other telephonic link number.

3.4 Where a document is served by fax or other electronic means, the party serving the document is not required in addition to send a copy by post or document exchange, but if he does not do so and the document is proved not to have been received then the court may, on any application arising out of that non-receipt, take account of the fact that a hard copy was not sent.

Service on certain individuals

Personal service on partners

4.1 Where partners are sued in the name of a partnership, service should be in accordance with rule 6.4(5) and the table set out in rule 6.5(5) where it refers to an "individual who is suing or being sued in the name of a firm".

4.2 A claim form or particulars of claim which are served by leaving them with a person at the principal or last known place of business of the partnership, must at the same time have served with them a notice as to whether that person is being served:

(1) as a partner,

(2) as a person having control or management of the partnership business, or

(3) as both.

Service on Members of H.M. Forces and United States Air Force

5 The Lord Chancellor's Office issued a memorandum on 26 July 1979 as to service on members of HM Forces and guidance notes as to service on members of the United States Air Force. The provisions annexed to this practice direction are derived from that memorandum and guidance notes.

Service generally

Personal service on a company or other corporation

6.1 Personal service on a registered company or corporation in accordance with rule 6.4(4) service is effected by leaving a document with 'a person holding a senior position'.

6.2 Each of the following persons is a person holding a senior position:

(1) in respect of a registered company or corporation, a director, the treasurer, secretary, chief executive, manager or other officer of the company or corporation, and

(2) in respect of a corporation which is not a registered company, in addition to those persons set out in (1), the mayor, chairman, president, town clerk or similar officer of the corporation.

Change of address

7   A party or his legal representative who changes his address for service shall give notice in writing of the change as soon as it has taken place to the court and every other party.

Service by the court

8.1 Where the court effects service of a document in accordance with rule 6.3(1) and (2), the method will normally be by first class post.

8.2 Where a party receives a notice of non-service of a document by the court, he should take steps to effect service of the document himself as the court is under no further duty to effect service.

Content of evidence

The following applications relating to service require evidence in support

9.1 An application for an order for service by an alternative method[3] should be supported by evidence stating:

(1) the reason an order for an alternative method of service is sought, and

(2) what steps have been taken to serve by other permitted means.

9.2 An application for service of a claim form relating to a contract on the agent of a principal who is overseas should be supported by evidence setting out:

(1) full details of the contract and that it was entered into within the jurisdiction with or through an agent who is either an individual residing or carrying on business within the jurisdiction, or a registered company or corporation having a registered office or a place of business within the jurisdiction,

(2) that the principal for whom the agent is acting was, at the time the contract was entered into and is at the time of making the application, neither an individual, registered company or corporation as described in (1) above, and

(3) why service out of the jurisdiction cannot be affected.

ANNEX

Service on Members of H.M. Forces

1.   The following information is for litigants and legal representatives who wish to serve legal documents in civil proceedings in the courts of England and Wales on parties to the proceedings who are (or who, at the material time, were) regular members of Her Majesty's Forces.

2.   The proceedings may take place in the county court or the High Court, and the documents to be served may be both originating claims, interim applications and pre-action applications. Proceedings for divorce or maintenance and proceedings in the Family Courts generally are subject to special rules as to service which are explained in a practice direction issued by the Senior District Judge of the Principal Registry on 26 June 1979.

3.   In these instructions, the person wishing to effect service is referred to as the 'claimant' and the person to be served is referred to as the 'serviceman'; the expression 'overseas' means outside the United Kingdom.

Enquiries as to address

4.   As a first step, the claimant's legal representative will need to find out where the serviceman is serving, if he does not already know. For this purpose he should write to the appropriate officer of the Ministry of Defence as specified in paragraph 10 below.

---

3   See rule 6.8.

5. The letter of enquiry should in every case show that the writer is a legal representative and that the enquiry is made solely with a view to the service of legal documents in civil proceedings.

6. In all cases the letter should give the full name, service number, rank or rating, and Ship, Arm or Trade, Regiment or Corps and Unit or as much of this information as is available. Failure to quote the service number and the rank or rating may result either in failure to identify the serviceman or in considerable delay.

7. The letter should contain an undertaking by the legal representative that, if the address is given, it will be used solely for the purpose of issuing and serving documents in the proceedings and that so far as is possible the legal representative will disclose the address only to the court and not to his client or to any other person or body. A legal representative in the service of a public authority or private company should undertake that the address will be used solely for the purpose of issuing and serving documents in the proceedings and that the address will not be disclosed so far as is possible to any other part of his employing organisation or to any other person but only to the court. Normally on receipt of the required information and undertaking the appropriate office will give the service address.

8. If the legal representative does not give the undertaking, the only information he will receive will be whether the serviceman is at that time serving in England or Wales, Scotland, Northern Ireland or overseas.

9. It should be noted that a serviceman's address which ends with a British Forces Post Office address and reference (BFPO) will nearly always indicate that he is serving overseas.

10. The letter of enquiry should be addressed as follows:

(a) *Royal Navy Officers*
The Naval Secretary
Room 161
Victory Building
HM Naval Base
Portsmouth
Hants PO1 3LS

RN Ratings
Commodore Naval Drafting
Centurion Building
Grange Road
Gosport
Hants PO13 9XA

RN Medical and Dental Officers
The Medical Director General
(Naval)
Room 114
Victory Building
HM Naval Base
Portsmouth
Hants PO1 3LS
Officers of Queen Alexandra's Royal Naval Nursing Service
The Matron-in-Chief
QARNNS
Room 139
Victory Building
HM Naval Base
Portsmouth
Hants PO1 3LS

Naval Chaplains
Director General Naval
Chaplaincy Service
Room 201
Victory Building
HM Naval Base
Portsmouth
Hants PO1 3LS

(b) *Royal Marine Officers and Ranks*
Personnel Section
West Battery
Whale Island
Portsmouth
Hants PO2 8DX

RM Ranks HQRM
(DRORM)
West Battery
Whale Island
Portsmouth
Hants PO2 8DX

(c) *Army Officers and other ranks*
Ministry of Defence
Army Personnel Centre
Secretariat, Public Enquiries
RM CD424
Kentigern House
65 Brown Street
Glasgow G2 8EH

(d) *Royal Air Force Officers and Other Ranks.*
Personnel Management Agency (RAF)
Building 248
RAF Innsworth
Gloucester GL3 1EZ

Assistance in serving documents on servicemen

11. Once the claimant's legal representative has learnt the serviceman's address, he may use that address as the address for service by post, in cases where this method of service is allowed by the Civil Procedure Rules. There are, however, some situations in which service of the proceedings, whether in the High Court or in the county court, has to be effected personally; in these cases an appointment will have to be sought, through the Commanding Officer of the Unit, Establishment or Ship concerned, for the purpose of effecting service. The procedure for obtaining an appointment is described below, and it applies whether personal service is to be effected by the claimant's legal representative or his agent or by a court bailiff, or, in the case of proceedings served overseas (with the leave of the court) through the British Consul or the foreign judicial authority.

12. The procedure for obtaining an appointment to effect personal service is by application to the Commanding Officer of the Unit, Establishment or Ship in which the serviceman is serving. The Commanding Officer may grant permission for the document server to enter the Unit, Establishment or Ship but if this is not appropriate he may offer arrangements for the

serviceman to attend at a place in the vicinity of the Unit, Establishment or Ship in order that he may be served. If suitable arrangements cannot be made the legal representative will have evidence that personal service is impracticable, which may be useful in an application for service by an alternative method.

General

13. Subject to the procedure outlined in paragraphs 11 and 12, there are no special arrangements to assist in the service of process when a serviceman is outside the United Kingdom. The appropriate office will however give an approximate date when the serviceman is likely to return to the United Kingdom.

14. It sometimes happens that a serviceman has left the service by the time that the enquiry is made. If the claimant's legal representative confirms that the proceedings result from an occurrence when the serviceman was in the Forces and he gives the undertaking referred to in paragraph 7, the last known private address after discharge will normally be provided. In no other case however will the Department disclose the private address of a member of H.M. Forces.

Service on members of United States Air Force

15. In addition to the information contained in the memorandum of 26 July 1979, the Lord Chancellor's Office, some doubts having been expressed as to the correct procedure to be followed by persons having civil claims against members of the United States Air Force in this country, issued the following notes for guidance with the approval of the appropriate United States authorities:

16. Instructions have been issued by the U.S. authorities to the commanding officers of all their units in this country that every facility is to be given for the service of documents in civil proceedings on members of the U.S. Air Force. The proper course to be followed by a creditor or other person having a claim against a member of the U.S. Air Force is for him to communicate with the commanding officer or, where the unit concerned has a legal officer, with the legal officer of the defendant's unit requesting him to provide facilities for the service of documents on the defendant. It is not possible for the U.S. authorities to act as arbitrators when a civil claim is made against a member of their forces. It is, therefore, essential that the claim should either be admitted by the defendant or judgment should be obtained on it, whether in the High Court or a county court. If a claim has been admitted or judgment has been obtained and the claimant has failed to obtain satisfaction within a reasonable period, his proper course is then to write to: Office of the Staff Judge Advocate, Headquarters, Third Air Force, R.A.F. Mildenhall, Suffolk, enclosing a copy of the defendant's written admission of the claim or, as the case may be, a copy of the judgment. Steps will then be taken by the Staff Judge Advocate to ensure that the matter is brought to the defendant's attention with a view to prompt satisfaction of the claim.

PRACTICE DIRECTION – SERVICE OUT OF THE JURISDICTION

THIS PRACTICE DIRECTION SUPPLEMENTS SECTION III OF PART 6

Service out of the jurisdiction where permission of the Court is not required

1.1 The usual form of words of the statement required by Rule 6.19(3) should be:–

"I state that the High Court of England and Wales has power under the Civil Jurisdiction and Judgments Act 1982 to hear this claim and that no proceedings are pending between the parties in Scotland, Northern Ireland or another Convention territory of any contracting state as defined by section 1(3) of the Act".

1.2 However, in proceedings to which Rule 6.19(1)(b)(ii) applies, the statement should be:–

"I state that the High Court of England and Wales has power under the Civil Jurisdiction and Judgments Act 1982, the claim having as its object rights in rem in immovable property or tenancies in immovable property (or otherwise in accordance with the provisions of Article 16 of Schedule 1, 3C or 4 to that Act) to which Article 16 of Schedule 1, 3C or 4 to that Act applies, to hear the claim and that no proceedings are pending between the parties in Scotland, Northern Ireland or another Convention territory of any contracting state as defined by Section 1(3) of the Act".

1.3 And in proceedings to which Rule 6.19(1)(b)(iii) applies, the statement should be:–

"I state that the High Court of England and Wales has power under the Civil Jurisdiction and Judgments Act 1982, the defendant being a party to an agreement conferring jurisdiction to which Article 17 of Schedule 1, 3C or 4 to that Act applies, to hear the claim and that no proceedings are pending between the parties in Scotland, Northern Ireland or another Convention territory of any contracting state as defined by Section 1(3) of the Act".

1.4 A claim form appearing to be for service on a defendant under the provisions of Rule 6.19 which does not include a statement in the form of 1.1, 1.2 or 1.3 above will be marked on issue "Not for service out of the jurisdiction".

1.5 Where a claim form is served without particulars of claim, it must be accompanied by a copy of Form N1C (notes for defendants).

Service out of the jurisdiction where permission is required

Documents to be filed under Rule 6.26(2)(d)

2.1 A complete set of the following documents must be provided for each party to be served out of the jurisdiction

(1) A copy of particulars of claim if not already incorporated in or attached to the claim.

(2) A duplicate of the claim form of the particulars of claim and of any documents accompanying the claim and of any translation required by Rule 6.28.

(3) Forms for responding to the claim;

(4) Any translation required under Rule 6.28 and paragraphs 4.1 and 4.2, in duplicate.

2.2 The documents to be served in certain countries require legalisation and the Foreign Process Section (Room E02), Royal Courts of Justice will advise on request. Some countries require legislation and some require a formal letter of request, see Form No. 34 to Table 2 of Practice Direction to Part 4 which must be signed by the Senior Master of the Queen's Bench Division irrespective of the Division of the High Court or any county court in which the order was made.

Service in Scotland, Northern Ireland, the Channel Islands, the Isle of Man, Commonwealth countries, United Kingdom Overseas Territories and the Republic of Ireland

3.1 The requirements of Section III of Part 6, do not apply to the countries listed in Rule 6.25(4) and service should be effected by the claimant or his agent direct except in the case of a Commonwealth State where the judicial authorities have required service to be in accordance with Rule 6.24(1)(b)(i). These are presently Malta and Singapore.

3.2 For the purposes of Rule 6.25(4)(c), the following countries are United Kingdom Overseas Territories:–

(a) Anguilla;

(b) Bermuda;

(c) British Antarctic Territory

(d) British Indian Ocean Territory

(e) Cayman Islands;

(f) Falklands Islands and Dependencies;

(g) Gibraltar;

(h) Monserrat;

(i) Pitcairn, Henderson, Ducie and Oeno;

(j) St. Helena and Dependencies;

(k) South Georgia and South Sandwich Islands;

(l) Sovereign Base Areas of Akrotiri and Dhekalia;

(m) Turks and Caicos Islands; and

(n) Virgin Islands.

Translations

4.1 Rule 6.28 applies to particulars of claim not included in a claim form as well as to claim forms.

4.2 Where a translation of a claim form is required under Rule 6.28, the claimant must also file a translation of all the forms that will accompany the claim form.

(It should be noted that English is not an official language in the Province of Quebec).

Service with the permission of the Court under certain Acts

5.1 Rule 6.20(18) provides that a claim form may be served out of the jurisdiction with the Court's permission if the claim is made under an enactment specified in the relevant Practice Direction.

5.2 These enactments are:

(1) The Nuclear Installations Act 1965,

(2) The Social Security Contributions and Benefits Act 1992,

(3) The Directive of the Council of the European Communities dated 15 March 1976 No. 76/308/EEC, where service is to be effected in a member state of the European Union,

(4) The Drug Trafficking Offences Act 1994,

(5) The Financial Services Act 1986,

(6) The Banking Act 1987,

(7) Part VI of the Criminal Justice Act 1988,

(8) The Immigration (Carriers' Liability) Act 1987.

5.3 Under the State Immunity Act 1978, the foreign state being served is allowed an additional two months over the normal period for filing an acknowledgment of service or defence or for filing or serving an admission allowed under paragraphs 7.3 and 7.4.

Service of petitions, application notices and orders

6.1 The provisions of Section III of Part 6 (special provisions about service out of the jurisdiction) apply to service out of the jurisdiction of a petition, application notice or order.

(Rule 6.30(1) contains special provisions relating to application notices).

6.2 Where an application notice is to be served out of the jurisdiction in accordance with Section III of Part 6 the Court must have regard to the country in which the application notice is to be served in setting the date for the hearing of the application and giving any direction about service of the respondent's evidence.

6.3 Where the permission of the Court is required for a claim form to be served out of the jurisdiction the permission of the Court, unless rule 6.30(3) applies, must also be obtained for service out of the jurisdiction of any other document to be served in the proceedings and the provisions of this Practice Direction will, so far as applicable to that other document, apply.

6.4 When particulars of claim are served out of the jurisdiction any statement as to the period for responding to the claim contained in any of the forms required by Rule 7.8 to accompany the particulars of claim must specify the period prescribed under Rule 6.22 or 6.23 or (as the case may be) by the order permitting service out of the jurisdiction (see Rule 6.21(4)).

Period for responding to a claim form

7.1 Where a claim form has been served out of the jurisdiction without permission under Rule 6.19 –

(1) Rule 6.22 sets out the period for filing an acknowledgment of service or filing or serving an admission;

(2) Rule 6.23 sets out the period for filing a defence.

7.2 Where an order grants permission to serve a claim form out of the jurisdiction, the periods within which the defendant may –

(1) file an acknowledgment of service

(2) file or serve an admission;

(3) file a defence

will be calculated in accordance with paragraphs 7.3 and 7.4 having regard to the Table below.

(Rule 6.21(4) requires an order giving permission for a claim form to be served out of the jurisdiction to specify the period within which the defendant may respond to the claim form).

7.3 The period for filing an acknowledgment of service under Part 10 or filing or serving an admission under Part 14 is –

(1) where the defendant is served with a claim form which states that particulars of claim are to follow, the number of days listed in the Table after service of the particulars of claim; and

(2) in any other case, the number of days listed in the Table after service of the claim form.

For example: where a defendant has been served with a claim form (accompanied by particulars of claim) in the Bahamas, the period for acknowledging service or admitting the claim is 22 days after service.

7.4 The period for filing a defence under Part 15 is –

(1) the number of days listed in the Table after service of the particulars of claim, or

(2) where the defendant has filed an acknowledgment of service, the number of days listed in the Table plus an additional 14 days after the service of the particulars of claim.

For example, where a defendant has been served with particulars of claim in Gibraltar and has acknowledged service, the period for filing a defence is 45 days after service of the particulars of claim.

Period for responding to an application notice

8.1 Where an application notice or order needs to be served out of the jurisdiction, the period for responding to service is 7 days less than the number of days listed in the Table.

Civil Jurisdiction and Judgment Act 1982

9.1 The following countries are parties to this Act:–

Austria	Italy
Belgium	Luxembourg
Denmark	Netherlands
France	Norway
Finland	Portugal
Germany	Scotland
Gibraltar	Spain
Greece	Switzerland
Iceland	Sweden
Ireland	

Address for service and further information

10.1 A defendant is required by Rule 6.5(2) to give an address for service within the jurisdiction.

10.2 Further information concerning service out of the jurisdiction can be obtained from the Foreign Process Section, Room E02, Royal Courts of Justice, Strand, London WC2A 2LL (telephone 020 7936 6691).

Table

Place or country	Number of days
Abu Dhabi	22
Afghanistan	23
Albania	25
Algeria	22
Angola	22
Anguilla	31
Antigua	23
Antilles (Netherlands)	31
Argentina	22

Armenia	21
Ascension	31
Australia	25
Austria	21
Azores	23
Bahamas	22
Bahrain	22
Balearic Islands	21
Bangladesh	23
Barbados	23
Belarus	21
Belgium	21
Belize	23
Benin	25
Bermuda	31
Bhutan	28
Bolivia	23
Bosnia–Hercegovina	21
Botswana	23
Brazil	22
Brunei	25
Bulgaria	23
Burkina Faso	23
Burma	23
Burundi	22
Cameroon	22
Canada	22
Canary Islands	22
Cape Verde Islands	25
Caroline Islands	31
Cayman Islands	31
Central African Republic	25
Chad	25
Chile	22
China	24
Christmas Island	27
Cocos (Keeling) Islands	41
Colombia	22
Comoros	23
Congo (People's Republic)	25
Corsica	21
Costa Rica	23
Croatia	21
Cuba	24
Cyprus	31
Cyrenaica (see Libya)	21
Czech Republic	21
Denmark	21
Djibouti	22
Dominica	23
Dominican Republic	23

Dubai	22
Ecuador	22
Egypt (Arab Republic)	22
El Salvador (Republic of)	25
Equatorial Guinea	23
Estonia	21
Ethiopia	22
Falkland Islands and Dependencies	31
Faroe Islands	31
Fiji	23
Finland	24
France	21
French Guiana	31
French Polynesia	31
French West Indies	31
Gabon	25
Gambia	22
Georgia	21
Germany	21
Ghana	22
Gibraltar	31
Greece	21
Greenland	31
Grenada	24
Guatemala	24
Guernsey	18
Guyana	22
Haiti	23
Holland (Netherlands)	21
Honduras	24
Hong Kong	31
Hungary	22
Iceland	22
India	23
Indonesia	22
Iran	22
Iraq	22
Ireland (Republic of)	21
Ireland (Northern)	21
Isle of Man	18
Israel	22
Italy	21
Ivory Coast	22
Jamaica	22
Japan	23
Jersey	18
Jordan	23
Kampuchea	38
Kazakhstan	21
Kenya	22
Kirgizstan	21

Korea (North)	28
Korea (South)	24
Kuwait	22
Laos	30
Latvia	21
Lebanon	22
Lesotho	23
Liberia	22
Libya	21
Liechtenstein	21
Lithuania	21
Luxembourg	21
Macau	31
Macedonia	21
Madagascar	23
Madeira	31
Malawi	23
Malaya	24
Maldive Islands	26
Mali	25
Malta	21
Mariana Islands	26
Marshall Islands	32
Mauritania	23
Mauritius	22
Mexico	23
Moldova	21
Monaco	21
Montserrat	31
Morocco	22
Mozambique	23
Nauru Island	36
Nepal	23
Netherlands	21
Nevis	24
New Caledonia	31
New Hebrides (now Vanuatu)	29
New Zealand	26
New Zealand Island Territories	50
Nicaragua	24
Niger (Republic of)	25
Nigeria	22
Norfolk Island	31
Norway	21
Oman (Sultanate of)	22
Pakistan	23
Panama (Republic of)	26
Papua New Guinea	26
Paraguay	22
Peru	22
Philippines	23

Pitcairn Island	31
Poland	21
Portugal	21
Portuguese Timor	31
Puerto Rico	23
Qatar	23
Reunion	31
Romania	22
Russia	21
Rwanda	23
Sabah	23
St. Helena	31
St. Kitts—Nevis	24
St. Lucia	24
St. Pierre and Miquelon	31
St. Vincent and the Grenadines	24
Samoa (U.S.A. Territory) (See also Western Samoa)	30
Sarawak	28
Saudi Arabia	24
Scotland	21
Senegal	22
Seychelles	22
Sharjah	24
Sierra Leone	22
Singapore	22
Slovakia	21
Slovenia	21
Society Islands	31
(French Polynesia) Solomon Islands	29
Somali Democratic Republic	22
South Africa (Republic of)	22
South Georgia (Falkland Island Dependencies)	31
South Orkneys	21
South Shetlands	21
Spain	21
Spanish Territories of North Africa	31
Sri Lanka	23
Sudan	22
Suriname	22
Swaziland	22
Sweden	21
Switzerland	21
Syria	23
Taiwan	23
Tajikistan	21
Tanzania	22
Thailand	23
Tibet	34
Tobago	23
Togo	22
Tonga	30

Tortola	31
Trinidad and Tobago	23
Tristan Da Cunha	31
Tunisia	22
Turkey	21
Turkmenistan	21
Turks and Caicos Islands	31
Uganda	22
Ukraine	21
United States of America	22
Uruguay	22
Uzbekistan	21
Vanuatu	29
Vatican City State	21
Venezuela	22
Vietnam	28
Virgin Islands – British (Tortola)	31
Virgin Islands – U.S.A	24
Wake Island	25
Western Samoa	34
Yemen (Republic of)	30
Yugoslavia (except for Bosnia-Hercegovina Croatia Macedonia and Slovenia)	21
Zaire	25
Zambia	23
Zimbabwe	22

PART 7

HOW TO START PROCEEDINGS – THE CLAIM FORM

Contents of this Part

Where to start proceedings

7.1   Restrictions on where proceedings may be started are set out in the relevant practice direction.

How to start proceedings

7.2 (1) Proceedings are started when the court issues a claim form at the request of the claimant.

(2) A claim form is issued on the date entered on the form by the court.

(A person who seeks a remedy from the court before proceedings are started or in relation to proceedings which are taking place, or will take place, in another jurisdiction must make an application under Part 23)

(Part 16 sets out what the claim form must include)

Right to use one claim form to start two or more claims

7.3　A claimant may use a single claim form to start all claims which can be conveniently disposed of in the same proceedings.

Particulars of claim

7.4 (1) Particulars of claim must –

(a) be contained in or served with the claim form; or

(b) subject to paragraph (2) be served on the defendant by the claimant within 14 days after service of the claim form.

(2) Particulars of claim must be served on the defendant no later than the latest time for serving a claim form.

(Rule 7.5 sets out the latest time for serving a claim form)

(3) Where the claimant serves particulars of claim separately from the claim form in accordance with paragraph (1)(b), he must, within 7 days of service on the defendant, file a copy of the particulars together with a certificate of service.

(Part 16 sets out what the particulars of claim must include)

(Part 22 requires particulars of claim to be verified by a statement of truth)

(Rule 6.10 makes provision for a certificate of service)

Service of a claim form

7.5 (1) After a claim form has been issued, it must be served on the defendant.

(2) The general rule is that a claim form must be served within 4 months after the date of issue.

(3) The period for service is 6 months where the claim form is to be served out of the jurisdiction.

Extension of time for serving a claim form

7.6 (1) The claimant may apply for an order extending the period within which the claim form may be served.

(2) The general rule is that an application to extend the time for service must be made –

(a) within the period for serving the claim form specified by rule 7.5; or

(b) where an order has been made under this rule, within the period for service specified by that order.

(3) If the claimant applies for an order to extend the time for service of the claim form after the end of the period specified by rule 7.5 or by an order made under this rule, the court may make such an order only if –

(a) the court has been unable to serve the claim form; or

(b) the claimant has taken all reasonable steps to serve the claim form but has been unable to do so; and

(c) in either case, the claimant has acted promptly in making the application.

(4) An application for an order extending the time for service –

    (a) must be supported by evidence; and

    (b) may be made without notice.

Application by defendant for service of claim form

7.7 (1) Where a claim form has been issued against a defendant, but has not yet been served on him, the defendant may serve a notice on the claimant requiring him to serve the claim form or discontinue the claim within a period specified in the notice.

(2) The period specified in a notice served under paragraph (1) must be at least 14 days after service of the notice.

(3) If the claimant fails to comply with the notice, the court may, on the application of the defendant –

    (a) dismiss the claim; or

    (b) make any other order it thinks just.

Form for defence etc must be served with particulars of claim

7.8 (1) When particulars of claim are served on a defendant, whether they are contained in the claim form, served with it or served subsequently, they must be accompanied by –

    (a) a form for defending the claim;

    (b) a form for admitting the claim; and

    (c) a form for acknowledging service.

(2) Where the claimant is using the procedure set out in Part 8 (alternative procedure for claims) –

    (a) paragraph (1) does not apply; and

    (b) a form for acknowledging service must accompany the claim form.

Fixed date and other claims

7.9   A practice direction –

    (a) may set out the circumstances in which the court may give a fixed date for a hearing when it issues a claim;

    (b) may list claims in respect of which there is a specific claim form for use and set out the claim form in question; and

    (c) may disapply or modify these Rules as appropriate in relation to the claims referred to in paragraphs (a) and (b).

Production centre for claims

7.10(1) There shall be a Production Centre for the issue of claim forms and other related matters.

(2) The relevant practice direction makes provision for –

    (a) which claimants may use the Production Centre;

    (b) the type of claims which the Production Centre may issue;

    (c) the functions which are to be discharged by the Production Centre;

    (d) the place where the Production Centre is to be located; and

    (e) other related matters.

(3) The relevant practice direction may disapply or modify these Rules as appropriate in relation to claims issued by the Production Centre.

PRACTICE DIRECTION –
HOW TO START PROCEEDINGS – THE CLAIM FORM
THIS PRACTICE DIRECTION SUPPLEMENTS CPR PART 7

General

1 Subject to the following provisions of this practice direction, proceedings which both the High Court and the county courts have jurisdiction to deal with may be started in the High Court or in a county court.

Where to start proceedings

2.1 Proceedings (whether for damages or for a specified sum) may not be started in the High Court unless the value of the claim is more than £15,000.

2.2 Proceedings which include a claim for damages in respect of personal injuries must not be started in the High Court unless the value of the claim is £50,000 or more (paragraph 9 of the High Court and County Courts Jurisdiction Order 1991 (S.I. 1991/724 as amended) describes how the value of a claim is to be determined).

2.3 A claim must be issued in the High Court or a county court if an enactment so requires.

2.4 Subject to paragraphs 2.1 and 2.2 above, a claim should be started in the High Court if by reason of:

(1) the financial value of the claim and the amount in dispute, and/or

(2) the complexity of the facts, legal issues, remedies or procedures involved, and/or

(3) the importance of the outcome of the claim to the public in general,

the claimant believes that the claim ought to be dealt with by a High Court judge.

(CPR Part 30 and the practice direction supplementing Part 30 contain provisions relating to the transfer to the county court of proceedings started in the High Court and vice-versa.)

2.5 A claim relating to Chancery business (which includes any of the matters specified in paragraph 1 of Schedule 1 to the Supreme Court Act 1981) may, subject to any enactment, rule or practice direction, be dealt with in the High Court or in a county court. The claim form should, if issued in the High Court, be marked in the top right hand corner 'Chancery Division' and, if issued in the county court, be marked 'Chancery Business'.

(For the equity jurisdiction of county courts, see section 23 of the County Courts Act 1984.)

2.6 A claim relating to any of the matters specified in sub-paragraphs (a) and (b) of paragraph 2 of Schedule 1 to the Supreme Court Act 1981 must be dealt with in the High Court and will be assigned to the Queen's Bench Division.

2.7 Practice directions which supplement CPR Part 49 (Specialist Proceedings) will contain provisions relating to the commencement and conduct of the specialist proceedings listed in that Part.

2.8 A claim in the High Court for which a jury trial is directed will, if not already being dealt with in the Queen's Bench Division, be transferred to that Division.

2.9 The following proceedings may not be started in a county court unless the parties have agreed otherwise in writing:

(1) a claim for damages or other remedy for libel or slander, and

(2) a claim in which the title to any toll, fair, market or franchise is in question.

The claim form

3.1 A claimant must use practice form N1 or practice form N208 (the Part 8 claim form) to start a claim (but see paragraphs 3.2 and 3.4 below).

3.2 Rule 7.9 deals with fixed date claims and rule 7.10 deals with the Production Centre for the issue of claims; there are separate practice directions supplementing rules 7.9 and 7.10.

3.3 If a claimant wishes his claim to proceed under Part 8, or if the claim is required to proceed under Part 8, the claim form should so state. Otherwise the claim will proceed under Part 7. But note that in respect of claims in specialist proceedings (listed in CPR Part 49) and claims brought under the RSC or CCR set out in the Schedule to the CPR (see CPR Part 50) the CPR will apply only to the extent that they are not inconsistent with the rules and practice directions that expressly apply to those claims.

3.4 To commence specialist proceedings (listed in CPR Part 49) it may be necessary to use the practice form approved for that purpose by the practice direction relating to the specialist proceedings in question. Reference should be made to that practice direction.

3.5 Where a claim which is to be served out of the jurisdiction is one which the court has power to deal with under the Civil Jurisdiction and Judgments Act 1982, the claim form and, when they are contained in a separate document, the particulars of claim should be endorsed with a statement that the court has power under that Act to deal with the claim and that no proceedings based on the same claim are pending between the parties in Scotland, Northern Ireland or another Convention territory[1].

3.6 If a claim for damages or for an unspecified sum is started in the High Court, the claim form must:

(1) state that the claimant expects to recover more than £15,000 (or £50,000 or more if the claim is for personal injuries) or

(2) state that some enactment provides that the claim may only be commenced in the High Court and specify that enactment or

(3) state that the claim is to be in one of the specialist High Court lists (see CPR Part 49) and specify that list.

3.7 If the contents of a claim form commencing specialist proceedings complies with the requirements of the specialist list in question the claim form will also satisfy paragraph 3.6 above.

3.8 If a claim for damages for personal injuries is started in the county court, the claim form must state whether or not the claimant expects to recover more than £1,000 in respect of pain, suffering and loss of amenity.

3.9 If a claim for housing disrepair which includes a claim for an order requiring repairs or other work to be carried out by the landlord is started in the county court, the claim form must state:

(1) whether or not the cost of the repairs or other work is estimated to be more than £1,000, and

(2) whether or not the claimant expects to recover more than £1,000 in respect of any claim for damages[2]. If either of the amounts mentioned in (1) and (2) is more than £1,000, the small claims track will not be the normal track for that claim.

Title of proceedings

4.1 The claim form and every other statement of case, must be headed with the title of the proceedings. The title should state:

(1) the number of proceedings,

(2) the court or Division in which they are proceeding,

(3) the full name of each party,

(4) his status in the proceedings (ie. claimant/defendant).

4.2 Where there is more than one claimant and/or more than one defendant, the parties should be described in the title as follows:-

(1) AB

(2) CD

(3) EF Claimants and

(1) GH

(2) IJ

(3) KL Defendants

---

1 'Convention territory' means the territory or territories of any Contracting State as defined by S.1(3) of the Civil Jurisdiction and Judgments Act 1982, to which the Brussels Conventions or Lugano Convention apply.

2 See rules 16.3(4) and 26.6.

[3 and 4 *Authors' note: Footnotes 3 and 4 seem to be missing from the printed version.*]

Start of proceedings

5.1 Proceedings are started when the court issues a claim form at the request of the claimant (see rule 7.2) but where the claim form as issued was received in the court office on a date earlier than the date on which it was issued by the court, the claim is 'brought' for the purposes of the Limitation Act 1980 and any other relevant statute on that earlier date.

5.2 The date on which the claim form was received by the court will be recorded by a date stamp either on the claim form held on the court file or on the letter that accompanied the claim form when it was received by the court.

5.3 An enquiry as to the date on which the claim form was received by the court should be directed to a court officer.

5.4 Parties proposing to start a claim which is approaching the expiry of the limitation period should recognise the potential importance of establishing the date the claim form was received by the court and should themselves make arrangements to record the date.

5.5 Where it is sought to start proceedings against the estate of a deceased defendant where probate or letters of administration have not been granted, the claimant should issue the claim against 'the personal representatives of A.B. deceased'. The claimant should then, before the expiry of the period for service of the claim form, apply to the court for the appointment of a person to represent the estate of the deceased.

Particulars of claim

6.1 Where the claimant does not include the particulars of claim in the claim form, particulars of claim may be served separately:

(1) either at the same time as the claim form, or

(2) within 14 days after service of the claim form provided that the service of the particulars of claim is within 4 months after the date of issue of the claim form[5] (or 6 months where the claim form is to be served out of the jurisdiction[6]).

6.2 If the particulars of claim are not included in or have not been served with the claim form, the claim form must contain a statement that particulars of claim will follow[7].

(These paragraphs do not apply where the Part 8 procedure is being used. For information on matters to be included in the claim form or the particulars of claim, see Part 16 (statements of case) and the practice direction which supplements it.)

Statement of truth

7.1 Part 22 requires the claim form and, where they are not included in the claim form, the particulars of claim, to be verified by a statement of truth.

7.2 The form of the statement of truth is as follows: '[I believe][the claimant believes] that the facts stated in [this claim form] [these particulars of claim] are true.'

7.3 Attention is drawn to rule 32.14 which sets out the consequences of verifying a statement of case containing a false statement without an honest belief in its truth.

(For information regarding statements of truth see Part 22 and the practice direction which supplements it.)

Extension of time

8.1 An application under rule 7.6 (for an extension of time for serving a claim form under rule 7.6(1)) must be made in accordance with Part 23 and supported by evidence.

8.2 The evidence should state:

(1) all the circumstances relied on,

(2) the date of issue of the claim,

---

5 See rules 7.4(2) and 7.5(2).
6 See rule 7.5(3).
7 See rule 16.2(2).

(3) the expiry date of any rule 7.6 extension, and

(4) a full explanation as to why the claim has not been served.

(For information regarding (1) written evidence see Part 32 and the practice direction which supplements it and (2) service of the claim form see Part 6 and the practice direction which supplements it.)

PRACTICE DIRECTION – CONSUMER CREDIT ACT CLAIM
THIS PRACTICE DIRECTION SUPPLEMENTS CPR RULE 7.9

1.1 In this practice direction 'the Act' means the Consumer Credit Act 1974, a section referred to by number means the section with that number in the Act, and expressions which are defined in the Act have the same meaning in this practice direction as they have in the Act.

1.2 'Consumer Credit Act procedure' means the procedure set out in this practice direction.

When to use the Consumer Credit Act procedure

2.1 A claimant must use the Consumer Credit Act procedure where he makes a claim under a provision of the Act to which paragraph 3 of this practice direction applies.

2.2 Where a claimant is using the Consumer Credit Act procedure the CPR are modified to the extent that they are inconsistent with the procedure set out in this practice direction.

2.3 The court may at any stage order the claim to continue as if the claimant had not used the Consumer Credit Act procedure, and if it does so the court may give any directions it considers appropriate.

2.4 This practice direction also sets out matters which must be included in the particulars of claim in certain types of claim, and restrictions on where certain types of claim may be started.

The provisions of the Act

3.1 Subject to paragraph 3.2 and 3.3 this practice direction applies to claims made under the following provisions of the Act:

(1) section 141 (claim by the creditor to enforce regulated agreement relating to goods etc),

(2) section 129 (claim by debtor or hirer for a time order),

(3) section 90 (creditor's claim for an order for recovery of protected goods),

(4) section 92(1) (creditor's or owner's claim to enter premises to take possession of goods),

(5) section 139(a) (debtor's claim for a credit agreement to be reopened as extortionate), and

(6) creditor's or owner's claim for a court order to enforce a regulated agreement relating to goods or money where the court order is required by –

   (a) section 65(1) (improperly-executed agreement),

   (b) section 86(2) of the Act (death of debtor or hirer where agreement is partly secured or unsecured),

   (c) section 111(2) (default notice etc not served on surety),

   (d) section 124(1) or (2) (taking of a negotiable instrument in breach of terms of section 123), or

   (e) section 105(7)(a) or (b) (security not expressed in writing, or improperly executed).

3.2 This practice direction does not apply to any claim made under the provisions listed in paragraph 3.1 above if that claim relates to the recovery of land.

(Provisions governing the procedure for such claims can be found in CPR Schedule 2, CCR Order 49 r. 4 and related rules about the matters to be included in the particulars of claim can be found in CPR Schedule 2, CCR Order 6.)

3.3 This practice direction also does not apply to a claim made by the creditor under section 141 of the Act to enforce a regulated agreement where the agreement relates only to money. Such a claim must be started by the issue of a Part 7 claim form.

Restrictions on where to start some Consumer Credit Act claims

4.1 Where the claim includes a claim to recover goods to which a regulated hire purchase agreement or conditional sale agreement relates, it may only be started in the county court for the district in which the debtor, or one of the debtors:

(1) resides or carries on business, or

(2) resided or carried on business at the date when the defendant last made a payment under the agreement.

4.2 In any other claim to recover goods, the claim may only be started in the court for the district:

(1) in which the defendant, or one of the defendants, resides or carries on business, or

(2) in which the goods are situated.

4.3 A claim of a debtor or hirer for an order under section 129(1)(b) of the Act (a time order) may only be started in the court where the claimant resides or carries on business.

(Costs rule 45.1(2)(b) allows the claimant to recover fixed costs in certain circumstances where such a claim is made.)

(Paragraph 7 sets out the matters the claimant must include in his particulars of claim where he is using the Consumer Credit Act procedure.)

The Consumer Credit Act procedure

5.1 In the types of claim to which paragraph 3 applies the court will fix a hearing date on the issue of the claim form.

5.2 The particulars of claim must be served with the claim form.

5.3 Where a claimant is using the Consumer Credit Act procedure, the defendant to the claim is not required to:

(1) serve an acknowledgment of service, or

(2) file a defence, although he may choose to do so.

5.4 Where a defendant intends to defend a claim, his defence should be filed within 14 days of service of the particulars of claim. If the defendant fails to file a defence within this period, but later relies on it, the court may take such a failure into account as a factor when deciding what order to make about costs.

5.5 Part 12 (default judgment) does not apply where the claimant is using the Consumer Credit Act procedure.

5.6 Each party must be given at least 28 days' notice of the hearing date.

5.7 Where the claimant serves the claim form, he must serve notice of the hearing date at the same time, unless the hearing date is specified in the claim form.

Powers of the court at the hearing

6.1 On the hearing date the court may dispose of the claim.

6.2 If the court does not dispose of the claim on the hearing date:

(1) if the defendant has filed a defence, the court will:

(a) allocate the claim to a track and give directions about the management of the case, or

(b) give directions to enable it to allocate the claim to a track,

(2) if the defendant has not filed a defence, the court may make any order or give any direction it considers appropriate.

6.3 Rule 26.5 (3) to (5) and rules 26.6 to 26.10 apply to the allocation of a claim under paragraph 6.2.

Matters which must be included in the particulars of claim

7.1 Where the Consumer Credit Act procedure is used, the claimant must state in his particulars of claim that the claim is a Consumer Credit Act claim.

7.2 A claimant making a claim for the delivery of goods to enforce a hire purchase agreement or conditional sale agreement which is:

(1) a regulated agreement for the recovery of goods, and

(2) let to a person other than a company or other corporation, must also state (in this order) in his particulars of claim:

    (a) the date of the agreement,

    (b) the parties to the agreement,

    (c) the number or other identification of the agreement (with enough information to allow the debtor to identify the agreement),

    (d) where the claimant was not one of the original parties to the agreement, the means by which the rights and duties of the creditor passed to him,

    (e) the place where the agreement was signed by the defendant (if known),

    (f) the goods claimed,

    (g) the total price of the goods,

    (h) the paid up sum,

    (i) the unpaid balance of the total price,

    (j) whether a default notice or a notice under section 76(1) or section 88(1) of the Act has been served on the defendant, and, if it has, the date and the method of service,

    (k) the date on which the right to demand delivery of the goods accrued,

    (l) the amount (if any) claimed as an alternative to the delivery of goods, and

    (m) the amount (if any) claimed in addition to –

        (i) the delivery of the goods, or

        (ii) any claim under sub paragraph (l) above with the grounds of each such claim.

7.3 A claimant who is a debtor or hirer making a claim for an order under section 129(1)(b) of the Act (a time order) must state (in the following order) in his particulars of claim:

    (1) the date of the agreement,

    (2) the parties to the agreement,

    (3) the number or other means of identifying the agreement,

    (4) details of any sureties,

    (5) if the defendant is not one of the original parties to the agreement then the name of the original party to the agreement,

    (6) the names and addresses of the persons intended to be served with the claim form,

    (7) the place where the claimant signed the agreement,

    (8) details of the notice served by the creditor or owner giving rise to the claim for the time order,

    (9) the total unpaid balance the claimant admits is due under the agreement, and –

        (a) the amount of any arrears (if known), and

        (b) the amount and frequency of the payments specified in the agreement, (10) the claimant's proposals for payments of any arrears and of future instalments together with details of his means;

    (11) where the claim relates to a breach of the agreement other than for the payment of money the claimant's proposals for remedying it.

7.4 (1) This paragraph applies where a claimant is required to obtain a court order to enforce a regulated agreement by:

    (a) section 65(1) (improperly-executed agreement),

    (b) section 105(7)(a) or (b) (security not expressed in writing, or improperly-executed),

    (c) section 111(2) (default notice etc. not served on surety),

    (d) section 124(1) or (2) (taking of a negotiable instrument in breach of terms of section 123), or

    (e) section 86(2) of the Act (death of debtor or hirer where agreement is partly secured or unsecured).

    (2) The claimant must state in his particulars of claim what the circumstances are that require him to obtain a court order for enforcement.

Admission of certain claims for recovery of goods under regulated agreements

8.1 In a claim to recover goods to which section 90(1)[1] applies:

(1) the defendant may admit the claim, and

(2) offer terms on which a return order should be suspended under section 135(1)(b).

8.2 He may do so by filing a request in practice form N9C.

8.3 He should do so within the period for making an admission specified in rule 14.2(b). If the defendant fails to file his request within this period, and later makes such a request, the court may take the failure into account as a factor when deciding what order to make about costs.

8.4 On receipt of the admission, the court will serve a copy on the claimant.

8.5 The claimant may obtain judgment by filing a request in practice form N228.

8.6 On receipt of the request for judgment, the court will enter judgment in the terms of the defendant's admission and offer and for costs.

8.7 If:

(1) the claimant does not accept the defendant's admission and offer, and

(2) the defendant does not appear on the hearing date fixed when the claim form was issued, the court may treat the defendant's admission and offer as evidence of the facts stated in it for the purposes of sections 129(2)(a)[2] and 135(2)[3].

Additional requirements about parties to the proceedings

9.1 The court may dispense with the requirement in section 141(5) (all parties to a regulated agreement and any surety to be parties to any proceedings) in any claim relating to the regulated agreement, if:

(1) the claim form has not been served on the debtor or the surety, and

(2) the claimant either before or at the hearing makes an application (which may be made without notice) for the court to make such an order.

9.2 In a claim relating to a regulated agreement where –

(1) the claimant was not one of the original parties to the agreement, and

(2) the former creditor's rights and duties under the agreement have passed to him by –

(a) operation of law, or

(b) assignment,

the requirement of section 141(5) (all parties to a regulated agreement and any surety to be parties to any proceedings) does not apply to the former creditor, unless the court otherwise orders.

9.3 Where a claimant who is a creditor or owner makes a claim for a court order under section 86(2) (death of debtor or hirer where agreement is partly secured or unsecured) the personal

---

1 Section 90(1) provides that-
"At any time when-
(a) the debtor is in breach of a regulated hire-purchase or a regulated conditional sale agreement relating to goods, and
(b) the debtor has paid to the creditor one-third or more of the total price of the goods, and
(c) the property in the goods remains in the creditor,
the creditor is not entitled to recover possession of the goods from the debtor except on an order of the court."

2 Section 129(2) provides that-
"A time order shall provide for one or both of the following, as the court considers just-
(a) the payment by the debtor or hirer or any surety of any sum owed under a regulated agreement or a security by such instalments, payable at such times, as the court, having regard to the means of the debtor or hirer and any surety, considers reasonable;
(b) the remedying by the debtor or hirer of any breach of a regulated agreement (other than non-payment of money) within such period as the court may specify."

3 Section 135(2) provides that-
"The court shall not suspend the operation of a term [in an order relating to a regulated agreement] requiring the delivery up of goods by any person unless satisfied that the goods are in his possession or control."

representatives of the deceased debtor or hirer must be parties to the proceedings in which the order is sought, unless no grant of representation has been made to the estate.

9.4 Where no grant of representation has been made to the estate of the deceased debtor or hirer, the claimant must make an application in accordance with Part 23 for directions about which persons (if any) are to be made parties to the claim as being affected or likely to be affected by the enforcement of the agreement.

9.5 The claimant's application under paragraph 9.4:

(a) may be made without notice, and

(b) should be made before the claim form is issued.

Notice to be given to re-open a consumer credit agreement

10.1 Where a debtor or any surety intends to apply for a consumer credit agreement to be reopened after a claim on or relating to the agreement has already begun, and:

(1) section 139(1)(b)[4] ; or

(2) section 139(1)(c),

applies, the debtor or surety must serve written notice of his intention on the court and every other party to the proceedings within 14 days of the service of the claim form on him.

10.2 If the debtor or surety (as the case may be) serves a notice under paragraph 10.1 he will be treated as having filed a defence for the purposes of the Consumer Credit Act procedure.

PRACTICE DIRECTION – PRODUCTION CENTRE

THIS PRACTICE DIRECTION SUPPLEMENTS CPR RULE 7.10.

General

1.1 In this Practice Direction

'the Centre' means the Production Centre.

'Centre user' means a person who is for the time being permitted to issue claims through the Centre, and includes a solicitor acting for such a person.

'officer' means the officer in charge of the Centre or another officer of the Centre acting on his behalf.

'national creditor code' means the number or reference allotted to a Centre user by the officer.

'Code of Practice' means any code of practice which may at any time be issued by the Court Service relating to the discharge by the Centre of its functions and the way in which a Centre user is to conduct business with the Centre.

'data' means any information which is required to be given to the court or which is to be contained in any document to be sent to the court or to any party.

1.2 For any purpose connected with the exercise of its functions, the Centre will be treated as part of the office of the court whose name appears on the claim form to which the functions relate, or in whose name the claim form is requested to be issued, and the officer will be treated as an officer of that court.

---

4   Section 139(1) provides that-

"(1)   A credit agreement may, if the court thinks just, be reopened on the ground that the credit bargain is extortionate-

(a) on an application for the purpose made by the debtor or any surety to the High Court, county court or sheriff court; or

(b) at the instance of the debtor or a surety in any proceedings to which the debtor and creditor are parties, being proceedings to enforce the credit agreement, any security relating to it or any linked transaction; or

(c) at the instance of the debtor or a surety in other proceedings in any court where the amount paid or payable under the credit agreement is relevant."

1.3 (1) The functions of the Centre include the provision of a facility which, through the use of information technology, enables a Centre user to have claim forms issued and served, whether or not those claim forms are to be treated as issued in the Northampton County Court or in another county court.

(2) If a Centre user issues claim forms in the name of Northampton County Court, the functions of the Centre also include:

(a) the handling of defences and admissions,

(b) the entry of judgment in default, on admission, on acceptance, or on determination,

(c) the registration of judgments,

(d) the issue of warrants of execution,

(e) the transfer to the defendant's home court of any case which is to continue following the filing of a defence or where a hearing is required before judgment, and

(f) the transfer to the defendant's home court, in the circumstances to which CCR Order 25 rule 2 (transfer for enforcement) applies, of any case for an oral examination or where enforcement of a judgment (other than by warrant of execution) is to follow.

1.4 (1) Where the officer is to take any step, any rule or Practice Direction which requires a document to be filed before he does so will be treated as complied with if the data which that document would contain is delivered to the Centre in computer readable form in accordance with the Code of Practice.

(2) Data relating to more than one case may be included in a single document or delivery of data.

(3) CPR Rule 6.3(3) (copies of documents to be served by court) does not apply to any document which is to be produced by electronic means from data supplied by a Centre user.

(4) Paragraph 10.3 of the practice direction supplementing CPR Part 16 (statements of case), which requires documentation to be attached to the particulars of contract claims, does not apply to claims to be issued by the Centre.

(5) The practice direction supplementing CPR Part 22 (statements of truth) is modified as follows:

(a) a single statement of truth may accompany each batch of requests to issue claim forms and may be in electronic form,

(b) the form of such a statement should be as follows: 'I believe that the facts stated in the attached claim forms are true.', and

(c) the signature of the appropriate person (as to which see section 3 of the practice direction supplementing CPR Part 22) may be in electronic form.

Claims which may not be issued through the centre

2.1 The Centre will not issue any claim form which is to be issued in the High Court.

2.2 The Centre will only issue a claim form if the claim is for a specified sum of money less than £100,000.

2.3 The Centre will not issue any of the following types of claim:

(1) a claim against more than two defendants,

(2) a claim against two defendants where a different sum is claimed against each of them,

(3) a claim where particulars of claim separate from the claim form are required,

(4) a claim against the Crown,

(5) a claim for an amount in a foreign currency,

(6) a claim where either party is known to be a child or patient within Part 21 of the Civil Procedure Rules,

(7) a claim where the claimant is a legally assisted person within the meaning of the Legal Aid Act 1988,

(8) a claim where the defendant's address for service as it appears on the claim form is not in England or Wales.

(9) a claim which is to be issued under Part 8 of the Civil Procedure Rules.

Centre users

3.1 Only a Centre user may issue or conduct claims through the Centre.

3.2 The officer may permit any person to be a Centre user.

3.3 The officer may withdraw the permission for any person to be a Centre user.

3.4 A Centre user must comply with the provisions of the Code of Practice in his dealings with the Centre.

3.5 The officer will allot a national creditor code to each Centre user.

The Code of Practice

4.1 The Code of Practice will contain provisions designed to ensure that the Centre can discharge its functions efficiently, and it may in particular provide for:

   (1) the forms of magnetic media that may be used,

   (2) the circumstances in which data may or must be supplied in magnetic form,

   (3) the circumstances in which data may or must be supplied in a document and the form that such a document must take,

   (4) how often data may be supplied,

   (5) the numbering of cases and data relating to cases,

   (6) data to be given to the Centre by the Centre user about cases which have been settled or paid or are otherwise not proceeding, and

   (7) accounting arrangements and the method of payment of fees.

4.2 The Court Service may change the Code of Practice from time to time.

Other modifications to the Civil Procedure Rules

Powers of the officer to make orders:-

5.1 The officer may make the following orders:

   (1) an order to set aside a default judgment where, after that judgment has been entered, the claim form in the case is returned by the Post Office as undelivered,

   (2) an order to set aside a judgment on application by a Centre user,

   (3) an order to transfer the case, in the circumstances to which CCR Order 25 rule 2 applies (transfer for enforcement or oral examination), of any case to another county court on the application of a Centre user. Procedure on the filing of a defence

5.2 (1) This paragraph applies where a Centre user has issued a claim in the Northampton County Court and the defendant has filed a defence to the claim or to part of the claim.

   (2) On the filing of the defence the officer will serve a notice on the Centre user requiring the Centre user to notify him within 28 days whether he wishes the claim to proceed.

   (3) If the Centre user does not notify the officer within the time specified in the notice that he wishes the claim to proceed the claim will be stayed, and the officer will notify the parties accordingly.

   (4) The proceedings will not be transferred to the defendant's home court under CPR rule 26.2, and no allocation questionnaires will be served under CPR rule 26.3(3) until the Centre user notifies the officer that he wishes the claim to continue.

PRACTICE DIRECTION – CLAIMS FOR THE RECOVERY OF TAXES
THIS PRACTICE DIRECTION SUPPLEMENTS CPR RULE 7.9

Scope

1.1 This practice direction applies to claims by the Inland Revenue for the recovery of–

   (a) Income Tax,

   (b) Corporation Tax,

   (c) Capital Gains Tax,

   (d) Interest, penalties and surcharges on Income Tax, Corporation Tax or Capital Gains Tax which by virtue of section 69 of the Taxes Management Act 1970 are to be treated as if they are taxes due and payable,

(e) National Insurance Contributions and interest, penalties and surcharges thereon.

Procedure

2.1 If a defence is filed, the court will fix a date for the hearing.

2.2 Part 26 (Case management - preliminary stage) apart from CPR rule 26.2 (automatic transfer) does not apply to claims to which this practice direction applies.

At the hearing

3.1 On the hearing date the court may dispose of the claim.

(Section 70 of the Taxes Management Act 1970 and section 118 of the Social Security Administration Act 1992 provide that a certificate of an officer of the Commissioners of Inland Revenue is sufficient evidence that a sum mentioned in such a certificate is unpaid and due to the Crown.)

3.2 But exceptionally, if the court does not dispose of the claim on the hearing date it may give case management directions, which may, if the defendant has filed a defence, include allocating the case.

PART 8

ALTERNATIVE PROCEDURE FOR CLAIMS

Contents of this Part

Types of claim in which Part 8 procedure may be followed	Rule 8.1
Contents of the claim form	Rule 8.2
Acknowledgment of service	Rule 8.3
Consequence of not filing an acknowledgment of service	Rule 8.4
Filing and serving written evidence	Rule 8.5
Evidence – general	Rule 8.6
Part 20 claims	Rule 8.7
Procedure where defendant objects to use of Part 8 procedure	Rule 8.8
Modifications to the general rules	Rule 8.9

Types of claim in which Part 8 procedure may be followed

8.1 (1) The Part 8 procedure is the procedure set out in this Part.

   (2) A claimant may use the Part 8 procedure where –

   (a) he seeks the court's decision on a question which is unlikely to involve a substantial dispute of fact; or

   (b) paragraph (6) applies.

   (3) The court may at any stage order the claim to continue as if the claimant had not used the Part 8 procedure and, if it does so, the court may give any directions it considers appropriate.

   (4) Paragraph (2) does not apply if a practice direction provides that the Part 8 procedure may not be used in relation to the type of claim in question.

   (5) Where the claimant uses the Part 8 procedure he may not obtain default judgment under Part 12.

   (6) A rule or practice direction may, in relation to a specified type of proceedings –

   (a) require or permit the use of the Part 8 procedure; and

   (b) disapply or modify any of the rules set out in this Part as they apply to those proceedings.

(Rule 8.9 provides for other modifications to the general rules where the Part 8 procedure is being used.)

Contents of the claim form

8.2 Where the claimant uses the Part 8 procedure the claim form must state –

    (a) that this Part applies;

    (b) (i) the question which the claimant wants the court to decide; or

        (ii) the remedy which the claimant is seeking and the legal basis for the claim to that remedy;

    (c) if the claim is being made under an enactment, what that enactment is;

    (d) if the claimant is claiming in a representative capacity, what that capacity is; and

    (e) if the defendant is sued in a representative capacity, what that capacity is.

(Part 22 provides for the claim form to be verified by a statement of truth.)

(Rule 7.5 provides for service of the claim form.)

Issue of claim form without naming defendants

8.2A (1) A practice direction may set out the circumstances in which the court may give permission for a claim form to be issued under this Part without naming a defendant.

    (2) An application for permission must be made by application notice before the claim form is issued.

    (3) The application notice for permission –

        (a) need not be served on any other person; and

        (b) must be accompanied by a copy of the claim form that the applicant proposes to issue.

    (4) Where the court gives permission it will give directions about the future management of the claim.

Acknowledgment of service

8.3 (1) The defendant must –

    (a) file an acknowledgment of service in the relevant practice form not more than 14 days after service of the claim form; and

    (b) serve the acknowledgment of service on the claimant and any other party.

    (2) The acknowledgment of service must state –

    (a) whether the defendant contests the claim; and

    (b) if the defendant seeks a different remedy from that set out in the claim form, what that remedy is.

    (3) The following rules of Part 10 (acknowledgment of service) apply –

    (a) rule 10.3(2) (exceptions to the period for filing an acknowledgment of service); and

    (b) rule 10.5 (contents of acknowledgment of service).

    (4) Part 11 (disputing the court's jurisdiction) applies subject to the modification that in rule 11(4)(a) and (5)(b) (time limit for application disputing court's jurisdiction) references to the period for filing a defence are treated as if they were references to a period of 14 days from the filing of an acknowledgment of service.

Consequence of not filing an acknowledgment of service

8.4 (1) This rule applies where –

    (a) the defendant has failed to file an acknowledgment of service; and

    (b) the time period for doing so has expired.

    (2) The defendant may attend the hearing of the claim but may not take part in the hearing unless the court gives permission.

Filing and serving written evidence

8.5 (1) The claimant must file any written evidence on which he intends to rely when he files his claim form.

(2) The claimant's evidence must be served on the defendant with the claim form.

(3) A defendant who wishes to rely on written evidence must file it when he files his acknowledgment of service.

(4) If he does so, he must also, at the same time, serve a copy of his evidence on the other parties.

(5) The claimant may, within 14 days of service of the defendant's evidence on him, file further written evidence in reply.

(6) If he does so, he must also, within the same time limit, serve a copy of his evidence on the other parties.

(7) The claimant may rely on the matters set out in his claim form as evidence under this rule if the claim form is verified by a statement of truth.

Evidence – general

8.6 (1) No written evidence may be relied on at the hearing of the claim unless –

(a) it has been served in accordance with rule 8.5; or

(b) the court gives permission.

(2) The court may require or permit a party to give oral evidence at the hearing.

(3) The court may give directions requiring the attendance for cross-examination$^{(GL)}$ of a witness who has given written evidence.

(Rule 32.1 contains a general power for the court to control evidence)

Part 20 claims

8.7 Where the Part 8 procedure is used, Part 20 (counterclaims and other additional claims) applies except that a party may not make a Part 20 claim (as defined by rule 20.2) without the court's permission.

Procedure where defendant objects to use of the Part 8 procedure

8.8 (1) Where the defendant contends that the Part 8 procedure should not be used because –

(a) there is a substantial dispute of fact; and

(b) the use of the Part 8 procedure is not required or permitted by a rule or practice direction,

he must state his reasons when he files his acknowledgment of service.

(Rule 8.5 requires a defendant who wishes to rely on written evidence to file it when he files his acknowledgment of service)

(2) When the court receives the acknowledgment of service and any written evidence it will give directions as to the future management of the case.

(Rule 8.1(3) allows the court to make an order that the claim continue as if the claimant had not used the Part 8 procedure)

Modifications to the general rules

8.9 Where the Part 8 procedure is followed –

(a) provision is made in this Part for the matters which must be stated in the claim form and the defendant is not required to file a defence and therefore –

(i) Part 16 (statements of case) does not apply;

(ii) Part 15 (defence and reply) does not apply;

(iii) any time limit in these Rules which prevents the parties from taking a step before a defence is filed does not apply;

(iv) the requirement under rule 7.8 to serve on the defendant a form for defending the claim does not apply;

(b) the claimant may not obtain judgment by request on an admission and therefore –

(i) rules 14.4 to 14.7 do not apply; and

(ii) the requirement under rule 7.8 to serve on the defendant a form for admitting the claim does not apply; and

(c) the claim shall be treated as allocated to the multi-track and therefore Part 26 does not apply.

PRACTICE DIRECTION – ALTERNATIVE PROCEDURE FOR CLAIMS
THIS PRACTICE DIRECTION SUPPLEMENTS CPR PART 8

Types of claim in which Part 8 procedure may be used

1.1 A claimant may use the Part 8 procedure where he seeks the court's decision on a question which is unlikely to involve a substantial dispute of fact.

1.2 A claimant may also use the Part 8 procedure if a practice direction permits or requires its use for the type of proceedings in question.

1.3 The practice directions referred to in paragraph 1.2 above may in some respects modify or disapply the Part 8 procedure and, where that is so, it is those practice directions that must be complied with.

1.4 The types of claim for which the Part 8 procedure may be used include:

(1) a claim by or against a child or patient which has been settled before the commencement of proceedings and the sole purpose of the claim is to obtain the approval of the court to the settlement,

(2) a claim for provisional damages which has been settled before the commencement of proceedings and the sole purpose of the claim is to obtain a consent judgment,

(3) provided there is unlikely to be a substantial dispute of fact, a claim for a summary order for possession against named or unnamed defendants occupying land or premises without the licence or consent of the person claiming possession.

1.5 Where it appears to a court officer that a claimant is using the Part 8 procedure inappropriately, he may refer the claim to a judge for the judge to consider the point.

1.6 The court may at any stage order the claim to continue as if the claimant had not used the Part 8 procedure and, if it does so, the court will allocate the claim to a track and give such directions as it considers appropriate[1].

Issuing the claim

2.1 Part 7 and the practice direction which supplements it contain a number of rules and directions applicable to all claims, including those to which Part 8 applies. Those rules and directions should be applied where appropriate.

2.2 Where a claimant uses the Part 8 procedure, the claim form (practice form N208) should be used and must state the matters set out in rule 8.2 and, if paragraphs 1.2 or 1.3 apply, must comply with the requirements of the practice direction in question. In particular, the claim form must state that Part 8 applies; a Part 8 claim form means a claim form which so states.

Responding to the claim

3.1 The provisions of Part 15 (defence and reply) do not apply where the claim form is a Part 8 claim form.

---

1   Rule 8.1(3).

3.2 Where a defendant who wishes to respond to a Part 8 claim form is required to file an acknowledgment of service, that acknowledgment of service should be in practice form N210[2] but can, alternatively, be given in an informal document such as a letter.

3.3 Rule 8.3 sets out provisions relating to an acknowledgment of service of a Part 8 claim form.

3.4 Rule 8.4 sets out the consequence of failing to file an acknowledgment of service.

3.5 The provisions of Part 12 (obtaining default judgment) do not apply where the claim form is a Part 8 claim form.

3.6 Where a defendant believes that the Part 8 procedure should not be used because there is a substantial dispute of fact or, as the case may be, because its use is not authorised by any rule or practice direction, he must state his reasons in writing when he files his acknowledgment of service[3]. If the statement of reasons includes matters of evidence it should be verified by a statement of truth.

Managing the claim

4.1 The court may give directions immediately a Part 8 claim form is issued either on the application of a party or on its own initiative. The directions may include fixing a hearing date where:

    (1) there is no dispute, such as in child and patient settlements, or

    (2) where there may be a dispute, such as in claims for mortgage possession or appointment of trustees, but a hearing date could conveniently be given.

4.2 Where the court does not fix a hearing date when the claim form is issued, it will give directions for the disposal of the claim as soon as practicable after the defendant has acknowledged service of the claim form or, as the case may be, after the period for acknowledging service has expired.

4.3 Certain applications, such as a consent application under section 38 of the Landlord and Tenant Act 1954, may not require a hearing.

4.4 The court may convene a directions hearing before giving directions.

Evidence

5.1 A claimant wishing to rely on written evidence should file it when his Part 8 claim form is issued[4] (unless the evidence is contained in the claim form itself).

5.2 Evidence will normally be in the form of a witness statement or an affidavit but a claimant may rely on the matters set out in his claim form provided that it has been verified by a statement of truth.

(For information about (1) statements of truth see Part 22 and the practice direction that supplements it, and (2) written evidence see Part 32 and the practice direction that supplements it.)

5.3 A defendant wishing to rely on written evidence, should file it with his acknowledgment of service[5].

5.4 Rule 8.5 sets out the times and provisions for filing and serving written evidence.

5.5 A party may apply to the court for an extension of time to serve and file evidence under Rule 8.5 or for permission to serve and file additional evidence under Rule 8.6(1).

(For information about applications see Part 23 and the practice direction that supplements it)

5.6 (1) The parties may, subject to the following provisions, agree in writing on an extension of time for serving and filing evidence under Rule 8.5(3) or Rule 8.5(5).

    (2) An agreement extending time for a defendant to file evidence under Rule 8.5(3) –

        (a) must be filed by the defendant at the same time as he files his acknowledgment of service; and

---

2   Rule 8.3(1)(a).

3   Rule 8.8(1).

4   Rule 8.5.

5   Rule 8.5(3).

(b) must not extend time by more than 14 days after the defendant files his acknowledgment of service.

(3) An agreement extending time for a claimant to file evidence in reply under Rule 8.5(5) must not extend time to more than 28 days after service of the defendant's evidence on the claimant.

PRACTICE DIRECTION – PART 8
THIS PRACTICE DIRECTION SUPPLEMENTS CPR PART 8, AND SCHEDULE 1 AND SCHEDULE 2 TO THE CPR

Terminology

1.1 In this practice direction "Schedule rules" means provisions contained in the Schedules to the CPR, which were previously contained in the Rules of the Supreme Court (1965) or the County Court Rules (1981).

Contents of this Practice Direction

2.1 This practice direction explains–
   (1) how to start the claims referred to in Sections A and B;
   (2) which form to use as the claim form;
   (3) the procedure which those claims will follow; and
   (4) how to start the appeals referred to in Section C.

(Further guidance about Forms other than claim forms can be found in the practice direction supplementing Part 4.)

(Forms to be used when making applications under Schedule 1, RSC.0.53 for judicial review and under Schedule RSC.0.54 for writs of habeas corpus are forms 86 and 87 (modified as necessary). Reference should be made to the relevant existing Crown Office practice directions for further guidance on procedure).

How to use this Practice Direction

3.1 This Practice direction is divided into three sections – Section A, Section B and Section C. Only one section will be relevant to how to make a particular claim or appeal.

3.2 If the claim is described in paragraph A.1 – use section A.

3.3 If the claim is described in paragraph B.1 – use section B.

3.4 If the appeal is described in paragraph C.1 – use section C.

Section A

Application

A.1 Section A applies if –
   (1) the claim is listed in Table 1 below;
   (2) an Act provides that a claim or application in the High Court is to be brought by originating summons; or
   (3) before 26 April 1999, a claim or application in the High Court would have been brought by originating summons, and is not listed in Section C, and no other method for bringing the claim or application on and after 26 April 1999 is specified in a Schedule rule or practice direction.

A.2 (1) The claimant must use the Part 8 procedure unless an Act, Schedule rule, or practice direction, makes any additional or contrary provision.
   (2) Where such additional or contrary provision is made the claimant must comply with it and modify the Part 8 procedure accordingly.

Claim form

A.3 The claimant must use the Part 8 claim form.

Table 1

RSC O.17, r.3(1)	Interpleader (Mode of application)
RSC O.50, r.9A	Charging orders, Stop orders etc., Enforcement of charging order by sale
RSC O.50, r.10(2)	Charging orders, Stop orders etc., Funds in court: Stop order
RSC O.50, r.14(4)	Charging orders, Stop orders etc., Withdrawal etc. of Stop Notice
RSC O.50, r.15(2)	Charging orders, Stop orders etc,. Order prohibiting transfer, etc., of securities
RSC O. 71, r. 2(1)	Reciprocal Enforcement of Judgments and Enforcement of European Community Judgments and Recommendations etc. under The Merchant Shipping (Liner Conferences) Act 1982 (I Reciprocal Enforcement: The Administration of Justice Act 1920 and the Foreign Judgments (Reciprocal Enforcement) Act 1933 – Application for registration)
RSC O. 71, r. 38	Reciprocal Enforcement of Judgments and Enforcement of European Community Judgments and Recommendations etc. under The Merchant Shipping (Liner Conferences) Act 1982 (III Reciprocal Enforcement: The Civil Jurisdiction and Judgments Act 1982 – Enforcement of United Kingdom Judgments in other Parts of the United Kingdom: Non-money Provisions)
RSC O. 71, r. 41	Reciprocal Enforcement of Judgments and Enforcement of European Community Judgments and Recommendations etc. under The Merchant Shipping (Liner Conferences) Act 1982 (IV Enforcement of Recommendations etc. under the Merchant Shipping (Liner Conferences) Act 1982 – Application for registration)
RSC O. 77, r. 11	Proceedings by and against the Crown (Interpleader: Application for order against Crown)
RSC O. 77, r. 16(2)	Proceedings by and against the Crown (Attachment of debts, etc.)
RSC O. 77, r. 17(1)	Proceedings by and against the Crown (Proceedings relating to postal packets)
RSC O. 77, r. 18(1)	Proceedings by and against the Crown (Applications under sections 17 and 29 of Crown Proceedings Act)
RSC O. 79, r. 8(2)	Criminal Proceedings (Estreat of recognizances)
RSC O. 79, r. 9(2)	Criminal Proceedings (Bail)
RSC O. 79, r. 10(2)	Criminal Proceedings (Issue of witness summons, etc.)
RSC O. 79, r. 11(1)	Criminal Proceedings (Application for warrant to arrest witness)
RSC O. 81, r. 10(1)	Partners (Applications for orders charging partner's interest in partnership property)
RSC O. 82, r. 8(2)	Defamation claims (Fulfilment of offer of amends under section 4 of the Defamation Act 1952)
RSC O. 88, r. 3	Mortgage claims (Commencement of claim)1 –RSC O. 92, r. 5(2) Lodgment, Investment etc. of Funds in Court: Chancery Division (Applications with respect to funds in court)
RSC O. 93, r. 5(2)	Applications and Appeals to High Court under Various Acts: Chancery Division (Applications under section 2(3) of the Public Order Act 1936)
RSC O. 93, r. 6(2)	Applications and Appeals to High Court under Various Acts: Chancery Division (Application under the Variation of Trusts Act 1958)
RSC O. 93, r. 18(2)	Applications and Appeals to High Court under Various Acts: Chancery Division (Proceedings under section 86 of the Civil Aviation Act 1982)

RSC O. 93, r. 20(2)	Applications and Appeals to High Court under Various Acts: Chancery Division (Proceedings under section 50 of the Administration of Justice Act 1985)
RSC O. 93, r. 21	Applications and Appeals to High Court under Various Acts: Chancery Division (Proceedings under section 48 of the Administration of Justice Act 1985)
RSC O. 93, r. 23(2)(a)	Applications and Appeals to High Court under Various Acts: Chancery Division (Proceedings under the Banking Act 1987: applications under sections 26(3), 71(3) and (5) and 77(3) and (5)).
RSC O. 94, r. 5	Applications and Appeals to High Court under Various Acts: Queen's Bench Division (Exercise of jurisdiction under Representation of the People Acts)
RSC O. 95, r. 2(1)	Bills of Sale Acts 1878 and 1882 and the Industrial and Provident Societies Act 1967 (Entry of satisfaction)
RSC O. 95, r. 3	Bills of Sale Acts 1878 and 1882 and the Industrial and Provident Societies Act 1967 (Restraining removal on sale of goods seized)
RSC O. 96, r. 1	The Mines (Working Facilities and Support) Act 1966 etc. (Assignment to Chancery Division)
RSC O. 96, r. 3	The Mines (Working Facilities and Support) Act 1966 etc. (Issue of claim form)
RSC O. 97, r. 2	The Landlord and Tenant Acts 1927, 1954 and 1987 (Assignment of proceedings to Chancery Division etc.)
RSC O. 97, r. 5	The Landlord and Tenant Acts 1927, 1954 and 1987 (Proceedings under Part I of the Act of 1927)
RSC O. 97, r. 6(1)	The Landlord and Tenant Acts 1927, 1954 and 1987 (Application for new tenancy under section 24 of the Act of 1954)
RSC O. 97, r. 6A(1)	The Landlord and Tenant Acts 1927, 1954 and 1987 (Application to authorise agreement)
RSC O. 97, r. 9A(1)(b)	The Landlord and Tenant Acts 1927, 1954 and 1987 (Application to determine interim rent)
RSC O. 97, r. 14	The Landlord and Tenant Acts 1927, 1954 and 1987 (Application under section 19 of the Act of 1987)
RSC O. 97, r. 15(3)	The Landlord and Tenant Acts 1927, 1954 and 1987 (Application for order under section 24 of the Act of 1987)
RSC O. 97, r. 16(3)	The Landlord and Tenant Acts 1927, 1954 and 1987 (Application for acquisition order under section 29 of the Act of 1987)
RSC O. 99, r. 3(1)	Inheritance (Provision for Family and Dependants) Act 1975 (Application for Financial Provision) (High Court and County Court Cases)
RSC O. 106, r. 3(2)	Proceedings Relating to Solicitors: The Solicitors Act 1974 (Power to order solicitor to deliver cash account etc.)
RSC O. 106, r. 6(2)	Proceedings Relating to Solicitors: The Solicitors Act 1974 (Applications under schedule 1 to the Act)
RSC O. 106, r. 8(1)	Proceedings Relating to Solicitors: The Solicitors Act 1974 (Interim order restricting payment out of banking account)
RSC 0109 r. 1(3)	Administration Act 1960 (Applications under Act)
RSC O. 113, r. 1	Summary proceedings for possession of land (Proceedings to be brought by claim form)

Section B

Application

B.1 Section B applies if the claim –

(1) is listed in Table 2;

(2) in the county court is for, or includes a claim for:
    (a) the recovery of possession of land; or
    (b) for damages for harassment under Section 3 of the Protection from Harassment Act 1997
(3) would have been brought before 26 April 1999 –
    (a) in the High Court, by originating motion and is not listed in Section C;
    (b) in the county court–
        (i) by originating application; or
        (ii) by petition, and
no other procedure is prescribed in an Act, a Schedule rule or a practice direction.

Table 2

Schedule Rule	Claim Form
RSC O. 56, r. 8(1)	Appeals, etc., to High Court by Case Stated: General (Application for order to state a case)
RSC O. 56, r. 10(1)	Appeals, etc., to High Court by Case Stated: General (Proceedings for determination of case)
RSC O. 71, r. 24 2	Reciprocal Enforcement of Judgments and Enforcement of European Community Judgments and Recommendations etc., under The Merchant Shipping (Liner Conferences) Act 1982, II Enforcement of European Community Judgments. (Application for enforcement of Euratom inspection order)
RSC O. 77, r. 8(2)3	Proceedings by and against the Crown (Summary applications to the court in certain revenue matters)
RSC O. 93, r. 19(1)	Applications and Appeals to High Court under Various Acts: (Proceedings under section 85(7) of the Fair Trading Act 1973 and the Control of Misleading Advertisements Regulations 1988)
RSC O. 93, r. 22(3)	Applications and Appeals to High Court under Various Acts: Chancery Division (Proceedings under the Financial Services Act 1986 (Applications by inspectors under section 94 or 178).
RSC O. 94, r. 1(2)	Applications and Appeals to High Court under Various Acts: Queens Bench Division (Jurisdiction of High Court to Quash Certain Orders, Schemes etc.)
RSC O. 94, r. 7(2)	Applications and Appeals to High Court under Various Acts: Queens Bench Division (Reference of Question of Law by Agricultural Land Tribunal)
RSC O. 94, r. 11(4)	Applications and Appeals to High Court under Various Acts: Queens Bench Division (Case stated by Mental Health Review Tribunal)
RSC O. 94, r. 12(5)(c)	Applications and Appeals to High Court under Various Acts: Queens Bench Division Applications for permission under section 289(6) of the Town and Country Planning Act 1990 and section 65(5) of the Planning (Listed Buildings and Conservation Areas) Act 1990
RSC O. 94, r. 13(5)	Applications and Appeals to High Court under Various Acts: Queens Bench Division Proceedings under sections 289 and 290 of the Town and Country Planning Act 1990 and under section 65 of the Planning (Listed Buildings and Conservation Areas) Act 1990

RSC O. 94, r. 14(2)	Applications and Appeals to High Court under Various Acts: Queens Bench Division Applications under section 13 of the Coroners Act 1988	
RSC O. 94, r. 15(2)	Applications and Appeals to High Court under Various Acts: Queens Bench Division Applications under section 42 of the Supreme Court Act 1981	
RSC O. 98, r. 2(1)	Local Government Finance Act 1982, Part III (Application by auditor for declaration)	
RSC 0.109, r. 2(4)	Administration of Justice Act 1960 (Appeals under section 13 of Act)	
RSC O. 114, r. 2(2)	References to the European Court (Making of order)	
RSC O. 115, r. 2B(1)	Confiscation and Forfeiture in Connection with Criminal Proceedings (I. Drug Trafficking Act 1994 and Criminal Justice (International Co-operation) Act 1990 –Application for confiscation Order)	
RSC O. 115, r. 3(1)	Confiscation and Forfeiture in Connection with Criminal Proceedings (I. Drug Trafficking Act 1994 and Criminal Justice (International Co-operation) Act 1990 –Application for restraint order or charging order)	
RSC O. 115, r. 7(1)	Confiscation and Forfeiture in Connection with Criminal Proceedings (I. Drug Trafficking Act 1994 and Criminal Justice (International Co-operation) Act 1990 –Realisation of property)	
RSC O. 115, r. 26 (1)	Confiscation and Forfeiture in Connection with Criminal Proceedings (III. Prevention of Terrorism (Temporary Provisions) Act 1989 – Application for restraint order)	
RSC 0.116, r 5(1)	The Criminal Procedure and Investigations Act 1996 (Application under section 54(3)).	
CCR O. 24, r.1(1)	Summary proceedings for the recovery of land (Part I – Land: proceedings to be by claim form)	N312
CCR O. 24, r. 10(2)(a)	Summary proceedings for the recovery of land – (Part II Interim possession orders – issue of the applications)	N130
CCR O. 31, r. 4(1)	Charging orders (Enforcement of charging order by sale)	
CCR O. 43, r. 2(1)	The Landlord and Tenant Acts 1927, 1954, 1985 and 1987 (Commencement of proceedings and answer)	
CCR O. 43, r. 4(1)	The Landlord and Tenant Acts 1927, 1954, 1985 and 1987 (Proceedings under Part I of the Act of 1927)	N394 N395 N396
CCR O.43, r 6(1)	The Landlord and Tenant Acts 1927, 1954, 1985 and 1987 (Application for a new tenancy under section 24 of the Act of 1954)	N397
CCR O.43, r 16	The Landlord and Tenant Acts 1927, 1954, 1985 and 1987 (Application under section 12(2) of the Act of 1985)	
CCR O. 43, r. 18(1)	The Landlord and Tenant Acts 1927, 1954, 1985 and 1987 (Application for order under section 24 of the Act of 1987)	

CCR O. 43, r. 19(1)	The Landlord and Tenant Acts 1927, 1954, 1985 and 1987 (Application for acquisition order under section 29 of the Act of 1987)	
CCR O.43, r. 20(1)	The Landlord and Tenant Acts 1927, 1954, 1985 and 1987 (Application for order under section 38 or 40 of the Act of 1987)	
CCR O.44, r 1(1)	The Agricultural Holdings Act 1986 (Special case stated by arbitrator)	
CCR O.44, r 3(1)	The Agricultural Holdings Act 1986 (Removal of arbitrator or setting aside award)	
CCR O. 45, r. 1(1)	The Representation of the People Act 1983 (Application for detailed assessment of returning officer's account)	N408
CCR O. 46, r. 1(1)	The Legitimacy Act 1976 (Manner of application))	
CCR O. 49, r. 1(2)	Miscellaneous Statutes: (Access to Neighbouring Land Act 1992)	
CCR O. 49, r. 4(5)	Miscellaneous Statutes: (Consumer Credit Act 1974 – claim relating to land (Application under section 129(1)(b)))	N440
CCR O. 49, r. 4(9)	Miscellaneous Statutes: (Consumer Credit Act 1974 – claim relating to land (Application for enforcement order))	
CCR O. 49, r. 4(14)	Miscellaneous Statutes: (Consumer Credit Act 1974 – claim relating to land (Application under section 139(1)(a) for a credit agreement to be reopened))	
CCR O. 49, r. 4(15)	Miscellaneous Statutes: (Consumer Credit Act 1974 – claim relating to land (proceedings as are mentioned in section 139(1)(b) or (c)))	
CCR O. 49, r. 5(1)	Miscellaneous Statutes: Fair Trading Act 1973 (Proceedings under section 35, 38 or 40)	
CCR O. 49, r.6(5)	Miscellaneous Statutes: Housing Act 1988: assured tenancies (application for accelerated possession)	N5A
CCR O. 49, r.6A(5)	Miscellaneous Statutes: Housing Act 1988: assured shorthold tenancies (application for accelerated possession)	N5B
CCR O. 49, r. 6B(1)	Miscellaneous Statutes: Housing Act 1996: Injunctions and Powers of Arrest (Application for injunction under section 152)	N16A
CCR O. 49, r. 7(2)	Miscellaneous Statutes: Injunctions to Prevent Environmental Harm: Town and Country Planning Act 1990 etc. (Application for injunction)	
CCR O. 49, r. 9(3)	Miscellaneous Statutes: Leasehold Reform, Housing and Urban Development Act 1993	
CCR O. 49, r. 10(3)	Miscellaneous Statutes: Local Government Finance Act 1982	
CCR O. 49, r. 12(2)	Miscellaneous Statutes: Mental Health Act 1983 (Application)	
CCR O. 49, r. 13(1)	Miscellaneous Statutes: Mobile Homes Act 1983 (Applications and questions)	
CCR O. 49, r. 15(1)	Miscellaneous Statutes: Post Office Act 1969 (Application under section 30(5))	

Special provisions take precedence

B.2 The claimant must first comply with any special provision set out in the Schedule rules, practice direction or any Act relating to the claim.

(In Schedule 2, CCR O.6 makes special provisions about particulars of claim and CCR O.7 makes special provision for service, for certain types of claim.)

B.3 Special provisions contained in Schedule rules or an Act may set out–

    (1) where the claim may be started;

    (2) the contents of the claim form;

    (3) whether a hearing is required;

    (4) the nature of evidence required in support of the claim, and when it must be filed or served;

    (5) the method of service of the claim form and evidence;

    (6) persons on whom service must or may be effected;

    (7) the form and content of Notices, and when they must or may be filed, and on whom served;

    (8) the form and content of any affidavit, answer, or reply and when they must or may be filed or served;

    (9) persons who may apply to be joined as parties to the claim;

    (10) minimum periods of notice before the hearing date.

B.4 Where a Schedule rule makes special provision for the contents of particulars of claim, those particulars must be attached to the claim form and served with it.

B.5 Subject to any special or contrary provision in an Act or Schedule rule, the claimant must use the procedure set out in the remainder of this section.

Restrictions on where to start the claim

B.6 Where the claimant is bringing a claim in a county court that claim may only be started–

    (1) in the county court for the district in which–

        (a) the defendants or one of the defendants lives or carries on business; or

        (b) the subject matter of the claim is situated; or

    (2) if there is no defendant named in the claim form, in the county court for the district in which the claimant or one of the claimants lives or carries on business.

B.7 Where the claimant is making a claim in the county court for –

    (1) the recovery of land;

    (2) the foreclosure or redemption of any mortgage;

    (3) enforcing any charge or lien on land;

    (4) the recovery of moneys secured by a mortgage or charge on land,

the claim must be started in the court for the district in which the land, or any part of it, is situated.

Claim form

B.8 This paragraph sets out which Form is to be used as the claim form–

    (1) where a claim form number is listed against a particular claim in Table 2, the claimant must use that numbered form as the claim form;

    (2) where the claimant intends to make a claim in the county court which is for, or includes, the recovery of possession of land, the claimant must use the claim form numbered in the practice direction supplementing Part 4 (Forms), and

    (3) in every other claim, the claimant must use the Part 8 claim form.

Court will fix a date

B.9 When the court issues the claim form it will–

    (1) fix a date for the hearing; and

    (2) prepare a notice of the hearing date for each party.

Service of the claim form

B.10 The claim form must be served not less than 21 days before the hearing date.

B.11 Where the claimant serves the claim form, he must serve notice of the hearing date at the same time, unless the hearing date is specified in the claim form.

Defendant is not required to respond

B.12 The defendant is not required to serve an acknowledgment of service.

At the hearing

B.13 The court may on the hearing date –

    (1) proceed to hear the case and dispose of the claim; or

    (2) give case management directions.

B.14 Case management directions given under paragraph B.13 will, if the defendant has filed a defence, include the allocation of a case to a track, or directions to enable the case to be allocated.

(A defended county court claim for possession of land, where it has been allocated to the multi-track, will not normally be transferred to the Civil Trial Centre: see paragraph 10(1) of the Part 26 (Case Management preliminary stages practice direction))

B.15 CPR rule 26.5(3) to (5) and CPR rules 26.6 to 26.10 apply to the allocation of a claim under paragraph B.14.

SECTION C

C.1 Section C applies if the appeal is listed in Table 3.

C.2 The Schedule rules provide –

    (1) that the appeal must be started by Notice of Appeal; and

    (2) the procedure the appeal should follow.

(Further information on the procedure to be followed, and the form of the Notice of Appeal for Appeals to the Court of Appeal can be found in the Practice Direction for the Court of Appeal (Civil Division).)

Table 3

Schedule Rule		Claim Form
RSC O. 55, r. 3(1)	Appeals, etc., to High Court from Court, Tribunal or person: general (Bringing of Appeal)	
RSC 0.59, r. 3(1)	Appeals to the Court of Appeal	
RSC 0.60, r. 1	Appeals to the Court of Appeal from Restrictive Practices Court	
RSC 0.61, r. 3(1)	Appeals from Tribunals to Court of Appeal by Case Stated. (Proceedings on case stated)	
RSC 0.91, r. 2(2)	Revenue proceedings (Appeal under section 222 of the Inheritance Tax Act 1984)	
RSC 0.93, r. 11(3)	Applications and Appeals to High Court under various Acts: Chancery Division (Appeal under section 17 of the Industrial Assurance Act)	
RSC 0.93, r. 12(1)	Applications and Appeals to High Court under Various Acts: Chancery Division (Appeals, etc., affecting Industrial and Provident Societies, etc.)	
RSC 0.93, r. 23(2)(b)	Applications and Appeals to High Court under Various Acts: Chancery Division Appeal (Proceedings under the Banking Appeal Act 1987 – appeals under section 31(1).)	
RSC O. 94, r. 10	Applications and Appeals to High Court under Various Acts: Queens Bench Division (Tribunals and Enquiries Act 1971: Appeal from Minister of Transport)	

RSC O. 94, r. 10A(2)	Applications and Appeals to High Court under Various Acts: Queens Bench Division (Consumer Credit Act 1974: Appeal from Secretary of State)
RSC O. 101, r. 4(1)	The Pensions Appeal Tribunals Act 1943 (Appeal)
RSC 0.106, r. 12(1)	Proceedings relating to Solicitors: The Solicitors Act 1974 (Title, service etc., of Notice of Appeal)
RSC 0.108, r. 5(2)	Proceedings relating to Charities: The Charities Act 1993 (Appeal against order, etc., of Commissioners)
RSC 0.111, r. 4(3)	Social Security Administration Act 1992 (Reference of question of law)

PART 9

RESPONDING TO PARTICULARS OF CLAIM – GENERAL

Contents of this Part

Scope of this Part

9.1 (1) This Part sets out how a defendant may respond to particulars of claim.

    (2) Where the defendant receives a claim form which states that particulars of claim are to follow, he need not respond to the claim until the particulars of claim have been served on him.

Defence, admission or acknowledgment of service

9.2 When particulars of claim are served on a defendant, the defendant may –

    (a) file or serve an admission in accordance with Part 14;

    (b) file a defence in accordance with Part 15, (or do both, if he admits only part of the claim); or

    (c) file an acknowledgment of service in accordance with Part 10.

(RSC Order 15 r.12A, in Schedule 1 makes special provision where the defendant in a derivative claim responds to particulars of claim.)

PART 10

ACKNOWLEDGMENT OF SERVICE

Contents of this Part

Acknowledgment of service

10.1(1) This Part deals with the procedure for filing an acknowledgment of service.

(2) Where the claimant uses the procedure set out in Part 8 (alternative procedure for claims) this Part applies subject to the modifications set out in rule 8.3.

(3) A defendant may file an acknowledgment of service if –

    (a) he is unable to file a defence within the period specified in rule 15.4; or

    (b) he wishes to dispute the court's jurisdiction.

(Part 11 sets out the procedure for disputing the court's jurisdiction.)

Consequence of not filing an acknowledgment of service

10.2 If –

    (a) a defendant fails to file an acknowledgment of service within the period specified in rule 10.3; and

    (b) does not within that period file a defence in accordance with Part 15 or serve or file an admission in accordance with Part 14,

the claimant may obtain default judgment if Part 12 allows it.

The period for filing an acknowledgment of service

10.3(1) The general rule is that the period for filing an acknowledgment of service is –

    (a) where the defendant is served with a claim form which states that particulars of claim are to follow, 14 days after service of the particulars of claim; and

    (b) in any other case, 14 days after service of the claim form.

(2) The general rule is subject to the following rules –

    (a) rule 6.22 (which specifies how the period for filing an acknowledgment of service is calculated where the claim form is served out of the jurisdiction); and

    (b) rule 6.16(4) (which requires the court to specify the period for responding to the particulars of claim when it makes an order under that rule).

Notice to claimant that defendant has filed an acknowledgment of service

10.4 On receipt of an acknowledgment of service, the court must notify the claimant in writing.

Contents of acknowledgment of service

10.5 An acknowledgment of service must –

    (a) be signed by the defendant or his legal representative; and

    (b) include the defendant's address for service.

(Rule 6.5 provides that an address for service must be within the jurisdiction.)

(RSC Order 81, in Schedule 1, makes special provision in relation to the acknowledgment of service in a claim against a firm.)

(The Contentious Probate Proceedings Practice Direction provides that a defendant who wishes to defend a contentious probate claim must file an acknowledgment of service.)

PRACTICE DIRECTION – ACKNOWLEDGMENT OF SERVICE
THIS PRACTICE DIRECTION SUPPLEMENTS CPR PART 10

Responding to the claim

1.1 Part 9 sets out how a defendant may respond to a claim.

1.2 Part 10 sets out the provisions for acknowledging service (but see rule 8.3 for information about acknowledging service of a claim under the Part 8 procedure).

The form of acknowledgment of service

2 A defendant who wishes to acknowledge service of a claim should do so by using form N9.

Address for service

3.1 The defendant must include in his acknowledgment of service an address for the service of documents[1].

3.2 Where the defendant is represented by a legal representative[2] and the legal representative has signed the acknowledgment of service form, the address must be the legal representative's business address; otherwise the address for service that is given should be as set out in rule 6.5 and the practice direction which supplements Part 6.

Signing the acknowledgment of service

4.1 An acknowledgment of service must be signed by the defendant or by his legal representative.

4.2 Where the defendant is a company or other corporation, a person holding a senior position in the company or corporation may sign the acknowledgment of service on the defendant's behalf, but must state the position he holds.

4.3 Each of the following persons is a person holding a senior position:

(1) in respect of a registered company or corporation, a director, the treasurer, secretary, chief executive, manager or other officer of the company or corporation, and

(2) in respect of a corporation which is not a registered company, in addition to those persons set out in (1), the mayor, chairman, president, town clerk or similar officer of the corporation.

4.4 Where the defendant is a partnership, the acknowledgment of service may be signed by:

(1) any of the partners, or

(2) a person having the control or management of the partnership business.

4.5 Children and patients may acknowledge service only by their litigation friend or his legal representative unless the court otherwise orders[3].

General

5.1 The defendant's name should be set out in full on the acknowledgment of service.

5.2 Where the defendant's name has been incorrectly set out in the claim form, it should be correctly set out on the acknowledgment of service followed by the words 'described as' and the incorrect name.

5.3 If two or more defendants to a claim acknowledge service of a claim through the same legal representative at the same time, only one acknowledgment of service need be used.

5.4 An acknowledgment of service may be amended or withdrawn only with the permission of the court.

5.5 An application for permission under paragraph 5.4 must be made in accordance with Part 23 and supported by evidence.

---

1 See rule 6.5.

2 See rule 2.3 for the definition of legal representative.

3 See Part 21.

PART 11

DISPUTING THE COURT'S JURISDICTION

Contents of this Part

Procedure for disputing the court's jurisdiction.   Rule 11

Procedure for disputing the court's jurisdiction

11 (1) A defendant who wishes to –

(a) dispute the court's jurisdiction to try the claim; or

(b) argue that the court should not exercise its jurisdiction,

may apply to the court for an order declaring that it has no such jurisdiction or should not exercise any jurisdiction which it may have.

(2) A defendant who wishes to make such an application must first file an acknowledgment of service in accordance with Part 10.

(3) A defendant who files an acknowledgment of service does not, by doing so, lose any right that he may have to dispute the court's jurisdiction.

(4) An application under this rule must –

(a) be made within the period for filing a defence; and

(b) be supported by evidence.

(Rule 15.4 sets out the period for filing a defence)

(5) If the defendant –

(a) files an acknowledgment of service; and

(b) does not make such an application within the period for filing a defence,

he is to be treated as having accepted that the court has jurisdiction to try the claim.

(6) An order containing a declaration that the court has no jurisdiction or will not exercise its jurisdiction may also make further provision including –

(a) setting aside the claim form;

(b) setting aside service of the claim form;

(c) discharging any order made before the claim was commenced or before the claim form was served; and

(d) staying$^{(GL)}$ the proceedings.

(7) If on an application under this rule the court does not make a declaration –

(a) the acknowledgment of service shall cease to have effect; and

(b) the defendant may file a further acknowledgment of service within 14 days or such other period as the court may direct.

(8) If the defendant files a further acknowledgment of service in accordance with paragraph (7)(b) he shall be treated as having accepted that the court has jurisdiction to try the claim.

(9) Where a defendant makes an application under this rule he need not file a defence before the hearing of the application.

(10) Where the claimant uses the procedure set out in Part 8 (alternative procedure for claims) this Part applies subject to the modifications set out in rule 8.3.

PART 12

DEFAULT JUDGMENT

Contents of this Part

Meaning of 'default judgment'

12.1   In these Rules, 'default judgment' means judgment without trial where a defendant –

    (a) has failed to file an acknowledgment of service; or

    (b) has failed to file a defence.

(Part 10 contains provisions about filing an acknowledgment of service and Part 15 contains provisions about filing a defence.)

Claims in which default judgment may not be obtained

12.2   A claimant may not obtain a default judgment –

    (a) on a claim for delivery of goods subject to an agreement regulated by the Consumer Credit Act 1974[15];

    (b) where he uses the procedure set out in Part 8 (alternative procedure for claims); or

    (c) in any other case where a practice direction provides that the claimant may not obtain default judgment.

Conditions to be satisfied

12.3 (1) The claimant may obtain judgment in default of an acknowledgment of service only if –

    (a) the defendant has not filed an acknowledgment of service or a defence to the claim (or any part of the claim); and

    (b) the relevant time for doing so has expired.

  (2) Judgment in default of defence may be obtained only –

    (a) where an acknowledgment of service has been filed but a defence has not been filed;

    (b) in a counterclaim made under rule 20.4, where a defence has not been filed,

  and, in either case, the relevant time limit for doing so has expired.

(Rule 20.4 makes general provision for a defendant's counterclaim against a claimant, and rule 20.4(3) provides that Part 10 (acknowledgment of service) does not apply to a counterclaim made under that rule.)

(15) 1974 c.39.

(3) The claimant may not obtain a default judgment if –

    (a) the defendant has applied –

        (i) to have the claimant's statement of case struck out under rule 3.4; or

        (ii) for summary judgment under Part 24,

        and, in either case, that application has not been disposed of;

    (b) the defendant has satisfied the whole claim (including any claim for costs) on which the claimant is seeking judgment; or

    (c) (i) the claimant is seeking judgment on a claim for money; and

        (ii) the defendant has filed or served on the claimant an admission under rule 14.4 or 14.7 (admission of liability to pay all of the money claimed) together with a request for time to pay.

(Part 14 sets out the procedure where a defendant admits a money claim and asks for time to pay.)

(Rule 6.14 provides that, where the claim form is served by the claimant, he may not obtain default judgment unless he has filed a certificate of service.)

Procedure for obtaining default judgment

12.4 (1) Subject to paragraph (2), a claimant may obtain a default judgment by filing a request in the relevant practice form where the claim is for –

    (a) a specified amount of money;

    (b) an amount of money to be decided by the court;

    (c) delivery of goods where the claim form gives the defendant the alternative of paying their value; or

    (d) any combination of these remedies.

(2) The claimant must make an application in accordance with Part 23 if he wishes to obtain a default judgment –

    (a) on a claim which consists of or includes a claim for any other remedy; or

    (b) where rule 12.9 or rule 12.10 so provides.

(3) Where a claimant –

    (a) claims any other remedy in his claim form in addition to those specified in paragraph (1); but

    (b) abandons that claim in his request for judgment,

    he may still obtain a default judgment by filing a request under paragraph (1).

Nature of judgment where default judgment obtained by filing a request

12.5 (1) Where the claim is for a specified sum of money, the claimant may specify in a request filed under rule 12.4(1) –

    (a) the date by which the whole of the judgment debt is to be paid; or

    (b) the times and rate at which it is to be paid by instalments.

(2) Except where paragraph (4) applies, a default judgment on a claim for a specified amount of money obtained on the filing of a request, will be judgment for the amount of the claim (less any payments made) and costs –

    (a) to be paid by the date or at the rate specified in the request for judgment; or

    (b) if none is specified, immediately.

(Interest may be included in a default judgment obtained by filing a request if the conditions set out in Rule 12.6 are satisfied.)

(Rule 45.4 provides for fixed costs on the entry of a default judgment.)

(3) Where the claim is for an unspecified amount of money a default judgment obtained on the filing of a request will be for an amount to be decided by the court and costs.

(4) Where the claim is for delivery of goods and the claim form gives the defendant the alternative of paying their value, a default judgment obtained on the filing of a request will be judgment requiring the defendant to –

    (a) deliver the goods or (if he does not do so) pay the value of the goods as decided by the court (less any payments made); and

    (b) pay costs.

(Rule 12.7 sets out the procedure for deciding the amount of a judgment or the value of the goods.)

(5) The claimant's right to enter judgment requiring the defendant to deliver goods is subject to rule 40.14 (judgment in favour of certain part owners relating to the detention of goods).

Interest

12.6 (1) A default judgment on a claim for a specified amount of money obtained on the filing of a request may include the amount of interest claimed to the date of judgment if –

    (a) the particulars of claim include the details required by rule 16.4;

    (b) where interest is claimed under section 35A of the Supreme Court Act 1981[16] or section 69 of the County Courts Act 1984[17], the rate is no higher than the rate of interest payable on judgment debts at the date when the claim form was issued; and

    (c) the claimant's request for judgment includes a calculation of the interest claimed for the period from the date up to which interest was stated to be calculated in the claim form to the date of the request for judgment.

(2) In any case where paragraph (1) does not apply, judgment will be for an amount of interest to be decided by the court.

(Rule 12.7 sets out the procedure for deciding the amount of interest.)

Procedure for deciding an amount or value

12.7 (1) This rule applies where the claimant obtains a default judgment on the filing of a request under rule 12.4(1) and judgment is for –

    (a) an amount of money to be decided by the court;

    (b) the value of goods to be decided by the court; or

    (c) an amount of interest to be decided by the court.

(2) Where the court enters judgment it will –

    (a) give any directions it considers appropriate; and

    (b) if it considers it appropriate, allocate the case.

Claim against more than one defendant

12.8 (1) A claimant may obtain a default judgment on request under this Part on a claim for money or a claim for delivery of goods against one of two or more defendants, and proceed with his claim against the other defendants.

---

(16) 1981 c.54. Section 35A was inserted by the Administration of Justice Act 1982 (c.53), section 15(1), Schedule 1, Part I.

(17) 1984 c.28. Section 69 was amended by the Courts and Legal Services Act 1990 (c.41), Schedule 18, paragraph 46.

(2) Where a claimant applies for a default judgment against one of two or more defendants –

    (a) if the claim can be dealt with separately from the claim against the other defendants –

        (i) the court may enter a default judgment against that defendant; and

        (ii) the claimant may continue the proceedings against the other defendants;

    (b) if the claim cannot be dealt with separately from the claim against the other defendants –

        (i) the court will not enter default judgment against that defendant; and

        (ii) the court must deal with the application at the same time as it disposes of the claim against the other defendants.

(3) A claimant may not enforce against one of two or more defendants any judgment obtained under this Part for possession of land or for delivery of goods unless –

    (a) he has obtained a judgment for possession or delivery (whether or not obtained under this Part) against all the defendants to the claim; or

    (b) the court gives permission.

Procedure for obtaining a default judgment for costs only

12.9 (1) Where a claimant wishes to obtain a default judgment for costs only –

    (a) if the claim is for fixed costs, he may obtain it by filing a request in the relevant practice form;

    (b) if the claim is for any other type of costs, he must make an application in accordance with Part 23.

(2) Where an application is made under this rule for costs only, judgment shall be for an amount to be decided by the court.

(Part 45 sets out when a claimant is entitled to fixed costs.)

Default judgment obtained by making an application

12.10   The claimant must make an application in accordance with Part 23 where –

    (a) the claim is –

        (i)   a claim against a child or patient;

        (ii) a claim in tort by one spouse against the other; or

        (iii) a claim against the Crown.

    (b) he wishes to obtain a default judgment where the defendant has failed to file an acknowledgment of service –

        (i)   against a defendant who has been served with the claim out of the jurisdiction under rule 6.19(1) (service without leave under the Civil Jurisdiction and Judgments Act 1982)[18];

        (ii) against a defendant domiciled in Scotland or Northern Ireland or in any other Convention territory;

        (iii) against a State;

        (iv) against a diplomatic agent who enjoys immunity from civil jurisdiction by virtue of the Diplomatic Privileges Act 1964[19]; or

(18) 1982 c.27.
(19) 1964 c.81.

(v) against persons or organisations who enjoy immunity from civil jurisdiction pursuant to the provisions of the International Organisations Acts 1968 and 1981[20].

Supplementary provisions where applications for default judgment are made

12.11(1) Where the claimant makes an application for a default judgment, judgment shall be such judgment as it appears to the court that the claimant is entitled to on his statement of case.

(2) Any evidence relied on by the claimant in support of his application need not be served on a party who has failed to file an acknowledgment of service.

(3) An application for a default judgment on a claim against a child or patient or a claim in tort between spouses must be supported by evidence.

(4) An application for a default judgment may be made without notice if –

(a) the claim was served in accordance with the Civil Jurisdiction and Judgments Act 1982;

(b) the defendant has failed to file an acknowledgment of service; and

(c) notice does not need to be given under any other provision of these Rules.

(5) Where an application is made against a State for a default judgment where the defendant has failed to file an acknowledgment of service –

(a) the application may be made without notice, but the court hearing the application may direct that a copy of the application notice be served on the State;

(b) if the court –

(i) grants the application; or

(ii) directs that a copy of the application notice be served on the State,

the judgment or application notice (and the evidence in support) may be served out of the jurisdiction without any further order;

(c) where paragraph (5)(b) permits a judgment or an application notice to be served out of the jurisdiction, the procedure for serving the judgment or the application notice is the same as for serving a claim form under Section III of Part 6 except where an alternative method of service has been agreed under section 12(6) of the State Immunity Act 1978[21].

(Rule 23.1 defines 'application notice'.)

(6) For the purposes of this rule and rule 12.10 –

(a) 'domicile' is to be determined in accordance with the provisions of sections 41 to 46 of the Civil Jurisdiction and Judgments Act 1982;

(b) 'Convention territory' means the territory or territories of any Contracting State, as defined by section 1(3) of the Civil Jurisdiction and Judgments Act 1982, to which the Brussels Conventions or Lugano Convention apply;

(c) 'State' has the meaning given by section 14 of the State Immunity Act 1978; and

(d) 'Diplomatic agent' has the meaning given by Article 1(e) of Schedule 1 to the Diplomatic Privileges Act 1964.

---

(20) 1968 c.48; 1981 c.9.
(21) 1978 c.33.

PRACTICE DIRECTION – DEFAULT JUDGMENT
THIS PRACTICE DIRECTION SUPPLEMENTS CPR PART 12

Default judgment

1.1 A default judgment is judgment without a trial where a defendant has failed to file either:

(1) an acknowledgment of service, or

(2) a defence.

For this purpose a defence includes any document purporting to be a defence.

(See Part 10 and the practice direction which supplements it for information about the acknowledgment of service, and Parts 15 and 16 and the practice directions which supplement them for information about the defence and what it should contain.)

1.2 A claimant may not obtain a default judgment under Part 12 (notwithstanding that no acknowledgment of service or defence has been filed) if:

(1) the procedure set out in Part 8 (Alternative Procedure for Claims) is being used, or

(2) the claim is for delivery of goods subject to an agreement regulated by the Consumer Credit Act 1974, or

(3) the claim is one to which RSC Order 88 (Schedule 1 to the CPR) (mortgage claims) applies or if proceeding in a county court, is a claim for money secured by mortgage, unless, in either case, the claimant obtains the permission of the court, or

(4) the claim is made in proceedings in respect of which, under CPR Part 49 and practice directions supplemental to that Part, either there is no requirement for an acknowledgment of service or a defence to be filed or special provision is made about the obtaining of a default judgment.

1.3 Examples of proceedings where default judgment under Part 12 cannot be obtained are:

(1) admiralty proceedings;

(2) arbitration proceedings;

(3) contentious probate proceedings;

(4) claims for provisional damages.

Obtaining default judgment

2.1 Rules 12.4(1) and 12.9(1) describe the claims in respect of which a default judgment may be obtained by filing a request in the appropriate practice form.

2.2 A default judgment on:

(1) the claims referred to in rules 12.9(1)(b) and 12.10, and

(2) claims other than those described in rule 12.4(1),

can only be obtained if an application for default judgment is made and cannot be obtained by filing a request.

2.3 The following are some of the types of claim which require an application for a default judgment:

(1) against children and patients[1],

(2) for costs (other than fixed costs) only[2],

(3) by one spouse against the other[3] on a claim in tort[4],

(4) for delivery up of goods where the defendant will not be allowed the alternative of paying their value,

(5) against the Crown, and

(6) against persons or organisations who enjoy immunity from civil jurisdiction under the

---

1 See rule 12.10(a)(i).

2 See rule 12.9(b).

3 See rule 12.10(a)(ii).

4 Tort may be defined as an act or a failure to do an act which causes harm or damage to another person and which gives the other person a right to claim compensation without having to rely on a contract with the person who caused the harm or damage.

provisions of the International Organisations Acts 1968 and 1981.

Default judgment by request

3 Requests for default judgment;

(1) in respect of a claim for a specified amount of money or for the delivery of goods where the defendant will be given the alternative of paying a specified sum representing their value, or for fixed costs only, must be in Form N205A or N225, and

(2) in respect of a claim where an amount of money (including an amount representing the value of goods) is to be decided by the court, must be in Form N205B or N227.

Evidence

4.1 Both on a request and on an application for default judgment the court must be satisfied that:

(1) the particulars of claim have been served on the defendant (a certificate of service on the court file will be sufficient evidence),

(2) either the defendant has not filed an acknowledgment of service or has not filed a defence and that in either case the relevant period for doing so has expired,

(3) the defendant has not satisfied the claim, and

(4) the defendant has not returned an admission to the claimant under rule or filed an admission with the court under rule 14.6.

4.2 On an application against a child or patient[5]:

(1) a litigation friend[6] to act on behalf of the child or patient must be appointed by the court before judgment can be obtained, and

(2) the claimant must satisfy the court by evidence that he is entitled to the judgment claimed.

4.3 On an application where the defendant was served with the claim either:

(1) outside the jurisdiction[7] without leave under the Civil Jurisdiction and Judgments Act 1982, or

(2) within the jurisdiction but when domiciled[8] in Scotland or Northern Ireland or in any other Convention territory[9],

and the defendant has not acknowledged service, the evidence must establish that:

(1) the claim is one that the court has power to hear and decide,

(2) no other court has exclusive jurisdiction under the Act to hear and decide the claim, and

(3) the claim has been properly served in accordance with Article 20 of Schedule 1, 3C or 4 of the Act.

4.4 On an application against a State[10] the evidence must:

(1) set out the grounds of the application,

(2) establish the facts proving that the State is excepted from the immunity conferred by section 1 of the State Immunity Act 1978,

(3) establish that the claim was sent through the Foreign and Commonwealth Office to the Ministry of Foreign Affairs of the State (unless the State agreed to a different form of service), and

(4) establish that the time for acknowledging service, which is extended to two months by section 12(2) of the Act, has expired.

(See rule 40.8 for when default judgment against a State takes effect.)

---

5 As defined in rule 21.1(2).

6 As defined in the practice direction which supplements Part 21.

7 As defined in rule 2.3.

8 As determined in accordance with the provisions of ss. 41 to 46 of the Civil Jurisdictions and Judgments Act 1982.

9 Means the territory of a Contracting State as defined in s.1(3) of the Civil Jurisdiction and Judgments Act 1982.

10 As defined in s.14 of the State Immunity Act 1978.

4.5 Evidence in support of an application referred to in paragraphs 4.3 and 4.4 above must be by affidavit.

4.6 On an application for judgment for delivery up of goods where the defendant will not be given the alternative of paying their value, the evidence must identify the goods and state where the claimant believes the goods to be situated and why their specific delivery up is sought.

General

5.1 On all applications to which this practice direction applies, other than those referred to in paragraphs 4.3 and 4.4 above[11], notice should be given in accordance with Part 23.

5.2 Where default judgment is given on a claim for a sum of money expressed in a foreign currency, the judgment should be for the amount of the foreign currency with the addition of 'or the Sterling equivalent at the time of payment'.

PART 13

SETTING ASIDE OR VARYING DEFAULT JUDGMENT

Contents of this Part

Scope of this Part

13.1 The rules in this Part set out the procedure for setting aside or varying judgment entered under Part 12 (default judgment).

(CCR Order 22 r.10 sets out the procedure for varying the rate at which a judgment debt must be paid.)

Cases where the court must set aside judgment entered under Part 12

13.2 The court must set aside$^{(GL)}$ a judgment entered under Part 12 if judgment was wrongly entered because –

(a) in the case of a judgment in default of an acknowledgment of service, any of the conditions in rule 12.3(1) and 12.3(3) was not satisfied;

(b) in the case of a judgment in default of a defence, any of the conditions in rule 12.3(2) and 12.3(3) was not satisfied; or

(c) the whole of the claim was satisfied before judgment was entered.

Cases where the court may set aside or vary judgment entered under Part 12

13.3(1) In any other case, the court may set aside$^{(GL)}$ or vary a judgment entered under Part 12 if –

(a) the defendant has a real prospect of successfully defending the claim; or

---

11 See rule 12.11(4) and (5).

   (b) it appears to the court that there is some other good reason why –
    (i) the judgment should be set aside or varied; or
    (ii) the defendant should be allowed to defend the claim.
  (2) In considering whether to set aside[GL] or vary a judgment entered under Part 12, the matters to which the court must have regard include whether the person seeking to set aside the judgment made an application to do so promptly.

(Rule 3.1(3) provides that the court may attach conditions when it makes an order.)

Application to set aside or vary judgment – procedure

13.4(1) Where –
   (a) the claim is for a specified amount of money;
   (b) the judgment was obtained in a court which is not the defendant's home court;
   (c) the claim has not been transferred to another defendant's home court under rule 14.12 (admission – determination of rate of payment by judge) or rule 26.2 (automatic transfer); and
   (d) the defendant is an individual
   the court will transfer an application by a defendant under this Part to set aside[GL] or vary judgment to the defendant's home court.
  (1A) In this rule, 'defendant's home court' has the meaning given to it by rule 2.3, except that reference to the defendant's address for service shall be a reference to that address shown on the last of the following documents to be filed at court giving an address for service for the defendant-
   (a) the application to set aside[GL];
   (b) any acknowledgment of service; and
   (c) the claim form.
  (2) Paragraph (1) does not apply where the claim was commenced in a specialist list.
  (3) An application under rule 13.3 (cases where the court may set aside[GL] or vary judgment) must be supported by evidence.

Claimant's duty to apply to set aside the judgment

13.5(1) This rule applies where –
   (a) the claimant has purported to serve particulars of claim; and
   (b) the claimant has entered judgment under Part 12 against the defendant to whom the particulars of claim were sent.
  (2) If a claimant who has entered judgment subsequently has good reason to believe that the particulars of claim did not reach the defendant before the claimant entered judgment, he must –
   (a) file a request for the judgment to be set aside[GL]; or
   (b) apply to the court for directions.
  (3) The claimant may take no further step in the proceedings for the enforcement of the judgment until the judgment has been set aside[GL] or the court has disposed of the application for directions.

Abandoned claim restored where default judgment set aside

13.6 Where –
   (a) the claimant claimed a remedy in addition to one specified in rule 12.4(1) (claims in respect of which the claimant may obtain default judgment by filing a request);

(b) the claimant abandoned his claim for that remedy in order to obtain default judgment on request in accordance with rule 12.4(3); and

(c) that default judgment is set aside^(GL) under this Part,

the abandoned claim is restored when the default judgment is set aside.

PART 14

ADMISSIONS

Contents of this Part

Making an admission

14.1(1) A party may admit the truth of the whole or any part of another party's case.

(2) He may do this by giving notice in writing (such as in a statement of case or by letter).

(3) Where the only remedy which the claimant is seeking is the payment of money, the defendant may also make an admission in accordance with –

(a) rule 14.4 (admission of whole claim for specified amount of money);

(b) rule 14.5 (admission of part of claim for specified amount of money);

(c) rule 14.6 (admission of liability to pay whole of claim for unspecified amount of money); or

(d) rule 14.7 (admission of liability to pay claim for unspecified amount of money where defendant offers a sum in satisfaction of the claim).

(4) Where the defendant makes an admission as mentioned in paragraph (3), the claimant has a right to enter judgment except where –

(a) the defendant is a child or patient; or

(b) the claimant is a child or patient and the admission is made under rule 14.5 or 14.7.

(Rule 21.10 provides that, where a claim is made by or on behalf of a child or patient or against a child or patient, no settlement, compromise or payment shall be valid, so far as it relates to that person's claim, without the approval of the court.)

(5) The court may allow a party to amend or withdraw an admission.

(Rule 3.1(3) provides that the court may attach conditions when it makes an order.)

Period for making an admission

14.2(1) The period for returning an admission under rule 14.4 or for filing it under rules 14.5, 14.6 or 14.7 is –

    (a) where the defendant is served with a claim form which states that particulars of claim will follow, 14 days after service of the particulars; and

    (b) in any other case, 14 days after service of the claim form.

(2) Paragraph (1) is subject to the following rules –

    (a) rule 6.22 (which specifies how the period for filing or returning an admission is calculated where the claim form is served out of the jurisdiction); and

    (b) rule 6.16(4) (which requires the court to specify the period for responding to the particulars of claim when it makes an order under that rule).

(3) A defendant may return an admission under rule 14.4 or file it under rules 14.5, 14.6 or 14.7 after the end of the period for returning or filing it specified in paragraph (1) if the claimant has not obtained default judgment under Part 12.

(4) If he does so, this Part shall apply as if he had made the admission within that period.

Admission by notice in writing – application for judgment

14.3(1) Where a party makes an admission under rule 14.1(2) (admission by notice in writing), any other party may apply for judgment on the admission.

(2) Judgment shall be such judgment as it appears to the court that the applicant is entitled to on the admission.

Admission of whole of claim for specified amount of money

14.4(1) This rule applies where –

    (a) the only remedy which the claimant is seeking is the payment of a specified amount of money; and

    (b) the defendant admits the whole of the claim.

(2) The defendant may admit the claim by returning to the claimant an admission in the relevant practice form.

(3) The claimant may obtain judgment by filing a request in the relevant practice form and, if he does so –

    (a) if the defendant has not requested time to pay, the procedure in paragraphs (4) to (6) will apply;

    (b) if the defendant has requested time to pay, the procedure in rule 14.9 will apply.

(4) The claimant may specify in his request for judgment –

    (a) the date by which the whole of the judgment debt is to be paid; or

    (b) the times and rate at which it is to be paid by instalments.

(5) On receipt of the request for judgment the court will enter judgment.

(6) Judgment will be for the amount of the claim (less any payments made) and costs –

    (a) to be paid by the date or at the rate specified in the request for judgment; or

    (b) if none is specified, immediately.

(Rule 14.14 deals with the circumstances in which judgment under this rule may include interest.)

Admission of part of claim for specified amount of money

14.5(1) This rule applies where –

    (a) the only remedy which the claimant is seeking is the payment of a specified amount of money; and

    (b) the defendant admits part of the claim.

(2) The defendant may admit part of the claim by filing an admission in the relevant practice form.

(3) On receipt of the admission, the court will serve a notice on the claimant requiring him to return the notice stating that –

    (a) he accepts the amount admitted in satisfaction of the claim;

    (b) he does not accept the amount admitted by the defendant and wishes the proceedings to continue; or

    (c) if the defendant has requested time to pay, he accepts the amount admitted in satisfaction of the claim, but not the defendant's proposals as to payment.

(4) The claimant must –

    (a) file the notice; and

    (b) serve a copy on the defendant,

within 14 days after it is served on him.

(5) If the claimant does not file the notice within 14 days after it is served on him, the claim is stayed(GL) until he files the notice.

(6) If the claimant accepts the amount admitted in satisfaction of the claim, he may obtain judgment by filing a request in the relevant practice form and, if he does so –

    (a) if the defendant has not requested time to pay, the procedure in paragraphs (7) to (9) will apply;

    (b) if the defendant has requested time to pay, the procedure in rule14.9 will apply.

(7) The claimant may specify in his request for judgment –

    (a) the date by which the whole of the judgment debt is to be paid; or

    (b) the time and rate at which it is to be paid by instalments.

(8) On receipt of the request for judgment, the court will enter judgment.

(9) Judgment will be for the amount admitted (less any payments made) and costs –

    (a) to be paid by the date or at the rate specified in the request for judgment; or

    (b) if none is specified, immediately.

(If the claimant files notice under paragraph (3) that he wishes the proceedings to continue, the procedure which then follows is set out in Part 26)

Admission of liability to pay whole of claim for unspecified amount of money

14.6(1) This rule applies where –

    (a) the only remedy which the claimant is seeking is the payment of money;

    (b) the amount of the claim is not specified; and

    (c) the defendant admits liability but does not offer to pay a specified amount of money in satisfaction of the claim.

(2) The defendant may admit the claim by filing an admission in the relevant practice form.

(3) On receipt of the admission, the court will serve a copy on the claimant.

(4) The claimant may obtain judgment by filing a request in the relevant practice form.

(5) If the claimant does not file a request for judgment within 14 days after service of the admission on him, the claim is stayed$^{(GL)}$ until he files the request.

(6) On receipt of the request for judgment the court will enter judgment.

(7) Judgment will be for an amount to be decided by the court and costs.

Admission of liability to pay claim for unspecified amount of money where defendant offers a sum in satisfaction of the claim

14.7(1) This rule applies where –
  (a) the only remedy which the claimant is seeking is the payment of money;
  (b) the amount of the claim is not specified; and
  (c) the defendant –
     (i) admits liability; and
     (ii) offers to pay a specified amount of money in satisfaction of the claim.

(2) The defendant may admit the claim by filing an admission in the relevant practice form.

(3) On receipt of the admission, the court will serve a notice on the claimant requiring him to return the notice stating whether or not he accepts the amount in satisfaction of the claim.

(4) If the claimant does not file the notice within 14 days after it is served on him, the claim is stayed$^{(GL)}$ until he files the notice.

(5) If the claimant accepts the offer he may obtain judgment by filing a request in the relevant practice form and if he does so –
  (a) if the defendant has not requested time to pay, the procedure in paragraphs (6) to (8) will apply;
  (b) if the defendant has requested time to pay, the procedure in rule 14.9 will apply.

(6) The claimant may specify in his request for judgment –
  (a) the date by which the whole of the judgment debt is to be paid; or
  (b) the times and rate at which it is to be paid by instalments.

(7) On receipt of the request for judgment, the court will enter judgment.

(8) Judgment will be for the amount offered by the defendant (less any payments made) and costs –
  (a) to be paid on the date or at the rate specified in the request for judgment; or
  (b) if none is specified, immediately.

(9) If the claimant does not accept the amount offered by the defendant, he may obtain judgment by filing a request in the relevant practice form.

(10) Judgment under paragraph (9) will be for an amount to be decided by the court and costs.

Allocation of claims in relation to outstanding matters

14.8 Where the court enters judgment under rule 14.6 or 14.7 for an amount to be decided by the court it will –
  (a) give any directions it considers appropriate; and
  (b) if it considers it appropriate, allocate the case.

Request for time to pay

14.9(1) A defendant who makes an admission under rules 14.4, 14.5 or 14.7 (admission relating to a claim for a specified amount of money or offering to pay a specified amount of money) may make a request for time to pay.

(2) A request for time to pay is a proposal about the date of payment or a proposal to pay by instalments at the times and rate specified in the request.

(3) The defendant's request for time to pay must be served or filed (as the case may be) with his admission.

(4) If the claimant accepts the defendant's request, he may obtain judgment by filing a request in the relevant practice form.

(5) On receipt of the request for judgment, the court will enter judgment.

(6) Judgment will be –
  (a) where rule 14.4 applies, for the amount of the claim (less any payments made) and costs;
  (b) where rule 14.5 applies, for the amount admitted (less any payments made) and costs; or
  (c) where rule 14.7 applies, for the amount offered by the defendant (less any payments made) and costs; and
  (in all cases) will be for payment at the time and rate specified in the defendant's request for time to pay.

(Rule 14.10 sets out the procedure to be followed if the claimant does not accept the defendant's request for time to pay.)

Determination of rate of payment

14.10 (1) This rule applies where the defendant makes a request for time to pay under rule 14.9.

(2) If the claimant does not accept the defendant's proposals for payment, he must file a notice in the relevant practice form.

(3) Where the defendant's admission was served direct on the claimant, a copy of the admission and the request for time to pay must be filed with the claimant's notice.

(4) When the court receives the claimant's notice, it will enter judgment for the amount admitted (less any payments made) to be paid at the time and rate of payment determined by the court.

Determination of rate of payment by court officer

14.11 (1) A court officer may exercise the powers of the court under rule 14.10(4) where the amount outstanding (including costs) is not more than £50,000.

(2) Where a court officer is to determine the time and rate of payment, he must do so without a hearing.

Determination of rate of payment by judge

14.12 (1) Where a judge is to determine the time and rate of payment, he may do so without a hearing.

(2) Where a judge is to determine the time and rate of payment at a hearing, the proceedings must be transferred automatically to the defendant's home court if –
  (a) the only claim is for a specified amount of money;
  (b) the defendant is an individual;

(c) the claim has not been transferred to another defendant's home court under rule 13.4 (application to set aside$^{(GL)}$ or vary default judgment – procedure) or rule 26.2 (automatic transfer);

(d) the claim was not started in the defendant's home court; and

(e) the claim was not started in a specialist list.

(Rule 2.3 explains which court is a defendant's home court)

(3) If there is to be a hearing to determine the time and rate of payment, the court must give each party at least 7 days' notice of the hearing.

Right of re-determination

14.13 (1)Where –

(a) a court officer has determined the time and rate of payment under rule 14.11; or

(b) a judge has determined the time and rate of payment under rule 14.12 without a hearing,

either party may apply for the decision to be re–determined by a judge.

(2) An application for re–determination must be made within 14 days after service of the determination on the applicant.

(3) Where an application for re–determination is made, the proceedings must be transferred to the defendant's home court if –

(a) the only claim (apart from a claim for interest or costs) is for a specified amount of money;

(b) the defendant is an individual;

(c) the claim has not been transferred to another defendant's home court under rule 13.4 (application to set aside$^{(GL)}$ or vary default judgment – procedure) or rule 26.2 (automatic transfer);

(d) the claim was not started in the defendant's home court; and

(e) the claim was not started in a specialist list.

(Rule 2.3 explains which court is a defendant's home court.)

Interest

14.14 (1) Judgment under rule 14.4 (admission of whole of claim for specified amount of money) shall include the amount of interest claimed to the date of judgment if –

(a) the particulars of claim include the details required by rule 16.4;

(b) where interest is claimed under section 35A of the Supreme Court Act 1981[22] or section 69 of the County Courts Act 1984[23], the rate is no higher than the rate of interest payable on judgment debts at the date when the claim form was issued; and

(c) the claimant's request for judgment includes a calculation of the interest claimed for the period from the date up to which interest was stated to be calculated in the claim form to the date of the request for judgment.

(2) In any case where judgment is entered under rule 14.4 and the conditions in paragraph (1) are not satisfied judgment shall be for an amount of interest to be decided by the court.

---

(22) 1981 c.54. Section 35A was inserted by the Administration of Justice Act 1982 (c.53), section 15(1), Schedule 1, Part I.

(23) 1984 c.28. Schedule 69 was amended by the Courts and Legal Services Act 1990 (c.41), section 125(3), Schedule 18, paragraph 46.

(3) Where judgment is entered for an amount of interest to be decided by the court, the court will give directions for the management of the case.

PRACTICE DIRECTION – ADMISSIONS

THIS PRACTICE DIRECTION SUPPLEMENTS CPR PART 14

Admissions generally

1.1 Rules 14.1 and 14.2 deal with the manner in which a defendant may make an admission of a claim or part of a claim.

1.2 Rules 14.3, 14.4, 14.5, 14.6 and 14.7 set out how judgment may be obtained on a written admission.

Forms

2.1 When particulars of claim are served on a defendant the forms for responding to the claim that will accompany them will include a form[1] for making an admission.

2.2 If the defendant is requesting time to pay he should complete as fully as possible the statement of means contained in the admission form, or otherwise give in writing the same details of his means as could have been given in the admission form.

Returning or filing the admission

3.1 If the defendant wishes to make an admission in respect of the whole of a claim for a specified amount of money, the admission form or other written notice of the admission should be completed and returned to the claimant within 14 days of service of the particulars of claim[2].

3.2 If the defendant wishes to make an admission in respect of a part of a claim for a specified amount of money, or in respect of a claim for an unspecified amount of money, the admission form or other written notice of admission should be completed and filed with the court within 14 days of service of the particulars of claim[3].

3.3 The defendant may also file a defence under rule 15.2.

Request for time to pay

4.1 A defendant who makes an admission in respect of a claim for a specified sum of money or offers to pay a sum of money in respect of a claim for an unspecified sum may, in the admission form, make a request for time to pay[4].

4.2 If the claimant accepts the defendant's request, he may obtain judgment by filing a request for judgment contained in Form N225A[5]; the court will then enter judgment for payment at the time and rate specified in the defendant's request[6].

4.3 If the claimant does not accept the request for time to pay, he should file notice to that effect by completing Form N225A; the court will then enter judgment for the amount of the admission (less any payments made) at a time and rate of payment decided by the court (see rule 14.10).

---

1 Practice forms N9A (specified amount) or N9C (unspecified amount).
2 Rules 14.2 and 14.4.
3 Rules 14.2, 14.5, 14.6 and 14.7.
4 Rule 14.9.
5 Rule 14.9(4).
6 Rule 14.9(5) and (6).

Determining the rate of payment

5.1 In deciding the time and rate of payment the court will take into account:

   (1) the defendant's statement of means set out in the admission form or in any other written notice of the admission filed,

   (2) the claimant's objections to the defendant's request set out in the claimant's notice[7], and

   (3) any other relevant factors.

5.2 The time and rate of payment may be decided:

   (1) by a judge with or without a hearing, or

   (2) by a court officer without a hearing provided that –

      (a) the only claim is for a specified sum of money, and

      (b) the amount outstanding is not more than £50,000 (including costs).

5.3 Where a decision has been made without a hearing whether by a court officer or by a judge, either party may apply for the decision to be re-determined by a judge[8].

5.4 If the decision was made by a court officer the re-determination may take place without a hearing, unless a hearing is requested in the application notice.

5.5 If the decision was made by a judge the re-determination must be made at a hearing unless the parties otherwise agree.

5.6 Rule 14.13(2) describes how to apply for a re-determination.

Varying the rate of payment

6.1 Either party may, on account of a change in circumstances since the date of the decision (or re-determination as the case may be) apply to vary the time and rate of payment of instalments still remaining unpaid.

6.2 An application to vary under paragraph 6.1 above should be made in accordance with Part 23.

PART 15

DEFENCE AND REPLY

Contents of this Part

Part not to apply where claimant uses Part 8 procedure

15.1 This Part does not apply where the claimant uses the procedure set out in Part 8 (alternative procedure for claims.)

---

7   Practice form N225A.

8   Rule 14.13(1).

Filing a defence

15.2   A defendant who wishes to defend all or part of a claim must file a defence.

(Part 14 contains further provisions which apply where the defendant admits a claim.)

Consequence of not filing a defence

15.3   If a defendant fails to file a defence, the claimant may obtain default judgment if Part 12 allows it.

The period for filing a defence

15.4(1) The general rule is that the period for filing a defence is –

(a) 14 days after service of the particulars of claim; or

(b) if the defendant files an acknowledgment of service under Part 10, 28 days after service of the particulars of claim.

(Rule 7.4 provides for the particulars of claim to be contained in or served with the claim form or served within 14 days of service of the claim form.)

(2) The general rule is subject to the following rules –

(a) rule 6.23 (which specifies how the period for filing a defence is calculated where the claim form is served out of the jurisdiction);

(b) rule 11 (which provides that, where the defendant makes an application disputing the court's jurisdiction, he need not file a defence before the hearing);

(c) rule 24.4(2) (which provides that, if the claimant applies for summary judgment before the defendant has filed a defence, the defendant need not file a defence before the summary judgment hearing); and

(d) rule 6.16(4) (which requires the court to specify the period for responding to the particulars of claim when it makes an order under that rule).

Agreement extending the period for filing a defence

15.5(1) The defendant and the claimant may agree that the period for filing a defence specified in rule 15.4 shall be extended by up to 28 days.

(2) Where the defendant and the claimant agree to extend the period for filing a defence, the defendant must notify the court in writing.

Service of copy of defence

15.6   A copy of the defence must be served on every other party.

(Part 16 sets out what a defence must contain.)

Making a counterclaim

15.7   Part 20 applies to a defendant who wishes to make a counterclaim.

Reply to defence

15.8   If a claimant files a reply to the defence, he must –

(a) file his reply when he files his allocation questionnaire; and

(b) serve his reply on the other parties at the same time as he files it.

(Rule 26.3(6) requires the parties to file allocation questionnaires and specifies the period for doing so.)

(Part 22 requires a reply to be verified by a statement of truth)

No statement of case after a reply to be filed without court's permission

15.9   A party may not file or serve any statement of case after a reply without the permission of the court.

Claimant's notice where defence is that money claimed has been paid

15.10 (1) Where –

    (a) the only claim (apart from a claim for costs and interest) is for a specified amount of money; and

    (b) the defendant states in his defence that he has paid to the claimant the amount claimed,

the court will send notice to the claimant requiring him to state in writing whether he wishes the proceedings to continue.

    (2) When the claimant responds, he must serve a copy of his response on the defendant.

    (3) If the claimant fails to respond under this rule within 28 days after service of the court's notice on him the claim shall be stayed$^{(GL)}$.

    (4) Where a claim is stayed under this rule any party may apply for the stay$^{(GL)}$ to be lifted.

(If the claimant files notice under this rule that he wishes the proceedings to continue, the procedure which then follows is set out in Part 26.)

Claim stayed if it is not defended or admitted

15.11 (1) Where –

    (a) at least 6 months have expired since the end of the period for filing a defence specified in rule 15.4;

    (b) no defendant has served or filed an admission or filed a defence or counterclaim; and

    (c) the claimant has not entered or applied for judgment under Part 12 (default judgment), or Part 24 (summary judgment),

the claim shall be stayed$^{(GL)}$.

    (2) Where a claim is stayed$^{(GL)}$ under this rule any party may apply for the stay to be lifted.

PRACTICE DIRECTION – DEFENCE AND REPLY
THIS PRACTICE DIRECTION SUPPLEMENTS CPR PART 15

Defending the claim

1.1 The provisions of Part 15 do not apply to claims in respect of which the Part 8 procedure is being used.

1.2 In relation to specialist proceedings (see CPR Part 49) in respect of which special provisions for defence and reply are made by the rules and practice directions applicable to those claims, the provisions of Part 15 apply only to the extent that they are not inconsistent with those rules and practice directions.

1.3 Form N9B (specified amount) or N9D (unspecified amount or non-money claims) may be used for the purpose of defence and is included in the response pack served on the defendant with the particulars of claim.

1.4 Attention is drawn to rule 15.3 which sets out a possible consequence of not filing a defence.

(Part 16 (statements of case) and the practice direction which supplements it contain rules and directions about the contents of a defence.)

Statement of truth

2.1 Part 22 requires a defence to be verified by a statement of truth.

2.2 The form of the statement of truth is as follows: '[I believe][the defendant believes] that the facts stated in this defence are true.'

2.3 Attention is drawn to rule 32.14 which sets out the consequences of verifying a statement of case containing a false statement without an honest belief in its truth.

(For information about statements of truth see Part 22 and the practice direction which supplements it.)

General

3.1 Where a defendant to a claim serves a counterclaim under Part 20, the defence and counterclaim should normally form one document with the counterclaim following on from the defence.

3.2 Where a claimant serves a reply and a defence to counterclaim, the reply and defence to counterclaim should normally form one document with the defence to counterclaim following on from the reply.

3.3 Where a claim has been stayed under rules 15.10(3) or 15.11(1) any party may apply for the stay to be lifted[1].

3.4 The application should be made in accordance with Part 23 and should give the reason for the applicant's delay in proceeding with or responding to the claim.

PART 16

STATEMENTS OF CASE

Contents of this Part

Part not to apply where claimant uses Part 8 procedure

16.1   This Part does not apply where the claimant uses the procedure set out in Part 8 (alternative procedure for claims).

Contents of the claim form

6.2 (1) The claim form must –

    (a) contain a concise statement of the nature of the claim;

    (b) specify the remedy which the claimant seeks;

    (c) where the claimant is making a claim for money, contain a statement of value in accordance with rule 16.3; and

    (d) contain such other matters as may be set out in a practice direction.

(2) If the particulars of claim specified in rule 16.4 are not contained in, or are not served with the claim form, the claimant must state on the claim form that the particulars of claim will follow.

(3) If the claimant is claiming in a representative capacity, the claim form must state what that capacity is.

---

1   Rules 15.10(4) and 15.11(2).

(4) If the defendant is sued in a representative capacity, the claim form must state what that capacity is.

(5) The court may grant any remedy to which the claimant is entitled even if that remedy is not specified in the claim form.

(Part 22 requires a claim form to be verified by a statement of truth.)

Statement of value to be included in the claim form

16.3(1) This rule applies where the claimant is making a claim for money.

(2) The claimant must, in the claim form, state –
  (a) the amount of money which he is claiming;
  (b) that he expects to recover –
    (i)   not more than £5,000;
    (ii) more than £5,000 but not more than £15,000; or
    (iii) more than £15,000; or
  (c) that he cannot say how much he expects to recover.

(3) In a claim for personal injuries, the claimant must also state in the claim form whether the amount which he expects to recover as general damages for pain, suffering and loss of amenity is –
  (a) not more than £1,000; or
  (b) more than £1,000.

(4) In a claim which includes a claim by a tenant of residential premises against his landlord where the tenant is seeking an order requiring the landlord to carry out repairs or other work to the premises, the claimant must also state in the claim form –
  (a) whether the estimated costs of those repairs or other work is-
    (i) not more than £1000; or
    (ii) more than £1000; and
  (b) whether the financial value of any other claim for damages is-
    (i) not more than £1000; or
    (ii) more than £1000.

(5) If the claim form is to be issued in the High Court it must, where this rule applies –
  (a) state that the claimant expects to recover more than £15,000;
  (b) state that some other enactment provides that the claim may be commenced only in the High Court and specify that enactment;
  (c) if the claim is a claim for personal injuries state that the claimant expects to recover £50,000 or more; or
  (d) state that the claim is to be in one of the specialist High Court lists and state which list.

(6) When calculating how much he expects to recover, the claimant must disregard any possibility –
  (a) that he may recover –
    (i) interest;
    (ii) costs;
  (b) that the court may make a finding of contributory negligence against him;
  (c) that the defendant may make a counterclaim or that the defence may include a set-off; or

(d) that the defendant may be liable to pay an amount of money which the court awards to the claimant to the Secretary of State for Social Security under section 6 of the Social Security (Recovery of Benefits) Act 1997[24].

(7) The statement of value in the claim form does not limit the power of the court to give judgment for the amount which it finds the claimant is entitled to.

Contents of the particulars of claim

16.4(1) Particulars of claim must include –

(a) a concise statement of the facts on which the claimant relies;

(b) if the claimant is seeking interest, a statement to that effect and the details set out in paragraph (2);

(c) if the claimant is seeking aggravated damages$^{(GL)}$ or exemplary damages$^{(GL)}$, a statement to that effect and his grounds for claiming them;

(d) if the claimant is seeking provisional damages, a statement to that effect and his grounds for claiming them; and

(e) such other matters as may be set out in a practice direction.

(2) If the claimant is seeking interest he must –

(a) state whether he is doing so –

(i) under the terms of a contract;

(ii) under an enactment and if so which; or

(iii) on some other basis and if so what that basis is; and

(b) if the claim is for a specified amount of money, state –

(i) the percentage rate at which interest is claimed;

(ii) the date from which it is claimed;

(iii) the date to which it is calculated, which must not be later than the date on which the claim form is issued;

(iv) the total amount of interest claimed to the date of calculation; and

(v) the daily rate at which interest accrues after that date.

(Part 22 requires particulars of claim to be verified by a statement of truth)

Contents of defence

16.5(1) In his defence, the defendant must state –

(a) which of the allegations in the particulars of claim he denies;

(b) which allegations he is unable to admit or deny, but which he requires the claimant to prove; and

(c) which allegations he admits.

(2) Where the defendant denies an allegation –

(a) he must state his reasons for doing so; and

(b) if he intends to put forward a different version of events from that given by the claimant, he must state his own version.

(3) A defendant who –

(a) fails to deal with an allegation; but

(b) has set out in his defence the nature of his case in relation to the issue to which that allegation is relevant, shall be taken to require that allegation to be proved.

---

(24) 1997 c.27.

(4) Where the claim includes a money claim, a defendant shall be taken to require that any allegation relating to the amount of money claimed be proved unless he expressly admits the allegation.

(5) Subject to paragraphs (3) and (4), a defendant who fails to deal with an allegation shall be taken to admit that allegation.

(6) If the defendant disputes the claimant's statement of value under rule16.3 he must –

(a) state why he disputes it; and

(b) if he is able, give his own statement of the value of the claim.

(7) If the defendant is defending in a representative capacity, he must state what that capacity is.

(8) If the defendant has not filed an acknowledgment of service under Part 10, he must give an address for service.

(Part 22 requires a defence to be verified by a statement of truth)

(Rule 6.5 provides that an address for service must be within the jurisdiction)

Defence of set-off

16.6   Where a defendant –

(a) contends he is entitled to money from the claimant; and

(b) relies on this as a defence to the whole or part of the claim,

the contention may be included in the defence and set off against the claim, whether or not it is also a Part 20 claim.

Reply to defence

16.7(1) A claimant who does not file a reply to the defence shall not be taken to admit the matters raised in the defence.

(2) A claimant who –

(a) files a reply to a defence; but

(b) fails to deal with a matter raised in the defence,

shall be taken to require that matter to be proved.

(Part 22 requires a reply to be verified by a statement of truth)

Court's power to dispense with statements of case

16.8   If a claim form has been –

(a) issued in accordance with rule 7.2; and

(b) served in accordance with rule 7.5,

the court may make an order that the claim will continue without any other statement of case.

(Other rules about the contents of statements of case can be found –

(a) in Schedule 1, in the following RSC – O.77 (proceedings against the Crown); O.88 (mortgage claims); O.97 (claims under section 1 of the Landlord and Tenant Act 1927); and

(b) in Schedule 2, in the following CCR – O.6 (recovery of land; mortgage claims; mortgage claims – dwelling house and hire purchase); O.42 (proceedings against the Crown); O.43 (applications under sections 13 or 24 of the Landlord and Tenant Act 1954 and sections 24, 29, 30 or 40 of the Landlord and Tenant Act 1987); O.49 (applications under various statutes).

PRACTICE DIRECTION – STATEMENTS OF CASE
THIS PRACTICE DIRECTION SUPPLEMENTS CPR PART 16

General

1.1 The provisions of Part 16 do not apply to claims in respect of which the Part 8 procedure is being used.

1.2 In relation to specialist proceedings (see CPR Part 49) in respect of which special provisions for statements of case are made by the rules and practice directions applicable to those claims, the provisions of Part 16 and of this practice direction apply only to the extent that they are not inconsistent with those rules and practice directions.

The claim form

2   Rule 16.2 refers to matters which the claim form must contain. Where the claim is for money, the claim form must also contain the statement of value referred to in rule 16.3.

(For information about how and where a claim may be started see Part 7 and the practice direction which supplements it)

Particulars of claim

3.1 If practicable, the particulars of claim should be set out in the claim form.

3.2 Where the claimant does not include the particulars of claim in the claim form, particulars of claim may be served separately:

(1) either at the same time as the claim form, or

(2) within 14 days after service of the claim form[1] provided that the service of the particulars of claim is not later than 4 months from the date of issue of the claim form[2] (or 6 months where the claim form is to be served out of the jurisdiction)[3].

3.3 If the particulars of claim are not included in or have not been served with the claim form, the claim form must also contain a statement that particulars of claim will follow[4].

3.4 Particulars of claim which are not included in the claim form must be verified by a statement of truth, the form of which is as follows: '[I believe][the claimant believes] that the facts stated in these particulars of claim are true.'

3.5 Attention is drawn to rule 32.14 which sets out the consequences of verifying a statement of case containing a false statement without an honest belief in its truth.

3.6 The full particulars of claim must include:

(1) the matters set out in rule 16.4, and

(2) where appropriate, the matters set out in practice directions relating to specific types of claims.

3.7 Attention is drawn to the provisions of rule 16.4(2) in respect of a claim for interest.

3.8 Particulars of claim served separately from the claim form must also contain:

(1) the name of the court in which the claim is proceeding,

(2) the claim number,

(3) the title of the proceedings, and

(4) the claimant's address for service.

Matters which must be included in the particulars of claim in certain types of claim

Personal injury claims

4.1 The particulars of claim must contain:

---

1   See rule 7.4(1)(b).
2   See rules 7.4(2) and 7.5(2).
3   See rule 7.5(3).
4   See rule 16.2(2).

(1) the claimant's date of birth, and

(2) brief details of the claimant's personal injuries.

4.2 The claimant must attach to his particulars of claim a schedule of details of any past and future expenses and losses which he claims.

4.3 Where the claimant is relying on the evidence of a medical practitioner the claimant must attach to or serve with his particulars of claim a report from a medical practitioner about the personal injuries which he alleges in his claim.

4.4 In a provisional damages claim the claimant must state in his particulars of claim:

(1) that he is seeking an award of provisional damages under either section 32A of the Supreme Court Act 1981 or section 51 of the County Courts Act 1984,

(2) that there is a chance that at some future time the claimant will develop some serious disease or suffer some serious deterioration in his physical or mental condition, and

(3) specify the disease or type of deterioration in respect of which an application may be made at a future date.

(Part 41 and the practice direction which supplements it contain information about awards for provisional damages.)

Fatal accident claims

5.1 In a fatal accident claim the claimant must state in his particulars of claim:

(1) that it is brought under the Fatal Accidents Act 1976,

(2) the dependents on whose behalf the claim is made,

(3) the date of birth of each dependent, and

(4) details of the nature of the dependency claim.

5.2 A fatal accident claim may include a claim for damages for bereavement.

5.3 In a fatal accident claim the claimant may also bring a claim under the Law Reform (Miscellaneous Provisions) Act 1934 on behalf of the estate of the deceased.

(For information on apportionment under the Law Reform (Miscellaneous Provisions) Act 1934 and the Fatal Accidents Act 1976 or between dependants see Part 37 and the practice direction which supplements it.)

Recovery of land

6 In a claim for recovery of land the particulars of claim must:

(1) identify the land sought to be recovered,

(2) state whether the claim relates to residential premises,

(3) if the claim relates to residential premises, and the tenancy is one which otherwise would be a protected tenancy within the meaning of the Rent Act 1977, state whether the rateable value of the premises on every day specified by section 4(2) of the Rent Act 1977 in relation to the premises exceeds the sum so specified or whether the rent for the time being payable in respect of the premises exceeds the sum specified in section 4(4)(b) of the Act,

(4) where the claim relates to residential premises and is for non-payment of rent, state –

(a) the amount due at the start of the proceedings,

(b) details of all payments which have been missed,

(c) details of any history of late or under-payment,

(d) any previous steps taken to recover the arrears of rent with full details of any court proceedings, and

(e) any relevant information about the defendant's circumstances, in particular whether any payments are made on his behalf directly to the claimant under the Social Security Contributions and Benefits Act 1992,

(5) give details about the agreement or tenancy, if any, under which the land was held, stating when it determined and the amount of money payable by way of rent or licence fee,

(6) in a case to which section 138 of the County Courts Act 1984 applies (forfeiture for non-payment of rent), state the daily rate at which the rent in arrear is to be calculated,

(7) state the ground on which possession is claimed whether statutory or otherwise, and

(8) in a case where the claimant knows of any person entitled to claim relief against forfeiture as underlessee (including a mortgagee) under section 146(4) of the Law of Property Act 1925 (or in accordance with section 38 of the Supreme Court Act 1981), give the name and address of that person.

(See also further rules about recovery of land in RSC Orders 88 and 113

(Schedule 1 to the CPR) and CCR Orders 6 and 24

(Schedule 2 to the CPR)).

Hire purchase claims

7.1 Where the claim is for the delivery of goods let under a hire-purchase agreement or conditional sale agreement to a person other than a company or other corporation, the claimant must state in the particulars of claim:

(1) the date of the agreement,

(2) the parties to the agreement,

(3) the number or other identification of the agreement,

(4) where the claimant was not one of the original parties to the agreement, the means by which the rights and duties of the creditor passed to him,

(5) whether the agreement is a regulated agreement, and if it is not a regulated agreement, the reason why,

(6) the place where the agreement was signed by the defendant,

(7) the goods claimed,

(8) the total price of the goods,

(9) the paid-up sum,

(10) the unpaid balance of the total price,

(11) whether a default notice or a notice under section 76(1) or 98(1) of the Consumer Credit Act 1974 has been served on the defendant, and if it has, the date and method of service,

(12) the date when the right to demand delivery of the goods accrued,

(13) the amount (if any) claimed as an alternative to the delivery of goods, and

(14) the amount (if any) claimed in addition to –

(a) the delivery of the goods, or

(b) any claim under (13) above,

with the grounds of each claim.

(If the agreement is a regulated agreement the procedure set out in the practice direction relating to consumer credit act claims (which supplements Part 7) should be used).

7.2 Where the claim is not for the delivery of goods, the claimant must state in his particulars of claim:

(1) the matters set out in paragraph 7.1(1) to (6) above,

(2) the goods let under the agreement,

(3) the amount of the total price,

(4) the paid-up sum,

(5) the amount (if any) claimed as being due and unpaid in respect of any instalment or instalments of the total price, and

(6) the nature and amount of any other claim and how it arises.

Other matters to be included in particulars of claim

8.1 Where a claim is made for an injunction or declaration in respect of or relating to any land or the possession, occupation, use or enjoyment of any land the particulars of claim must:

(1) state whether or not the injunction or declaration relates to residential premises, and

(2) identify the land (by reference to a plan where necessary).

8.2 Where a claim is brought to enforce a right to recover possession of goods the particulars of claim must contain a statement showing the value of the goods.

8.3 Where a claim is based upon a written agreement:

(1) a copy of the contract or documents constituting the agreement should be attached to or served with the particulars of claim and the original(s) should be available at the hearing, and

(2) any general conditions of sale incorporated in the contract should also be attached (but where the contract is or the documents constituting the agreement are bulky this practice direction is complied with by attaching or serving only the relevant parts of the contract or documents).

8.4 Where a claim is based upon an oral agreement, the particulars of claim should set out the contractual words used and state by whom, to whom, when and where they were spoken.

8.5 Where a claim is based upon an agreement by conduct, the particulars of claim must specify the conduct relied on and state by whom, when and where the acts constituting the conduct were done.

8.6 In a claim issued in the High Court relating to a Consumer Credit Agreement, the particulars of claim must contain a statement that the action is not one to which section 141 of the Consumer Credit Act 1974 applies.

Matters which must be specifically set out in the particulars of claim if relied on

9.1 A claimant who wishes to rely on evidence:

(1) under section 11 of the Civil Evidence Act 1968 of a conviction of an offence, or

(2) under section 12 of the above-mentioned Act of a finding or adjudication of adultery or paternity,

must include in his particulars of claim a statement to that effect and give the following details:

(1) the type of conviction, finding or adjudication and its date,

(2) the court or Court-Martial which made the conviction, finding or adjudication, and

(3) the issue in the claim to which it relates.

9.2 The claimant must specifically set out the following matters in his particulars of claim where he wishes to rely on them in support of his claim:

(1) any allegation of fraud,

(2) the fact of any illegality,

(3) details of any misrepresentation,

(4) details of all breaches of trust,

(5) notice or knowledge of a fact,

(6) details of unsoundness of mind or undue influence,

(7) details of wilful default, and

(8) any facts relating to mitigation of loss or damage.

General

10.1 Where a claim is for a sum of money expressed in a foreign currency it must expressly state:

(1) that the claim is for payment in a specified foreign currency,

(2) why it is for payment in that currency,

(3) the Sterling equivalent of the sum at the date of the claim, and

(4) the source of the exchange rate relied on to calculate the Sterling equivalent.

10.2 A subsequent statement of case must not contradict or be inconsistent with an earlier one; for example a reply to a defence must not bring in a new claim. Where new matters have come to light the appropriate course may be to seek the court's permission to amend the statement of case.

The defence

General

11.1 Rule 16.5 deals with the contents of the defence.

11.2 A defendant should deal with every allegation in accordance with rule 16.5(1) and (2).

11.3 Rule 16.5(3), (4) and (5) sets out the consequences of not dealing with an allegation.

Statement of truth

12.1 Part 22 requires a defence to be verified by a statement of truth.

12.2 The form of the statement of truth is as follows: '[I believe][the defendant believes] that the facts stated in the defence are true.'

12.3 Attention is drawn to rule 32.14 which sets out the consequences of verifying a statement of case containing a false statement without an honest belief in its truth.

Matters which must be included in the defence

Personal injury claims

13.1 Where the claim is for personal injuries and the claimant has attached a medical report in respect of his alleged injuries, the defendant should:

 (1) state in his defence whether he –

   (a) agrees,

   (b) disputes, or

   (c) neither agrees nor disputes but has no knowledge of,

  the matters contained in the medical report,

 (2) where he disputes any part of the medical report, give in his defence his reasons for doing so, and

 (3) where he has obtained his own medical report on which he intends to rely, attach it to his defence.

13.2 Where the claim is for personal injuries and the claimant has included a schedule of past and future expenses and losses, the defendant should include in or attach to his defence a counter-schedule stating:

 (1) which of those items he –

   (a) agrees,

   (b) disputes, or

   (c) neither agrees nor disputes but has no knowledge of, and

 (2) where any items are disputed, supplying alternative figures where appropriate.

Other matters

14.1 The defendant must give details of the expiry of any relevant limitation period relied on.

14.2 Rule 37.3 and paragraph 2 of the practice direction which supplements Part 37 contains information about a defence of tender.

14.3 A party may:

 (1) refer in his statement of case to any point of law on which his claim or defence, as the case may be, is based,

 (2) give in his statement of case the name of any witness he proposes to call, and

 (3) attach to or serve with this statement of case a copy of any document which he considers is necessary to his claim or defence, as the case may be (including any expert's report to be filed in accordance with Part 35).

Competition Act 1998

15 A party who wishes to rely on a finding of the Director General of Fair Trading as provided by section 58 of the Competition Act 1998 must include in his statement of case a statement to that effect and identify the Director's finding on which he seeks to rely.

PART 17

AMENDMENTS TO STATEMENTS OF CASE

Contents of this Part

Amendments to statements of case

7.1 (1) A party may amend his statement of case at any time before it has been served on any other party.

   (2) If his statement of case has been served, a party may amend it only –

     (a) with the written consent of all the other parties; or

     (b) with the permission of the court.

   (3) If a statement of case has been served, an application to amend it by removing, adding or substituting a party must be made in accordance with rule 19.4.

(Part 22 requires amendments to a statement of case to be verified by a statement of truth unless the court orders otherwise.)

Power of court to disallow amendments made without permission

17.2(1) If a party has amended his statement of case where permission of the court was not required, the court may disallow the amendment.

   (2) A party may apply to the court for an order under paragraph (1) within 14 days of service of a copy of the amended statement of case on him.

Amendments to statements of case with the permission of the court

17.3(1) Where the court gives permission for a party to amend his statement of case, it may give directions as to –

     (a) amendments to be made to any other statement of case; and

     (b) service of any amended statement of case.

   (2) The power of the court to give permission under this rule is subject to –

     (a) rule 19.1 (change of parties – general);

     (b) rule 19.4 (special provisions about adding or substituting parties after the end of a relevant limitation period)(GL); and

     (c) rule 17.4 (amendments of statement of case after the end of a relevant limitation period).

Amendments to statements of case after the end of a relevant limitation period

17.4(1) This rule applies where –

     (a) a party applies to amend his statement of case in one of the ways mentioned in this rule; and

     (b) a period of limitation has expired under –

       (i) the Limitation Act 1980[25];

       (ii) the Foreign Limitation Periods Act 1984[26];

(25) 1980 c.58.
(26) 1984 c.16.

(iii) section 190 of the Merchant Shipping Act 1995[27]; or

(iv) any other statutory provision

(2) The court may allow an amendment whose effect will be to add or substitute a new claim, but only if the new claim arises out of the same facts or substantially the same facts as a claim in respect of which the party applying for permission has already claimed a remedy in the proceedings.

(3) The court may allow an amendment to correct a mistake as to the name of a party, but only where the mistake was genuine and not one which would cause reasonable doubt as to the identity of the party in question.

(4) The court may allow an amendment to alter the capacity in which a party claims if the new capacity is one which that party had when the proceedings started or has since acquired.

(Rule 19.4 specifies the circumstances in which the court may allow a new party to be added or substituted after the end of a relevant limitation period[GL].)

PRACTICE DIRECTION – AMENDMENTS TO STATEMENTS OF CASE
THIS PRACTICE DIRECTION SUPPLEMENTS CPR PART 17

A party applying for an amendment will usually be responsible for the costs of and arising from the amendment.

Applications to amend where the permission of the court is required

1.1 The application may be dealt with at a hearing or, if rule 23.8 applies, without a hearing.

1.2 When making an application to amend a statement of case, the applicant should file with the court:

(1) the application notice, and

(2) a copy of the statement of case with the proposed amendments.

1.3 Where permission to amend has been given, the applicant should within 14 days of the date of the order, or within such other period as the court may direct, file with the court the amended statement of case.

1.4 If the substance of the statement of case is changed by reason of the amendment, the statement of case should be re-verified by a statement of truth[1].

1.5 A copy of the order and the amended statement of case should be served on every party to the proceedings, unless the court orders otherwise.

General

2.1 The amended statement of case and the court copy of it should be endorsed as follows:

(1) where the court's permission was required: 'Amended [Particulars of Claim or as may be] by Order of [Master ....][District Judge .... or as may be] dated...............'

(2) Where the court's permission was not required: 'Amended [Particulars of Claim or as may be] under CPR [rule 17.1(1) or (2)(a)] dated.................'

2.2 The statement of case in its amended form need not show the original text. However, where the court thinks it desirable for both the original text and the amendments to be shown, the court may direct that the amendments should be shown either:

---

(27) 1995 c.21.

---

1   See Part 22 for information about the statement of truth.

(1) by coloured amendments, either manuscript or computer generated, or

(2) by use of a numerical code in a monochrome computer generated document.

2.3 Where colour is used, the text to be deleted should be struck through in colour and any text replacing it should be inserted or underlined in the same colour.

2.4 The order of colours to be used for successive amendments is; (1) red, (2) green, (3) violet and (4) yellow.

(For information about changes to parties see Part 19 and the practice direction which supplements it.)

PART 18

FURTHER INFORMATION

Contents of this Part

Obtaining further information

18.1 (1) The court may at any time order a party to –

    (a) clarify any matter which is in dispute in the proceedings; or

    (b) give additional information in relation to any such matter, whether or not the matter is contained or referred to in a statement of case.

  (2) Paragraph (1) is subject to any rule of law to the contrary.

  (3) Where the court makes an order under paragraph (1), the party against whom it is made must –

    (a) file his response; and

    (b) serve it on the other parties, within the time specified by the court.

(Part 22 requires a response to be verified by a statement of truth)

(Part 53 (defamation) restricts requirements for providing further information about sources of information in defamation claims).

Restriction on the use of further information

18.2   The court may direct that information provided by a party to another party (whether given voluntarily or following an order made under rule 18.1) must not be used for any purpose except for that of the proceedings in which it is given.

PRACTICE DIRECTION – FURTHER INFORMATION
THIS PRACTICE DIRECTION SUPPLEMENTS CPR PART 18

Attention is also drawn to Part 22 (Statements of Truth).

Preliminary request for further information or clarification

1.1 Before making an application to the court for an order under Part 18, the party seeking clarification or information (the first party) should first serve on the party from whom it is sought (the second party) a written request for that clarification or information (a Request) stating a date by which the response to the Request should be served. The date must allow the second party a reasonable time to respond.

1.2 A Request should be concise and strictly confined to matters which are reasonably necessary and proportionate to enable the first party to prepare his own case or to understand the case he has to meet.

1.3 Requests must be made as far as possible in a single comprehensive document and not piecemeal.

1.4 A Request may be made by letter if the text of the Request is brief and the reply is likely to be brief; otherwise the Request should be made in a separate document.

1.5 If a Request is made in a letter, the letter should, in order to distinguish it from any other that might routinely be written in the course of a case,

    (1) state that it contains a Request made under Part 18, and

    (2) deal with no matters other than the Request.

1.6 (1) A Request (whether made by letter or in a separate document) must –

    (a) be headed with the name of the court and the title and number of the claim,

    (b) in its heading state that it is a Request made under Part 18, identify the first party and the second party and state the date on which it is made,

    (c) set out in a separate numbered paragraph each request for information or clarification,

    (d) where a Request relates to a document, identify that document and (if relevant) the paragraph or words to which it relates,

    (e) state the date by which the first party expects a response to the Request,

    (2) (a) A Request which is not in the form of a letter may, if convenient, be prepared in such a way that the response may be given on the same document.

    (b) To do this the numbered paragraphs of the Request should appear on the left hand half of each sheet so that the paragraphs of the response may then appear on the right.

    (c) Where a Request is prepared in this form an extra copy should be served for the use of the second party.

Responding to a request

2.1 A response to a Request must be in writing, dated and signed by the second party or his legal representative.

2.2 (1) Where the Request is made in a letter the second party may give his response in a letter or in a formal reply.

    (2) Such a letter should identify itself as a response to the Request and deal with no other matters than the response.

2.3 (1) Unless the Request is in the format described in paragraph 1.6(2) and the second party uses the document supplied for the purpose, a response must:

    (a) be headed with the name of the court and the title and number of the claim,

    (b) in its heading identify itself as a response to that Request,

    (c) repeat the text of each separate paragraph of the Request and set out under each paragraph the response to it,

    (d) refer to and have attached to it a copy of any document not already in the possession of the first party which forms part of the response.

    (2) A second or supplementary response to a Request must identify itself as such in its heading.

2.4 The second party must when he serves his response on the first party serve on every other party and file with the court a copy of the Request and of his response.

Statements of truth

3   Attention is drawn to Part 22 and to the definition of a statement of case in Part 2 of the rules; a response should be verified by a statement of truth.

General matters

4.1 (1) If the second party objects to complying with the Request or part of it or is unable to do so at all or within the time stated in the Request he must inform the first party promptly and in any event within that time.

(2) He may do so in a letter or in a separate document (a formal response), but in either case he must give reasons and, where relevant, give a date by which he expects to be able to comply.

4.2 (1) There is no need for a second party to apply to the court if he objects to a Request or is unable to comply with it at all or within the stated time. He need only comply with paragraph 4.1(1) above.

(2) Where a second party considers that a Request can only be complied with at disproportionate expense and objects to comply for that reason he should say so in his reply and explain briefly why he has taken that view.

Applications for orders under Part 18

5.1 Attention is drawn to Part 23 (Applications) and to the Practice Direction which supplements that Part.

5.2 An application notice for an order under Part 18 should set out or have attached to it the text of the order sought and in particular should specify the matter or matters in respect of which the clarification or information is sought.

5.3 (1) If a Request under paragraph 1 for the information or clarification has not been made, the application notice should, in addition, explain why not.

(2) If a Request for clarification or information has been made, the application notice or the evidence in support should describe the response, if any.

5.4 Both the first party and the second party should consider whether evidence in support of or in opposition to the application is required.

5.5 (1) Where the second party has made no response to a Request served on him, the first party need not serve the application notice on the second party, and the court may deal with the application without a hearing.

(2) Sub-paragraph (1) above only applies if at least 14 days have passed since the Request was served and the time stated in it for a response has expired.

5.6 Unless paragraph 5.5 applies the application notice must be served on the second party and on all other parties to the claim.

5.7 An order made under Part 18 must be served on all parties to the claim.

5.8 Costs:

(1) Attention is drawn to the Costs Practice Direction and in particular the court's power to make a summary assessment of costs.

(2) Attention is also drawn to rule 43.5(5) which provides that if an order does not mention costs no party is entitled to costs relating to that order.

PART 19

ADDITION AND SUBSTITUTION OF PARTIES

Contents of this Part

Parties - general

19.1   Any number of claimants or defendants may be joined as parties to a claim.

I   Addition and substitution of parties

Change of parties – general

19.2(1) This rule applies where a party is to be added or substituted except where the
         case falls within rule 19.5 (special provisions about changing parties after the
         end of a relevant limitation period$^{(GL)}$).

  (2) The court may order a person to be added as a new party if –

       (a) it is desirable to add the new party so that the court can resolve all the
           matters in dispute in the proceedings; or

       (b) there is an issue involving the new party and an existing party which is
           connected to the matters in dispute in the proceedings, and it is desirable
           to add the new party so that the court can resolve that issue.

  (3) The court may order any person to cease to be a party if it is not desirable for
       that person to be a party to the proceedings.

  (4) The court may order a new party to be substituted for an existing one if –

       (a) the existing party's interest or liability has passed to the new party; and

       (b) it is desirable to substitute the new party so that the court can resolve the
           matters in dispute in the proceedings.

Provisions applicable where two or more persons are jointly entitled to a remedy

19.3(1) Where a claimant claims a remedy to which some other person is jointly
         entitled with him, all persons jointly entitled to the remedy must be parties
         unless the court orders otherwise.

  (2) If any person does not agree to be a claimant, he must be made a defendant,
       unless the court orders otherwise.

  (3) This rule does not apply in probate proceedings.

Procedure for adding and substituting parties

19.4(1) The court's permission is required to remove, add or substitute a party, unless
         the claim form has not been served.

  (2) An application for permission under paragraph (1) may be made by –

       (a) an existing party; or

(b) a person who wishes to become a party.

(3) An application for an order under rule 19.2(4) (substitution of a new party where existing party's interest or liability has passed) –

    (a) may be made without notice; and

    (b) must be supported by evidence.

(4) Nobody may be added or substituted as a claimant unless –

    (a) he has given his consent in writing; and

    (b) that consent has been filed with the court.

(5) An order for the removal, addition or substitution of a party must be served on –

    (a) all parties to the proceedings; and

    (b) any other person affected by the order.

(6) When the court makes an order for the removal, addition or substitution of a party, it may give consequential directions about –

    (a) filing and serving the claim form on any new defendant;

    (b) serving relevant documents on the new party; and

    (c) the management of the proceedings.

Special provisions about adding or substituting parties after the end of a relevant limitation period

19.5(1) This rule applies to a change of parties after the end of a period of limitation under –

    (a) the Limitation Act 1980[28];

    (b) the Foreign Limitation Periods Act 1984[29];

    (c) section 190 of the Merchant Shipping Act 1995[30]; or

    (d) any other statutory provision.

(2) The court may add or substitute a party only if –

    (a) the relevant limitation period[GL] was current when the proceedings were started; and

    (b) the addition or substitution is necessary.

(3) The addition or substitution of a party is necessary only if the court is satisfied that –

    (a) the new party is to be substituted for a party who was named in the claim form in mistake for the new party;

    (b) the claim cannot properly be carried on by or against the original party unless the new party is added or substituted as claimant or defendant; or

    (c) the original party has died or had a bankruptcy order made against him and his interest or liability has passed to the new party.

(4) In addition, in a claim for personal injuries the court may add or substitute a party where it directs that –

    (a) (i) section 11 (special time limit for claims for personal injuries); or

        (ii) section 12 (special time limit for claims under fatal accidents legislation), of the Limitation Act 1980 shall not apply to the claim by or against the new party; or

(28) 1980 c.58.

(29) 1984 c.16.

(30) 1995 c.21.

(b) the issue of whether those sections apply shall be determined at trial.

(Rule 17.4 deals with other changes after the end of a relevant limitation period$^{(GL)}$.)

II Representative parties

Representative parties with same interest

19.6(1) Where more than one person has the same interest in a claim –

    (a) the claim may be begun; or

    (b) the court may order that the claim be continued,

by or against one or more of the persons who have the same interest as representatives of any other persons who have that interest.

(2) The court may direct that a person may not act as a representative.

(3) Any party may apply to the court for an order under paragraph (2).

(4) Unless the court otherwise directs any judgment or order given in a claim in which a party is acting as a representative under this rule –

    (a) is binding on all persons represented in the claim; but

    (b) may only be enforced by or against a person who is not a party to the claim with the permission of the court.

(5) This rule does not apply to a claim to which rule 19.7 applies.

Representation of interested persons who cannot be ascertained etc

19.7(1) This rule applies to claims about –

    (a) the estate of a deceased person;

    (b) property subject to a trust; or

    (c) the meaning of a document, including a statute.

(2) The court may make an order appointing a person to represent any other person or persons in the claim where the person or persons to be represented –

    (a) are unborn;

    (b) cannot be found;

    (c) cannot easily be ascertained; or

    (d) are a class of persons who have the same interest in a claim and –

        (i) one or more members of that class are within sub-paragraphs (a), (b) or (c); or

        (ii) to appoint a representative would further the overriding objective.

(3) An application for an order under paragraph (2) –

    (a) may be made by –

        (i) any person who seeks to be appointed under the order; or

        (ii) any party to the claim; and

    (b) may be made at any time before or after the claim has started.

(4) An application notice for an order under paragraph (2) must be served on –

    (a) all parties to the claim, if the claim has started;

    (b) the person sought to be appointed, if that person is not the applicant or a party to the claim; and

    (c) any other person as directed by the court.

(5) The court's approval is required to settle a claim in which a party is acting as a representative under this rule.

(6) The court may approve a settlement where it is satisfied that the settlement is for the benefit of all the represented persons.

(7) Unless the court otherwise directs, any judgment or order given in a claim in which a party is acting as a representative under this rule –

    (a) is binding on all persons represented in the claim; but

    (b) may only be enforced by or against a person who is not a party to the claim with the permission of the court.

Death

19.8(1) Where a person who had an interest in a claim has died and that person has no personal representative the court may order –

    (a) the claim to proceed in the absence of a person representing the estate of the deceased; or

    (b) a person to be appointed to represent the estate of the deceased.

(2) Where a defendant against whom a claim could have been brought has died and –

    (a) a grant of probate or administration has been made, the claim must be brought against the persons who are the personal representatives of the deceased;

    (b) a grant of probate or administration has not been made –

        (i) the claim must be brought against "the estate of" the deceased; and

        (ii) the claimant must apply to the court for an order appointing a person to represent the estate of the deceased in the claim.

(3) A claim shall be treated as having been brought against "the estate of" the deceased in accordance with paragraph (2)(b)(i) where –

    (a) the claim is brought against the "personal representatives" of the deceased but a grant of probate or administration has not been made; or

    (b) the person against whom the claim was brought was dead when the claim was started.

(4) Before making an order under this rule, the court may direct notice of the application to be given to any other person with an interest in the claim.

(5) Where an order has been made under paragraphs (1) or (2)(b)(ii) any judgment or order made or given in the claim is binding on the estate of the deceased.

Derivative claims

19.9(1) This rule applies where a company, other incorporated body or trade union is alleged to be entitled to claim a remedy and a claim is made by one or more members of the company, body or trade union for it to be given that remedy (a "derivative claim").

(2) The company, body or trade union for whose benefit a remedy is sought must be a defendant to the claim.

(3) After the claim form has been issued the claimant must apply to the court for permission to continue the claim and may not take any other step in the proceedings except –

    (a) except as provided by paragraph (5); or

    (b) where the court gives permission.

(4) An application in accordance with paragraph (3) must be supported by written evidence.

(5) The –

    (a) claim form;

    (b) application notice; and

    (c) written evidence in support of the application,

must be served on the defendant within the period within which the claim form must be served and, in any event, at least 14 days before the court is to deal with the application.

(6) If the court gives the claimant permission to continue the claim, the time within which the defence must be filed is 14 days after the date on which the permission is given or such period as the court may specify.

(7) The court may order the company, body or trade union to indemnify the claimant against any liability in respect of costs incurred in the claim.

III Group litigation

Definition

19.10   A Group Litigation Order ("GLO") means an order made under rule 19.11 to provide for the case management of claims which give rise to common or related issues of fact or law (the "GLO issues").

Group litigation order

19.11 (1) The court may make a GLO where there are or are likely to be a number of claims giving rise to the GLO issues.

(The practice direction provides the procedure for applying for a GLO)

(2) A GLO must –

(a) contain directions about the establishment of a register (the 'group register') on which the claims managed under the GLO will be entered;

(b) specify the GLO issues which will identify the claims to be managed as a group under the GLO; and

(c) specify the court (the "management court") which will manage the claims on the group register.

(3) A GLO may –

(a) in relation to claims which raise one or more of the GLO issues –

(i)   direct their transfer to the management court;

(ii) order their stay$^{(GL)}$ until further order; and

(iii) direct their entry on the group register;

(b) direct that from a specified date claims which raise one or more of the GLO issues should be started in the management court and entered on the group register; and

(c) give directions for publicising the GLO.

Effect of the GLO

19.12 (1) Where a judgment or order is given or made in a claim on the group register in relation to one or more GLO issues –

(a) that judgment or order is binding on the parties to all other claims that are on the group register at the time the judgment is given or the order is made unless the court orders otherwise; and

(b) the court may give directions as to the extent to which that judgment or order is binding on the parties to any claim which is subsequently entered on the group register.

(2) Unless paragraph (3) applies, any party who is adversely affected by a judgment or order which is binding on him may seek permission to appeal the order.

(3) A party to a claim which was entered on the group register after a judgment or order which is binding on him was given or made may not –

    (a) apply for the judgment or order to be set aside$^{(GL)}$, varied or stayed$^{(GL)}$; or

    (b) appeal the judgment or order,

but may apply to the court for an order that the judgment or order is not binding on him.

(4) Unless the court orders otherwise, disclosure of any document relating to the GLO issues by a party to a claim on the group register is disclosure of that document to all parties to claims –

    (a) on the group register; and

    (b) which are subsequently entered on the group register.

Case management

19.13   Directions given by the management court may include directions –

    (a) varying the GLO issues;

    (b) providing for one or more claims on the group register to proceed as test claims;

    (c) appointing the solicitor of one or more parties to be the lead solicitor for the claimants or defendants;

    (d) specifying the details to be included in a statement of case in order to show that the criteria for entry of the claim on the group register have been met;

    (e) specifying a date after which no claim may be added to the group register unless the court gives permission; and

    (f) for the entry of any particular claim which meets one or more of the GLO issues on the group register.

(Part 3 contains general provisions about the case management powers of the court.)

Removal from the register

19.14(1) A party to a claim entered on the group register may apply to the management court for the claim to be removed from the register.

(2) If the management court orders the claim to be removed from the register it may give directions about the future management of the claim.

Test claims

19.15 (1) Where a direction has been given for a claim on the group register to proceed as a test claim and that claim is settled, the management court may order that another claim on the group register be substituted as the test claim.

(2) Where an order is made under paragraph (1), any order made in the test claim before the date of substitution is binding on the substituted claim unless the court orders otherwise.

PRACTICE DIRECTION – ADDITION
AND SUBSTITUTION OF PARTIES
THIS PRACTICE DIRECTION SUPPLEMENTS CPR PART 19

A party applying for an amendment will usually be responsible for the costs of and arising from the amendment.

Changes of parties

General

1.1 Parties may be removed, added or substituted in existing proceedings either on the court's own initiative or on the application of either an existing party or a person who wishes to become a party.

1.2 The application may be dealt with without a hearing where all the existing parties and the proposed new party are in agreement.

1.3 The application to add or substitute a new party should be supported by evidence setting out the proposed new party's interest in or connection with the claim.

1.4 The application notice should be filed in accordance with rule 23.3 and, unless the application is made under rule 19.1(4)[1], be served in accordance with rule 23.4.

1.5 An order giving permission to amend will, unless the court orders otherwise, be drawn up. It will be served by the court unless the parties wish to serve it or the court orders them to do so.

Addition or Substitution of Claimant

2.1 Where an application is made to the court to add or to substitute a new party to the proceedings as claimant, the party applying must file:

(1) the application notice,

(2) the proposed amended claim form and particulars of claim, and

(3) the signed, written consent of the new claimant to be so added or substituted.

2.2 Where the court makes an order adding or substituting a party as claimant but the signed, written consent of the new claimant has not been filed:

(1) the order, and

(2) the addition or substitution of the new party as claimant,

will not take effect until the signed, written consent of the new claimant is filed.

2.3 Where the court has made an order adding or substituting a new claimant, the court may direct:

(1) a copy of the order to be served on every party to the proceedings and any other person affected by the order,

(2) copies of the statements of case and of documents referred to in any statement of case to be served on the new party,

(3) the party who made the application to file within 14 days an amended claim form and particulars of claim.

Addition or substitution of defendant

3.1 The Civil Procedure Rules apply to a new defendant who has been added or substituted as they apply to any other defendant (see in particular the provisions of Parts 9, 10, 11 and 15).

3.2 Where the court has made an order adding or substituting a defendant whether on its own initiative or on an application, the court may direct:

(1) the claimant to file with the court within 14 days (or as ordered) an amended claim form and particulars of claim for the court file,

(2) a copy of the order to be served on all parties to the proceedings and any other person affected by it,

(3) the amended claim form and particulars of claim, forms for admitting, defending and acknowledging the claim and copies of the statements of case and any other documents referred to in any statement of case to be served on the new defendant.

---

1   See rule 19.3(2)(a).

(4) unless the court orders otherwise, the amended claim form and particulars of claim to be served on any other defendants.

3.3 A new defendant does not become a party to the proceedings until the amended claim form has been served on him[2].

Removal of party

4 Where the court makes an order for the removal of a party from the proceedings:

(1) the claimant must file with the court an amended claim form and particulars of claim, and

(2) a copy of the order must be served on every party to the proceedings and on any other person affected by the order.

Transfer of interest or liability

5.1 Where the interest or liability of an existing party has passed to some other person, application should be made to the court to add or substitute that person[3].

5.2 The application must be supported by evidence showing the stage the proceedings have reached and what change has occurred to cause the transfer of interest or liability.

(For information about making amendments generally, see the practice direction supplementing Part 17.)

PRACTICE DIRECTION –GROUP LITIGATION
THIS PRACTICE DIRECTION SUPPLEMENTS SECTION III OF PART 19.

Introduction

1 This practice direction deals with group litigation where the multiple parties are claimants. Section III of Part 19 (group litigation orders) also applies where the multiple parties are defendants. The court will give such directions in such a case as are appropriate.

Preliminary steps

2.1 Before applying for a Group Litigation Order ("GLO") the solicitor acting for the proposed applicant should consult the Law Society's Multi Party Action Information Service in order to obtain information about other cases giving rise to the proposed GLO issues.

2.2 It will often be convenient for the claimants' solicitors to form a Solicitors' Group and to choose one of their number to take the lead in applying for the GLO and in litigating the GLO issues. The lead solicitor's role and relationship with the other members of the Solicitors' Group should be carefully defined in writing and will be subject to any directions given by the court under CPR 19.13(c).

2.3 In considering whether to apply for a GLO, the applicant should consider whether any other order would be more appropriate. In particular he should consider whether, in the circumstances of the case, it would be more appropriate for–

(1) the claims to be consolidated; or

(2) the rules in Section II of Part 19 (representative parties) to be used.

Application for a GLO

3.1 An application for a GLO must be made in accordance with CPR Part 23, may be made at any time before or after any relevant claims have been issued and may be made either by a claimant or by a defendant.

---

2 *Kettleman v Hansel Properties Ltd* (1987) AC 189, HL.

3 See rule 19.1(4).

3.2 The following information should be included in the application notice or in written evidence filed in support of the application:

(1) a summary of the nature of the litigation;

(2) the number and nature of claims already issued;

(3) the number of parties likely to be involved;

(4) the common issues of fact or law (the "GLO issues") that are likely to arise in the litigation; and

(5) whether there are any matters that distinguish smaller groups of claims within the wider group.

3.3 A GLO may not be made in the Queen's Bench Division without the consent of the Lord Chief Justice or in the Chancery Division or a county court without the consent of the Vice-Chancellor.

3.4 The court to which the application for a GLO is made will, if minded to make the GLO, send to the Lord Chief Justice or the Vice-Chancellor (as the case may be) a copy of the application notice, a copy of any relevant written evidence and a written statement as to why a GLO is thought to be desirable. These steps may be taken either before or after a hearing of the application.

High Court in London

3.5 The application for the GLO should be made to the Senior Master in the Queen's Bench Division or the Chief Chancery Master in the Chancery Division. For claims that are proceeding or are likely to proceed in a specialist list, the application should be made to the senior judge of that list.

High Court outside London

3.6 Outside London, the application should be made to a Presiding Judge or a Chancery Supervising Judge of the Circuit in which the District Registry which has issued the application notice is situated.

County courts

3.7 The application should be made to the Designated Civil Judge for the area in which the county court which has issued the application notice is situated.

3.8 The applicant for a GLO should request the relevant court to refer the application notice to the judge by whom the application will be heard as soon as possible after the application notice has been issued. This is to enable the judge to consider whether to follow the practice set out in paragraph 3.4 above prior to the hearing of the application.

3.9 The directions under paragraphs 3.5, 3.6 and 3.7 above do not prevent the judges referred to from making arrangements for other judges to hear applications for GLOs when they themselves are unavailable.

GLO made by court of its own initiative

4 Subject to obtaining the appropriate consent referred to in paragraph 3.3 and the procedure set out in paragraph 3.4, the court may make a GLO of its own initiative. (CPR 3.3 deals with the procedure that applies when a court proposes to make an order of its own initiative.)

The GLO

5 CPR 19.11(2) and (3) set out rules relating to the contents of GLOs.

The Group Register

6.1 Once a GLO has been made a Group Register will be established on which will be entered such details as the court may direct of the cases which are to be subject to the GLO.

6.2 An application for details of a case to be entered on a Group Register may be made by any party to the case.

6.3 An order for details of the case to be entered on the Group Register will not be made unless the case gives rise to at least one of the GLO issues.

(CPR 19.10 defines GLO issues.)

6.4 The court, if it is not satisfied that a case can be conveniently case managed with the other cases on the Group Register, or if it is satisfied that the entry of the case on the Group Register would adversely affect the case management of the other cases, may refuse to allow details of the case to be entered on the Group Register, or order their removal from the Register if already entered, although the case gives rise to one or more of the Group issues.

6.5 The Group Register will normally be maintained by and kept at the court but the court may direct this to be done by the solicitor for one of the parties to a case entered on the Register.

6.6 (1) Rule 5.4 (supply of documents from court records) applies where the register is maintained by the court. A party to a claim on the group register may request documents relating to any other claim on the group register in accordance with rule 5.4(1) as if he were a party to those proceedings.

(2) Where the register is maintained by a solicitor, any person may inspect the Group Register during normal business hours and upon giving reasonable notice to the solicitor; the solicitor may charge a fee not exceeding the fee prescribed for a search at the court office.

6.7 In this paragraph, "the court" means the management court specified in the GLO.

Allocation to track

7 Once a GLO has been made and unless the management court directs otherwise:

(1) every claim in a case entered on the Group Register will be automatically allocated, or re-allocated (as the case may be), to the multi-track;

(2) any case management directions that have already been given in any such case otherwise than by the management court will be set aside; and

(3) any hearing date already fixed otherwise than for the purposes of the group litigation will be vacated.

Managing judge

8 A judge ("the managing judge") will be appointed for the purpose of the GLO as soon as possible. He will assume overall responsibility for the management of the claims and will generally hear the GLO issues. A Master or a District Judge may be appointed to deal with procedural matters, which he will do in accordance with any directions given by the managing judge. A costs judge may be appointed and may be invited to attend case management hearings.

Claims to be started in management court

9.1 The management court may order that as from a specified date all claims that raise one or more of the GLO issues shall be started in the management court.

9.2 Failure to comply with an order made under paragraph 9.1 will not invalidate the commencement of the claim but the claim should be transferred to the management court and details entered on the Group Register as soon as possible. Any party to the claim may apply to the management court for an order under CPR 19.14 removing the case from the Register or, as the case may be, for an order that details of the case be not entered on the Register.

Transfer

10 Where the management court is a county court and a claim raising one or more of the GLO issues is proceeding in the High Court, an order transferring the case to the management court and directing the details of the case to be entered on the Group Register can only be made in the High Court.

Publicising the GLO

11 After a GLO has been made, a copy of the GLO should be supplied—

(1) to the Law Society, 113 Chancery Lane, London WC2A 1PL; and

(2) to the Senior Master, Queen's Bench Division, Royal Courts of Justice, Strand, London WC2A 2LL.

Case management

12.1 The management court may give case management directions at the time the GLO is made or subsequently. Directions given at a case management hearing will generally be binding on all claims that are subsequently entered on the Group Register (see CPR 19.12(1)).

12.2 Any application to vary the terms of the GLO must be made to the management court.

12.3 The management court may direct that one or more of the claims are to proceed as test claims.

12.4 The management court may give directions about how the costs of resolving common issues or the costs of claims proceeding as test claims are to be borne or shared as between the claimants on the Group Register.

Cut-off dates

13 The management court may specify a date after which no claim may be added to the Group Register unless the court gives permission. An early cut-off date may be appropriate in the case of "instant disasters" (such as transport accidents). In the case of consumer claims, and particularly pharmaceutical claims, it may be necessary to delay the ordering of a cut-off date.

Statements of case

14.1 The management court may direct that the GLO claimants serve "Group Particulars of Claim" which set out the various claims of all the claimants on the Group Register at the time the particulars are filed. Such particulars of claim will usually contain–

(1) general allegations relating to all claims; and

(2) a schedule containing entries relating to each individual claim specifying which of the general allegations are relied on and any specific facts relevant to the claimant.

14.2 The directions given under paragraph 14.1 should include directions as to whether the Group Particulars should be verified by a statement or statements of truth and, if so, by whom.

14.3 The specific facts relating to each claimant on the Group Register may be obtained by the use of a questionnaire. Where this is proposed, the management court should be asked to approve the questionnaire. The management court may direct that the questionnaires completed by individual claimants take the place of the schedule referred to in paragraph 14.1(2).

14.4 The management court may also give directions about the form that particulars of claim relating to claims which are to be entered on the Group Register should take.

The trial

15.1 The management court may give directions–

(1) for the trial of common issues; and

(2) for the trial of individual issues.

15.2 Common issues and test claims will normally be tried at the management court. Individual issues may be directed to be tried at other courts whose locality is convenient for the parties.

Costs

16.1 CPR 48 contains rules about costs where a GLO has been made.

16.2 Where the court has made an order about costs in relation to any application or hearing which involved both–

(1) one or more of the GLO issues; and

(2) an issue or issues relevant only to individual claims;

and the court has not directed the proportion of the costs that is to relate to common costs and the proportion that is to relate to individual costs in accordance with rule 48.[ ](5), the costs judge will make a decision as to the relevant proportions at or before the commencement of the detailed assessment of costs.

PART 20

COUNTERCLAIMS AND OTHER ADDITIONAL CLAIMS

Contents of this Part

Purpose of Part 20

20.1   The purpose of Part 20 is to enable Part 20 claims to be managed in the most convenient and effective manner.

Meaning of 'Part 20 claim'

20.2 (1) A Part 20 claim is any claim other than a claim by a claimant against a defendant and includes –

(a) a counterclaim by a defendant against the claimant or against the claimant and some other person;

(b) a claim by a defendant against any person (whether or not already a party) for contribution$^{(GL)}$ or indemnity$^{(GL)}$ or some other remedy; and

(c) where a Part 20 claim has been made against a person who is not already a party, any claim made by that person against any other person (whether or not already a party).

(2) In this Part 'Part 20 claimant' means a person who makes a Part 20 claim.

Part 20 claim to be treated as a claim for the purposes of the rules

20.3 (1) A Part 20 claim shall be treated as if it were a claim for the purposes of these Rules, except as provided by this Part.

(2) The following rules do not apply to Part 20 claims –

(a) rules 7.5 and 7.6 (time within which a claim form may be served);

(b) rule 16.3(5) (statement of value where claim to be issued in the High Court); and

(c) Part 26 (case management – preliminary stage).

(3) Part 12 (default judgment) applies to a Part 20 claim only if it is a counterclaim.

(4) With the exception of –

(a) rules 14.1(1) and 14.1(2) (which provide that a party may admit the truth of another party's case in writing); and

(b) rule 14.(3) (admission by notice in writing – application for judgment),

which apply to all Part 20 claims, Part 14 (admissions) applies to a Part 20 claim only if it is a counterclaim.

(Rule 12.3 (2) sets out how to obtain judgment in default of defence where the Part 20 claim is a counterclaim against the claimant, and rule 20.11 makes special provision for default judgment in some categories of Part 20 claims)

Defendant's counterclaim against the claimant

20.4 (1) A defendant may make a counterclaim against a claimant by filing particulars of the counterclaim.

(2) A defendant may make a counterclaim against a claimant –

    (a) without the court's permission if he files it with his defence; or

    (b) at any other time with the court's permission.

(Part 15 makes provision for a defence to a claim and applies to a defence to a counterclaim by virtue of rule 20.3)

(3) Part 10 (acknowledgment of service) does not apply to a claimant who wishes to defend a counterclaim.

Counterclaim against a person other than the claimant

20.5 (1) A defendant who wishes to counterclaim against a person other than the claimant must apply to the court for an order that that person be added as defendant to the counterclaim.

(2) An application for an order under paragraph (1) may be made without notice unless the court directs otherwise.

(3) Where the court makes an order under paragraph (1), it will give directions as to the management of the case.

Defendant's claim for contribution or indemnity from co-defendant

20.6 A defendant who has filed an acknowledgment of service or a defence may make a Part 20 claim for contribution$^{(GL)}$ or indemnity$^{(GL)}$ against another defendant by –

    (a) filing a notice containing a statement of the nature and grounds of his claim; and

    (b) serving that notice on the other defendant.

Procedure for making any other Part 20 claim

20.7 (1) This rule applies to any Part 20 claim except –

    (a) a counterclaim; and

    (b) a claim for contribution$^{(GL)}$ or indemnity$^{(GL)}$ made in accordance with rule 20.6.

(2) A Part 20 claim is made when the court issues a Part 20 claim form.

(3) A defendant may make a Part 20 claim –

    (a) without the court's permission if the Part 20 claim is issued before or at the same time as he files his defence;

    (b) at any other time with the court's permission.

(Rule 15.4 sets out the period for filing a defence)

(4) Particulars of a Part 20 claim must be contained in or served with the Part 20 claim.

(5) An application for permission to make a Part 20 claim may be made without notice, unless the court directs otherwise.

Service of a Part 20 claim form

20.8 (1) Where a Part 20 claim may be made without the court's permission, the Part 20 claim form must –

> (a) in the case of a counterclaim, be served on every other party when a copy of the defence is served;
>
> (b) in the case of any other Part 20 claim, be served on the person against whom it is made within 14 days after the date on which the party making the Part 20 claim files his defence.

(2) Paragraph (1) does not apply to a claim for contribution$^{(GL)}$ or indemnity$^{(GL)}$ made in accordance with rule 20.6.

(3) Where the court gives permission to make a Part 20 claim it will at the same time give directions as to the service of the Part 20 claim.

Matters relevant to question of whether a Part 20 claim should be separate from main claim

20.9 (1) This rule applies where the court is considering whether to –

> (a) permit a Part 20 claim to be made;
>
> (b) dismiss a Part 20 claim; or
>
> (c) require a Part 20 claim to be dealt with separately from the claim by the claimant against the defendant.

(Rule 3.1(2)(e) and (j) deal respectively with the court's power to order that part of proceedings be dealt with as separate proceedings and to decide the order in which issues are to be tried)

(2) The matters to which the court may have regard include –

> (a) the connection between the Part 20 claim and the claim made by the claimant against the defendant;
>
> (b) whether the Part 20 claimant is seeking substantially the same remedy which some other party is claiming from him; and
>
> (c) whether the Part 20 claimant wants the court to decide any question connected with the subject matter of the proceedings –
>
> > (i) not only between existing parties but also between existing parties and a person not already a party; or
> >
> > (ii) against an existing party not only in a capacity in which he is already a party but also in some further capacity.

Effect of service of a Part 20 claim

20.10 (1) A person on whom a Part 20 claim is served becomes a party to the proceedings if he is not a party already.

(2) When a Part 20 claim is served on an existing party for the purpose of requiring the court to decide a question against that party in a further capacity, that party also becomes a party in the further capacity specified in the Part 20 claim.

Special provisions relating to default judgment on a Part 20 claim other than a counterclaim or a contribution or indemnity notice

20.11 (1) This rule applies if –

> (a) the Part 20 claim is not –
>
> > (i) a counterclaim; or
> >
> > (ii) a claim by a defendant for contribution$^{(GL)}$ or indemnity$^{(GL)}$ against another defendant under rule 20.6; and
>
> (b) the party against whom a Part 20 claim is made fails to file an acknowledgment of service or defence in respect of the Part 20 claim.

(2) The party against whom the Part 20 claim is made –

   (a) is deemed to admit the Part 20 claim, and is bound by any judgment or decision in the main proceedings in so far as it is relevant to any matter arising in the Part 20 claim;

   (b) subject to paragraph (3), if default judgment under Part 12 is given against the Part 20 claimant, the Part 20 claimant may obtain judgment in respect of the Part 20 claim by filing a request in the relevant practice form.

(3) A Part 20 claimant may not enter judgment under paragraph (2)(b) without the court's permission if –

   (a) he has not satisfied the default judgment which has been given against him; or

   (b) he wishes to obtain judgment for any remedy other than a contribution$^{(GL)}$ or indemnity$^{(GL)}$.

(4) An application for the court's permission under paragraph (3) may be made without notice unless the court directs otherwise.

(5) The court may at any time set aside$^{(GL)}$ or vary a judgment entered under paragraph (2)(b).

Procedural steps on service of a Part 20 claim form on a non-party

20.12 (1) Where a Part 20 claim form is served on a person who is not already a party it must be accompanied by –

   (a) a form for defending the claim;

   (b) a form for admitting the claim;

   (c) a form for acknowledging service; and

   (d) a copy of –

      (i) every statement of case which has already been served in the proceedings; and

      (ii) such other documents as the court may direct.

(2) A copy of the Part 20 claim form must be served on every existing party.

Case management where there is a defence to a Part 20 claim form

20.13 (1) Where a defence is filed to a Part 20 claim the court must consider the future conduct of the proceedings and give appropriate directions.

(2) In giving directions under paragraph (1) the court must ensure that, so far as practicable, the Part 20 claim and the main claim are managed together.

(CCR Order 42, in Schedule 2, makes provision for a Part 20 claim against the Crown where the Crown is not a party)

PRACTICE DIRECTION – COUNTERCLAIMS AND OTHER PART 20 CLAIMS
THIS PRACTICE DIRECTION SUPPLEMENTS CPR PART 20

A Part 20 claim is any claim other than the claim by the claimant against the defendant.

Cases where court's permission to make a Part 20 claim is required

1.1 Rules 20.4(2)(b), 20.5(1) and 20.7(3)(b) set out the circumstances in which the court's permission will be needed for making a Part 20 claim.

1.2 Where an application is made for permission to make a Part 20 claim the application notice should be filed together with a copy of the proposed Part 20 claim.

Applications for permission to issue a Part 20 claim

2.1 An application for permission to make a Part 20 claim must be supported by evidence stating:

(1) the stage which the action has reached,

(2) the nature of the claim to be made by the Part 20 claimant or details of the question or issue which needs to be decided,

(3) a summary of the facts on which the Part 20 claim is based, and

(4) the name and address of the proposed Part 20 defendant.

(For further information regarding evidence see the practice direction which supplements Part 32.)

2.2 Where delay has been a factor contributing to the need to apply for permission to make a Part 20 claim an explanation of the delay should be given in evidence.

2.3 Where possible the applicant should provide a timetable of the action to date.

2.4 Rules 20.5(2) and 20.7(5) allow applications to be made to the court without notice unless the court otherwise directs.

General

3 The Civil Procedure Rules apply generally to Part 20 claims as if they were claims[1]. Parties should be aware that the provisions relating to failure to respond will apply.

Statement of truth

4.1 The contents of a Part 20 claim should be verified by a statement of truth. Part 22 requires a statement of case to be verified by a statement of truth.

4.2 The form of the statement of truth should be as follows: '[I believe][the [Part 20 claimant]★ believes] that the facts stated in this statement of case are true, ★(For the purpose of this practice direction the Part 20 claimant means any party making a Part 20 claim.)

4.3 Attention is drawn to rule 32.14 which sets out the consequences of verifying a statement of case containing a false statement without an honest belief in its truth.

(For information regarding statements of truth see Part 22 and the practice direction which supplements it.)

Case management where there is a Part 20 defence

5.1 Where the Part 20 defendant files a defence, other than to a counterclaim, the court will arrange a hearing to consider case management of the Part 20 claim.

5.2 The court will give notice of the hearing to each party likely to be affected by any order made at the hearing.

5.3 At the hearing the court may:

(1) treat the hearing as a summary judgment hearing,

(2) order that the Part 20 proceedings be dismissed,

(3) give directions about the way any claim, question or issue set out in or arising from the Part 20 claim should be dealt with,

(4) give directions as to the part, if any, the Part 20 defendant will take at the trial of the claim,

(5) give directions about the extent to which the Part 20 defendant is to be bound by any judgment or decision to be made in the claim.

5.4 The court may make any of the orders in 5.3(1) to (5) either before or after any judgment in the claim has been entered by the claimant against the defendant.

Form of counterclaim

6.1 Where a defendant to a claim serves a counterclaim under this Part, the defence and counterclaim should normally form one document with the counterclaim following on from the defence.

---

1   Rule 20.3 but note the exceptions set out in rule 20.3 (2) and (3).

6.2 Where a claimant serves a reply and a defence to counterclaim, the reply and the defence to counterclaim should normally form one document with the defence to counterclaim following on from the reply.

Titles of proceedings where there are Part 20 claims

7.1 The title of every Part 20 claim should include:

    (1) the full name of each party, and

    (2) his status in the proceedings (e.g. claimant, defendant, Part 20 claimant, Part 20 defendant etc.). For example: AB Claimant CD Defendant/Part 20 Claimant EF Part 20 Defendant

7.2 Where a defendant makes a counterclaim not only against the claimant but also against a non-party the title should show this as follows: AB Claimant/Part 20 Defendant CD Defendant/Part 20 Claimant and XY Part 20 Defendant

7.3 Where there is more than one Part 20 claim, the parties to the first Part 20 claim should be described as 'Part 20 Claimant (1st claim)' and 'Part 20 Defendant (1st claim)', the parties to the second Part 20 claim should be described as 'Part 20 Claimant (2nd claim)' and 'Part 20 Defendant (2nd claim)', and so on. For example: AB Claimant and Part 20 Defendant (2nd claim) CD Defendant and Part 20 Claimant (1st claim) EF Part 20 Defendant (1st claim) and Part 20 Claimant (2nd claim) GH Part 20 Defendant (2nd claim)

7.4 Where the full name of a party is lengthy it must appear in the title but thereafter in the statement of case it may be identified by an abbreviation such as initials or a recognised shortened name.

7.5 Where a party to proceedings has more than one status eg. Claimant and Part 20 Defendant (2nd claim) or Part 20 Defendant (1st claim) and Part 20 Claimant (2nd claim) the combined status must appear in the title but thereafter it may be convenient to refer to the party by name, e.g. Mr Smith or, if paragraph 7.4 applies, by initials or a shortened name.

7.6 Paragraph 4 of the practice direction supplementing Part 7 contains further directions regarding the title to proceedings.

PART 21

CHILDREN AND PATIENTS

Contents of this Part

Scope of this Part

21.1 (1) This Part –

    (a) contains special provisions which apply in proceedings involving children and patients; and

(b) sets out how a person becomes a litigation friend.

(2) In this Part –

(a) 'child' means a person under 18; and

(b) 'patient' means a person who by reason of mental disorder within the meaning of the Mental Health Act 1983[31] is incapable of managing and administering his own affairs.

(Rule 6.6 contains provisions about the service of documents on children and patients)

(Rule 48.5 deals with costs where money is payable by or to a child or patient)

Requirement for litigation friend in proceedings by or against children and patients

21.2 (1) A patient must have a litigation friend to conduct proceedings on his behalf.

(2) A child must have a litigation friend to conduct proceedings on his behalf unless the court makes an order under paragraph (3).

(3) The court may make an order permitting the child to conduct proceedings without a litigation friend.

(4) An application for an order under paragraph (3) –

(a) may be made by the child;

(b) if the child already has a litigation friend, must be made on notice to the litigation friend; and

(c) if the child has no litigation friend, may be made without notice.

(5) Where –

(a) the court has made an order under paragraph (3); and

(b) it subsequently appears to the court that it is desirable for a litigation friend to conduct the proceedings on behalf of the child,

the court may appoint a person to be the child's litigation friend.

Stage of proceedings at which a litigation friend becomes necessary

21.3 (1) This rule does not apply where the court has made an order under rule 21.2(3).

(2) A person may not, without the permission of the court –

(a) make an application against a child or patient before proceedings have started; or

(b) take any step in proceedings except –

(i) issuing and serving a claim form; or

(ii) applying for the appointment of a litigation friend under rule 21.6,

until the child or patient has a litigation friend.

(3) If a party becomes a patient during proceedings, no party may take any step in the proceedings without the permission of the court until the patient has a litigation friend.

(4) Any step taken before a child or patient has a litigation friend shall be of no effect unless the court otherwise orders.

Who may be a litigation friend without a court order

21.4 (1) This rule does not apply if the court has appointed a person to be a litigation friend.

(2) A person authorised under Part VII of the Mental Health Act 1983 to conduct legal proceedings in the name of a patient or on his behalf is entitled to be the

---

(31) 1983 c.20.

litigation friend of the patient in any proceedings to which his authority extends.

(3) If nobody has been appointed by the court or, in the case of a patient, authorised under Part VII, a person may act as a litigation friend if he –

    (a) can fairly and competently conduct proceedings on behalf of the child or patient;

    (b) has no interest adverse to that of the child or patient; and

    (c) where the child or patient is a claimant, undertakes to pay any costs which the child or patient may be ordered to pay in relation to the proceedings, subject to any right he may have to be repaid from the assets of the child or patient.

How a person becomes a litigation friend without a court order

21.5 (1) If the court has not appointed a litigation friend, a person who wishes to act as a litigation friend must follow the procedure set out in this rule.

(2) A person authorised under Part VII of the Mental Health Act 1983 must file an official copy$^{(GL)}$ of the order or other document which constitutes his authorisation to act.

(3) Any other person must file a certificate of suitability stating that he satisfies the conditions specified in rule 21.4(3).

(4) A person who is to act as a litigation friend for a claimant must file –

    (a) the authorisation; or

    (b) the certificate of suitability,

at the time when the claim is made.

(5) A person who is to act as a litigation friend for a defendant must file –

    (a) the authorisation; or

    (b) the certificate of suitability,

at the time when he first takes a step in the proceedings on behalf of the defendant.

(6) The litigation friend must –

    (a) serve the certificate of suitability on every person on whom, in accordance with rule 6.6 (service on parent, guardian etc.), the claim form should be served; and

    (b) file a certificate of service when he files the certificate of suitability.

(Rule 6.10 sets out the details to be contained in a certificate of service.)

How a person becomes a litigation friend by court order

21.6 (1) The court may make an order appointing a litigation friend.

(2) An application for an order appointing a litigation friend may be made by –

    (a) a person who wishes to be the litigation friend; or

    (b) a party.

(3) Where –

    (a) a person makes a claim against a child or patient;

    (b) the child or patient has no litigation friend;

    (c) the court has not made an order under rule 21.2(3) (order that a child can act without a litigation friend); and

    (d) either –

        (i) someone who is not entitled to be a litigation friend files a defence; or

        (ii) the claimant wishes to take some step in the proceedings, the claimant must apply to the court for an order appointing a litigation friend for the child or patient.

(4) An application for an order appointing a litigation friend must be supported by evidence.

(5) The court may not appoint a litigation friend under this rule unless it is satisfied that the person to be appointed complies with the conditions specified in rule 21.4(3).

Court's power to change litigation friend and to prevent person acting as litigation friend

21.7 (1) The court may –
   (a) direct that a person may not act as a litigation friend;
   (b) terminate a litigation friend's appointment;
   (c) appoint a new litigation friend in substitution for an existing one.

(2) An application for an order under paragraph (1) must be supported by evidence.

(3) The court may not appoint a litigation friend under this rule unless it is satisfied that the person to be appointed complies with the conditions specified in rule 21.4(3).

Appointment of litigation friend by court order – supplementary

21.8 (1) An application for an order under rule 21.6 or 21.7 must be served on every person on whom, in accordance with rule 6.6 (service on parent, guardian etc), the claim form should be served.

(2) Where an application for an order under rule 21.6 is in respect of a patient, the application must also be served on the patient unless the court orders otherwise.

(3) An application for an order under rule 21.7 must also be served on –
   (a) the person who is the litigation friend, or who is purporting to act as the litigation friend, when the application is made; and
   (b) the person who it is proposed should be the litigation friend, if he is not the applicant.

(4) On an application for an order under rule 21.6 or 21.7, the court may appoint the person proposed or any other person who complies with the conditions specified in rule 21.4(3).

Procedure where appointment of litigation friend ceases

21.9 (1) When a child who is not a patient reaches the age of 18, a litigation friend's appointment ceases.

(2) When a party ceases to be a patient, the litigation friend's appointment continues until it is ended by a court order.

(3) An application for an order under paragraph (2) may be made by –
   (a) the former patient;
   (b) the litigation friend; or
   (c) a party.

(4) The child or patient in respect of whom the appointment to act has ceased must serve notice on the other parties –
   (a) stating that the appointment of his litigation friend to act has ceased;
   (b) giving his address for service; and
   (c) stating whether or not he intends to carry on the proceedings.

(5) If he does not do so within 28 days after the day on which the appointment of the litigation friend ceases the court may, on application, strike out(GL) any claim or defence brought by him.

(6) The liability of a litigation friend for costs continues until –

    (a) the person in respect of whom his appointment to act has ceased serves the notice referred to in paragraph (4); or

    (b) the litigation friend serves notice on the parties that his appointment to act has ceased.

Compromise etc by or on behalf of child or patient

21.10 (1) Where a claim is made –

    (a) by or on behalf of a child or patient; or

    (b) against a child or patient,

no settlement, compromise or payment and no acceptance of money paid into court shall be valid, so far as it relates to the claim by, on behalf of or against the child or patient, without the approval of the court.

  (2) Where –

    (a) before proceedings in which a claim is made by or on behalf of, or against a child or patient (whether alone or with any other person) are begun, an agreement is reached for the settlement of the claim; and

    (b) the sole purpose of proceedings on that claim is to obtain the approval of the court to a settlement or compromise of the claim, the claim must –

      (i) be made using the procedure set out in Part 8 (alternative procedure for claims); and

      (ii) include a request to the court for approval of the settlement or compromise.

(Rule 48.5 contains provisions about costs where money is payable to a child or patient.)

Control of money recovered by or on behalf of child or patient

21.11 (1) Where in any proceedings –

    (a) money is recovered by or on behalf of or for the benefit of a child or patient; or

    (b) money paid into court is accepted by or on behalf of a child or patient, the money shall be dealt with in accordance with directions given by the court under this rule and not otherwise.

  (2) Directions given under this rule may provide that the money shall be wholly or partly paid into court and invested or otherwise dealt with.

Appointment of guardian of child's estate

21.12 (1) The court may appoint the Official Solicitor to be a guardian of a child's estate where –

    (a) money is paid into court on behalf of the child in accordance with directions given under rule 21.11 (control of money received by a child or patient);

    (b) the Criminal Injuries Compensation Board or the Criminal Injuries Compensation Authority notifies the court that it has made or intends to make an award to the child;

    (c) a court or tribunal outside England and Wales notifies the court that it has ordered or intends to order that money be paid to the child;

    (d) the child is absolutely entitled to the proceeds of a pension fund; or

(e) in any other case, such an appointment seems desirable to the court.

(2) The court may not appoint the Official Solicitor under this rule unless –

    (a) the persons with parental responsibility (within the meaning of section 3 of the Children Act 1989[(32)]) agree; or

    (b) the court considers that their agreement can be dispensed with.

(3) The Official Solicitor's appointment may continue only until the child reaches 18.

PRACTICE DIRECTION – CHILDREN AND PATIENTS
THIS PRACTICE DIRECTION SUPPLEMENTS CPR PART 21

General

1.1 In this practice direction 'child' means a person under 18 years old and 'patient' means a person who by reason of mental disorder within the meaning of the Mental Health Act 1983 is incapable of managing and administering his own affairs[1].

1.2 A patient must bring or defend proceedings by a litigation friend (see paragraph 2 below for the definition of a litigation friend).

1.3 In the proceedings referred to in paragraph 1.2 above the patient should be referred to in the title as 'A.B. (by C.D. his litigation friend)'.

1.4 A child must bring or defend proceedings by a litigation friend unless the court has made an order permitting the child to do so on his own behalf[2].

1.5 Where:

    (1) the child has a litigation friend, the child should be referred to in the title to proceedings as 'A.B. (a child by C.D. his litigation friend)', and

    (2) the child is conducting proceedings on his own behalf, the child should be referred to in the title as 'A.B. (a child)'.

1.6 The approval of the court must be obtained if a settlement of a claim by or against a child or patient[3] is to be valid. A settlement includes an agreement on a sum to be apportioned to a dependant child under the Fatal Accidents Act 1976.

1.7 The approval of the court must also be obtained before making a voluntary interim payment to a child or patient.

(Rule 39.2(3) provides for a hearing or part of a hearing to be in private.)

The litigation friend

2.1 It is the duty of a litigation friend fairly and competently to conduct proceedings on behalf of a child or patient. He must have no interest in the proceedings adverse to that of the child or patient and all steps and decisions he takes in the proceedings must be taken for the benefit of the child or patient.

2.2 A person may become a litigation friend:

    (1) of a child –

        (a) without a court order under the provisions of rule 21.5, or

        (b) by a court order under rule 21.6, and

---

(32) 1989 c.41.

---

1   See rule 21.1(2).
2   See rule 21.2(3).
3   See rule 21.10.

(2) of a patient
    (a) by authorisation under Part VII of the Mental Health Act 1983, or
    (b) by a court order under rule 21.6.

2.3 In order to become a litigation friend without a court order the person who wishes to act as litigation friend must:

    (1) if he wishes to act on behalf of a patient, file an official copy of the order or other document which constitutes the authorisation referred to in paragraph 2.2(2)(a) above, or

    (2) if he wishes to act on behalf of a child, or on behalf of a patient without the authorisation referred to in (1) above, file a certificate of suitability[4] –

        (a) stating that he consents to act,

        (b) stating that he knows or believes that the [claimant] [defendant] is a [child][patient],

        (c) in the case of a patient, stating the grounds of his belief and if his belief is based upon medical opinion attaching any relevant document to the certificate,

        (d) stating that he can fairly and competently conduct proceedings on behalf of the child or patient and has no interest adverse to that of the child or patient,

        (e) where the child or patient is a claimant, undertaking to pay any costs which the child or patient may be ordered to pay in relation to the proceedings, subject to any right he may have to be repaid from the assets of the child or patient, and

        (f) which he has signed in verification of its contents.

2.4 The litigation friend must serve a certificate of suitability[5]:

    (1) in the case of a child (who is not also a patient) on one of the child's parents or guardians or if there is no parent or guardian, on the person with whom the child resides or in whose care the child is, and

    (2) in the case of a patient on the person authorised under Part VII of the Mental Health Act 1983 to conduct proceedings on behalf of the patient or if there is no person so authorised, on the person with whom the patient resides or in whose care the patient is.

2.4A The litigation friend is not required to serve the documents referred to in paragraph 2.3(2)(c) when he serves a certificate of suitability on the person to be served under paragraph 2.4.

2.5 The litigation friend must file either the certificate of suitability together with a certificate of service[6] of it, or the authorisation referred to in paragraph 2.3(1) above:

    (1) where the litigation friend is acting on behalf of a claimant, when the claim form is issued, and

    (2) where the litigation friend is acting on behalf of a defendant, when he first takes a step in the action.

Application for a court order appointing a litigation friend

3.1 Rule 21.6 sets out who may apply for an order appointing a litigation friend.

3.2 An application should be made in accordance with Part 23 and must be supported by evidence[7].

3.3 The application notice must be served:

    (1) on the persons referred to in paragraph 2.4 above, and

    (2) where the application is in respect of a patient, on the patient unless the court orders otherwise.

3.4 The evidence in support must satisfy the court that the proposed litigation friend:

    (1) consents to act,

    (2) can fairly and competently conduct proceedings on behalf of the child or patient,

    (3) has no interest adverse to that of the child or patient, and

    (4) where the child or patient is a claimant, undertakes to pay any costs which the child or

---

4   See rule 21.5(3).
5   See rule 21.5(6) and rule 6.9 (service).
6   See rule 6.10 for the certificate of service.
7   See rule 21.6(4).

patient may be ordered to pay in relation to the proceedings, subject to any right he may have to be repaid from the assets of the child or patient.

3.5 Where a claimant wishes to take a step in proceedings against a child or patient who does not have a litigation friend he must apply to the court for an order appointing a litigation friend.

3.6 The proposed litigation friend must satisfy the conditions in paragraph 3.4(1), (2) and (3) above and may be one of the persons referred to in paragraph 2.4 above where appropriate, or otherwise may be the Official Solicitor. Where it is sought to appoint the Official Solicitor, provision should be made for payment of his charges.

Change of litigation friend and prevention of person acting as litigation friend

4.1 Rule 21.7(1) states that the court may:

   (1) direct that a person may not act as a litigation friend,

   (2) terminate a litigation friend's appointment,

   (3) substitute a new litigation friend for an existing one.

4.2 Where an application is made for an order under rule 21.7(1), the application notice must set out the reasons for seeking it. The application must be supported by evidence.

4.3 If the order sought is the substitution of a new litigation friend for an existing one, the evidence must satisfy the court of the matters set out in paragraph 3.4 above.

4.4 The application notice must be served:

   (1) on the persons referred to in paragraph 2.4 above, and

   (2) on the litigation friend or person purporting to act as litigation friend.

Procedure where need for a litigation friend has come to an end

5.1 Rule 21.9 deals with the situation where the need for a litigation friend comes to an end during the proceedings because either:

   (1) a child who is not also a patient reaches the age of 18 (full age) during the proceedings, or

   (2) a patient ceases to be a patient (recovers).

5.2 A child on reaching full age must serve on the other parties to the proceedings and file with the court a notice:

   (1) stating that he has reached full age,

   (2) stating that his litigation friend's appointment has ceased[8],

   (3) giving an address for service[9], and

   (4) stating whether or not he intends to carry on with or continue to defend the proceedings.

5.3 If the notice states that the child intends to carry on with or continue to defend the proceedings he shall subsequently be described in the proceedings as;

     'A.B. (formerly a child but now of full age)'

5.4 Whether or not a child having reached full age serves a notice in accordance with rule 21.9(4)(a) and paragraph 5.2(2) above, a litigation friend may at any time after the child has reached full age serve a notice on the other parties that his appointment has ceased.

5.5 The liability of a litigation friend for costs continues until a notice that his appointment to act has ceased is served on the other parties[10].

5.6 Where a patient recovers, an application under rule 21.9(3) must be made for an order under rule 21.9(2) that the litigation friend's appointment has ceased.

5.7 The application must be supported by the following evidence:

   (1) a medical report indicating that the patient has recovered and that he is capable of managing and administering his property and affairs,

   (2) where the patient's affairs were under the control of the Court of Protection, a copy of the order or notice discharging the receiver, and

   (3) if the application is made by the patient, a statement whether or not he intends to carry on with or continue to defend the proceedings.

---

8   Rule 21.9(4)(a).

9   See rule 6.5.

10 Rule 21.9(6).

5.8 An order under rule 21.9(2) must be served on the other parties to the proceedings. The patient must file with the court a notice;

(1) stating that his litigation friend's appointment has ceased,

(2) giving an address for service[11], and

(3) stating whether or not he intends to carry on with or continue to defend the proceedings.

Settlement or compromise by or on behalf of a child or patient

6.1 Where a claim by or on behalf of a child or patient has been dealt with by agreement prior to the start of proceedings and only the approval of the court to the agreement is sought, the claim:

(1) must be made using the Part 8 procedure,

(2) must include a request for approval of the settlement or compromise, and

(3) in addition to the details of the claim, must set out the terms of the settlement or compromise or have attached to it a draft consent order in practice form N292.

6.2 In order to approve the settlement or compromise, the information concerning the claim that the court will require will include:

(1) whether and to what extent the defendant admits liability,

(2) the age and occupation (if any) of the child or patient,

(3) the litigation friend's approval of the proposed settlement or compromise, and

(4) in a personal injury case arising from an accident –

    (a) the circumstances of the accident,

    (b) any medical reports,

    (c) where appropriate, a schedule of any past and future expenses and losses claimed and any other relevant information relating to personal injury as set out in the practice direction which supplements Part 16 (statements of case), and

    (d) where considerations of liability are raised –

        (i) any evidence or police reports in any criminal proceedings or in an inquest, and

        (ii) details of any prosecution brought.

6.3 (1) An opinion on the merits of the settlement or compromise given by counsel or solicitor acting for the child or patient should, except in very clear cases, be obtained.

(2) A copy of the opinion and, unless the instructions on which it was given are sufficiently set out in it, a copy of the instructions, must also be supplied to the court.

6.4 Applications for the approval of a settlement or compromise will normally be heard by a Master or district judge.

(For information about structured settlements see the practice direction on structured settlements supplementing Part 40 (judgments and orders))

(For information about provisional damages claims see Part 41 and the practice direction which supplements it)

Apportionments under the Fatal Accidents Act 1976

7.1 A judgment on or settlement in respect of a claim under the Fatal Accidents Act 1976 must be apportioned between the persons by or on whose behalf the claim has been brought.

7.2 Where a claim is brought on behalf of a dependent child or children, the money apportioned to any child must be invested on his behalf in accordance with rules 21.10 and 21.11 and paragraphs 8 and 9 below.

7.3 In order to approve an apportionment of money to a dependent child, the court will require the following information;

(1) the matters set out in paragraph 6.2(1),(2) above, and

(2) in respect of the deceased

    (a) where death was caused by an accident, the matters set out in paragraph 6.2(3)(a),(b) and (c) above, and

---

11   See rule 6.5.

    (b) his future loss of earnings, and

(3) the extent and nature of the dependency.

Control of money recovered by or on behalf of a child or patient

8.1 Money recovered or paid into court on behalf of or for the benefit of a child or patient shall be dealt with in accordance with directions of the court under rule 21.11.

8.2 The court:

  (1) may direct the money to be paid into the High Court for investment,

  (2) may also direct that certain sums be paid direct to the child or patient, his litigation friend or his legal representative[12] for the immediate benefit of the child or patient or for expenses incurred on his behalf, and

  (3) may direct the applications in respect of the investment of the money be transferred to a local district registry.

8.3 The Master or district judge will consider the general aims to be achieved for the money in court (the fund) by investment and will give directions as to the type of investment.

8.4 Where a child is also a patient, and likely to remain so on reaching full age, his fund should be administered as a patient's fund.

8.5 Where a child or patient is legally aided the fund will be subject to a first charge under s. 16 of the Legal Aid Act 1988 (the legal aid charge) and an order for the investment of money on the child or patient's behalf must contain a direction to that effect.

Guardian's accounts

9   Paragraph 8 of the practice direction supplementing Part 40 (Judgments and Orders) deals with the approval of the accounts of a guardian of assets of a child.

Investments on behalf of a child

10.1 At the hearing of the application for the approval of the agreement the litigation friend or his legal representative should provide a CFO form 320 (request for investment) for completion by the Master or district judge.

10.2 On receipt of that form in the Court Funds Office the investment managers of the Public Trust Office will make the appropriate investment.

10.3 Where an award of damages for a child is made at trial the trial judge may direct:

  (1) the money to be paid into court and placed in the special investment account, and

  (2) the litigation friend to make an application to a Master or district judge for further investment directions.

10.4 If the money to be invested is very small the court may order it to be paid direct to the litigation friend to be put into a building society account (or similar) for the child's use.

10.5 If the money is invested in court it must be paid out to the child when he reaches full age.

Investments on behalf of a patient

11.1 The Court of Protection is responsible for protecting the property of patients and is given extensive powers to do so under the Mental Health Act 1983. Fees are charged for the administration of funds by the Court of Protection and these should be provided for in any settlement.

11.2 Where the sum to be administered is:

  (1) over £30,000, the order approving the settlement will contain a direction to the litigation friend to apply to the Court of Protection for the appointment of a receiver, after which the fund will be transferred to the Court of Protection,

  (2) under £20,000, it may be retained in court and invested in the same way as the fund of a child, or

  (3) in intermediate cases the advice of the Master of the Court of Protection should be sought.

---

12 See rule 2.3 for a definition of legal representative.

11.3 A form of order transferring the fund to the Court of Protection is set out in practice form N292.

11.4 In order for the Court Funds Office to release a fund which is subject to the legal aid charge to the Court of Protection the litigation friend or his legal representative should provide the appropriate area office of the Legal Aid Board with an undertaking in respect of a sum to cover their costs, following which the area office will advise the Court Funds Office in writing of that sum, enabling them to transfer the balance to the Court of Protection on receipt of a CFO form 200 payment schedule authorised by the court.

11.5 The CFO form 200 should be completed and presented to the court where the settlement or trial took place for authorisation, subject to paragraphs 11.6 and 11.7 below.

11.6 Where the settlement took place in the Royal Courts of Justice the CFO form 200 should be completed and presented for authorisation:

(1) on behalf of a child, in the Masters' Secretary's Office, Room E214, and

(2) on behalf of a patient, in the Action Department, Room E15.

11.7 Where the trial took place in the Royal Courts of Justice the CFO form 200 is completed and authorised by the court officer.

Payment out of funds in court

12.1 Applications to a Master or district judge;

(1) for payment out of money from the fund for the benefit of the child, or

(2) to vary an investment strategy, may be dealt with without a hearing unless the court directs otherwise.

12.2 When the child reaches full age, his fund in court:

(1) where it is a sum of money will be paid out to him, and

(2) where it is in the form of investments other than money (for example shares or unit trusts), will be transferred into his name.

12.3 An application for payment out of funds being administered by the Court of Protection must be made to the Court of Protection.

(For further information on payments into and out of court see the practice directions supplementing Parts 36 and 37.)

PART 22

STATEMENTS OF TRUTH

Contents of this Part

Documents to be verified by a statement of truth

22.1 (1) The following documents must be verified by a statement of truth –

(a) a statement of case;

(b) a response complying with an order under rule 18.1 to provide further information; and

(c) a witness statement.

(2) Where a statement of case is amended, the amendments must be verified by a statement of truth unless the court orders otherwise.

(Part 17 provides for amendments to statements of case.)

(3) If an applicant wishes to rely on matters set out in his application notice as evidence, the application notice must be verified by a statement of truth.

(4) Subject to paragraph (5), a statement of truth is a statement that –

    (a) the party putting forward the document; or

    (b) in the case of a witness statement, the maker of the witness statement,

believes the facts stated in the document are true.

(5) If a party is conducting proceedings with a litigation friend, the statement of truth in –

    (a) a statement of case;

    (b) a response; or

    (c) an application notice,

is a statement that the litigation friend believes the facts stated in the document being verified are true.

(6) The statement of truth must be signed by –

    (a) in the case of a statement of case, a response or an application –

        (i) the party or litigation friend; or

        (ii) the legal representative on behalf of the party or litigation friend; and

    (b) in the case of a witness statement, the maker of the statement.

(7) A statement of truth which is not contained in the document which it verifies, must clearly identify that document.

(8) A statement of truth in a statement of case may be made by –

    (a) a person who is not a party; or

    (b) by two parties jointly,

where this is permitted by a relevant practice direction.

Failure to verify a statement of case

22.2 (1) If a party fails to verify his statement of case by a statement of truth –

    (a) the statement of case shall remain effective unless struck out; but

    (b) the party may not rely on the statement of case as evidence of any of the matters set out in it.

(2) The court may strike out$^{(GL)}$ a statement of case which is not verified by a statement of truth.

(3) Any party may apply for an order under paragraph (2).

Failure to verify a witness statement

22.3   If the maker of a witness statement fails to verify the witness statement by a statement of truth the court may direct that it shall not be admissible as evidence.

Power of the court to require a document to be verified

22.4 (1) The court may order a person who has failed to verify a document in accordance with rule 22.1 to verify the document.

(2) Any party may apply for an order under paragraph (1).

PRACTICE DIRECTION – STATEMENTS OF TRUTH
THIS PRACTICE DIRECTION SUPPLEMENTS CPR PART 22

Documents to be verified by a statement of truth

1.1 Rule 22.1(1) sets out the documents which must be verified by a statement of truth. The documents include:

(1) a statement of case,

(2) a response complying with an order under rule 18.1 to provide further information, and

(3) a witness statement.

1.2 If an applicant wishes to rely on matters set out in his application notice as evidence, the application notice must be verified by a statement of truth[1].

1.3 An expert's report should also be verified by a statement of truth. For the form of the statement of truth verifying an expert's report (which differs from that set out below) see the practice direction which supplements Part 35.

1.4 In addition, a notice of objections to an account being taken by the court should be verified by a statement of truth unless verified by an affidavit or a witness statement[2].

1.5 The statement of truth may be contained in the document it verifies or it may be in a separate document served subsequently, in which case it must identify the document to which it relates.

1.6 Where the form to be used includes a jurat for the content to be verified by an affidavit then a statement of truth is not required in addition.

Form of the statement of truth

2.1 The form of the statement of truth verifying a statement of case, a response, an application notice or a notice of objections should be as follows:

'[I believe][the (claimant or as may be) believes] that the facts stated in this [name document being verified] are true.'

2.2 The form of the statement of truth verifying a witness statement should be as follows:

'I believe that the facts stated in this witness statement are true.'

2.3 Where the statement of truth is contained in a separate document, the document containing the statement of truth must be headed with the title of the proceedings and the claim number. The document being verified should be identified in the statement of truth as follows:

(1) claim form: 'the claim form issued on [date]',

(2) particulars of claim: 'the particulars of claim issued on [date]',

(3) statement of case: 'the [defence or as may be] served on the [name of party] on [date]',

(4) application notice: 'the application notice issued on [date] for [set out the remedy sought]',

(5) witness statement: 'the witness statement filed on [date] or served on [party] on [date]'.

Who may sign the statement of truth

3.1 In a statement of case, a response or an application notice, the statement of truth must be signed by:

(1) the party or his litigation friend[3], or

(2) the legal representative[4] of the party or litigation friend.

3.2 A statement of truth verifying a witness statement must be signed by the witness.

3.3 A statement of truth verifying a notice of objections to an account must be signed by the objecting party or his legal representative.

---

1   See rule 22.1(3).

2   See the Accounts and Enquiries practice direction supplementing Part 40 (judgments and orders).

3   See Part 21 (children and patients).

4   See rule 2.3 for the definition of legal representative.

3.4 Where a document is to be verified on behalf of a company or other corporation, subject to paragraph 3.7 below, the statement of truth must be signed by a person holding a senior position[5] in the company or corporation. That person must state the office or position he holds.

3.5 Each of the following persons is a person holding a senior position:

(1) in respect of a registered company or corporation, a director, the treasurer, secretary, chief executive, manager or other officer of the company or corporation, and

(2) in respect of a corporation which is not a registered company, in addition to those persons set out in (1), the mayor, chairman, president or town clerk or other similar officer of the corporation.

3.6 Where the document is to be verified on behalf of a partnership, those who may sign the statement of truth are:

(1) any of the partners, or

(2) a person having the control or management of the partnership business.

3.6A An insurer or the Motor Insurers' Bureau may sign a statement of truth in a statement of case on behalf of a party where the insurer or the Motor Insurers' Bureau has a financial interest in the result of proceedings brought wholly or partially by or against that party.

3.7 Where a party is legally represented, the legal representative may sign the statement of truth on his behalf. The statement signed by the legal representative will refer to the client's belief, not his own. In signing he must state the capacity in which he signs and the name of his firm where appropriate.

3.8 Where a legal representative has signed a statement of truth, his signature will be taken by the court as his statement:

(1) that the client on whose behalf he has signed had authorised him to do so,

(2) that before signing he had explained to the client that in signing the statement of truth he would be confirming the client's belief that the facts stated in the document were true, and

(3) that before signing he had informed the client of the possible consequences to the client if it should subsequently appear that the client did not have an honest belief in the truth of those facts (see rule 32.14).

3.9 The individual who signs a statement of truth must print his full name clearly beneath his signature.

3.10 A legal representative who signs a statement of truth must sign in his own name and not that of his firm or employer.

3.11 The following are examples of the possible application of this practice direction describing who may sign a statement of truth verifying statements in documents other than a witness statement. These are only examples and not an indication of how a court might apply the practice direction to a specific situation.

Managing Agent	An agent who manages property or investments for the party cannot sign a statement of truth. It must be signed by the party or by the legal representative of the party.
Trusts	Where some or all of the trustees comprise a single party one, some or all of the trustees comprising the party may sign a statement of truth. The legal representative of the trustees may sign it.
Insurers and the Motor Insurers Bureau	If an insurer has a financial interest in a claim involving its insured then, if the' insured is the party, the insurer may sign a statement of truth in a statement of case for the insured claimant. Paragraphs 3.4 and 3.5 apply to the insurer if it is a company. The claims manager employed by the insurer responsible for handling the insurance claim

---

5   See rule 6.4(4).

	or managing the staff handling the claim may sign the statement of truth for the insurer (see next example). The position for the Motor Insurers' Bureau is similar.
Companies	Paragraphs 3.4 and 3.5 apply. The word manager will be construed in the context of the phrase "a person holding a senior position" which it is used to define. The court will consider the size of the company and the size and nature of the claim. It would expect the manager signing the statement of truth to have personal knowledge of the content of the document or to be responsible for managing those who have that knowledge of the content. A small company may not have a manager, apart from the directors, who holds a senior position. A large company will have many such managers. In a larger company with specialist claims, insurance or legal departments the statement may be signed by the manager of such a department if he or she is responsible for handling the claim or managing the staff handling it.
In-house legal representatives	Legal representative is defined in rule 2.3(1). A legal representative employed by a party may sign a statement of truth. However a person who is not a solicitor, barrister or other authorised litigator, but who is employed by the company and is managed by such a person, is not employed by that person and so cannot sign a statement of truth. (This is unlike the employee of a solicitor in private practice who would come within the definition of legal representative.) However such a person may be a manager and able to sign the statement on behalf of the company in that capacity.

Consequences of failure to verify

4.1 If a statement of case is not verified by a statement of truth, the statement of case will remain effective unless it is struck out[6], but a party may not rely on the contents of a statement of case as evidence until it has been verified by a statement of truth.

4.2 Any party may apply to the court for an order that unless within such period as the court may specify the statement of case is verified by the service of a statement of truth, the statement of case will be struck out.

4.3 The usual order for the costs of an application referred to in paragraph 4.2 will be that the costs be paid by the party who had failed to verify in any event and forthwith.

Penalty

5 Attention is drawn to rule 32.14 which sets out the consequences of verifying a statement of case containing a false statement without an honest belief in its truth.

---

6   See rule 22.2(1).

PART 23

GENERAL RULES ABOUT APPLICATIONS FOR COURT ORDERS

Contents of this Part

Meaning of 'application notice' and 'respondent'

23.1   In this Part –

'application notice' means a document in which the applicant states his intention to seek a court order; and

'respondent' means –

(a) the person against whom the order is sought; and

(b) such other person as the court may direct.

Where to make an application

23.2 (1) The general rule is that an application must be made to the court where the claim was started.

(2) If a claim has been transferred to another court since it was started, an application must be made to the court to which the claim has been transferred.

(3) If the parties have been notified of a fixed date for the trial, an application must be made to the court where the trial is to take place.

(4) If an application is made before a claim has been started, it must be made to the court where it is likely that the claim to which the application relates will be started unless there is good reason to make the application to a different court.

(5) If an application is made after proceedings to enforce judgment have begun, it must be made to any court which is dealing with the enforcement of the judgment unless any rule or practice direction provides otherwise.

Application notice to be filed

23.3 (1) The general rule is that an applicant must file an application notice.

(2) An applicant may make an application without filing an application notice if –

(a) this is permitted by a rule or practice direction; or

(b) the court dispenses with the requirement for an application notice.

Notice of an application

23.4 (1) The general rule is that a copy of the application notice must be served on each respondent.

(2) An application may be made without serving a copy of the application notice if this is permitted by –

(a) a rule;

(b) a practice direction; or

(c) a court order.

(Rule 23.7 deals with service of a copy of the application notice.)

Time when an application is made

23.5   Where an application must be made within a specified time, it is so made if the application notice is received by the court within that time.

What an application notice must include

23.6   An application notice must state –

(a) what order the applicant is seeking; and

(b) briefly, why the applicant is seeking the order.

(Part 22 requires an application notice to be verified by a statement of truth if the applicant wishes to rely on matters set out in his application notice as evidence)

Service of a copy of an application notice

23.7 (1) A copy of the application notice –

(a) must be served as soon as practicable after it is filed; and

(b) except where another time limit is specified in these Rules or a practice direction, must in any event be served at least 3 days before the court is to deal with the application.

(2) If a copy of the application notice is to be served by the court, the applicant must, when he files the application notice, file a copy of any written evidence in support.

(3) When a copy of an application notice is served it must be accompanied by –

(a) a copy of any written evidence in support; and

(b) a copy of any draft order which the applicant has attached to his application.

(4) If –

(a) an application notice is served; but

(b) the period of notice is shorter than the period required by these Rules or a practice direction,

the court may direct that, in the circumstances of the case, sufficient notice has been given and hear the application.

(5) This rule does not require written evidence –

(a) to be filed if it has already been filed; or

(b) to be served on a party on whom it has already been served.

(Part 6 contains the general rules about service of documents including who must serve a copy of the application notice)

Applications which may be dealt with without a hearing

23.8   The court may deal with an application without a hearing if –

(a) the parties agree as to the terms of the order sought;

(b) the parties agree that the court should dispose of the application without a hearing, or

(c) the court does not consider that a hearing would be appropriate.

Service of application where application made without notice

23.9 (1) This rule applies where the court has disposed of an application which it permitted to be made without service of a copy of the application notice.

(2) Where the court makes an order, whether granting or dismissing the application, a copy of the application notice and any evidence in support must, unless the court orders otherwise, be served with the order on any party or other person –

(a) against whom the order was made; and

(b) against whom the order was sought.

(3) The order must contain a statement of the right to make an application to set aside$^{(GL)}$ or vary the order under rule 23.10.

Application to set aside or vary order made without notice

23.10 (1) A person who was not served with a copy of the application notice before an order was made under rule 23.9, may apply to have the order set aside$^{(GL)}$ or varied.

(2) An application under this rule must be made within 7 days after the date on which the order was served on the person making the application.

Power of the court to proceed in the absence of a party

23.11 (1) Where the applicant or any respondent fails to attend the hearing of an application, the court may proceed in his absence.

(2) Where –

(a) the applicant or any respondent fails to attend the hearing of an application; and

(b) the court makes an order at the hearing,

the court may, on application or of its own initiative, re-list the application.

(Part 40 deals with service of orders)

PRACTICE DIRECTION – APPLICATIONS
THIS PRACTICE DIRECTION SUPPLEMENTS CPR PART 23

Reference to a judge

1 A Master or district judge may refer to a judge any matter which he thinks should properly be decided by a judge, and the judge may either dispose of the matter or refer it back to the Master or district judge.

Application notices

2.1 An application notice must, in addition to the matters set out in rule 23.6, be signed and include:

(1) the title of the claim,

(2) the reference number of the claim,

(3) the full name of the applicant,

(4) where the applicant is not already a party, his address for service, and

(5) either a request for a hearing or a request that the application be dealt with without a hearing.

(Practice Form N244 may be used.)

2.2 On receipt of an application notice containing a request for a hearing the court will notify the applicant of the time and date for the hearing of the application.

2.3 On receipt of an application notice containing a request that the application be dealt with without a hearing, the application notice will be sent to a Master or district judge so that he may decide whether the application is suitable for consideration without a hearing.

2.4 Where the Master or district judge agrees that the application is suitable for consideration without a hearing, the court will so inform the applicant and the respondent and may give directions for the filing of evidence. (Rules 23.9 and 23.10 enable a party to apply for an order made without a hearing to be set aside or varied.)

2.5 Where the Master or district judge does not agree that the application is suitable for consideration without a hearing, the court will notify the applicant and the respondent of the time, date and place for the hearing of the application and may at the same time give directions as to the filing of evidence.

2.6 If the application is intended to be made to a judge, the application notice should so state. In that case, paragraphs 2.3, 2.4 and 2.5 will apply as though references to the Master or district judge were references to a judge.

2.7 Every application should be made as soon as it becomes apparent that it is necessary or desirable to make it.

2.8 Applications should wherever possible be made so that they can be considered at any other hearing for which a date has already been fixed or for which a date is about to be fixed. This is particularly so in relation to case management conferences, allocation and listing hearings and pre-trial reviews fixed by the court.

2.9 The parties must anticipate that at any hearing the court may wish to review the conduct of the case as a whole and give any necessary case management directions. They should be ready to assist the court in doing so and to answer questions the court may ask for this purpose.

2.10 Where a date for a hearing has been fixed and a party wishes to make an application at that hearing but he does not have sufficient time to serve an application notice he should inform the other party and the court (if possible in writing) as soon as he can of the nature of the application and the reason for it. He should then make the application orally at the hearing.

Applications without service of application notice

3 An application may be made without serving an application notice only:
(1) where there is exceptional urgency,
(2) where the overriding objective is best furthered by doing so,
(3) by consent of all parties,
(4) with the permission of the court,
(5) where paragraph 2.10 above applies, or
(6) where a court order, rule or practice direction permits.

Giving notice of an application

4.1 Unless the court otherwise directs or paragraph 3 of this practice direction applies the application notice must be served as soon as practicable after it has been issued and, if there is to be a hearing, at least 3 clear days before the hearing date (rule 23.7(1)(b)).

4.2 Where an application notice should be served but there is not sufficient time to do so, informal notification of the application should be given unless the circumstances of the application require secrecy.

Pre-action applications

5 All applications made before a claim is commenced should be made under Part 23 of the Civil Procedure Rules. Attention is drawn in particular to rule 23.2(4).

Telephone hearings

6.1 The court may order than an application or part of an application be dealt with by a telephone hearing.

6.2 An order under 6.1 will not normally be made unless every party entitled to be given notice of the application and to be heard at the hearing has consented to the order.

6.3 (1) Where a party entitled to be heard at the hearing of the application is acting in person, the court –

    (a) may not make an order under 6.1 except on condition that arrangements will be made for the party acting in person to be attended at the telephone hearing by a responsible person to whom the party acting in person is known and who can confirm to the court the identity of the party; and

    (b) may not give effect to an order under 6.1 unless the party acting in person is accompanied by a responsible person who at the commencement of the hearing confirms to the court the identity of the party.

    (2) The "responsible person" may be a barrister, solicitor, legal executive, doctor, clergyman, police officer, prison officer or other person of comparable status.

    (3) If the court makes an order under 6.1 it will give any directions necessary for the telephone hearing.

6.4 No representative of a party to an application being heard by telephone may attend the judge in person while the application is being heard unless the other party to the application has agreed that he may do so.

6.5 If an application is to be heard by telephone the following directions will apply, subject to any direction to the contrary:

    (1) The applicant's legal representative must arrange the telephone conference by the British Telecom conference call 'call out' system or by some other comparable system for precisely the time fixed by the court.

    (2) He must tell the operator the telephone numbers of all those participating in the conference call and the sequence in which they are to be called.

    (3) It is the responsibility of the applicant's legal representative to ascertain from all the other parties whether they have instructed counsel and, if so the identity of counsel, and whether the legal representative and counsel will be on the same or different telephone numbers.

    (4) The sequence in which they are to be called will be:

        (a) the applicant's legal representative and (if on a different number) his counsel,

        (b) the legal representative (and counsel) for all other parties, and

        (c) the judge.

    (5) The applicant's legal representative must arrange for the conference to be recorded on tape by the telecommunications provider whose system is being used and must send the tape to the court.

    (6) Each speaker is to remain on the line after being called by the operator setting up the conference call. The call may be 2 or 3 minutes before the time fixed for the application.

    (7) When the judge has been connected the applicant's legal representative (or his counsel) will introduce the parties in the usual way.

    (8) If the use of a 'speakerphone' by any party causes the judge or any other party any difficulty in hearing what is said the judge may require that party to use a hand held telephone.

    (9) The telephone charges debited to the account of the party initiating the conference call will be treated as part of the costs of the application.

Video conferencing

7 Where the parties to a matter wish to use video conferencing facilities, and those facilities are available in the relevant court, they should apply to the Master or district judge for directions.

Note of proceedings

8 The procedural judge should keep, either by way of a note or a tape recording, brief details of all proceedings before him, including the dates of the proceedings and a short statement of the decision taken at each hearing.

Evidence

9.1 The requirement for evidence in certain types of applications is set out in some of the rules and practice directions. Where there is no specific requirement to provide evidence it should be borne in mind that, as a practical matter, the court will often need to be satisfied by evidence of the facts that are relied on in support of or for opposing the application.

9.2 The court may give directions for the filing of evidence in support of or opposing a particular application. The court may also give directions for the filing of evidence in relation to any hearing that it fixes on its own initiative. The directions may specify the form that evidence is to take and when it is to be served.

9.3 Where it is intended to rely on evidence which is not contained in the application itself, the evidence, if it has not already been served, should be served with the application.

9.4 Where a respondent to an application wishes to rely on evidence which has not yet been served he should serve it as soon as possible and in any event in accordance with any directions the court may have given.

9.5 If it is necessary for the applicant to serve any evidence in reply it should be served as soon as possible and in any event in accordance with any directions the court may have given.

9.6 Evidence must be filed with the court as well as served on the parties. Exhibits should not be filed unless the court otherwise directs.

9.7 The contents of an application notice may be used as evidence (otherwise than at trial) provided the contents have been verified by a statement of truth[1].

Consent orders

10.1 Rule 40.6 sets out the circumstances where an agreed judgment or order may be entered and sealed.

10.2 Where all parties affected by an order have written to the court consenting to the making of the order a draft of which has been filed with the court, the court will treat the draft as having been signed in accordance with rule 40.6(7).

10.3 Where a consent order must be made by a judge (i.e. rule 40.6(2) does not apply) the order must be drawn so that the judge's name and judicial title can be inserted.

10.4 The parties to an application for a consent order must ensure that they provide the court with any material it needs to be satisfied that it is appropriate to make the order. Subject to any rule or practice direction a letter will generally be acceptable for this purpose.

10.5 Where a judgment or order has been agreed in respect of an application or claim where a hearing date has been fixed, the parties must inform the court immediately. (note that parties are reminded that under rules 28.4 and 29.5 the case management timetable cannot be varied by written agreement of the parties.)

Other applications considered without a hearing

11.1 Where rule 23.8(b) applies the parties should so inform the court in writing and each should confirm that all evidence and other material on which he relies has been disclosed to the other parties to the application.

11.2 Where rule 23.8(c) applies the court will treat the application as if it were proposing to make an order on its own initiative.

Miscellaneous

12.1 Except in the most simple application the applicant should bring to any hearing a draft of the order sought. If the case is proceeding in the Royal Courts of Justice and the order is unusually long or complex it should also be supplied on disk for use by the court office [The current word processing system to be used is WordPerfect 5.1].

12.2 Where rule 23.11 applies, the power to re-list the application in rule 23.11(2) is in addition to any other powers of the court with regard to the order (for example to set aside, vary, discharge or suspend the order).

---

1   See Part 22.

Costs

13.1 Attention is drawn to the costs practice direction and, in particular, to the court's power to make a summary assessment of costs.

13.2 Attention is also drawn to rule 44.13(i) which provides that if an order makes no mention of costs, none are payable in respect of the proceedings to which it relates.

PART 24

SUMMARY JUDGMENT

Contents of this Part

Scope of this Part

24.1 This Part sets out a procedure by which the court may decide a claim or a particular issue without a trial.

(Part 53 makes special provision about summary disposal of defamation claims in accordance with the Defamation Act 1996[33].)

Grounds for summary judgment

24.2 The court may give summary judgment against a claimant or defendant on the whole of a claim or on a particular issue if –

  (a) it considers that –

     (i) that claimant has no real prospect of succeeding on the claim or issue; or

     (ii) that defendant has no real prospect of successfully defending the claim or issue; and

  (b) there is no other reason why the case or issue should be disposed of at a trial.

(Rule 3.4 makes provision for the court to strike out[GL] a statement of case or part of a statement of case if it appears that it discloses no reasonable grounds for bringing or defending a claim)

Types of proceedings in which summary judgment is available

24.3(1) The court may give summary judgment against a claimant in any type of proceedings.

  (2) The court may give summary judgment against a defendant in any type of proceedings except –

    (a) proceedings for possession of residential premises against–

      (i) a mortgagor; or

---

(33) 1196 c.31

(ii) a tenant or a person holding over after the end of his tenancy whose occupancy is protected within the meaning of the Rent Act 1977[34] or the Housing Act 1988[35] and;

(b) proceedings for an admiralty claim in rem; and

(c) contentious probate proceedings.

Procedure

24.4(1) A claimant may not apply for summary judgment until the defendant against whom the application is made has filed –

(a) an acknowledgment of service; or

(b) a defence,

unless –

(i) the court gives permission; or

(ii) a practice direction provides otherwise.

(Rule 10.3 sets out the period for filing an acknowledgment of service and rule 15.4 the period for filing a defence)

(2) If a claimant applies for summary judgment before a defendant against whom the application is made has filed a defence, that defendant need not file a defence before the hearing.

(3) Where a summary judgment hearing is fixed, the respondent (or the parties where the hearing is fixed of the court's own initiative) must be given at least 14 days' notice of –

(a) the date fixed for the hearing; and

(b) the issues which it is proposed that the court will decide at the hearing.

(4) A practice direction may provide for a different period of notice to be given.

(Part 23 contains the general rules about how to make an application)

(Rule 3.3 applies where the court exercises its powers of its own initiative)

Evidence for the purposes of a summary judgment hearing

24.5(1) If the respondent to an application for summary judgment wishes to rely on written evidence at the hearing, he must –

(a) file the written evidence; and

(b) serve copies on every other party to the application,

at least 7 days before the summary judgment hearing.

(2) If the applicant wishes to rely on written evidence in reply, he must –

(a) file the written evidence; and

(b) serve a copy on the respondent,

at least 3 days before the summary judgment hearing.

(3) Where a summary judgment hearing is fixed by the court of its own initiative –

(a) any party who wishes to rely on written evidence at the hearing must –

(i) file the written evidence; and

(ii) unless the court orders otherwise, serve copies on every other party to the proceedings,

at least 7 days before the date of the hearing;

---

(34) 1977 c.42

(35) 1988 c.50

(b) any party who wishes to rely on written evidence at the hearing in reply to any other party's written evidence must –

    (i) file the written evidence in reply; and

    (ii) unless the court orders otherwise serve copies on every other party to the proceedings,

at least 3 days before the date of the hearing.

(4) This rule does not require written evidence –

    (a) to be filed if it has already been filed; or

    (b) to be served on a party on whom it has already been served.

Court's powers when it determines a summary judgment application

24.6   When the court determines a summary judgment application it may –

    (a) give directions as to the filing and service of a defence;

    (b) give further directions about the management of the case.

(Rule 3.1(3) provides that the court may attach conditions when it makes an order)

**PRACTICE DIRECTION – THE SUMMARY DISPOSAL OF CLAIMS
THIS PRACTICE DIRECTION SUPPLEMENTS CPR PART 24**

Applications for summary judgment under Part 24

1.1 Attention is drawn to Part 24 itself and to:

Part 3, in particular rule 3.1(3)and (5),

Part 22,

Part 23, in particular rule 23.6,

Part 32, in particular rule 32.6(2).

1.2 In this paragraph, where the context so admits, the word 'claim' includes:

    (1) a part of a claim, and

    (2) an issue on which the claim in whole or part depends.

1.3 An application for summary judgment under rule 24.2 may be based on:

    (1) a point of law (including a question of construction of a document),

    (2) the evidence which can reasonably be expected to be available at trial or the lack of it, or

    (3) a combination of these.

1.4 Rule 24.4(1) deals with the stage in the proceedings at which an application under Part 24 can be made (but see paragraph 7.1 below).

Procedure for making an application

2   (1) Attention is drawn to rules 24.4(3) and 23.6.

    (2) The application notice must include a statement that it is an application for summary judgment made under Part 24.

    (3) The application notice or the evidence contained or referred to in it or served with it must –

        (a) identify concisely any point of law or provision in a document on which the applicant relies, and/or

        (b) state that it is made because the applicant believes that on the evidence the respondent has no real prospect of succeeding on the claim or issue or (as the case may be) of successfully defending the claim or issue to which the application relates,

    and in either case state that the applicant knows of no other reason why the disposal of the claim or issue should await trial.

    (4) Unless the application notice itself contains all the evidence (if any) on which the applicant relies, the application notice should identify the written evidence on which the

applicant relies. This does not affect the applicant's right to file further evidence under rule 24.5(2).

(5) The application notice should draw the attention of the respondent to rule 24.5(1).

The hearing

3 (1) The hearing of the application will normally take place before a Master or a district judge.

(2) The Master or district judge may direct that the application be heard by a High Court Judge (if the case is in the High Court) or a circuit judge (if the case is in a county court).

The court's approach

4 Where it appears to the court possible that a claim or defence may succeed but improbable that it will do so, the court may make a conditional order, as described below.

Orders the court may make

5.1 The orders the court may make on an application under Part 24 include:

(1) judgment on the claim,

(2) the striking out or dismissal of the claim,

(3) the dismissal of the application,

(4) a conditional order.

5.2 A conditional order is an order which requires a party:

(1) to pay a sum of money into court, or

(2) to take a specified step in relation to his claim or defence, as the case may be, and provides that that party's claim will be dismissed or his statement of case will be struck out if he does not comply.

(Note – the court will not follow its former practice of granting leave to a defendant to defend a claim, whether conditionally or unconditionally.)

Accounts and inquiries

6 If a remedy sought by a claimant in his claim form includes, or necessarily involves, taking an account or making an inquiry, an application can be made under Part 24 by any party to the proceedings for an order directing any necessary accounts or inquiries to be taken or made.

(This paragraph replaces RSC Order 43, rule 1, but applies to county court proceedings as well as to High Court proceedings. The Accounts practice direction supplementing Part 40 contains further provisions as to orders for accounts and inquiries.)

Specific performance

7.1 (1) If a remedy sought by a claimant in his claim form includes a claim–

(a) for specific performance of an agreement (whether in writing or not) for the sale, purchase, exchange, mortgage or charge of any property, or for the grant or assignment of a lease or tenancy of any property, with or without an alternative claim for damages, or

(b) for rescission of such an agreement, or

(c) for the forfeiture or return of any deposit made under such an agreement,

the claimant may apply under Part 24 for judgment.

(2) The claimant may do so at any time after the claim form has been served, whether or not the defendant has acknowledged service of the claim form, whether or not the time for acknowledging service has expired and whether or not any particulars of claim have been served.

7.2 The application notice by which an application under paragraph 7.1 is made must have attached to it the text of the order sought by the claimant.

7.3 The application notice and a copy of every affidavit or witness statement in support and of any exhibit referred to therein must be served on the defendant not less than 4 days before the hearing of the application. (note – the 4 days replaces for these applications the 14 days specified in rule 24.4(3). Rule 24.5 cannot, therefore, apply.)

(This paragraph replaces RSC Order 86, rules 1 and 2 but applies to county court proceedings as well as to High Court proceedings.)

Setting aside order for summary judgment

8.1 If an order for summary judgment is made against a respondent who does not appear at the hearing of the application, the respondent may apply for the order to be set aside or varied (see also rule 23.11).

8.2 On the hearing of an application under paragraph 8.1 the court may make such order as it thinks just.

Costs

9.1 Attention is drawn to Part 44 (fixed costs).

9.2 Attention is drawn to the Costs Practice Direction and in particular to the court's power to make a summary assessment of costs.

9.3 Attention is also drawn to rule 43.5(5) which provides that if an order does not mention costs no party is entitled to costs relating to that order.

Case management

10 Where the court dismisses the application or makes an order that does not completely dispose of the claim, the court will give case management directions as to the future conduct of the case.

PART 25

INTERIM REMEDIES

Contents of this Part

I Interim remedies

I Interim remedies

Orders for interim remedies

25.1(1) The court may grant the following interim remedies –

    (a) an interim injunction$^{(GL)}$;

    (b) an interim declaration;

(c) an order –

    (i) for the detention, custody or preservation of relevant property;

    (ii) for the inspection of relevant property;

    (iii) for the taking of a sample of relevant property;

    (iv) for the carrying out of an experiment on or with relevant property;

    (v) for the sale of relevant property which is of a perishable nature or which for any other good reason it is desirable to sell quickly; and

    (vi) for the payment of income from relevant property until a claim is decided;

(d) an order authorising a person to enter any land or building in the possession of a party to the proceedings for the purposes of carrying out an order under sub-paragraph (c);

(e) an order under section 4 of the Torts (Interference with Goods) Act 1977[36] to deliver up goods;

(f) an order (referred to as a 'freezing injunction[GL]') –

    (i) restraining a party from removing from the jurisdiction assets located there; or

    (ii) restraining a party from dealing with any assets whether located within the jurisdiction or not;

(g) an order directing a party to provide information about the location of relevant property or assets or to provide information about relevant property or assets which are or may be the subject of an application for a freezing injunction[GL];

(h) an order (referred to as a 'search order') under section 7 of the Civil Procedure Act 1997[37] (order requiring a party to admit another party to premises for the purpose of preserving evidence etc.);

(i) an order under section 33 of the Supreme Court Act 1981[38] or section 52 of the County Courts Act 1984[39] (order for disclosure of documents or inspection of property before a claim has been made);

(j) an order under section 34 of the Supreme Court Act 1981[40] or section 53 of the County Courts Act 1984[41] (order in certain proceedings for disclosure of documents or inspection of property against a non-party);

(k) an order (referred to as an order for interim payment) under rule 25.6 for payment by a defendant on account of any damages, debt or other sum (except costs) which the court may hold the defendant liable to pay;

(l) an order for a specified fund to be paid into court or otherwise secured, where there is a dispute over a party's right to the fund;

(m) an order permitting a party seeking to recover personal property to pay money into court pending the outcome of the proceedings and directing that, if he does so, the property shall be given up to him; and

---

(36) 1977 c.32; section 4 was amended by the Supreme Court Act 1981 (c.54), section 152(1), Schedule 5; by the County Courts Act 1984 (c.28), section 148(1), Schedule 2, Part V, paragraph 64 and by S.I. 1980/397 (NI3).

(37) 1997 c.12.

(38) 1981 c.54. Section 33 was amended by S.I. 1998/2940.

(39) 1984 c.28. Section 52 was amended by the Courts and Legal Services Act 1990 (c.41), Schedule 18, paragraph 43 and by S.I. 1998/2940.

(40) 1981 c.54. Section 34 was amended by S.I. 1998/2940.

(41) 1984 c.28. Section 53 was amended by the Courts and Legal Services Act 1990 (c.41), Schedule 18, paragraph 44 and by S.I. 1998/2940.

(n) an order directing a party to prepare and file accounts relating to the dispute.

(Rule 34.2 provides for the court to issue a witness summons requiring a witness to produce documents to the court at the hearing or on such date as the court may direct)

(2) In paragraph (1)(c) and (g), 'relevant property' means property (including land) which is the subject of a claim or as to which any question may arise on a claim.

(3) The fact that a particular kind of interim remedy is not listed in paragraph (1) does not affect any power that the court may have to grant that remedy.

(4) The court may grant an interim remedy whether or not there has been a claim for a final remedy of that kind.

Time when an order for an interim remedy may be made

25.2 (1) An order for an interim remedy may be made at any time, including –

(a) before proceedings are started; and

(b) after judgment has been given.

(Rule 7.2 provides that proceedings are started when the court issues a claim form)

(2) However –

(a) paragraph (1) is subject to any rule, practice direction or other enactment which provides otherwise;

(b) the court may grant an interim remedy before a claim has been made only if –

(i) the matter is urgent; or

(ii) it is otherwise desirable to do so in the interests of justice; and

(c) unless the court otherwise orders, a defendant may not apply for any of the orders listed in rule 25.1(1) before he has filed either an acknowledgment of service or a defence.

(Part 10 provides for filing an acknowledgment of service and Part 15 for filing a defence)

(3) Where the court grants an interim remedy before a claim has been commenced, it may give directions requiring a claim to be commenced.

(4) In particular, the court need not direct that a claim be commenced where the application is made under section 33 of the Supreme Court Act 1981 or section 52 of the County Courts Act 1984 (order for disclosure, inspection etc. before commencement of a claim).

How to apply for an interim remedy

25.3 (1) The court may grant an interim remedy on an application made without notice if it appears to the court that there are good reasons for not giving notice.

(2) An application for an interim remedy must be supported by evidence, unless the court orders otherwise.

(3) If the applicant makes an application without giving notice, the evidence in support of the application must state the reasons why notice has not been given.

(Part 3 lists general powers of the court)

(Part 23 contains general rules about making an application)

Application for an interim remedy where there is no related claim

25.4 (1) This rule applies where a party wishes to apply for an interim remedy but –

(a) the remedy is sought in relation to proceedings which are taking place, or will take place, outside the jurisdiction; or

(b) the application is made under section 33 of the Supreme Court Act 1981 or section 52 of the County Courts Act 1984 (order for disclosure, inspection etc. before commencement) before a claim has been commenced.

(2) An application under this rule must be made in accordance with the general rules about applications contained in Part 23.

(The following provisions are also relevant –

- Rule 25.5 (inspection of property before commencement or against a non-party)
- Rule 31.16 (orders for disclosure of documents before proceedings start)
- Rule 31.17 (orders for disclosure of documents against a person not a party))

Inspection of property before commencement or against a non-party

25.5 (1) This rule applies where a person makes an application under –

(a) section 33(1) of the Supreme Court Act 1981 or section 52(1) of the County Courts Act 1984 (inspection etc. of property before commencement);

(b) section 34(3) of the Supreme Court Act 1981 or section 53(3) of the County Courts Act 1984 (inspection etc. of property against a non-party).

(2) The evidence in support of such an application must show, if practicable by reference to any statement of case prepared in relation to the proceedings or anticipated proceedings, that the property –

(a) is or may become the subject matter of such proceedings; or

(b) is relevant to the issues that will arise in relation to such proceedings.

(3) A copy of the application notice and a copy of the evidence in support must be served on –

(a) the person against whom the order is sought; and

(b) in relation to an application under section 34(3) of the Supreme Court Act 1981 or section 53(3) of the County Courts Act 1984, every party to the proceedings other than the applicant.

Interim payments – general procedure

25.6 (1) The claimant may not apply for an order for an interim payment before the end of the period for filing an acknowledgment of service applicable to the defendant against whom the application is made.

(Rule 10.3 sets out the period for filing an acknowledgment of service)

(Rule 25.1(1)(k) defines an interim payment)

(2) The claimant may make more than one application for an order for an interim payment.

(3) A copy of an application notice for an order for an interim payment must –

(a) be served at least 14 days before the hearing of the application; and

(b) be supported by evidence.

(4) If the respondent to an application for an order for an interim payment wishes to rely on written evidence at the hearing, he must –

(a) file the written evidence; and

(b) serve copies on every other party to the application,

at least 7 days before the hearing of the application.

(5) If the applicant wishes to rely on written evidence in reply, he must –

(a) file the written evidence; and

(b) serve a copy on the respondent,

at least 3 days before the hearing of the application.

(6) This rule does not require written evidence –

    (a) to be filed if it has already been filed; or

    (b) to be served on a party on whom it has already been served.

(7) The court may order an interim payment in one sum or in instalments.

(Part 23 contains general rules about applications)

Interim payments – conditions to be satisfied and matters to be taken into account

25.7 (1) The court may make an order for an interim payment only if –

    (a) the defendant against whom the order is sought has admitted liability to pay damages or some other sum of money to the claimant;

    (b) the claimant has obtained judgment against that defendant for damages to be assessed or for a sum of money (other than costs) to be assessed;

    (c) except where paragraph (3) applies, it is satisfied that, if the claim went to trial, the claimant would obtain judgment for a substantial amount of money (other than costs) against the defendant from whom he is seeking an order for an interim payment; or

    (d) the following conditions are satisfied –

        (i) the claimant is seeking an order for possession of land (whether or not any other order is also sought); and

        (ii) the court is satisfied that, if the case went to trial, the defendant would be held liable (even if the claim for possession fails) to pay the claimant a sum of money for the defendant's occupation and use of the land while the claim for possession was pending.

(2) In addition, in a claim for personal injuries the court may make an order for an interim payment of damages only if –

    (a) the defendant is insured in respect of the claim;

    (b) the defendant's liability will be met by –

        (i) an insurer under section 151 of the Road Traffic Act 1988[42]; or

        (ii) an insurer acting under the Motor Insurers Bureau Agreement, or the Motor Insurers Bureau where it is acting itself; or

    (c) the defendant is a public body.

(3) In a claim for personal injuries where there are two or more defendants, the court may make an order for the interim payment of damages against any defendant if –

    (a) it is satisfied that, if the claim went to trial, the claimant would obtain judgment for substantial damages against at least one of the defendants (even if the court has not yet determined which of them is liable); and

    (b) paragraph (2) is satisfied in relation to each of the defendants.

(4) The court must not order an interim payment of more than a reasonable proportion of the likely amount of the final judgment.

(5) The court must take into account –

    (a) contributory negligence; and

    (b) any relevant set-off or counterclaim.

---

(42) 1988 c.52. Section 151 was amended by the Road Traffic Act 1991 (c.40), section 83, Schedule 8.

Powers of court where it has made an order for interim payment

25.8(1) Where a defendant has been ordered to make an interim payment, or has in fact made an interim payment (whether voluntarily or under an order), the court may make an order to adjust the interim payment.

(2) The court may in particular –

(a) order all or part of the interim payment to be repaid;

(b) vary or discharge the order for the interim payment;

(c) order a defendant to reimburse, either wholly or partly, another defendant who has made an interim payment.

(3) The court may make an order under paragraph (2)(c) only if –

(a) the defendant to be reimbursed made the interim payment in relation to a claim in respect of which he has made a claim against the other defendant for a contribution$^{(GL)}$, indemnity$^{(GL)}$ or other remedy; and

(b) where the claim or part to which the interim payment relates has not been discontinued or disposed of, the circumstances are such that the court could make an order for interim payment under rule 25.7.

(4) The court may make an order under this rule without an application by any party if it makes the order when it disposes of the claim or any part of it.

(5) Where –

(a) a defendant has made an interim payment; and

(b) the amount of the payment is more than his total liability under the final judgment or order,

the court may award him interest on the overpaid amount from the date when he made the interim payment.

Restriction on disclosure of an interim payment

25.9 The fact that a defendant has made an interim payment, whether voluntarily or by court order, shall not be disclosed to the trial judge until all questions of liability and the amount of money to be awarded have been decided unless the defendant agrees.

Interim injunction to cease if claim is stayed

25.10 If –

(a) the court has granted an interim injunction$^{(GL)}$; and

(b) the claim is stayed$^{(GL)}$ other than by agreement between the parties,

the interim injunction$^{(GL)}$ shall be set aside$^{(GL)}$ unless the court orders that it should continue to have effect even though the claim is stayed.

Interim injunction to cease after 14 days if claim struck out

25.11(1) If–

(a) the court has granted an interim injunction$^{(GL)}$; and

(b) the claim is struck out under rule 3.7 (sanctions for non-payment of certain fees),

the interim injunction shall cease to have effect 14 days after the date that the claim is struck out unless paragraph (2) applies.

(2) If the claimant applies to reinstate the claim before the interim injunction ceases to have effect under paragraph (1), the injunction shall continue until the hearing of the application unless the court orders otherwise.

II Security for costs

25.12(1) A defendant to any claim may apply under this Section of this Part for security for his costs of the proceedings.

(Part 3 provides for the court to order payment of sums into court in other circumstances. Rule 20.3 provides for this Section of this Part to apply to Part 20 claims.)

    (2) An application for security for costs must be supported by written evidence.

    (3) Where the court makes an order for security for costs, it will –

        (a) determine the amount of security; and

        (b) direct –

            (i) the manner in which; and

            (ii) the time within which the

security must be given.

Conditions to be satisfied

25.13(1) The court may make an order for security for costs under rule 25.12 if –

        (a) it is satisfied, having regard to all the circumstances of the case, that it is just to make such an order; and

        (b) (i) one or more of the conditions in paragraph (2) applies, or

            (ii) an enactment permits the court to require security for costs.

    (2) The conditions are –

        (a) the claimant is an individual –

            (i) who is ordinarily resident out of the jurisdiction; and

            (ii) is not a person against whom a claim can be enforced under the Brussels Conventions or the Lugano Convention, as defined by section 1(1) of the Civil Jurisdiction and Judgments Act 1982[43];

        (b) the claimant is a company or other incorporated body –

            (i) which is ordinarily resident out of the jurisdiction; and

            (ii) is not a body against whom a claim can be enforced under the Brussels Conventions or the Lugano Convention;

        (c) the claimant is a company or other body (whether incorporated inside or outside Great Britain) and there is reason to believe that it will be unable to pay the defendant's costs if ordered to do so;

        (d) the claimant has changed his address since the claim was commenced with a view to evading the consequences of the litigation;

        (e) the claimant failed to give his address in the claim form, or gave an incorrect address in that form;

        (f) the claimant is acting as a nominal claimant, other than as a representative claimant under Part 19, and there is reason to believe that he will be unable to pay the defendant's costs if ordered to do so;

        (g) the claimant has taken steps in relation to his assets that would make it difficult to enforce an order for costs against him.

(Rule 3.4 allows the court to strike out a statement of case and Part 24 for it to give summary judgment.)

---

(43) 1982 c.27; section 1(1) was amended by the Civil Jurisdiction and Judgment Act 1991 (c.12), section 2(2) and 2(3).

Security for costs other than from the claimant

25.14(1) The defendant may seek an order against someone other than the claimant, and the court may make an order for security for costs against that person if –

    (a) it is satisfied, having regard to all the circumstances of the case, that it is just to make such an order; and

    (b) one or more of the conditions in paragraph (2) applies.

  (2) The conditions are that the person –

    (a) has assigned the right to the claim to the claimant with a view to avoiding the possibility of a costs order being made against him; or

    (b) has contributed or agreed to contribute to the claimant's costs in return for a share of any money or property which the claimant may recover in the proceedings; and

    is a person against whom a costs order may be made.

(Rule 48.2 makes provision for costs orders against non-parties.)

Security for costs of an appeal

25.15(1) The court may order security for costs of an appeal against-

    (a) an appellant;

    (b) a respondent who also appeals,

    on the same grounds as it may order security for costs against a claimant under this Part.

  (2) The court may also make an order under paragraph (1) where the appellant, or the respondent who also appeals, is a limited company and there is reason to believe it will be unable to pay the costs of the other parties to the appeal should its appeal be unsuccessful.

PRACTICE DIRECTION – INTERIM INJUNCTIONS
THIS PRACTICE DIRECTION SUPPLEMENTS CPR PART 25

Jurisdiction

1.1 High Court Judges and any other Judge duly authorised may grant 'search orders'[1] and 'freezing injunctions'[2].

1.2 In a case in the High Court, Masters and district judges have the power to grant injunctions:

    (1) by consent,

    (2) in connection with charging orders and appointments of receivers,

    (3) in aid of execution of judgments.

1.3 In any other case any judge who has jurisdiction to conduct the trial of the action has the power to grant an injunction in that action.

1.4 A Master or district judge has the power to vary or discharge an injunction granted by any Judge with the consent of all the parties.

Making an application

2.1 The application notice must state:

    (1) the order sought, and

    (2) the date, time and place of the hearing.

---

1   Rule 25.1(1)(g).
2   Rule 25.1(1)(f).

2.2 The application notice and evidence in support must be served as soon as practicable after issue and in any event not less than 3 days before the court is due to hear the application[3].

2.3 Where the court is to serve, sufficient copies of the application notice and evidence in support for the court and for each respondent should be filed for issue and service.

2.4 Whenever possible a draft of the order sought should be filed with the application notice and a disk containing the draft should also be available to the court. This will enable the court officer to arrange for any amendments to be incorporated and for the speedy preparation and sealing of the order. The current word processing system to be used is WordPerfect 5.1.

Evidence

3.1 Applications for search orders and freezing injunctions must be supported by affidavit evidence.

3.2 Applications for other interim injunctions must be supported by evidence set out in either:

(1) a witness statement, or

(2) a statement of case provided that it is verified by a statement of truth[4], or

(3) the application provided that it is verified by a statement of truth,

unless the court, an Act, a rule or a practice direction requires evidence by affidavit.

3.3 The evidence must set out the facts on which the applicant relies for the claim being made against the respondent, including all material facts of which the court should be made aware.

3.4 Where an application is made without notice to the respondent, the evidence must also set out why notice was not given.

(See Part 32 and the practice direction that supplements it for information about evidence.)

Urgent applications and applications without notice

4.1 These fall into two categories:

(1) applications where a claim form has already been issued, and

(2) applications where a claim form has not yet been issued,

and, in both cases, where notice of the application has not been given to the respondent.

4.2 These applications are normally dealt with at a court hearing but cases of extreme urgency may be dealt with by telephone.

4.3 Applications dealt with at a court hearing after issue of a claim form:

(1) the application notice, evidence in support and a draft order (as in 2.4 above) should be filed with the court two hours before the hearing wherever possible,

(2) if an application is made before the application notice has been issued, a draft order (as in 2.4 above) should be provided at the hearing, and the application notice and evidence in support must be filed with the court on the same or next working day or as ordered by the court, and

(3) except in cases where secrecy is essential, the applicant should take steps to notify the respondent informally of the application.

4.4 Applications made before the issue of a claim form:

(1) in addition to the provisions set out at 4.3 above, unless the court orders otherwise, either the applicant must undertake to the court to issue a claim form immediately or the court will give directions for the commencement of the claim[5],

(2) where possible the claim form should be served with the order for the injunction,

(3) an order made before the issue of a claim form should state in the title after the names of the applicant and respondent 'the Claimant and Defendant in an Intended Action'.

4.5 Applications made by telephone:

(1) where it is not possible to arrange a hearing, application can be made between 10.00 a.m.

---

3   Rule 23.7(1) and (2) and see rule 23.7(4) (short service).

4   See Part 22.

5   Rule 25.2(3).

6   [*Authors' note: Apparently missing!*]

and 5.00 p.m. weekdays by telephoning the Royal Courts of Justice on 0171 936 6000 and asking to be put in contact with a High Court Judge of the appropriate Division available to deal with an emergency application in a High Court matter. The appropriate district registry may also be contacted by telephone. In county court proceedings, the appropriate county court should be contacted,

(2) where an application is made outside those hours the applicant should either –

    (a) telephone the Royal Courts of Justice on 0171 936 6000 where he will be put in contact with the clerk to the appropriate duty judge in the High Court (or the appropriate area Circuit Judge where known), or

    (b) the Urgent Court Business Officer of the appropriate Circuit who will contact the local duty judge.

(3) where the facility is available it is likely that the judge will require a draft order to be faxed to him,

(4) the application notice and evidence in support must be filed with the court on the same or next working day or as ordered, together with two copies of the order for sealing,

(5) injunctions will be heard by telephone only where the applicant is acting by counsel or solicitors.

Orders for injunctions

5.1 Any order for an injunction, unless the court orders otherwise, must contain:

(1) an undertaking by the applicant to the court to pay any damages which the respondent(s) (or any other party served with or notified of the order) sustain which the court considers the applicant should pay,

(2) if made without notice to any other party, an undertaking by the applicant to the court to serve on the respondent the application notice, evidence in support and any order made as soon as practicable,

(3) if made without notice to any other party, a return date for a further hearing at which the other party can be present,

(4) if made before filing the application notice, an undertaking to file and pay the appropriate fee on the same or next working day, and

(5) if made before issue of a claim form –

    (a) an undertaking to issue and pay the appropriate fee on the same or next working day, or

    (b) directions for the commencement of the claim.

5.2 An order for an injunction made in the presence of all parties to be bound by it or made at a hearing of which they have had notice, may state that it is effective until trial or further order.

5.3 Any order for an injunction must set out clearly what the respondent must do or not do.

Freezing injunctions

Orders to restrain disposal of assets worldwide and within England and Wales

6   Examples of Freezing Injunctions are annexed to this practice direction.

Search orders

Orders for the preservation of evidence and property

7.1 The following provisions apply to search orders in addition to those listed above.

The Supervising Solicitor

7.2 The Supervising Solicitor must be experienced in the operation of search orders. A Supervising Solicitor may be contacted either through the Law Society or, for the London area, through the London Solicitors Litigation Association.

7.3 Evidence:

(1) the affidavit must state the name, firm and its address, and experience of the Supervising Solicitor, also the address of the premises and whether it is a private or business address, and

(2) the affidavit must disclose very fully the reason the order is sought, including the probability that relevant material would disappear if the order were not made.

7.4 Service:

(1) the order must be served personally by the Supervising Solicitor, unless the court otherwise orders, and must be accompanied by the evidence in support and any documents capable of being copied,

(2) confidential exhibits need not be served but they must be made available for inspection by the respondent in the presence of the applicant's solicitors while the order is carried out and afterwards be retained by the respondent's solicitors on their undertaking not to permit the respondent –

(a) to see them or copies of them except in their presence, and

(b) to make or take away any note or record of them,

(3) the Supervising Solicitor may be accompanied only by the persons mentioned in the order,

(4) the Supervising Solicitor must explain the terms and effect of the order to the respondent in every day language and advise him of his right to –

(a) legal advice, and

(b) apply to vary or discharge the order,

(5) where the Supervising Solicitor is a man and the respondent is likely to be an unaccompanied woman, at least one other person named in the order must be a woman and must accompany the Supervising Solicitor, and

(6) the order may only be served between 9.30 a.m. and 5.30 p.m. Monday to Friday unless the court otherwise orders.

7.5 Search and custody of materials:

(1) no material shall be removed unless clearly covered by the terms of the order,

(2) the premises must not be searched and no items shall be removed from them except in the presence of the respondent or a person who appears to be a responsible employee of the respondent,

(3) where copies of documents are sought, the documents should be retained for no more than 2 days before return to the owner,

(4) where material in dispute is removed pending trial, the applicant's solicitors should place it in the custody of the respondent's solicitors on their undertaking to retain it in safekeeping and to produce it to the court when required,

(5) in appropriate cases the applicant should insure the material retained in the respondent's solicitors' custody,

(6) the Supervising Solicitor must make a list of all material removed from the premises and supply a copy of the list to the respondent,

(7) no material shall be removed from the premises until the respondent has had reasonable time to check the list,

(8) if any of the listed items exists only in computer readable form, the respondent must immediately give the applicant's solicitors effective access to the computers, with all necessary passwords, to enable them to be searched, and cause the listed items to be printed out,

(9) the applicant must take all reasonable steps to ensure that no damage is done to any computer or data,

(10) the applicant and his representatives may not themselves search the respondent's computers unless they have sufficient expertise to do so without damaging the respondent's system,

(11) the Supervising Solicitor shall provide a report on the carrying out of the order to the applicant's solicitors,

(12) as soon as the report is received the applicant's solicitors shall –

(a) serve a copy of it on the respondent, and

(b) file a copy of it with the court, and

(13) where the Supervising Solicitor is satisfied that full compliance with paragraph 7.5(7) and (8) above is impracticable, he may permit the search to proceed and items to be removed without compliance with the impracticable requirements.

General

8.1 The Supervising Solicitor must not be an employee or member of the applicant's firm of solicitors.

8.2 If the court orders that the order need not be served by the Supervising Solicitor, the reason for so ordering must be set out in the order.

8.3 The search order must not be carried out at the same time as a police search warrant.

8.4 There is no privilege against self incrimination in Intellectual Property cases (see the Supreme Court Act 1981, section 72) therefore in those cases, paragraph (4) of the Respondent's Entitlements and any other references to incrimination in the Search Order, should be removed.

8.5 Applications in intellectual property cases should be made in the Chancery Division.

8.6 An example of a Search Order is annexed to this Practice Direction.

ANNEX

Freezing Injunction	IN THE [HIGH COURT OF JUSTICE]
Order to restrain assets in England and Wales	[CHANCERY DIVISION]
	[Strand, London WC2A 2LL]

Before The Honourable Mr Justice   [   ]

Claim No.

Dated

Applicant

Seal

Respondent

Name, address and reference of Respondent

PENAL NOTICE

IF YOU THE WITHIN NAMED [   ] DISOBEY THIS ORDER YOU MAY BE HELD TO BE IN CONTEMPT OF COURT AND LIABLE TO IMPRISONMENT OR FINED OR YOUR ASSETS SEIZED

IMPORTANT

NOTICE TO THE RESPONDENT

You should read the terms of the Order and the Guidance Notes very carefully. You are advised to consult a Solicitor as soon as possible.

This Order prohibits you, the Respondent, from dealing with your assets up to the amount stated in the Order, but subject to any exceptions set out at the end of the Order. You have a right to ask the Court to vary or discharge this Order.

If you disobey this Order you may be found guilty of Contempt of Court and may be sent to prison or fined. In the case of a Corporate Respondent, it may be fined, its Directors may be sent to prison or fined or its assets may be seized.

THE ORDER

An application was made today [*date*] by [Counsel][Solicitors][or as may be] for the Applicant to Mr Justice [   ] who heard the application. The Judge read the affidavits listed in Schedule A and accepted the undertakings set out in Schedule B at the end of this Order. As a result of the application **IT IS ORDERED** that until [[   ] ('the return date')] [or further Order of the Court]:-

1   The Respondent must not remove from England and Wales or in any way dispose of or deal with or diminish the value of any of his assets which are in England and Wales whether in his own name or not and whether solely or jointly owned up to the value of £   .

This prohibition includes the following assets in particular:—

   (a)   the property known as [title/address] or the net sale money after payment of any mortgages if it has been sold;

   (b)   the property and assets of the Respondent's business known as (or carried on at [address]) or the sale money if any of them have been sold; and

   (c)   any money in the account numbered [a/c number] at [title/address].

2   If the total unencumbered value of the Respondent's assets in England and Wales exceeds £   , the Respondent may remove any of those assets from England and Wales or may dispose of or deal with them so long as the total unencumbered value of his assets still in England and Wales remains above £   .

3   Exceptions to this Order:-

   (1)   This Order does not prohibit the Respondent from spending

          £   a week towards his ordinary living expenses [and £   a week towards his ordinary and proper business expenses] and also   £   a week [or a reasonable sum] on legal advice and representation. But before spending any money the Respondent must tell the Applicant's legal representatives[7] where the money is to come from.

   [(2)   This Order does not prohibit the Respondent from dealing with or disposing of any of his assets in the ordinary and proper course of business.]

   (3)   The Respondent may agree with the Applicant's legal representatives that the above spending limits should be increased or that this Order should be varied in any other respect, but any agreement must be in writing.

   (4)   The Respondent may cause this Order to cease to have effect if the Respondent provides security by paying the sum of £   into Court or makes provision for security in that sum by another method agreed with the Applicant's legal representatives.

4   The Respondent must:-

   (1)   Inform the Applicant in writing at once of all his assets in England and Wales and whether in his own name or not and whether solely or jointly owned, giving the value, location and details of all such assets. [The Respondent may be entitled to refuse to provide some or all of this information on the grounds that it may

---

7   For the definition of legal representative see the glossary in Part 2.

incriminate him. *This sentence may be inserted in cases not covered by the Theft Act 1968, s.31.*]

(2) Confirm the information in an affidavit which must be served on the Applicant's legal representatives within [   ] days after this Order has been served on the Respondent.

[5 *Where an Order for service by an alternative means or service out of the jurisdiction has been made –*

(1) The Applicant may issue and serve a Claim Form on the Respondent at [address] by [method of service].

(2) If the Respondent wishes to defend the Claim where the Claim Form states that Particulars of Claim are to follow he must complete and return the Acknowledgment of Service within [   ] days of being served with the Claim Form. Where the Particulars of Claim are served with the Claim Form, and the Respondent wishes to defend part or all of the Claim he must complete and return an Acknowledgment of Service within [   ] days of being served with the Claim Form or a Defence within [   ] days.

GUIDANCE NOTES

EFFECT OF THIS ORDER

(1) A respondent who is an individual who is ordered not to do something must not do it himself or in any other way. He must not do it through others acting on his behalf or on his instructions or with his encouragement.

(2) A respondent which is a corporation and which is ordered not to do something must not do it itself or by its directors, officers, employees or agents or in any other way.

VARIATION OR DISCHARGE OF THIS ORDER

The Respondent (or anyone notified of this Order) may apply to the court at any time to vary or discharge this Order (or so much of it as affects that person), but anyone wishing to do so must first inform the Applicant's legal representatives.

PARTIES OTHER THAN THE APPLICANT AND RESPONDENT

(1) Effect of this Order:

It is a Contempt of Court for any person notified of this Order knowingly to assist in or permit a breach of this Order. Any person doing so may be sent to prison, fined or have his assets seized.

(2) Set off by banks:

This injunction does not prevent any bank from exercising any right of set off it may have in respect of any facility which it gave to the respondent before it was notified of this Order.

(3) Withdrawals by the Respondent:

No bank need enquire as to the application or proposed application of any money withdrawn by the Respondent if the withdrawal appears to be permitted by this Order.

INTERPRETATION OF THIS ORDER

(1) In this Order, where there is more than one Respondent, (unless otherwise stated), references to 'the Respondent' means both or all of them.

(2) A requirement to serve on 'the Respondent' means on each of them. However, the Order is effective against any Respondent on whom it is served.

(3) An Order requiring 'the Respondent' to do or not to do anything applies to all Respondents.

COMMUNICATIONS WITH THE COURT

All communications to the Court about this Order should be sent, where the Order is made in the Chancery Division, to [Room TM 510], Royal Courts of Justice, Strand, London WC2A 2LL quoting the case number. The telephone number is 0171 936 [6827]; and where the order is made in the Queen's Bench Division, to Room W11 (0171 936 6009). The offices are open between 10 a.m. and 4.30 p.m. Monday to Friday.

SCHEDULE A

AFFIDAVITS

The Applicant relied on the following affidavits:

    [name]   *[number of affidavit]*   *[date sworn]*   *[filed on behalf of]*

(1)

(2)

SCHEDULE B

UNDERTAKINGS GIVEN TO THE COURT BY THE APPLICANT

(1) If the Court later finds that this Order has caused loss to the Respondent, and decides that the Respondent should be compensated for that loss, the Applicant will comply with any Order the Court may make.

(2) The Applicant will on or before *[date]* cause a written guarantee in the sum of £   to be issued from a bank having a place of business within England or Wales, such guarantee being in respect of any Order the Court may make pursuant to paragraph (1) above. The Applicant will further, forthwith upon issue of the guarantee, cause a copy of it to be served on the Respondent.

(3) As soon as practicable the Applicant will [issue and serve on the Respondent a Claim Form in the form of the draft produced to the Court] [serve on the Respondent the Claim Form] claiming the appropriate relief, together with this Order.

(4) The Applicant will cause an affidavit to be sworn and filed [substantially in the terms of the draft affidavit produced to the Court] [confirming the substance of what was said to the Court by the Applicant's Counsel/Solicitors].

[(5) *Where a return date has been given* – As soon as practicable the Applicant will serve on the Respondent an Application for the return date together with a copy of the affidavits and exhibits containing the evidence relied on by the Applicant.]

(6) Anyone notified of this Order will be given a copy of it by the Applicant's legal representatives.

(7) The Applicant will pay the reasonable costs of anyone other than the Respondent which have been incurred as a result of this Order including the costs of ascertaining whether that person holds any of the Respondent's assets and if the Court later finds that this Order has caused such person loss, and decides that such person should be compensated for that loss, the Applicant will comply with any Order the Court may make.

(8) If for any reason this Order ceases to have effect (including in particular where the Respondent provides security as provided for above or the Applicant does not provide a bank guarantee as provided for above), the Applicant will forthwith take all reasonable steps to inform, in writing, any person or company to whom he has given notice of this Order, or who he has reasonable grounds for supposing may act upon this Order, that it has ceased to have effect.

NAME AND ADDRESS OF APPLICANT'S LEGAL REPRESENTATIVES

The Applicant's Legal Representatives are:-

[Name, address, reference, fax and telephone numbers both in and out of office hours.]

ANNEX

★★Freezing Injunction★★
Order to restrain assets worldwide

Before The Honourable Mr Justice

IN THE [HIGH COURT OF JUSTICE]
[CHANCERY DIVISION]
[Strand, London WC2A 2LL]
[   ]

Claim No.

Dated

Applicant

Seal

Respondent

Name, address and reference of Respondent

PENAL NOTICE

IF YOU THE WITHIN NAMED [   ] DISOBEY THIS ORDER YOU MAY BE HELD TO BE IN CONTEMPT OF COURT AND LIABLE TO IMPRISONMENT OR FINED OR YOUR ASSETS SEIZED

IMPORTANT

NOTICE TO THE RESPONDENT

You should read the terms of the Order and the Guidance Notes very carefully. You are advised to consult a Solicitor as soon as possible.

This Order prohibits you, the Respondent, from dealing with your assets up to the amount stated in the Order, but subject to any exceptions set out at the end of the Order. You have a right to ask the Court to vary or discharge this Order.

If you disobey this Order you may be found guilty of Contempt of Court and may be sent to prison or fined. In the case of a Corporate Respondent, it may be fined, its Directors may be sent to prison or fined or its assets may be seized.

THE ORDER

An application was made today [date] by [Counsel][Solicitors][or as may be] for the Applicant to Mr Justice [   ] who heard the application. The Judge read the affidavits listed in Schedule A and accepted the undertakings set out in Schedule B at the end of this Order. As a result of the application IT IS ORDERED that until [[   ] ('the return date')] [further Order of the Court]:-1 The Respondent must not:-

(1) remove from England and Wales or in any way dispose of or deal with or diminish the value of any of his assets which are in England and Wales whether in his own name or not and whether solely or jointly owned up to the value of £   ,or

(2) in any way dispose of or deal with or diminish the value of any of his assets whether they are in or outside England or Wales whether in his own name or not and whether solely or jointly owned up to the same value. This prohibition includes the following assets in particular:-

    (a) the property known as [*title/address*] or the net sale money after payment of any mortgages if it has been sold;

    (b) the property and assets of the Respondent's business known as (or carried on at [*address*]) or the sale money if any of them have been sold; and

    (c) any money in the account numbered [*a/c number*] at [*title/address*].

2   (1) If the total unencumbered value of the Respondent's assets in England and Wales exceeds £   , the Respondent may remove any of those assets from England and Wales or may dispose of or deal with them so long as the total unencumbered value of his assets still in England and Wales remains above £   .

    (2) If the total unencumbered value of the Respondent's assets in England and Wales does not exceed £   , the Respondent must not remove any of those assets from England and Wales and must not dispose of or deal with any of them, but if he has other assets outside England and Wales the Respondent may dispose of or deal with those assets so long as the total unencumbered value of all his assets whether in or outside England and Wales remains above £   .

3   Exceptions to this Order:-

    (1) This Order does not prohibit the Respondent from spending £   a week towards his ordinary living expenses [and £   a week towards his ordinary and proper business expenses] and also £   a week [or a reasonable sum] on legal advice and representation. But before spending any money the Respondent must tell the Applicant's legal representatives where the money is to come from.

    [(2) This Order does not prohibit the Respondent from dealing with or disposing of any of his assets in the ordinary and proper course of business.]

    (3) The Respondent may agree with the Applicant's legal representatives that the above spending limits should be increased or that this Order should be varied in any other respect, but any agreement must be in writing.

    (4) The Respondent may cause this Order to cease to have effect if the Respondent provides security by paying the sum of £   into Court or makes provision for security in that sum by another method agreed with the Applicant's legal representatives.

4   The Respondent must:-
   (1) Inform the Applicant in writing at once of all his assets whether in or outside England and Wales and whether in his own name or not and whether solely or jointly owned, giving the value, location and details of all such assets. [The Respondent may be entitled to refuse to provide some or all of this information on the grounds that it may incriminate him. *This sentence may be inserted in cases not covered by the Theft Act 1968, s.31.*]
   (2) Confirm the information in an affidavit which must be served on the Applicant's legal representatives within [   ] days after this Order has been served on the Respondent.

[5   *Where an Order for service by an alternative means or service out of the jurisdiction has been made –*
   (1) The Applicant may issue and serve a Claim Form on the Respondent at [address] by [method of service]
   (2) If the Respondent wishes to defend the Claim he must complete and return the Notice of Intention to Defend within [   ] days of being served with the Claim Form.]

GUIDANCE NOTES

EFFECT OF THIS ORDER

(1) A Respondent who is an individual who is ordered not to do something must not do it himself or in any other way. He must not do it through others acting on his behalf or on his instructions or with his encouragement.

(2) A Respondent which is a corporation and which is ordered not to do something must not do it itself or by its directors, officers, employees or agents or in any other way.

VARIATION OR DISCHARGE OF THIS ORDER

The Respondent (or anyone notified of this Order) may apply to the Court at any time to vary or discharge this Order (or so much of it as affects that person), but anyone wishing to do so must first inform the Applicant's legal representatives.

PARTIES OTHER THAN THE APPLICANT AND RESPONDENT

(1) Effect of this Order:-

It is a Contempt of Court for any person notified of this Order knowingly to assist in or permit a breach of this Order. Any person doing so may be sent to prison, fined or have his assets seized.

(2) Effect of this Order outside England and Wales:-

The terms of this Order do not affect or concern anyone outside the jurisdiction of this Court until it is declared enforceable by or is enforced by a Court in the relevant country and then they are to affect him only to the extent they have been declared enforceable or have been enforced UNLESS the person is:

  (i)   a person to whom this Order is addressed or an officer or an agent appointed by power of attorney of that person; or

  (ii) a person who is subject to the jurisdiction of this Court and (a) has been given written notice of this Order at his residence or place of business within the jurisdiction of this Court and (b) is able to prevent acts or omissions outside the jurisdiction of this Court which constitute or assist in a breach of the terms of this Order.

(3) Set off by Banks:-

This injunction does not prevent any bank from exercising any right of set off it may have in respect of any facility which it gave to the Respondent before it was notified of this Order.

(4) Withdrawals by the Respondent:-

No bank need enquire as to the application or proposed application of any money withdrawn by the Respondent if the withdrawal appears to be permitted by this Order.

INTERPRETATION OF THIS ORDER

(1) In this Order, where there is more than one Respondent, (unless otherwise stated) references to 'the Respondent' means both or all of them.

(2) A requirement to serve on 'the Respondent' means on each of them. However, the Order is effective against any Respondent on whom it is served.

(3) An Order requiring 'the Respondent' to do or not to do anything applies to all Respondents.

COMMUNICATIONS WITH THE COURT

All communications to the Court about this Order should be sent, where the Order is made in the Chancery Division, to [Room TM 510], Royal Courts of Justice, Strand, London WC2A 2LL quoting the case number. The telephone number is 0171 936 [6827]; and where the order is made in the Queen's Bench Division, to Room W11 (0171 936 6009). The offices are open between 10 a.m. and 4.30 p.m. Monday to Friday.

SCHEDULE A

AFFIDAVITS

The Applicant relied on the following affidavits:

    [name]   [number of affidavit]   [date sworn]   [filed on behalf of]

    (1)

    (2)

SCHEDULE B

UNDERTAKINGS GIVEN TO THE COURT BY THE APPLICANT

(1) If the Court later finds that this Order has caused loss to the Respondent, and decides that the Respondent should be compensated for that loss, the Applicant will comply with any Order the Court may make.

(2) The Applicant will on or before [date] cause a written guarantee in the sum of £   to be issued from a bank having a place of business within England or Wales, such guarantee being in respect of any Order the Court may make pursuant to paragraph (1) above. The Applicant will further, forthwith upon issue of the guarantee, cause a copy of it to be served on the Respondent.

[(3) As soon as practicable the Applicant will [issue and serve on the Respondent a Claim Form in the form of the draft produced to the Court] [serve on the Respondent the Claim Form] claiming the appropriate relief, together with this Order.]

(4) The Applicant will cause an affidavit to be sworn and filed [substantially in the terms of the draft affidavit produced to the Court] [confirming the substance of what was said to the Court by the Applicant's Counsel/Solicitors].

[(5) Where a return date has been given– As soon as practicable the Applicant will serve on the Respondent an application for the return date together with a copy of the affidavits and exhibits containing the evidence relied on by the Applicant.]

(6) Anyone notified of this Order will be given a copy of it by the Applicant's legal representatives.

(7) The Applicant will pay the reasonable costs of anyone other than the Respondent which have been incurred as a result of this Order including the costs of ascertaining whether that person holds any of the Respondent's assets and if the Court later finds that this Order has caused such person loss, and decides that such person should be compensated for that loss, the Applicant will comply with any Order the Court may make.

(8) If for any reason this Order ceases to have effect (including in particular where the Respondent provides security as provided for above or the Applicant does not provide a bank guarantee as provided for above), the Applicant will forthwith take all reasonable steps to inform, in writing, any person or company to whom he has given notice of this Order, or

who he has reasonable grounds for supposing may act upon this Order, that it has ceased to have effect.

[(9) The Applicant will not without the leave of the Court begin proceedings against the Respondent in any other jurisdiction or use information obtained as a result of an Order of the Court in this jurisdiction for the purpose of civil or criminal proceedings in any other jurisdiction.]

[(10) The Applicant will not without the leave of the Court seek to enforce this Order in any country outside England and Wales [or seek an Order of a similar nature including Orders conferring a charge or other security against the Respondent or the Respondent's assets].]

NAME AND ADDRESS OF APPLICANT'S LEGAL REPRESENTATIVES

The Applicant's Legal Representatives are:-

[Name, address, reference, fax and telephone numbers both in and out of office hours.]

ANNEX

★★Search Order★★ Order to preserve evidence and property Before The Honourable Mr Justice	IN THE [HIGH COURT OF JUSTICE] [CHANCERY DIVISION] [Strand, London WC2A 2LL] [ ]

Claim No.

Dated

Applicant

Seal

Respondent

Name, address and reference of Respondent

PENAL NOTICE

IF YOU THE WITHIN NAMED [•   ] DISOBEY THIS ORDER YOU MAY BE HELD TO BE IN CONTEMPT OF COURT AND LIABLE TO IMPRISONMENT OR FINED OR YOUR ASSETS SEIZED

IMPORTANT

NOTICE TO THE RESPONDENT

You should read the terms of the Order and the Guidance Notes very carefully. You are advised to consult a Solicitor as soon as possible.

This Order orders you, the Respondent, to allow the persons mentioned in the Order to enter the premises described in the Order and to search for, examine and remove or copy the articles specified in the Order. The persons so named will have no right to enter the premises or, having entered, to remain at the premises, unless you give your consent to their doing so. If, however, you withhold your consent you will be in breach of this Order and may be held to be in Contempt of Court.

The Order also requires you to hand over any of such articles which are under your control and to provide information to the Applicant's Solicitors, and prohibits you from doing certain acts.

If you, the Respondent, disobey this Order you may be found guilty of contempt of Court and may be sent to prison or fined. In the case of a Corporate Respondent, it may be fined, its Directors may be sent to prison or fined or its assets may be seized.

THE ORDER

AN APPLICATION was made today [*date*] by [Counsel] [Solicitors] for the Applicant to Mr Justice [   ] who heard the application. The Judge read the affidavits listed in Schedule F at the end of this Order and accepted the undertakings by the Applicant, the Applicant's Solicitors and the Supervising Solicitor set forth in the Schedules at the end of this Order. As a result of the application IT IS ORDERED that until [[   ] ('the return date')] [or further Order of the Court]:-

1. (1) The Respondent must allow Mr/Mrs/Miss [   ] ('the Supervising Solicitor'), together with Mr [   ] a Solicitor of the Supreme Court, and a partner in the firm of [   ] the Applicant's Solicitors and up to [   ] other persons being [*their capacity*] accompanying them, to enter the premises mentioned in Schedule A to this Order and any other premises of the Respondent disclosed under paragraph 4(1) below and any vehicles under the Respondent's control on or around the premises so that they can search for, inspect, photograph or photocopy, and deliver into the safekeeping of the Applicant's Solicitors all the documents and articles which are listed in Schedule B to this Order ('the listed items') or which Mr [   ] believes to be listed items.

(2) The Respondent must allow those persons to remain on the premises until the search is complete, and to re-enter the premises on the same or the following day in order to complete the search.

2. (1) No item may be removed from the premises until a list of the items to be removed has been prepared, and a copy of the list has been supplied to the person served with the Order, and he has been given a reasonable opportunity to check the list.

(2) The premises must not be searched, and items must not be removed from them, except in the presence of the Respondent or a person appearing to be a responsible employee of the Respondent or in control of the premises.

(3) If the Supervising Solicitor is satisfied that full compliance with paragraph 2(1) or (2) above is impracticable, he may permit the search to proceed and items to be removed without compliance with the impracticable requirements.

3. (1) The Respondent must immediately hand over to the Applicant's Solicitors any of the listed items which are in his possession or under his control save for any computer or hard disk integral to any computer.

(2) If any of the listed items exists only in computer readable form, the Respondent must immediately give the Applicant's Solicitors effective access to the computers, with all necessary passwords, to enable them to be searched, and cause the listed items to be printed out. A print-out of the items must be given to the Applicant's Solicitors or displayed on the computer screen so that they can be read and copied. All reasonable steps shall be taken by the Applicant to ensure that no damage is done to any computer or data. The Applicant and his representatives may not themselves search the Respondent's computers unless they have sufficient expertise to do so without damaging the Respondent's system.

4. (1) The Respondent must immediately inform the Applicant's Solicitors:—
    (a) where all the listed items are; and
    (b) so far as he is aware —
        (i)   the name and address of everyone who has supplied him, or offered to supply him, with listed items,
        (ii) the name and address of everyone to whom he has supplied, or offered to supply, listed items, and
        (iii) full details of the dates and quantities of every such supply and offer.
    (2) Within [   ] days after being served with this Order the Respondent must swear an affidavit setting out the above information.

5. (1) Except for the purpose of obtaining legal advice, the Respondent or anyone else with knowledge of this Order must not directly or indirectly inform anyone of these proceedings or of the contents of this Order, or warn anyone that proceedings have been or may be brought against him by the Applicant until [[   ] the return date] [or further Order of the Court].
    (2) The Respondent must not destroy, tamper with, cancel or part with possession, power, custody or control of the listed items otherwise than in accordance with the terms of this Order.
    (3) [*Insert any negative injunction.*]
[6 *Insert any further order.*]

GUIDANCE NOTES

EFFECT OF THIS ORDER

(1) A Respondent who is an individual who is ordered not to do something must not do it himself or in any other way. He must not do it through others acting on his behalf or on his instructions or with his encouragement.

(2) A Respondent which is a corporation and which is ordered not to do something must not do it itself or by its directors officers employees or agents or in any other way.

(3) This Order must be complied with either by the Respondent himself or by an employee of the Respondent or other person appearing to be in control of the premises and having authority to permit the premises to be entered and the search to proceed.

(4) This Order requires the Respondent or his employee or other person appearing to be in control of the premises and having that authority to permit entry to the premises immediately the Order is served upon him, except as stated in paragraph 6 below.

RESPONDENT'S ENTITLEMENTS

(1) Before you the Respondent or the person appearing to be in control of the premises allow anybody onto the premises to carry out this Order you are entitled to have the solicitor who serves you with this Order explain to you what it means in everyday language.

(2) You are entitled to insist that there is nobody [or nobody except Mr] present who could gain commercially from anything he might read or see on your premises.

(3) You are entitled to refuse to permit entry before 9:30 a.m. or after 5:30 p.m. or at all on Saturday and Sunday unless the Court has ordered otherwise.

(4) Except in certain cases, you may be entitled to refuse to permit disclosure of any documents which may incriminate you ('incriminating documents') or to answer any questions if to do so may incriminate you. It may be prudent to take advice, because if you so refuse, your refusal may be taken into account by the Court at a later stage.

(5) You are entitled to refuse to permit disclosure of any documents passing between you and your Solicitors or Patent or Trade Mark Agents for the purpose of obtaining advice ('privileged documents').

(6) You are entitled to seek legal advice, and to ask the Court to vary or discharge this Order, provided you do so at once, and provided you do not disturb or move anything in the interim and that meanwhile you permit the Supervising Solicitor (who is a Solicitor acting independently of the Applicant) to enter, but not start to search.

(7) Before permitting entry to the premises by any person other than the Supervising Solicitor, you (or any other person appearing to be in control of the premises) may gather together any

documents you believe may be [incriminating or] privileged and hand them to the Supervising Solicitor for the Supervising Solicitor to assess whether they are [incriminating or] privileged as claimed. If the Supervising Solicitor concludes that any of the documents may be [incriminating or] privileged documents or if there is any doubt as to their status the Supervising Solicitor shall exclude them from the search and shall retain the documents of doubtful status in his possession pending further order of the Court. While this is being done, you may refuse entry to the premises by any other person, and may refuse to permit the search to begin, for a short time (not to exceed two hours, unless the Supervising Solicitor agrees to a longer period). If you wish to take legal advice and gather documents as permitted, you must first inform the Supervising Solicitor and keep him informed of the steps being taken.

RESTRICTIONS ON SERVICE

Paragraph 1 of the Order is subject to the following restrictions:–

(1) This Order may only be served between 9:30 a.m. and 5:30 p.m. on a weekday unless the Court has ordered otherwise.

(2) This Order may not be carried out at the same time as a police search warrant.

(3) This Order must be served by the Supervising Solicitor, and paragraph 1 of the Order must be carried out in his presence and under his supervision. Where the premises are likely to be occupied by an unaccompanied woman and the Supervising Solicitor is a man, at least one of the persons accompanying him as provided by paragraph 1 of the Order shall be a woman.

(4) This Order does not require the person served with the Order to allow anyone [or anyone except Mr] to enter the premises who in the view of the Supervising Solicitor could gain commercially from anything he might read or see on the premises if the person served with the Order objects.

VARIATION OR DISCHARGE OF THIS ORDER

The Respondent (or anyone notified of this Order) may apply to the Court at any time to vary or discharge this Order (or so much of it as affects that person), but anyone wishing to do so must first inform the Applicant's Solicitors.

INTERPRETATION OF THIS ORDER

(1) In this Order, where there is more than one Respondent, references to 'the Respondent' means both or all of them.

(2) A requirement to serve on 'the Respondent' means on each of them. However, the Order is effective against any Respondent on whom it is served.

(3) An Order requiring 'the Respondent' to do or not to do anything applies to all Respondents.

(4) Any other requirement that something shall be done to or in the presence of 'the Respondent' means to or in the presence of any one of them or in the case of a firm or company a director or a person appearing to the Supervising Solicitor to be a responsible employee.

COMMUNICATIONS WITH THE COURT

All communications to the Court about this Order should be sent, where the Order is made in the Chancery Division, to [Room TM 510], Royal Courts of Justice, Strand, London, WC2A 2LL quoting the case number. The telephone number is 0171 936 [6827]; and where the order is made in the Queen's Bench Division, to Room W11 (0171 936 6009). The offices are open between 10 a.m. and 4.30 p.m. Monday to Friday.

SCHEDULE A

The premises

SCHEDULE B

The listed items

SCHEDULE C

UNDERTAKINGS GIVEN TO THE COURT BY THE APPLICANT

(1) If the Court later finds that this Order or carrying it out has caused loss to the Respondent, and decides that the Respondent should be compensated for that loss, the Applicant will comply with any Order the Court may make. Further, if the carrying out of this Order has been in breach of the terms of this Order or otherwise in a manner inconsistent with the Applicant's Solicitors' duties as Officers of the Court the Applicant will comply with any order for damages the Court may make.

[(2) As soon as practicable to issue a Claim Form [in the form of the draft produced to the Court] [claiming appropriate relief.]]

[(3) To [swear and file an affidavit] [cause an affidavit to be sworn and filed] [substantially in the terms of the draft produced to the Court] [confirming the substance of what was said to the Court by the Applicant's Counsel/Solicitors].]

(4) To serve on the Respondent at the same time as this Order is served upon him:

    (i)   the Claim Form, or if not issued, the draft produced to the Court,

    (ii) an Application for hearing on [*date*],

    (iii) copies of the affidavits [or draft affidavits] and exhibits capable of being copied containing the evidence relied on by the Applicant [Copies of the confidential exhibits need not be served, but they must be made available for inspection by or on behalf of the Respondent in the presence of the Applicant's Solicitors while the Order is carried out. Afterwards they must be provided to a Solicitor representing the Respondent who gives a written undertaking not to permit the Respondent to see them or copies of them except in his presence and not to permit the Respondent to make or take away any note or record of the exhibits.], and

    (iv) a note of any allegation of fact made orally to the Judge where such allegation is not contained in the affidavits or draft affidavits read by the Judge.

(5) To serve on the Respondent a copy of the Supervising Solicitor's report on the carrying out of this Order as soon as it is received.

(6) Not, without the leave of the Court, to use any information or documents obtained as a result of carrying out this Order nor to inform anyone else of these proceedings except for the purposes of these proceedings (including adding further Respondents) or commencing civil proceedings in relation to the same or related subject matter to these proceedings until after the return date.

[(7) To maintain pending further order the sum of £   in an account controlled by the Applicant's Solicitors.]

[(8) To insure the items removed from the premises.]

SCHEDULE D

UNDERTAKINGS GIVEN BY THE APPLICANT'S SOLICITORS

(1) To answer at once to the best of their ability any question whether a particular item is a listed item.

(2) To return the originals of all documents obtained as a result of this Order (except original documents which belong to the Applicant) as soon as possible and in any event within two working days of their removal.

(3) While ownership of any item obtained as a result of this Order is in dispute, to deliver the article into the keeping of Solicitors acting for the Respondent within two working days from receiving a written undertaking by them to retain the article in safe keeping and to produce it to the Court when required.

(4) To retain in their own safe keeping all other items obtained as a result of this Order until the Court directs otherwise.

SCHEDULE E

UNDERTAKINGS GIVEN BY THE SUPERVISING SOLICITOR

(1) To offer to explain to the person served with the Order its meaning and effect fairly and in everyday language, and to inform him of his right to seek legal advice (such advice to include

an explanation that the Respondent may be entitled to avail himself of [the privilege against self-incrimination or] [legal professional privilege]) and apply to vary or discharge the Order as mentioned in the Respondent's Entitlements above.

(2) To make and provide to the Applicant's Solicitors and to the Judge who made this Order (for the purposes of the Court file) a written report on the carrying out of the Order.

SCHEDULE F

AFFIDAVITS

The Applicant relied on the following affidavits:-

[name] [number of affidavit] [date sworn] [filed on behalf of]

NAME AND ADDRESS OF APPLICANT'S SOLICITORS

The Applicant's Solicitors are:-

[Name, address, reference, fax and telephone numbers both in and out of office hours.]

PRACTICE DIRECTION – INTERIM PAYMENTS
THIS PRACTICE DIRECTION SUPPLEMENTS CPR PART 25

General

1.1 Rule 25.7 sets out the conditions to be satisfied and matters to be taken into account before the court will make an order for an interim payment.

1.2 The permission of the court must be obtained before making a voluntary interim payment in respect of a claim by a child or patient.

Evidence

2.1 An application for an interim payment of damages must be supported by evidence dealing with the following:
  (1) the sum of money sought by way of an interim payment,
  (2) the items or matters in respect of which the interim payment is sought,
  (3) the sum of money for which final judgment is likely to be given,
  (4) the reasons for believing that the conditions set out in rule 25.7 are satisfied,
  (5) any other relevant matters,
  (6) in claims for personal injuries, details of special damages and past and future loss, and
  (7) in a claim under the Fatal Accidents Act 1976, details of the person(s) on whose behalf the claim is made and the nature of the claim.

2.2 Any documents in support of the application should be exhibited, including, in personal injuries claims, the medical report(s).

2.3 If a respondent to an application for an interim payment wishes to rely on written evidence at the hearing he must comply with the provisions of rule 25.6(4).

2.4 If the applicant wishes to rely on written evidence in reply he must comply with the provisions of rule 25.6(5).

Instalments

3 Where an interim payment is to be paid in instalments the order should set out:
  (1) the total amount of the payment,
  (2) the amount of each instalment,
  (3) the number of instalments and the date on which each is to be paid, and
  (4) to whom the payment should be made.

Compensation recovery payments

4.1 Where in a claim for personal injuries there is an application for an interim payment of damages:

(1) which is other than by consent,

(2) which falls under the heads of damage set out in column 1 of Schedule 2 of the Social Security (Recovery of Benefits) Act 1997 in respect of recoverable benefits received by the claimant set out in column 2 of that Schedule, and

(3) where the defendant is liable to pay recoverable benefits to the Secretary of State,

the defendant should obtain from the Secretary of State a certificate of recoverable benefits.

4.2 A copy of the certificate should be filed at the hearing of the application for an interim payment.

4.3 The order will set out the amount by which the payment to be made to the claimant has been reduced according to the Act and the Social Security Recovery of Benefits) Regulations 1997.

4.4 The payment made to the claimant will be the net amount but the interim payment for the purposes of paragraph 5 below will be the gross amount.

Adjustment of final judgment figure

5.1 In this paragraph 'judgment' means:

(1) any order to pay a sum of money,

(2) a final award of damages,

(3) an assessment of damages.

5.2 In a final judgment where an interim payment has previously been made which is less than the total amount awarded by the judge, the order should set out in a preamble:

(1) the total amount awarded by the judge, and

(2) the amounts and dates of the interim payment(s).

5.3 The total amount awarded by the judge should then be reduced by the total amount of any interim payments, and an order made for entry of judgment and payment of the balance.

5.4 In a final judgment where an interim payment has previously been made which is more than the total amount awarded by the judge, the order should set out in a preamble:

(1) the total amount awarded by the judge, and

(2) the amounts and dates of the interim payment(s).

5.5 An order should then be made for repayment, reimbursement, variation or discharge under rule 25.8(2) and for interest on an overpayment under rule 25.8(5).

5.6 A practice direction supplementing Part 40 provides further information concerning adjustment of the final judgment sum.

PRACTICE DIRECTION – ACCOUNTS AND INQUIRIES
THIS PRACTICE DIRECTION SUPPLEMENTS CPR PART 25

An application for an order for accounts and inquiries may also be made under Part 24 (summary judgment). Reference should be made to paragraph 6 of the practice direction that supplements that Part.

1. The remedies that the court may grant under Part 25 include orders directing accounts to be taken and inquiries to be made.

2. The court may, on application or on its own initiative, at any stage in the proceedings, whether before or after judgment, make an order directing any necessary accounts to be taken or inquiries to be made.

3. Every direction for an account to be taken or an inquiry to be made shall be numbered in the order so that, as far as possible, each distinct account and inquiry is given its own number.

(This practice direction replaces RSC Order 43, rule 2 and applies to county court proceedings as well as to High Court proceedings.)

(The accounts and inquiries practice direction supplementing Part 40 contains provisions regarding the taking of an account or conduct of an inquiry after the order for the account or inquiry has been made.)

PART 26

CASE MANAGEMENT – PRELIMINARY STAGE

Contents of this Part

Scope of this Part

26.1(1) This Part provides for –

    (a) the automatic transfer of some defended cases between courts; and

    (b) the allocation of defended cases to case management tracks.

  (2) There are three tracks –

    (a) the small claims track;

    (b) the fast track; and

    (c) the multi-track.

(Rule 26.6 sets out the normal scope of each track. Part 27 makes provision for the small claims track. Part 28 makes provision for the fast track. Part 29 makes provision for the multi-track.)

Automatic transfers

26.2(1) This rule applies to proceedings where –

    (a) the claim is for a specified amount of money;

    (b) the claim was commenced in a court which is not the defendant's home court;

    (c) the claim has not been transferred to another defendant's home court under rule 13.4 (application to set aside$^{(GL)}$ or vary default judgment – procedure) or rule 14.12 (admission – determination of rate of payment by judge); and

    (d) the defendant is an individual.

  (2) This rule does not apply where the claim was commenced in a specialist list$^{(GL)}$.

  (3) Where this rule applies, the court will transfer the proceedings to the defendant's home court when a defence is filed, unless paragraph (4) applies.

(Rule 2.3 defines 'defendant's home court'.)

  (4) Where the claimant notifies the court under rule 15.10 or rule 14.5 that he wishes the proceedings to continue, the court will transfer the proceedings to the defendant's home court when it receives that notification from the claimant.

(Rule 15.10 deals with a claimant's notice where the defence is that money claimed has been paid.)

(Rule 14.5 sets out the procedure where the defendant admits part of a claim for a specified amount of money.)

(5) Where –

(a) the claim is against two or more defendants with different home courts; and

(b) the defendant whose defence is filed first is an individual,

proceedings are to be transferred under this rule to the home court of that defendant.

(6) The time when a claim is automatically transferred under this rule may be varied by a practice direction in respect of claims issued by the Production Centre.

(Rule 7.10 makes provision for the Production Centre.)

Allocation questionnaire

26.3(1) When a defendant files a defence the court will serve an allocation questionnaire on each party unless –

(a) rule 15.10 or rule 14.5 applies; or

(b) the court dispenses with the need for a questionnaire.

(2) Where there are two or more defendants and at least one of them files a defence, the court will serve the allocation questionnaire under paragraph (1) –

(a) when all the defendants have filed a defence; or

(b) when the period for the filing of the last defence has expired,

whichever is the sooner.

(Rule 15.4 specifies the period for filing a defence.)

(3) Where proceedings are automatically transferred to the defendant's home court under rule 26.2, the court in which the proceedings have been commenced will serve an allocation questionnaire before the proceedings are transferred.

(4) Where –

(a) rule 15.10 or rule 14.5 applies; and

(b) the proceedings are not automatically transferred to the defendant's home court under rule 26.2,

the court will serve an allocation questionnaire on each party when the claimant files a notice indicating that he wishes the proceedings to continue.

(5) The court may, on the application of the claimant, serve an allocation questionnaire earlier than it would otherwise serve it under this rule.

(6) Each party must file the completed allocation questionnaire no later than the date specified in it, which shall be at least 14 days after the date when it is deemed to be served on the party in question.

(7) The time when the court serves an allocation questionnaire under this rule may be varied by a practice direction in respect of claims issued by the Production Centre.

(Rule 7.10 makes provision for the Production Centre.)

(Rule 6.7 specifies when a document is deemed to be served.)

Stay to allow for settlement of the case

26.4(1) A party may, when filing the completed allocation questionnaire, make a written request for the proceedings to be stayed[(GL)] while the parties try to settle the case by alternative dispute resolution[(GL)] or other means.

(2) Where –

    (a) all parties request a stay$^{(GL)}$ under paragraph (1); or

    (b) the court, of its own initiative, considers that such a stay would be appropriate,

the court will direct that the proceedings be stayed for one month.

(3) The court may extend the stay$^{(GL)}$ until such date or for such specified period as it considers appropriate.

(4) Where the court stays$^{(GL)}$ the proceedings under this rule, the claimant must tell the court if a settlement is reached.

(5) If the claimant does not tell the court by the end of the period of the stay$^{(GL)}$ that a settlement has been reached, the court will give such directions as to the management of the case as it considers appropriate.

Allocation

26.5(1) The court will allocate the claim to a track –

    (a) when every defendant has filed an allocation questionnaire, or

    (b) when the period for filing the allocation questionnaires has expired,

whichever is the sooner, unless it has –

      (i) stayed$^{(GL)}$ the proceedings under rule 26.4; or

      (ii) dispensed with the need for allocation questionnaires.

(Rules 12.7 and 14.8 provide for the court to allocate a claim to a track where the claimant obtains default judgment on request or judgment on admission for an amount to be decided by the court)

(2) If the court has stayed$^{(GL)}$ the proceedings under rule 26.4, it will allocate the claim to a track at the end of the period of the stay.

(3) Before deciding the track to which to allocate proceedings or deciding whether to give directions for an allocation hearing to be fixed, the court may order a party to provide further information about his case.

(4) The court may hold an allocation hearing if it thinks it is necessary.

(5) If a party fails to file an allocation questionnaire, the court may give any direction it considers appropriate.

Scope of each track

26.6(1) The small claims track is the normal track for –

    (a) any claim for personal injuries where –

      (i) the financial value of the claim is not more than £5,000; and

      (ii) the financial value of any claim for damages for personal injuries is not more than £1,000;

    (b) any claim which includes a claim by a tenant of residential premises against his landlord where –

      (i) the tenant is seeking an order requiring the landlord to carry out repairs or other work to the premises (whether or not the tenant is also seeking some other remedy);

      (ii) the cost of the repairs or other work to the premises is estimated to be not more than £1,000; and

      (iii) the financial value of any other claim for damages is not more than £1,000.

(Rule 2.3 defines 'claim for personal injuries' as proceedings in which there is a claim for damages in respect of personal injuries to the claimant or any other person or in respect of a person's death.)

(2) For the purposes of paragraph (1) 'damages for personal injuries' means damages claimed as compensation for pain, suffering and loss of amenity and does not include any other damages which are claimed.

(3) Subject to paragraph (1), the small claims track is the normal track for any claim which has a financial value of not more than £5,000.

(Rule 26.7(4) provides that the court will not allocate to the small claims track certain claims in respect of harassment or unlawful eviction.)

(4) Subject to paragraph (5), the fast track is the normal track for any claim –

    (a) for which the small claims track is not the normal track; and

    (b) which has a financial value of not more than £15,000.

(5) The fast track is the normal track for the claims referred to in paragraph (4) only if the court considers that –

    (a) the trial is likely to last for no longer than one day; and

    (b) oral expert evidence at trial will be limited to –

        (i) one expert per party in relation to any expert field; and

        (ii) expert evidence in two expert fields.

(6) The multi-track is the normal track for any claim for which the small claims track or the fast track is not the normal track.

General rule for allocation

26.7(1) In considering whether to allocate a claim to the normal track for that claim under rule 26.6, the court will have regard to the matters mentioned in rule 26.8(1).

(2) The court will allocate a claim which has no financial value to the track which it considers most suitable having regard to the matters mentioned in rule 26.8(1).

(3) The court will not allocate proceedings to a track if the financial value of the claim, assessed by the court under rule 26.8, exceeds the limit for that track unless all the parties consent to the allocation of the claim to that track.

(4) The court will not allocate a claim to the small claims track, if it includes a claim by a tenant of residential premises against his landlord for a remedy in respect of harassment or unlawful eviction.

Matters relevant to allocation to a track

26.8(1) When deciding the track for a claim, the matters to which the court shall have regard include –

    (a) the financial value, if any, of the claim;

    (b) the nature of the remedy sought;

    (c) the likely complexity of the facts, law or evidence;

    (d) the number of parties or likely parties;

    (e) the value of any counterclaim or other Part 20 claim and the complexity of any matters relating to it;

    (f) the amount of oral evidence which may be required;

    (g) the importance of the claim to persons who are not parties to the proceedings;

(h) the views expressed by the parties; and

(i) the circumstances of the parties.

(2) It is for the court to assess the financial value of a claim and in doing so it will disregard –

(a) any amount not in dispute;

(b) any claim for interest;

(c) costs; and

(d) any contributory negligence.

(3) Where –

(a) two or more claimants have started a claim against the same defendant using the same claim form; and

(b) each claimant has a claim against the defendant separate from the other claimants,

the court will consider the claim of each claimant separately when it assesses financial value under paragraph (1).

Notice of allocation

26.9(1) When it has allocated a claim to a track, the court will serve notice of allocation on every party.

(2) When the court serves notice of allocation on a party, it will also serve –

(a) a copy of the allocation questionnaires filed by the other parties; and

(b) a copy of any further information provided by another party about his case (whether by order or not).

(Rule 26.5 provides that the court may, before allocating proceedings, order a party to provide further information about his case)

Re-allocation

26.10 The court may subsequently re-allocate a claim to a different track.

PRACTICE DIRECTION – CASE MANAGEMENT – PRELIMINARY STAGE: ALLOCATION AND RE-ALLOCATION THIS PRACTICE DIRECTION SUPPLEMENTS CPR PART 26

Reminders of important rule provisions other than Parts 26–29

Attention is drawn in particular to the following provisions of the Civil Procedure Rules:

Part 1	The Overriding Objective (defined in Rule 1.1).
	The duty of the court to further that objective by actively managing cases (set out in Rule 1.4).
	The requirement that the parties help the court to further that objective (set out in Rule 1.3).
Part 3	The court's case management powers (which may be exercised on application or on its own initiative) and the sanctions which it may impose.
Part 24	The court's power to grant summary judgment.
Parts 32–35	Evidence, especially the court's power to control evidence.

Attention is also drawn to the practice directions which supplement those Parts and Parts 27–29, and to those which relate to the various specialist jurisdictions.

The allocation questionnaire

2.1 *Form*

The allocation questionnaire referred to in Part 26 will be in Form N150.

Attention is drawn to the Costs Practice Direction 43, paragraph 4.5(1) which requires an estimate of costs to be filed and served when an allocation questionnaire is filed.

2.2 *Provision of Extra Information*

(1) This paragraph sets out what a party should do when he files his allocation questionnaire if he wishes to give the court information about matters which he believes may affect its decision about allocation or case management.

(2) The general rule is that the court will not take such information into account unless the document containing it either:

    (a) confirms that all parties have agreed that the information is correct and that it should be put before the court, or

    (b) confirms that the party who has sent the document to the court has delivered a copy to all the other parties.

(3) The following are examples of information which will be likely to help the court:

    (a) a party's intention to apply for summary judgment or some other order that may dispose of the case or reduce the amount in dispute or the number of issues remaining to be decided,

    (b) a party's intention to issue a Part 20 claim or to add another party,

    (c) the steps the parties have taken in the preparation of evidence (in particular expert evidence), the steps they intend to take and whether those steps are to be taken in co-operation with any other party,

    (d) the directions the party believes will be appropriate to be given for the management of the case,

    (e) about any particular facts that may affect the timetable the court will set,

    (f) any facts which may make it desirable for the court to fix an allocation hearing or a hearing at which case management directions will be given.

2.3 *Consultation*

(1) The parties should consult one another and co-operate in completing the allocation questionnaires and giving other information to the court.

(2) They should try to agree the case management directions which they will invite the court to make. Further details appear in the practice directions which supplement Parts 28 and 29.

(3) The process of consultation must not delay the filing of the allocation questionnaires.

2.4 *Hearings Before Allocation*

Where a court hearing takes place (for example on an application for an interim injunction or for summary judgment under Part 24) before the claim is allocated to a track, the court may at that hearing:

(1) dispense with the need for the parties to file allocation questionnaires, treat the hearing as an allocation hearing, make an order for allocation and give directions for case management, or

(2) fix a date for allocation questionnaires to be filed and give other directions.

2.5 *Consequences of Failure to File an Allocation Questionnaire*

(1) If no party files an allocation questionnaire within the time specified by Form N152:

    (a) the file will be referred to a judge for his directions,

    (b) the judge will usually order that unless an allocation questionnaire is filed within 3 days from service of that order the claim and any counterclaim will be struck out, but he may make a different order.

(2) Where a party files an allocation questionnaire but another party does not, the court may:

    (a) allocate the claim to a track if it considers that it has enough information to do so, or

    (b) order that an allocation hearing is listed and that all or any parties must attend.

Stay to allow for settlement of the case

3.1 *Procedure for the parties to apply to extend the stay*

    (1) (a) The court will generally accept a letter from any party or from the solicitor for any party as an application to extend the stay under rule 26.4.

        (b) The letter should –

            (i) confirm that the application is made with the agreement of all parties, and

            (ii) explain the steps being taken and identify any mediator or expert assisting with the process.

    (2) (a) An order extending the stay must be made by a judge.

        (b) The extension will generally be for no more than 4 weeks unless clear reasons are given to justify a longer time.

    (3) More than one extension of the stay may be granted.

3.2 *Position at the end of the stay if no settlement is reached*

    (1) At the end of the stay the file will be referred to a judge for his directions.

    (2) He will consider whether to allocate the claim to a track and what other directions to give, or may require any party to give further information or fix an allocation hearing.

3.3 Any party may apply for a stay to be lifted.

3.4 *Position where settlement is reached during a stay*

Where the whole of the proceedings are settled during a stay, the taking of any of the following steps will be treated as an application for the stay to be lifted:

    (1) an application for a consent order (in any form) to give effect to the settlement,

    (2) an application for the approval of a settlement where a party is a person under a disability,

    (3) giving notice of acceptance of money paid into court in satisfaction of the claim or applying for money in court to be paid out.

Allocation, Re-allocation and case management

4.1 *The court's general approach*

The Civil Procedure Rules lay down the overriding objective, the powers and duties of the court and the factors to which it must have regard in exercising them. The court will expect to exercise its powers as far as possible in co-operation with the parties and their legal representatives so as to deal with the case justly in accordance with that objective.

4.2 *Allocation to track*

    (1) In most cases the court will expect to have enough information from the statements of case and allocation questionnaires to be able to allocate the claim to a track and to give case management directions.

    (2) If the court does not have enough information to allocate the claim it will generally make an order under rule 26.5(3) requiring one or more parties to provide further information within 14 days.

    (3) Where there has been no allocation hearing the notice of allocation will be in Forms N154 (fast track), N155 (multi-track) or N157–160 (small claims).

    (4) (a) The general rule is that the court will give brief reasons for its allocation decision, and these will be set out in the notice of allocation.

        (b) The general rule does not apply where all the allocation questionnaires which have been filed have expressed the wish for the claim to be allocated to the track to which the court has allocated it.

    (5) Paragraph 6 of this practice direction deals with allocation hearings and Paragraph 7 deals with allocation principles.

    (6) Paragraph 11 of this practice direction deals with re-allocation.

4.3 The practice directions supplementing Parts 27, 28 and 29 contain further information about the giving of case management directions at the allocation stage.

Summary judgment or other early termination

5.1 Part of the court's duty of active case management is the summary disposal of issues which do not need full investigation and trial (rule 1.4(2)(c)),

5.2 The court's powers to make orders to dispose of issues in that way include:

(a) under rule 3.4, striking out a statement of case, or part of a statement of case, and

(b) under Part 24, giving summary judgment where a claimant or a defendant has no reasonable prospect of success. The court may use these powers on an application or on its own initiative. The practice direction 'Summary Disposal of Claims' contains further information.

5.3 (1) A party intending to make such an application should do so before or when filing his allocation questionnaire.

(2) Where a party makes an application for such an order before a claim has been allocated to a track the court will not normally allocate the claim before the hearing of the application.

(3) Where a party files an allocation questionnaire stating that he intends to make such an application but has not done so, the judge will usually direct that an allocation hearing is listed.

(4) The application may be heard at that allocation hearing if the application notice has been issued and served in sufficient time.

5.4 (1) This paragraph applies where the court proposes to make such an order of its own initiative.

(2) The court will not allocate the claim to a track but instead it will either:

(a) fix a hearing, giving the parties at least 14 days notice of the date of the hearing and of the issues which it is proposed that the court will decide, or

(b) make an order directing a party to take the steps described in the order within a stated time and specifying the consequence of not taking those steps.

5.5 Where the court decides at the hearing of an application or a hearing fixed under paragraph 5.4(2)(a) that the claim (or part of the claim) is to continue it may:

(1) treat that hearing as an allocation hearing, allocate the claim and give case management directions, or

(2) give other directions.

Allocation hearings

6.1 *General Principle*

The court will only hold an allocation hearing on its own initiative if it considers that it is necessary to do so.

6.2 *Procedure*

Where the court orders an allocation hearing to take place:

(1) it will give the parties at least 7 days notice of the hearing in Form N153, and

(2) Form N153 will give a brief explanation of the decision to order the hearing.

6.3 *Power to treat another hearing as an allocation hearing*

Where the court may treat another hearing as an allocation hearing it does not need to give notice to any party that it proposes to do so.

6.4 The notice of allocation after an allocation hearing will be in Forms N154, N155 or N157.

6.5 *Representation*

A legal representative who attends an allocation hearing should, if possible, be the person responsible for the case and must in any event be familiar with the case, be able to provide the court with the information it is likely to need to take its decisions about allocation and case management, and have sufficient authority to deal with any issues that are likely to arise.

6.6 *Sanctions*

(1) This paragraph sets out the sanctions that the court will usually impose for default in connection with the allocation procedure, but the court may make a different order.

(2) (a) Where an allocation hearing takes place because a party has failed to file an allocation questionnaire or to provide further information which the court has ordered, the court will usually order that party to pay on the indemnity basis the costs of any

other party who has attended the hearing, summarily assess the amount of those costs, and order them to be paid forthwith or within a stated period.

(b) The court may order that if the party does not pay those costs within the time stated his statement of case will be struck out.

(3) Where a party whose default has led to a fixing of an allocation hearing is still in default and does not attend the hearing the court will usually make an order specifying the steps he is required to take and providing that unless he takes them within a stated time his statement of case will be struck out.

Allocation principles

7.1 *Rules 26.6, 26.7 and 26.8*

(1) Rule 26.6 sets out the scope of each track,

(2) Rule 26.7 states the general rule for allocation, and

(3) Rule 26.8 sets out the matters relevant to allocation to a track.

7.2 *Objective of this paragraph*

The object of this paragraph is to explain what will be the court's general approach to some of the matters set out in rule 26.8.

7.3 *'the financial value of the claim'*

(1) Rule 26.8(2) provides that it is for the court to assess the financial value of a claim.

(2) Where the court believes that the amount the claimant is seeking exceeds what he may reasonably be expected to recover it may make an order under rule 26.5(3) directing the claimant to justify the amount.

7.4 *'any amount not in dispute'*

In deciding, for the purposes of rule 26.8(2), whether an amount is in dispute the court will apply the following general principles:

(1) Any amount for which the defendant does not admit liability is in dispute,

(2) Any sum in respect of an item forming part of the claim for which judgment has been entered (for example a summary judgment) is not in dispute,

(3) Any specific sum claimed as a distinct item and which the defendant admits he is liable to pay is not in dispute,

(4) Any sum offered by the defendant which has been accepted by the claimant in satisfaction of any item which forms a distinct part of the claim is not in dispute.

It follows from these provisions that if, in relation to a claim the value of which is above the small claims track limit of £5,000, the defendant makes, before allocation, an admission that reduces the amount in dispute to a figure below £5,000 (see CPR Part 14), the normal track for the claim will be the small claims track. As to recovery of pre-allocation costs, the claimant can, before allocation, apply for judgment with costs on the amount of the claim that has been admitted (see CPR rule 14.3 but see also paragraph 5.1(3) of the Costs Directions relating to CPR Part 44 under which the court has a discretion to allow pre-allocation costs).

7.5 *'the views expressed by the parties'*

The court will treat these views as an important factor, but the allocation decision is one for the court, to be taken in the light of all the circumstances, and the court will not be bound by any agreement or common view of the parties.

7.6 *'the circumstances of the parties'*

See paragraph 8.

7.7 *'the value of any counterclaim or other Part 20 claim'*

Where the case involves more than one money claim (for example where there is a Part 20 claim or there is more than one claimant each making separate claims) the court will not generally aggregate the claims. Instead it will generally regard the largest of them as determining the financial value of the claims.

The small claims track – allocation and case management

8.1 *Allocation*

(1) (a) The small claims track is intended to provide a proportionate procedure by which most straightforward claims with a financial value of not more than £5,000 can be decided, without the need for substantial pre-hearing preparation and the formalities of a traditional trial, and without incurring large legal costs. (Rule 26.6 provides for a lower financial value in certain types of case.)

(b) The procedure laid down in Part 27 for the preparation of the case and the conduct of the hearing are designed to make it possible for a litigant to conduct his own case without legal representation if he wishes.

(c) Cases generally suitable for the small claims track will include consumer disputes, accident claims, disputes about the ownership of goods and most disputes between a landlord and tenant other than those for possession.

(d) A case involving a disputed allegation of dishonesty will not usually be suitable for the small claims track.

(2) *Rule 26.7(3) and rule 27.14(5)*

(a) These rules allow the parties to consent to the allocation to the small claims track of a claim the value of which is above the limits mentioned in rule 26.6(2) and, in that event, the rules make provision about costs.

(b) The court will not allocate such a claim to the small claims track, notwithstanding that the parties have consented to the allocation, unless it is satisfied that it is suitable for that track.

(c) The court will not normally allow more than one day for the hearing of such a claim.

(d) The court will give case management directions to ensure that the case is dealt with in as short a time as possible. These may include directions of a kind that are not usually given in small claim cases, for example, for Scott Schedules.

8.2 *Case management*

(1) Directions for case management of claims allocated to the small claims track will generally be given by the court on allocation.

(2) Rule 27.4 contains further provisions about directions and the practice direction supplementing Part 27 sets out the standard directions which the court will usually give.

The fast track

9.1 *Allocation*

(1) Where the court is to decide whether to allocate to the fast track or the multi-track a claim for which the normal track is the fast track, it will allocate the claim to the fast track unless it believes that it cannot be dealt with justly on that track.

(2) The court will, in particular, take into account the limits likely to be placed on disclosure, the extent to which expert evidence may be necessary and whether the trial is likely to last more than a day.

(3) (a) When it is considering the likely length of the trial the court will regard a day as being a period of 5 hours, and will consider whether that is likely to be sufficient time for the case to be heard.

(b) The court will also take into account the case management directions (including the fixing of a trial timetable) that are likely to be given and the court's powers to control evidence and to limit cross-examination.

(c) The possibility that a trial might last longer than one day is not necessarily a conclusive reason for the court to allocate or to re-allocate a claim to the multi-track.

(d) A claim may be allocated to the fast track or ordered to remain on that track although there is to be a split trial.

(e) Where the case involves a counterclaim or other Part 20 claim that will be tried with the claim and as a result the trial will last more than a day, the court may not allocate it to the fast track.

9.2 *Case management*

   (1) Directions for the case management of claims which have been allocated to the fast track will be given at the allocation stage or at the listing stage (in either case with or without a hearing) or at both, and if necessary at other times. The trial judge may, at or before the trial, give directions for its conduct.

   (2) The practice direction supplementing Part 28 contains further provisions and contains standard directions which the court may give.

The multi-track

10.1 The following paragraphs do not apply to—

   (1) a claim for possession of land in the county court, where the defendant has filed a defence;

   (2) any claim which is being dealt with at the Royal Courts of Justice.

10.2 *Venue for allocation and case management*

   (1) The case management of a claim which is allocated to the multi-track will normally be dealt with at a Civil Trial Centre.

   (2) In the case of a claim to which Part 49 (specialist proceedings) applies, case management must be dealt with at a Civil Trial Centre. Sub-paragraphs (4) to (10) do not apply to such a claim. The claim will be allocated to the multi-track irrespective of its value, and must be transferred to a Civil Trial Centre for allocation and case management if not already there.

   (3) Where a claim is issued in or automatically transferred to a Civil Trial Centre it will be allocated and managed at that court.

   (4) The following sub-paragraphs apply to a claim which is issued in or automatically transferred to a court which is not a Civil Trial Centre. Such a court is referred to as a 'feeder court'.

   (5) Where a judge sitting at a feeder court decides, on the basis of the allocation questionnaires and any other documents filed by the parties, that the claim should be dealt with on the multi-track he will normally make an order:

      (a) allocating the claim to that track,

      (b) giving case management directions, and

      (c) transferring the claim to a Civil Trial Centre.

   (6) If he decides that an allocation hearing or some pre-allocation hearing is to take place (for example to strike out a statement of case under Part 3 of the Rules) that hearing will take place at the feeder court.

   (7) If, before allocation, a hearing takes place at a feeder court and in exercising his powers under paragraph 2.4(1) above the judge allocates the claim to the multi-track, he will also normally make an order transferring the claim to a Civil Trial Centre.

   (8) A judge sitting at a feeder court may, rather than making an allocation order himself, transfer the claim to a Civil Trial Centre for the decision about allocation to be taken there.

   (9) When, following an order for transfer, the file is received at the Civil Trial Centre, a judge sitting at that Centre will consider it and give any further directions that appear necessary or desirable.

   (10) Where there is reason to believe that more than one case management conference may be needed and the parties or their legal advisers are located inconveniently far from the Civil Trial Centre, a judge sitting at a feeder court may, with the agreement of the Designated Civil Judge and notwithstanding the allocation of the case to the multi-track, decide that in the particular circumstances of the case it should not be transferred to a Civil Trial Centre, but should be case managed for the time being at the feeder court.

   (11) A Designated Civil Judge may at any time make an order transferring a claim from a feeder court to a Civil Trial Centre and he may do so irrespective of the track, if any, to which it has been allocated.

   (12) No order will be made by a feeder court fixing a date for a hearing at a Civil Trial Centre

unless that date has been given or confirmed by a judge or listing officer of that Centre.

10.3 *Case management*

Part 29 of the Rules and the practice direction supplementing that Part set out the procedure to be adopted.

Re-allocation of claims and the variation of directions

11.1(1) Where a party is dissatisfied with an order made allocating the claim to a track he may appeal or apply to the court to re-allocate the claim.

(2) He should appeal if the order was made at a hearing at which he was present or represented, or of which he was given due notice.

(3) In any other case he should apply to the court to re-allocate the claim.

11.2 Where there has been a change in the circumstances since an order was made allocating the claim to a track the court may re-allocate the claim. It may do so on application or on its own initiative.

The practice directions supplementing Parts 28 and 29 contain provisions about the variation of case management directions.

Allocation and case management of assessments of damages and allied proceedings

12.1 *Scope*

(1) In the following paragraphs a 'relevant order' means an order or judgment of the court which requires the amount of money to be paid by one party to another to be decided by the court.

(2) A relevant order may have been obtained:

(a) by a judgment in default under Part 12,

(b) by a judgment on an admission under Part 14,

(c) on the striking out of a statement of case under Part 3,

(d) on a summary judgment application under Part 24,

(e) on the determination of a preliminary issue or on a trial as to liability, or

(f) at trial.

(3) A relevant order includes an order for an amount of damages or interest to be decided by the court, an order for the taking of an account or the making of an inquiry as to any sum due, and any similar order.

(4) A relevant order does not include an order for the assessment of costs except where the court has made an order for the assessment of costs payable under a contract other than a contract between a solicitor and client for legal services.

12.2 *Directions*

(1) Directions which may be given under the following paragraphs may include:

(a) a direction allocating or re-allocating the claim,

(b) a direction that allocation questionnaires be filed by a specified date,

(c) a direction that a date be fixed for a hearing or a further hearing,

(d) an order that the claim be stayed while the parties try to settle the case by alternative dispute resolution or other means.

(2) Directions may specify the level or type of judge before whom a hearing or a further hearing will take place and the nature and purpose of that hearing.

12.3 *Allocation*

Where a claim has not been allocated to a track at the time a relevant order is made, the court will not normally consider it to be appropriate to allocate it to a track (other than the small claims track) unless the amount payable appears to be genuinely disputed on grounds which appear to be substantial. It may instead direct that a disposal hearing (referred to in paragraph 12.8) be listed.

12.4 *Orders and judgments made at hearings*

Where a relevant order is made by a judge at a hearing, the judge should at the same time give such directions as the information about the case available to him enables him to give.

12.5 *Orders made by consent without a hearing*

(1) Where a relevant order is made by consent without a hearing a judge will give directions.

(2) The parties should where possible file with the draft consent order agreed directions which they invite the court to give.

12.6 *Judgments entered on admissions without a hearing*

(1) Where a relevant order is a judgment entered without a hearing under Part 14 the court will give directions.

(2) The court may in particular direct that a disposal hearing be listed.

12.7 *Judgments entered in default*

(1) This paragraph applies where the relevant order is a judgment entered under Part 12 without a hearing.

(2) On the entry of the judgment the court will list a disposal hearing.

12.8 *Disposal hearings*

(1) At a disposal hearing the court may give directions or decide the amount payable in accordance with this sub-paragraph.

(2) If the financial value of the claim (determined in accordance with Part 26) is such that the claim would, if defended, be allocated to the small claims track, the court will normally allocate it to that track and may treat the disposal hearing as a final hearing in accordance with Part 27.

(3) If the court does not give directions and does not allocate the claim to the small claims track, it may nonetheless order that the amount payable is to be decided there and then without allocating the claim to another track.

(4) Rule 32.6 applies to evidence at a disposal hearing unless the court otherwise directs.

(5) The court will not exercise its powers under sub-paragraph 12.8(3) unless any written evidence on which the claimant relies has been served on the defendant at least 3 days before the disposal hearing.

12.9 *Costs*

(1) Attention is drawn to the costs practice directions and in particular to the court's power to make a summary assessment of costs.

(2) Attention is drawn to rule 44.13(1) which provides that if an order makes no mention of costs, none are payable in respect of the proceedings to which it relates.

(3) Attention is drawn to rule 27.14 (special rules about costs in cases allocated to the small claims track).

(4) Attention is drawn to Part 46 (fixed trial costs in cases which have been allocated to the fast track). Part 46 (Fast track trial costs) will not apply to a case dealt with at a disposal hearing whatever the financial value of the claim. So the costs of a disposal hearing will be in the discretion of the court.

12.10 *Jurisdiction of Masters and district judges*

Unless the court otherwise directs, a Master or a district judge may decide the amount payable under a relevant order irrespective of the financial value of the claim and of the track to which the claim may have been allocated.

PART 27

THE SMALL CLAIMS TRACK

Contents of this Part

Scope of this Part

27.1(1) This Part –

    (a) sets out the special procedure for dealing with claims which have been allocated to the small claims track under Part 26; and

    (b) limits the amount of costs that can be recovered in respect of a claim which has been allocated to the small claims track.

(Rule 27.14 deals with costs on the small claims track)

    (2) A claim being dealt with under this Part is called a small claim.

(Rule 26.6 provides for the scope of the small claims track. A claim for a remedy for harassment or unlawful eviction relating, in either case, to residential premises shall not be allocated to the small claims track whatever the financial value of the claim. Otherwise, the small claims track will be the normal track for –

- any claim which has a financial value of not more than £5,000 subject to the special provisions about claims for personal injuries and housing disrepair claims;
- any claim for personal injuries which has a financial value of not more than £5,000 where the claim for damages for personal injuries is not more than £1,000; and
- any claim which includes a claim by a tenant of residential premises against his landlord for repairs or other work to the premises where the estimated cost of the repairs or other work is not more than £1000 and the financial value of any other claim for damages is not more than £1,000)

Extent to which other Parts apply

27.2(1) The following Parts of these Rules do not apply to small claims –

    (a) Part 25 (interim remedies) except as it relates to interim injunctions[GL];

    (b) Part 31 (disclosure and inspection);

    (c) Part 32 (evidence) except rule 32.1 (power of court to control evidence);

    (d) Part 33 (miscellaneous rules about evidence);

    (e) Part 35 (experts and assessors) except rules 35.1 (duty to restrict expert evidence), 35.3 (experts – overriding duty to the court), 35.7 (court's power to direct that evidence is to be given by single joint expert) and 35.8 (instructions to a single joint expert);

    (f) Part 18 (further information);

    (g) Part 36 (offers to settle and payments into court); and

    (h) Part 39 (hearings) except rule 39.2 (general rule – hearing to be in public).

    (2) The other Parts of these Rules apply to small claims except to the extent that a rule limits such application.

Court's power to grant a final remedy

27.3 The court may grant any final remedy in relation to a small claim which it could grant if the proceedings were on the fast track or the multi-track.

Preparation for the hearing

27.4(1) After allocation the court will –

    (a) give standard directions and fix a date for the final hearing;

    (b) give special directions and fix a date for the final hearing;

    (c) give special directions and direct that the court will consider what further directions are to be given no later than 28 days after the date the special directions were given;

    (d) fix a date for a preliminary hearing under rule 27.6; or

    (e) give notice that it proposes to deal with the claim without a hearing under rule 27.10 and invite the parties to notify the court by a specified date if they agree the proposal.

  (2) The court will –

    (a) give the parties at least 21 days' notice of the date fixed for the final hearing, unless the parties agree to accept less notice; and

    (b) inform them of the amount of time allowed for the final hearing.

  (3) In this rule –

    (a) 'standard directions' means –

      (i) a direction that each party shall, at least 14 days before the date fixed for the final hearing, file and serve on every other party copies of all documents (including any expert's report) on which he intends to rely at the hearing; and

      (ii) any other standard directions set out in the relevant practice direction; and

    (b) 'special directions' means directions given in addition to or instead of the standard directions.

Experts

27.5 No expert may give evidence, whether written or oral, at a hearing without the permission of the court.

(Rule 27.14(3)(d) provides for the payment of an expert's fees)

Preliminary hearing

27.6 (1) The court may hold a preliminary hearing for the consideration of the claim, but only –

    (a) where –

      (i) it considers that special directions, as defined in rule 27.4, are needed to ensure a fair hearing; and

      (ii) it appears necessary for a party to attend at court to ensure that he understands what he must do to comply with the special directions; or

    (b) to enable it to dispose of the claim on the basis that one or other of the parties has no real prospect of success at a final hearing; or

    (c) to enable it to strike out[(GL)] a statement of case or part of a statement of case on the basis that the statement of case, or the part to be struck out, discloses no reasonable grounds for bringing or defending the claim.

  (2) When considering whether or not to hold a preliminary hearing, the court must have regard to the desirability of limiting the expense to the parties of attending court.

  (3) Where the court decides to hold a preliminary hearing, it will give the parties at least 14 days' notice of the date of the hearing.

(4) The court may treat the preliminary hearing as the final hearing of the claim if all the parties agree.

(5) At or after the preliminary hearing the court will –

(a) fix the date of the final hearing (if it has not been fixed already) and give the parties at least 21 days' notice of the date fixed unless the parties agree to accept less notice;

(b) inform them of the amount of time allowed for the final hearing; and

(c) give any appropriate directions.

Power of court to add to, vary or revoke directions

27.7   The court may add to, vary or revoke directions.

Conduct of the hearing

27.8 (1) The court may adopt any method of proceeding at a hearing that it considers to be fair.

(2) Hearings will be informal.

(3) The strict rules of evidence do not apply.

(4) The court need not take evidence on oath.

(5) The court may limit cross-examination$^{(GL)}$.

(6) The court must give reasons for its decision.

Non-attendance of parties at a final hearing

27.9 (1) If a party who does not attend a final hearing –

(a) has given the court written notice at least 7 days before the date of the hearing that he will not attend; and

(b) has, in that notice, requested the court to decide the claim in his absence,

the court will take into account that party's statement of case and any other documents he has filed when it decides the claim.

(2) If a claimant does not –

(a) attend the hearing; and

(b) give the notice referred to in paragraph (1),

the court may strike out$^{(GL)}$ the claim.

(3) If –

(a) a defendant does not –

(i) attend the hearing; or

(ii) give the notice referred to in paragraph (1); and

(b) the claimant either –

(i) does attend the hearing; or

(ii) gives the notice referred to in paragraph (1),

the court may decide the claim on the basis of the evidence of the claimant alone.

(4) If neither party attends or gives the notice referred to in paragraph (1), the court may strike out$^{(GL)}$ the claim and any defence and counterclaim.

Disposal without a hearing

27.10   The court may, if all parties agree, deal with the claim without a hearing.

Setting judgment aside and re-hearing

27.11(1) A party –

(a) who was neither present nor represented at the hearing of the claim; and

    (b) who has not given written notice to the court under rule 27.9(1),

may apply for an order that a judgment under this Part shall be set aside$^{(GL)}$ and the claim re-heard.

  (2) A party who applies for an order setting aside a judgment under this rule must make the application not more than 14 days after the day on which notice of the judgment was served on him.

  (3) The court may grant an application under paragraph (2) only if the applicant –

    (a) had a good reason for not attending or being represented at the hearing or giving written notice to the court under rule 27.9(1); and

    (b) has a reasonable prospect of success at the hearing.

  (4) If a judgment is set aside$^{(GL)}$ –

    (a) the court must fix a new hearing for the claim; and

    (b) the hearing may take place immediately after the hearing of the application to set the judgment aside and may be dealt with by the judge who set aside$^{(GL)}$ the judgment.

  (5) A party may not apply to set aside$^{(GL)}$ a judgment under this rule if the court dealt with the claim without a hearing under rule 27.10.

Right of appeal under Part 27

27.12(1) A party may appeal against an order under this Part only on the grounds that –

    (a) there was serious irregularity affecting the proceedings; or

    (b) the court made a mistake of law.

  (2) On an appeal the court may make any order it considers appropriate.

  (3) The court may dismiss an appeal without a hearing.

  (4) This rule does not limit any right of appeal arising under any Act.

Procedure for making an appeal

27.13(1) A party who wishes to appeal must file a notice of appeal not more than 14 days after the day on which notice of the order was served on him.

  (2) Notice of appeal –

    (a) must be filed at the court which made the order; and

    (b) must set out the grounds for the appeal with particulars of the serious irregularity or mistake of law alleged.

Costs on the small claims track

27.14(1) This rule applies to any case which has been allocated to the small claims track unless paragraph (5) applies.

(Rules 44.9 and 44.11 make provision in relation to orders for costs made before a claim has been allocated to the small claims track)

  (2) The court may not order a party to pay a sum to another party in respect of that other party's costs except –

    (a) the fixed costs attributable to issuing the claim which–

      (i) are payable under Part 45; or

      (ii) would be payable under Part 45 if that Part applied to the claim;

    (b) in proceedings which included a claim for an injunction$^{(GL)}$ or an order for specific performance a sum not exceeding the amount specified in the relevant practice direction for legal advice and assistance relating to that claim;

(c) costs assessed by the summary procedure in relation to an appeal under rule 27.12; and

(d) such further costs as the court may assess by the summary procedure and order to be paid by a party who has behaved unreasonably.

(3) The court may also order a party to pay all or part of –

(a) any court fees paid by another party;

(b) expenses which a party or witness has reasonably incurred in travelling to and from a hearing or in staying away from home for the purposes of attending a hearing;

(c) a sum not exceeding the amount specified in the relevant practice direction for any loss of earnings by a party or witness due to attending a hearing or to staying away from home for the purpose of attending a hearing; and

(d) a sum not exceeding the amount specified in the relevant practice direction for an expert's fees.

(4) The limits on costs imposed by this rule also apply to any fee or reward for acting on behalf of a party to the proceedings charged by a person exercising a right of audience by virtue of an order under section 11 of the Courts and Legal Services Act 1990[44] (a lay representative).

(5) Where –

(a) the financial value of a claim exceeds the limit for the small claims track; but

(b) the claim has been allocated to the small claims track in accordance with rule 26.7(3),

the claim shall be treated, for the purposes of costs, as if it were proceeding on the fast track except that trial costs shall be in the discretion of the court and shall not exceed the amount set out for the value of the claim in rule 46.2 (amount of fast track trial costs).

(Rule 26.7(3) allows the parties to consent to a claim being allocated to a track where the financial value of the claim exceeds the limit for that track)

Claim re-allocated from the small claims track to another track

27.15 Where a claim is allocated to the small claims track and subsequently re-allocated to another track, rule 27.14 (costs on the small claims track) will cease to apply after the claim has been re-allocated and the fast track or multi-track costs rules will apply from the date of re-allocation.

PRACTICE DIRECTION – THE SMALL CLAIMS TRACK
THIS PRACTICE DIRECTION SUPPLEMENTS CPR PART 27

Judges

1 The functions of the court described in Part 27 which are to be carried out by a judge will generally be carried out by a district judge but may be carried out by a Circuit Judge.

Case management directions

2.1 Rule 27.4 explains how directions will be given, and rule 27.6 contains provisions about the holding of a preliminary hearing and the court's powers at such a hearing.

2.2 Appendix A sets out the Standard Directions which the court may give.

---

(44) 1990 c.41.

Representation at a hearing

3.1 In this paragraph:

(1) a lawyer means a barrister, a solicitor or a legal executive employed by a solicitor, and

(2) a lay representative means any other person.

3.2 (1) A party may present his own case at a hearing or a lawyer or lay representative may present it for him.

(2) The Lay Representatives (Right of Audience) Order 1999 provides that a lay representative may not exercise any right of audience:–

(a) where his client does not attend the hearing;

(b) at any stage after judgment; or

(c) on any appeal brought against any decision made by the district judge in the proceedings.

(3) However the court, exercising its general discretion to hear anybody, may hear a lay representative even in circumstances excluded by the Order.

(4) Any of its officers or employees may represent a corporate party.

Small claim hearing

4.1 (1) The general rule is that a small claim hearing will be in public.

(2) The judge may decide to hold it in private if:

(a) the parties agree, or

(b) a ground mentioned in rule 39.2(3) applies.

(3) A hearing or part of a hearing which takes place other than at the court, for example at the home or business premises of a party, will not be in public.

4.2 A hearing that takes place at the court will generally be in the judge's room but it may take place in a courtroom.

4.3 Rule 27.8 allows the court to adopt any method of proceeding that it considers to be fair and to limit cross-examination. The judge may in particular:

(1) ask questions of any witness himself before allowing any other person to do so,

(2) ask questions of all or any of the witnesses himself before allowing any other person to ask questions of any witnesses,

(3) refuse to allow cross-examination of any witness until all the witnesses have given evidence in chief,

(4) limit cross-examination of a witness to a fixed time or to a particular subject or issue, or both.

Recording evidence and the giving of reasons

5.1 The judge may direct that all or any part of the proceedings will be tape recorded by the court. A party may obtain a transcript of such a recording on payment of the proper transcriber's charges.

5.2 Attention is drawn to section 9 of the Contempt of Court Act 1981 (which deals with the unauthorised use of tape recorders in court) and to the Practice Direction ([1981] 1 WLR 1526) which relates to it.

5.3 The judge will make a note of the central points of the oral evidence unless it is tape recorded by the court.

5.4 The judge will make a note of the central reasons for his judgment unless it is given orally and tape recorded by the court.

5.5 (1) The judge may give his reasons as briefly and simply as the nature of the case allows.

(2) He will normally do so orally at the hearing, but he may give them later either in writing or at a hearing fixed for him to do so.

5.6 Where the judge decides the case without a hearing under rule 27.10 or a party who has given notice under rule 27.9(1) does not attend the hearing, the judge will prepare a note of his reasons and the court will send a copy to each party.

5.7 A party is entitled to a copy of any note made by the judge under sub-paragraphs 5.3 or 5.4.

5.8 Nothing in this practice direction affects the duty of a judge at the request of a party to make a note of the matters referred to in section 80 of the County Courts Act 1984.

Non-attendance of a party at a hearing

6.1 Attention is drawn to rule 27.9 (which enables a party to give notice that he will not attend a final hearing and sets out the effect of his giving such notice and of not doing so), and to paragraph 3 above.

6.2 Nothing in those provisions affects the general power of the court to adjourn a hearing, for example where a party who wishes to attend a hearing on the date fixed cannot do so for a good reason.

Costs

7.1 Attention is drawn to Rule 27.14 which contains provisions about the costs which may be ordered to be paid by one party to another.

7.2 The amount which a party may be ordered to pay under rule 27.14(2)(b) (for legal advice and assistance in claims including an injunction or specific performance) is a sum not exceeding £260.

7.3 The amounts which a party may be ordered to pay under rule 27.14(3)(c) (loss of earnings) and (d) (experts' fees) are:

   (1) for the loss of earnings of each party or witness due to attending a hearing or staying away from home for the purpose of attending a hearing, a sum not exceeding £50 per day for each person, and

   (2) for expert's fees, a sum not exceeding £200 for each expert.

(As to recovery of pre-allocation costs in a case in which an admission by the defendant has reduced the amount in dispute to a figure below £5,000, reference should be made to paragraph 7.4 of the Practice Direction supplementing CPR Part 26 and to paragraph 5.1(3) of the Costs Directions relating to CPR Part 44)

Appeals from decisions of district judges

8.1 An appeal from a decision of a district judge under Part 27 will be dealt with by a Circuit Judge.

8.2 Attention is drawn to rule 27.12 and 13 and in particular to the limited grounds of appeal and the time limits for giving notice of appeal.

8.3 A notice of appeal must set out particulars of the serious irregularity or mistake of law relied on.

8.4 When a notice of appeal is filed it will be put before a Circuit Judge as soon as possible after it is filed and he will decide how to deal with the appeal.

8.5 The court will serve a copy of the notice on all other parties.

8.6 The Circuit Judge may either:

   (1) dismiss the appeal without a hearing if no sufficient ground is shown in the notice of appeal, or

   (2) order that the appeal is to be listed for hearing.

8.7 The Circuit Judge will give any necessary directions:

   (1) about the filing of any evidence concerning any allegation of serious irregularity, and

   (2) about the supply to the parties of copies of any document (including any note made by the judge who heard the case) which he has taken or may have taken into account in dealing with the appeal.

8.8 Where the Circuit Judge dismisses the appeal without a hearing his order will contain brief reasons for his decision.

8.9 Where the Circuit Judge directs that the appeal is to be listed for hearing the court will give at least seven days notice of the hearing to all parties.

8.10 If the appeal is allowed, the Circuit Judge will if possible dispose of the case at the same time without ordering the claim to be reheard. He may do so without hearing further evidence.

APPENDIX A
FORM A – THE STANDARD DIRECTIONS

(for use where the district judge specifies no other directions)

THE COURT DIRECTS

1. Each party shall deliver to every other party and to the court office copies of all documents (including any experts' report) on which he intends to rely at the hearing no later than [   ] [14 days before the hearing].

2. The original documents shall be brought to the hearing.

3. [Notice of hearing date and time allowed.]

4. The court must be informed immediately if the case is settled by agreement before the hearing date.

FORM B – STANDARD DIRECTIONS FOR USE IN CLAIMS ARISING OUT OF ROAD ACCIDENTS

THE COURT DIRECTS

1. Each party shall deliver to every other party and to the court office copies of all documents on which he intends to rely at the hearing. These may include:
   - experts' reports (including medical reports where damages for personal injury are claimed),
   - witness statements,
   - invoices and estimates for repairs,
   - documents which relate to other losses, such as loss of earnings,
   - sketch plans and photographs.

2. The copies shall be delivered no later than [   ] [14 days before the hearing].

3. The original documents shall be brought to the hearing.

4. Before the date of the hearing the parties shall try to agree the cost of the repairs and any other losses claimed subject to the court's decision about whose fault the accident was.

5. Signed statements setting out the evidence of all witnesses on whom each party intends to rely shall be prepared and copies included in the documents mentioned in paragraph 1. This includes the evidence of the parties themselves and of any other witness, whether or not he is going to come to court to give evidence.

6. The parties should note that:
   (a) In deciding the case the court will find it very helpful to have a sketch plan and photographs of the place where the accident happened,
   (b) The court may decide not to take into account a document or the evidence of a witness if no copy of that document or no copy of a statement or report by that witness has been supplied to the other parties.

7. [Notice of hearing date and time allowed.]

8. The court must be informed immediately if the case is settled by agreement before the hearing date.

FORM C – STANDARD DIRECTIONS FOR USE IN CLAIMS ARISING OUT OF BUILDING DISPUTES, VEHICLE REPAIRS AND SIMILAR CONTRACTUAL CLAIMS

THE COURT DIRECTS

1. Each party shall deliver to every other party and to the court office copies of all documents on which he intends to rely at the hearing. These may include:
   - the contract,
   - witness statements,
   - experts' reports,
   - photographs,
   - invoices for work done or goods supplied,
   - estimates for work to be done.

2. The copies shall be delivered no later than [   ] [14 days before the hearing].

3. The original documents shall be brought to the hearing.

4. [The   shall deliver to the   and to the court office [no later than   ] [with his copy documents] a list showing all items of work which he complains about and why, and the amount claimed for putting each item right.]

5. [The   shall deliver to the   and to the court office [no later than   ] [with his copy documents] a breakdown of the amount he is claiming showing all work done and materials supplied.]

6. Before the date of the hearing the parties shall try to agree about the nature and cost of any remedial work required, subject to the court's decision about any other issue in the case.

7. [Signed statements setting out the evidence of all witnesses on whom each party intends to rely shall be prepared and included in the documents mentioned in paragraph 1. This includes the evidence of the parties themselves and of any other witness, whether or not he is going to come to court to give evidence.]

8. The parties should note that:
   (a) in deciding the case the judge may find it helpful to have photographs showing the work in question,

   (b) the judge may decide not to take into account a document or the evidence of a witness if no copy of that document or no copy of a statement or report by that witness has been supplied to the other parties.

9. [Notice of hearing date and time allowed.]
10. The court must be informed immediately if the case is settled by agreement before the hearing date.

FORM D – TENANTS' CLAIMS FOR THE RETURN OF DEPOSITS/LANDLORDS CLAIMS FOR DAMAGE CAUSED

THE COURT DIRECTS

1. Each party shall deliver to every other party and to the court office copies of all documents on which he intends to rely at the hearing. These may include:
   - the tenancy agreement and any inventory,
   - the rent book or other evidence of rent and other payments made by the   to the   ,
   - photographs,
   - witness statements,
   - invoices or estimates for work and goods.

2. The copies shall be delivered no later than [   ] [14 days before the hearing].

3. The original documents shall be brought to the hearing.

4. The   shall deliver with his copy documents a list showing each item of loss or damage for which he claims the   ought to pay, and the amount he claims for the replacement or repair.

5. The parties shall before the hearing date try to agree about the nature and cost of any repairs and replacements needed, subject to the court's decision about any other issue in the case.

6. [Signed statements setting out the evidence of all witnesses on whom each party intends to rely shall be prepared and included in the documents mentioned in paragraph 1. This includes the evidence of the parties themselves and of any other witness whether or not he is going to come to court to give evidence.]

7. The parties should note that: a) in deciding the case the judge may find it helpful to have photographs showing the condition of the property, b) the judge may decide not to take into account a document or the evidence of a witness if no copy of that document or no copy of a statement or report by that witness has been supplied to the other parties.

8. [Notice of hearing date and time allowed.]

9. The court must be informed immediately if the case is settled by agreement before the hearing date.

FORM E – HOLIDAY AND WEDDING CLAIMS

THE COURT DIRECTS

1. Each party shall deliver to every other party and to the court office copies of all documents on which he intends to rely at the hearing. These may include:
   - any written contract, brochure or booking form,
   - photographs,
   - documents showing payments made,
   - witness statements
   - letters.

2. The copies shall be delivered no later than [   ] [14 days before the hearing].

3. The original documents shall be brought to the hearing.

4. Signed statements setting out the evidence of all witnesses on whom each party intends to rely shall be prepared and copies included in the documents mentioned in paragraph 1. This includes the evidence of the parties themselves and of any other witness, whether or not he is going to come to court to give evidence.

5. If either party intends to show a video as evidence he must:
   (a) contact the court at once to make arrangements for him to do so, because the court may not have the necessary equipment, and
   (b) provide the other party with a copy of the video or the opportunity to see it (if he asks) at least 2 weeks before the hearing.

6. The parties should note that the court may decide not to take into account a document or the evidence of a witness or a video if these directions have not been complied with.

7. [Notice of hearing date and time allowed.]

8. The court must be told immediately if the case is settled by agreement before the hearing date.

FORM F – SOME SPECIAL DIRECTIONS

The   must clarify his case. He must do this by delivering to the court office and to the
                       no later than

[a list of   ]

[details of   ]

[   ]

The   shall allow the   to inspect   by
appointment within   days of receiving a request to do so.

The hearing will not take place at the court but at   .

The   must bring to court at the hearing the   .

Signed statements setting out the evidence of all witnesses on whom each party intends to rely shall be prepared and copies included in the documents mentioned in paragraph 1. This includes the evidence of the parties themselves and of any other witness, whether or not he is going to come to court to give evidence.

The court may decide not to take into account a document [or video] or the evidence of a witness if these directions have not been complied with.

If he does not [do so] [   ] his [Claim] [Defence] [and Counterclaim] and will be struck out and [(specify consequence)]. It appears to the court that expert evidence is necessary on the issue of [   ] and that that evidence should be given by a single expert [   ] to be instructed by the parties jointly. If the parties cannot agree about who to chose and what arrangements to make about paying his fee, either party may apply to the court for further directions. If either party intends to show a video as evidence he must

(a) contact the court at once to make arrangements for him to do so, because the court may not have the necessary equipment, and

(b) provide the other party with a copy of the video or the opportunity to see it at least [   ] before the hearing.

PART 28

THE FAST TRACK

Contents of this Part

Scope of this Part

28.1   This Part contains general provisions about management of cases allocated to the fast track and applies only to cases allocated to that track.

(Part 27 sets out the procedure for claims allocated to the small claims track)

(Part 29 sets out the procedure for claims allocated to the multi-track)

General provisions

28.2 (1) When it allocates a case to the fast track, the court will give directions for the management of the case and set a timetable for the steps to be taken between the giving of the directions and the trial.

(2) When it gives directions, the court will –

(a) fix the trial date; or

(b) fix a period, not exceeding 3 weeks, within which the trial is to take place.

(3) The trial date or trial period will be specified in the notice of allocation.

(4) The standard period between the giving of directions and the trial will be not more than 30 weeks.

(5) The court's power to award trial costs is limited in accordance with Part 46.

Directions

28.3 (1) The matters to be dealt with by directions under rule 28.2(1) include –

(a) disclosure of documents;

(b) service of witness statements; and

(c) expert evidence.

(2) If the court decides not to direct standard disclosure, it may –

(a) direct that no disclosure take place; or

(b) specify the documents or the classes of documents which the parties must disclose.

(Rule 31.6 explains what is meant by standard disclosure)

(Rule 26.6(5) deals with limitations in relation to expert evidence and the likely length of trial in fast track cases)

Variation of case management timetable

28.4 (1) A party must apply to the court if he wishes to vary the date which the court has fixed for –

(a) the return of a listing questionnaire under rule 28.5;

(b) the trial; or

(c) the trial period.

(2) Any date set by the court or these Rules for doing any act may not be varied by the parties if the variation would make it necessary to vary any of the dates mentioned in paragraph (1).

(Rule 2.11 allows the parties to vary a date by written agreement except where the rules provide otherwise or the court orders otherwise)

Listing questionnaire

28.5 (1) The court will send the parties a listing questionnaire for completion and return by the date specified in the notice of allocation unless it considers that the claim can be listed for trial without the need for a listing questionnaire.

(2) The date specified for filing a listing questionnaire will not be more than 8 weeks before the trial date or the beginning of the trial period.

(3) If –

(a) a party fails to file the completed questionnaire by the date specified;

(b) a party has failed to give all the information requested by the listing questionnaire; or

(c) the court considers that a hearing is necessary to enable it to decide what directions to give in order to complete preparation of the case for trial,

the court may fix a listing hearing or give such other directions as it thinks appropriate.

Fixing or confirming the trial date and giving directions

28.6 (1) As soon as practicable after the date specified for filing a completed listing questionnaire the court will –

(a) fix the date for the trial (or, if it has already done so, confirm that date);

(b) give any directions for the trial, including a trial timetable, which it considers appropriate; and

(c) specify any further steps that need to be taken before trial.

(2) The court will give the parties at least 3 weeks' notice of the date of the trial unless, in exceptional circumstances, the court directs that shorter notice will be given.

Conduct of trial

28.7 Unless the trial judge otherwise directs, the trial will be conducted in accordance with any order previously made.

PRACTICE DIRECTION – THE FAST TRACK
THIS PRACTICE DIRECTION SUPPLEMENTS CPR PART 28

General

1.1 Attention is drawn in particular to the following Parts of the Civil Procedure Rules:

Part 1	The overriding objective
Part 3	The court's case management powers
Part 26	Case management – preliminary stage
Part 31	Disclosure and inspection of documents
Parts 32-34	Evidence
Part 35	Experts and assessors and to the practice directions which relate to those Parts.

and to the practice directions which relate to those Parts.

1.2 Attention is also drawn to:

Rule 26.6(5) – which makes provision about limitations on expert evidence and the length of trial in fast track cases.

Part 46 – Fast Track Trial Costs

Case management

2.1 Case management of cases allocated to the fast track will generally be by directions given at two stages in the case:

(1) at allocation to the track, and

(2) on the filing of listing questionnaires.

2.2 The court will seek whenever possible to give directions at those stages only and to do so without the need for a hearing to take place. It will expect to do so with the co-operation of the parties.

2.3 The court will however hold a hearing to give directions whenever it appears necessary or desirable to do so, and where this happens because of the default of a party or his legal representative it will usually impose a sanction.

2.4 The court may give directions at any hearing on the application of a party or on its own initiative.

2.5 When any hearing has been fixed it is the duty of the parties to consider what directions the court should be asked to give and to make any application that may be appropriate to be dealt with at that hearing.

2.6 When the court fixes a hearing to give directions it will give the parties at least 3 days notice of the hearing.

2.7 Appendix A contains forms of directions. When making an order the court will as far as possible base its order on those forms. Agreed directions which the parties file and invite the court to make should also be based on those forms.

2.8 Where a party needs to apply for a direction of a kind not included in the case management timetable which has been set (for example to amend his statement of case or for further information to be given by another party) he must do so as soon as possible so as to minimise the need to change that timetable.

2.9 Courts will make arrangements to ensure that applications and other hearings are listed promptly to avoid delay in the conduct of cases.

Directions on allocation

3.1 Attention is drawn to the court's duty under rule 28.2(2) to set a case management timetable and to fix a trial date or a trial period, and to the matters which are to be dealt with by directions under Rule 28.3(1).

3.2 The court will seek to tailor its directions to the needs of the case and the steps of which it is aware that the parties have already taken to prepare the case. In particular it will have regard to the extent to which any pre-action protocol has or (as the case may be) has not been complied with.

3.3 At this stage the court's first concern will be to ensure that the issues between the parties be identified and that the necessary evidence is prepared and disclosed.

3.4 The court may have regard to any document filed by a party with his allocation questionnaire containing further information provided that the document states either that its contents have been agreed with every other party or that it has been served on every other party and when it was served.

3.5 If:

(1) the parties have filed agreed directions for the management of the case, and

(2) the court considers that the proposals are suitable,

it may approve them and give directions in the terms proposed.

3.6 (1) To obtain the court's approval the agreed directions must:

(a) set out a timetable by reference to calendar dates for the taking of steps for the preparation of the case,

   (b) include a date or a period (the trial period) when it is proposed that the trial will take place,

   (c) include provision about disclosure of documents, and

   (d) include provision about both factual and expert evidence.

(2) The latest proposed date for the trial or the end of the trial period must be not later than 30 weeks from the date the directions order is made.

(3) The trial period must not be longer than 3 weeks.

(4) The provision in (1)(c) above may:

   (a) limit disclosure to standard disclosure between all parties or to less than that, and/or

   (b) direct that disclosure will take place by the supply of copy documents without a list, but it must in that case either direct that the parties must serve a disclosure statement with the copies or record that they have agreed to disclose in that way without such a statement.

(5) The provision in (1)(d) may be to the effect that no expert evidence is required.

3.7 Directions agreed by the parties should also where appropriate contain provisions about:

(1) the filing of any reply or amended statement of case that may be required,

(2) dates for the service of requests for further information under the practice direction supplementing Part 18 and questions to experts under rule 35.6 and when they are to be dealt with,

(3) the disclosure of evidence,

(4) the use of a single joint expert, or in cases where the use of a single expert has not been agreed the exchange and agreement of expert evidence (including whether exchange is to be simultaneous or sequential) and without prejudice discussions of the experts.

3.8 If the court does not approve the agreed directions filed by the parties but decides that it will give directions on its own initiative without a hearing, it will take them into account in deciding what directions to give.

3.9 Where the court is to give directions on its own initiative and it is not aware of any steps taken by the parties other than the service of statements of case, its general approach will be:

(1) to give directions for the filing and service of any further information required to clarify either party's case,

(2) to direct standard disclosure between the parties,

(3) to direct the disclosure of witness statements by way of simultaneous exchange,

(4) to give directions for a single joint expert unless there is good reason not to do so,

(5) in cases where directions for a single expert are not given:

   (a) to direct disclosure of experts' reports by way of simultaneous exchange, and

   (b) if experts' reports are not agreed, to direct a discussion between the experts for the purpose set out in rule 35.12(1) and the preparation of a report under rule 35.12(3).

3.10(1) If it appears to the court that the claim is one which will be allocated to the fast track but that it cannot properly give directions on its own initiative or approve agreed directions that have been filed, the court may either:

   (a) allocate the claim to the fast track, fix a trial date or trial period and direct that a case management hearing is to be listed and give directions at that hearing, or

   (b) direct that an allocation hearing is to be listed and give directions at that hearing.

(2) In either case the hearing will be listed as promptly as possible.

3.11 Where the court is proposing on its own initiative to make an order under rule 35.15 (which gives the court power to appoint an assessor), the court must, unless the parties have consented in writing to the order, list a directions hearing.

3.12 The table set out below contains a typical timetable the court may give for the preparation of the case.

Disclosure	4 weeks
Exchange of witness statements	10 weeks
Exchange of experts' reports	14 weeks
Sending of listing questionnaires by the court	20 weeks

Filing of completed listing questionnaires	22 weeks
Hearing	30 weeks

These periods will run from the date of the notice of allocation.

3.13(1) Where it considers that some or all of the steps in that timetable are not necessary the court may omit them and direct an earlier trial.

(2) This may happen where the court is informed that a pre-action protocol has been complied with or that steps which it would otherwise order to be taken have already been taken.

(3) It may also happen where an application (for example for summary judgment or for an injunction) has been heard before allocation and little or no further preparation is required. In such a case the court may dispense with the need for a listing questionnaire.

Variation of directions

4.1 This paragraph deals with the procedure to be adopted:

(1) where a party is dissatisfied with a direction given by the court,

(2) where the parties agree about changes they wish made to the directions given, or

(3) where a party wishes to apply to vary a direction.

4.2 (1) It is essential that any party who wishes to have a direction varied takes steps to do so as soon as possible.

(2) The court will assume for the purposes of any later application that a party who did not appeal and who made no application to vary within 14 days of service of the order containing the directions was content that they were correct in the circumstances then existing.

4.3 (1) Where a party is dissatisfied with a direction given or other order made by the court he may appeal or apply to the court for it to reconsider its decision.

(2) He should appeal if the direction was given or the order was made at a hearing at which he was present or represented, or of which he had due notice.

(3) In any other case he should apply to the court to reconsider its decision.

(4) If an application is made for the court to reconsider its decision:

(a) it will usually be heard by the judge who gave the directions or another judge of the same level,

(b) the court will give all parties at least 3 days notice of the hearing, and

(c) the court may confirm its decision or make a different order.

4.4 Where there has been a change in the circumstances since the order was made the court may set aside or vary any direction it has given. It may do so on application or on its own initiative.

4.5 Where the parties agree about changes to be made to the directions given:

(1) If rule 2.11 (variation by agreement of a date set by the court for doing any act other than those stated in the note to that rule) or rule 31.5, 31.10(8) or 31.13 (agreements about disclosure) applied the parties need not file the written agreement.

(2) (a) In any other case the parties must apply for an order by consent.

(b) The parties must file a draft of the order sought and an agreed statement of the reasons why the variation is sought.

(c) The court may make an order in the agreed terms or in other terms without a hearing, but it may direct that a hearing is to be listed.

Failure to comply with case management directions

5.1 Where a party has failed to comply with a direction given by the court any other party may apply for an order to enforce compliance or for a sanction to be imposed or both of these.

5.2 The party entitled to apply for such an order must do so without delay but should first warn the other party of his intention to do so.

5.3 The court may take any such delay into account when it decides whether to make an order imposing a sanction or whether to grant relief from a sanction imposed by the rules or any practice direction.

5.4 (1) The court will not allow a failure to comply with directions to lead to the postponement of the trial unless the circumstances of the case are exceptional.

(2) If it is practicable to do so the court will exercise its powers in a manner that enables the case to come on for trial on the date or within the period previously set.

(3) In particular the court will assess what steps each party should take to prepare the case for trial, direct that those steps are taken in the shortest possible time and impose a sanction for non-compliance. Such a sanction may, for example, deprive a party of the right to raise or contest an issue or to rely on evidence to which the direction relates.

(4) Where it appears that one or more issues are or can be made ready for trial at the time fixed while others cannot, the court may direct that the trial will proceed on the issues which are or will then be ready, and order that no costs will be allowed for any later trial of the remaining issues or that those costs will be paid by the party in default.

(5) Where the court has no option but to postpone the trial it will do so for the shortest possible time and will give directions for the taking of the necessary steps in the meantime as rapidly as possible.

(6) Litigants and lawyers must be in no doubt that the court will regard the postponement of a trial as an order of last resort. The court may exercise its power to require a party as well as his legal representative to attend court at a hearing where such an order is to be sought.

Listing questionnaires and listing

6.1 (1) The listing questionnaire will be in Form N170.

(2) Unless it has dispensed with listing questionnaires, the court will send Forms N170 and N171 (Notice of date for return of the listing questionnaire) to each party no later than 2 weeks before the date specified in the notice of allocation or in any later direction of the court for the return of the completed questionnaires.

(3) When all the listing questionnaires have been filed or when the time for filing them has expired the file will be placed before a judge for his directions.

(4) Although the Rules do not require the parties to exchange copies of the questionnaires before they are filed they are encouraged to do so to avoid the court being given conflicting or incomplete information.

Attention is drawn to the Costs Practice Direction, paragraph 4.5(2), which requires a costs estimate to be filed and served at the same time as the listing questionnaire is filed.

6.2 Attention is drawn to rule 28.6(1) (which sets out the court's duty at the listing questionnaire stage) and to rule 28.5(3) (which sets out circumstances in which the court may decide to hold a listing hearing).

6.3 Where the judge decides to hold a listing hearing the court will fix a date which is as early as possible and the parties will be given at least 3 days' notice of the date. The notice of a listing hearing will be in Form N153.

6.4 The court's general approach will be as set out in the following paragraphs. The court may however decide to make other orders, and in particular the court will take into account the steps, if any, which the parties have taken to prepare the case for trial.

6.5 (1) Where no party files a listing questionnaire the court will normally make an order that if no listing questionnaire is filed by any party within 3 days from service of the order the claim and any counterclaim will be struck out.

(2) Where a party files a listing questionnaire but another party does not do so, the court normally will give listing directions. These will usually fix or confirm the trial date and provide for steps to be taken to prepare the case for trial.

Directions the court will give on listing

7.1 Directions the court must give:

(1) The court must confirm or fix the trial date, specify the place of trial and give a time estimate. The trial date must be fixed and the case listed on the footing that the hearing will end on the same calendar day as that on which it commenced.

(2) The court will serve a notice of hearing on the parties at least 3 weeks before the hearing unless they agree to accept shorter notice or the court authorises shorter service under rule 28.6(2), and

(3) The notice of hearing will be in Form N172.

7.2 Other directions:

(1) The parties should seek to agree directions and may file the proposed order. The court may make an order in those terms or it may make a different order.

(2) Agreed directions should include provision about:

   (a) evidence,

   (b) a trial timetable and time estimate,

   (c) the preparation of a trial bundle,

   (d) any other matter needed to prepare the case for trial.

(3) The court will include such of these provisions as are appropriate in any order that it may make, whether or not the parties have filed agreed directions.

(4) (a) A direction giving permission to use expert evidence will say whether it gives permission for oral evidence or reports or both and will name the experts concerned.

   (b) The court will not make a direction giving permission for an expert to give oral evidence unless it believes it is necessary in the interests of justice to do so.

   (c) Where no 'without prejudice' meeting or other discussion between experts has taken place the court may grant that permission conditionally on such a discussion taking place and a report being filed before the trial.

7.3 The principles set out in paragraph 4 of this practice direction about the variation of directions apply also to directions given at this stage.

The trial

8.1 The trial will normally take place at the court where the case is being managed, but it may be at another court if it is appropriate having regard to the needs of the parties and the availability of court resources.

8.2 The judge will generally have read the papers in the trial bundle and may dispense with an opening address.

8.3 The judge may confirm or vary any timetable given previously, or if none has been given set his own.

8.4 Attention is drawn to the provisions in Part 32 and the following parts of the Rules about evidence, and in particular –

(1) to rule 32.1 (court's power to control evidence and to restrict cross-examination), and

(2) to rule 32.5(2) (witness statements to stand as evidence in chief).

8.5 At the conclusion of the trial the judge will normally summarily assess the costs of the claim in accordance with rule 44.7 and Part 46 (fast track trial costs). Attention is drawn to the steps the practice directions about costs requires the parties to take.

8.6 Where a trial is not finished on the day for which it is listed the judge will normally sit on the next court day to complete it.

APPENDIX
FAST TRACK STANDARD DIRECTIONS

FURTHER STATEMENTS OF CASE

The   must file a   and serve a copy on   no later than   .

REQUESTS FOR FURTHER INFORMATION

Any request for clarification or further information based on another party's statement of case shall be served no later than   .

[Any such request shall be dealt with no later than [   ]

DISCLOSURE OF DOCUMENTS

[No disclosure of documents is required]

[[Each party] [The   ]
shall give [to the   ]
[to every other party] standard disclosure of documents [relating to
                                                                                                          ]

by serving copies together with a disclosure statement no

later than   ].

[Disclosure shall take place as follows:

[Each party shall give standard discovery to every other party by list]

[Disclosure is limited to [standard] [disclosure by the

to the   ] [of documents relating to damage] [the following documents
                        ]

[The latest date for delivery of the lists is   ]

[The latest date for service of any request to inspect or for a copy of a document is
                        ]]

WITNESSES OF FACT

Each party shall serve on every other party the witness statements of all witnesses of fact on whom he intends to rely. There shall be simultaneous exchange of such statements no later than
.

EXPERT EVIDENCE

[No expert evidence being necessary, no party has permission to call or rely on expert evidence].

[On it appearing to the court that expert evidence is necessary on the issue of [
                        ] and that that evidence should be given by the report of a single expert instructed jointly by the parties, the   shall no later than inform the court whether or not such an expert has been instructed].

[The expert evidence on the issue of   shall be   limited to a single expert jointly instructed by the parties.

If the parties cannot agree by who that expert is to be and about the payment of his fees either party may apply for further directions.

Unless the parties agree in writing or the court orders otherwise, the fees and expenses of such an expert shall be paid to him [by the parties equally] [   ] and be limited to £.

[The report of the expert shall be filed at the court no later than   ].

[No party shall be entitled to recover by way of costs from any other party more than £ for the fees or expenses of an expert].

The parties shall exchange reports setting out the substance of any expert evidence on which they intend to rely.

[The exchange shall take place simultaneously no later than   ].

[The   shall serve his report(s) no later than the   and the
                        shall serve his reports no later than the   ].

[The exchange of reports relating to [causation] [   ] shall take place simultaneously no later than   . The   shall serve his report(s) relating to [damage] [   ] no later than   and the shall serve his reports relating to it no later than   ].

Reports shall be agreed if possible no later than [days after service] [   ].

[If the reports are not agreed within that time there shall be a without prejudice discussion between the relevant experts no later than   to identify the issues between them and to reach agreement if possible.

The experts shall prepare for the court a statement of the issues on which they agree and on which they disagree with a summary of their reasons, and that statement shall be filed with the court [no later than   ] [with] [no later than the date for filing] [the listing questionnaire].

[Each party has permission to use [   ] as expert witness(es) to give [oral] evidence [in the form of a   report] at the trial in the field of   provided that the substance of the evidence to be given has been disclosed as above and has not been agreed].

[Each party has permission to use in evidence   experts' report(s) [and the court will consider when the claim is listed for trial whether expert oral evidence will be allowed].]

QUESTIONS TO EXPERTS

The time for service on another party of any question addressed to an expert instructed by that party is not later than   days after service of that expert's report.

Any such question shall be answered within   days of service.

REQUESTS FOR INFORMATION ETC.

Each party shall serve any request for clarification or further information based on any document disclosed or statement served by another party no later than   days after disclosure or service.

Any such request shall be dealt with within   days of service.

DOCUMENTS TO BE FILED WITH LISTING QUESTIONNAIRES

The parties must file with their listing questionnaires copies of [their experts' reports] [witness statements] [replies to requests for further information]

DATES FOR FILING LISTING QUESTIONNAIRES AND THE TRIAL

Each party must file a completed listing questionnaire no later than   .
The trial of this case will take place [on   ] [on a date to be fixed between   and   ].

DIRECTIONS FOLLOWING FILING OF LISTING QUESTIONNAIRE

Expert Evidence
The parties have permission to rely at the trial on expert evidence as follows:

The claimant: Oral evidence –
                     Written evidence –
The defendant: Oral evidence –
                     Written evidence –

Trial Timetable
The time allowed for the trial is

[The timetable for the trial may be agreed by the parties, subject to the approval of the trial judge].

[The timetable for the trial (subject to the approval of the trial judge) will be that
].

[The evidence in chief for each party will be contained in witness statements and reports, the time allowed for cross-examination by the defendant is limited to   and the time allowed for cross-examination by the claimant is limited to   ].

[The time allowed for the claimant's evidence is   . The time allowed for the defendant's evidence is   ].

The time allowed for the submissions on behalf of each party is   .

The remainder of the time allowed for the trial (being   ) is reserved for the judge to consider and give the judgment and to deal with costs].

Trial Bundle Etc.

The claimant shall lodge an indexed bundle of documents contained in a ring binder and with each page clearly numbered at the court not more than 7 days and not less than 3 days before the start of the trial. [A case summary (which should not exceed 250 words) outlining the matters still in issue, and referring where appropriate to the relevant documents shall be included in the bundle for the assistance of the judge in reading the papers before the trial]. [The parties shall seek to agree the contents of the trial bundle and the case summary].

Settlement

Each party must inform the court immediately if the claim is settled whether or not it is then possible to file a draft consent order to give effect to their agreement.

PART 29

THE MULTI-TRACK

Contents of this Part

Scope of this Part

29.1   This Part contains general provisions about management of cases allocated to the multi-track and applies only to cases allocated to that track.

(Part 27 sets out the procedure for claims allocated to the small claims track.)

(Part 28 sets out the procedure for claims allocated to the fast track.)

Case management

29.2 (1) When it allocates a case to the multi-track, the court will –

    (a) give directions for the management of the case and set a timetable for the steps to be taken between the giving of directions and the trial; or

    (b) fix –

        (i) a case management conference; or

        (ii) a pre-trial review,

    or both, and give such other directions relating to the management of the case as it sees fit.

  (2) The court will fix the trial date or the period in which the trial is to take place as soon as practicable.

  (3) When the court fixes the trial date or the trial period under paragraph (2), it will –

    (a) give notice to the parties of the date or period; and

    (b) specify the date by which the parties must file a listing questionnaire.

Case management conference and pre-trial review

29.3 (1) The court may fix –

    (a) a case management conference; or

    (b) a pre-trial review,

    at any time after the claim has been allocated.

  (2) If a party has a legal representative, a representative –

    (a) familiar with the case; and

    (b) with sufficient authority to deal with any issues that are likely to arise,

    must attend case management conferences and pre-trial reviews.

(Rule 3.1(2)(c) provides that the court may require a party to attend the court)

Steps taken by the parties

29.4   If –

    (a) the parties agree proposals for the management of the proceedings (including a proposed trial date or period in which the trial is to take place); and

    (b) the court considers that the proposals are suitable,

    it may approve them without a hearing and give directions in the terms proposed.

Variation of case management timetable

29.5 (1) A party must apply to the court if he wishes to vary the date which the court has fixed for –

    (a) a case management conference;

    (b) a pre-trial review;

    (c) the return of a listing questionnaire under rule 29.6;

    (d) the trial; or

    (e) the trial period.

  (2) Any date set by the court or these Rules for doing any act may not be varied by the parties if the variation would make it necessary to vary any of the dates mentioned in paragraph (1).

(Rule 2.11 allows the parties to vary a date by written agreement except where the rules provide otherwise or the court orders otherwise)

Listing questionnaire

29.6 (1) The court will send the parties a listing questionnaire for completion and return by the date specified in directions given under rule 29.2(3) unless it considers that the claim can be listed for trial without the need for a listing questionnaire.

(2) Each party must file the completed listing questionnaire by the date specified by the court.

(3) If –

    (a) a party fails to file the completed questionnaire by the date specified;

    (b) a party has failed to give all the information requested by the listing questionnaire; or

    (c) the court considers that a hearing is necessary to enable it to decide what directions to give in order to complete preparation of the case for trial,

the court may fix a date for a listing hearing or give such other directions as it thinks appropriate.

Pre-trial review

29.7 If, on receipt of the parties' listing questionnaires, the court decides –

    (a) to hold a pre-trial review; or

    (b) to cancel a pre-trial review which has already been fixed,

it will serve notice of its decision at least 7 days before the date fixed for the hearing or, as the case may be, the cancelled hearing.

Setting a trial timetable and fixing or confirming the trial date or week

29.8 As soon as practicable after –

    (a) each party has filed a completed listing questionnaire;

    (b) the court has held a listing hearing under rule 29.6(3); or

    (c) the court has held a pre-trial review under rule 29.7,

the court will –

    (i) set a timetable for the trial unless a timetable has already been fixed, or the court considers that it would be inappropriate to do so;

    (ii) fix the date for the trial or the week within which the trial is to begin (or, if it has already done so, confirm that date); and

    (iii) notify the parties of the trial timetable (where one is fixed under this rule) and the date or trial period.

Conduct of trial

29.9 Unless the trial judge otherwise directs, the trial will be conducted in accordance with any order previously made.

PRACTICE DIRECTION – THE MULTI-TRACK
THIS PRACTICE DIRECTION SUPPLEMENTS CPR PART 29

General

1.1 Attention is drawn in particular to the following Parts of the Civil Procedure Rules:

    Part 1   The overriding objective

    Part 3   The court's case management powers

    Part 26   Case management – preliminary stage

Part 31   Disclosure and inspection of documents

Parts 32 to 34   Evidence

Part 35   Experts and assessors

and to the practice directions which relate to those Parts.

1.2 Attention is also drawn to Part 49 of the Rules (Specialist Jurisdictions) and to the practice directions which apply to those jurisdictions.

Case management in the Royal Courts of Justice

2.1 This part of the practice direction applies to claims begun by claim form issued in the Central Office or Chancery Chambers in the Royal Courts of Justice.

2.2 A claim with an estimated value of less than £50,000 will generally, unless:

(a) it is required by an enactment to be tried in the High Court,

(b) it falls within a specialist list (as defined in CPR Part 49), or

(c) it falls within one of the categories specified in 2.6 below or is otherwise within the criteria of article 7(5) of the High Court and County Courts Jurisdiction Order 1991,

be transferred to a county court.

2.3 Paragraph 2.2 is without prejudice to the power of the court in accordance with Part 30 to transfer to a county court a claim with an estimated value that exceeds £50,000.

2.4 The decision to transfer may be made at any stage in the proceedings but should, subject to paragraph 2.5, be made as soon as possible and in any event not later than the date for the filing of listing questionnaires.

2.5 If an application is made under rule 3.4 (striking out) or under Part 24 (summary judgment) or under Part 25 (interim remedies), it will usually be convenient for the application to be dealt with before a decision to transfer is taken.

2.6 Each party should state in his allocation questionnaire whether he considers the claim should be managed and tried at the Royal Courts of Justice and, if so, why. Claims suitable for trial in the Royal Courts of Justice include:

(1) professional negligence claims,

(2) Fatal Accident Act claims,

(3) fraud or undue influence claims,

(4) defamation claims,

(5) claims for malicious prosecution or false imprisonment,

(6) claims against the police,

(7) contentious probate claims.

Such claims may fall within the criteria of article 7(5) of the High Court and County Courts Jurisdiction Order 1991.

2.7 Attention is drawn to the practice direction on transfer (Part 30).

Case management – general provisions

3.1 (1) Case management of a claim which is proceeding at the Royal Courts of Justice will be undertaken there.

(2) (a) Case management of any other claim which has been allocated to the multi-track will normally be undertaken at a Civil Trial Centre.

(b) The practice direction supplementing Part 26 provides for what will happen in the case of a claim which is issued in or transferred to a court which is not a Civil Trial Centre.

3.2 The hallmarks of the multi-track are:

(1) the ability of the court to deal with cases of widely differing values and complexity, and

(2) the flexibility given to the court in the way it will manage a case in a way appropriate to its particular needs.

3.3 (1) On allocating a claim to the multi-track the court may give directions without a hearing, including fixing a trial date or a period in which the trial will take place,

(2) Alternatively, whether or not it fixes a trial date or period, it may either –

     (a) give directions for certain steps to be taken and fix a date for a case management conference or a pre-trial review to take place after they have been taken, or

     (b) fix a date for a case management conference.

(3) Attention is drawn to rule 29.2(2) which requires the court to fix a trial date or period as soon as practicable.

3.4 The court may give or vary directions at any hearing which may take place on the application of a party or of its own initiative.

3.5 When any hearing has been fixed it is the duty of the parties to consider what directions the court should be asked to give and to make any application that may be appropriate to be dealt with then.

3.6 The court will hold a hearing to give directions whenever it appears necessary or desirable to do so, and where this happens because of the default of a party or his legal representative it will usually impose a sanction.

3.7 When the court fixes a hearing to give directions it will give the parties at least 3 days' notice of the hearing unless rule 29.7 applies (7 days notice to be given in the case of a pre-trial review).

3.8 Where a party needs to apply for a direction of a kind not included in the case management timetable which has been set (for example to amend his statement of case or for further information to be given by another party) he must do so as soon as possible so as to minimise the need to change that timetable.

3.9 Courts will make arrangements to ensure that applications and other hearings are listed promptly to avoid delay in the conduct of cases.

3.10(1) Case management will generally be dealt with by:

     (a) a Master in cases proceeding in the Royal Courts of Justice,

     (b) a district judge in cases proceeding in a District Registry of the High Court, and

     (c) a district judge or a Circuit Judge in cases proceeding in a county court.

(2) A Master or a district judge may consult and seek the directions of a judge of a higher level about any aspect of case management.

(3) A member of the court staff who is dealing with the listing of a hearing may seek the directions of any judge about any aspect of that listing.

Directions on allocation

4.1 Attention is drawn to the court's duties under Rule 29.2.

4.2 The court will seek to tailor its directions to the needs of the case and the steps which the parties have already taken to prepare the case of which it is aware. In particular it will have regard to the extent to which any pre-action protocol has or (as the case may be) has not been complied with.

4.3 At this stage the court's first concern will be to ensure that the issues between the parties are identified and that the necessary evidence is prepared and disclosed.

4.4 The court may have regard to any document filed by a party with his allocation questionnaire containing further information, provided that the document states either that its contents has been agreed with every other party or that it has been served on every other party, and when it was served.

4.5 On the allocation of a claim to the multi-track the court will consider whether it is desirable or necessary to hold a case management conference straight away, or whether it is appropriate instead to give directions on its own initiative.

4.6 The parties and their advisers are encouraged to try to agree directions and to take advantage of rule 29.4 which provides that if:

(1) the parties agree proposals for the management of the proceedings (including a proposed trial date or period in which the trial is to take place), and

(2) the court considers that the proposals are suitable,

it may approve them without a hearing and give directions in the terms proposed.

4.7 (1) To obtain the court's approval the agreed directions must –

     (a) set out a timetable by reference to calendar dates for the taking of steps for the preparation of the case,

    (b) include a date or a period (the trial period) when it is proposed that the trial will take place,

    (c) include provision about disclosure of documents, and

    (d) include provision about both factual and expert evidence.

(2) The court will scrutinise the timetable carefully and in particular will be concerned to see that any proposed date or period for the trial and (if provided for) for a case management conference is no later than is reasonably necessary.

(3) The provision in (1)(c) above may –

    (a) limit disclosure to standard disclosure or less than that, and/or

    (b) direct that disclosure will take place by the supply of copy documents without a list, but it must in that case say either that the parties must serve a disclosure statement with the copies or that they have agreed to disclose in that way without such a statement.

(4) The provision in (1)(d) about expert evidence may be to the effect that none is required.

4.8 Directions agreed by the parties should also where appropriate contain provisions about:

(1) the filing of any reply or amended statement of case that may be required,

(2) dates for the service of requests for further information under the practice direction supplementing Part 18 and of questions to experts under rule 35.6 and by when they are to be dealt with,

(3) the disclosure of evidence,

(4) the use of a single joint expert, or in cases where it is not agreed, the exchange of expert evidence (including whether exchange is to be simultaneous or sequential) and without prejudice discussions between experts.

4.9 If the court does not approve the agreed directions filed by the parties but decides that it will give directions of its own initiative without fixing a case management conference, it will take them into account in deciding what directions to give.

4.10 Where the court is to give directions on its own initiative without holding a case management conference and it is not aware of any steps taken by the parties other than the exchange of statements of case, its general approach will be:

(1) to give directions for the filing and service of any further information required to clarify either party's case,

(2) to direct standard disclosure between the parties,

(3) to direct the disclosure of witness statements by way of simultaneous exchange,

(4) to give directions for a single joint expert on any appropriate issue unless there is a good reason not to do so,

(5) unless paragraph 4.11 (below) applies, to direct disclosure of experts' reports by way of simultaneous exchange on those issues where a single joint expert is not directed,

(6) if experts' reports are not agreed, to direct a discussion between experts for the purpose set out in rule 35.12(1) and the preparation of a statement under rule 35.12(3),

(7) to list a case management conference to take place after the date for compliance with those directions, and (8) to specify a trial period.

4.11 If it appears that expert evidence will be required both on issues of liability and on the amount of damages, the court may direct that the exchange of those reports that relate to liability will be exchanged simultaneously but that those relating to the amount of damages will be exchanged sequentially.

4.12 (1) If it appears to the court that it cannot properly give directions on its own initiative and no agreed directions have been filed which it can approve, the court will direct a case management conference to be listed.

    (2) The conference will be listed as promptly as possible.

4.13 Where the court is proposing on its own initiative to make an order under rule 35.7 (which gives the court power to direct that evidence on a particular issue is to be given by a single expert) or under rule 35.15 (which gives the court power to appoint an assessor), the court must, unless the parties have consented in writing to the order, list a case management conference.

Case management conferences

5.1 The court will at any case management conference:

(1) review the steps which the parties have taken in the preparation of the case, and in particular their compliance with any directions that the court may have given,

(2) decide and give directions about the steps which are to be taken to secure the progress of the claim in accordance with the overriding objective, and

(3) ensure as far as it can that all agreements that can be reached between the parties about the matters in issue and the conduct of the claim are made and recorded.

5.2 (1) Rule 29.3(2) provides that where a party has a legal representative, a representative familiar with the case and with sufficient authority to deal with any issues that are likely to arise must attend case management conferences and pre-trial reviews.

(2) That person should be someone who is personally involved in the conduct of the case, and who has the authority and information to deal with any matter which may reasonably be expected to be dealt with at such a hearing, including the fixing of the timetable, the identification of issues and matters of evidence.

(3) Where the inadequacy of the person attending or of his instructions leads to the adjournment of a hearing, the court will expect to make a wasted costs order.

5.3 The topics the court will consider at a case management conference are likely to include:

(1) whether the claimant has made clear the claim he is bringing, in particular the amount he is claiming, so that the other party can understand the case he has to meet,

(2) whether any amendments are required to the claim, a statement of case or any other document,

(3) what disclosure of documents, if any, is necessary,

(4) what expert evidence is reasonably required in accordance with rule 35.1 and how and when that evidence should be obtained and disclosed,

(5) what factual evidence should be disclosed,

(6) what arrangements should be made about the giving of clarification or further information and the putting of questions to experts, and

(7) whether it will be just and will save costs to order a split trial or the trial of one or more preliminary issues.

5.4 In all cases the court will set a timetable for the steps it decides are necessary to be taken. These steps may include the holding of a case management conference or a pre-trial review, and the court will be alert to perform its duty to fix a trial date or period as soon as it can.

5.5 (1) The court will not at this stage give permission to use expert evidence unless it can identify each expert by name or field in its order and say whether his evidence is to be given orally or by the use of his report.

(2) A party who obtains expert evidence before obtaining a direction about it does so at his own risk as to costs, except where he obtained the evidence in compliance with a pre-action protocol.

5.6 To assist the court, the parties and their legal advisers should:

(1) ensure that all documents that the court is likely to ask to see (including witness statements and experts' reports) are brought to the hearing,

(2) consider whether the parties should attend,

(3) consider whether a case summary will be useful, and

(4) consider what orders each wishes to be made and give notice of them to the other parties.

5.7 (1) A case summary:

(a) should be designed to assist the court to understand and deal with the questions before it,

(b) should set out a brief chronology of the claim, the issues of fact which are agreed or in dispute and the evidence needed to decide them,

(c) should not normally exceed 500 words in length, and

(d) should be prepared by the claimant and agreed with the other parties if possible.

5.8 (1) Where a party wishes to obtain an order not routinely made at a case management conference and believes that his application will be opposed, he should issue and serve the application in time for it to be heard at the case management conference.

(2) If the time allowed for the case management conference is likely to be insufficient for the application to be heard he should inform the court at once so that a fresh date can be fixed.

(3) A costs sanction may be imposed on a party who fails to comply with sub-paragraph (1) or (2).

5.9 At a case management conference the court may also consider whether the case ought to be tried by a High Court judge or by a judge who specialises in that type of claim and how that question will be decided. In that case the claim may need to be transferred to another court.

Variation of directions

6.1 This paragraph deals with the procedure to be adopted:
   (1) where a party is dissatisfied with a direction given by the court,
   (2) where the parties have agreed about changes they wish made to the directions given, or
   (3) where a party wishes to apply to vary a direction.

6.2 (1) It is essential that any party who wishes to have a direction varied takes steps to do so as soon as possible.
   (2) The court will assume for the purposes of any later application that a party who did not appeal, and who made no application to vary within 14 days of service of the order containing the directions, was content that they were correct in the circumstances then existing.

6.3 (1) Where a party is dissatisfied with a direction given or other order made by the court he may appeal or apply to the court for it to reconsider its decision.
   (2) Unless paragraph 6.4 applies, a party should appeal if the direction was given or the order was made at a hearing at which he was present, or of which he had due notice.
   (3) In any other case he should apply to the court to reconsider its decision.
   (4) If an application is made for the court to reconsider its decision:
      (a) it will usually be heard by the judge who gave the directions or another judge of the same level,
      (b) the court will give all parties at least 3 days notice of the hearing, and
      (c) the court may confirm its directions or make a different order.

6.4 Where there has been a change in the circumstances since the order was made the court may set aside or vary a direction it has given. It may do so on application or on its own initiative.

6.5 Where the parties agree about changes they wish made to the directions given:
   (1) If rule 2.11 (variation by agreement of a date set by the court for doing any act other than those stated in the note to that rule) or rule 31.5, 31.10(8) or 31.13 (agreements about disclosure) applies the parties need not file the written agreement.
   (2) (a) In any other case the parties must apply for an order by consent.
      (b) The parties must file a draft of the order sought and an agreed statement of the reasons why the variation is sought.
      (c) The court may make an order in the agreed terms or in other terms without a hearing, but it may direct that a hearing is to be listed.

Failure to comply with case management directions

7.1 Where a party fails to comply with a direction given by the court any other party may apply for an order that he must do so or for a sanction to be imposed or both of these.

7.2 The party entitled to apply for such an order must do so without delay but should first warn the other party of his intention to do so.

7.3 The court may take any such delay into account when it decides whether to make an order imposing a sanction or to grant relief from a sanction imposed by the rules or any other practice direction.

7.4 (1) The court will not allow a failure to comply with directions to lead to the postponement of the trial unless the circumstances are exceptional.
   (2) If it is practical to do so the court will exercise its powers in a manner that enables the case to come on for trial on the date or within the period previously set.

(3) In particular the court will assess what steps each party should take to prepare the case for trial, direct that those steps are taken in the shortest possible time and impose a sanction for non-compliance. Such a sanction may, for example, deprive a party of the right to raise or contest an issue or to rely on evidence to which the direction relates.

(4) Where it appears that one or more issues are or can be made ready for trial at the time fixed while others cannot, the court may direct that the trial will proceed on the issues which are then ready, and direct that no costs will be allowed for any later trial of the remaining issues or that those costs will be paid by the party in default.

(5) Where the court has no option but to postpone the trial it will do so for the shortest possible time and will give directions for the taking of the necessary steps in the meantime as rapidly as possible.

(6) Litigants and lawyers must be in no doubt that the court will regard the postponement of a trial as an order of last resort. Where it appears inevitable the court may exercise its power to require a party as well as his legal representative to attend court at the hearing where such an order is to be sought.

(7) The court will not postpone any other hearing without a very good reason, and for that purpose the failure of a party to comply on time with directions previously given will not be treated as a good reason.

Listing questionnaires and listing

8.1 (1) The listing questionnaire will be in Form N170.

(2) Unless it dispenses with listing questionnaires and orders an early trial on a fixed date, the court will specify the date for filing completed listing questionnaires when it fixes the trial date or trial period under rule 29.2(2).

(3) The date for filing the completed listing questionnaires will be not later than 8 weeks before the trial date or the start of the trial period.

(4) The court will serve the listing questionnaires on the parties at least 14 days before that date.

(5) Although the rules do not require the parties to exchange copies of the questionnaires before they are filed they are encouraged to do so to avoid the court being given conflicting or incomplete information.

(6) The file will be placed before a judge for his directions when all the questionnaires have been filed or when the time for filing them has expired.

8.2 The court's general approach will be as set out in the following paragraphs. The court may however decide to make other orders, and in particular the court will take into account the steps, if any, of which it is aware which the parties have taken to prepare the case for trial.

8.3 (1) Where no party files a listing questionnaire the court will normally make an order that if no listing questionnaire is filed by any party within 3 days from service of the order, the claim and any counterclaim will be struck out.

(2) Where a party files a listing questionnaire but another party (the defaulting party) does not do so, the court will fix a listing hearing. Whether or not the defaulting party attends the hearing, the court will normally fix or confirm the trial date and make other orders about the steps to be taken to prepare the case for trial.

8.4 Where the court decides to hold a listing hearing the court will fix a date which is as early as possible and the parties will be given at least 3 days notice of the date.

8.5 Where the court decides to hold a pre-trial review (whether or not this is in addition to a listing hearing) the court will give the parties at least 7 days notice of the date.

Directions the court will give on listing

9.1 *Directions the court must give*

The court must fix the trial date or week, give a time estimate and fix the place of trial.

9.2 *Other directions*

(1) The parties should seek to agree directions and may file an agreed order. The court may make an order in those terms or it may make a different order.

(2) Agreed directions should include provision about:

(a) evidence especially expert evidence,

(b) a trial timetable and time estimate,

(c) the preparation of a trial bundle, and

(d) any other matter needed to prepare the case for trial.

(3) The court will include such of these provisions as are appropriate in any order that it may make, whether or not the parties have filed agreed directions.

(4) Unless a direction doing so has been given before, a direction giving permission to use expert evidence will say whether it gives permission to use oral evidence or reports or both and will name the experts concerned.

9.3 The principles set out in paragraph 6 of this practice direction about variation of directions applies equally to directions given at this stage.

The trial

10.1 The trial will normally take place at a Civil Trial Centre but it may be at another court if it is appropriate having regard to the needs of the parties and the availability of court resources.

10.2 The judge will generally have read the papers in the trial bundle and may dispense with an opening address.

10.3 The judge may confirm or vary any timetable given previously, or if none has been given set his own.

10.4 Attention is drawn to the provisions in Part 32 and the following parts of the Rules about evidence, and in particular:

(1) to rule 32.1 (court's power to control evidence and to restrict cross-examination), and

(2) to rule 32.5(2) statements and reports to stand as evidence in chief.

10.5 In an appropriate case the judge may summarily assess costs in accordance with rule 44.7. Attention is drawn to the practice directions about costs and the steps the parties are required to take.

10.6 Once the trial of a multi-track claim has begun, the judge will normally sit on consecutive court days until it has been concluded.

PART 30

TRANSFER

Contents of this Part

Scope of this Part

30.1 This Part deals with the transfer of proceedings between county courts, between the High Court and the county courts and within the High Court.

(Rule 26.2 provides for automatic transfer in certain cases)

Transfer between county courts and within the High Court

30.2 (1) A county court may order proceedings before that court, or any part of them (such as a counterclaim or an application made in the proceedings), to be transferred to another county court if it is satisfied that –

    (a) an order should be made having regard to the criteria in rule 30.3; or

    (b) proceedings for –

       (i) the detailed assessment of costs; or

       (ii) the enforcement of a judgment or order,

    could be more conveniently or fairly taken in that other county court.

(2) If proceedings have been started in the wrong county court, a judge of the county court may order that the proceedings –

    (a) be transferred to the county court in which they ought to have been started;

    (b) continue in the county court in which they have been started; or

    (c) be struck out.

(3) An application for an order under paragraph (1) or (2) must be made to the county court where the claim is proceeding.

(4) The High Court may, having regard to the criteria in rule 30.3, order proceedings in the Royal Courts of Justice or a district registry, or any part of such proceedings (such as a counterclaim or an application made in the proceedings), to be transferred –

    (a) from the Royal Courts of Justice to a district registry; or

    (b) from a district registry to the Royal Courts of Justice or to another district registry.

(5) A district registry may order proceedings before it for the detailed assessment of costs to be transferred to another district registry if it is satisfied that the proceedings could be more conveniently or fairly taken in that other district registry.

(6) An application for an order under paragraph (4) or (5) must, if the claim is proceeding in a district registry, be made to that registry.

(7) Where some enactment, other than these Rules, requires proceedings to be started in a particular county court, neither paragraphs (1) nor (2) give the court power to order proceedings to be transferred to a county court which is not the court in which they should have been started or to order them to continue in the wrong court.

(8) Probate proceedings may only be transferred under paragraph (4) to the Chancery Division at the Royal Courts of Justice or to one of the Chancery district registries.

Criteria for a transfer order

30.3 (1) Paragraph (2) sets out the matters to which the court must have regard when considering whether to make an order under –

    (a) section 40(2), 41(1) or 42(2) of the County Courts Act 1984[45] (transfer between the High Court and a county court);

    (b) rule 30.2(1) (transfer between county courts); or

    (c) rule 30.2(4) (transfer between the Royal Courts of Justice and the district registries).

(2) The matters to which the court must have regard include –

---

(45) 1984 c.28. Section 40 was substituted by section 2(1) of the Courts and Legal Services Act 1990 (c.41). Section 41 was amended by the Matrimonial and Family Proceedings Act 1984 (c.42), Schedule 1, paragraph 31 and by section 2(2) of the Courts and Legal Services Act 1990. Section 42 was substituted by section 2(3) of the Courts and Legal Services Act 1990.

(a) the financial value of the claim and the amount in dispute, if different;

(b) whether it would be more convenient or fair for hearings (including the trial) to be held in some other court;

(c) the availability of a judge specialising in the type of claim in question;

(d) whether the facts, legal issues, remedies or procedures involved are simple or complex;

(e) the importance of the outcome of the claim to the public in general;

(f) the facilities available at the court where the claim is being dealt with and whether they may be inadequate because of any disabilities of a party or potential witness.

Procedure

30.4 (1) Where the court orders proceedings to be transferred, the court from which they are to be transferred must give notice of the transfer to all the parties.

(2) An order made before the transfer of the proceedings shall not be affected by the order to transfer.

Transfer between divisions and to and from a specialist list

30.5 (1) The High Court may order proceedings in any Division of the High Court to be transferred to another Division.

(2) The court may order proceedings to be transferred to or from a specialist list.

(3) An application for the transfer of proceedings to or from a specialist list must be made to a judge dealing with claims in that list.

Power to specify place where hearings are to be held

30.6 The court may specify the place (for instance, a particular county court) where the trial or some other hearing in any proceedings is to be held and may do so without ordering the proceedings to be transferred.

Transfer of control of money in court

30.7 The court may order that control of any money held by it under rule 21.11 (control of money recovered by or on behalf of a child or patient) be transferred to another court if that court would be more convenient.

Certiorari or prohibition

30.8 A party obtaining from the High Court, on an application made without notice, an order giving permission to make an application for –

(a) an order of certiorari to remove proceedings from a county court; or

(b) an order of prohibition to any county court,

must immediately serve a copy of the order on the other parties and on the court officer of the county court.

(Other rules about transfer can be found in Schedule 2 in the following CCR – O.25 (transfer of proceedings for enforcement); O.30 (transfer of garnishee proceedings))

PRACTICE DIRECTION – TRANSFER
THIS PRACTICE DIRECTION SUPPLEMENTS CPR PART 30

Value of a case and transfer

1 In addition to the criteria set out in Rule 30.3(2) attention is drawn to the financial limits set out in the High Court and County Courts Jurisdiction Order 1991, as amended.

2 Attention is also drawn to paragraph 2 of the Practice Direction on Part 29 (the multi-track).

Date of transfer

3 Where the court orders proceedings to be transferred, the order will take effect from the date it is made by the court.

Procedure on transfer

4.1 Where an order for transfer has been made the transferring court will immediately send notice of the transfer to the receiving court. The notice will contain:

(1) the name of the case, and

(2) the number of the case.

4.2 At the same time as the transferring court notifies the receiving court it will also notify the parties of the transfer under rule 30.4(1).

Procedure for an appeal against order of transfer

5.1 An appeal against an order that proceedings be transferred:

(1) where either the transferring court or the receiving court is the High Court, and the order was made by a Master or district judge, should be made in the High Court,

(2) where the order was made in proceedings in the High Court by a High Court judge, should be made in the Court of Appeal,

(3) where both the transferring and receiving courts are county courts, and the order was made by a district judge, should be made in the receiving court,

(4) where the order was made in county court proceedings by a circuit judge, should be made in the Court of Appeal.

5.2 Where paragraph 5.1(3) applies, the receiving court may, if it is convenient to the parties, remit the appeal to the transferring court to be dealt with there.

5.3 An appeal made under 5.1(1) or 5.1(3) above must be begun by the issue of an application notice in accordance with Part 23 of the Rules and the practice direction which supplements Part 23.

5.4 An appeal made under 5.1(2) or 5.1(4) above must be begun by the issue of a notice of appeal in accordance with the provisions of RSC Order 59 (see Part 50 and Schedule 1 to the Rules).

Applications to set aside

6.1 Where a party may apply to set aside an order for transfer (e.g. under rule 23.10) the application should be made to the court which made the order.

6.2 Such application should be made in accordance with Part 23 of the Rules and the practice direction which supplements it.

PART 31

DISCLOSURE AND INSPECTION OF DOCUMENTS

Contents of this Part

Scope of this Part

31.1 (1) This Part sets out rules about the disclosure and inspection of documents.

　(2) This Part applies to all claims except a claim on the small claims track.

Meaning of disclosure

31.2　A party discloses a document by stating that the document exists or has existed.

Right of inspection of a disclosed document

31.3 (1) A party to whom a document has been disclosed has a right to inspect that document except where –

　(a) the document is no longer in the control of the party who disclosed it;

　(b) the party disclosing the document has a right or a duty to withhold inspection of it; or

　(c) paragraph (2) applies.

(Rule 31.8 sets out when a document is in the control of a party.)

(Rule 31.19 sets out the procedure for claiming a right or duty to withhold inspection.)

　(2)　Where a party considers that it would be disproportionate to the issues in the case to permit inspection of documents within a category or class of document disclosed under rule 31.6(b) –

　(a) he is not required to permit inspection of documents within that category or class; but

(b) he must state in his disclosure statement that inspection of those documents will not be permitted on the grounds that to do so would be disproportionate.

(Rule 31.6 provides for standard disclosure.)

(Rule 31.10 makes provision for a disclosure statement.)

(Rule 31.12 provides for a party to apply for an order for specific inspection of documents.)

Meaning of document

31.4   In this Part –

'document' means anything in which information of any description is recorded; and

'copy', in relation to a document, means anything onto which information recorded in the document has been copied, by whatever means and whether directly or indirectly.

Disclosure limited to standard disclosure

31.5 (1) An order to give disclosure is an order to give standard disclosure unless the court directs otherwise.

(2) The court may dispense with or limit standard disclosure.

(3) The parties may agree in writing to dispense with or to limit standard disclosure.

(The court may make an order requiring standard disclosure under rule 28.3 which deals with directions in relation to cases on the fast track and under rule 29.2 which deals with case management in relation to cases on the multi-track.)

Standard disclosure – what documents are to be disclosed

31.6   Standard disclosure requires a party to disclose only –

(a) the documents on which he relies; and

(b) the documents which –

(i)   adversely affect his own case;

(ii) adversely affect another party's case; or

(iii) support another party's case; and

(c) the documents which he is required to disclose by a relevant practice direction.

Duty of search

31.7 (1) When giving standard disclosure, a party is required to make a reasonable search for documents falling within rule 31.6(b) or (c).

(2) The factors relevant in deciding the reasonableness of a search include the following –

(a) the number of documents involved;

(b) the nature and complexity of the proceedings;

(c) the ease and expense of retrieval of any particular document; and

(d) the significance of any document which is likely to be located during the search.

(3) Where a party has not searched for a category or class of document on the grounds that to do so would be unreasonable, he must state this in his disclosure statement and identify the category or class of document.

(Rule 31.10 makes provision for a disclosure statement.)

Duty of disclosure limited to documents which are or have been in a party's control

31.8 (1) A party's duty to disclose documents is limited to documents which are or have been in his control.

(2) For this purpose a party has or has had a document in his control if –

(a) it is or was in his physical possession;

(b) he has or has had a right to possession of it; or

(c) he has or has had a right to inspect or take copies of it.

Disclosure of copies

31.9 (1) A party need not disclose more than one copy of a document.

(2) A copy of a document that contains a modification, obliteration or other marking or feature –

(a) on which a party intends to rely; or

(b) which adversely affects his own case or another party's case or supports another party's case;

shall be treated as a separate document.

(Rule 31.4 sets out the meaning of a copy of a document)

Procedure for standard disclosure

31.10 (1) The procedure for standard disclosure is as follows.

(2) Each party must make and serve on every other party, a list of documents in the relevant practice form.

(3) The list must identify the documents in a convenient order and manner and as concisely as possible.

(4) The list must indicate –

(a) those documents in respect of which the party claims a right or duty to withhold inspection; and

(b) (i) those documents which are no longer in the party's control; and

(ii) what has happened to those documents.

(Rule 31.19 (3) and (4) require a statement in the list of documents relating to any documents inspection of which a person claims he has a right or duty to withhold.)

(5) The list must include a disclosure statement.

(6) A disclosure statement is a statement made by the party disclosing the documents –

(a) setting out the extent of the search that has been made to locate documents which he is required to disclose;

(b) certifying that he understands the duty to disclose documents; and

(c) certifying that to the best of his knowledge he has carried out that duty.

(7) Where the party making the disclosure statement is a company, firm, association or other organisation, the statement must also –

(a) identify the person making the statement; and

(b) explain why he is considered an appropriate person to make the statement.

(8) The parties may agree in writing –

(a) to disclose documents without making a list; and

(b) to disclose documents without the disclosing party making a disclosure statement.

(9) A disclosure statement may be made by a person who is not a party where this is permitted by a relevant practice direction.

Duty of disclosure continues during proceedings

31.11 (1) Any duty of disclosure continues until the proceedings are concluded.

(2) If documents to which that duty extends come to a party's notice at any time during the proceedings, he must immediately notify every other party.

Specific disclosure or inspection

31.12 (1) The court may make an order for specific disclosure or specific inspection.

(2) An order for specific disclosure is an order that a party must do one or more of the following things –

(a) disclose documents or classes of documents specified in the order;

(b) carry out a search to the extent stated in the order;

(c) disclose any documents located as a result of that search.

(3) An order for specific inspection is an order that a party permit inspection of a document referred to in rule 31.3(2).

(Rule 31.3(2) allows a party to state in his disclosure statement that he will not permit inspection of a document on the grounds that it would be disproportionate to do so.)

Disclosure in stages

31.13 The parties may agree in writing, or the court may direct, that disclosure or inspection or both shall take place in stages.

Documents referred to in statements of case etc.

31.14 A party may inspect a document mentioned in –

(a) a statement of case;

(b) a witness statement;

(c) a witness summary;

(d) an affidavit(GL); or

(e) subject to rule 35.10(4), an expert's report.

(Rule 35.10(4) makes provision in relation to instructions referred to in an expert's report.)

Inspection and copying of documents

31.15 Where a party has a right to inspect a document –

(a) that party must give the party who disclosed the document written notice of his wish to inspect it;

(b) the party who disclosed the document must permit inspection not more than 7 days after the date on which he received the notice; and

(c) that party may request a copy of the document and, if he also undertakes to pay reasonable copying costs, the party who disclosed the document must supply him with a copy not more than 7 days after the date on which he received the request.

(Rule 31.3 and 31.14 deal with the right of a party to inspect a document.)

Disclosure before proceedings start

31.16 (1) This rule applies where an application is made to the court under any Act for disclosure before proceedings have started[46].

---

[46] An application for disclosure before proceedings have started is permitted under section 33 of the Supreme Court Act 1981 (c.54) or section 52 of the County Courts Act 1984 (c.28).

(2) The application must be supported by evidence.

(3) The court may make an order under this rule only where –

    (a) the respondent is likely to be a party to subsequent proceedings;

    (b) the applicant is also likely to be a party to those proceedings;

    (c) if proceedings had started, the respondent's duty by way of standard disclosure, set out in rule 31.6, would extend to the documents or classes of documents of which the applicant seeks disclosure; and

    (d) disclosure before proceedings have started is desirable in order to –

        (i) dispose fairly of the anticipated proceedings;

        (ii) assist the dispute to be resolved without proceedings; or

        (iii) save costs.

(4) An order under this rule must –

    (a) specify the documents or the classes of documents which the respondent must disclose; and

    (b) require him, when making disclosure, to specify any of those documents –

        (i) which are no longer in his control; or

        (ii) in respect of which he claims a right or duty to withhold inspection.

(5) Such an order may –

    (a) require the respondent to indicate what has happened to any documents which are no longer in his control; and

    (b) specify the time and place for disclosure and inspection.

Orders for disclosure against a person not a party

31.17 (1) This rule applies where an application is made to the court under any Act for disclosure by a person who is not a party to the proceedings[47].

(2) The application must be supported by evidence.

(3) The court may make an order under this rule only where –

    (a) the documents of which disclosure is sought are likely to support the case of the applicant or adversely affect the case of one of the other parties to the proceedings; and

    (b) disclosure is necessary in order to dispose fairly of the claim or to save costs.

(4) An order under this rule must –

    (a) specify the documents or the classes of documents which the respondent must disclose; and

    (b) require the respondent, when making disclosure, to specify any of those documents –

        (i) which are no longer in his control; or

        (ii) in respect of which he claims a right or duty to withhold inspection.

(5) Such an order may –

    (a) require the respondent to indicate what has happened to any documents which are no longer in his control; and

    (b) specify the time and place for disclosure and inspection.

---

(47) An application for disclosure against a person who is not a party to proceedings is permitted under section 34 of the Supreme Court Act 1981 (c.54) or section 53 of the County Courts Act 1984 (c.28).

Rules not to limit other powers of the court to order disclosure

31.18 Rules 31.16 and 31.17 do not limit any other power which the court may have to order –

(a) disclosure before proceedings have started; and

(b) disclosure against a person who is not a party to proceedings.

Claim to withhold inspection or disclosure of a document

31.19 (1) A person may apply, without notice, for an order permitting him to withhold disclosure of a document on the ground that disclosure would damage the public interest.

(2) Unless the court orders otherwise, an order of the court under paragraph (1) –

(a) must not be served on any other person; and

(b) must not be open to inspection by any person.

(3) A person who wishes to claim that he has a right or a duty to withhold inspection of a document, or part of a document, must state in writing –

(a) that he has such a right or duty; and

(b) the grounds on which he claims that right or duty.

(4) The statement referred to in paragraph (3) must be made –

(a) in the list in which the document is disclosed; or

(b) if there is no list, to the person wishing to inspect the document.

(5) A party may apply to the court to decide whether a claim made under paragraph (3) should be upheld.

(6) For the purpose of deciding an application under paragraph (1) (application to withhold disclosure) or paragraph (3) (claim to withhold inspection) the court may –

(a) require the person seeking to withhold disclosure or inspection of a document to produce that document to the court; and

(b) invite any person, whether or not a party, to make representations.

(7) An application under paragraph (1) or paragraph (5) must be supported by evidence.

(8) This Part does not affect any rule of law which permits or requires a document to be withheld from disclosure or inspection on the ground that its disclosure or inspection would damage the public interest.

Restriction on use of a privileged document inspection of which has been inadvertently allowed

31.20 Where a party inadvertently allows a privileged(GL) document to be inspected, the party who has inspected the document may use it or its contents only with the permission of the court.

Consequence of failure to disclose documents or permit inspection

31.21 A party may not rely on any document which he fails to disclose or in respect of which he fails to permit inspection unless the court gives permission.

Subsequent use of disclosed documents

31.22 (1) A party to whom a document has been disclosed may use the document only for the purpose of the proceedings in which it is disclosed, except where –

(a) the document has been read to or by the court, or referred to, at a hearing which has been held in public;

(b) the court gives permission; or

(c) the party who disclosed the document and the person to whom the document belongs agree.

(2) The court may make an order restricting or prohibiting the use of a document which has been disclosed, even where the document has been read to or by the court, or referred to, at a hearing which has been held in public.

(3) An application for such an order may be made –

(a) by a party; or

(b) by any person to whom the document belongs.

False disclosure statements

31.23(1) Proceedings for contempt of court may be brought against a person if he makes, or causes to be made, a false disclosure statement, without an honest belief in its truth.

(2) Proceedings under this rule may be brought only –

(a) by the Attorney General; or

(b) with the permission of the court.

PRACTICE DIRECTION – DISCLOSURE AND INSPECTION
THIS PRACTICE DIRECTION SUPPLEMENTS CPR PART 31

General

1.1 The normal order for disclosure will be an order that the parties give standard disclosure.

1.2 In order to give standard disclosure the disclosing party must make a reasonable search for documents falling within the paragraphs of rule 31.6.

1.3 Having made the search the disclosing party must (unless rule 31.10(8) applies) make a list of the documents of whose existence the party is aware that fall within those paragraphs and which are or have been in the party's control (see rule 31.8).

1.4 The obligations imposed by an order for standard disclosure may be dispensed with or limited either by the court or by written agreement between the parties. Any such written agreement should be lodged with the court.

The search

2 The extent of the search which must be made will depend upon the circumstances of the case including, in particular, the factors referred to in rule 31.7(2). The parties should bear in mind the overriding principle of proportionality (see rule 1.1(2)(c)). It may, for example, be reasonable to decide not to search for documents coming into existence before some particular date, or to limit the search to documents in some particular place or places, or to documents falling into particular categories.

The list

3.1 The list should be in Form N265.

3.2 In order to comply with rule 31.10(3) it will normally be necessary to list the documents in date order, to number them consecutively and to give each a concise description (eg. letter, claimant to defendant). Where there is a large number of documents all falling into a particular category the disclosing party may list those documents as a category rather than individually e.g. 50 bank statements relating to account number _ at _ Bank, _19_ to _19_; or, 35 letters passing between _ and _ between _19_ and _19_.

3.3 The obligations imposed by an order for disclosure will continue until the proceedings come to an end. If, after a list of documents has been prepared and served, the existence of further documents to which the order applies comes to the attention of the disclosing party, the party must prepare and serve a supplemental list.

Disclosure statement

4.1 A list of documents must (unless rule 31.10(8)(b) applies) contain a disclosure statement complying with rule 31.10. The form of disclosure statement is set out in the Annex to this practice direction.

4.2 The disclosure statement should:

(1) expressly state that the disclosing party believes the extent of the search to have been reasonable in all the circumstances, and

(2) in setting out the extent of the search (see rule 31.10(6)) draw attention to any particular limitations on the extent of the search which were adopted for proportionality reasons and give the reasons why the limitations were adopted, e.g. the difficulty or expense that a search not subject to those limitations would have entailed or the marginal relevance of categories of documents omitted from the search.

4.3 Where rule 31.10(7) applies, the details given in the disclosure statement about the person making the statement must include his name and address and the office or position he holds in the disclosing party.

4.4 If the disclosing party has a legal representative acting for him, the legal representative must endeavour to ensure that the person making the disclosure statement (whether the disclosing party or, in a case to which rule 31.10(7) applies, some other person) understands the duty of disclosure under rule 31.

4.5 If the disclosing party wishes to claim that he has a right or duty to withhold a document, or part of a document, in his list of documents from inspection (see rule 31.19(3)), he must state in writing:

(1) that he has such a right or duty, and

(2) the grounds on which he claims that right or duty.

4.6 The statement referred to in paragraph 4.5 above should normally be included in the disclosure statement and must indicate the document, or part of a document, to which the claim relates.

4.7 An insurer or the Motor Insurers' Bureau may sign a disclosure statement on behalf of a party where the insurer or the Motor Insurers' Bureau has a financial interest in the result of proceedings brought wholly or partially by or against that party. Rule 31.10(7) and paragraph 4.3 above shall apply to the insurer or the Motor Insurers' Bureau making such a statement.

Specific disclosure

5.1 If a party believes that the disclosure of documents given by a disclosing party is inadequate he may make an application for an order for specific disclosure (see rule 31.12).

5.2 The application notice must specify the order that the applicant intends to ask the court to make and must be supported by evidence (see rule 31.12(2) which describes the orders the court may make).

5.3 The grounds on which the order is sought may be set out in the application notice itself but if not there set out must be set out in the evidence filed in support of the application.

5.4 In deciding whether or not to make an order for specific disclosure the court will take into account all the circumstances of the case and, in particular, the overriding objective described in Part 1. But if the court concludes that the party from whom specific disclosure is sought has failed adequately to comply with the obligations imposed by an order for disclosure (whether by failing to make a sufficient search for documents or otherwise) the court will usually make such order as is necessary to ensure that those obligations are properly complied with.

Claims to withhold disclosure or inspection of a document

6.1 A claim to withhold inspection of a document, or part of a document, disclosed in a list of documents does not require an application to the court. Where such a claim has been made, a party who wishes to challenge it must apply to the court (see rule 31.19(5)).

6.2 Rule 31.19(1) and (6) provide a procedure enabling a party to apply for an order permitting disclosure of the existence of a document to be withheld.

Inspection of documents mentioned in expert's report (Rule 31.14(e))

7. Reference should be made to the practice direction supplementing Part 35 (Experts and Assessors) for provisions dealing with applications to inspect these documents.

ANNEX

DISCLOSURE STATEMENT

I, the above named claimant [or defendant] [if party making disclosure is a company, firm or other organisation identify here who the person making the disclosure statement is and why he is the appropriate person to make it] state that I have carried out a reasonable and proportionate search to locate all the documents which I am required to disclose under the order made by the court on day of . I did not search:

(1) for documents predating .... ,
(2) for documents located elsewhere than .... ,
(3) for documents in categories other than ....

I certify that I understand the duty of disclosure and to the best of my knowledge I have carried out that duty. I certify that the list above is a complete list of all documents which are or have been in my control and which I am obliged under the said order to disclose.

PART 32

EVIDENCE

Contents of this Part

Power of court to control evidence

32.1 (1) The court may control the evidence by giving directions as to –

(a) the issues on which it requires evidence;

(b) the nature of the evidence which it requires to decide those issues; and

(c) the way in which the evidence is to be placed before the court.

(2) The court may use its power under this rule to exclude evidence that would otherwise be admissible.

(3) The court may limit cross-examination(GL).

Evidence of witnesses – general rule

32.2 (1) The general rule is that any fact which needs to be proved by the evidence of witnesses is to be proved –

  (a) at trial, by their oral evidence given in public; and

  (b) at any other hearing, by their evidence in writing.

(2) This is subject –

  (a) to any provision to the contrary contained in these Rules or elsewhere; or

  (b) to any order of the court.

Evidence by video link or other means

32.3 The court may allow a witness to give evidence through a video link or by other means.

Requirement to serve witness statements for use at trial

32.4 (1) A witness statement is a written statement signed by a person which contains the evidence which that person would be allowed to give orally.

(2) The court will order a party to serve on the other parties any witness statement of the oral evidence which the party serving the statement intends to rely on in relation to any issues of fact to be decided at the trial.

(3) The court may give directions as to –

  (a) the order in which witness statements are to be served; and

  (b) whether or not the witness statements are to be filed.

Use at trial of witness statements which have been served

32.5 (1) If –

  (a) a party has served a witness statement; and

  (b) he wishes to rely at trial on the evidence of the witness who made the statement,

  he must call the witness to give oral evidence unless the court orders otherwise or he puts the statement in as hearsay evidence.

(Part 33 contains provisions about hearsay evidence.)

(2) Where a witness is called to give oral evidence under paragraph (1), his witness statement shall stand as his evidence in chief(GL) unless the court orders otherwise.

(3) A witness giving oral evidence at trial may with the permission of the court –

  (a) amplify his witness statement; and

  (b) give evidence in relation to new matters which have arisen since the witness statement was served on the other parties.

(4) The court will give permission under paragraph (3) only if it considers that there is good reason not to confine the evidence of the witness to the contents of his witness statement.

(5) If a party who has served a witness statement does not –

  (a) call the witness to give evidence at trial; or

  (b) put the witness statement in as hearsay evidence,

  any other party may put the witness statement in as hearsay evidence.

Evidence in proceedings other than at trial

32.6 (1) Subject to paragraph (2), the general rule is that evidence at hearings other than the trial is to be by witness statement unless the court, a practice direction or any other enactment requires otherwise.

   (2) At hearings other than the trial, a party may, rely on the matters set out in –
   (a) his statement of case; or
   (b) his application notice,
   if the statement of case or application notice is verified by a statement of truth.

Order for cross-examination

32.7 (1) Where, at a hearing other than the trial, evidence is given in writing, any party may apply to the court for permission to cross-examine the person giving the evidence.

   (2) If the court gives permission under paragraph (1) but the person in question does not attend as required by the order, his evidence may not be used unless the court gives permission.

Form of witness statement

32.8   A witness statement must comply with the requirements set out in the relevant practice direction.

(Part 22 requires a witness statement to be verified by a statement of truth.)

Witness summaries

32.9 (1) A party who –
   (a) is required to serve a witness statement for use at trial; but
   (b) is unable to obtain one,
   may apply, without notice, for permission to serve a witness summary instead.
   (2) A witness summary is a summary of –
   (a) the evidence, if known, which would otherwise be included in a witness statement; or
   (b) if the evidence is not known, the matters about which the party serving the witness summary proposes to question the witness.
   (3) Unless the court orders otherwise, a witness summary must include the name and address of the intended witness.
   (4) Unless the court orders otherwise, a witness summary must be served within the period in which a witness statement would have had to be served.
   (5) Where a party serves a witness summary, so far as practicable rules 32.4 (requirement to serve witness statements for use at trial), 32.5(3) (amplifying witness statements), and 32.8 (form of witness statement) shall apply to the summary.

Consequence of failure to serve witness statement or summary

32.10   If a witness statement or a witness summary for use at trial is not served in respect of an intended witness within the time specified by the court, then the witness may not be called to give oral evidence unless the court gives permission.

Cross-examination on a witness statement

32.11   Where a witness is called to give evidence at trial, he may be cross-examined on his witness statement whether or not the statement or any part of it was referred to during the witness's evidence in chief[(GL)].

Use of witness statements for other purposes

32.12 (1) Except as provided by this rule, a witness statement may be used only for the purpose of the proceedings in which it is served.

(2) Paragraph (1) does not apply if and to the extent that –

(a) the witness gives consent in writing to some other use of it;

(b) the court gives permission for some other use; or

(c) the witness statement has been put in evidence at a hearing held in public.

Availability of witness statements for inspection

32.13 (1) A witness statement which stands as evidence in chief(GL) is open to inspection unless the court otherwise directs during the course of the trial.

(2) Any person may ask for a direction that a witness statement is not open to inspection.

(3) The court will not make a direction under paragraph (2) unless it is satisfied that a witness statement should not be open to inspection because of –

(a) the interests of justice;

(b) the public interest;

(c) the nature of any expert medical evidence in the statement;

(d) the nature of any confidential information (including information relating to personal financial matters) in the statement; or

(e) the need to protect the interests of any child or patient.

(4) The court may exclude from inspection words or passages in the statement.

False statements

32.14 (1) Proceedings for contempt of court may be brought against a person if he makes, or causes to be made, a false statement in a document verified by a statement of truth without an honest belief in its truth.

(Part 22 makes provision for a statement of truth)

(2) Proceedings under this rule may be brought only –

(a) by the Attorney General; or

(b) with the permission of the court.

Affidavit evidence

32.15 (1) Evidence must be given by affidavit(GL) instead of or in addition to a witness statement if this is required by the court, a provision contained in any other rule, a practice direction or any other enactment.

(2) Nothing in these Rules prevents a witness giving evidence by affidavit(GL) at a hearing other than the trial if he chooses to do so in a case where paragraph (1) does not apply, but the party putting forward the affidavit(GL) may not recover the additional cost of making it from any other party unless the court orders otherwise.

Form of affidavit

32.16 An affidavit(GL) must comply with the requirements set out in the relevant practice direction.

Affidavit made outside the jurisdiction

32.17 A person may make an affidavit(GL) outside the jurisdiction in accordance with –

(a) this Part; or

(b) the law of the place where he makes the affidavit(GL).

Notice to admit facts

32.18 (1) A party may serve notice on another party requiring him to admit the facts, or the part of the case of the serving party, specified in the notice.

(2) A notice to admit facts must be served no later than 21 days before the trial.

(3) Where the other party makes any admission in response to the notice, the admission may be used against him only –

(a) in the proceedings in which the notice to admit is served; and

(b) by the party who served the notice.

(4) The court may allow a party to amend or withdraw any admission made by him on such terms as it thinks just.

Notice to admit or produce documents

32.19 (1) A party shall be deemed to admit the authenticity of a document disclosed to him under Part 31 (disclosure and inspection of documents) unless he serves notice that he wishes the document to be proved at trial.

(2) A notice to prove a document must be served –

(a) by the latest date for serving witness statements; or

(b) within 7 days of disclosure of the document,

whichever is later.

PRACTICE DIRECTION – WRITTEN EVIDENCE
THIS PRACTICE DIRECTION SUPPLEMENTS CPR PART 32

Evidence in general

1.1 Rule 32.2 sets out how evidence is to be given and facts are to be proved.

1.2 Evidence at a hearing other than the trial should normally be given by witness statement[1] (see paragraph 17 onwards). However a witness may give evidence by affidavit if he wishes to do so[2] (and see paragraph 1.4 below).

1.3 Statements of case (see paragraph 26 onwards) and application notices[3] may also be used as evidence provided that their contents have been verified by a statement of truth[4].

(For information regarding evidence by deposition see Part 34 and the practice direction which supplements it.)

1.4 Affidavits must be used as evidence in the following instances:

(1) where sworn evidence is required by an enactment[5], Statutory Instrument, rule[6], order or practice direction,

(2) in any application for a search order, a freezing injunction, or an order requiring an occupier to permit another to enter his land, and

(3) in any application for an order against anyone for alleged contempt of court.

1.5 If a party believes that sworn evidence is required by a court in another jurisdiction for any

---

1   See rule 32.6(1).

2   See rule 32.15(2).

3   See Part 23 for information about making an application.

4   Rule 32.6(2) and see Part 22 for information about the statement of truth.

5   See, e.g., s. 3(5)(a) of the Protection from Harassment Act 1997.

6   See, e.g., RSC O.115 rr.(2B), (14) and others (Confiscation and Forfeiture in Connection with Criminal Proceedings) and RSC O.110 r.(3) (Environmental Control Proceedings – injunctions 'in rem' against unknown Defendant).

purpose connected with the proceedings, he may apply to the court for a direction that evidence shall be given only by affidavit on any pre-trial applications.

1.6 The court may give a direction under rule 32.15 that evidence shall be given by affidavit instead of or in addition to a witness statement or statement of case:

(1) on its own initiative, or

(2) after any party has applied to the court for such a direction.

1.7 An affidavit, where referred to in the Civil Procedure Rules or a practice direction, also means an affirmation unless the context requires otherwise.

Affidavits

Deponent

2 A deponent is a person who gives evidence by affidavit or affirmation.

Heading

3.1 The affidavit should be headed with the title of the proceedings (see paragraph 4 of the practice direction supplementing Part 7 and paragraph 7 of the practice direction supplementing Part 20); where the proceedings are between several parties with the same status it is sufficient to identify the parties as follows:

Number:

A.B. (and others)	Claimants/Applicants
C.D. (and others)	Defendants/Respondents

(as appropriate)

3.2 At the top right hand corner of the first page (and on the backsheet) there should be clearly written:

(1) the party on whose behalf it is made,

(2) the initials and surname of the deponent,

(3) the number of the affidavit in relation to that deponent,

(4) the identifying initials and number of each exhibit referred to, and

(5) the date sworn.

Body of Affidavit

4.1 The affidavit must, if practicable, be in the deponent's own words, the affidavit should be expressed in the first person and the deponent should:

(1) commence 'I (full name) of (address) state on oath......',

(2) if giving evidence in his professional, business or other occupational capacity, give the address at which he works in (1) above, the position he holds and the name of his firm or employer,

(3) give his occupation or, if he has none, his description, and

(4) state if he is a party to the proceedings or employed by a party to the proceedings, if it be the case.

4.2 An affidavit must indicate:

(1) which of the statements in it are made from the deponent's own knowledge and which are matters of information or belief, and

(2) the source for any matters of information or belief.

4.3 Where a deponent:

(1) refers to an exhibit or exhibits, he should state 'there is now shown to me marked "..." the (description of exhibit)', and

(2) makes more than one affidavit (to which there are exhibits) in the same proceedings, the numbering of the exhibits should run consecutively throughout and not start again with each affidavit.

Jurat

5.1 The jurat of an affidavit is a statement set out at the end of the document which authenticates the affidavit.

5.2 It must:

    (1) be signed by all deponents,

    (2) be completed and signed by the person before whom the affidavit was sworn whose name and qualification must be printed beneath his signature,

    (3) contain the full address of the person before whom the affidavit was sworn, and

    (4) follow immediately on from the text and not be put on a separate page.

Format of Affidavits

6.1 An affidavit should:

    (1) be produced on durable quality A4 paper with a 3.5cm margin,

    (2) be fully legible and should normally be typed on one side of the paper only,

    (3) where possible, be bound securely in a manner which would not hamper filing, or otherwise each page should be endorsed with the case number and should bear the initials of the deponent and of the person before whom it was sworn,

    (4) have the pages numbered consecutively as a separate document (or as one of several documents contained in a file),

    (5) be divided into numbered paragraphs,

    (6) have all numbers, including dates, expressed in figures, and

    (7) give in the margin the reference to any document or documents mentioned.

6.2 It is usually convenient for an affidavit to follow the chronological sequence of events or matters dealt with; each paragraph of an affidavit should as far as possible be confined to a distinct portion of the subject.

Inability of Deponent to read or sign Affidavit

7.1 Where an affidavit is sworn by a person who is unable to read or sign it, the person before whom the affidavit is sworn must certify in the jurat that:

    (1) he read the affidavit to the deponent,

    (2) the deponent appeared to understand it, and

    (3) the deponent signed or made his mark, in his presence.

7.2 If that certificate is not included in the jurat, the affidavit may not be used in evidence unless the court is satisfied that it was read to the deponent and that he appeared to understand it. Two versions of the form of jurat with the certificate are set out at Annex 1 to this practice direction.

Alterations to Affidavits

8.1 Any alteration to an affidavit must be initialled by both the deponent and the person before whom the affidavit was sworn.

8.2 An affidavit which contains an alteration that has not been initialled may be filed or used in evidence only with the permission of the court.

Who may administer oaths and take Affidavits

9.1 Only the following may administer oaths and take affidavits:

    (1) Commissioners for oaths[7],

    (2) Practising solicitors[8],

    (3) other persons specified by statute[9],

    (4) certain officials of the Supreme Court[10],

    (5) a circuit judge or district judge[11],

    (6) any justice of the peace[12], and

---

7   Commissioner for Oaths Act 1889 and 1891.

8   Section 81 of the Solicitors Act 1974.

9   Section 65 of the Administration of Justice Act 1985, s.113 of the Courts and Legal Services Act 1990 and the Commissioners for Oaths (Prescribed Bodies) Regulations 1994 and 1995.

10   Section 2 of the Commissioners for Oaths Act 1889.

11   Section 58 of the County Courts Act 1984.

12   Section 58 as above.

(7) certain officials of any county court appointed by the judge of that court for the purpose[13].

9.2 An affidavit must be sworn before a person independent of the parties or their representatives.

Filing of Affidavits

10.1 If the court directs that an affidavit is to be filed[14], it must be filed in the court or Division, or Office or Registry of the court or Division where the action in which it was or is to be used, is proceeding or will proceed.

10.2 Where an affidavit is in a foreign language:

(1) the party wishing to rely on it –

    (a) must have it translated, and

    (b) must file the foreign language affidavit with the court, and

(2) the translator must make and file with the court an affidavit verifying the translation and exhibiting both the translation and a copy of the foreign language affidavit.

Exhibits

Manner of Exhibiting Documents

11.1 A document used in conjunction with an affidavit should be:

(1) produced to and verified by the deponent, and remain separate from the affidavit, and

(2) identified by a declaration of the person before whom the affidavit was sworn.

11.2 The declaration should be headed with the name of the proceedings in the same way as the affidavit.

11.3 The first page of each exhibit should be marked:

(1) as in paragraph 3.2 above, and

(2) with the exhibit mark referred to in the affidavit.

Letters

12.1 Copies of individual letters should be collected together and exhibited in a bundle or bundles. They should be arranged in chronological order with the earliest at the top, and firmly secured.

12.2 When a bundle of correspondence is exhibited, the exhibit should have a front page attached stating that the bundle consists of original letters and copies. They should be arranged and secured as above and numbered consecutively. 14 Rules 32.1(3) and 32.4(3)(b).

Other documents

13.1 Photocopies instead of original documents may be exhibited provided the originals are made available for inspection by the other parties before the hearing and by the judge at the hearing.

13.2 Court documents must not be exhibited (official copies of such documents prove themselves).

13.3 Where an exhibit contains more than one document, a front page should be attached setting out a list of the documents contained in the exhibit; the list should contain the dates of the documents.

Exhibits other than documents

14.1 Items other than documents should be clearly marked with an exhibit number or letter in such a manner that the mark cannot become detached from the exhibit.

14.2 Small items may be placed in a container and the container appropriately marked.

General provisions

15.1 Where an exhibit contains more than one document:

(1) the bundle should not be stapled but should be securely fastened in a way that does not hinder the reading of the documents, and

(2) the pages should be numbered consecutively at bottom centre.

15.2 Every page of an exhibit should be clearly legible; typed copies of illegible documents should be included, paginated with 'a' numbers.

---

13 Section 58 as above.
14 Rules 32.1(3) and 32.4(3)(b).

15.3 Where affidavits and exhibits have become numerous, they should be put into separate bundles and the pages numbered consecutively throughout.

15.4 Where on account of their bulk the service of exhibits or copies of exhibits on the other parties would be difficult or impracticable, the directions of the court should be sought as to arrangements for bringing the exhibits to the attention of the other parties and as to their custody pending trial.

Affirmations

16 All provisions in this or any other practice direction relating to affidavits apply to affirmations with the following exceptions:

(1) the deponent should commence 'I (name) of (address) do solemnly and sincerely affirm.......', and

(2) in the jurat the word 'sworn' is replaced by the word 'affirmed'.

Witness statements

Heading

17.1 The witness statement should be headed with the title of the proceedings (see paragraph 4 of the practice direction supplementing Part 7 and paragraph 7 of the practice direction supplementing Part 20); where the proceedings are between several parties with the same status it is sufficient to identify the parties as follows:

Number:

| A.B. (and others) | Claimants/Applicants |
| C.D. (and others) | Defendants/Respondents |

(as appropriate)

17.2 At the top right hand corner of the first page there should be clearly written:

(1) the party on whose behalf it is made,

(2) the initials and surname of the witness,

(3) the number of the statement in relation to that witness,

(4) the identifying initials and number of each exhibit referred to, and

(5) the date the statement was made.

Body of witness statement

18.1 The witness statement must, if practicable, be in the intended witness's own words, the statement should be expressed in the first person and should also state:

(1) the full name of the witness,

(2) his place of residence or, if he is making the statement in his professional, business or other occupational capacity, the address at which he works, the position he holds and the name of his firm or employer,

(3) his occupation, or if he has none, his description, and

(4) the fact that he is a party to the proceedings or is the employee of such a party if it be the case.

18.2 A witness statement must indicate:

(1) which of the statements in it are made from the witness's own knowledge and which are matters of information or belief, and

(2) the source for any matters of information or belief.

18.3 An exhibit used in conjunction with a witness statement should be verified and identified by the witness and remain separate from the witness statement.

18.4 Where a witness refers to an exhibit or exhibits, he should state 'I refer to the (description of exhibit) marked "...".

18.5 The provisions of paragraphs 11.3 to 15.4 (exhibits) apply similarly to witness statements as they do to affidavits.

18.6 Where a witness makes more than one witness statement to which there are exhibits, in the same proceedings, the numbering of the exhibits should run consecutively throughout and not start again with each witness statement.

Format of witness statement

19.1 A witness statement should:

(1) be produced on durable quality A4 paper with a 3.5cm margin,

(2) be fully legible and should normally be typed on one side of the paper only,

(3) where possible, be bound securely in a manner which would not hamper filing, or otherwise each page should be endorsed with the case number and should bear the initials of the witness,

(4) have the pages numbered consecutively as a separate statement (or as one of several statements contained in a file),

(5) be divided into numbered paragraphs,

(6) have all numbers, including dates, expressed in figures, and

(7) give in the margin the reference to any document or documents mentioned.

19.2 It is usually convenient for a witness statement to follow the chronological sequence of the events or matters dealt with, each paragraph of a witness statement should as far as possible be confined to a distinct portion of the subject.

Statement of Truth

20.1 A witness statement is the equivalent of the oral evidence which that witness would, if called, give in evidence; it must include a statement by the intended witness that he believes the facts in it are true[15].

20.2 To verify a witness statement the statement of truth is as follows: 'I believe that the facts stated in this witness statement are true'

20.3 Attention is drawn to rule 32.14 which sets out the consequences of verifying a witness statement containing a false statement without an honest belief in its truth.

Inability of witness to read or sign statement

21.1 Where a witness statement is made by a person who is unable to read or sign the witness statement, it must contain a certificate made by an authorised person.

21.2 An authorised person is a person able to administer oaths and take affidavits but need not be independent of the parties or their representatives.

21.3 The authorised person must certify:

(1) that the witness statement has been read to the witness,

(2) that the witness appeared to understand it and approved its content as accurate,

(3) that the declaration of truth has been read to the witness,

(4) that the witness appeared to understand the declaration and the consequences of making a false witness statement, and

(5) that the witness signed or made his mark in the presence of the authorised person.

21.4 The form of the certificate is set out at Annex 2 to this practice direction.

Alterations to witness statements

22.1 Any alteration to a witness statement must be initialled by the person making the statement or by the authorised person where appropriate (see paragraph 21).

22.2 A witness statement which contains an alteration that has not been initialled may be used in evidence only with the permission of the court.

Filing of witness statements

23.1 If the court directs that a witness statement is to be filed[16], it must be filed in the court or Division, or Office or Registry of the court or Division where the action in which it was or is to be used, is proceeding or will proceed.

23.2 Where the court has directed that a witness statement in a foreign language is to be filed:

(1) the party wishing to rely on it must –

(a) have it translated, and

(b) file the foreign language witness statement with the court, and

---

15 See Part 22 for information about the statement of truth.

16 Rule 32.4(3)(b).

    (2) the translator must make and file with the court an affidavit verifying the translation and exhibiting both the translation and a copy of the foreign language witness statement.

Certificate of court officer

24.1 Where the court has ordered that a witness statement is not to be open to inspection by the public[17] or that words or passages in the statement are not to be open to inspection[18] the court officer will so certify on the statement and make any deletions directed by the court under rule 32.13(4).

Defects in affidavits, witness statements and exhibits

25.1 Where:

    (1) an affidavit,

    (2) a witness statement, or

    (3) an exhibit to either an affidavit or a witness statement,

does not comply with Part 32 or this practice direction in relation to its form, the court may refuse to admit it as evidence and may refuse to allow the costs arising from its preparation.

25.2 Permission to file a defective affidavit or witness statement or to use a defective exhibit may be obtained from a judge [19] in the court where the case is proceeding.

Statements of case

26.1 A statement of case may be used as evidence in an interim application provided it is verified by a statement of truth[20].

26.2 To verify a statement of case the statement of truth should be set out as follows: '[I believe][the (party on whose behalf the statement of case is being signed) believes] that the facts stated in the statement of case are true'.

26.3 Attention is drawn to rule 32.14 which sets out the consequences of verifying a witness statement containing a false statement without an honest belief in its truth.

(For information regarding statements of truth see Part 22 and the practice direction which supplements it.)

(Practice directions supplementing Parts 7, 9 and 17 provide further information concerning statements of case.)

ANNEX 1

CERTIFICATE TO BE USED WHERE A DEPONENT TO AN AFFIDAVIT IS UNABLE TO READ OR SIGN IT

Sworn at ....this......day of................. Before me, I having first read over the contents of this affidavit to the deponent [if there are exhibits, add 'and explained the nature and effect of the exhibits referred to in it'] who appeared to understand it and approved its content as accurate, and made his mark on the affidavit in my presence.

Or; (after, Before me) the witness to the mark of the deponent having been first sworn that he had read over etc. (as above) and that he saw him make his mark on the affidavit. (Witness must sign).

CERTIFICATE TO BE USED WHERE A DEPONENT TO AN AFFIRMATION IS UNABLE TO READ OR SIGN IT

Affirmed at...............this.........day of.............. Before me, I having first read over the contents of this affirmation to the deponent [if there are exhibits, add 'and explained the nature and effect of the exhibits referred to in it'] who appeared to understand it and approved its content as accurate, and made his mark on the affirmation in my presence.

---

17   Rule 32.13(2).

18   Rule 32.13(4).

19   Rule 2.3(1); definition of judge.

20   See rule 32.6(2)(a).

Or, (after, Before me) the witness to the mark of the deponent having been first sworn that he had read over etc. (as above) and that he saw him make his mark on the affirmation. (Witness must sign).

ANNEX 2

CERTIFICATE TO BE USED WHERE A WITNESS IS UNABLE TO READ OR SIGN A WITNESS STATEMENT

I certify that I [name and address of authorised person] have read over the contents of this witness statement and the declaration of truth to the witness [if there are exhibits, add 'and explained the nature and effect of the exhibits referred to in it'] who appeared to understand (a) the statement and approved its content as accurate and (b) the declaration of truth and the consequences of making a false witness statement, and made his mark in my presence.

PART 33

MISCELLANEOUS RULES ABOUT EVIDENCE

Contents of this Part

Introductory

33.1   In this Part –

(a) 'hearsay' means a statement made, otherwise than by a person while giving oral evidence in proceedings, which is tendered as evidence of the matters stated; and

(b) references to hearsay include hearsay of whatever degree.

Notice of intention to rely on hearsay evidence

33.2(1)   Where a party intends to rely on hearsay evidence at trial and either –

(a) that evidence is to be given by a witness giving oral evidence; or

(b) that evidence is contained in a witness statement of a person who is not being called to give oral evidence;

that party complies with section 2(1)(a) of the Civil Evidence Act 1995[(48)] by serving a witness statement on the other parties in accordance with the court's order.

(2)   Where paragraph (1)(b) applies, the party intending to rely on the hearsay evidence must, when he serves the witness statement –

---

(48) 1995 c.38. Section 2 provides that a party proposing to bring hearsay evidence must notify any other party of that fact and, on request, give particulars of or relating to the evidence.

(a) inform the other parties that the witness is not being called to give oral evidence; and

(b) give the reason why the witness will not be called.

(3) In all other cases where a party intends to rely on hearsay evidence at trial, that party complies with section 2(1)(a) of the Civil Evidence Act 1995 by serving a notice on the other parties which –

(a) identifies the hearsay evidence;

(b) states that the party serving the notice proposes to rely on the hearsay evidence at trial; and

(c) gives the reason why the witness will not be called.

(4) The party proposing to rely on the hearsay evidence must –

(a) serve the notice no later than the latest date for serving witness statements; and

(b) if the hearsay evidence is to be in a document, supply a copy to any party who requests him to do so.

Circumstances in which notice of intention to rely on hearsay evidence is not required

33.3 Section 2(1) of the Civil Evidence Act 1995 (duty to give notice of intention to rely on hearsay evidence) does not apply –

(a) to evidence at hearings other than trials;

(aa) to an affidavit or witness statement which is to be used at trial but which does not contain hearsay evidence;

(b) to a statement which a party to a probate action wishes to put in evidence and which is alleged to have been made by the person whose estate is the subject of the proceedings; or

(c) where the requirement is excluded by a practice direction.

Power to call witness for cross-examination on hearsay evidence

33.4(1) Where a party –

(a) proposes to rely on hearsay evidence; and

(b) does not propose to call the person who made the original statement to give oral evidence,

the court may, on the application of any other party, permit that party to call the maker of the statement to be cross-examined on the contents of the statement.

(2) An application for permission to cross-examine under this rule must be made not more than 14 days after the day on which a notice of intention to rely on the hearsay evidence was served on the applicant.

Credibility

33.5 (1) Where a party –

(a) proposes to rely on hearsay evidence; but

(b) does not propose to call the person who made the original statement to give oral evidence; and

(c) another party wishes to call evidence to attack the credibility of the person who made the statement,

the party who so wishes must give notice of his intention to the party who proposes to give the hearsay statement in evidence.

(2) A party must give notice under paragraph (1) not more than 14 days after the day on which a hearsay notice relating to the hearsay evidence was served on him.

Use of plans, photographs and models as evidence

33.6 (1) This rule applies to evidence (such as a plan, photograph or model) which is not –

    (a) contained in a witness statement, affidavit(GL) or expert's report;

    (b) to be given orally at trial; or

    (c) evidence of which prior notice must be given under rule 33.2.

(2) This rule includes documents which may be received in evidence without further proof under section 9 of the Civil Evidence Act 1995[49].

(3) Unless the court orders otherwise the evidence shall not be receivable at a trial unless the party intending to put it in evidence has given notice to the other parties in accordance with this rule.

(4) Where the party intends to use the evidence as evidence of any fact then, except where paragraph (6) applies, he must give notice not later than the latest date for serving witness statements.

(5) He must give notice at least 21 days before the hearing at which he proposes to put in the evidence, if –

    (a) there are not to be witness statements; or

    (b) he intends to put in the evidence solely in order to disprove an allegation made in a witness statement.

(6) Where the evidence forms part of expert evidence, he must give notice when the expert's report is served on the other party.

(7) Where the evidence is being produced to the court for any reason other than as part of factual or expert evidence, he must give notice at least 21 days before the hearing at which he proposes to put in the evidence.

(8) Where a party has given notice that he intends to put in the evidence, he must give every other party an opportunity to inspect it and to agree to its admission without further proof.

Evidence of finding on question of foreign law

33.7 (1) This rule sets out the procedure which must be followed by a party who intends to put in evidence a finding on a question of foreign law by virtue of section 4(2) of the Civil Evidence Act 1972[50]).

(2) He must give any other party notice of his intention.

(3) He must give the notice –

    (a) if there are to be witness statements, not later than the latest date for serving them; or

    (b) otherwise, not less than 21 days before the hearing at which he proposes to put the finding in evidence.

(4) The notice must –

    (a) specify the question on which the finding was made; and

    (b) enclose a copy of a document where it is reported or recorded.

---

(49) Section 9 of the Civil Evidence Act 1995 provides that documents that form part of the records of a business or public authority, as defined in that section, may be received in evidence without further proof.

(50) 1972 c.30.

Evidence of consent of trustee to act

33.8 A document purporting to contain the written consent of a person to act as trustee and to bear his signature verified by some other person is evidence of such consent.

PRACTICE DIRECTION – CIVIL EVIDENCE ACT 1995
THIS PRACTICE DIRECTION SUPPLEMENTS CPR PART 33

1. Section 16(3A) of the Civil Evidence Act 1995 (c. 38.) (as amended) provides that transitional provisions for the application of the provisions of the Civil Evidence Act 1995 to proceedings begun before 31st January 1997 may be made by practice direction.

2. Except as provided for by paragraph 3, the provisions of the Civil Evidence Act 1995 apply to claims commenced before 31st January 1997.

3. The provisions of the Civil Evidence Act 1995 do not apply to claims commenced before 31 January 1997 if, before 26 April 1999:
   (a) directions were given, or orders were made, as to the evidence to be given at the trial or hearing; or
   (b) the trial or hearing had begun.

PART 34

DEPOSITIONS AND COURT ATTENDANCE BY WITNESSES

Contents of this Part

Scope of this Part

34.1 (1) This Part provides –
   (a) for the circumstances in which a person may be required to attend court to give evidence or to produce a document; and
   (b) for a party to obtain evidence before a hearing to be used at the hearing.
   (2) In this Part, reference to a hearing includes a reference to the trial.

Witness summons

34.2 (1) A witness summons is a document issued by the court requiring a witness to –

    (a) attend court to give evidence; or

    (b) produce documents to the court.

(2) A witness summons must be in the relevant practice form.

(3) There must be a separate witness summons for each witness.

(4) A witness summons may require a witness to produce documents to the court either –

    (a) on the date fixed for a hearing; or

    (b) on such date as the court may direct.

(5) The only documents that a summons under this rule can require a person to produce before a hearing are documents which that person could be required to produce at the hearing.

Issue of a witness summons

34.3 (1) A witness summons is issued on the date entered on the summons by the court.

(2) A party must obtain permission from the court where he wishes to –

    (a) have a summons issued less than 7 days before the date of the trial;

    (b) have a summons issued for a witness to attend court to give evidence or to produce documents on any date except the date fixed for the trial; or

    (c) have a summons issued for a witness to attend court to give evidence or to produce documents at any hearing except the trial.

(3) A witness summons must be issued by –

    (a) the court where the case is proceeding; or

    (b) the court where the hearing in question will be held.

(4) The court may set aside[GL] or vary a witness summons issued under this rule.

Witness summons in aid of inferior court or of tribunal

34.4 (1) The court may issue a witness summons in aid of an inferior court or of a tribunal.

(2) The court which issued the witness summons under this rule may set it aside.

(3) In this rule, 'inferior court or tribunal' means any court or tribunal that does not have power to issue a witness summons in relation to proceedings before it.

Time for serving a witness summons

34.5 (1) The general rule is that a witness summons is binding if it is served at least 7 days before the date on which the witness is required to attend before the court or tribunal.

(2) The court may direct that a witness summons shall be binding although it will be served less than 7 days before the date on which the witness is required to attend before the court or tribunal.

(3) A witness summons which is –

    (a) served in accordance with this rule; and

    (b) requires the witness to attend court to give evidence,

is binding until the conclusion of the hearing at which the attendance of the witness is required.

Who is to serve a witness summons

34.6 (1) A witness summons is to be served by the court unless the party on whose behalf it is issued indicates in writing, when he asks the court to issue the summons, that he wishes to serve it himself.

(2) Where the court is to serve the witness summons, the party on whose behalf it is issued must deposit, in the court office, the money to be paid or offered to the witness under rule 34.7.

Right of witness to travelling expenses and compensation for loss of time

34.7 At the time of service of a witness summons the witness must be offered or paid –

(a) a sum reasonably sufficient to cover his expenses in travelling to and from the court; and

(b) such sum by way of compensation for loss of time as may be specified in the relevant practice direction.

Evidence by deposition

34.8 (1) A party may apply for an order for a person to be examined before the hearing takes place.

(2) A person from whom evidence is to be obtained following an order under this rule is referred to as a 'deponent' and the evidence is referred to as a 'deposition'.

(3) An order under this rule shall be for a deponent to be examined on oath before –

(a) a judge;

(b) an examiner of the court; or

(c) such other person as the court appoints.

(Rule 34.15 makes provision for the appointment of examiners of the court)

(4) The order may require the production of any document which the court considers is necessary for the purposes of the examination.

(5) The order must state the date, time and place of the examination.

(6) At the time of service of the order the deponent must be offered or paid –

(a) a sum reasonably sufficient to cover his expenses in travelling to and from the place of examination; and

(b) such sum by way of compensation for loss of time as may be specified in the relevant practice direction.

(7) Where the court makes an order for a deposition to be taken, it may also order the party who obtained the order to serve a witness statement or witness summary in relation to the evidence to be given by the person to be examined.

(Part 32 contains the general rules about witness statements and witness summaries.)

Conduct of examination

34.9 (1) Subject to any directions contained in the order for examination, the examination must be conducted in the same way as if the witness were giving evidence at a trial.

(2) If all the parties are present, the examiner may conduct the examination of a person not named in the order for examination if all the parties and the person to be examined consent.

(3) The examiner may conduct the examination in private if he considers it appropriate to do so.

(4) The examiner must ensure that the evidence given by the witness is recorded in full.

(5) The examiner must send a copy of the deposition –

    (a) to the person who obtained the order for the examination of the witness; and

    (b) to the court where the case is proceeding.

(6) The party who obtained the order must send each of the other parties a copy of the deposition which he receives from the examiner.

Enforcing attendance of witness

34.10 (1) If a person served with an order to attend before an examiner –

    (a) fails to attend; or

    (b) refuses to be sworn for the purpose of the examination or to answer any lawful question or produce any document at the examination,

a certificate of his failure or refusal, signed by the examiner, must be filed by the party requiring the deposition.

(2) On the certificate being filed, the party requiring the deposition may apply to the court for an order requiring that person to attend or to be sworn or to answer any question or produce any document, as the case may be.

(3) An application for an order under this rule may be made without notice.

(4) The court may order the person against whom an order is made under this rule to pay any costs resulting from his failure or refusal.

Use of deposition at a hearing

34.11(1) A deposition ordered under rule 34.8 may be given in evidence at a hearing unless the court orders otherwise.

(2) A party intending to put in evidence a deposition at a hearing must serve notice of his intention to do so on every other party.

(3) He must serve the notice at least 21 days before the day fixed for the hearing.

(4) The court may require a deponent to attend the hearing and give evidence orally.

(5) Where a deposition is given in evidence at trial, it shall be treated as if it were a witness statement for the purposes of rule 32.13 (availability of witness statements for inspection).

Restrictions on subsequent use of deposition taken for the purpose of any hearing except the trial

34.12(1) Where the court orders a party to be examined about his or any other assets for the purpose of any hearing except the trial, the deposition may be used only for the purpose of the proceedings in which the order was made.

(2) However, it may be used for some other purpose –

    (a) by the party who was examined;

    (b) if the party who was examined agrees; or

    (c) if the court gives permission.

Where a person to be examined is out of the jurisdiction – letter of request

34.13(1) Where a party wishes to take a deposition from a person outside the jurisdiction, the High Court may order the issue of a letter of request to the judicial authorities of the country in which the proposed deponent is.

(2) A letter of request is a request to a judicial authority to take the evidence of that person, or arrange for it to be taken.

(3) The High Court may make an order under this rule in relation to county court proceedings.

(4) If the government of a country allows a person appointed by the High Court to examine a person in that country, the High Court may make an order appointing a special examiner for that purpose.

(5) A person may be examined under this rule on oath or affirmation or in accordance with any procedure permitted in the country in which the examination is to take place.

(6) If the High Court makes an order for the issue of a letter of request, the party who sought the order must file –

    (a) the following documents and, except where paragraph (7) applies, a translation of them –

        (i) a draft letter of request;

        (ii) a statement of the issues relevant to the proceedings;

        (iii) a list of questions or the subject matter of questions to be put to the person to be examined; and

    (b) an undertaking to be responsible for the Secretary of State's expenses.

(7) There is no need to file a translation if –

    (a) English is one of the official languages of the country where the examination is to take place; or

    (b) a practice direction has specified that country as a country where no translation is necessary.

Fees and expenses of examiner of the court

34.14(1) An examiner of the court may charge a fee for the examination.

(2) He need not send the deposition to the court unless the fee is paid.

(3) The examiner's fees and expenses must be paid by the party who obtained the order for examination.

(4) If the fees and expenses due to an examiner are not paid within a reasonable time, he may report that fact to the court.

(5) The court may order the party who obtained the order for examination to deposit in the court office a specified sum in respect of the examiner's fees and, where it does so, the examiner will not be asked to act until the sum has been deposited.

(6) An order under this rule does not affect any decision as to the party who is ultimately to bear the costs of the examination.

Examiners of the court

34.15 (1) The Lord Chancellor shall appoint persons to be examiners of the court.

(2) The persons appointed shall be barristers or solicitor-advocates who have been practising for a period of not less than three years.

(3) The Lord Chancellor may revoke an appointment at any time.

(Other relevant rules can be found in Schedule 1, in the following RSC – O.70 (obtaining evidence for foreign court); O.79 (issue of witness summons in relation to criminal proceedings in the High Court).)

PRACTICE DIRECTION – DEPOSITIONS AND COURT ATTENDANCE BY WITNESSES
THIS PRACTICE DIRECTION SUPPLEMENTS CPR PART 34

Witness summonses

Issue of witness summons

1.1 A witness summons may require a witness to:
    (1) attend court to give evidence,
    (2) produce documents to the court, or
    (3) both, on either a date fixed for the hearing or such date as the court may direct[1].

1.2 Two copies of the witness summons[2] should be filed with the court for sealing, one of which will be retained on the court file.

1.3 A mistake in the name or address of a person named in a witness summons may be corrected if the summons has not been served.

1.4 The corrected summons must be re-sealed by the court and marked 'Amended and Re-Sealed'.

Witness summons issued in aid of an inferior court or tribunal

2.1 A witness summons may be issued in the High Court or a county court in aid of a court or tribunal which does not have the power to issue a witness summons in relation to the proceedings before it[3].

2.2 A witness summons referred to in paragraph 2.1 may be set aside by the court which issued it[4].

2.3 An application to set aside a witness summons referred to in paragraph 2.1 will be heard:
    (1) in the High Court by a Master at the Royal Courts of Justice or by a district judge in a District Registry, and
    (2) in a county court by a district judge.

2.4 Unless the court otherwise directs, the applicant must give at least 2 days' notice to the party who issued the witness summons of the application, which will normally be dealt with at a hearing.

Travelling expenses and compensation for loss of time

3.1 When a witness is served with a witness summons he must be offered a sum to cover his travelling expenses to and from the court and compensation for his loss of time[5].

3.2 If the witness summons is to be served by the court, the party issuing the summons must deposit with the court:
    (1) a sum sufficient to pay for the witness's expenses in travelling to the court and in returning to his home or place of work, and
    (2) a sum in respect of the period during which earnings or benefit are lost, or such lesser sum as it may be proved that the witness will lose as a result of his attendance at court in answer to the witness summons.

3.3 The sum referred to in 3.2(2) is to be based on the sums payable to witnesses attending the Crown Court[6].

3.4 Where the party issuing the witness summons wishes to serve it himself[7], he must:
    (1) notify the court in writing that he wishes to do so, and
    (2) at the time of service offer the witness the sums mentioned in paragraph 3.2 above.

---

1   Rule 34.2(4).
2   in Practice form N20.
3   Rule 34.4(1).
4   Rule 34.4(2).
5   Rule 34.7.
6   Fixed pursuant to the Prosecution of Offences Act 1985 and the Costs in Criminal Cases General Regulations 1986.
7   Rule 34.6(1).

Depositions

To be taken in England and Wales for use as evidence in proceedings in courts in England and Wales

4.1 A party may apply for an order for a person to be examined on oath before:

(1) a judge,

(2) an examiner of the court, or

(3) such other person as the court may appoint[8].

4.2 The party who obtains an order for the examination of a deponent[9] before an examiner of the court[10] must:

(1) apply to the Foreign Process Section of the Masters' Secretary's Department at the Royal Courts of Justice for the allocation of an examiner,

(2) when allocated, provide the examiner with copies of all documents in the proceedings necessary to inform the examiner of the issues, and

(3) pay the deponent a sum to cover his travelling expenses to and from the examination and compensation for his loss of time[11].

4.3 In ensuring that the deponent's evidence is recorded in full, the court or the examiner may permit it to be recorded on audiotape or videotape, but the deposition[12] must always be recorded in writing by him or by a competent shorthand writer or stenographer.

4.4 If the deposition is not recorded word for word, it must contain, as nearly as may be, the statement of the deponent; the examiner may record word for word any particular questions and answers which appear to him to have special importance.

4.5 If a deponent objects to answering any question or where any objection is taken to any question, the examiner must:

(1) record in the deposition or a document attached to it –

(a) the question,

(b) the nature of and grounds for the objection, and

(c) any answer given, and

(2) give his opinion as to the validity of the objection and must record it in the deposition or a document attached to it.

The court will decide as to the validity of the objection and any question of costs arising from it.

4.6 Documents and exhibits must:

(1) have an identifying number or letter marked on them by the examiner, and

(2) be preserved by the party or his legal representative[13] who obtained the order for the examination, or as the court or the examiner may direct.

4.7 The examiner may put any question to the deponent as to:

(1) the meaning of any of his answers, or

(2) any matter arising in the course of the examination.

4.8 Where a deponent:

(1) fails to attend the examination, or

(2) refuses to:

(a) be sworn, or

(b) answer any lawful question, or

(c) produce any document,

---

8   Rule 34.8(3).

9   See rule 34.8(2) for explanation of 'deponent' and 'deposition'.

10 For the appointment of examiners of the court see rule 34.15.

11 Rule 34.8(6).

12 See rule 34.8(2) for explanation of 'deponent' and 'deposition'.

13 For the definition of legal representative see rule 2.3.

the examiner will sign a certificate[14] of such failure or refusal and may include in his certificate any comment as to the conduct of the deponent or of any person attending the examination.

4.9 The party who obtained the order for the examination must file the certificate with the court and may apply for an order that the deponent attend for examination or as may be[15]. The application may be made without notice[16].

4.10 The court will make such order on the application as it thinks fit including an order for the deponent to pay any costs resulting from his failure or refusal[17].

4.11 A deponent who wilfully refuses to obey an order made against him under Part 34 may be proceeded against for contempt of court.

4.12 A deposition must:

(1) be signed by the examiner,

(2) have any amendments to it initialled by the examiner and the deponent,

(3) be endorsed by the examiner with –

(a) a statement of the time occupied by the examination, and

(b) a record of any refusal by the deponent to sign the deposition and of his reasons for not doing so, and

(4) be sent by the examiner to the court where the proceedings are taking place for filing on the court file.

4.13 Rule 34.14 deals with the fees and expenses of an examiner.

Depositions to be taken abroad for use as evidence in proceedings before courts in England and Wales

5.1 Where a party wishes to take a deposition from a person outside the jurisdiction, the High Court may order the issue of a letter of request to the judicial authorities of the country in which the proposed deponent is[18].

5.2 An application for an order referred to in paragraph 5.1 should be made by application notice in accordance with Part 23.

5.3 The documents which a party applying for an order for the issue of a letter of request must file with his application notice are set out in rule 34.13(6). They are as follows:

(1) a draft letter of request in the form set out in Annex A to this practice direction,

(2) a statement of the issues relevant to the proceedings,

(3) a list of questions or the subject matter of questions to be put to the proposed deponent,

(4) a translation of the documents in (1), (2) and (3) above unless the proposed deponent is in a country –

(a) of which English is one of the official languages, or

(b) listed at Annex B to this practice direction, unless the particular circumstances of the case require a translation,

(5) an undertaking to be responsible for the expenses of the Secretary of State, and

(6) a draft order.

5.4 The above documents should be filed with the Masters' Secretary in Room E214, Royal Courts of Justice, Strand, London WC2A 2LL.

5.5 The application will be dealt with by the Senior Master of the Queen's Bench Division of the High Court who will, if appropriate, sign the letter of request.

5.6 Attention is drawn to the provisions of rule 23.10 (application to vary or discharge an order made without notice).

---

14 Rule 34.10.
15 Rule 34.10(2) and (3).
16 Rule 34.10(3).
17 Rule 34.10(4).
18 Rule 34.13(1).

5.7 If parties are in doubt as to whether a translation under paragraph 5.3(4) above is required, they should seek guidance from the Foreign Process Section of the Masters' Secretary's Department.

5.8 A special examiner appointed under rule 34.13(4) may be the British Consul or the Consul-General or his deputy in the country where the evidence is to be taken if:

(1) there is in respect of that country a Civil Procedure Convention providing for the taking of evidence in that country for the assistance of proceedings in the High Court or other court in this country, or

(2) with the consent of the Secretary of State.

5.9 The provisions of paragraphs 4.1 to 4.12 above apply to the depositions referred to in this paragraph.

Depositions to be taken in England and Wales for use as evidence in proceedings before courts abroad pursuant to letters of request

6.1 Schedule 1 to Part 50 (RSC Order 70) relating to obtaining evidence for foreign courts applies to letters of request and should be read in conjunction with this part of the practice direction.

6.2 The Evidence (Proceedings in Other Jurisdictions) Act 1975 applies to these depositions.

6.3 Where a foreign court sends a letter of request under which it is proposed that an application to give effect to the request be made by an agent in England or Wales of a party to the foreign proceedings, the application should be made by an application notice (see CPR Part 23) and should be supported by a witness statement or affidavit exhibiting:

(1) the letter of request;

(2) a statement of the issues relevant to the proceedings;

(3) a list of questions or the subject matter of questions to be put to the proposed deponent;

(4) a translation of the documents in (1), (2) and (3) above if necessary; and

(5) a draft order.

6.4 Where the application to give effect to the request is made by the Treasury Solicitor (see RSC Order 70 rule 3), he must provide to the court:

(1) a statement of the issues relevant to the proceedings;

(2) a list of questions or the subject matter of questions to be put to the proposed deponent;

(3) a translation of

(a) the documents in (1) and (2) above and

(b) the letter of request, if necessary; and

(4) a draft order.

6.5 The order for the deponent to attend and be examined together with the evidence upon which the order was made must be served on the deponent.

6.6 Attention is drawn to the provisions of rule 23.10 (application to vary or discharge an order made without notice).

6.7 Arrangements for the examination to take place at a specified time and place before an examiner of the court or such other person as the court may appoint shall be made by the applicant for the order (ie. the agent referred to in paragraph 6.3 or the Treasury Solicitor) and approved by the Senior Master.

6.8 The provisions of paragraph 4.2 to 4.12 apply to the depositions referred to in this paragraph, except that the examiner must send the deposition to the Senior Master.

(For further information about evidence see Part 32 and the practice direction which supplements it.)

ANNEX A

DRAFT LETTER OF REQUEST

To the Competent Judicial Authority of   in the   of

I [name] Senior Master of the Queen's Bench Division of the Supreme Court of England and Wales respectfully request the assistance of your court with regard to the following matters.

1. A claim is now pending in the   Division of the High Court of Justice in England and Wales entitled as follows

    [set out full title and claim number]

    in which [name] of [address] is the claimant and [name] of [address] is the defendant.

2. The names and addresses of the representatives or agents of [set out names and addresses of representatives of the parties].

3. The claim by the claimant is for:-

    (a) [set out the nature of the claim]

    (b) [the relief sought, and]

    (c) [a summary of the facts.]

4. It is necessary for the purposes of justice and for the due determination of the matters in dispute between the parties that you cause the following witnesses, who are resident within your jurisdiction, to be examined. The names and addresses of the witnesses are as follows:-

5. The witnesses should be examined on oath or if that is not possible within your laws or is impossible of performance by reason of the internal practice and procedure of your court or by reason of practical difficulties, they should be examined in accordance with whatever procedure your laws provide for in these matters.

6. Either/

The witnesses should be examined in accordance with the list of questions annexed hereto.

Or/

The witnesses should be examined regarding [set out full details of evidence sought]

N.B. Where the witness is required to produce documents, these should be clearly identified.

7. I would ask that you cause me, or the agents of the parties (if appointed), to be informed of the date and place where the examination is to take place.

8. Finally, I request that you will cause the evidence of the said witnesses to be reduced into writing and all documents produced on such examinations to be duly marked for identification and that you will further be pleased to authenticate such examinations by the seal of your court or in such other way as is in accordance with your procedure and return the written evidence and documents produced to me addressed as follows:-

    Senior Master of the Queen's Bench Division

    Royal Courts of Justice

    Strand

    London WC2A 2LL

    England

ANNEX B

Countries where the translation referred to in paragraph 5.3(4) above should not be required:

    Australia

    Canada (other than Quebec)

    Holland

    New Zealand

    The United States of America

PRACTICE DIRECTION – FEES FOR EXAMINERS OF THE COURT
THIS PRACTICE DIRECTION SUPPLEMENTS CPR PART 34

Scope

1.1 This practice direction sets out–
  (1) how to calculate the fees an examiner of the court ("an examiner") may charge; and
  (2) the expenses he may recover.

(CPR Rule 34.8 (3) (b) provides that the court may make an order for evidence to be obtained by the examination of a witness before an examiner of the court).

1.2 The party who obtained the order for the examination must pay the fees and expenses of the examiner.

(CPR rule 34.14 permits an examiner to charge a fee for the examination and contains other provisions about his fees and expenses, and rule 34.15 provides who may be appointed as an examiner of the court).

The examination fee

2.1 An examiner may charge an hourly rate for each hour (or part of an hour) that he is engaged in examining the witness.

2.2 The hourly rate is to be calculated by reference to the formula set out in paragraph 3.

2.3 The examination fee will be the hourly rate multiplied by the number of hours the examination has taken. For example-Examination fee = hourly rate x number of hours.

How to calculate the hourly rate – the formula

3.1 Divide the amount of the minimum annual salary of a post within Group 7 of the judicial salary structure as designated by the Review Body on Senior Salaries[1] , by 220 to give 'x'; and then divide 'x' by 6 to give the hourly rate.

For example:

$$\frac{\text{minimum annual salary}}{220} = x$$

$$\frac{x}{6} = \text{hourly rate}$$

Single fee chargeable on making the appointment for examination

4.1 An examiner of court is also entitled to charge a single fee of twice the hourly rate (calculated in accordance with paragraph 3 above) as "the appointment fee" when the appointment for the examination is made.

4.2 The examiner is entitled to retain the appointment fee where the witness fails to attend on the date and time arranged.

4.3 Where the examiner fails to attend on the date and time arranged he may not charge a further appointment fee for arranging a subsequent appointment.

(The examiner need not send the deposition to the court until his fees are paid – see CPR rule 34.14 (2)).

Examiners' expenses

5.1 The examiner of court is also entitled to recover the following expenses-
  (1) all reasonable travelling expenses;
  (2) any other expenses reasonably incurred; and
  (3) subject to paragraph 5.2, any reasonable charge for the room where the examination takes place.

---

1   The Report of the Review Body on Senior Salaries is published annually by the Stationery Office.

5.2 No expenses may be recovered under sub-paragraph (3) above if the examination takes place at the examiner's usual business address.

(If the examiner's fees and expenses are not paid within a reasonable time he may report the fact to the court, see CPR Rule 34.14 (4) and (5)).

PART 35

EXPERTS AND ASSESSORS

Contents of this Part

Duty to restrict expert evidence

35.1   Expert evidence shall be restricted to that which is reasonably required to resolve the proceedings.

Interpretation

35.2   A reference to an 'expert' in this Part is a reference to an expert who has been instructed to give or prepare evidence for the purpose of court proceedings.

Experts – overriding duty to the court

35.3 (1) It is the duty of an expert to help the court on the matters within his expertise.

(2) This duty overrides any obligation to the person from whom he has received instructions or by whom he is paid.

Court's power to restrict expert evidence

35.4 (1) No party may call an expert or put in evidence an expert's report without the court's permission.

(2) When a party applies for permission under this rule he must identify –

(a) the field in which he wishes to rely on expert evidence; and

(b) where practicable the expert in that field on whose evidence he wishes to rely.

(3) If permission is granted under this rule it shall be in relation only to the expert named or the field identified under paragraph (2).

(4) The court may limit the amount of the expert's fees and expenses that the party who wishes to rely on the expert may recover from any other party.

General requirement for expert evidence to be given in a written report

35.5 (1) Expert evidence is to be given in a written report unless the court directs otherwise.

(2) If a claim is on the fast track, the court will not direct an expert to attend a hearing unless it is necessary to do so in the interests of justice.

Written questions to experts

35.6 (1) A party may put to –

(a) an expert instructed by another party; or

(b) a single joint expert appointed under rule 35.7,

written questions about his report.

(2) Written questions under paragraph (1) –

(a) may be put once only;

(b) must be put within 28 days of service of the expert's report; and

(c) must be for the purpose only of clarification of the report,

unless in any case –

(i) the court gives permission; or

(ii) the other party agrees.

(3) An expert's answers to questions put in accordance with paragraph (1) shall be treated as part of the expert's report.

(4) Where –

(a) a party has put a written question to an expert instructed by another party in accordance with this rule; and

(b) the expert does not answer that question,

the court may make one or both of the following orders in relation to the party who instructed the expert –

(i) that the party may not rely on the evidence of that expert; or

(ii) that the party may not recover the fees and expenses of that expert from any other party.

Court's power to direct that evidence is to be given by a single joint expert

35.7 (1) Where two or more parties wish to submit expert evidence on a particular issue, the court may direct that the evidence on that issue is to given by one expert only.

(2) The parties wishing to submit the expert evidence are called 'the instructing parties'.

(3) Where the instructing parties cannot agree who should be the expert, the court may –

(a) select the expert from a list prepared or identified by the instructing parties; or

(b) direct that the expert be selected in such other manner as the court may direct.

Instructions to a single joint expert

35.8 (1) Where the court gives a direction under rule 35.7 for a single joint expert to be used, each instructing party may give instructions to the expert.

(2) When an instructing party gives instructions to the expert he must, at the same time, send a copy of the instructions to the other instructing parties.

(3) The court may give directions about –

(a) the payment of the expert's fees and expenses; and

(b) any inspection, examination or experiments which the expert wishes to carry out.

(4) The court may, before an expert is instructed –

(a) limit the amount that can be paid by way of fees and expenses to the expert; and

(b) direct that the instructing parties pay that amount into court.

(5) Unless the court otherwise directs, the instructing parties are jointly and severally liable(GL) for the payment of the expert's fees and expenses.

Power of court to direct a party to provide information

35.9 Where a party has access to information which is not reasonably available to the other party, the court may direct the party who has access to the information to –

(a) prepare and file a document recording the information; and

(b) serve a copy of that document on the other party.

Contents of report

35.10 (1) An expert's report must comply with the requirements set out in the relevant practice direction.

(2) At the end of an expert's report there must be a statement that –

(a) the expert understands his duty to the court; and

(b) he has complied with that duty.

(3) The expert's report must state the substance of all material instructions, whether written or oral, on the basis of which the report was written.

(4) The instructions referred to in paragraph (3) shall not be privileged(GL) against disclosure but the court will not, in relation to those instructions –

(a) order disclosure of any specific document; or

(b) permit any questioning in court, other than by the party who instructed the expert,

unless it is satisfied that there are reasonable grounds to consider the statement of instructions given under paragraph (3) to be inaccurate or incomplete.

Use by one party of expert's report disclosed by another

35.11 Where a party has disclosed an expert's report, any party may use that expert's report as evidence at the trial.

Discussions between experts

35.12 (1) The court may, at any stage, direct a discussion between experts for the purpose of requiring the experts to –

(a) identify the issues in the proceedings; and

(b) where possible, reach agreement on an issue.

(2) The court may specify the issues which the experts must discuss.

(3) The court may direct that following a discussion between the experts they must prepare a statement for the court showing –

(a) those issues on which they agree; and

(b) those issues on which they disagree and a summary of their reasons for disagreeing.

(4) The content of the discussion between the experts shall not be referred to at the trial unless the parties agree.

(5) Where experts reach agreement on an issue during their discussions, the agreement shall not bind the parties unless the parties expressly agree to be bound by the agreement.

Consequence of failure to disclose expert's report

35.13   A party who fails to disclose an expert's report may not use the report at the trial or call the expert to give evidence orally unless the court gives permission.

Expert's right to ask court for directions

35.14 (1) An expert may file a written request for directions to assist him in carrying out his function as an expert.

(2) An expert may request directions under paragraph (1) without giving notice to any party.

(3) The court, when it gives directions, may also direct that a party be served with –

   (a) a copy of the directions; and

   (b) a copy of the request for directions.

Assessors

35.15 (1) This rule applies where the court appoints one or more persons (an 'assessor') under section 70 of the Supreme Court Act 1981[51] or section 63 of the County Courts Act 1984[52].

(2) The assessor shall assist the court in dealing with a matter in which the assessor has skill and experience.

(3) An assessor shall take such part in the proceedings as the court may direct and in particular the court may –

   (a) direct the assessor to prepare a report for the court on any matter at issue in the proceedings; and

   (b) direct the assessor to attend the whole or any part of the trial to advise the court on any such matter.

(4) If the assessor prepares a report for the court before the trial has begun –

   (a) the court will send a copy to each of the parties; and

   (b) the parties may use it at trial.

(5) The remuneration to be paid to the assessor for his services shall be determined by the court and shall form part of the costs of the proceedings.

(6) The court may order any party to deposit in the court office a specified sum in respect of the assessor's fees and, where it does so, the assessor will not be asked to act until the sum has been deposited.

(7) Paragraphs (5) and (6) do not apply where the remuneration of the assessor is to be paid out of money provided by Parliament.

---

(51) 1981 c.54.
(52) 1984 c.28. Section 63 was amended by S.I. 1998/2940.

PRACTICE DIRECTION – EXPERTS AND ASSESSORS
THIS PRACTICE DIRECTION SUPPLEMENTS CPR PART 35

Part 35 is intended to limit the use of oral expert evidence to that which is reasonably required. In addition, where possible, matters requiring expert evidence should be dealt with by a single expert. Permission of the court is always required either to call an expert or to put an expert's report in evidence.

Form and content of expert's reports

1.1 An expert's report should be addressed to the court and not to the party from whom the expert has received his instructions.

1.2 An expert's report must:

(1) give details of the expert's qualifications,

(2) give details of any literature or other material which the expert has relied on in making the report,

(3) say who carried out any test or experiment which the expert has used for the report and whether or not the test or experiment has been carried out under the expert's supervision,

(4) give the qualifications of the person who carried out any such test or experiment, and

(5) where there is a range of opinion on the matters dealt with in the report –

    (i) summarise the range of opinion, and

    (ii) give reasons for his own opinion,

(6) contain a summary of the conclusions reached,

(7) contain a statement that the expert understands his duty to the court and has complied with that duty (rule 35.10(2)), and

(8) contain a statement setting out the substance of all material instructions (whether written or oral). The statement should summarise the facts and instructions given to the expert which are material to the opinions expressed in the report or upon which those opinions are based (rule 35.10(3)).

1.3 An expert's report must be verified by a statement of truth as well as containing the statements required in paragraph 1.2 (7) and (8) above.

1.4 The form of the statement of truth is as follows: ' I believe that the facts I have stated in this report are true and that the opinions I have expressed are correct.'

1.5 Attention is drawn to rule 32.14 which sets out the consequences of verifying a document containing a false statement without an honest belief in its truth.

(For information about statements of truth see Part 22 and the practice direction which supplements it.)

1.6 In addition, an expert's report should comply with the requirements of any approved expert's protocol.

Information

2 Under Part 35.9 the court may direct a party with access to information which is not reasonably available to another party to serve on that other party a document which records the information. The document served must include sufficient details of all the facts, tests, experiments and assumptions which underlie any part of the information to enable the party on whom it is served to make, or to obtain, a proper interpretation of the information and an assessment of its significance.

Instructions

3 The instructions referred to in paragraph 1.2(8) will not be protected by privilege (see rule 35.10(4)). But cross-examination of the expert on the contents of his instructions will not be allowed unless the court permits it (or unless the party who gave the instructions consents to it). Before it gives permission the court must be satisfied that there are reasonable grounds to consider that the statement in the report of the substance of the instructions is inaccurate or incomplete. If the court is so satisfied, it will allow the cross-examination where it appears to be in the interests of justice to do so.

QUESTIONS TO EXPERTS

4.1 Questions asked for the purpose of clarifying the expert's report (see rule 35.6) should be put, in writing, to the expert not later than 28 days after receipt of the expert's report (see paragraphs 1.2 to 1.5 above as to verification).

4.2 Where a party sends a written question or questions direct to an expert and the other party is represented by solicitors, a copy of the questions should, at the same time, be sent to those solicitors.

4.3 The party or parties instructing the expert must pay any fees charged by that expert for answering questions put under rule 35.6. This does not affect any decision of the court as to the party who is ultimately to bear the expert's costs.

SINGLE EXPERT

5 Where the court has directed that the evidence on a particular issue is to be given by one expert only (rule 35.7) but there are a number of disciplines relevant to that issue, a leading expert in the dominant discipline should be identified as the single expert. He should prepare the general part of the report and be responsible for annexing or incorporating the contents of any reports from experts in other disciplines.

ASSESSORS

6.1 An assessor may be appointed to assist the court under rule 35.15. Not less than 21 days before making any such appointment, the court will notify each party in writing of the name of the proposed assessor, of the matter in respect of which the assistance of the assessor will be sought and of the qualifications of the assessor to give that assistance.

6.2 Where any person has been proposed for appointment as an assessor, objection to him, either personally or in respect of his qualification, may be taken by any party.

6.3 Any such objection must be made in writing and filed with the court within 7 days of receipt of the notification referred to in paragraph 6.1 and will be taken into account by the court in deciding whether or not to make the appointment (section 63(5) of the County Courts Act 1984).

6.4 Copies of any report prepared by the assessor will be sent to each of the parties but the assessor will not give oral evidence or be open to cross-examination or questioning.

PART 36

OFFERS TO SETTLE AND PAYMENTS INTO COURT

Contents of this Part

Scope of this Part

36.1 (1) This Part contains rules about –

    (a) offers to settle and payments into court; and

    (b) the consequences where an offer to settle or payment into court is made in accordance with this Part.

  (2) Nothing in this Part prevents a party making an offer to settle in whatever way he chooses, but if that offer is not made in accordance with this Part, it will only have the consequences specified in this Part if the court so orders.

(Part 36 applies to Part 20 claims by virtue of rule 20.3.)

Part 36 offers and Part 36 payments – general provisions

36.2 (1) An offer made in accordance with the requirements of this Part is called –

    (a) if made by way of a payment into court, 'a Part 36 payment';

    (b) otherwise 'a Part 36 offer'.

(Rule 36.3 sets out when an offer has to be made by way of a payment into court)

  (2) The party who makes an offer is the 'offeror'.

  (3) The party to whom an offer is made is the 'offeree'.

  (4) A Part 36 offer or a Part 36 payment –

    (a) may be made at any time after proceedings have started; and

    (b) may be made in appeal proceedings.

  (5) A Part 36 offer or a Part 36 payment shall not have the consequences set out in this Part while the claim is being dealt with on the small claims track unless the court orders otherwise.

(Part 26 deals with allocation to the small claims track.)

(Rule 27.2 provides that Part 36 does not apply to small claims.)

A defendant's offer to settle a money claim requires a Part 36 payment

36.3 (1) Subject to rules 36.5(5) and 36.23, an offer by a defendant to settle a money claim will not have the consequences set out in this Part unless it is made by way of a Part 36 payment.

  (2) A Part 36 payment may only be made after proceedings have started.

(Rule 36.5(5) permits a Part 36 offer to be made by reference to an interim payment.)

(Rule 36.10 makes provision for an offer to settle a money claim before the commencement of proceedings.)

(Rule 36.23 makes provision for where benefit is recoverable under the Social Security (Recovery of Benefit) Act 1997[53].)

Defendant's offer to settle the whole of a claim which includes both a money claim and a non-money claim

36.4(1) This rule applies where a defendant to a claim which includes both a money claim and a non-money claim wishes –

    (a) to make an offer to settle the whole claim which will have the consequences set out in this Part; and

    (b) to make a money offer in respect of the money claim and a non-money offer in respect of the non-money claim.

  (2) The defendant must –

    (a) make a Part 36 payment in relation to the money claim; and

    (b) make a Part 36 offer in relation to the non-money claim.

  (3) The Part 36 payment notice must –

    (a) identify the document which sets out the terms of the Part 36 offer; and

    (b) state that if the claimant gives notice of acceptance of the Part 36 payment he will be treated as also accepting the Part 36 offer.

(Rule 36.6 makes provision for a Part 36 payment notice.)

  (4) If the claimant gives notice of acceptance of the Part 36 payment, he shall also be taken as giving notice of acceptance of the Part 36 offer in relation to the non-money claim.

Form and content of a Part 36 offer

36.5(1) A Part 36 offer must be in writing.

  (2) A Part 36 offer may relate to the whole claim or to part of it or to any issue that arises in it.

  (3) A Part 36 offer must –

    (a) state whether it relates to the whole of the claim or to part of it or to an issue that arises in it and if so to which part or issue;

    (b) state whether it takes into account any counterclaim; and

    (c) if it is expressed not to be inclusive of interest, give the details relating to interest set out in rule 36.22(2).

  (4) A defendant may make a Part 36 offer limited to accepting liability up to a specified proportion.

  (5) A Part 36 offer may be made by reference to an interim payment.

(Part 25 contains provisions relating to interim payments)

  (6) A Part 36 offer made not less than 21 days before the start of the trial must –

    (a) be expressed to remain open for acceptance for 21 days from the date it is made; and

    (b) provide that after 21 days the offeree may only accept it if –

      (i) the parties agree the liability for costs; or

      (ii) the court gives permission.

  (7) A Part 36 offer made less than 21 days before the start of the trial must state that the offeree may only accept it if –

    (a) the parties agree the liability for costs; or

    (b) the court gives permission.

---

(53) 1997 c.27.

(Rule 36.8 makes provision for when a Part 36 offer is treated as being made.)

(8) If a Part 36 offer is withdrawn it will not have the consequences set out in this Part.

Notice of a Part 36 payment

36.6(1) A Part 36 payment may relate to the whole claim or part of it or to an issue that arises in it.

(2) A defendant who makes a Part 36 payment must file with the court a notice ('Part 36 payment notice') which –

(a) states the amount of the payment;

(b) states whether the payment relates to the whole claim or to part of it or to any issue that arises in it and if so to which part or issue;

(c) states whether it takes into account any counterclaim;

(d) if an interim payment has been made, states that the defendant has taken into account the interim payment; and

(e) if it is expressed not to be inclusive of interest, gives the details relating to interest set out in rule 36.22(2).

(Rule 25.6 makes provision for an interim payment.)

(Rule 36.4 provides for further information to be included where a defendant wishes to settle the whole of a claim which includes a money claim and a non-money claim.)

(Rule 36.23 makes provision for extra information to be included in the payment notice in a case where benefit is recoverable under the Social Security (Recovery of Benefit) Act 1997.)

(3) The court will serve the Part 36 payment notice on the offeree unless the offeror informs the court, when the money is paid into court, that the offeror will serve the notice.

(4) Where the offeror serves the Part 36 payment notice he must file a certificate of service.

(Rule 6.10 specifies what must be contained in a certificate of service.)

(5) A Part 36 payment may be withdrawn only with the permission of the court.

Offer to settle a claim for provisional damages

36.7(1) A defendant may make a Part 36 payment in respect of a claim which includes a claim for provisional damages.

(2) Where he does so, the Part 36 payment notice must specify whether or not the defendant is offering to agree to the making of an award of provisional damages.

(3) Where the defendant is offering to agree to the making of an award of provisional damages the payment notice must also state –

(a) that the sum paid into court is in satisfaction of the claim for damages on the assumption that the injured person will not develop the disease or suffer the type of deterioration specified in the notice;

(b) that the offer is subject to the condition that the claimant must make any claim for further damages within a limited period; and

(c) what that period is.

(4) Where a Part 36 payment is –

(a) made in accordance with paragraph (3); and

(b) accepted within the relevant period in rule 36.11,

the Part 36 payment will have the consequences set out in rule 36.13, unless the court orders otherwise.

(5) If the claimant accepts the Part 36 payment he must, within 7 days of doing so, apply to the court for an order for an award of provisional damages under rule 41.2.

(Rule 41.2 provides for an order for an award of provisional damages.)

(6) The money in court may not be paid out until the court has disposed of the application made in accordance with paragraph (5).

Time when a Part 36 offer or a Part 36 payment is made and accepted

36.8(1) A Part 36 offer is made when received by the offeree.

(2) A Part 36 payment is made when written notice of the payment into court is served on the offeree.

(3) An improvement to a Part 36 offer will be effective when its details are received by the offeree.

(4) An increase in a Part 36 payment will be effective when notice of the increase is served on the offeree.

(5) A Part 36 offer or Part 36 payment is accepted when notice of its acceptance is received by the offeror.

Clarification of a Part 36 offer or a Part 36 payment notice

36.9(1) The offeree may, within 7 days of a Part 36 offer or payment being made, request the offeror to clarify the offer or payment notice.

(2) If the offeror does not give the clarification requested under paragraph (1) within 7 days of receiving the request, the offeree may, unless the trial has started, apply for an order that he does so.

(3) If the court makes an order under paragraph (2), it must specify the date when the Part 36 offer or Part 36 payment is to be treated as having been made.

Court to take into account offer to settle made before commencement of proceedings

36.10(1) If a person makes an offer to settle before proceedings are begun which complies with the provisions of this rule, the court will take that offer into account when making any order as to costs.

(2) The offer must –

(a) be expressed to be open for at least 21 days after the date it was made;

(b) if made by a person who would be a defendant were proceedings commenced, include an offer to pay the costs of the offeree incurred up to the date 21 days after the date it was made; and

(c) otherwise comply with this Part.

(3) If the offeror is a defendant to a money claim –

(a) he must make a Part 36 payment within 14 days of service of the claim form; and

(b) the amount of the payment must be not less than the sum offered before proceedings began.

(4) An offeree may not, after proceedings have begun, accept –

(a) an offer made under paragraph (2); or

(b) a Part 36 payment made under paragraph (3),

without the permission of the court.

(5) An offer under this rule is made when it is received by the offeree.

Time for acceptance of a defendant's Part 36 offer or Part 36 payment

36.11 (1) A claimant may accept a Part 36 offer or a Part 36 payment made not less than 21 days before the start of the trial without needing the court's permission if he gives the defendant written notice of acceptance not later than 21 days after the offer or payment was made.

(Rule 36.13 sets out the costs consequences of accepting a defendant's offer or payment without needing the permission of the court.)

(2) If –

   (a) a defendant's Part 36 offer or Part 36 payment is made less than 21 days before the start of the trial; or

   (b) the claimant does not accept it within the period specified in paragraph (1) –

      (i) if the parties agree the liability for costs, the claimant may accept the offer or payment without needing the permission of the court;

      (ii) if the parties do not agree the liability for costs the claimant may only accept the offer or payment with the permission of the court.

(3) Where the permission of the court is needed under paragraph (2) the court will, if it gives permission, make an order as to costs.

Time for acceptance of a claimant's Part 36 offer

36.12 (1) A defendant may accept a Part 36 offer made not less than 21 days before the start of the trial without needing the court's permission if he gives the claimant written notice of acceptance not later than 21 days after the offer was made.

(Rule 36.14 sets out the costs consequences of accepting a claimant's offer without needing the permission of the court)

(2) If –

   (a) a claimant's Part 36 offer is made less than 21 days before the start of the trial; or

   (b) the defendant does not accept it within the period specified in paragraph (1) –

      (i) if the parties agree the liability for costs, the defendant may accept the offer without needing the permission of the court;

      (ii) if the parties do not agree the liability for costs the defendant may only accept the offer with the permission of the court.

(3) Where the permission of the court is needed under paragraph (2) the court will, if it gives permission, make an order as to costs.

Costs consequences of acceptance of a defendant's Part 36 offer or Part 36 payment

36.13 (1) Where a Part 36 offer or a Part 36 payment is accepted without needing the permission of the court the claimant will be entitled to his costs of the proceedings up to the date of serving notice of acceptance.

(2) Where –

   (a) a Part 36 offer or a Part 36 payment relates to part only of the claim; and

   (b) at the time of serving notice of acceptance the claimant abandons the balance of the claim,

the claimant will be entitled to his costs of the proceedings up to the date of serving notice of acceptance, unless the court orders otherwise.

(3) The claimant's costs include any costs attributable to the defendant's counterclaim if the Part 36 offer or the Part 36 payment notice states that it takes into account the counterclaim.

(4) Costs under this rule will be payable on the standard basis if not agreed.

Costs consequences of acceptance of a claimant's Part 36 offer

36.14   Where a claimant's Part 36 offer is accepted without needing the permission of the court the claimant will be entitled to his costs of the proceedings up to the date upon which the defendant serves notice of acceptance.

The effect of acceptance of a Part 36 offer or a Part 36 payment

36.15(1) If a Part 36 offer or Part 36 payment relates to the whole claim and is accepted, the claim will be stayed$^{(GL)}$.

(2) In the case of acceptance of a Part 36 offer which relates to the whole claim –
   (a) the stay$^{(GL)}$ will be upon the terms of the offer; and
   (b) either party may apply to enforce those terms without the need for a new claim.

(3) If a Part 36 offer or a Part 36 payment which relates to part only of the claim is accepted –
   (a) the claim will be stayed$^{(GL)}$ as to that part; and
   (b) unless the parties have agreed costs, the liability for costs shall be decided by the court.

(4) If the approval of the court is required before a settlement can be binding, any stay$^{(GL)}$ which would otherwise arise on the acceptance of a Part 36 offer or a Part 36 payment will take effect only when that approval has been given.

(5) Any stay$^{(GL)}$ arising under this rule will not affect the power of the court –
   (a) to enforce the terms of a Part 36 offer;
   (b) to deal with any question of costs (including interest on costs) relating to the proceedings;
   (c) to order payment out of court of any sum paid into court.

(6) Where –
   (a) a Part 36 offer has been accepted; and
   (b) a party alleges that –
      (i) the other party has not honoured the terms of the offer; and
      (ii) he is therefore entitled to a remedy for breach of contract,
   the party may claim the remedy by applying to the court without the need to start a new claim unless the court orders otherwise.

Payment out of a sum in court on the acceptance of a Part 36 payment

36.16   Where a Part 36 payment is accepted the claimant obtains payment out of the sum in court by making a request for payment in the practice form.

Acceptance of a Part 36 offer or a Part 36 payment made by one or more, but not all, defendants

36.17(1) This rule applies where the claimant wishes to accept a Part 36 offer or a Part 36 payment made by one or more, but not all, of a number of defendants.

(2) If the defendants are sued jointly or in the alternative, the claimant may accept the offer or payment without needing the permission of the court in accordance with rule 36.11(1) if –
   (a) he discontinues his claim against those defendants who have not made the offer or payment; and

(b) those defendants give written consent to the acceptance of the offer or payment.

(3) If the claimant alleges that the defendants have a several liability$^{(GL)}$ to him the claimant may –

(a) accept the offer or payment in accordance with rule 36.11(1); and

(b) continue with his claims against the other defendants if he is entitled to do so.

(4) In all other cases the claimant must apply to the court for –

(a) an order permitting a payment out to him of any sum in court; and

(b) such order as to costs as the court considers appropriate.

Other cases where a court order is required to enable acceptance of a Part 36 offer or a Part 36 payment

36.18(1) Where a Part 36 offer or a Part 36 payment is made in proceedings to which rule 21.10 applies –

(a) the offer or payment may be accepted only with the permission of the court; and

(b) no payment out of any sum in court shall be made without a court order.

(Rule 21.10 deals with compromise etc. by or on behalf of a child or patient.)

(2) Where the court gives a claimant permission to accept a Part 36 offer or payment after the trial has started –

(a) any money in court may be paid out only with a court order; and

(b) the court must, in the order, deal with the whole costs of the proceedings.

(3) Where a claimant accepts a Part 36 payment after a defence of tender before claim$^{(GL)}$ has been put forward by the defendant, the money in court may be paid out only after an order of the court.

(Rule 37.3 requires a defendant who wishes to rely on a defence of tender before claim$^{(GL)}$ to make a payment into court.)

Restriction on disclosure of a Part 36 offer or a Part 36 payment

36.19(1) A Part 36 offer will be treated as 'without prejudice$^{(GL)}$ except as to costs'.

(2) The fact that a Part 36 payment has been made shall not be communicated to the trial judge until all questions of liability and the amount of money to be awarded have been decided.

(3) Paragraph (2) does not apply –

(a) where the defence of tender before claim$^{(GL)}$ has been raised;

(b) where the proceedings have been stayed$^{(GL)}$ under rule 36.15 following acceptance of a Part 36 offer or Part 36 payment; or

(c) where –

(i) the issue of liability has been determined before any assessment of the money claimed; and

(ii) the fact that there has or has not been a Part 36 payment may be relevant to the question of the costs of the issue of liability.

Costs consequences where claimant fails to do better than a Part 36 offer or a Part 36 payment

36.20(1) This rule applies where at trial a claimant –

(a) fails to better a Part 36 payment; or

(b) fails to obtain a judgment which is more advantageous than a defendant's Part 36 offer.

(2) Unless it considers it unjust to do so, the court will order the claimant to pay any costs incurred by the defendant after the latest date on which the payment or offer could have been accepted without needing the permission of the court.

(Rule 36.11 sets out the time for acceptance of a defendant's Part 36 offer or Part 36 payment.)

Costs and other consequences where claimant does better than he proposed in his Part 36 offer

36.21(1) This rule applies where at trial –

(a) a defendant is held liable for more; or

(b) the judgment against a defendant is more advantageous to the claimant,

than the proposals contained in a claimant's Part 36 offer.

(2) The court may order interest on the whole or part of any sum of money (excluding interest) awarded to the claimant at a rate not exceeding 10% above base rate$^{(GL)}$ for some or all of the period starting with the latest date on which the defendant could have accepted the offer without needing the permission of the court.

(3) The court may also order that the claimant is entitled to –

(a) his costs on the indemnity basis from the latest date when the defendant could have accepted the offer without needing the permission of the court; and

(b) interest on those costs at a rate not exceeding 10% above base rate$^{(GL)}$.

(4) Where this rule applies, the court will make the orders referred to in paragraphs (2) and (3) unless it considers it unjust to do so.

(Rule 36.12 sets out the latest date when the defendant could have accepted the offer)

(5) In considering whether it would be unjust to make the orders referred to in paragraphs (2) and (3) above, the court will take into account all the circumstances of the case including –

(a) the terms of any Part 36 offer;

(b) the stage in the proceedings when any Part 36 offer or Part 36 payment was made;

(c) the information available to the parties at the time when the Part 36 offer or Part 36 payment was made; and

(d) the conduct of the parties with regard to the giving or refusing to give information for the purposes of enabling the offer or payment into court to be made or evaluated.

(6) The power of the court under this rule is in addition to any other power it may have to award interest.

Interest

36.22(1) Unless –

(a) a claimant's Part 36 offer which offers to accept a sum of money; or

(b) a Part 36 payment notice,

indicates to the contrary, any such offer or payment will be treated as inclusive of all interest until the last date on which it could be accepted without needing the permission of the court.

(2) Where a claimant's Part 36 offer or Part 36 payment notice is expressed not to be inclusive of interest, the offer or notice must state –

(a) whether interest is offered; and

(b) if so, the amount offered, the rate or rates offered and the period or periods for which it is offered.

Deduction of benefits

36.23(1) This rule applies where a payment to a claimant following acceptance of a Part 36 offer or Part 36 payment into court would be a compensation payment as defined in section 1 of the Social Security (Recovery of Benefits) Act 1997[54].

(2) A defendant to a money claim may make an offer to settle the claim which will have the consequences set out in this Part, without making a Part 36 payment if –

(a) at the time he makes the offer he has applied for, but not received, a certificate of recoverable benefit; and

(b) he makes a Part 36 payment not more than 7 days after he receives the certificate.

(Section 1 of the 1997 Act defines 'recoverable benefit'.)

(3) A Part 36 payment notice must state –

(a) the amount of gross compensation;

(b) the name and amount of any benefit by which that gross amount is reduced in accordance with section 8 and Schedule 2 to the 1997 Act; and

(c) that the sum paid in is the net amount after deduction of the amount of benefit.

(4) For the purposes of rule 36.20, a claimant fails to better a Part 36 payment if he fails to obtain judgment for more than the gross sum specified in the Part 36 payment notice.

(5) Where –

(a) a Part 36 payment has been made; and

(b) application is made for the money remaining in court to be paid out,

the court may treat the money in court as being reduced by a sum equivalent to any further recoverable benefits paid to the claimant since the date of payment into court and may direct payment out accordingly.

PRACTICE DIRECTION – OFFERS TO SETTLE AND PAYMENTS INTO COURT
THIS PRACTICE DIRECTION SUPPLEMENTS CPR PART 36

Part 36 offers and Part 36 payments

1.1 A written offer to settle a claim[1] or part of a claim or any issue that arises in it made in accordance with the provisions of Part 36 is called:

(1) if made by way of a payment into court, a Part 36 payment[2], or

(2) if made otherwise, a Part 36 offer[3].

---

(54) 1997 c.27.

---

1 Includes Part 20 claims.
2 See rule 36.2(1)(a).
3 See rule 36.2(1)(b).

1.2 A Part 36 offer or Part 36 payment has the costs and other consequences set out in rules 36.13, 36.14, 36.20 and 36.21.

1.3 An offer to settle which is not made in accordance with Part 36 will only have the consequences specified in that Part if the court so orders and will be given such weight on any issue as to costs as the court thinks appropriate[4].

Parties and Part 36 offers

2.1 A Part 36 offer, subject to paragraph 3 below, may be made by any party.

2.2 The party making an offer is the 'offeror' and the party to whom it is made is the 'offeree'.

2.3 A Part 36 offer may consist of a proposal to settle for a specified sum or for some other remedy.

2.4 A Part 36 offer is made when received by the offeree[5].

2.5 An improvement to a Part 36 offer is effective when its details are received by the offeree[6].

Parties and Part 36 payments

3.1 An offer to settle for a specified sum made by a defendant[7] must, in order to comply with Part 36, be made by way of a Part 36 payment into court[8].

3.2 A Part 36 payment is made when the Part 36 payment notice is served on the claimant[9].

3.3 An increase to a Part 36 payment will be effective when notice of the increase is served on the claimant[10].

(For service of the Part 36 payment notice see rule 36.6(3) and (4).)

3.4 A defendant who wishes to withdraw or reduce a Part 36 payment must obtain the court's permission to do so.

3.5 Permission may be obtained by making an application in accordance with Part 23 stating the reasons giving rise to the wish to withdraw or reduce the Part 36 payment.

Making a Part 36 payment

4.1 To make a Part 36 payment the defendant must file the following documents:

(1) where that court is a county court or a district registry –

  (a) the Part 36 payment notice, and

  (b) the payment, usually a cheque made payable to Her Majesty's Paymaster General,

with the court, and

(2) where that court is the Royal Courts of Justice –

  (a) the Part 36 payment notice with the court, and

  (b) the payment, usually a cheque made payable to the Accountant General of the Supreme Court, and

  (c) a sealed copy of the Claim Form,

  (d) the Court Funds Office form 100 with the Court Funds Office.

Part 36 offers and Part 36 payments – general provisions

5.1 A Part 36 offer or a Part 36 payment notice must:

(1) state that it is a Part 36 offer or that the payment into court is a Part 36 payment, and

---

4   See rule 36.1(2).
5   See rule 36.8(1).
6   See rule 36.8(3).
7   Includes a respondent to a claim or issue.
8   See rule 36.3(1).
9   See rule 36.8(2).
10   See rule 36.8(4).
11   Rule 36.4. [*Authors' note: This footnote does not actually appear in the text of the printed version.*]
12   Practice form N242A. [*Authors' note: This footnote does not actually appear in the text of the printed version.*]

(2) be signed by the offeror or his legal representative[13].

5.2 The contents of a Part 36 offer must also comply with the requirements of rule 36.5(3), (5) and (6).

5.3 The contents of a Part 36 payment notice must comply with rule 36.6(2) and, if rule 36.23 applies, with rule 36.23(3).

5.4 A Part 36 offer or Part 36 payment will be taken to include interest unless it is expressly stated in the offer or the payment notice that interest is not included, in which case the details set out in rule 36.22(2) must be given.

5.5 Where a Part 36 offer is made by a company or other corporation, a person holding a senior position in the company or corporation may sign the offer on the offeror's behalf, but must state the position he holds.

5.6 Each of the following persons is a person holding a senior position:

(1) in respect of a registered company or corporation, a director, the treasurer, secretary, chief executive, manager or other officer of the company or corporation, and

(2) in respect of a corporation which is not a registered company, in addition to those persons set out in (1), the mayor, chairman, president, town clerk or similar officer of the corporation.

Clarification of Part 36 offer or payment

6.1 An offeree may apply to the court for an order requiring the offeror to clarify the terms of a Part 36 offer or Part 36 payment notice (a clarification order) where the offeror has failed to comply within 7 days with a request for clarification[14].

6.2 An application for a clarification order should be made in accordance with Part 23.

6.3 The application notice should state the respects in which the terms of the Part 36 offer or Part 36 payment notice, as the case may be, are said to need clarification.

Acceptance of a Part 36 offer or payment

7.1 The times for accepting a Part 36 offer or a Part 36 payment are set out in rules 36.11 and 36.12.

7.2 The general rule is that a Part 36 offer or Part 36 payment made more than 21 days before the start of the trial may be accepted within 21 days after it was made without the permission of the court. The costs consequences set out in rules 36.13 and 36.14 will then come into effect.

7.3 A Part 36 offer or Part 36 payment made less than 21 days before the start of the trial cannot be accepted without the permission of the court unless the parties agree what the costs consequences of acceptance will be.

7.4 The permission of the court may be sought:

(1) before the start of the trial, by making an application in accordance with Part 23, and

(2) after the start of the trial, by making an application to the trial judge.

7.5 If the court gives permission it will make an order dealing with costs and may order that, in the circumstances, the costs consequences set out in rules 36.13 and 36.14 will apply.

7.6 Where a Part 36 offer or Part 36 payment is accepted in accordance with rule 36.11(1) or rule 36.12(1) the notice of acceptance must be sent to the offeror and filed with the court.

7.7 The notice of acceptance:

(1) must set out –

(a) the claim number, and

(b) the title of the proceedings,

(2) must identify the Part 36 offer or Part 36 payment notice to which it relates, and

(3) must be signed by the offeree or his legal representative (see paragraphs 6.5 and 6.6 above).

---

13 For the definition of legal representative see rule 2.3.

14 See rule 36.9(1) and (2).

7.8 Where:

(1) the court's approval, or

(2) an order for payment of money out of court, or

(3) an order apportioning money in court –

(a) between the Fatal Accidents Act 1976 and the Law Reform (Miscellaneous Provisions) Act 1934, or

(b) between the persons entitled to it under the Fatal Accidents Act 1976,

is required for acceptance of a Part 36 offer or Part 36 payment, application for the approval or the order should be made in accordance with Part 23.

7.9 The court will include in any order made under paragraph 7.8 above a direction for;

(1) the payment out of the money in court, and

(2) the payment of interest.

7.10 Unless the parties have agreed otherwise:

(1) interest accruing up to the date of acceptance will be paid to the offeror, and

(2) interest accruing as from the date of acceptance until payment out will be paid to the offeree.

7.11 A claimant may not accept a Part 36 payment which is part of a defendant's offer to settle the whole of a claim consisting of both a money and a non-money claim unless at the same time he accepts the offer to settle the whole of the claim. Therefore:

(1) if a claimant accepts a Part 36 payment which is part of a defendant's offer to settle the whole of the claim, or

(2) if a claimant accepts a Part 36 offer which is part of a defendant's offer to settle the whole of the claim,

the claimant will be deemed to have accepted the offer to settle the whole of the claim[15].

(See paragraph 8 below for the method of obtaining money out of court.)

PAYMENT OUT OF COURT

8.1 To obtain money out of court following acceptance of a Part 36 payment, the claimant should file a request for payment with the court[16].

8.2 The request for payment should contain the following details:

(1) where the party receiving the payment –

(a) is legally represented –

(i) the name, business address and reference of the legal representative, and

(ii) the name of the bank and the sort code number, the title of the account and the account number where the payment is to be transmitted, and

(2) where the party is acting in person –

(a) his name and address, and

(b) his bank account details as in (ii) above.

8.3 Where the request for payment is made to the Royal Courts of Justice, the claimant should also complete Court Funds Office form 201 and file it in the Court Funds Office.

8.4 Subject to paragraph 9.5(1) and (2), if a party does not wish the payment to be transmitted into his bank account or if he does not have a bank account, he may send a written request to the Accountant-General for the payment to be made to him by cheque.

8.5 Where a party seeking payment out of court has provided the necessary information, the payment:

(1) where a party is legally represented, must be made to the legal representative,

(2) if the party is not legally represented but is, or has been, in receipt of legal aid in respect of the proceedings and a notice to that effect has been filed, should be made to the Legal Aid Board by direction of the court,

---

15 See rule 36.4.

16 In practice form N243.

(3) where a person entitled to money in court dies without having made a will and the court is satisfied –

    (a) that no grant of administration of his estate has been made, and

    (b) that the assets of his estate, including the money in court, do not exceed in value the amount specified in any order in force under section 6 of the Administration of Estates (Small Payments) Act 1965,

may be ordered to be made to the person appearing to have the prior right to a grant of administration of the estate of the deceased, e.g. a widower, widow, child, father, mother, brother or sister of the deceased.

Foreign currency

9.1 Money may be paid into court in a foreign currency:

    (1) where it is a Part 36 payment and the claim is in a foreign currency, or

    (2) under a court order.

9.2 The court may direct that the money be placed in an interest bearing account in the currency of the claim or any other currency.

9.3 Where a Part 36 payment is made in a foreign currency and has not been accepted within 21 days, the defendant may apply for an order that the money be placed in an interest bearing account.

9.4 The application should be made in accordance with Part 23 and should state:

    (1) that the payment has not been accepted in accordance with rule 36.11, and

    (2) the type of currency on which interest is to accrue.

Compensation recovery

10.1 Where a defendant makes a Part 36 payment in respect of a claim for a sum or part of a sum:

    (1) which falls under the heads of damage set out in column 1 of Schedule 2 of the Social Security (Recovery of Benefits) Act 1997 in respect of recoverable benefits received by the claimant as set out in column 2 of that Schedule, and

    (2) where the defendant is liable to pay recoverable benefits to the Secretary of State,

the defendant should obtain from the Secretary of State a certificate of recoverable benefits and file the certificate with the Part 36 payment notice.

10.2 If a defendant wishes to offer to settle a claim where he has applied for but not yet received a certificate of recoverable benefits, he may, provided that he makes a Part 36 payment not more than 7 days after he has received the certificate, make a Part 36 offer which will have the costs and other consequences set out in rules 36.13 and 36.20.

10.3 The Part 36 payment notice should state in addition to the requirements set out in rule 36.6(2):

    (1) the total amount represented by the Part 36 payment (the gross compensation),

    (2) that the defendant has reduced this sum by £   , in accordance with section 8 of and Schedule 2 to the Social Security (Recovery of Benefits) Act 1997, which was calculated as follows:

    Name of benefit   Amount

and

    (3) that the amount paid in, being the sum of £   is the net amount after the deduction of the amount of benefit.

10.4 On acceptance of a Part 36 payment to which this paragraph relates, a claimant will receive the sum in court which will be net of the recoverable benefits.

10.5 In establishing at trial whether a claimant has bettered or obtained a judgment more advantageous than a Part 36 payment to which this paragraph relates, the court will base its decision on the gross sum specified in the Part 36 payment notice.

General

11.1 Where a party on whom a Part 36 offer, a Part 36 payment notice or a notice of acceptance is to be served is legally represented, the Part 36 offer, Part 36 payment notice and notice of acceptance must be served on the legal representative.

11.2 In a claim arising out of an accident involving a motor vehicle on a road or in a public place:

(1) where the damages claimed include a sum for hospital expenses, and

(2) the defendant or his insurer pays that sum to the hospital under section 157 of the Road Traffic Act 1988,

the defendant must give notice of that payment to the court and all the other parties to the proceedings.

11.3 Money paid into court:

(1) as a Part 36 payment which is not accepted by the claimant, or

(2) under a court order,

will be placed after 21 days in a basic account[17] (subject to paragraph 11.4 below) for interest to accrue.

11.4 Where money referred to in paragraph 11.3 above is paid in in respect of a child or patient it will be placed in a special investment account[18] for interest to accrue.

(A practice direction supplementing Part 21 contains information about the investment of money in court in respect of a child or patient.)

(Practice directions supplementing Part 40 contain information about adjustment of the judgment sum in respect of recoverable benefits, and about structured settlements.)

(A practice direction supplementing Part 41 contains information about provisional damages awards.)

PART 37

MISCELLANEOUS PROVISIONS ABOUT PAYMENTS INTO COURT

Contents of this Part

Money paid into court under a court order – general

37.1(1) When a party makes a payment into court under a court order, the court will give notice of the payment to every other party.

(2) Money paid into court under a court order may not be paid out without the court's permission except where –

(a) the defendant treats the money as a Part 36 payment under rule 37.2; and

(b) the claimant accepts the Part 36 payment without needing the permission of the court.

(Rule 36.11 sets out when the claimant can accept a Part 36 payment without needing the permission of the court.)

---

17 See rule 26 of the Court Funds Office Rules 1987.

18 See rule 26 as above.

Money paid into court may be treated as a Part 36 payment

37.2(1) Where a defendant makes a payment into court following an order made under rule 3.1(3) or 3.1(5) he may choose to treat the whole or any part of the money paid into court as a Part 36 payment.

(Rule 36.2 defines a Part 36 payment.)

(2) To do this he must file a Part 36 payment notice.

(Rule 36.6 sets out what a Part 36 payment notice must contain and provides for the court to serve it on the other parties.)

(3) If he does so Part 36 applies to the money as if he had paid it into court as a Part 36 payment.

Money paid into court where defendant wishes to rely on defence of tender before claim

37.3(1) Where a defendant wishes to rely on a defence of tender before claim(GL) he must make a payment into court of the amount he says was tendered.

(2) If the defendant does not make a payment in accordance with paragraph (1) the defence of tender before claim(GL) will not be available to him until he does so.

(3) Where the defendant makes such payment into court –

(a) he may choose to treat the whole or any part of the money paid into court as a Part 36 payment; and

(b) if he does so, he must file a Part 36 payment notice.

Proceedings under Fatal Accidents Act 1976[55] and Law Reform (Miscellaneous Provisions) Act 1934[56] – apportionment by court

37.4(1) Where –

(a) a claim includes claims arising under –

(i) the Fatal Accidents Act 1976; and

(ii) the Law Reform (Miscellaneous Provisions) Act 1934;

(b) a single sum of money is paid into court in satisfaction of those claims; and

(c) the money is accepted,

the court shall apportion the money between the different claims.

(2) The court shall apportion money under paragraph (1) –

(a) when it gives directions under rule 21.11 (control of money received by a child or patient); or

(b) if rule 21.11 does not apply, when it gives permission for the money to be paid out of court.

(3) Where, in an action in which a claim under the Fatal Accidents Act 1976 is made by or on behalf of more than one person –

(a) a sum in respect of damages is ordered or agreed to be paid in satisfaction of the claim; or

(b) a sum of money is accepted in satisfaction of the claim,

the court shall apportion it between the persons entitled to it unless it has already been apportioned by the court, a jury, or agreement between the parties.

---

(55) 1976 c.30.
(56) 1934 c.41.

(Other rules about payments into court can be found –

(a) in Schedule 1, in the following RSC – O.49 (garnishee proceedings); O.50 (stop orders in funds in court); O.92 (payments into court in particular circumstances); and

(b) in Schedule 2, in the following CCR – O.30 (garnishee proceedings); O.49 (payment in under various statutes).)

PRACTICE DIRECTION – MISCELLANEOUS PROVISIONS ABOUT PAYMENTS INTO COURT
THIS PRACTICE DIRECTION SUPPLEMENTS CPR PART 37

For information about payments into and out of court in relation to offers to settle see Part 36 and the practice direction which supplements it.

Payments into court under an order

1.1 Where money is paid into court under an order, the party making the payment should:
   (1) lodge his payment, and
   (2) file a copy of the order directing payment into court.
1.2 Where the order is made in a county court or district registry the payment will usually be made by cheque payable to Her Majesty's Paymaster General.
1.3 Where the order is made in the Royal Courts of Justice, the payment will usually be made by cheque payable to the Accountant General of the Supreme Court, and should be;
   (1) accompanied by
      (a) a completed Court Funds Office forms 100 or 101, and
      (b) a sealed copy of the order, and
   (2) lodged in the Court Fund Office. A copy of the Court Funds Office receipt should be filed in the appropriate court office in the Royal Courts of Justice.

Defence of tender

2.1 A defendant paying a sum of money into court in support of a defence of tender[1] should do so when filing his defence and should at the same time complete and file:
   (1) a notice of payment into court, and
   (2) where the defence is filed in the Royal Courts of Justice, Court Funds Office form 100.
2.2 A defence of tender will not be available to a defendant until he has complied with paragraph 2.1.

General

3.1 Where money is paid into court:
   (1) under an order permitting a defendant to defend or to continue to defend under rule 37.2(1), or
   (2) in support of a defence of tender under rule 37.3, the party making the payment may, if a defendant, choose to treat the whole or any part of the money as a Part 36 payment[2].
3.2 In order to do so the defendant must file a Part 36 payment notice in accordance with rule 36.6 (see also paragraph 6 of the practice direction which supplements Part 36).
3.3 Rule 37.4 deals with the apportionment of money paid into court in respect of claims arising under:
   (1) the Fatal Accidents Act 1976, and

---

1   Rule 37.3.
2   Rules 37.2(2) and 37.3(3).

(2) the Law Reform (Miscellaneous Provisions) Act 1934.

(See also paragraph 8.8 of the practice direction supplementing Part 36.)

Payment out of court

4.1 Except where money which has been paid into court is treated as a Part 36 payment and can be accepted by the claimant without needing the court's permission, the court's permission is required to take the money out of court.

4.2 Permission may be obtained by making an application in accordance with Part 23. The application notice must state the grounds on which the order for payment out is sought. Evidence of any facts on which the applicant relies may also be necessary.

4.3 To obtain the money out of court the applicant must comply with the provisions of paragraph 9 of the practice direction supplementing Part 36 where they apply.

Foreign currency

5 For information on payments into court made in a foreign currency, see paragraph 9 of the practice direction supplementing Part 36.

PART 38

DISCONTINUANCE

Contents of this Part

Scope of this Part

38.1 (1) The rules in this Part set out the procedure by which a claimant may discontinue all or part of a claim.

(2) A claimant who –

(a) claims more than one remedy; and

(b) subsequently abandons his claim to one or more of the remedies but continues with his claim for the other remedies,

is not treated as discontinuing all or part of a claim for the purposes of this Part.

(The procedure for amending a statement of case, set out in Part 17, applies where a claimant abandons a claim for a particular remedy but wishes to continue with his claim for other remedies.)

Right to discontinue claim

38.2 (1) A claimant may discontinue all or part of a claim at any time.

(2) However –

(a) a claimant must obtain the permission of the court if he wishes to discontinue all or part of a claim in relation to which –

     (i) the court has granted an interim injunction^(GL) ; or

     (ii) any party has given an undertaking to the court;

  (b) where the claimant has received an interim payment in relation to a claim (whether voluntarily or pursuant to an order under Part 25), he may discontinue that claim only if –

     (i) the defendant who made the interim payment consents in writing; or

     (ii) the court gives permission;

  (c) where there is more than one claimant, a claimant may not discontinue unless –

     (i) every other claimant consents in writing; or

     (ii) the court gives permission.

(3) Where there is more than one defendant, the claimant may discontinue all or part of a claim against all or any of the defendants.

Procedure for discontinuing

38.3 (1) To discontinue a claim or part of a claim, a claimant must –

  (a) file a notice of discontinuance; and

  (b) serve a copy of it on every other party to the proceedings.

(2) The claimant must state in the notice of discontinuance which he files that he has served notice of discontinuance on every other party to the proceedings.

(3) Where the claimant needs the consent of some other party, a copy of the necessary consent must be attached to the notice of discontinuance.

(4) Where there is more than one defendant, the notice of discontinuance must specify against which defendants the claim is discontinued.

Right to apply to have notice of discontinuance set aside

38.4 (1) Where the claimant discontinues under rule 38.2(1) the defendant may apply to have the notice of discontinuance set aside^(GL) .

(2) The defendant may not make an application under this rule more than 28 days after the date when the notice of discontinuance was served on him.

When discontinuance takes effect where permission of the court is not needed

38.5 (1) Discontinuance against any defendant takes effect on the date when notice of discontinuance is served on him under rule 38.3(1).

(2) Subject to rule 38.4, the proceedings are brought to an end as against him on that date.

(3) However, this does not affect proceedings to deal with any question of costs.

Liability for costs

38.6 (1) Unless the court orders otherwise, a claimant who discontinues is liable for the costs which a defendant against whom he discontinues incurred on or before the date on which notice of discontinuance was served on him.

(2) If proceedings are only partly discontinued –

  (a) the claimant is liable under paragraph (1) for costs relating only to the part of the proceedings which he is discontinuing; and

  (b) unless the court orders otherwise, the costs which the claimant is liable to pay must not be assessed until the conclusion of the rest of the proceedings.

(3) This rule does not apply to claims allocated to the small claims track.

(Rule 44.12 provides for the basis of assessment where right to costs arises on discontinuance.)

Discontinuance and subsequent proceedings

38.7   A claimant who discontinues a claim needs the permission of the court to make another claim against the same defendant if –

(a) he discontinued the claim after the defendant filed a defence; and

(b) the other claim arises out of facts which are the same or substantially the same as those relating to the discontinued claim.

Stay of remainder of partly discontinued proceedings where costs not paid

38.8 (1) This rule applies where –

(a) proceedings are partly discontinued;

(b) a claimant is liable to pay costs under rule 38.6; and

(c) the claimant fails to pay those costs within 21 days of –

(i) the date on which the parties agreed the sum payable by the claimant; or

(ii) the date on which the court ordered the costs to be paid.

(2) Where this rule applies, the court may stay^(GL) the remainder of the proceedings until the claimant pays the whole of the costs which he is liable to pay under rule 38.6.

PART 39

MISCELLANEOUS PROVISIONS
RELATING TO HEARINGS

Contents of this Part

Interpretation

39.1   In this Part, reference to a hearing includes a reference to the trial.

General rule – hearing to be in public

39.2 (1) The general rule is that a hearing is to be in public.

(2) The requirement for a hearing to be in public does not require the court to make special arrangements for accommodating members of the public.

(3) A hearing, or any part of it, may be in private if –

(a) publicity would defeat the object of the hearing;

(b) it involves matters relating to national security;

(c) it involves confidential information (including information relating to personal financial matters) and publicity would damage that confidentiality;

    (d) a private hearing is necessary to protect the interests of any child or patient;

    (e) it is a hearing of an application made without notice and it would be unjust to any respondent for there to be a public hearing;

    (f) it involves uncontentious matters arising in the administration of trusts or in the administration of a deceased person's estate; or

    (g) the court considers this to be necessary, in the interests of justice.

(4) The court may order that the identity of any party or witness must not be disclosed if it considers non-disclosure necessary in order to protect the interests of that party or witness.

(RSC Order 52, in Schedule 1, provides that a committal hearing may be in private.)

Failure to attend the trial

39.3 (1) The court may proceed with a trial in the absence of a party but –

    (a) if no party attends the trial, it may strike out$^{(GL)}$ the whole of the proceedings;

    (b) if the claimant does not attend, it may strike out his claim and any defence to counterclaim; and

    (c) if a defendant does not attend, it may strike out his defence or counterclaim (or both).

(2) Where the court strikes out proceedings, or any part of them, under this rule, it may subsequently restore the proceedings, or that part.

(3) Where a party does not attend and the court gives judgment or makes an order against him, the party who failed to attend may apply for the judgment or order to be set aside$^{(GL)}$.

(4) An application under paragraph (2) or paragraph (3) for an order to restore proceedings must be supported by evidence.

(5) Where an application is made under paragraph (2) or (3) by a party who failed to attend the trial, the court may grant the application only if the applicant –

    (a) acted promptly when he found out that the court had exercised its power to strike out$^{(GL)}$ or to enter judgment or make an order against him;

    (b) had a good reason for not attending the trial; and

    (c) has a reasonable prospect of success at the trial.

Timetable for trial

39.4   When the court sets a timetable for a trial in accordance with rule 28.6 (fixing or confirming the trial date and giving directions – fast track) or rule 29.8 (setting a trial timetable and fixing or confirming the trial date or week – multi-track) it will do so in consultation with the parties.

Trial bundles

39.5 (1) Unless the court orders otherwise, the claimant must file a trial bundle containing documents required by –

    (a) a relevant practice direction; and

    (b) any court order.

(2) The claimant must file the trial bundle not more than 7 days and not less than 3 days before the start of the trial.

Representation at trial of companies or other corporations

39.6   A company or other corporation may be represented at trial by an employee if –

(a) the employee has been authorised by the company or corporation to appear at trial on its behalf; and

(b) the court gives permission.

Impounded documents

39.7 (1) Documents impounded by order of the court must not be released from the custody of the court except in compliance –

(a) with a court order; or

(b) with a written request made by a Law Officer or the Director of Public Prosecutions.

(2) A document released from the custody of the court under paragraph(1)(b) must be released into the custody of the person who requested it.

(3) Documents impounded by order of the court, while in the custody of the court, may not be inspected except by a person authorised to do so by a court order.

PRACTICE DIRECTION – MISCELLANEOUS PROVISIONS RELATING TO HEARINGS
THIS PRACTICE DIRECTION SUPPLEMENTS CPR PART 39

Hearings

1.1 In Part 39, reference to a hearing includes reference to the trial[1].

1.2 The general rule is that a hearing is to be in public[2].

1.3 Rule 39.2(3) sets out the type of proceedings which may be dealt with in private.

1.4 The decision as to whether to hold a hearing in public or in private must be made by the judge conducting the hearing having regard to any representations which may have been made to him.

1.4A The judge should also have regard to Article 6(1) of the European Convention for Human Rights. This requires that, in general, court hearings are to be held in public, but the press and public may be excluded in the circumstances specified in that Article. Article 6(1) will usually be relevant, for example, where a party applies for a hearing which would normally be held in public to be held in private as well as where a hearing would normally be held in private. The judge may need to consider whether the case is within any of the exceptions permitted by Article 6(1).

1.5 The hearings set out below shall in the first instance be listed by the court as hearings in private under rule 39.2(3)(c), namely:

(1) a claim by a mortgagee against one or more individuals for an order for possession of land,

(2) a claim by a landlord against one or more tenants or former tenants for the repossession of a dwelling house based on the non-payment of rent,

(3) an application to suspend a warrant of execution or a warrant of possession or to stay execution where the court is being invited to consider the ability of a party to make payments to another party,

(4) a redetermination under rule 14.13 or an application to vary or suspend the payment of a judgment debt by instalments,

(5) an application for a charging order (including an application to enforce a charging order), garnishee order, attachment of earnings order, administration order, or the appointment of a receiver,

---

1   Rule 39.1.
2   Rule 39.2(1).

(6)   an oral examination,

(7)   the determination of an assisted person's liability for costs under regulation 127 of the Civil Legal Aid (General) Regulations 1989,

(8)   an application for security for costs under section 726(1) of the Companies Act 1985, and

(9)   proceedings brought under the Consumer Credit Act 1974, the Inheritance (Provision for Family and Dependants) Act 1975 or the Protection from Harassment Act 1997,

(10) an application by a trustee or personal representative for directions as to bringing or defending legal proceedings, and

(11) an application under the Variation of Trusts Act 1958 where there are no facts in dispute.

1.6   Rule 39.2(3)(d) states that a hearing may be in private where it involves the interests of a child or patient. This includes the approval of a compromise or settlement on behalf of a child or patient or an application for the payment of money out of court to such a person.

1.7   Attention is drawn to paragraph 5.1 of the practice direction which supplements Part 27 (relating to the hearing of claims in the small claims track), which provides that the judge may decide to hold a small claim hearing in private if the parties agree or if a ground mentioned in rule 39.2(3) applies. A hearing of a small claim in premises other than the court will not be a hearing in public.

1.8   Nothing in this practice direction prevents a judge ordering that a hearing taking place in public shall continue in private, or vice-versa.

1.9   If the court or judge's room in which the proceedings are taking place has a sign on the door indicating that the proceedings are private, members of the public who are not parties to the proceedings will not be admitted unless the court permits.

1.10 Where there is no such sign on the door of the court or judge's room, members of the public will be admitted where practicable. The judge may, if he thinks it appropriate, adjourn the proceedings to a larger room or court.

1.11 When a hearing takes place in public, members of the public may obtain a transcript of any judgment given or a copy of any order made, subject to payment of the appropriate fee.

1.12 When a judgment is given or an order is made in private, if any member of the public who is not a party to the proceedings seeks a transcript of the judgment or a copy of the order, he must seek the leave of the judge who gave the judgment or made the order.

1.13 A judgment or order given or made in private, when drawn up, must have clearly marked in the title:

'Before [title and name of judge] sitting in Private'

1.14 References to hearings being in public or private or in a judge's room contained in the Civil Procedure Rules (including the Rules of the Supreme Court and the County Court Rules scheduled to Part 50) and the practice directions which supplement them do not restrict any existing rights of audience or confer any new rights of audience in respect of applications or proceedings which under the rules previously in force would have been heard in court or in chambers respectively.

1.15 Where the court lists a hearing of a claim by a mortgagee for an order for possession of land under paragraph 1.5(1) above to be in private, any fact which needs to be proved by the evidence of witnesses may be proved by evidence in writing.

(CPR rule 32.2 sets out the general rule as to how evidence is to be given and facts are to be proved.)

Failure to attend the trial

2.1   Rule 39.3 sets out the consequences of a party's failure to attend the trial.

2.2   The court may proceed with a trial in the absence of a party[3]. In the absence of:

(1)   the defendant, the claimant may –

(a)   prove his claim at trial and obtain judgment on his claim and for costs, and

(b)   seek the striking out of any counterclaim,

---

3   Rule 39.3(1).

(2) the claimant, the defendant may –
    (a) prove any counterclaim at trial and obtain judgment on his counterclaim and for costs, and
    (b) seek the striking out of the claim, or
(3) both parties, the court may strike out the whole of the proceedings.

2.3 Where the court has struck out proceedings, or any part of them, on the failure of a party to attend, that party may apply in accordance with Part 23 for the proceedings, or that part of them, to be restored and for any judgment given against that party to be set aside[4].

2.4 The application referred to in paragraph 2.3 above must be supported by evidence giving reasons for the failure to attend court and stating when the applicant found out about the order against him.

Bundles of documents for hearings or trial

3.1 Unless the court orders otherwise, the claimant must file the trial bundle not more than 7 days and not less than 3 days before the start of the trial.

3.2 Unless the court orders otherwise, the trial bundle should include a copy of:
    (1) the claim form and all statements of case,
    (2) a case summary and/or chronology where appropriate,
    (3) requests for further information and responses to the requests,
    (4) all witness statements to be relied on as evidence,
    (5) any witness summaries,
    (6) any notices of intention to rely on hearsay evidence under rule 32.2,
    (7) any notices of intention to rely on evidence (such as a plan, photograph etc.) under rule 33.6 which is not –
        (a) contained in a witness statement, affidavit or experts report,
        (b) being given orally at trial,
        (c) hearsay evidence under rule 33.2,
    (8) any medical reports and responses to them,
    (9) any experts' reports and responses to them,
    (10) any order giving directions as to the conduct of the trial, and
    (11) any other necessary documents.

3.3 The originals of the documents contained in the trial bundle, together with copies of any other court orders should be available at the trial.

3.4 The preparation and production of the trial bundle, even where it is delegated to another person, is the responsibility of the legal representative[5] who has conduct of the claim on behalf of the claimant.

3.5 The trial bundle should be paginated (continuously) throughout, and indexed with a description of each document and the page number. Where the total number of pages is more than 100, numbered dividers should be placed at intervals between groups of documents.

3.6 The bundle should normally be contained in a ring binder or lever arch file. Where more than one bundle is supplied, they should be clearly distinguishable, for example, by different colours or letters. If there are numerous bundles, a core bundle should be prepared containing the core documents essential to the proceedings, with references to the supplementary documents in the other bundles.

3.7 For convenience, experts' reports may be contained in a separate bundle and cross referenced in the main bundle.

3.8 If a document to be included in the trial bundle is illegible, a typed copy should be included in the bundle next to it, suitably cross-referenced.

3.9 The contents of the trial bundle should be agreed where possible. The parties should also agree where possible:

---

4 Rule 39.3(2) and (3).
5 For the definition of legal representative see rule 2.3.

(1) that the documents contained in the bundle are authentic even if not disclosed under Part 31, and

(2) that documents in the bundle may be treated as evidence of the facts stated in them even if a notice under the Civil Evidence Act 1995 has not been served.

Where it is not possible to agree the contents of the bundle, a summary of the points on which the parties are unable to agree should be included.

3.10 The party filing the trial bundle should supply identical bundles to all the parties to the proceedings and for the use of the witnesses.

Settlement or discontinuance after the trial date is fixed

4.1 Where:

(1) an offer to settle a claim is accepted,

(2) or a settlement is reached, or

(3) a claim is discontinued,

which disposes of the whole of a claim for which a date or 'window' has been fixed for the trial, the parties must ensure that the listing officer for the trial court is notified immediately.

4.2 If an order is drawn up giving effect to the settlement or discontinuance, a copy of the sealed order should be filed with the listing officer.

Representation at hearings

5.1 At any hearing, a written statement containing the following information should be provided for the court:

(1) the name and address of each advocate,

(2) his qualification or entitlement to act as an advocate, and

(3) the party for whom he so acts.

5.2 Where a party is a company or other corporation and is to be represented at a hearing by an employee the written statement should contain the following additional information:

(1) The full name of the company or corporation as stated in its certificate of registration.

(2) The registered number of the company or corporation.

(3) The position or office in the company or corporation held by the representative.

(4) The date on which and manner in which the representative was authorised to act for the company or corporation, e.g.   19   : written authority from managing director; or   19   : Board resolution dated   19   .

5.3 Rule 39.6 is intended to enable a company or other corporation to represent itself as a litigant in person. Permission under rule 39.6(b) should therefore be given by the court unless there is some particular and sufficient reason why it should be withheld. In considering whether to grant permission the matters to be taken into account include the complexity of the issues and the experience and position in the company or corporation of the proposed representative.

5.4 Permission under rule 39.6(b) should be obtained in advance of the hearing from, preferably, the judge who is to hear the case, but may, if it is for any reason impracticable or inconvenient to do so, be obtained from any judge by whom the case could be heard.

5.5 The permission may be obtained informally and without notice to the other parties. The judge who gives the permission should record in writing that he has done so and supply a copy to the company or corporation in question and to any other party who asks for one.

5.5 Permission should not normally be granted under Rule 39.6:

(a) in jury trials;

(b) in contempt proceedings.

Recording of proceedings

6.1 At any hearing, whether in the High Court or a county court, the judgment (and any summing up given by the judge) will be recorded unless the judge directs otherwise. Oral evidence will normally be recorded also.

6.2 No party or member of the public may use unofficial recording equipment in any court or judge's room without the permission of the court. To do so without permission constitutes a contempt of court[6].

6.3 Any party or person may require a transcript or transcripts of the recording of any trial or hearing to be supplied to him, upon payment of the charges authorised by any scheme in force for the making of the recording or the transcript.

6.4 Where the person requiring the transcript or transcripts is not a party to the proceedings and the trial or hearing or any part of it was held in private under CPR rule 39.2, paragraph 6.3 does not apply unless the court so orders.

6.5 Attention is drawn to paragraph 7.9 of the Court of Appeal (Civil Division) Practice Direction which deals with the provision of transcripts for use in the Court of Appeal at public expense.

Exhibits at trial

7 Exhibits which are handed in and proved during the course of the trial should be recorded on an exhibit list and kept in the custody of the court until the conclusion of the trial, unless the judge directs otherwise. At the conclusion of the trial it is the parties' responsibility to obtain the return of those exhibits which they handed in and to preserve them for the period in which any appeal may take place.

PRACTICE DIRECTION – COURT SITTINGS
THIS PRACTICE DIRECTION SUPPLEMENTS CPR PART 39

Court sittings

1.1 (1) The sittings of the Court of Appeal and of the High Court shall be four in every year, that is to say

    (a) the Michaelmas sittings which shall begin on 1st October and end on 21st December;

    (b) the Hilary sittings which shall begin on 11th January and end on the Wednesday before Easter Sunday;

    (c) the Easter sittings which shall begin on the second Tuesday after Easter Sunday and end on the Friday before the spring holiday; and

    (d) the Trinity sittings which shall begin on the second Tuesday after the spring holiday and end on 31st July.

  (2) In the above paragraph "spring holiday" means the bank holiday falling on the last Monday in May or any day appointed instead of that day under section 1(2) of the Banking and Financial Dealings Act 1971.

Vacations

The Court of Appeal

2 Attention is drawn to paragraph 11.2 of the Court of Appeal (Civil Division) Practice Direction which deals with the sittings of the Court of Appeal during vacations.

The High Court

3.1 (1) One or more judges of each Division of the High Court shall sit in vacation on such days as the senior judge of that Division may from time to time direct, to hear such cases, claims, matters or applications as require to be immediately or promptly heard and to hear other cases, claims, matters or applications if the senior judge of that Division determines that sittings are necessary for that purpose.

---

6   Section 9 of the Contempt of Court Act 1981.

(2) Any party to a claim or matter may at any time apply to the Court for an order that such claim or matter be heard in vacation and, if the Court is satisfied that the claim or matter requires to be immediately or promptly heard, it may make an order accordingly and fix a date for the hearing.

(3) Any judge of the High Court may hear such other cases, claims, matters or applications in vacation as the Court may direct.

3.2 The directions in paragraph 3.1 shall not apply in relation to the trial or hearing of cases, claims, matters or applications outside the Royal Courts of Justice but the senior Presiding Judge of each Circuit, with the concurrence of the Senior Presiding Judge, and the Vice-Chancellor of the County Palatine of Lancaster and the Chancery Supervising Judge for Birmingham, Bristol and Cardiff, with the concurrence of the Vice-Chancellor, may make such arrangements for vacation sittings in the courts for which they are respectively responsible as they think desirable.

3.3 (1) Subject to the discretion of the Judge, any appeal and any application normally made to a Judge may be made in the month of September.

(2) In the month of August, save with the permission of a Judge or under arrangements for vacation sittings in courts outside the Royal Courts of Justice, appeals to a Judge will be limited to the matters set out in paragraph 3.5 below, and only applications or real urgency will be dealt with, for example urgent applications in respect of injunctions or for possession under RSC Order 113 (Schedule 1 to the CPR).

(3) It is desirable, where this is practical, that applications or appeals are submitted to a Master, District Judge or Judge prior to the hearing of the application or appeal so that they can be marked "fit for August" or "fit for vacation." If they are so marked, then normally the Judge will be prepared to hear the application or appeal in August, if marked "fit for August" or in September if marked "fit for vacation". A request to have the papers so marked should normally be made in writing, shortly setting out the nature of the application or appeal and the reasons why it should be dealt with in August or in September, as the case may be.

Chancery Masters

3.4 There is no distinction between term time and vacation so far as business before the Chancery Masters is concerned. The Masters will deal with all types of business throughout the year, and when a Master is on holiday his list will normally be taken by a Deputy Master.

Queen's Bench Masters

3.5 (1) An application notice may, without permission, be issued returnable before a Master in the month of August for any of the following purposes:

to set aside a claim form or particulars of claim, or service of a claim form or particulars of claim;

to set aside judgment; for stay of execution;

for any order by consent;

for judgment or permission to enter judgment;

for approval of settlements or for interim payment;

for relief from forfeiture; for charging order; for garnishee order;

for appointment or discharge of a receiver;

for relief by way of sheriff's interpleader;

for transfer to a county court or for trial by Master;

for time where time is running in the month of August;

(2) In any case of urgency any other type of application notice (that is other than those for the purposes in (1) above), may, with the permission of a Master be issued returnable before a Master during the month of August.

PART 40

JUDGMENTS, ORDERS, SALE OF LAND, ETC

Contents of this Part

I   Judgments and orders

Scope of this Part

40.1   This Section sets out rules about judgments and orders which apply except where any other of these Rules makes a different provision in relation to the judgment or order in question.

Standard requirements

40.2 (1) Every judgment or order must state the name and judicial title of the person who made it, unless it is –

   (a) default judgment entered under rule 12.4(1) (entry of default judgment where judgment is entered by a court officer) or a default costs certificate obtained under rule 47.11;

   (b) judgment entered under rule 14.4, 14.5, 14.6, 14.7 and 14.9 (entry of judgment on admission where judgment is entered by a court officer); or

   (c) a consent order under rule 40.6(2) (consent orders made by court officers).

   (2) Every judgment or order must –

   (a) bear the date on which it is given or made; and

   (b) be sealed^(GL) by the court.

Drawing up and filing of judgments and orders

40.3 (1) Every judgment or order will be drawn up by the court unless –

    (a) the court orders a party to draw it up;

    (b) a party, with the permission of the court, agrees to draw it up;

    (c) the court dispenses with the need to draw it up; or

    (d) it is a consent order under rule 40.6.

  (2) The court may direct that –

    (a) a judgment or an order drawn up by a party must be checked by the court before it is sealed$^{(GL)}$; or

    (b) before a judgment or an order is drawn up by the court, the parties must file an agreed statement of its terms.

  (3) Where a judgment or an order is to be drawn up by a party –

    (a) he must file it no later than 7 days after the date on which the court ordered or permitted him to draw it up so that it can be sealed$^{(GL)}$ by the court; and

    (b) if he fails to file it within that period, any other party may draw it up and file it.

Service of judgments and orders

40.4 (1) Where a judgment or an order has been drawn up by a party and is to be served by the court –

    (a) the party who drew it up must file a copy to be retained at court and sufficient copies for service on him and on the other parties; and

    (b) once it has been sealed$^{(GL)}$, the court must serve a copy of it on each party to the proceedings.

  (2) Unless the court directs otherwise, any order made otherwise than at trial must be served on –

    (a) the applicant and the respondent; and

    (b) any other person on whom the court orders it to be served.

(Rule 6.3 specifies who must serve judgments and orders.)

(RSC Order 44 in Schedule 1 contains rules about the service of notice of certain judgments.)

Power to require judgment or order to be served on a party as well as his solicitor

40.5   Where the party on whom a judgment or order is to be served is acting by a solicitor, the court may order the judgment or order to be served on the party as well as on his solicitor.

Consent judgments and orders

40.6 (1) This rule applies where all the parties agree the terms in which a judgment should be given or an order should be made.

  (2) A court officer may enter and seal$^{(GL)}$ an agreed judgment or order if –

    (a) the judgment or order is listed in paragraph (3);

    (b) none of the parties is a litigant in person; and

    (c) the approval of the court is not required by these Rules, a practice direction or any enactment before an agreed order can be made.

  (3) The judgments and orders referred to in paragraph (2) are –

    (a) a judgment or order for –

      (i) the payment of an amount of money (including a judgment or order for damages or the value of goods to be decided by the court); or

      (ii) the delivery up of goods with or without the option of paying the value of the goods or the agreed value.

  (b) an order for –

      (i) the dismissal of any proceedings, wholly or in part;

      (ii) the stay$^{(GL)}$ of proceedings on agreed terms, disposing of the proceedings, whether those terms are recorded in a schedule to the order or elsewhere;

      (iii) the stay$^{(GL)}$ of enforcement of a judgment, either unconditionally or on condition that the money due under the judgment is paid by instalments specified in the order;

      (iv) the setting aside under Part 13 of a default judgment which has not been satisfied;

      (v) the payment out of money which has been paid into court;

      (vi) the discharge from liability of any party;

      (vii) the payment, assessment or waiver of costs, or such other provision for costs as may be agreed.

(4) Rule 40.3 (drawing up and filing of judgments and orders) applies to judgments and orders entered and sealed$^{(GL)}$ by a court officer under paragraph (2) as it applies to other judgments and orders.

(5) Where paragraph (2) does not apply, any party may apply for a judgment or order in the terms agreed.

(6) The court may deal with an application under paragraph (5) without a hearing.

(7) Where this rule applies –

  (a) the order which is agreed by the parties must be drawn up in the terms agreed;

  (b) it must be expressed as being 'By Consent';

  (c) it must be signed by the legal representative acting for each of the parties to whom the order relates or, where paragraph (5) applies, by the party if he is a litigant in person.

When judgment or order takes effect

40.7 (1) A judgment or order takes effect from the day when it is given or made, or such later date as the court may specify.

  (2) This rule applies to all judgments and orders except those to which rule 40.10 (judgment against a State) applies.

Time from which interest begins to run

40.8 (1) Where interest is payable on a judgment pursuant to section 17 of the Judgments Act 1838$^{(57)}$ or section 74 of the County Courts Act 1984$^{(58)}$, the interest shall begin to run from the date that judgment is given unless –

  (a) a rule in another Part or a practice direction makes different provision; or

  (b) the court orders otherwise.

---

(57) 1838 c.110. Section 17 was amended by S.I. 1998/2940.

(58) 1984 c.28. Section 74 was amended by section 2 of the Private International Law (Miscellaneous Provisions) Act 1995 (c.42).

(2) The court may order that interest shall begin to run from a date before the date that judgment is given.

Who may apply to set aside or vary a judgment or order

40.9   A person who is not a party but who is directly affected by a judgment or order may apply to have the judgment or order set aside or varied.

Judgment against a State in default of acknowledgment of service

40.10 (1) Where the claimant obtains default judgment under Part 12 on a claim against a State where the defendant has failed to file an acknowledgment of service, the judgment does not take effect until 2 months after service on the State of –

(a) a copy of the judgment; and

(b) a copy of the evidence in support of the application for permission to enter default judgment (unless the evidence has already been served on the State in accordance with an order made under Part 12).

(2) In this rule, 'State' has the meaning given by section 14 of the State Immunity Act 1978[59].

Time for complying with a judgment or order

40.11   A party must comply with a judgment or order for the payment of an amount of money (including costs) within 14 days of the date of the judgment or order, unless –

(a) the judgment or order specifies a different date for compliance (including specifying payment by instalments);

(b) any of these Rules specifies a different date for compliance; or

(c) the court has stayed the proceedings or judgment.

(Parts 12 and 14 specify different dates for complying with certain default judgments and judgments on admissions.)

Correction of errors in judgments and order

40.12 (1) The court may at any time correct an accidental slip or omission in a judgment or order.

(2) A party may apply for a correction without notice.

Cases where court gives judgment both on claim and counterclaim

40.13 (1) This rule applies where the court gives judgment for specified amounts both for the claimant on his claim and against the claimant on a counterclaim.

(2) If there is a balance in favour of one of the parties, it may order the party whose judgment is for the lesser amount to pay the balance.

(3) In a case to which this rule applies, the court may make a separate order as to costs against each party.

Judgment in favour of certain part owners relating to the detention of goods

40.14 (1) In this rule 'part owner' means one of two or more persons who have an interest in the same goods.

(2) Where –

(a) a part owner makes a claim relating to the detention of the goods; and

(b) the claim is not based on a right to possession,

any judgment or order given or made in respect of the claim is to be for the

---

(59) 1978 c.33.

payment of damages only, unless the claimant had the written authority of every other part owner of the goods to make the claim on his behalf as well as for himself.

(3) This rule applies notwithstanding anything in subsection (3) of section 3 of the Torts (Interference with Goods) Act 1977[60], but does not affect the remedies and jurisdiction mentioned in subsection (8) of that section.

II Sale of land etc and conveyancing counsel

Scope of this section

40.15(1) This Section –

    (a) deals with the court's power to order the sale, mortgage, partition or exchange of land; and

    (b) contains provisions about conveyancing counsel.

(Section 131 of the Supreme Court Act 1981[61] (provides for the appointment of the conveyancing counsel of the Supreme Court.)

    (2) In this Section "land" includes any interest in, or right over, land.

Power to order sale etc.

40.16 In any proceedings relating to land, the court may order the land, or part of it, to be –

    (a) sold;

    (b) mortgaged;

    (c) exchanged; or

    (d) partitioned.

Power to order delivery up of possession etc.

40.17 Where the court has made an order under rule 40.16, it may order any party to deliver up to the purchaser or any other person –

    (a) possession of the land;

    (b) receipt of rents or profits relating to it; or

    (c) both.

Reference to conveyancing counsel

40.18(1) The court may direct conveyancing counsel to investigate and prepare a report on the title of any land or to draft any document.

    (2) The court may take the report on title into account when it decides the issue in question.

(Provisions dealing with the fees payable to conveyancing counsel are set out in the practice direction relating to Part 44.)

Party may object to report

40.19(1) Any party to the proceedings may object to the report on title prepared by conveyancing counsel.

    (2) Where there is an objection, the issue will be referred to a judge for determination.

(Part 23 contains general rules about making an application.)

---

(60) 1977 c.32.

(61) 1981 c.54; section 131 was amended by the Courts and Legal Services Act 1990 (c.41),

PRACTICE DIRECTION – ACCOUNTS, INQUIRIES ETC.
THIS PRACTICE DIRECTION SUPPLEMENTS CPR PART 40

Section 1 contains provisions as to taking accounts and conducting inquiries under a judgment or order. Section 2 contains provisions formerly in CCR Order 23.

As to obtaining an interim or summary order for accounts or inquiries, attention is drawn to the Accounts & Inquiries Practice Direction that supplements CPR Part 25 and to paragraph 6 of the Summary Judgment Practice Direction that supplements CPR Part 24.

Section 1

Accounts and inquiries: general

1.1 Where the court orders any account to be taken or any inquiry to be made, it may, by the same or a subsequent order, give directions as to the manner in which the account is to be taken and verified or the inquiry is to be conducted.

1.2 In particular, the court may direct that in taking an account, the relevant books of account shall be evidence of their contents but that any party may take such objections to the contents as he may think fit.

1.3 Any party may apply to the court in accordance with CPR Part 23 for directions as to the taking of an account or the conduct of an inquiry or for the variation of directions already made.

1.4 Every direction for the taking of an account or the making of an inquiry shall be numbered in the order so that, as far as possible, each distinct account and inquiry is given its own separate number.

Verifying the account

2. Subject to any order to the contrary:
   (1) the accounting party must make out his account and verify it by an affidavit or witness statement to which the account is exhibited,
   (2) the accounting party must file the account with the court and at the same time notify the other parties that he has done so and of the filing of any affidavit or witness statement verifying or supporting the account.

Objections

3.1 Any party who wishes to contend:
   (a) that an accounting party has received more than the amount shown by the account to have been received, or
   (b) that the accounting party should be treated as having received more than he has actually received, or
   (c) that any item in the account is erroneous in respect of amount, or
   (d) that in any other respect the account is inaccurate, must, unless the court directs otherwise, give written notice to the accounting party of his objections.

3.2 The written notice referred to in paragraph 3.1 must, so far as the objecting party is able to do so:
   (a) state the amount by which it is contended that the account understates the amount received by the accounting party,
   (b) state the amount which it is contended that the accounting party should be treated as having received in addition to the amount he actually received,
   (c) specify the respects in which it is contended that the account is inaccurate, and
   (d) in each case, give the grounds on which the contention is made.

3.3 The contents of the written notice must, unless the notice contains a statement of truth, be verified by either an affidavit or a witness statement to which the notice is an exhibit.

(Part 22 and the Practice Direction that supplements it contain provisions about statements of truth).

Allowances

4.   In taking any account all just allowances shall be made without any express direction to that effect.

Management of proceedings

5.   The court may at any stage in the taking of an account or in the course of an inquiry direct a hearing in order to resolve an issue that has arisen and for that purpose may order that points of claim and points of defence be served and give any necessary directions.

Delay

6.1 If it appears to the court that there is undue delay in the taking of any account or the progress of any inquiry the court may require the accounting party or the party with the conduct of the inquiry, as the case may be, to explain the delay and may then make such order for the management of the proceedings (including a stay) and for costs as the circumstances may require.

6.2 The directions the court may give under paragraph 6.1 include a direction that the Official Solicitor take over the conduct of the proceedings and directions providing for the payment of the Official Solicitor's costs.

Distribution

7.   Where some of the persons entitled to share in a fund are known but there is, or is likely to be, difficulty or delay in ascertaining other persons so entitled, the court may direct, or allow, immediate payment of their shares to the known persons without reserving any part of those shares to meet the subsequent costs of ascertaining the other persons.

Guardian's accounts

8.   The accounts of a person appointed guardian of the property of a child (defined in CPR 21.1(2)) must be verified and approved in such manner as the court may direct.

Section 2

Application of RSC Order 44 to County Court proceedings

9.1 The provision of rules 1 to 10 of RSC 44 (see Part 50 and Schedule 1 to the CPR) relating to proceedings under a judgment or order in the Chancery Division shall apply to proceedings under a judgment or order made in a County Court –

   (a)   in proceedings for:-
      (i)   the administration of the estate of a deceased person; or
      (ii)   the execution of a trust; or
      (iii) the sale of any property; or
   (b)   in any other proceedings in the exercise of its equity jurisdiction.

9.2 Where a judgment or order directs an account to be taken or an inquiry to be made and does not otherwise provide, the account shall be taken or the inquiry made by a Master or district judge (if the proceedings are in the High Court) or a district judge (if the proceedings are in the county court).

10. The court shall give to every creditor or other person whose claim or any part of whose claim has been allowed or disallowed, and who did not attend when the claim was disposed of, a notice informing him of that fact.

11. Rule 11 of RSC 44 (Schedule 1 to the CPR) shall apply to proceedings in a county court as if references to "the Master" were references to a district judge.

12. An appeal shall lie to the judge from any order made by a district judge under rules 1 to 10 of RSC Order 44 (including an order giving directions as to the further conduct of the proceedings) and the provisions about an appeal in rule 12 of RSC 44 shall apply.

PRACTICE DIRECTION – JUDGMENTS AND ORDERS
THIS PRACTICE DIRECTION SUPPLEMENTS CPR PART 40

Drawing up and filing of judgments and orders

1.1 Rule 40.2 sets out the standard requirements for judgments and orders and rule 40.3 deals with how judgments and orders should be drawn up.

1.2 A party who has been ordered or given permission to draw up an order must file it for sealing within 7 days of being ordered or permitted to do so[1]. If he fails to do so, any other party may draw it up and file it[2].

1.3 If the court directs that a judgment or order which is being drawn up by a party must be checked by the court before it is sealed, the party responsible must file the draft within 7 days of the date the order was made with a request that the draft be checked before it is sealed.

1.4 If the court directs the parties to file an agreed statement of terms of an order which the court is to draw up[3], the parties must do so no later than 7 days from the date the order was made, unless the court directs otherwise.

1.5 If the court requires the terms of an order which is being drawn up by the court to be agreed by the parties the court may direct;

(1) a copy of the draft order to be sent to all parties for their agreement to be endorsed on it and returned to the court before the order is sealed, or

(2) a copy of the draft order together with notice of an appointment to attend before the court to agree the terms of the order.

Preparation of deeds or documents under an order

2.1 Where a judgment or order directs any deed or document to be prepared, executed or signed, the order will state:

(1) the person who is to prepare the deed or document, and

(2) if the deed or document is to be approved, the person who is to approve it.

2.2 If the parties are unable to agree the form of the deed or document, any party may apply in accordance with Part 23 for the form of the deed or document to be settled.

2.3 In such case the judge may:

(1) settle the deed or document himself, or

(2) refer it to

    (a) a master, or

    (b) a district judge, or

    (c) a conveyancing counsel of the Supreme Court to settle.

(See also the Sale of Land practice direction supplementing CPR Part 40)

Consent orders

3.1 Rule 40.6(3) sets out the types of consent judgments and orders which may be entered and sealed by a court officer. The court officer may do so in those cases provided that:

(1) none of the parties is a litigant in person, and

(2) the approval of the court is not required by the Rules, a practice direction or any enactment[4].

3.2 If a consent order filed for sealing appears to be unclear or incorrect the court officer may refer it to a judge for consideration[5].

---

1   Rule 40.3(3)(a).
2   Rule 40.3(3)(b).
3   Rule 40.3(2)(b).
4   Rule 40.6(2).
5   Rule 3.2.

3.3 Where a consent judgment or order does not come within the provisions of rule 40.6(2):

(1) an application notice requesting a judgment or order in the agreed terms should be filed with the draft judgment or order to be entered or sealed, and

(2) the draft judgment or order must be drawn so that the judge's name and judicial title can be inserted.

3.4 A consent judgment or order must:

(1) be drawn up in the terms agreed,

(2) bear on it the words "By Consent", and

(3) be signed by

(a) solicitors or counsel acting for each of the parties to the order, or

(b) where a party is a litigant in person, the litigant[6].

3.5 Where the parties draw up a consent order in the form of a stay of proceedings on agreed terms, disposing of the proceedings[7], and where the terms are recorded in a schedule to the order, any direction for:

(1) payment of money out of court, or

(2) payment and assessment of costs should be contained in the body of the order and not in the schedule.

Correction of errors in judgments and orders

4.1 Where a judgment or order contains an accidental slip or omission a party may apply for it to be corrected[8].

4.2 The application notice (which may be an informal document such as a letter) should describe the error and set out the correction required. An application may be dealt with without a hearing:

(1) where the applicant so requests,

(2) with the consent of the parties, or

(3) where the court does not consider that a hearing would be appropriate.

4.3 The judge may deal with the application without notice if the slip or omission is obvious or may direct notice of the application to be given to the other party or parties.

4.4 If the application is opposed it should, if practicable, be listed for hearing before the judge who gave the judgment or made the order.

4.5 The court has an inherent power to vary its own orders to make the meaning and intention of the court clear.

Adjustment of final judgment figure in respect of compensation recovery payments

5.1 In a final judgment[9] where some or all of the damages awarded:

(1) fall under the heads of damage set out in column 1 of Schedule 2 to the Social Security (Recovery of Benefits) Act 1997 in respect of recoverable benefits received by the claimant set out in column 2 of that Schedule and

(2) where the defendant has paid to the Secretary of State the recoverable benefits in accordance with the certificate of recoverable benefits,

there should be stated in a preamble to the judgment or order the amount awarded under each head of damage and the amount by which it has been reduced in accordance with section 8 and Schedule 2 to the Social Security (Recovery of Benefits) Act 1997.

5.2 The judgment or order should then provide for entry of judgment and payment of the balance.

---

6 Rule 40.6(7).

7 Rule 40.6(3)(b)(ii).

8 Rule 40.10.

9 In this paragraph final "judgment" includes any order to pay a sum of money, a final award of damages and an assessment of damages.

Adjustment of final judgment figure in respect of an interim payment

6.1 In a final judgment[10] where an interim payment has previously been made which is less than the total amount awarded by the judge, the judgment or order should set out in a preamble:

(1) the total amount awarded by the judge, and

(2) the amount and date of the interim payment(s).

6.2 The total amount awarded by the judge should then be reduced by the total amount of any interim payments, and the judgment or order should then provide for entry of judgment and payment of the balance.

6.3 In a final judgment where an interim payment has previously been made which is more than the total amount awarded by the judge, the judgment or order should set out in a preamble;

(1) the total amount awarded by the judge, and

(2) the amount and date of the interim payment(s).

6.4 An order should then be made for repayment, reimbursement, variation or discharge under rule 25.8(2) and for interest on an overpayment under rule 25.8(5).

Statement as to service of a claim form

7.1 Where a party to proceedings which have gone to trial requires a statement to be included in the judgment as to where, and by what means the claim form issued in those proceedings was served, application should made to the trial judge when judgment is given.

7.2 If the judge so orders, the statement will be included in a preamble to the judgment as entered.

Orders requiring an act to be done

8.1 An order which requires an act to be done (other than a judgment or order for the payment of an amount of money) must specify the time within which the act should be done.

8.2 The consequences of failure to do an act within the time specified may be set out in the order. In this case the wording of the following examples suitably adapted must be used:

(1) Unless the [claimant][defendant] serves his list of documents by 4.00pm on Friday, January 22, 1999 his [claim][defence] will be struck out and judgment entered for the [defendant][claimant]., or

(2) Unless the [claimant][defendant] serves his list of documents within 14 days of service of this order his [claim][defence] will be struck out and judgment entered for the [defendant][claimant].

Example (1) should be used wherever possible.

Non-compliance with a judgment or order

9.1 An order which restrains a party from doing an act or requires an act to be done should, if disobedience is to be dealt with by an application to bring contempt of court proceedings, have the penal notice endorsed on it as follows: "If you the within-named [   ] do not comply with this order you may be held to be in contempt of court and imprisoned or fined, or [in the case of a company or corporation] your assets may be seized."

9.2 The provisions of paragraph 8.1 above also apply to an order which contains an undertaking by a party to do or not do an act, subject to paragraph 8.3 below.

9.3 The court has the power to decline to:

(1) accept an undertaking, and

(2) deal with disobedience in respect of an undertaking by contempt of court proceedings,

unless the party giving the undertaking has made a signed statement to the effect that he understands the terms of his undertaking and the consequences of failure to comply with it.

9.4 The statement may be endorsed on the [court copy of the] order containing the undertaking or may be filed in a separate document such as a letter.

---

10   As in Note 9 above.

Foreign currency

10. Where judgment is ordered to be entered in a foreign currency, the order should be in the following form: "It is ordered that the defendant pay the claimant (state the sum in the foreign currency) or the Sterling equivalent at the time of payment."

Costs

11.1 Attention is drawn to the costs practice direction and, in particular, to the court's power to make a summary assessment of costs.

11.2 Attention is also drawn to costs rule 43.5(5) which provides that if an order makes no mention of costs, none are payable in respect of the proceedings to which it relates.

Judgments paid by instalments

12. Where a judgment is to be paid by instalments, the judgment should set out:
    (1) the total amount of the judgment,
    (2) the amount of each instalment,
    (3) the number of instalments and the date on which each is to be paid, and
    (4) to whom the instalments should be paid.

Order to make an order of the House of Lords an order of the High Court

13.1 Application may be made in accordance with Part 23 for an order to make an order of the House of Lords an order of the High Court. The application should be made to the procedural judge of the Division, District Registry or court in which the proceedings are taking place and may be made without notice unless the court directs otherwise.

13.2 The application must be supported by the following evidence:
    (1) details of the order which was the subject of the appeal to the House of Lords,
    (2) details of the order of the House of Lords, with a copy annexed, and
    (3) a copy annexed of the certificate of the Clerk of Parliaments of the assessment of the costs of the appeal to the House of Lords in the sum of £..............

13.3 The order to make an order of the House of Lords an order of the High Court should be in form no PF68.

Examples of forms of trial judgment

14.1 The following general forms may be used;
    (1) judgment after trial before judge without jury – form no 45,
    (2) judgment after trial before judge with jury – form no 46,
    (3) judgment after trial before a Master or district judge – form no 47,
    (4) judgment after trial before a judge of the Technology and Construction court – form no 47 but with any necessary modifications.

14.2 A trial judgment should, in addition to the matters set out in paragraphs 5, 6 and 7 above, have the following matters set out in a preamble:
    (1) the questions put to a jury and their answers to those questions,
    (2) the findings of a jury and whether unanimous or by a majority,
    (3) any order made during the course of the trial concerning the use of evidence,
    (4) any matters that were agreed between the parties prior to or during the course of the trial in respect of
        (a) liability,
        (b) contribution,
        (c) the amount of the damages or part of the damages, and
    (5) the findings of the judge in respect of each head of damage in a personal injury case.

14.3 Form no 49 should be used for a trial judgment against an Estate.

The forms referred to in this practice direction are listed in the practice direction which supplements Part 4 (Forms).

For information about

(1) Orders for provisional damages: see Part 41 and the practice direction which supplements it.

(2) Orders in respect of children and patients: see Part 22 and the practice direction which supplements it.

(3) Orders containing directions for payment of money out of court: see Parts 36 and 37 and the practice directions which supplement them.

(4) Structured settlement orders: see the separate practice direction supplementing Part 40.

(5) Taking accounts and conducting inquiries under a judgment or order: see the separate practice direction supplementing Part 40.

PRACTICE DIRECTION–STRUCTURED SETTLEMENTS
THIS PRACTICE DIRECTION SUPPLEMENTS CPR PART 40

Structured settlements:

1.1 A structured settlement is a means of paying a sum awarded to or accepted by a claimant by way of instalments for the remainder of the claimant's life. The payments are either funded by an annuity from an insurance company or, where the party paying is a government body, by payments direct from that body.

1.2 The agreed sum which purchases the annuity or provides for payments (including any sum to be retained as capital for contingencies) is based on the sum offered or awarded on a conventional basis, less an amount representing the tax benefits obtained by the structure.

1.3 This type of order may be used both on settlement of a claim and after trial where the judge has found in favour of the claimant. In the latter case the claimant or his legal representative should ask the judge:

(1) not to provide for entry of judgment,

(2) to state the total amount to which the judge has found the claimant to be entitled, and

(3) for an adjournment to enable advice to be sought as to the formulation of a structured settlement based on that amount.

1.4 Where a claim settles before trial, an application should be made in accordance with CPR Part 23 for the consent order embodying the structured settlement to be made, and for the approval of the structured settlement where the claimant is a child or patient 1 .

1.5 If the claimant is not a child or patient, the consent order may be made without a hearing.

1.6 Where a hearing is required and as the annuity rate applicable to the structure may only remain available for a short time, the claimant's legal representative on issue of his application notice, should immediately seek an early date for the hearing.

1.7 At such a hearing the court will require the following documents and evidence to be filed not later than midday on the day before the hearing is to take place:

(1) Counsel's or the legal representative's opinion of the value of the claim on the basis of a conventional award (unless approval on that basis has already been given or the judge has stated the amount as in paragraph 1.3(2) above),

(2) a report of forensic accountants setting out the effect of a structured settlement bearing in mind the claimant's life expectancy and the anticipated cost of future care,

(3) a draft of the proposed structure agreement,

(4) sufficient information to satisfy the court that –

(a) enough of the agreed sum is retained as a contingency fund for anticipated future needs, and

(b) the structured settlement is secure and the annuities are payable by established insurers,

(5) details of any assets available to the claimant other than the agreed sum which is the subject of the application, and

(6) where the claimant is a patient, the approval or consent of the Court of Protection.

1.8 To obtain the approval of the Court of Protection the claimant's legal representative should lodge the documents and information set out in paragraph 1.7(1) to (5) above together with a copy of the claim form and any statements of case filed in the proceedings in the Enquiries and Acceptances Branch of the Public Trust Office, Stewart House, 24 Kingsway, London WC2B 6JH by midday on the fourth day before the hearing.

1.9 If an application for the appointment of a receiver by the Court of Protection has not already been made:

(1) two copies of the application seeking his appointment (form CP1),

(2) a certificate of family and property (form CP5), and

(3) a medical certificate (form CP3)

should be lodged at the same time as the documents and information mentioned in paragraph 1.8 above. Forms CP1, 3 and 5 may be obtained from the address set out in paragraph 1.8.

1.10 Wherever possible a draft order should also be filed at the same time as the documents in paragraph 1.7 above.

1.11 Examples of structured settlement orders are set out in an Annex to this practice direction which may be adapted for use after trial or as the individual circumstances require. It should be noted that the reference in the second paragraph of the Part 2 – structured settlement order to the "defendant's insurers" means the Life Insurer providing the annuity on behalf of the defendant.

1.12 Where it is necessary to obtain immediate payment out of money in court upon the order being made, the claimant's legal representatives should:

(1) contact the officer in charge of funds in court at the Court Funds Office at least 2 days before the hearing, and arrange for a cheque for the appropriate sum made payable to the insurers or government body to be ready for collection,

(2) notify the court office the day before the hearing so that the court is aware of the urgency, and

(3) bring to the hearing a completed Court Funds Office form 200 for authentication by the court upon the order being made.

ANNEX
PART 1- STRUCTURED SETTLEMENT ORDER

(Order to settle for conventional sum and for an adjournment to seek advice on the formulation of a structured settlement)

Title of Claim

UPON HEARING (Counsel/solicitor) for the claimant and (Counsel/solicitor) for the defendant

AND UPON the defendant by (Counsel/solicitor) having undertaken to keep open an offer of £............... in full and final settlement of the claim and the claimant having undertaken to limit the claim to £....................

AND UPON the claimant's solicitors undertaking to instruct appropriate advisers to advise upon a structured settlement and to use their best endeavours promptly to make proposals to the defendant's solicitors as to the most equitable formulation of a structured settlement and after to seek (further directions/approval) from the court if necessary

IT IS ORDERED that this claim is adjourned with permission to both parties to apply in respect of the further hearing relating to further directions providing for a structured settlement as undertaken by the claimant's solicitors and that these proceedings be reserved to the (trial judge) unless otherwise ordered

AND IT IS ORDERED that the costs of these proceedings together with the costs relating to any proposal for a structured settlement be (as ordered).

PART 2– STRUCTURED SETTLEMENT ORDER

(*Order giving effect to and approval of a structured settlement*)

Title of Claim

UPON HEARING (Counsel/solicitor) for the claimant and (Counsel/solicitor) for the defendant

AND the claimant and defendant having agreed to the terms set forth in the Schedule to this order in which the claimant accepts the sum of £.............. (overall sum) in satisfaction of the claim of which the sum of £................ is to be used by the [defendant's insurers for the purchase of an annuity][defendant for the provision of the appropriate payments]

AND UPON the Judge having approved the terms of the draft minute of order, the agreement and the schedule to this order

AND UPON the claimant and the insurer (name) undertaking to execute the agreement this day

BY CONSENT

IT IS ORDERED

(1) that of the sum of £.............. (total sum in court) now in court standing to the credit of this claim the sum of £................ be paid out to (insurers/payee) on behalf of the defendant for the purchase of an annuity as specified in the payment schedule to this order

(2) (other relevant orders)

( ) that all further proceedings in this claim be stayed except for the purpose of carrying the terms into effect

( ) that the parties have permission to apply to carry the terms into effect

SCHEDULE

(Attach draft agreement and set out any other terms of the settlement.)

PRACTICE DIRECTION –
1. COURT'S POWERS IN RELATION TO LAND.
2. CONVEYANCING COUNSEL OF THE COURT.
THIS PRACTICE DIRECTION SUPPLEMENTS CPR PART 40.

PART 1 - COURT'S POWERS IN RELATION TO LAND

Application to the court where land subject to an incumbrance

1.1 In this paragraph 'incumbrance' has the same meaning as it has in section 205(1) of the Law of Property Act 1925.

1.2 Where land subject to any incumbrance is sold or exchanged any party to the sale or exchange may apply to the court for a direction under section 50 of the Law of Property Act 1925 (discharge of incumbrances by the court on sales or exchanges).

1.3 The directions a court may give on such an application include a direction for the payment into court of a sum of money that the court considers sufficient to meet–

(1) the value of the incumbrance; and

(2) further costs, expenses and interest that may become due on or in respect of the incumbrance.

(Section 50(1) of the Law of Property Act 1925 contains provisions relating to the calculation of these amounts)

1.4 Where a payment into court has been made in accordance with a direction under section 50(1) the court may–

    (1) declare the land to be freed from the incumbrance; and

    (2) make any order it considers appropriate for giving effect to an order made under rule 40.16 or relating to the money in court and the income thereof.

1.5 An application under section 50 should

    (1) if made in existing proceedings, be made in accordance with CPR Part 23;

    (2) otherwise, be made by claim form under CPR Part 8.

Directions about the sale etc.

2 Where the court has made an order under rule 40.16 it may give any other directions it considers appropriate for giving effect to the order. In particular the court may give directions–

    (1) appointing a party or other person to conduct the sale;

    (2) for obtaining evidence of the value of the land;

    (3) as to the manner of sale;

    (4) settling the particulars and conditions of the sale;

    (5) fixing a minimum or reserve price;

    (6) as to the fees and expenses to be allowed to an auctioneer or estate agent;

    (7) for the purchase money to be paid

        (a) into court;

        (b) to trustees; or

        (c) to any other person;

    (8) for the result of a sale to be certified;

    (9) under rule 40.18.

Application for permission to bid

3.1 Where–

    (1) the court has made an order under rule 40.16 for land to be sold; and

    (2) a party wishes to bid for the land,

he should apply to the court for permission to do so.

3.2 An application for permission to bid must be made before the sale takes place.

3.3 If the court gives permission to all the parties to bid, it may appoint an independent person to conduct the sale.

3.4 "Bid" in this paragraph includes submitting a tender or other offer to buy.

Certifying sale result

4.1 If–

    (1) the court has directed the purchase money to be paid into court; or

    (2) the court has directed that the result of the sale be certified

the result of the sale must be certified by the person having conduct of the sale.

4.2 Unless the court directs otherwise, the certificate must give details of

    (1) the amount of the purchase price;

    (2) the amount of the fees and expenses payable to any auctioneer or estate agent;

    (3) the amount of any other expenses of the sale;

    (4) the net amount received in respect of the sale;

and must be verified by a statement of truth.

(Part 22 sets out requirements about statements of truth)

4.3 The certificate must be filed

    (1) if the proceedings are being dealt with in the Royal Courts of Justice, in Chancery Chambers;

(2) if the proceedings are being dealt with anywhere else, in the court where the proceedings are being dealt with.

Fees and expenses of auctioneers and estate agents

5.1 (1 Where the court has ordered the sale of land under rule 40.16, auctioneer's and estate agent's charges may, unless the court orders otherwise, include
  (a) commission;
  (b) fees for valuation of the land;
  (c) charges for advertising the land;
  (d) other expenses and disbursements but not charges for surveys.
  (2) The court's authorisation is required for charges relating to surveys.

5.2 If the total amount of the auctioneer's and estate agent's charges authorised under paragraph 5.1(1)
  (1) does not exceed 2.5% of the sale price; and
  (2) does not exceed the rate of commission that that agent would normally charge on a sole agency basis

the charges may, unless the court orders otherwise and subject to paragraph 5.3(3) and (4), be met by deduction of the amount of the charges from the proceeds of sale without the need for any further authorisation from the court.

5.3 If–
  (1) a charge made by an auctioneer or estate agent (whether in respect of fees or expenses or both) is not authorised under paragraph 5.1(1);
  (2) the total amount of the charges so authorised exceeds the limits set out in paragraph 5.2;
  (3) the land is sold in lots or by valuation; or
  (4) the sale is of investment property, business property or farm property

an application must be made to the court for approval of the fees and expenses to be allowed.

5.4 An application under paragraph 5.3 may be made by any party or, if he is not a party, by the person having conduct of the sale, and may be made either before or after the sale has taken place.

PART 2 – CONVEYANCING COUNSEL OF THE COURT

Reference to conveyancing counsel

6.1 When the court refers a matter under rule 40.18, the court may specify a particular conveyancing counsel.

6.2 If the court does not specify a particular conveyancing counsel, references will be distributed among conveyancing counsel in accordance with arrangements made by the Chief Chancery Master.

6.3 Notice of every reference under rule 40.18 must be given to the Chief Chancery Master.

6.4 The court will send a copy of the order, together with all other necessary documents, to conveyancing counsel.

6.5 A court order sent to conveyancing counsel under paragraph 6.4 will be sufficient authority for him to prepare his report or draft the document.

6.6 (1) An objection under rule 40.19 to a report on title prepared by conveyancing counsel must be made by application notice.
  (2) The application notice must state–
    (a) the matters the applicant objects to; and
    (b) the reason for the objection.

PART 41

PROVISIONAL DAMAGES

Contents of this Part

Application and definitions

41.1 (1) This Part applies to proceedings to which SCA s.32A or CCA s.51 applies.

     (2) In this Part –

         (a) 'SCA s.32A' means section 32A of the Supreme Court Act 1981[62];

         (b) 'CCA s.51' means section 51 of the County Courts Act 1984[63]; and

         (c) 'award of provisional damages' means an award of damages for personal injuries under which –

            (i) damages are assessed on the assumption referred to in SCA s.32A or CCA s.51 that the injured person will not develop the disease or suffer the deterioration; and

            (ii) the injured person is entitled to apply for further damages at a future date if he develops the disease or suffers the deterioration.

Order for an award of provisional damages

41.2 (1) The court may make an order for an award of provisional damages if –

         (a) the particulars of claim include a claim for provisional damages; and

         (b) the court is satisfied that SCA s.32A or CCA s.51 applies.

(Rule 16.4(1)(d) sets out what must be included in the particulars of claim where the claimant is claiming provisional damages.)

     (2) An order for an award of provisional damages –

         (a) must specify the disease or type of deterioration in respect of which an application may be made at a future date;

         (b) must specify the period within which such an application may be made; and

         (c) may be made in respect of more than one disease or type of deterioration and may, in respect of each disease or type of deterioration, specify a different period within which a subsequent application may be made.

     (3) The claimant may make more than one application to extend the period specified under paragraph (2)(b) or (2)(c).

Application for further damages

41.3 (1) The claimant may not make an application for further damages after the end of the period specified under rule 41.2(2), or such period as extended by the court.

     (2) Only one application for further damages may be made in respect of each disease or type of deterioration specified in the award of provisional damages.

---

(62) 1981 c.54. Section 32A was inserted by section 6(1) of the Administration of Justice Act 1982 (c.53).

(63) 1984 c.28.

(3) The claimant must give at least 28 days' written notice to the defendant of his intention to apply for further damages.

(4) If the claimant knows –

  (a) that the defendant is insured in respect of the claim; and

  (b) the identity of the defendant's insurers,

  he must also give at least 28 days' written notice to the insurers.

(5) Within 21 days after the end of the 28 day notice period referred to in paragraphs (3) and (4), the claimant must apply for directions.

(6) The rules in Part 25 about the making of an interim payment apply where an application is made under this rule.

PRACTICE DIRECTION – PROVISIONAL DAMAGES
THIS PRACTICE DIRECTION SUPPLEMENTS CPR PART 41 CLAIMS FOR PROVISIONAL DAMAGES

1.1 CPR Part 16 and the practice direction which supplements it set out information which must be included in the particulars of claim if a claim for provisional damages is made.

Judgment for an award of provisional damages

2.1 When giving judgment at trial the judge will:

  (1) specify the disease or type of deterioration, or diseases or types of deterioration, which

    (a) for the purpose of the award of immediate damages it has been assumed will not occur, and

    (b) will entitle the claimant to further damages if it or they do occur at a future date,

  (2) give an award of immediate damages,

  (3) specify the period or periods within which an application for further damages may be made in respect of each disease or type of deterioration, and

  (4) direct what documents are to be filed and preserved as the case file in support of any application for further damages.

2.2 The claimant may make an application or applications to extend the periods referred to in paragraph 2.1(3) above 1 .

2.3 A period specified under paragraph 2.1(3) may be expressed as being for the duration of the life of the claimant.

2.4 The documents to be preserved as the case file ("the case file documents") referred to in paragraph 2.1(4) will be set out in a schedule to the judgment as entered.

2.5 Causation of any further damages within the scope of the order shall be determined when any application for further damages is made.

2.6 A form for a provisional damages judgment is set out in the Annex to this practice direction.

The case file

3.1 The case file documents must be preserved until the expiry of the period or periods specified or of any extension of them.

3.2 The case file documents will normally include:

  (1) the judgment as entered,

  (2) the statements of case,

  (3) a transcript of the judge's oral judgment,

  (4) all medical reports relied on, and

  (5) a transcript of any parts of the claimant's own evidence which the judge considers necessary.

3.3 The associate/court clerk will:

  (1) ensure that the case file documents are provided by the parties where necessary and filed on the court file,

(2) endorse the court file

    (a) to the effect that it contains the case file documents, and

    (b) with the period during which the case file documents must be preserved, and

(3) preserve the case file documents in the court office where the proceedings took place.

3.4 Any subsequent order:

    (1) extending the period within which an application for further damages may be made, or

    (2) of the Court of Appeal discharging or varying the provisions of the original judgment or of any subsequent order under sub-paragraph (1) above,

will become one of the case file documents and must be preserved accordingly and any variation of the period within which an application for further damages may be made should be endorsed on the court file containing the case file documents.

3.5 On an application to extend the periods referred to in paragraph 2.1(3) above a current medical report should be filed.

3.6 Legal representatives are reminded that it is their duty to preserve their own case file.

Consent orders

4.1 An application to give effect to a consent order for provisional damages should be made in accordance with CPR Part 23. If the claimant is a child or patient 2 the approval of the court must also be sought and the application for approval will normally be dealt with at a hearing.

4.2 The order should be in the form of a consent judgment and should contain;

    (1) the matters set out in paragraph 2.1(1) to (3) above, and

    (2) a direction as to the documents to be preserved as the case file documents, which will normally be

        (a) the consent judgment,

        (b) any statements of case,

        (c) an agreed statement of facts, and

        (d) any agreed medical report(s).

4.3 The claimant or his legal representative must lodge the case file documents in the court office where the proceedings are taking place for inclusion in the court file. The court file should be endorsed as in paragraph 3.3(2) above, and the case file documents preserved as in paragraph 3.3(3) above.

Default judgment

5.1 Where a defendant:

    (1) fails to file an acknowledgment of service in accordance with CPR Part 10, and

    (2) fails to file a defence in accordance with CPR Part 15,

within the time specified for doing so, the claimant may not, unless he abandons his claim for provisional damages, enter judgment in default but should make an application in accordance with CPR Part 23 for directions.

5.2 The Master or district judge will normally direct the following issues to be decided:

    (1) whether the claim is an appropriate one for an award of provisional damages and if so, on what terms, and

    (2) the amount of immediate damages.

5.3 If the judge makes an award of provisional damages, the provisions of paragraph 3 above apply.

ANNEX
(EXAMPLE OF AN AWARD OF PROVISIONAL DAMAGES AFTER TRIAL)

(Title of proceedings)

THIS CLAIM having been tried before [title and name of judge] without a jury at [the Royal Courts of Justice or as may be] and [title and name of judge] having ordered that judgment as set out below be entered for the claimant

IT IS ORDERED —

(1) that the defendant pay the claimant by way of immediate damages the sum of £...............
(being (i) £.............. for special damages and £............. [agreed interest][interest at the rate of
...... from...........to............] (ii) £.............. for general damages and £............. [agreed
interest][interest at the rate of 2% from......... to...........] and (iii) £.............. for loss of future
earnings and/or earning capacity) on the assumption that the claimant would not at a future
date as a result of the act or omission giving rise to the claim develop the following
disease/type of deterioration namely [set out disease or type of deterioration]

(2) that if the claimant at a further date does develop that [disease][type of deterioration] he should
be entitled to apply for further damages provided that the application is made on or before [set
out period]

(3) that the documents set out in the schedule to this order be filed on the court file and preserved
as the case file until the expiry of the period set out in paragraph (2) above or of any extension
of that period which has been ordered

(4) (costs)

SCHEDULE

(list documents referred to in paragraph (3))

PART 42

CHANGE OF SOLICITOR

Contents of this Part

Solicitor acting for a party

42.1   Where the address for service of a party is the business address of his solicitor,
the solicitor will be considered to be acting for that party until the provisions of
this Part have been complied with.

(Part 6 contains provisions about the address for service.)

Change of solicitor – duty to give notice

42.2(1)   This rule applies where –

    (a) a party for whom a solicitor is acting wants to change his solicitor;

    (b) a party, after having conducted the claim in person, appoints a solicitor to
act on his behalf (except where the solicitor is appointed only to act as an
advocate for a hearing); or

    (c) a party, after having conducted the claim by a solicitor, intends to act in
person.

    (2) Where this rule applies, the party or his solicitor (where one is acting) must –

        (a) file notice of the change; and

        (b) serve notice of the change on every other party and, where paragraph
(1)(a) or (c) applies, on the former solicitor.

(3) The notice must state the party's new address for service.

(4) The notice filed at court must state that notice has been served as required by paragraph (2)(b).

(5) Subject to paragraph (6), where a party has changed his solicitor or intends to act in person, the former solicitor will be considered to be the party's solicitor unless and until –

    (a) notice is served in accordance with paragraph (1); or

    (b) the court makes an order under rule 42.3 and the order is served as required by paragraph (3) of that rule.

(6) Where the certificate of an assisted person within the meaning of the Civil Legal Aid (General) Regulations 1989[64] is revoked or discharged –

    (a) the solicitor who acted for the assisted person shall cease to be the solicitor acting in the case as soon as his retainer is determined under regulation 83 of those Regulations; and

    (b) if the assisted person wishes to continue –

        (i) where he appoints a solicitor to act on his behalf paragraph (2) will apply as if he had previously conducted the claim in person; and

        (ii) where he wants to act in person he must give an address for service.

(Rule 6.5 deals with a party's address for service)

Order that a solicitor has ceased to act

42.3(1) A solicitor may apply for an order declaring that he has ceased to be the solicitor acting for a party.

(2) Where an application is made under this rule –

    (a) notice of the application must be given to the party for whom the solicitor is acting, unless the court directs otherwise; and

    (b) the application must be supported by evidence.

(3) Where the court makes an order that a solicitor has ceased to act –

    (a) a copy of the order must be served on every party to the proceedings; and

    (b) if it is served by a party or the solicitor, the party or the solicitor (as the case may be) must file a certificate of service.

Removal of solicitor who has ceased to act on application of another party

42.4(1) Where –

    (a) a solicitor who has acted for a party –

        (i) has died;

        (ii) has become bankrupt;

        (iii) has ceased to practice; or

        (iv) cannot be found; and

    (b) the party has not given notice of a change of solicitor or notice of intention to act in person as required by rule 42.2(2),

any other party may apply for an order declaring that the solicitor has ceased to be the solicitor acting for the other party in the case.

(2) Where an application is made under this rule, notice of the application must be given to the party to whose solicitor the application relates unless the court directs otherwise.

---

(64) SI 1989/339, to which there are amendments not relevant to these Rules.

(3) Where the court makes an order made under this rule –

    (a) a copy of the order must be served on every other party to the proceedings; and

    (b) where it is served by a party, that party must file a certificate of service.

PRACTICE DIRECTION – CHANGE OF SOLICITOR
THIS PRACTICE DIRECTION SUPPLEMENTS PART 42 OF THE CIVIL PROCEDURE RULES

Solicitor acting for a party

1.1 Rule 42.1 states that where the address for service of a party is the business address[1] of his solicitor, the solicitor will be considered to be acting for that party until the provisions of Part 42 have been complied with.

1.2 Subject to rule 42.2(6) (where the certificate of an assisted person within the meaning of the Civil Legal Aid (General) Regulations 1989 is revoked or discharged), where a party has changed his solicitor or intends to act in person, the former solicitor will be considered to be the party's solicitor unless or until;

    (1) a notice of the change is

        (a) filed with the court[2], and

        (b) served on every other party[3], or

    (2) the court makes an order under rule 42.3 and the order is served on every other party[4]. The notice should not be filed until every other party has been served.

1.3 A solicitor appointed to represent a party only as an advocate at a hearing will not be considered to be acting for that party within the meaning of Part 42.

Notice of change of solicitor

2.1 Rule 42.2(1) sets out the circumstances following which a notice of the change must be filed and served.

2.2 A notice of the change giving the last known address of the former assisted person must also be filed and served on every party where, under rule 42.2(6):

    (1) the certificate of an assisted person within the meaning of the Civil Legal Aid (General) Regulations 1989 is revoked or discharged,

    (2) the solicitor who acted for the assisted person has ceased to act on determination of his retainer under regulation 83 of those Regulations, and

    (3) the assisted person wishes either to act in person or appoint another solicitor to act on his behalf.

2.3 In addition, where a party or solicitor changes his address for service, a notice of that change should be filed and served on every party.

2.4 A party who, having conducted a claim by a solicitor, intends to act in person must give in his notice an address for service that is within the jurisdiction[5].

2.5 Practice form N434 should be used to give notice of any change. The notice should be filed in the court office in which the claim is proceeding.

2.6 Where the claim is proceeding in the High Court the notice should be filed either in the appropriate District Registry or if the claim is proceeding in the Royal Courts of Justice, as follows;

---

1   Rule 6.5 and the Practice Direction supplementing Part 6 contain information about the business address.

2   Rule 42.2(2)(a)

3   Rule 42.2(2)(b)

4   Rule 42.2(5)

5   See rule 6.5(3).

(1) a claim proceeding in the Queen's Bench Division – in the Action Department of the Central Office,

(2) a claim proceeding in the Chancery Division – in Chancery Chambers,

(3) a claim proceeding in the Crown Office – in the Crown Office,

(4) a claim proceeding in the Admiralty and Commercial Registry – in the Admiralty and Commercial Registry, and

(5) a claim proceeding in the Technology and Construction Court – in the Registry of the Technology and Construction Court.

2.7 Where the claim is the subject of an appeal to the Court of Appeal, the notice should also be filed in the Civil Appeals Office.

Application for an order that a solicitor has ceased to act

3.1 A solicitor may apply under rule 42.3 for an order declaring that he has ceased to be the solicitor acting for a party.

3.2 The application should be made in accordance with Part 23[6] and must be supported by evidence[7]. Unless the court directs otherwise the application notice must be served on the party[8].

3.3 An order made under rule 42.3 must be served on every party and takes effect when it is served. Where the order is not served by the court, the person serving must file a certificate of service in practice form N215.

Application by another party to remove a solicitor

4.1 Rule 42.4 sets out circumstances in which any other party may apply for an order declaring that a solicitor has ceased to be the solicitor acting for another party in the proceedings.

4.2 The application should be made in accordance with Part 23 and must be supported by evidence. Unless the court directs otherwise the application notice must be served on the party to whose solicitor the application relates.

4.3 An order made under rule 42.4 must be served on every other party to the proceedings. Where the order is not served by the court, the person serving must file a certificate of service in practice form N215.

PART 43

SCOPE OF COST RULES AND DEFINITIONS

Contents of this Part

Scope of this Part

43.1 This Part contains definitions and interpretation of certain matters set out in the rules about costs contained in Parts 44 to 48.

---

6   See Part 23 and the Practice Direction which supplements it.

7   See Part 32 and the Practice Direction which supplements it for information about evidence.

8   Rule 42.3(2).

(Part 44 contains general rules about costs; Part 45 deals with fixed costs; Part 46 deals with fast track trial costs; Part 47 deals with the detailed assessment of costs and related appeals and Part 48 deals with costs payable in special cases.)

Definitions and application

43.2 (1) In Parts 44 to 48, unless the context otherwise requires –

    (a) 'costs' includes fees, charges, disbursements, expenses, remuneration, reimbursement allowed to a litigant in person under rule 48.6 and any fee or reward charged by a lay representative for acting on behalf of a party in proceedings allocated to the small claims track;

    (b) 'costs judge' means a taxing master of the Supreme Court;

    (c) 'costs officer' means –

        (i) a costs judge;

        (ii) a district judge; and

        (iii) an authorised court officer;

    (d) 'authorised court officer' means any officer of –

        (i) a county court;

        (ii) a district registry;

        (iii) the Principal Registry of the Family Division; or

        (iv) the Supreme Court Costs Office,

    whom the Lord Chancellor has authorised to assess costs.

    (e) 'fund' includes any estate or property held for the benefit of any person or class of person and any fund to which a trustee or personal representative is entitled in his capacity as such;

    (f) 'receiving party' means a party entitled to be paid costs;

    (g) 'paying party' means a party liable to pay costs;

    (h) 'assisted person' means an assisted person within the statutory provisions relating to legal aid; and

    (i) 'fixed costs' means the amounts which are to be allowed in respect of solicitors' charges in the circumstances set out in Part 45.

    (2) The costs to which Parts 44 to 48 apply include –

    (a) the following costs where those costs may be assessed by the court –

        (i) costs of proceedings before an arbitrator or umpire;

        (ii) costs of proceedings before a tribunal or other statutory body; and

        (iii) costs payable by a client to his solicitor; and

    (b) costs which are payable by one party to another party under the terms of a contract, where the court makes an order for an assessment of those costs.

Meaning of summary assessment

43.3 'Summary assessment' means the procedure by which the court, when making an order about costs, orders payment of a sum of money instead of fixed costs or 'detailed assessment'.

Meaning of detailed assessment

43.4 'Detailed assessment' means the procedure by which the amount of costs is decided by a costs officer in accordance with Part 47.

PRACTICE DIRECTION ABOUT COSTS
SUPPLEMENTING PARTS 43 TO 48 OF THE CIVIL PROCEDURE RULES

Introduction

1. This Practice Direction supplements Parts 43 to 48 of the Civil Procedure Rules. It applies to all proceedings to which those Parts apply.

2. Section III of the Directions Relating to Part 48 deals with transitional provisions affecting proceedings about costs which were pending before 26 April 1999.

3. Attention is drawn to the powers to make orders about costs conferred on the Supreme Court and any county court by Section 51 of the Supreme Court Act 1981.

4. In these Directions:

   "counsel" means a barrister or other person with a right of audience in relation to all proceedings in the High Court or in the County Courts in which he is instructed to act.

   "solicitor" means a solicitor of the Supreme Court or other person with a right of audience in relation to proceedings, who is conducting the claim or defence (as the case may be) on behalf of a party to the proceedings and, where the context admits, includes a patent agent.

5. In respect of any document which is required by these Directions to be signed by a party or his legal representative the Practice Direction supplementing Part 22 will apply as if the document in question was a statement of truth. (The Practice Direction supplementing Part 22 makes provision for cases in which a party is a child, a patient or a company or other corporation and cases in which a document is signed on behalf of a partnership).

DIRECTIONS RELATING TO PART 43
SCOPE OF COSTS RULES AND DEFINITIONS
SECTION 1 MODEL FORMS FOR CLAIMS FOR COSTS

RULE 43.3 MEANING OF SUMMARY ASSESSMENT

1.1 Rule 43.3 defines summary assessment.

1.2 Form 1 of the Schedule of Costs Forms annexed to this Direction is a model form of Statement of Costs to be used for summary assessments.

1.3 Further details about Statements of Costs are given in paragraph 4 of the Directions Relating to Rule 44.7 (Procedure for assessing costs).

RULE 43.4 MEANING OF DETAILED ASSESSMENT

1.4 Rule 43.4 defines detailed assessment.

1.5 Form 2 of the Schedule of Costs Forms annexed to this Practice Direction is a model form of bill of costs to be used for detailed assessments.

1.6 Further details about bills of costs are given in the next section of these Directions and in paragraph 2.7 of the Directions Relating to Part 47 (Procedure for detailed assessment of costs and default provisions).

1.7 Form 2 of the Schedule of Costs Forms and the next section of this practice direction both refer to the model form of bills of costs. The use of the model form is not compulsory, but is encouraged. A party wishing to rely upon a bill which departs from the model form should include in the background information of the bill an explanation for that departure.

1.8 In any order of the court (whether made before or after 26 April 1999) the word "taxation" will be taken to mean "detailed assessment" and the words "to be taxed" will be taken to mean "to be decided by detailed assessment" unless in either case the context otherwise requires.

SECTION 2 FORM AND CONTENTS OF BILLS OF COSTS

2.1 A bill of costs may consist of such of the following sections as may be appropriate:-

   (1) title page;

   (2) background information;

    (3) items of costs claimed under the headings specified in paragraph 2.5;

    (4) summary showing the total costs claimed on each page of the bill;

    (5) schedules of time spent on non-routine attendances; and

    (6) the certificates referred to in paragraph 2.14.

2.2 Where it is necessary or convenient to do so, a bill of costs may be divided into two or more parts, each part containing sections (2), (3) and (4) above. A division into parts will be necessary or convenient in the following circumstances:-

    (1) Where the receiving party acted in person during the course of the proceedings (whether or not he also had a legal representative at that time) the bill should be divided into different parts so as to distinguish between;

        (a) the costs claimed for work done by the legal representative; and

        (b) the costs claimed for work done by the receiving party in person.

    (2) Where the receiving party was represented by different solicitors during the course of the proceedings, the bill should be divided into different parts so as to distinguish between the costs payable in respect of each solicitor.

    (3) Where the receiving party obtained legal aid in respect of all or part of the proceedings the bill should be divided into separate parts so as to distinguish between;

        (a) costs claimed before legal aid was granted;

        (b) costs claimed against another party after legal aid was granted;

        (c) costs claimed against the Legal Aid Board only; and

        (d) any costs claimed after legal aid ceased.

    (4) Where value added tax (VAT) is claimed and there was a change in the rate of VAT during the course of the proceedings, the bill should be divided into separate parts so as to distinguish between;

        (a) costs claimed at the old rate of VAT; and

        (b) costs claimed at the new rate of VAT.

    (5) Where the bill covers costs payable under two or more orders under which there are different paying parties the bill should be divided into parts so as to deal separately with the costs payable by each paying party.

2.3 The title page of the bill of costs must set out:-

    (1) the full title of the proceedings;

    (2) the name of the party whose bill it is and a description of the document showing the right to assessment (as to which see paragraph 4.5 of the Directions Relating to Part 47);

    (3) if VAT is included as part of the claim for costs, the VAT number of the legal representative or other person in respect of whom VAT is claimed;

    (4) details of all legal aid certificates and legal aid amendment certificates in respect of which claims for costs are included in the bill.

2.4 The background information included in the bill of costs should set out:-

    (1) a brief description of the proceedings up to the date of the notice of commencement;

    (2) A statement of the status of the solicitor or solicitor's employee in respect of whom costs are claimed and (if those costs are calculated on the basis of hourly rates) the hourly rates claimed for each such person.

        It should be noted that "legal executive" means a Fellow of the Institute of Legal Executives.

        Other clerks who are fee earners of equivalent experience, may be entitled to similar rates. It should be borne in mind that Fellows of the Institute of Legal Executives will have spent approximately 6 years in practice, and taken both general and specialist examinations. The Fellows have therefore acquired considerable practical and academic experience. Clerks without the equivalent experience of legal executives will normally be treated as being the equivalent of trainee solicitors and para-legals.

    (3) a brief explanation of any agreement or arrangement between the receiving party and his solicitors which affects the costs claimed in the bill.

2.5 The bill of costs may consist of items under such of the following heads as may be appropriate:-

(1) attendances on the court and counsel up to the date of the notice of commencement;

(2) attendances on and communications with the receiving party;

(3) attendances on and communications with witnesses including any expert witness;

(4) attendances to inspect any property or place for the purposes of the proceedings;

(5) searches and enquiries made at offices of public records, the Companies Registry and similar searches and enquiries;

(6) attendances on and communications with other persons;

(7) communications with the court and with counsel;

(8) work done in connection with arithmetical calculations of compensation and/or interest;

(9) work done on documents: preparing and considering documentation which was of and incidental to the proceedings, including time spent on pre-action protocols where appropriate and time spent collating documents;

(10) work done in connection with mediation, alternative dispute resolution and negotiations with a view to settlement if not already covered in the heads listed above;

(11) attendances on and communications with London and other agents and work done by them;

(12) other work done which was of or incidental to the proceedings and which is not already covered in the heads listed above.

2.6 In respect of each of the heads of costs:-

(1) "communications" means letters out and telephone calls;

(2) communications which are not routine communications must be set out in chronological order;

(3) routine communications should be set out as a single item at the end of each head;

2.7 Each item claimed in the bill of costs must be consecutively numbered.

2.8 In each part of the bill of costs which claims items under head (1) (attendances on court and counsel) a note should be made of:

(1) all relevant events, including events which do not constitute chargeable items;

(2) any orders for costs which the court made (whether or not a claim is made in respect of those costs in this bill of costs).

2.10 The numbered items of costs may be set out on paper divided into five columns, of which the last two columns should be left blank. The five columns should be headed as follows: Item, Amount claimed, VAT, Amount allowed, VAT.

2.11 In respect of heads (2) to (12) in paragraph 2.5 above, if the number of attendances and communications other than routine communications is twenty or more, the claim for the costs of those items in that section of the bill of costs should be for the total only and should refer to a schedule in which the full record of dates and details is set out. If the bill of costs contains more than one schedule each schedule should be numbered consecutively.

2.12 The bill of costs must not contain any claims in respect of costs or court fees which relate solely to the detailed assessment proceedings other than costs claimed for preparing and checking the bill.

2.13 The summary must show the total profit costs and disbursements claimed separately from the total VAT claimed. Where the bill of costs is divided into parts the summary must also give totals for each part. If each page of the bill gives a page total the summary must also set out the page totals for each page.

2.14 The bill of costs must contain such of the certificates, the texts of which are set out in Form 4 of the Schedule of Costs Forms annexed to this Practice Direction, as are appropriate.

2.15 The following provisions relate to work done by solicitors:

(1) Routine letters out and routine telephone calls will in general be allowed on a unit basis of 6 minutes each, the charge being calculated by reference to the appropriate hourly rate. The unit charge for letters out will include perusing and considering the relevant letters in and no separate charge should be made for in-coming letters.

(2) E-mails received or sent by solicitors will not normally be allowed but the court may, in its discretion, allow an actual time charge for preparation of e-mails sent by solicitors which properly amount to attendances provided that the time taken has been recorded.

The court may also, in its discretion, allow a sum in respect of e-mails sent to the client or others where it is satisfied that, had e-mails not been sent, the number of communications which it would have been reasonable to allow would have been substantially greater than the number actually claimed.

(3) Local travelling expenses incurred by solicitors will not be allowed. The definition of "local" is a matter for the discretion of the court. While no absolute rule can be laid down, as a matter of guidance, "local" will, in general, be taken to mean within a radius of 10 miles from the court dealing with the case at the relevant time. Where travelling and waiting time is claimed, this should be allowed at the rate agreed with the client unless this is more than the hourly rate on the assessment.

(4) The cost of postage, couriers, out-going telephone calls, fax and telex messages will in general not be allowed but the court may exceptionally in its discretion allow such expenses in unusual circumstances or where the cost is unusually heavy.

(5) The cost of making copies of documents will not in general be allowed but the court may exceptionally in its discretion make an allowance for copying in unusual circumstances or where the documents copied are unusually numerous in relation to the nature of the case. Where this discretion is invoked the number of copies made, their purpose and the costs claimed for them must be set out in the bill.

(6) Agency charges as between a principal solicitor and his agent will be dealt with on the principle that such charges, where appropriate, form part of the principal solicitor's charges. Where these charges relate to head (1) in paragraph 2.5 (attendances at court and on counsel) they should be included in their chronological order in that head. In other cases they should be included in head (11) (attendances on London and other agents).

Costs of preparing the bill

2.16 A claim may be made for the reasonable costs of preparing and checking the bill of costs.

SECTION 3 SPECIAL PROVISIONS RELATING TO VAT

3.1 This section deals with claims for value added tax (VAT) which are made in respect of costs being dealt with by way of summary assessment or detailed assessment.

VAT Registration Number

3.2 The number allocated by HM Customs and Excise to every person registered under the Value Added Tax Act 1983 (except a Government Department) must appear in a prominent place at the head of every statement, bill of costs, fee sheet, account or voucher on which VAT is being included as part of a claim for costs.

Entitlement to VAT on Costs

3.3 VAT should not be included in a claim for costs if the receiving party is able to recover the VAT as input tax. Where the receiving party is able to obtain credit from HM Customs and Excise for a proportion of the VAT as input tax, only that proportion which is not eligible for credit should be included in the claim for costs.

3.4 The receiving party has responsibility for ensuring that VAT is claimed only when the receiving party is unable to recover the VAT or a proportion thereof as input tax.

3.5 Where there is a dispute as to whether VAT is properly claimed the receiving party must provide a certificate signed by the solicitors or the auditors of the receiving party in the form in the Schedule of Certificates annexed to this Practice Direction. Where the receiving party is a litigant in person who is claiming VAT, reference should be made by him to HM Customs and Excise and wherever possible a Statement to similar effect produced at the hearing at which the costs are assessed.

3.6 Where there is a dispute as to whether any service in respect of which a charge is proposed to be made in the bill is zero rated or exempt, reference should be made to HM Customs and Excise and wherever possible the view of HM Customs and Excise obtained and made known at the hearing at which the costs are assessed. Such application should be made by the receiving party. In the case of a bill from a solicitor to his own client such application should be made by the client.

Form of bill of costs where VAT rate changes

3.7 Where there is a change in the rate of VAT, suppliers of goods and services are entitled by ss.88(1) and 88(2) of the VAT Act 1994 in most circumstances to elect whether the new or the old rate of VAT should apply to a supply where the basic and actual tax points span a period during which there has been a change in VAT rates.

3.8 It will be assumed, unless a contrary indication is given in writing, that an election to take advantage of the provisions mentioned in paragraph 3.7 above and to charge VAT at the lower rate has been made. In any case in which an election to charge at the lower rate is not made, such a decision must be justified to the court assessing the costs.

Apportionment

3.9 All bills of costs, fees and disbursements on which VAT is included must be divided into separate parts so as to show work done before, on and after the date or dates from which any change in the rate of VAT takes effect. Where, however, a lump sum charge is made for work which spans a period during which there has been a change in VAT rates, and paragraphs 3.7 and 3.8 above do not apply, reference should be made to paragraphs 8 and 9 of Appendix F of Customs' Notice 700 (or any revised edition of that notice), a copy of which should be in the possession of every registered trader. If necessary, the lump sum should be apportioned. The totals of profit costs and disbursements in each part must be carried separately to the summary.

3.10 Should there be a change in the rate between the conclusion of a detailed assessment and the issue of the final costs certificate, any interested party may apply for the detailed assessment to be varied so as to take account of any increase or reduction in the amount of tax payable. Once the final costs certificate has been issued, no variation under this paragraph will be permitted.

Disbursements

3.11 Petty (or general) disbursements such as postage, fares etc which are normally treated as part of a solicitor's overheads and included in his profit costs should be charged with VAT even though they bear no tax when the solicitor incurs them. The cost of travel by public transport on a specific journey for a particular client where it forms part of the service rendered by a solicitor to his client and is charged in his bill of costs, attracts VAT.

3.12 Reference is made to the criteria set out in the VAT Guide (Customs and Excise Notice 700 – 1st August 1991 edition paragraph 83, or any revised edition of that Notice), as to expenses which are not subject to VAT. Charges for the cost of travel by public transport, postage, telephone calls and telegraphic transfers where these form part of the service rendered by the solicitor to his client are examples of charges which do not satisfy these criteria and are thus liable to VAT at the standard rate.

Legal Aid

3.13 VAT will be payable in respect of every supply made pursuant to a Legal Aid Certificate provided only that the person making the supply is a taxable person and that the assisted person is not resident outside the European Union. Where the assisted person is registered for VAT and the legal services paid for by the Legal Aid Board are in connection with the assisted person's business, the VAT on those services will be payable by the Legal Aid Board only.

3.14 In Legal Aid cases the legal aid summary must be drawn so as to show the total VAT on Counsel's fees as a separate item from the VAT on other disbursements and the VAT on profit costs.

Tax invoice

3.15 A bill of costs filed for detailed assessment is always retained by the Court. Accordingly if a solicitor waives his solicitor and client costs and accepts the costs certified by the court as payable by the unsuccessful party in settlement, it will be necessary for a short statement as to the amount of the certified costs and the VAT thereon to be prepared for use as the tax invoice.

Vouchers

3.16 Where receipted accounts for disbursements made by the solicitor or his client are retained as tax invoices a photostat copy of any such receipted account may be produced and will be accepted as sufficient evidence of payment when disbursements are vouched.

Certificates

3.17 In non legal aid cases the total VAT allowed will be shown in the final costs certificate as a separate item. In legal aid cases the VAT on Counsel's fees will be shown separately from the remaining VAT.

Litigants acting in person

3.18 Where a litigant acts in litigation on his own behalf he is not treated for the purposes of VAT as having supplied services and therefore no VAT is chargeable on that litigant's costs (even where, for example, that litigant is a solicitor or other legal representative).

3.19 Consequently in the circumstances described in the preceding paragraph, a bill of costs presented for agreement or assessment should not claim any VAT which will not be allowed on assessment.

Government Departments

3.20 On an assessment between parties, where costs are being paid to a Government Department in respect of services rendered by its legal staff, VAT should not be added.

SECTION 4 ESTIMATES OF COSTS

4.1 This section sets out certain steps which parties must take in order to keep the other parties informed about their potential liability in respect of costs and in order to assist the court to decide what, if any, order to make about costs and about case management.

4.2 In this section an estimate of costs means an estimate of those costs already incurred and, if appropriate, to be incurred by the party who gives it which he intends, if he is successful in the case, to seek to recover from any other party under an order for costs.

4.3 The court may at any stage in a case order any party to file an estimate of costs and to serve copies of the estimate on all other parties. The court may direct that the estimate be prepared in such a way as to demonstrate the likely effects of giving or not giving a particular case management direction which the court is considering, for example a direction for a split trial or for the trial of a preliminary issue. The court may specify a time limit for filing and serving the estimate. However, if no time limit is specified the estimate should be filed and served within 28 days of the date of the order.

4.4 An estimate of costs should be substantially in the form of a Statement of Costs as illustrated in Form 1 of the Schedule of Costs Forms annexed to this Practice Direction.

4.5 (1) When a party to a claim which is outside the financial scope of the small claims track, files an allocation questionnaire, he must also file an estimate of costs and serve a copy of it on every other party, unless the court otherwise directs. The legal representative must in addition serve a copy of the estimate upon the client.

(2) Where a party to a claim is being dealt with on the fast track or the multi track, or under Part 8 files a listing questionnaire, he must also file an estimate of costs and serve a copy of it on every other party, unless the court otherwise directs. Where a party is represented, the legal representative must in addition serve a copy of the estimate on the client.

(3) This paragraph does not apply to litigants in person.

PART 44

GENERAL RULES ABOUT COSTS

Contents of this Part

Scope of this Part

44.1   This Part contains general rules about costs and entitlement to costs.

(The definitions contained in Part 43 are relevant to this Part.)

Solicitor's duty to notify client

44.2   Where –

(a) the court makes a costs order against a legally represented party; and

(b) the party is not present when the order is made,

the party's solicitor must notify his client in writing of the costs order no later than 7 days after the solicitor receives notice of the order.

Court's discretion and circumstances to be taken into account when exercising its discretion as to costs

44.3(1)   The court has discretion as to –

(a) whether costs are payable by one party to another;

(b) the amount of those costs; and

(c) when they are to be paid.

(2) If the court decides to make an order about costs –

(a) the general rule is that the unsuccessful party will be ordered to pay the costs of the successful party; but

(b) the court may make a different order.

(3) The general rule does not apply to the following proceedings –

(a) proceedings in the Court of Appeal on an application or appeal made in connection with proceedings in the Family Division; or

(b) proceedings in the Court of Appeal from a judgment, direction, decision or order given or made in probate proceedings or family proceedings.

(4) In deciding what order (if any) to make about costs, the court must have regard to all the circumstances, including –

(a) the conduct of all the parties;

(b) whether a party has succeeded on part of his case, even if he has not been wholly successful; and

(c) any payment into court or admissible offer to settle made by a party which is drawn to the court's attention (whether or not made in accordance with Part 36).

(Part 36 contains further provisions about how the court's discretion is to be exercised where a payment into court or an offer to settle is made under that Part.)

(5) The conduct of the parties includes –

(a) conduct before, as well as during, the proceedings and in particular the extent to which the parties followed any relevant pre-action protocol;

(b) whether it was reasonable for a party to raise, pursue or contest a particular allegation or issue;

(c) the manner in which a party has pursued or defended his case or a particular allegation or issue; and

(d) whether a claimant who has succeeded in his claim, in whole or in part, exaggerated his claim.

(6) The orders which the court may make under this rule include an order that a party must pay –

(a) a proportion of another party's costs;

(b) a stated amount in respect of another party's costs;

(c) costs from or until a certain date only;

(d) costs incurred before proceedings have begun;

(e) costs relating to particular steps taken in the proceedings;

(f) costs relating only to a distinct part of the proceedings; and

(g) interest on costs from or until a certain date, including a date before judgment.

(7) Where the court would otherwise consider making an order under paragraph (6)(f), it must instead, if practicable, make an order under paragraph (6)(a) or (c).

(8) Where the court has ordered a party to pay costs, it may order an amount to be paid on account before the costs are assessed.

(9) Where a party entitled to costs is also liable to pay costs the court may assess the costs which that party is liable to pay and either –

(a) set off the amount assessed against the amount the party is entitled to be paid and direct him to pay any balance; or

(b) delay the issue of a certificate for the costs to which the party is entitled until he has paid the amount which he is liable to pay.

Basis of assessment

44.4 (1) Where the court is to assess the amount of costs (whether by summary or detailed assessment) it will assess those costs –

(a) on the standard basis; or

(b) on the indemnity basis,

but the court will not in either case allow costs which have been unreasonably incurred or are unreasonable in amount.

(Rule 48.3 sets out how the court decides the amount of costs payable under a contract.)

(2) Where the amount of costs is to be assessed on the standard basis, the court will –

(a) only allow costs which are proportionate to the matters in issue; and

(b) resolve any doubt which it may have as to whether costs were reasonably incurred or reasonable and proportionate in amount in favour of the paying party.

(Factors which the court may take into account are set out in rule 44.5.)

(3) Where the amount of costs is to be assessed on the indemnity basis, the court will resolve any doubt which it may have as to whether costs were reasonably incurred or were reasonable in amount in favour of the receiving party.

(4) Where –
(a) the court makes an order about costs without indicating the basis on which the costs are to be assessed; or
(b) the court makes an order for costs to be assessed on a basis other than the standard basis or the indemnity basis,
the costs will be assessed on the standard basis.

(5) This rule and Part 47 (detailed assessment of costs by a costs officer) do not apply to the extent that regulations made under the Legal Aid Act 1988[65] determine the amount payable.

(6) Where the amount of a solicitor's remuneration in respect of non-contentious business is regulated by any general orders made under the Solicitors Act 1974[66], the amount of the costs to be allowed in respect of any such business which falls to be assessed by the court will be decided in accordance with those general orders rather than this rule and rule 44.5.

Factors to be taken into account in deciding the amount of costs

44.5 (1) The court is to have regard to all the circumstances in deciding whether costs were –
(a) if it is assessing costs on the standard basis –
(i) proportionately and reasonably incurred; or
(ii) were proportionate and reasonable in amount, or
(b) if it is assessing costs on the indemnity basis –
(i) unreasonably incurred; or
(ii) unreasonable in amount.

(2) In particular the court must give effect to any orders which have already been made.

(3) The court must also have regard to –
(a) the conduct of all the parties, including in particular –
(i) conduct before, as well as during, the proceedings; and
(ii) the efforts made, if any, before and during the proceedings in order to try to resolve the dispute;
(b) the amount or value of any money or property involved;
(c) the importance of the matter to all the parties;
(d) the particular complexity of the matter or the difficulty or novelty of the questions raised;
(e) the skill, effort, specialised knowledge and responsibility involved;
(f) the time spent on the case; and
(g) the place where and the circumstances in which work or any part of it was done.

(65) 1988 c.34.
(66) 1974 c.47.

(Rule 35.4(4) gives the court power to limit the amount that a party may recover with regard to the fees and expenses of an expert)

Fixed costs

44.6   A party may recover the fixed costs specified in Part 45 in accordance with that Part.

Procedure for assessing costs

44.7   Where the court orders a party to pay costs to another party (other than fixed costs) it may either –

(a) make a summary assessment of the costs; or

(b) order detailed assessment of the costs by a costs officer,

unless any rule, practice direction or other enactment provides otherwise.

(The costs practice direction sets out the factors which will affect the court's decision under this rule)

Time for complying with an order for costs

44.8   A party must comply with an order for the payment of costs within 14 days of –

(a) the date of the judgment or order if it states the amount of those costs; or

(b) if the amount of those costs (or part of them) is decided later in accordance with Part 47, the date of the certificate which states the amount.

(Part 47 sets out the procedure for detailed assessment of costs)

Costs on the small claims track and fast track

44.9(1) Part 27 (small claims) and Part 46 (fast track trial costs) contain special rules about –

(a) liability for costs;

(b) the amount of costs which the court may award; and

(c) the procedure for assessing costs.

(2) Once a claim is allocated to a particular track, those special rules shall apply to the period before, as well as after, allocation except where the court or a practice direction provides otherwise.

Limitation on amount court may allow where a claim allocated to the fast track settles before trial

44.10(1) Where the court –

(a) assesses costs in relation to a claim which –

(i)   has been allocated to the fast track; and

(ii) settles before the start of the trial; and

(b) is considering the amount of costs to be allowed in respect of a party's advocate for preparing for the trial,

it may not allow, in respect of those advocate's costs, an amount that exceeds the amount of fast track trial costs which would have been payable in relation to the claim had the trial taken place.

(2) When deciding the amount to be allowed in respect of the advocate's costs, the court shall have regard to –

(a) when the claim was settled; and

(b) when the court was notified that the claim had settled.

(3) In this rule, 'advocate' and 'fast track trial costs' have the meanings given to them by Part 46.

(Part 46 sets out the amount of fast track trial costs which may be awarded.)

Costs following allocation and re-allocation

44.11(1) Any costs orders made before a claim is allocated will not be affected by allocation.

(2) Where –

    (a) a claim is allocated to a track; and

    (b) the court subsequently re-allocates that claim to a different track,

  then unless the court orders otherwise, any special rules about costs applying –

      (i) to the first track, will apply to the claim up to the date of re-allocation; and

      (ii) to the second track, will apply from the date of re-allocation.

(Part 26 deals with the allocation and re-allocation of claims between tracks.)

Cases where costs orders deemed to have been made

44.12(1) Where a right to costs arises under –

    (a) rule 3.7 (defendant's right to costs where claim struck out for non-payment of fees);

    (b) rule 36.13(1) (claimant's right to costs where he accepts defendant's Part 36 offer or Part 36 payment);

    (c) rule 36.14 (claimant's right to costs where defendant accepts the claimant's Part 36 offer); or

    (d) rule 38.6 (defendant's right to costs where claimant discontinues),

  a costs order will be deemed to have been made on the standard basis.

(2) Interest payable pursuant to section 17 of the Judgments Act 1838[67] or section 74 of the County Courts Act 1984[68] on the costs deemed to have been ordered under paragraph (1) shall begin to run from the date on which the event which gave rise to the entitlement to costs occurred.

Special situations

44.13 (1) Where the court makes an order which does not mention costs no party is entitled to costs in relation to that order.

(2) The court hearing an appeal may, unless it dismisses the appeal, make orders about the costs of the proceedings giving rise to the appeal as well as the costs of the appeal.

(3) Where proceedings are transferred from one court to another, the court to which they are transferred may deal with all the costs, including the costs before the transfer.

(4) Paragraph (3) is subject to any order of the court which ordered the transfer.

Court's powers in relation to misconduct

44.14 (1) The court may make an order under this rule where –

    (a) a party or his legal representative fails to conduct detailed assessment proceedings in accordance with Part 47 or any direction of the court; or

    (b) it appears to the court that the conduct of a party or his legal representative, before or during the proceedings which gave rise to the assessment proceedings, was unreasonable or improper.

---

(67) 1838 c.110. Section 17 was amended by S.I. 1998/2940.

(68) 1984 c.28. Section 74 was amended by section 2 of the Private International Law (Miscellaneous Provisions) Act 1995 (c.42).

(2) Where paragraph (1) applies, the court may –

    (a) disallow all or part of the costs which are being assessed; or

    (b) order the party at fault or his legal representative to pay costs which he has caused any other party to incur.

(3) Where –

    (a) the court makes an order under paragraph (2) against a legally represented party; and

    (b) the party is not present when the order is made,

the party's solicitor must notify his client in writing of the order no later than 7 days after the solicitor receives notice of the order.

(Other rules about costs can be found –

    (a) in Schedule 1, in the following RSC – O.45 (court may order act to be done at the expense of disobedient party); O.47 (writ of fieri facias to enforce payment of costs); and

    (b) in Schedule 2, in the following CCR – O.27 (attachment of earnings – judgment creditor's entitlement to costs); O.28 (costs on judgment summons); O.30 (garnishee proceedings – judgment creditor's entitlement to costs); O.49 (costs incurred in making a payment in under section 63 of the Trustee Act 1925 to be assessed by the detailed procedure)).

[Authors' note: For the general Introduction to the Costs Practice Direction, see after Part 43 above.]

DIRECTIONS RELATING TO PART 44
GENERAL RULES ABOUT COSTS

RULE 44.2 SOLICITOR'S DUTY TO NOTIFY CLIENT

1.1 For the purposes of rule 44.2 "client" includes a party for whom a solicitor is acting and any other person (for example an insurer or a trade union) who has instructed the solicitor to act or who is liable to pay his fees.

1.2 Where a solicitor notifies a client of an order under that rule, he must also explain why the order came to be made.

1.3 Although rule 44.2 does not specify any sanction for breach of the rule the court may, either in the order for costs itself or in a subsequent order, require the solicitor to produce to the court evidence showing that he took reasonable steps to comply with the rule.

RULE 44.3 COURT'S DISCRETION AND CIRCUMSTANCES TO BE TAKEN INTO ACCOUNT WHEN EXERCISING ITS DISCRETION AS TO COSTS

2.1 Attention is drawn to the factors set out in this rule which may lead the court to depart from the general rule stated in rule 44.3(2) and to make a different order about costs.

2.2 In a probate claim where a defendant has in his defence given notice that he requires the will to be proved in solemn form (see paragraph 8.3 of the Contentious Probate Practice Direction Supplementing Part 49), the court will not make an order for costs against the defendant unless it appears that there was no reasonable ground for opposing the will. The term "probate claim" is defined in paragraph 1.2 of the Contentious Probate Practice Direction.

2.3 (1) The court may make an order about costs at any stage in a case.

    (2) In particular the court may make an order about costs when it deals with any application, makes any order or holds any hearing and that order about costs may relate to the costs of that application, order or hearing.

2.4 In deciding what order to make about costs the court is required to have regard to all the circumstances including any payment into court or admissible offer to settle made by a party which is drawn to the court's attention (whether or not it is made in accordance with Part

36). Where a claimant has made a Part 36 offer and fails to obtain a judgment which is more advantageous than that offer that circumstance alone will not lead to a reduction in the costs awarded to the claimant under this rule.

2.5 There are certain costs orders which the court will commonly make in proceedings before trial. The following table sets out the general effect of these orders. The table is not an exhaustive list of the orders which the court may make.

Term	Effect
• Costs • Costs in any event	The party in whose favour the order is made is entitled to the costs in respect of the part of the proceedings to which the order relates, whatever other costs orders are made in the proceedings.
• Costs in the case • Costs in the application	The party in whose favour the court makes an order for costs at the end of the proceedings is entitled to his costs of the part of the proceedings to which the order relates.
• Costs reserved	The decision about costs is deferred to a later occasion, but if no later order is made the costs will be costs in the case.
• Claimant's/ Defendant's costs in the case/ application	If the party in whose favour the costs order is made is awarded costs at the end of the proceedings, that party is entitled to his costs of the part of the proceedings to which the order relates. If any other party is awarded costs at the end of the proceedings, the party in whose favour the final costs order is made is not liable to pay the costs of any other party in respect of the part of the proceedings to which the order relates.
• Costs thrown away	Where, for example, a judgment or order is set aside, the party in whose favour the costs order is made is entitled to the costs which have been incurred as a consequence. This includes the costs of – a) preparing for and attending any hearing at which the judgment or order which has been set aside was made; b) preparing for and attending any hearing to set aside the judgment or order in question; c) preparing for and attending any hearing at which the court orders the proceedings or the part in question to be adjourned; d) any steps taken to enforce a judgment or order which has subsequently been set aside.
• Costs of and caused by	Where, for example, the court makes this order on an application to amend a statement of case, the party in whose favour the costs order is made is entitled to the costs of preparing for and attending the application and the costs of any consequential amendment to his own statement of case.
• Costs here and below	The party in whose favour the costs order is made is entitled not only his costs in respect of the proceedings in which the court makes the order but also to his costs of the proceedings in any lower court. In the case of an appeal from a Divisional Court the party is not entitled to costs incurred in any court below the Divisional Court.
• No order as to costs • Each party to pay his own costs	Each party is to bear his own costs of the part of the proceedings to which the order relates whatever costs order the court makes at the end of the proceedings.

2.6 Where, under rule 44.3(8), the court orders an amount to be paid before costs are assessed–
   (1) the order will state that amount, and
   (2) if no other date for payment is specified in the order rule 44.8 (Time for complying with an order for costs) will apply.

Fees of counsel

2.7 (1) This paragraph applies where the court orders the detailed assessment of the costs of a hearing at which one or more counsel appeared for a party.

(2) Where an order for costs states the opinion of the court as to whether or not the hearing was fit for the attendance of one or more counsel, a costs officer conducting a detailed assessment of costs to which that order relates will have regard to the opinion stated.

Fees payable to conveyancing counsel appointed by the court to assist it

2.8 (1) Where the court refers any matter to the conveyancing counsel of the court the fees payable to counsel in respect of the work done or to be done will be assessed by the court in accordance with rule 44.3.

(2) An appeal from a decision of the court in respect of the fees of such counsel will be dealt with under the general rules as to appeals unless the appeal is against the decision of a costs officer when the appeal will be dealt with in accordance with Part 47 Section VIII. In either case the decision of the appellate court is final.

RULE 44.5 FACTORS TO BE TAKEN INTO ACCOUNT IN DECIDING THE AMOUNT OF COSTS

3.1 In applying the test of proportionality the court will have regard to rule 1.1(2)(c). The relationship between the total of the costs incurred and the financial value of the claim may not be a reliable guide. A fixed percentage cannot be applied in all cases to the value of the claim in order to ascertain whether or not the costs are proportionate.

3.2 In any proceedings there will be costs which will inevitably be incurred and which are necessary for the successful conduct of the case. Solicitors are not required to conduct litigation at rates which are uneconomic. Thus in a modest claim the proportion of costs is likely to be higher than in a large claim, and may even equal or possibly exceed the amount in dispute.

3.3 Where a trial takes place, the time taken by the court in dealing with a particular issue may not be an accurate guide to the amount of time properly spent by the legal or other representatives in preparation for the trial of that issue.

RULE 44.7 PROCEDURE FOR ASSESSING COSTS

4.1 Where the court does not order fixed costs (or no fixed costs are provided for) the amount of costs payable will be assessed by the court. This rule allows the court making an order about costs either

(a) to make a summary assessment of the amount of the costs, or

(b) to order the amount to be decided in accordance with Part 47 (a detailed assessment).

4.2 An order for costs will be treated as an order for the amount of costs to be decided by a detailed assessment unless the order otherwise provides.

Summary Assessment

4.3 Whenever a court makes an order about costs which does not provide for fixed costs to be paid the court should consider whether to make a summary assessment of costs.

4.4 (1) The general rule is that the court should make a summary assessment of the costs:

(a) at the conclusion of the trial of a case which has been dealt with on the fast track, in which case the order will deal with the costs of the whole claim, and

(b) at the conclusion of any other hearing, which has lasted not more than one day, in which case the order will deal with the costs of the application or matter to which the hearing related. If this hearing disposes of the claim, the order may deal with the costs of the whole claim;

unless there is good reason not to do so e.g. where the paying party shows substantial grounds for disputing the sum claimed for costs that cannot be dealt with summarily or there is insufficient time to carry out a summary assessment.

(2) The general rule in paragraph 1 does not apply to a mortgagee's costs incurred in mortgage possession proceedings or other proceedings relating to a mortgage unless the

mortgagee asks the court to make an order for his costs to be paid by another party. Section 1 of the directions relating to Part 48 deals in more detail with costs relating to mortgages.

(3) The general rule is that no summary assessment of costs will be made if the court has ordered that the costs in question will be treated as costs in the case (as to which see paragraph 2.4 above).

(4) Where an application has been made and the parties to the application agree an order by consent without any party attending, the parties should agree a figure for costs to be inserted in the consent order or agree that there should be no order for costs. If the parties cannot agree the costs position attendance on the appointment will be necessary but unless good reason can be shown for the failure to deal with costs as set out above no costs will be allowed for that attendance.

4.5 (1) It is the duty of the parties and their legal representatives to assist the judge in making a summary assessment of costs in any case to which paragraph 4.4 above applies, in accordance with the following paragraphs.

(2) Each party who intends to claim costs must prepare a written statement of the costs he intends to claim showing separately in the form of a schedule:

   (a) the number of hours to be claimed,

   (b) the hourly rate to be claimed,

   (c) the grade of fee earner;

   (d) the amount and nature of any disbursement to be claimed, other than counsel's fee for appearing at the hearing,

   (e) the amount of solicitor's costs to be claimed for attending or appearing at the hearing,

   (f) the fees of counsel to be claimed in respect of the hearing, and

   (g) any Value Added Tax to be claimed on these amounts.

(3) The statement of costs should follow as closely as possible Form 1 of the Schedule of Costs Forms annexed to this practice direction and must be signed by the party or his legal representative. Where a litigant is represented by a solicitor in his employment the statement of costs need not include the certificate appended at the end of Form 1.

(4) The statement of costs must be filed at court and copies of it must be served on any party against whom an order for payment of those costs is intended to be sought. The statement of costs should be filed and the copies of it should be served as soon as possible and in any event not less than 24 hours before the date fixed for the hearing.

4.6 The failure by a party, without reasonable excuse, to comply with the foregoing paragraphs will be taken into account by the court in deciding what order to make about the costs of the claim, hearing or application, and about the costs of any further hearing or detailed assessment hearing that may be necessary as a result of that failure.

4.7 If the court makes a summary assessment of the costs the court will specify the amount payable as a single figure which will include

   (a) all sums in respect of profit costs, disbursements and VAT which is allowed, and

   (b) the amount which is awarded under Part 46 (Fast Track Trial Costs).

4.8 The court awarding costs cannot make an order for a summary assessment of costs by a costs officer. If a summary assessment of costs is appropriate but the court awarding costs is unable to do so on the day, the court must give directions as to a further hearing.

4.9 (1) The court will not make a summary assessment of the costs of a receiving party who is an assisted person within the meaning of the Legal Aid Act 1988.

(2) A summary assessment of costs payable by an assisted person is not by itself a determination of the assisted person's liability to pay those costs (as to which see Section 17 of the Legal Aid Act 1988). Accordingly the court may make a summary assessment of costs payable by an assisted person.

(3) The court will not make a summary assessment of the costs of a receiving party who is a child or patient within the meaning of Part 21 unless the solicitor acting for the child or patient has waived the right to further costs (see paragraph 1.2(c) of the Direction relating to Part 48).

(4) The court may make a summary assessment of costs payable by a child or patient.

4.10 The court will not endorse disproportionate and unreasonable costs. Accordingly:

(a) When the amount of the costs to be paid has been agreed, the court will make this clear by saying that the order is by consent;

(b) If the judge is to make an order which is not by consent, the judge will, so far as possible, ensure that the final figure is not disproportionate and/or unreasonable having regard to Part 1 of the CPR. The judge will retain this responsibility notwithstanding the absence of challenge to individual items in the make-up of the figure sought. The fact that the paying party is not disputing the amount of costs can however be taken as some indication that the amount is proportionate and reasonable. The judge will therefore intervene only if satisfied that the costs are so disproportionate that it is right to do so.

Payments on account of costs

4.11 Whenever the court awards costs to be assessed by way of detailed assessment it should consider whether to exercise the power in rule 44.3(8) (Courts Discretion as to Costs) to order the paying party to pay such sum of money as it thinks just on account of those costs.

RULE 44.9 COSTS ON THE SMALL CLAIMS TRACK AND FAST TRACK

5.1 (1) Before a claim is allocated to one of those tracks the court is not restricted by any of the special rules that apply to that track.

(2) Where a claim has been allocated to one of those tracks, the special rules which relate to that track will apply to work done before as well as after allocation save to the extent (if any) that an order for costs in respect of that work was made before allocation.

(3) (i) This paragraph applies where a claim issued for a sum in excess of the normal financial scope of the small claims track is allocated to that track only because an admission of part of the claim by the defendant reduces the amount in dispute to a sum within the normal scope of that track.

(See also paragraph 7.4 of the practice direction supplementing CPR Part 26)

(ii) On entering judgment for the admitted part before allocation of the balance of the claim the court may allow costs in respect of the proceedings down to that date.

RULE 44.11 COSTS FOLLOWING ALLOCATION AND RE-ALLOCATION

6.1 This paragraph applies where the court is about to make an order to re-allocate a claim from the small claims track to another track.

6.2 Before making the order to re-allocate the claim, the court must decide whether any party is to pay costs to any other party down to the date of the order to re-allocate in accordance with the rules about costs contained in Part 27 (The Small Claims Track).

6.3 If it decides to make such an order about costs, the court will make a summary assessment of those costs in accordance with that Part.

RULE 44.14 COURT'S POWERS IN RELATION TO MISCONDUCT

7.1 Before making an order under rule 44.14 the court must give the party or legal representative in question a reasonable opportunity to attend a hearing to give reasons why it should not make such an order.

7.2 Conduct before or during the proceedings which gave rise to the assessment which is unreasonable or improper includes steps which are calculated to prevent or inhibit the court from furthering the overriding objective.

7.3 Although rule 44.14(3) does not specify any sanction for breach of the obligation imposed by the rule the court may, either in the order under paragraph (2) or in a subsequent order, require the solicitor to produce to the court evidence that he took reasonable steps to comply with the obligation.

PART 45

FIXED COSTS

Contents of this Part

Scope of this Part

45.1 (1) This Part sets out the amounts which, unless the court orders otherwise, are to be allowed in respect of solicitors' charges in the cases to which this Part applies.

(The definitions contained in Part 43 are relevant to this Part.)

(2) This Part applies where –

    (a) the only claim is a claim for a specified sum of money and –

        (i) judgment in default is obtained under rule 12.4(1);

        (ii) judgment on admission is obtained under rule 14.4(3);

        (iii) judgment on admission on part of the claim is obtained under rule 14.5(6);

        (iv) summary judgment is given under Part 24;

        (v) the court has made an order to strike out[GL] a defence under rule 3.4(2)(a) as disclosing no reasonable grounds for defending the claim; or

        (vi) rule 45.3 applies; or

    (b) the only claim is a claim where the court gave a fixed date for the hearing when it issued the claim and judgment is given for the delivery of goods,

    and in either case the value of the claim exceeds £25.

(The practice direction supplementing rule 7.9 sets out the types of case where a court may give a fixed date for a hearing when it issues a claim.)

(3) The rules in this Part do not apply to the extent that regulations under the Legal Aid Act 1988[69] determine the amount of costs payable to legal representatives.

(4) Any appropriate court fee will be allowed in addition to the costs set out in this Part.

Amount of fixed commencement costs

45.2 (1) The claim form may include a claim for fixed commencement costs.

(2) The amount of fixed commencement costs which the claim form may include shall be calculated by reference to the following table (Table 1).

(3) Additional costs may also be claimed in the circumstances specified in Table 3.

(4) The amount claimed, or the value of the goods claimed if specified, in the claim form is to be used for determining the band in the table that applies to the claim.

---

69 1988 c.34.

Table 1

Fixed costs on commencement of a claim

Relevant band	Where the claim form is served by the court or by any method other than by the claimant	Where • the claim form is served personally by the claimant; and • there is only one defendant	Where there is more than one defendant, for each additional defendant personally served at separate addresses by the claimant
Where – • the value of the claim exceeds £25 but does not exceed £500	£50	£60	£15
Where – • the value of the claim exceeds £500 but does not exceed £1,000	£70	£80	£15
Where – • the value of the claim exceeds £1,000 but does not exceed £5,000; or • the only claim is for delivery of goods and no value is specified or stated on the claim form	£80	£90	£15
Where – • the value of the claim exceeds £5,000	£100	£110	£15

When defendant only liable for fixed commencement costs

45.3 (1) Where –

    (a) the only claim is for a specified sum of money; and

    (b) the defendant pays the money claimed within 14 days after service of particulars of claim on him, together with the fixed commencement costs stated in the claim form,

the defendant is not liable for any further costs unless the court orders otherwise.

  (2) Where –

    (a) the claimant gives notice of acceptance of a payment into court in satisfaction of the whole claim;

    (b) the only claim is for a specified sum of money; and

    (c) the defendant made the payment into court within 14 days after service of the particulars of claim on him, together with the fixed costs stated in the claim form,

the defendant is not liable for any further costs unless the court orders otherwise.

Costs on entry of judgment

45.4 Where –

(a) the claimant has claimed fixed commencement costs under rule 45.2; and

(b) judgment is entered in the circumstances specified in the table in this rule (Table 2), the amount to be included in the judgment in respect of the claimant's solicitor's charges is the aggregate of –

(i) the fixed commencement costs; and

(ii) the relevant amount shown in Table 2.

Table 2

Fixed costs on entry of judgment

	Where the amount of the judgment exceeds £25 but does not exceed £5,000	Where the amount of the judgment exceeds £5,000
Where judgment in default of an acknowledgment of service is entered under rule 12.4(1) (entry of judgment by request on claim for money only)	£22	£30
Where judgment in default of a defence is entered under rule 12.4(1) (entry of judgment by request on claim for money only)	£25	£35
Where judgment is entered under rule 14.4 (judgment on admission), or rule 14.5 (judgment on admission of part of claim) and claimant accepts the defendant's proposal as to the manner of payment	£40	£55
Where judgment is entered under rule 14.4 (judgment on admission), or rule 14.5 (judgment on admission on part of claim) and court decides the date or times of payment	£55	£70
Where summary judgment is given under Part 24 or the court strikes out a defence under rule 3.4(2)(a), in either case, on application by a party	£175	£210
Where judgment is given on a claim for delivery of goods under a regulated agreement within the meaning of the Consumer Credit Act 1974[70] and no other entry in this table applies	£60	£85

(70) 1974 c.39.

Miscellaneous fixed costs

45.5   The table in this rule (Table 3) shows the amount to be allowed in respect of solicitor's charges in the circumstances mentioned.

Table 3

Miscellaneous fixed costs

For service by a party of any document required to be served personally including preparing and copying a certificate of service for each individual served	£15
Where service by an alternative method is permitted by an order under rule 6.8 for each individual served	£25
Where a document is served out of the jurisdiction – (a) in Scotland, Northern Ireland, the Isle of Man or the Channel Islands; (b) in any other place	£65 £75

(Other rules which provide for situations where fixed costs may be allowed can be found in Schedule 1 in RSC Order 62 and in Schedule 2 in CCR Order 38, Appendix B.)

(For opening sections of the Costs Practice Direction, see after Part 43 above.)

[Authors' note: For the general Introduction to the Costs Practice Direction, see after Part 43 above.]

DIRECTIONS RELATING TO PART 45
FIXED COSTS

FIXED COSTS IN SMALL CLAIMS

1.1 Under Rule 27.14 the costs which can be awarded to a claimant in a small claims track case include the fixed costs payable under Part 45 attributable to issuing the claim.

1.2 Those fixed costs shall be the sum of
   (a) the fixed commencement costs calculated in accordance with Table 1 of Rule 45.2 and;
   (b) the appropriate court fee or fees paid by the claimant.

FIXED COSTS ON THE ISSUE OF A DEFAULT COSTS CERTIFICATE

2.1 Unless paragraph 2.2 applies or unless the court orders otherwise, the fixed costs to be included in a default costs certificate are £80 plus a sum equal to any appropriate court fee payable on the issue of the certificate.

2.2 The fixed costs included in a certificate must not exceed the maximum sum specified for costs and court fee in the notice of commencement.

PART 46

FAST TRACK TRIAL COSTS

Contents of this Part

Scope of this Part

46.1 (1) This Part deals with the amount of costs which the court may award as the costs of an advocate for preparing for and appearing at the trial of a claim in the fast track (referred to in this rule as 'fast track trial costs').

(2) For the purposes of this Part –

(a) 'advocate' means a person exercising a right of audience as a representative of, or on behalf of, a party;

(b) 'fast track trial costs' means the costs of a party's advocate for preparing for and appearing at the trial, but does not include –

(i) any other disbursements; or

(ii) any value added tax payable on the fees of a party's advocate; and

(c) 'trial' includes a hearing where the court decides an amount of money or the value of goods following a judgment under Part 12 (default judgment) or Part 14 (admissions) but does not include –

(i) the hearing of an application for summary judgment under Part 24; or

(ii) the court's approval of a settlement or other compromise under rule 21.10.

(Part 21 deals with claims made by or on behalf of, or against, children and patients.)

Amount of fast track trial costs

46.2 (1) The following table shows the amount of fast track trial costs which the court may award (whether by summary or detailed assessment).

Value of the claim	Amount of fast track trial costs which the court may award
Up to £3,000	£350
More than £3,000 but not more than £10,000	£500
More than £10,000	£750

(2) The court may not award more or less than the amount shown in the table except where –

(a) it decides not to award any fast track trial costs; or

(b) rule 46.3 applies,

but the court may apportion the amount awarded between the parties to reflect their respective degrees of success on the issues at trial.

(3) Where the only claim is for the payment of money –
    (a) for the purpose of quantifying fast track trial costs awarded to a claimant, the value of the claim is the total amount of the judgment excluding –
        (i) interest and costs; and
        (ii) any reduction made for contributory negligence.
    (b) for the purpose of the quantifying fast track trial costs awarded to a defendant, the value of the claim is –
        (i) the amount specified in the claim form (excluding interest and costs);
        (ii) if no amount is specified, the maximum amount which the claimant reasonably expected to recover according to the statement of value included in the claim form under rule 16.3; or
        (iii) more than £10,000, if the claim form states that the claimant cannot reasonably say how much he expects to recover.
(4) Where the claim is only for a remedy other than the payment of money the value of the claim is deemed to be more than £3,000 but not more than £10,000, unless the court orders otherwise.
(5) Where the claim includes both a claim for the payment of money and for a remedy other than the payment of money, the value of the claim is deemed to be the higher of –
    (a) the value of the money claim decided in accordance with paragraph (3); or
    (b) the deemed value of the other remedy decided in accordance with paragraph (4),
unless the court orders otherwise.
(6) Where –
    (a) a defendant has made a counterclaim against the claimant;
    (b) the counterclaim has a higher value than the claim; and
    (c) the claimant succeeds at trial both on his claim and the counterclaim,
for the purpose of quantifying fast track trial costs awarded to the claimant, the value of the claim is the value of the defendant's counterclaim calculated in accordance with this rule.
(Rule 20.4 sets out how a defendant may make a counterclaim.)

Power to award more or less than the amount of fast track trial costs

46.3 (1) This rule sets out when a court may award –
    (a) an additional amount to the amount of fast track trial costs shown in the table in rule 46.2(1); and
    (b) less than those amounts.
(2) If –
    (a) in addition to the advocate, a party's legal representative attends the trial;
    (b) the court considers that it was necessary for a legal representative to attend to assist the advocate; and
    (c) the court awards fast track trial costs to that party,
the court may award an additional £250 in respect of the legal representative's attendance at the trial.
(Legal representative is defined in rule 2.3.)
    (3) If the court considers that it is necessary to direct a separate trial of an issue then the court may award an additional amount in respect of the separate trial but that amount is limited in accordance with paragraph (4) of this rule.

(4) The additional amount the court may award under paragraph 3 must not exceed two-thirds of the amount payable for that claim, subject to a minimum award of £350.

(5) Where the party to whom fast track trial costs are to be awarded is a litigant in person, the court will award –

    (a) if the litigant in person can prove financial loss, two-thirds of the amount that would otherwise be awarded; or

    (b) if the litigant in person fails to prove financial loss, an amount in respect of the time spent reasonably doing the work at the rate specified in the costs practice direction.

(6) Where a defendant has made a counterclaim against the claimant, and –

    (a) the claimant has succeeded on his claim; and

    (b) the defendant has succeeded on his counterclaim,

the court will quantify the amount of the award of fast track trial costs to which –

    (i) but for the counterclaim, the claimant would be entitled for succeeding on his claim; and

    (ii) but for the claim, the defendant would be entitled for succeeding on his counterclaim,

and make one award of the difference, if any, to the party entitled to the higher award of costs.

(7) Where the court considers that the party to whom fast track trial costs are to be awarded has behaved unreasonably or improperly during the trial, it may award that party an amount less than would otherwise be payable for that claim, as it considers appropriate.

(8) Where the court considers that the party who is to pay the fast track trial costs has behaved improperly during the trial the court may award such additional amount to the other party as it considers appropriate.

Fast track trial costs where there is more than one claimant or defendant

46.4 (1) Where the same advocate is acting for more than one party –

    (a) the court may make only one award in respect of fast track trial costs payable to that advocate; and

    (b) the parties for whom the advocate is acting are jointly entitled to any fast track trial costs awarded by the court.

(2) Where –

    (a) the same advocate is acting for more than one claimant; and

    (b) each claimant has a separate claim against the defendant,

the value of the claim, for the purpose of quantifying the award in respect of fast track trial costs is to be ascertained in accordance with paragraph (3).

(3) The value of the claim in the circumstances mentioned in paragraph (2)   is –

    (a) where the only claim of each claimant is for the payment of money –

        (i) if the award of fast track trial costs is in favour of the claimants, the total amount of the judgment made in favour of all the claimants jointly represented; or

        (ii) if the award is in favour of the defendant, the total amount claimed by the claimants,

and in either case, quantified in accordance with rule 46.2(3);

(b) where the only claim of each claimant is for a remedy other than the payment of money, deemed to be more than £3,000 but not more than £10,000; and

(c) where claims of the claimants include both a claim for the payment of money and for a remedy other than the payment of money, deemed to be –

    (i) more than £3,000 but not more than £10,000; or

    (ii) if greater, the value of the money claims calculated in accordance with sub paragraph (a) above.

(4) Where –

    (a) there is more than one defendant; and

    (b) any or all of the defendants are separately represented,

the court may award fast track trial costs to each party who is separately represented.

(5) Where –

    (a) there is more than one claimant; and

    (b) a single defendant,

the court may make only one award to the defendant of fast track trial costs, for which the claimants are jointly and severally liable[GL].

(6) For the purpose of quantifying the fast track trial costs awarded to the single defendant under paragraph (5), the value of the claim is to be calculated in accordance with paragraph (3) of this rule.

(For opening sections of the Costs Practice Direction, see after Part 43 above.)

[Authors' note: For the general Introduction to the Costs Practice Direction, see after Part 43 above.]

DIRECTIONS RELATING TO PART 46
FAST TRACK TRIAL COSTS

RULE 46.1 SCOPE OF PART 46

1.1 Part 46 applies to the costs of an advocate for preparing for and appearing at the trial of a claim in the fast track.

1.2 It applies only where, at the date of the trial, the claim is allocated to the fast track. It does not apply in any other case, irrespective of the financial value of the claim.

1.3 In particular it does not apply to:

    (a) the hearing of a claim which is allocated to the small claims track with the consent of the parties given under rule 26.7(3); or

    (b) a disposal hearing at which the amount to be paid under a judgment or order is decided by the court (see paragraph 12.8 of the Practice Direction which supplements Part 26 (Case Management – Preliminary Stage)).

Cases which settle before trial

1.4 Attention is drawn to rule 44.10 (limitation on amount court may award where a claim allocated to the fast track settles before trial).

PART 47

PROCEDURE FOR DETAILED ASSESSMENT OF COSTS AND DEFAULT PROVISIONS

Contents of this Part

(The definitions contained in Part 43 are relevant to this Part)

I General rules about detailed assessment

Time when detailed assessment may be carried out

47.1   The general rule is that the costs of any proceedings or any part of the proceedings are not to be assessed by the detailed procedure until the conclusion of the proceedings but the court may order them to be assessed immediately.

(The costs practice direction gives further guidance about when proceedings are concluded for the purpose of this rule.)

No stay of detailed assessment where there is an appeal

47.2   Detailed assessment is not stayed pending an appeal unless the court so orders.

Powers of an authorised court officer

47.3 (1) An authorised court officer has all the powers of the court when making a detailed assessment, except –

    (a) power to make a wasted costs order as defined in rule 48.7;

    (b) power to make an order under –

        (i) rule 44.14 (powers in relation to misconduct);

        (ii) rule 47.8 (sanction for delay in commencing detailed assessment proceedings);

        (iii) paragraph (2) (objection to detailed assessment by authorised court officer); and

    (c) power to make a detailed assessment of costs payable to a solicitor by his client, unless the costs are being assessed under rule 48.5 (costs where money is payable to a child or patient).

  (2) Where a party objects to the detailed assessment of costs being made by an authorised court officer, the court may order it to be made by a costs judge or a district judge.

(The costs practice direction sets out the relevant procedure.)

Venue for detailed assessment proceedings

47.4 (1) All applications and requests in detailed assessment proceedings must be made to or filed at the appropriate office.

(The costs practice direction sets out the meaning of 'appropriate office' in any particular case)

  (2) The court may direct that the appropriate office is to be the Supreme Court Costs Office.

  (3) A county court may direct that another county court is to be the appropriate office.

  (4) A direction under paragraph (3) may be made without proceedings being transferred to that court.

(Rule 30.2 makes provision for any county court to transfer the proceedings to another county court for detailed assessment of costs.)

II Costs payable by one party to another – commencement of detailed assessment proceedings

Application of this section

47.5   This section of Part 47 applies where a costs officer is to make a detailed assessment of costs which are payable by one party to another.

Commencement of detailed assessment proceedings

47.6 (1) Detailed assessment proceedings are commenced by the receiving party serving on the paying party –

    (a) notice of commencement in the relevant practice form; and

(b) a copy of the bill of costs.

(Rule 47.7 sets out the period for commencing detailed assessment proceedings.)

(2) The receiving party must also serve a copy of the notice of commencement and the bill on any other relevant persons specified in the costs practice direction.

(3) A person on whom a copy of the notice of commencement is served under paragraph (2) is a party to the detailed assessment proceedings (in addition to the paying party and the receiving party).

(The costs practice direction deals with –

- other documents which the party must file when he requests detailed assessment;
- the court's powers where it considers that a hearing may be necessary;
- the form of a bill; and
- the length of notice which will be given if a hearing date is fixed.)

Period for commencing detailed assessment proceedings

47.7 The following table shows the period for commencing detailed assessment proceedings.

Source of right to detailed assessment proceedings must be commenced	Time by which detailed assessment
Judgment, direction, order, award or other determination	3 months after the date of the judgment etc. Where detailed assessment is stayed pending an appeal, 3 months after the date of the order lifting the stay.
Discontinuance under Part 38	3 months after the date of service of notice of discontinuance under rule 38.3; or 3 months after the date of the dismissal of application to set the notice of discontinuance aside under rule 38.4
Acceptance of an offer to settle or a payment into court under Part 36	3 months after the date when the right to costs arose.

Sanction for delay in commencing detailed assessment proceedings

47.8 (1) Where the receiving party fails to commence detailed assessment proceedings within the period specified –

(a) in rule 47.7; or

(b) by any direction of the court,

the paying party may apply for an order requiring the receiving party to commence detailed assessment proceedings within such time as the court may specify.

(2) On an application under paragraph (1), the court may direct that, unless the receiving party commences detailed assessment proceedings within the time specified by the court, all or part of the costs to which the receiving party would otherwise be entitled will be disallowed.

(3) If –

(a) the paying party has not made an application in accordance with paragraph (1); and

(b) the receiving party commences the proceedings later than the period specified in rule 47.7, the court may disallow all or part of the interest otherwise payable to the receiving party under –

(i) section 17 of the Judgments Act 1838[71]; or

(ii) section 74 of the County Courts Act 1984[72],

but must not impose any other sanction except in accordance with rule 44.14 (powers in relation to misconduct).

(4) Where the costs to be assessed in a detailed assessment are payable out of the Legal Aid Fund, this rule applies as if the receiving party were the solicitor to whom the costs are payable and the paying party were the Legal Aid Board.

Points of dispute and consequence of not serving

47.9(1) The paying party and any other party to the detailed assessment proceedings may dispute any item in the bill of costs by serving points of dispute on –

(a) the receiving party; and

(b) every other party to the detailed assessment proceedings.

(2) The period for serving points of dispute is 21 days after the date of service of the notice of commencement.

(3) If a party serves points of dispute after the period set out in paragraph (2), he may not be heard further in the detailed assessment proceedings unless the court gives permission.

(The costs practice direction sets out requirements about the form of points of dispute.)

(4) The receiving party may file a request for a default costs certificate if –

(a) the period set out in rule 47.9 (2) for serving points of dispute has expired; and

(b) he has not been served with any points of dispute.

(5) If any party (including the paying party) serves points of dispute before the issue of a default costs certificate the court may not issue the default costs certificate.

(Section IV of this Part sets out the procedure to be followed after points of dispute have been filed)

Procedure where costs are agreed

47.10(1) If the paying party and the receiving party agree the amount of costs, either party may apply for a costs certificate (either interim or final) in the amount agreed.

(Rule 47.15 and rule 47.16 contain further provisions about interim and final costs certificates respectively.)

(2) An application for a certificate under paragraph (1) must be made –

(a) where the right to detailed assessment arises from a judgment or court order –

(i) to the court where the judgment or order was given or made, if the proceedings have not been transferred since then; or

(ii) to the court to which the proceedings have been transferred; and

(b) in any other case, to the court which would be the venue for detailed assessment proceedings under rule 47.4.

---

(71) 1838 c.110. Section 17 was amended by S.I. 1998/2940.

(72) 1984 c.28. Section 74 was amended by section 2 of the Private International Law (Miscellaneous Provisions) Act 1995 (c.42).

III Costs payable by one party to another – default provisions

47.11(1) Where the receiving party is permitted by rule 47.9 to obtain a default costs certificate, he does so by filing a request in the relevant practice form.

(The costs practice direction deals with the procedure by which the receiving party may obtain a default costs certificate.)

    (2) A default costs certificate will include an order to pay the costs to which it relates.

    (3) Where a receiving party obtains a default costs certificate, the costs payable to him for the commencement of detailed assessment proceedings shall be the sum set out in the costs practice direction.

Setting aside default costs certificate

47.12(1) The court must set aside a default costs certificate if the receiving party was not entitled to it.

    (2) In any other case, the court may set aside or vary a default costs certificate if it appears to the court that there is some good reason why the detailed assessment proceedings should continue.

    (3) Where –

        (a) the receiving party has purported to serve the notice of commencement on the paying party;

        (b) a default costs certificate has been issued; and

        (c) the receiving party subsequently discovers that the notice of commencement did not reach the paying party at least 21 days before the default costs certificate was issued,

    the receiving party must –

        (i) file a request for the default costs certificate to be set aside; or

        (ii) apply to the court for directions.

    (4) Where paragraph (3) applies, the receiving party may take no further step in –

        (a) the detailed assessment proceedings; or

        (b) the enforcement of the default costs certificate,

    until the certificate has been set aside or the court has given directions.

(The costs practice direction contains further details about the procedure for setting aside a default costs certificate and the matters which the court must take into account.)

IV Costs payable by one party to another – procedure where points of dispute are served

Optional reply

47.13(1) Where any party to the detailed assessment proceedings serves points of dispute, the receiving party may serve a reply on the other parties to the assessment proceedings.

    (2) He may do so within 21 days after service on him of the points of dispute to which his reply relates.

Detailed assessment hearing

47.14(1) Where points of dispute are served in accordance with this Part, the receiving party must file a request for a detailed assessment hearing.

    (2) He must file the request within 3 months of the expiry of the period for commencing detailed assessment proceedings as specified –

    (a) in rule 47.7; or

    (b) by any direction of the court.

(3) Where the receiving party fails to file a request in accordance with paragraph (2), the paying party may apply for an order requiring the receiving party to file the request within such time as the court may specify.

(4) On an application under paragraph (3), the court may direct that, unless the receiving party requests a detailed assessment hearing within the time specified by the court, all or part of the costs to which the receiving party would otherwise be entitled will be disallowed.

(5) If –

    (a) the paying party has not made an application in accordance with paragraph (3); and

    (b) the receiving party files a request for a detailed assessment hearing later than the period specified in paragraph (2),

    the court may disallow all or part of the interest otherwise payable to the receiving party under –

        (i) section 17 of the Judgments Act 1838[73]; or

        (ii) section 74 of the County Courts Act 1984[74],

    but must not impose any other sanction except in accordance with rule 44.14 (powers in relation to misconduct).

(6) No person other than –

    (a) the receiving party;

    (b) the paying party; and

    (c) any party who has served points of dispute under rule 47.9,

    may be heard at the detailed assessment hearing unless the court gives permission.

(7) Only items specified in the points of dispute may be raised at the hearing, unless the court gives permission.

(The costs practice direction specifies other documents which must be filed with the request for hearing and the length of notice which the court will give when it fixes a hearing date.)

V Interim costs certificate and final costs certificate

Power to issue an interim certificate

47.15(1) The court may at any time after the receiving party has filed a request for a detailed assessment hearing –

    (a) issue an interim costs certificate for such sum as it considers appropriate;

    (b) amend or cancel an interim certificate.

(2) An interim certificate will include an order to pay the costs to which it relates, unless the court orders otherwise.

(3) The court may order the costs certified in an interim certificate to be paid into court.

---

(73) 1838 c.110. Section 17 was amended by SI 1998/2940.

(74) 1984 c.28. Section 74 was amended by section 2 of the Private International Law (Miscellaneous Provisions) Act 1995 (c.42).

Final costs certificate

47.16(1) In this rule a completed bill means a bill calculated to show the amount due following the detailed assessment of the costs.

(2) The period for filing the completed bill is 14 days after the end of the detailed assessment hearing.

(3) When a completed bill is filed the court will issue a final costs certificate and serve it on the parties to the detailed assessment proceedings.

(4) Paragraph (3) is subject to any order made by the court that a certificate is not to be issued until other costs have been paid.

(5) A final costs certificate will include an order to pay the costs to which it relates, unless the court orders otherwise.

(The costs practice direction deals with the form of a final costs certificate.)

VI Detailed assessment procedure for costs of an assisted person where costs are payable out of the legal aid fund

Detailed assessment procedure for costs of an assisted person where costs are payable out of the legal aid fund

47.17(1) Where the court is to assess costs of an assisted person which are payable out of the legal aid fund, the assisted person's solicitor may commence detailed assessment proceedings by filing a request in the relevant practice form.

(2) A request under paragraph (1) must be filed within 3 months after the date when the right to detailed assessment arose.

(3) The solicitor must also serve a copy of the request for detailed assessment on the assisted person, if notice of the assisted person's interest has been given to the court in accordance with legal aid regulations.

(4) Where the solicitor has certified that the assisted person wishes to attend an assessment hearing, the court will, on receipt of the request for assessment, fix a date for the assessment hearing.

(5) Where paragraph (3) does not apply, the court will, on receipt of the request for assessment provisionally assess the costs without the attendance of the solicitor, unless it considers that a hearing is necessary.

(6) After the court has provisionally assessed the bill, it will return the bill to the solicitor.

(7) The court will fix a date for an assessment hearing if the solicitor informs the court, within 14 days after he receives the provisionally assessed bill, that he wants the court to hold such a hearing.

VII Costs of detailed assessment proceedings

Liability for costs of detailed assessment proceedings

47.18(1) The receiving party is entitled to his costs of the detailed assessment proceedings except where –

(a) the provisions of any Act, any of these Rules or any relevant practice direction provide otherwise; or

(b) the court makes some other order in relation to all or part of the costs of the detailed assessment proceedings.

(2) In deciding whether to make some other order, the court must have regard to all the circumstances, including –

(a) the conduct of all the parties;

(b) the amount, if any, by which the bill of costs has been reduced; and

(c) whether it was reasonable for a party to claim the costs of a particular item or to dispute that item.

Offers to settle without prejudice save as to costs of the detailed assessment proceedings

47.19(1) Where –

(a) a party (whether the paying party or the receiving party) makes a written offer to settle the costs of the proceedings which gave rise to the assessment proceedings; and

(b) the offer is expressed to be without prejudice$^{(GL)}$ save as to the costs of the detailed assessment proceedings,

the court will take the offer into account in deciding who should pay the costs of those proceedings.

(2) The fact of the offer must not be communicated to the costs officer until the question of costs of the detailed assessment proceedings falls to be decided.

(The costs practice direction provides that rule 47.19 does not apply where the receiving party is an assisted person.)

VIII   Appeals from authorised court officers in detailed assessment proceedings

Right to appeal

47.20   Any party to detailed assessment proceedings may appeal against a decision of an authorised court officer in those proceedings.

(Part 52 sets out general rules about appeals)

Court to hear appeal

47.21   An appeal against a decision of an authorised court officer is to a costs judge or a district judge of the High Court.

Appeal procedure

47.22(1) The appellant must file an appeal notice within 14 days after the date of the decision he wishes to appeal against.

(2) On receipt of the appeal notice, the court will –

(a) serve a copy of the notice on the parties to the detailed assessment proceedings; and

(b) give notice of the appeal to those parties.

Powers of the court on appeal

47.23   On an appeal from an authorised court officer the court will –

(a) re-hear the proceedings which gave rise to the decision appealed against; and

(b) make any order and give any directions as it considers appropriate.

(For opening sections of the Costs Practice Direction, see after Part 43 above.)

[Authors' note: For the general Introduction to the Costs Practice Direction, see after Part 43 above.]

DIRECTIONS RELATING TO PART 47
PROCEDURE FOR DETAILED ASSESSMENT OF COSTS AND DEFAULT PROVISIONS

SECTION I – GENERAL RULES ABOUT DETAILED ASSESSMENT

RULE 47.1 TIME WHEN ASSESSMENT MAY BE CARRIED OUT

1.1 (1) For the purposes of this rule, proceedings are concluded when the court has finally determined the matters in issue in the claim, whether or not there is an appeal.

(2) For the purposes of this rule, the making of an award of provisional damages under Part 41 will be treated as a final determination of the matters in issue.

(3) (a) A party who is served with a notice of commencement (see paragraph 2.3 below) may apply to a costs judge or a district judge to determine whether the party who served it is entitled to commence detailed assessment proceedings.

(b) On hearing such an application the orders which the court may make include: an order allowing the detailed assessment proceedings to continue, or an order setting aside the notice of commencement.

(4) A costs judge or a district judge may make an order allowing detailed assessment proceedings to be commenced where there is no realistic prospect of the claim continuing.

RULE 47.2 NO STAY OF DETAILED ASSESSMENT WHERE THERE IS AN APPEAL

1.2 (1) Rule 47.2 provides that detailed assessment is not stayed pending an appeal unless the court so orders.

(2) An application to stay the detailed assessment of costs pending an appeal may be made to the court whose order is being appealed or to the court who will hear the appeal.

RULE 47.3 POWERS OF AN AUTHORISED COURT OFFICER

1.3 (1) The court officers authorised by the Lord Chancellor to assess costs in the Supreme Court Costs Office and the Principal Registry of the Family Division are authorised to deal with claims for costs not exceeding £17,500 (excluding VAT) in the case of senior executive officers and £35,000 (excluding VAT) in the case of principal officers.

(2) Where the receiving party, paying party and any other party to the detailed assessment proceedings who has served points of dispute are agreed that the assessment should not be made by an authorised court officer, the receiving party should so inform the court when requesting a hearing date. The court will then list the hearing before a costs judge or a district judge.

(3) In any other case a party who objects to the assessment being made by an authorised court officer must make an application to the costs judge or district judge under Part 23 (General Rules about Applications for Court Orders) setting out the reasons for the objection and if sufficient reason is shown the court will direct that the bill be assessed by a costs judge or district judge.

RULE 47.4 VENUE FOR DETAILED ASSESSMENT PROCEEDINGS

1.4 For the purposes of rule 47.4(1) the "appropriate office" means

(1) the district registry or county court in which the case was being dealt with when the judgment or order was made or the event occurred which gave rise to the right to assessment, or to which it has subsequently been transferred; or

(2) the Principal Registry of the Family Division if the costs in question are the costs of any proceedings which were being dealt with in that registry when the judgment or order was made or when the event occurred which gave rise to the right to assessment, or which have subsequently been transferred to that registry; or

(3) In the case of appeals from the Principal Registry of the Family Division, a District Registry or a county court in respect of family proceedings, the Principal Registry of the Family Division.

(4) in all other cases, the Supreme Court Costs Office.

1.5 (1) A direction under rule 47.4(2) or (3) specifying a particular court, registry or office as the appropriate office may be given on application or on the court's own initiative.

(2) Before making such a direction on its own initiative the court will give the parties the opportunity to make representations.

(3) Unless the Supreme Court Costs Office is the appropriate office for the purposes of Rule 47.4(1) an order directing that an assessment is to take place at the Supreme Court Costs Office will be made only if it is appropriate to do so having regard to the size of the bill of costs, the difficulty of the issues involved, the likely length of the hearing, the cost to the parties and any other relevant matter.

SECTION II – COSTS PAYABLE BY ONE PARTY TO ANOTHER – COMMENCEMENT OF DETAILED ASSESSMENT PROCEEDINGS

RULE 47.6 COMMENCEMENT OF DETAILED ASSESSMENT PROCEEDINGS

2.1 Form 2 of the Schedule of Costs Forms annexed to this Practice Direction is a model form bill of costs for detailed assessment. Further information about bills of costs is set out in Sections 2 and 3 of the Directions Relating to Part 43.

2.2 The receiving party must serve on the paying party and all other relevant persons the following documents:

(1) a notice of commencement;

(2) a copy of the bill of costs;

(3) copies of the fee notes of counsel and of any expert in respect of fees claimed in the bill;

(4) written evidence as to any other disbursement which is claimed and which exceeds £250;

(5) a statement giving the name and address for service of any person upon whom the receiving party intends to serve the notice of commencement.

2.3 (1) The notice of commencement must be in Form 5 of the Schedule of Costs Forms annexed to this Practice Direction.

(2) Before it is served it must be completed to show as separate items

(a) the total amount of the bill of costs as drawn;

(b) the additional amounts which will be payable by way of fixed costs and court fees if a default costs certificate is obtained.

(3) The fixed costs payable in respect of solicitors' charges on the issue of a default costs certificate are £80.

2.4 (1) This paragraph applies where the notice of commencement is to be served outside England and Wales.

(2) The date to be inserted in the notice of commencement for the paying party to send points of dispute is a date (not less than 21 days from the date of service of the notice) which must be calculated by reference to the Practice Direction supplementing Section III of Part 6 as if the notice were a claim form and as if the date to be inserted was the date for the filing of a defence.

2.5 (1) For the purposes of rule 47.6(2) a "relevant person" means:

(a) any person who has taken part in the proceedings which gave rise to the assessment and who is directly liable under an order for costs made against him;

(b) any person who has given to the receiving party notice in writing that he has a financial interest in the outcome of the assessment and wishes to be a party accordingly;

(c) any other person whom the court orders to be treated as such.

(2) Where a party is unsure whether a person is or is not a relevant person, that party may apply to the appropriate office for directions.

(3) The court will generally not make an order that the person in respect of whom the application is made will be treated as a relevant person, unless within a specified time he applies to the court to be joined as a party to the assessment proceedings in accordance with Part 19 (Addition and Substitution of Parties).

2.6 (1) This paragraph applies in cases in which the bill of costs is capable of being copied onto a computer disk.

(2) If, before the detailed assessment hearing, a paying party requests a disk copy of a bill to which this paragraph applies, the receiving party must supply him with a copy free of charge not more than 7 days after the date on which he received the request.

RULE 47.7 PERIOD FOR COMMENCING DETAILED ASSESSMENT PROCEEDINGS

2.7 The parties may agree under rule 2.11 (Time limits may be varied by parties) to extend or shorten the time specified by rule 47.7 for commencing the detailed assessment proceedings.

2.8 A party may apply to the appropriate office for an order under rule 3.1(2)(a) to extend or shorten that time.

2.9 Attention is drawn to rule 47.6(1). The detailed assessment proceedings are commenced by service of the documents referred to.

2.10 Permission to commence assessment proceedings out of time is not required.

RULE 47.8 SANCTION FOR DELAY IN COMMENCING DETAILED ASSESSMENT PROCEEDINGS

2.11 (1) An application for an order under rule 47.8 must be made in writing and be issued in the appropriate office.

(2) The application notice must be served at least 7 days before the hearing.

RULE 47.9 POINTS OF DISPUTE AND CONSEQUENCES OF NOT SERVING

2.12 The parties may agree under rule 2.11 (Time limits may be varied by parties) to extend or shorten the time specified by rule 47.9 for service of points of dispute. A party may apply to the appropriate office for an order under rule 3.1(2)(a) to extend or shorten that time.

2.13 Points of dispute should be short and to the point and should follow as closely as possible Form 6 of the Schedule of Costs Forms annexed to this Practice Direction.

2.14 Points of dispute must–

(1) identify each item in the bill of costs which is disputed,

(2) in each case state concisely the nature and grounds of dispute,

(3) where practicable suggest a figure to be allowed for each item in respect of which a reduction is sought, and

(4) be signed by the party serving them or his solicitor.

2.15 (1) The normal period for serving points of dispute is 21 days after the date of service of the notice of commencement.

(2) Where a notice of commencement is served on a party outside England and Wales the period within which that party should serve points of dispute is to be calculated by reference to Section III of Part 6 as if the notice of commencement was a claim form and as if the period for serving points of dispute were the period for filing a defence.

2.16 A party who serves points of dispute on the receiving party must at the same time serve a copy on every other party to the detailed assessment proceedings, whose name and address for service appears on the statement served by the receiving party in accordance with paragraph 2.2(5) above.

2.17 (1) This paragraph applies in cases in which Points of Dispute are capable of being copied onto a computer disk.

(2) If, within 14 days of the receipt of the Points of Dispute, the receiving party requests a disk copy of them, the paying party must supply him with a copy free of charge not more than 7 days after the date on which he received the request.

RULE 47.10 PROCEDURE WHERE COSTS ARE AGREED

2.18 Where the parties have agreed terms as to the issue of a costs certificate (either interim or final) they should apply under rule 40.6 (Consent judgments and orders) for an order that a certificate be issued in terms set out in the application. Such an application may be dealt with by a court officer, who may issue the certificate.

2.19 Where the receiving party claims that the paying party has agreed to pay costs but that he will neither pay those costs nor join in a consent application under paragraph 2.18, the receiving party may apply under Part 23 (General Rules about Applications for Court Orders) for a certificate either interim or final to be issued.

2.20 An application under paragraph 2.19 must be supported by evidence and will be heard by a costs judge or a district judge. The respondent to the application must file and serve any evidence he relies on at least two days before the hearing date.

2.21 Nothing in rule 47.10 prevents parties who seek a judgment or order by consent from including in the draft a term that a party shall pay to another party a specified sum in respect of costs.

2.22 (1) The receiving party may discontinue the detailed assessment proceedings in accordance with Part 38 (Discontinuance).

(2) Where the receiving party discontinues the detailed assessment proceedings before a detailed assessment hearing has been requested, the paying party may apply to the appropriate office for an order about the costs of the detailed assessment proceedings.

(3) Where a detailed assessment hearing has been requested the receiving party may not discontinue unless the court gives permission.

(4) A bill of costs may be withdrawn by consent whether or not a detailed assessment hearing has been requested.

SECTION III – COSTS PAYABLE BY ONE PARTY TO ANOTHER – DEFAULT PROVISIONS

RULE 47.11 DEFAULT COSTS CERTIFICATE

3.1 A request for the issue of a default costs certificate must be made in Form 7 of the Schedule of Costs Forms annexed to this Practice Direction and must be signed by the receiving party or his solicitor.

3.2 The request must be filed at the appropriate office.

3.3 A default costs certificate will be in Form 9 or Form 10 of the Schedule of Costs Forms annexed to this Practice Direction.

3.4 Attention is drawn to Rules 40.3 (Drawing up and Filing of Judgments and Orders) and 40.4 (Service of Judgments and Orders) which apply to the preparation and service of a default costs certificate. The receiving party will be treated as having permission to draw up a default costs certificate by virtue of this Practice Direction.

3.5 The issue of a default costs certificate does not prohibit, govern or affect any detailed assessment of the same costs which is made pursuant to the Legal Aid Act 1988.

3.6 An application for an order staying enforcement of a default costs certificate may be made either–

(1) to a costs judge or district judge of the court office which issued the certificate; or

(2) to the court (if different) which has general jurisdiction to enforce the certificate.

3.7 Proceedings for enforcement of default costs certificates may not be issued in the Supreme Court Costs Office.

RULE 47.12 SETTING ASIDE DEFAULT COSTS CERTIFICATE

3.8 (1) A court officer may set aside a default costs certificate at the request of the receiving party under rule 47.12(3).

(2) A costs judge or a district judge will make any other order or give any directions under this rule.

3.9 (1) An application for an order under rule 47.12(2) to set aside or vary a default costs certificate must be supported by evidence.

(2) In deciding whether to set aside or vary a certificate under rule 47.12(2) the matters to which the court must have regard include whether the party seeking the order made the application promptly.

(3) As a general rule a default costs certificate will be set aside under rule 47.12(2) only if the applicant shows a good reason for the court to do so and if he files with his application a draft of the points of dispute he proposes to serve if his application is granted.

3.10(1) Attention is drawn to rule 3.1(3) (which enables the court when making an order to make it subject to conditions) and to rule 44.3(8) (which enables the court to order a party whom it has ordered to pay costs to pay an amount on account before the costs are assessed).

(2) A costs judge or a district judge may exercise the power of the court to make an order under rule 44.3(8) although he did not make the order about costs which led to the issue of the default costs certificate.

3.11 If a default costs certificate is set aside the court will give directions for the management of the detailed assessment proceedings.

SECTION IV COSTS PAYABLE BY ONE PARTY TO ANOTHER – PROCEDURE WHERE POINTS OF DISPUTE ARE SERVED

RULE 47.13 OPTIONAL REPLY

4.1 (1) Where the receiving party wishes to serve a reply, he must also serve a copy on every other party to the detailed assessment proceedings. The time for doing so is within 21 days after service of the points of dispute.

(2) A reply means:–
   (i) a separate document prepared by the receiving party; or
   (ii) his written comments added to the points of dispute.

(3) A reply must be signed by the party serving it or his solicitor.

RULE 47.14 DETAILED ASSESSMENT HEARING

4.2 The time for requesting a detailed assessment hearing is within 3 months of the expiry of the period for commencing detailed assessment proceedings.

4.3 The request for a detailed assessment hearing must be in form 8 of the Schedule of Costs Forms annexed to this Practice Direction. The request must be accompanied by:

(a) a copy of the notice of commencement of detailed assessment proceedings;

(b) a copy of the bill of costs;

(c) the document giving the right to detailed assessment (see paragraph 4.5 below);

(d) a copy of the points of dispute, annotated as necessary in order to show which items have been agreed and their value and to show which items remain in dispute and their value;

(e) as many copies of the points of dispute so annotated as there are persons who have served points of dispute;

(f) a copy of any replies served;

(g) a copy of all orders made by the court relating to the costs which are to be assessed;

(h) copies of the fee notes and other written evidence as served on the paying party in accordance with paragraph (2.2) above;

(i) where there is a dispute as to the receiving party's liability to pay costs to the solicitors who acted for the receiving party, any letter or other written information provided by the solicitor to his client explaining how the solicitor's charges are to be calculated;

(j) a statement signed by the receiving party or his solicitor giving the name, address for service, reference and telephone number and fax number, if any, of–
   (i) the receiving party;
   (ii) the paying party;
   (iii) any other person who has served points of dispute or who has given notice to the receiving party under paragraph 2.5 above;
   and giving an estimate of the length of time the detailed assessment hearing will take;

(k) where the application for a detailed assessment hearing is made by a party other than the receiving party, such of the documents set out in this paragraph as are in the possession of that party;

(l) where the court is to assess the costs of an assisted person–

    (i) the legal aid certificate, any amendment certificates, any authorities and any certificates of discharge or revocation of legal aid;

    (ii) a certificate, in Form 4(2) of the Schedule of Costs Forms annexed to this Practice Direction;

    (iii) if the assisted person has a financial interest in the detailed assessment hearing and wishes to attend, the postal address of that person to which the court will send notice of any hearing;

    (iv) if the rates payable out of the legal aid fund are prescribed rates, a schedule to the bill of costs setting out all the items in the bill which are claimed against other parties calculated at the legal aid prescribed rates with or without any claim for enhancement: (further information as to this schedule is set out in Section IX (Legal aid costs at prescribed rates below));

    (v) a copy of any default costs certificate in respect of costs claimed in the bill of costs.

4.4 (1) This paragraph applies to any document described in paragraph 4.3(i) above which the receiving party has filed in the appropriate office. The document must be the latest relevant version and in any event have been filed not more than 2 years before filing the request for a detailed assessment hearing.

    (2) In respect of any documents to which this paragraph applies, the receiving party may, instead of filing a copy of it, specify in the request for a detailed assessment hearing the case number under which a copy of the document was previously filed.

4.5 "The document giving the right to detailed assessment" means such one or more of the following documents as are appropriate to the detailed assessment proceedings:

(a) a copy of the judgment or order of the court giving the right to detailed assessment;

(b) a copy of the notice served under rule 3.7 (sanctions for non-payment of certain fees) where a claim is struck out under that rule;

(c) a copy of the notice of acceptance where an offer to settle is accepted under Part 36 (Offers to settle and payments into court);

(d) a copy of the notice of discontinuance in a case which is discontinued under Part 38 (Discontinuance);

(e) a copy of the award made on an arbitration under any Act or pursuant to an agreement, where no court has made an order for the enforcement of the award;

(f) a copy of the order, award or determination of a statutorily constituted tribunal or body;

(g) in a case under the Sheriffs Act 1887, the sheriff's bill of fees and charges, unless a court order giving the right to detailed assessment has been made;

(h) a notice of revocation or discharge under Regulation 82 of the Civil Legal Aid (General) Regulations 1989.

(j) In the county courts certain Acts and Regulations provide for costs incurred in proceedings under those Acts and Regulations to be assessed in the county court if so ordered on application. Where such an application is made, a copy of the order.

4.6 On receipt of the request for a detailed assessment hearing the court will fix a date for the hearing, or, if the costs officer so decides, will give directions or fix a date for a preliminary appointment.

4.7 (1) The court will give at least 14 days notice of the time and place of the detailed assessment hearing to every person named in the statement referred to in paragraph 4.3(j) above.

    (2) The court will when giving notice, give each person who has served points of dispute a copy of the points of dispute annotated by the receiving party in compliance with paragraph 4.3(d) above.

    (3) Attention is drawn to rule 47.14(6)&(7): apart from the receiving party, only those who have served points of dispute may be heard on the detailed assessment unless the court gives permission, and only items specified in the points of dispute may be raised unless the court gives permission.

4.8 (1) If the receiving party does not file a request for a detailed assessment hearing within the prescribed time, the paying party may apply to the court to fix a time within which the receiving party must do so. The sanction, for failure to request a detailed assessment hearing within the time specified by the court, is that all or part of the costs may be disallowed (see rule 47.8(2)).

(2) Where the receiving party requests a detailed assessment hearing after the time specified in the rules but before the paying party has made an application to the court to specify a time, the only sanction which the court may impose is to disallow all or part of the interest which would otherwise be payable for the period of delay, unless the court exercises its powers under rule 44.14 (court's powers in relation to misconduct).

4.9 If either party wishes to make an application in the detailed assessment proceedings the provisions of Part 23 (General Rules about Applications for Court Orders) apply.

4.10(1) This paragraph deals with the procedure to be adopted where a date has been given by the court for a detailed assessment hearing and

(a) the detailed assessment proceedings are settled; or

(b) a party to the detailed assessment proceedings wishes to apply to vary the date which the court has fixed; or

(c) the parties to the detailed assessment proceedings agree about changes they wish to make to any direction given for the management of the detailed assessment proceedings.

(2) If detailed assessment proceedings are settled, the receiving party must give notice of that fact to the court immediately, preferably by fax.

(3) A party who wishes to apply to vary a direction must do so in accordance with Part 23 (General Rules about Applications for Court Orders).

(4) If the parties agree about changes they wish to make to any direction given for the management of the detailed assessment proceedings–

(a) they must apply to the court for an order by consent; and

(b) they must file a draft of the directions sought and an agreed statement of the reasons why the variation is sought; and

(c) the court may make an order in the agreed terms or in other terms without a hearing, but it may direct that a hearing is to be listed.

4.11(1) If a party wishes to vary his bill of costs, points of dispute or a reply, an amended or supplementary document must be filed with the court and copies of it must be served on all other relevant parties.

(2) Permission is not required to vary a bill of costs, points of dispute or a reply but the court may disallow the variation or permit it only upon conditions, including conditions as to the payment of any costs caused or wasted by the variation.

4.12 Unless the court directs otherwise the receiving party must file with the court the papers in support of the bill not less than 7 days before the date for the detailed assessment hearing and not more than 14 days before that date.

4.13 The papers to be filed in support of the bill and the order in which they are to be arranged, are as follows:

(i) instructions and briefs to counsel arranged in chronological order together with all advices, opinions and drafts received in response to such instructions;

(ii) reports and opinions of medical and other experts arranged in chronological order;

(iii) correspondence files and attendance notes;

(iv) any other relevant papers;

(v) in detailed assessment proceedings to which rule 48.9 (Conditional Fees) applies, a copy of the conditional fee agreements;

(vi) in detailed assessment proceedings in proceedings which commenced before 26 April 1999, a full set of any relevant pleadings which have been served by the parties but not filed at court.

4.14 Once the detailed assessment hearing has ended it is the responsibility of the legal representative appearing for the receiving party or, as the case may be, the receiving party in person to remove the papers filed in support of the bill.

SECTION V INTERIM COSTS CERTIFICATE AND FINAL COSTS CERTIFICATE

RULE 47.15 POWER TO ISSUE AN INTERIM CERTIFICATE

5.1 (1) A party wishing to apply for an interim certificate may do so by making an application in accordance with Part 23 (General Rules about Applications for Court Orders).

(2) Attention is drawn to the fact that the court's power to issue an interim certificate arises only after the receiving party has filed a request for a detailed assessment hearing.

RULE 47.16 FINAL COSTS CERTIFICATE

5.2 At the detailed assessment hearing the court will indicate any disallowance or reduction in the sums claimed in the bill of costs by making an appropriate note on the bill.

5.3 Where the bill of costs is in the form illustrated in Form 2 of the Schedule of Costs Forms annexed to this Practice Direction, the receiving party must, in order to complete the bill after the detailed assessment hearing, enter in the fourth and fifth columns of the bill, the correct figures agreed or allowed in respect of each item and must re-calculate the summary of the bill appropriately.

5.4 The completed bill of costs must be filed with the court no later than 14 days after the detailed assessment hearing.

5.5 At the same time as filing the completed bill of costs, the party whose bill it is must also produce receipted fee notes and receipted accounts in respect of all disbursements except those covered by a certificate in Form 4(4) in the Schedule of Costs Forms annexed to this Practice Direction.

5.6 No final costs certificate will be issued until all relevant court fees payable on the assessment of costs have been paid.

5.7 If the receiving party fails to file a completed bill in accordance with rule 47.16 the paying party may make an application under Part 23 (General Rules about Applications for Court Orders) seeking an appropriate order under rule 3.1 (The court's general powers of management).

5.8 A final costs certificate will show:

(a) the amount of any costs which have been agreed between the parties or which have been allowed on detailed assessment;

(b) where applicable the amount agreed or allowed in respect of VAT on the costs agreed or allowed.

This provision is subject to any contrary provision made by the statutory provisions relating to legal aid.

5.9 A final costs certificate will include disbursements in respect of the fees of counsel only if receipted fee notes or accounts in respect of those disbursements have been produced to the court and only to the extent indicated by those receipts.

5.10 Where the certificate relates to costs payable between parties a separate certificate will be issued for each party entitled to costs.

5.11 Model forms of an interim costs certificate (Form 11) and final costs certificates (Forms 12 and 13) are included in the Schedule of Costs Forms annexed to this Practice Direction.

5.12 An application for an order staying enforcement of a interim costs certificate or final costs certificate may be made either:

(1) to a costs judge or district judge of the court office which issued the certificate; or

(2) to the court (if different) which has general jurisdiction to enforce the certificate.

5.13 Proceedings for enforcement of interim costs certificates or final costs certificates may not be issued in the Supreme Court Costs Office.

SECTION VI DETAILED ASSESSMENT PROCEDURE FOR COSTS OF AN ASSISTED PERSON PAYABLE OUT OF THE LEGAL AID FUND

RULE 47.17 DETAILED ASSESSMENT PROCEDURE WHERE COSTS ARE PAYABLE OUT OF THE LEGAL AID FUND

6.1 The provisions of this section apply where the court is to assess costs which are payable only out of the legal aid fund. Sections IV and IX apply in cases involving costs by another person as well as costs payable only out of the legal aid fund.

6.2 The time for requesting a detailed assessment of legal aid costs is within 3 months after the date when the right to detailed assessment arose.

6.3 The request for a detailed assessment of legal aid costs must be in Form 8 of the Schedule of Costs forms annexed to this Practice Direction. The request must be accompanied by:

    (a) a copy of the bill of costs;

    (b) the document giving the right to detailed assessment (for further information as to this document, see paragraph 4.5 above);

    (c) a copy of all orders made by the court relating to the costs which are to be assessed;

    (d) copies of any fee notes of counsel and any expert in respect of fees claimed in the bill;

    (e) written evidence as to any other disbursement which is claimed and which exceeds £250;

    (f) the legal aid certificates, any amendment certificates, any authorities and any certificates of discharge or revocation of legal aid;

    (g) In the Supreme Court Costs Office the relevant papers in support of the bill as described in paragraph 4.13 above; in cases proceeding in District Registries and county courts this provision does not apply and the papers should only be lodged if requested by the costs officer.

    (h) a statement signed by the solicitor giving his name, address for service reference, telephone number and fax number if any and, if the assisted person has a financial interest in the detailed assessment and wishes to attend, giving the postal address of that person, to which the court will send notice of any hearing:

6.4 Rule 47.17 provides that the court will hold a detailed assessment hearing if the assisted person has a financial interest in the detailed assessment and wishes to attend. The court may also hold a detailed assessment hearing in any other case, instead of provisionally assessing a bill of costs, where it considers that a hearing is necessary. Before deciding whether a hearing is necessary under this rule, the court may require the solicitor whose bill it is, to provide further information relating to the bill.

6.5 Where the court has provisionally assessed a bill of costs it will send to the solicitor a notice, in Form 14 in the Schedule of Costs Forms annexed to this practice direction, of the amount of costs which the court proposes to allow together with the bill itself. The legal representative should, if the provisional assessment is to be accepted, then complete the bill.

6.6 The court will fix a date for a detailed assessment hearing if the solicitor informs the court within 14 days after he receives the notice of the amount allowed on the provisional assessment that he wants the court to hold such a hearing.

6.7 The court will give at least 14 days notice of the time and place of the detailed assessment hearing to the solicitor and, if the assisted person has a financial interest in the detailed assessment and wishes to attend, to the assisted person.

6.8 If the solicitor whose bill it is, or any other party wishes to make an application in the detailed assessment proceedings, the provisions of Part 23 (General Rules about Applications for Court Orders) applies.

6.9 It is the responsibility of the legal representative to complete the bill by entering in the bill the correct figures allowed in respect of each item, recalculating the summary of the bill appropriately and completing the legal aid assessment certificate (Form 15).

SECTION VII COSTS OF DETAILED ASSESSMENT PROCEEDINGS

RULE 47.18 LIABILITY FOR COSTS OF DETAILED ASSESSMENT PROCEEDINGS.

7.1 As a general rule the court will assess the receiving party's costs of the detailed assessment proceedings and add them to the bill of costs.

7.2 If the costs of the detailed assessment proceedings are awarded to the paying party, the court will either assess those costs by summary assessment or make an order for them to be decided by detailed assessment.

7.3 Attention is drawn to the fact that in deciding what order to make about the costs of detailed assessment proceedings the court must have regard to the conduct of all parties, the amount by which the bill of costs has been reduced and whether it was reasonable for a party to claim the costs of a particular item or to dispute that item.

RULE 47.19 OFFERS TO SETTLE WITHOUT PREJUDICE SAVE AS TO THE COSTS OF THE DETAILED ASSESSMENT PROCEEDINGS.

7.4 Rule 47.19 allows the court to take into account offers to settle, without prejudice save as to the costs of detailed assessment proceedings, when deciding who is liable for the costs of those proceedings. The rule does not specify a time within which such an offer should be made. An offer made by the paying party should usually be made within 14 days after service of the notice of commencement on that party. If the offer is made by the receiving party it should normally be made within 14 days after the service of points of dispute by the paying party. Offers made after these periods are likely to be given less weight by the court in deciding what order as to costs to make unless there is good reason for the offer not being made until the later time.

7.5 Where an offer to settle is made it should specify whether or not it is intended to be inclusive of the cost of preparation of the bill, interest and VAT. The offer may include or exclude some or all of these items but the position must be made clear on the face of the offer so that the offeree is clear about the terms of the offer when it is being considered. Unless the offer states otherwise, the offer will be treated as being inclusive of all these items.

7.6 Where an offer to settle is accepted, an application may be made for a certificate in agreed terms, or the bill of costs may be withdrawn, in accordance with rule 47.10 (Procedure where costs are agreed).

7.7 Where the receiving party is an assisted person, an offer to settle without prejudice save as to the costs of the detailed assessment proceedings will not have the consequences specified under rule 47.19 unless the court so orders.

SECTION VIII APPEAL AGAINST DECISIONS IN DETAILED ASSESSMENT PROCEEDINGS
RULE 47.23 DUTY TO SEEK REASONS

8.1 A party wishing to appeal must request written reasons for the decision in accordance with Rule 47.23 and obtain the court's permission in accordance with Rule 47.24 unless the court otherwise orders. The request must be made in writing and filed at the end of the detailed assessment hearing, or subsequently in accordance with Rule 47.23(2) and (3). A copy of the request for written reasons must at the same time be served on all other parties to the detailed assessment hearing. A request for written reasons made by one party will be treated as a request made by all parties.

8.2 Attention is drawn to the time limits for requesting written reasons. In the case of the receiving party this is 14 days after the detailed assessment hearing (ie. when the completed bill of costs is filed). In the case of the paying party it is within 7 days after the detailed assessment hearing.

8.3 A request for written reasons must clearly identify the particular parts of the decision for which reasons are requested.

8.4 Before it gives written reasons the court may require the party seeking reasons to file a note of the decision in question and of the reasons which the court gave for it at the hearing.

8.5 Where a party requests written reasons the court may refuse the request. Such a refusal will usually be made only where the reasons underlying the decision are sufficiently recorded on the bill itself or in a note of the hearing which has been approved by the court.

8.6 The court will usually direct that written reasons are not necessary where the decision to be appealed against was a case management decision rather than a decision on the substance of the assessment proceedings.

8.7 A case management decision is one which does not decide the merits of the assessment proceedings. Examples are a decision to allow or refuse an extension of time, to adjourn proceedings or to add a party to the proceedings.

8.8 Where the court exercises any of its general case management powers under Part 3 the decision will generally be a case management decision.

8.9 Where written reasons are given the court will serve a copy of them on every party to the detailed assessment proceedings.

RULE 47.24 OBTAINING THE COURT'S PERMISSION TO APPEAL

8.10 The party may request permission to appeal by letter delivered to the court and copies to the other parties. The letter must correctly set out the title of the action and the court reference. It must also set out the basis upon which permission is sought. As a general rule the request should first be made to the judge who made the decision which is sought to be appealed. Where the same judge is unavailable, or states that he is unable to deal with the request for permission, the request may be made direct to the appellate court.

8.11 As a general rule the court will not rule upon a request for permission to appeal without first providing written reasons for the decision to which the request relates or without first dispensing with the need for written reasons.

8.12 Attention is drawn to the time limits for seeking permission to appeal ie. 14 days after receiving written reasons; or, if the court directs that no written reasons are required, within 7 days after service of that direction.

8.13 The time limit for seeking permission to appeal will be calculated without taking into account the day upon which the letter requesting permission was delivered to the court, the day upon which the party wishing to appeal received the court's reply to that letter or any day in between those days. (See rule 2.8(time)).

8.14 In considering an application for permission to appeal the court will take into account:

(1) whether the ground of appeal has a reasonable prospect of success;

(2) whether the costs of the appeal are likely to be disproportionate; this factor is particularly relevant where the appeal is as to quantum only;

(3) if the appeal is against a case management decision, whether an appeal at that stage in the proceedings is appropriate.

RULE 47.25 APPEAL PROCEDURE

8.15 The time for filing notice of appeal is set out at rule 47.25. Attention is drawn to the fact that permission is not required to appeal against the decision of an authorised court officer or in respect of a decision of a Costs Judge or District Judge against a legal representative in relation to misconduct or in respect of wasted costs.

8.16 A notice of appeal against the decision of a Costs Officer must be in Form 16 of the Schedule of Costs Forms annexed to this Practice Direction. The Notice must set out the grounds of appeal.

8.17 (1) If it is necessary to obtain the court's permission to appeal and the Costs Officer refuses to give permission, the party wishing to appeal must, before filing a notice of appeal, apply to the High Court Judge or Circuit Judge, as the case may be, on notice requesting permission.

(2) A copy of that notice must be served on all other parties who may be affected by the appeal.

(3) If the Judge who deals with the application grants permission to appeal, the order made will extend the time for appealing.

(4) The extended period will be as stated in the order, or, if no period is stated will be the period up to 7 days after the date of the Judge's decision to give permission to appeal.

8.18 Where a decision of a costs judge or district judge on an appeal from an authorised court officer is taken on further appeal to a High Court Judge or a Circuit Judge, the appellant must, before the hearing of the further appeal, file a note of the decision given by the costs judge or district judge. The note filed must be agreed (if possible) with the other parties to the appeal and must be approved by the costs judge or district judge.

SECTION IX LEGAL AID COSTS AT PRESCRIBED RATES

9.1 This section applies to a bill of costs of an assisted person which is payable by another person where the costs which can be claimed out of the legal aid fund are restricted to legal aid prescribed rates (with or without enhancement).

9.2 Where this section applies, the solicitor of the assisted person must file a legal aid schedule in accordance with Paragraph 4.3(l) above. The schedule should follow as closely as possible Form 3 of the Schedule of Costs Forms annexed to this Practice Direction.

9.3 The schedule must set out by reference to the item numbers in the bill of costs, all the costs claimed as payable by another person, but the arithmetic in the schedule should claim those items at prescribed rates only (with or without any claim for enhancement).

9.4 Where there has been a change in the prescribed rates during the period covered by the bill of costs, the schedule (as opposed to the bill) should be divided into separate parts, so as to deal separately with each change of rate. The schedule must also be divided so as to correspond with any divisions in the bill of costs.

9.5 The detailed assessment of the legal aid schedule will take place immediately after the detailed assessment of the bill of costs.

9.6 Attention is drawn to the possibility that, on occasions, the court may decide to conduct the detailed assessment of the legal aid schedule separately from any detailed assessment of the bill of costs. This will occur, for example, where a default costs certificate is obtained as between the parties but that certificate is not set aside at the time of the detailed assessment pursuant to the Legal Aid Act 1988.

9.7 Where costs have been assessed at prescribed rates it is the responsibility of the legal representative to enter the correct figures allowed in respect of each item and to recalculate the summary of the legal aid schedule referred to in paragraph 9.2 above.

PART 48

COSTS – SPECIAL CASES

Contents of this Part

I Costs payable by or to particular persons

(The definitions contained in Part 43 are relevant to this Part.)

I Costs payable by or to particular persons

Pre-commencement disclosure and orders for disclosure against a person who is not a party

48.1 (1) This paragraph applies where a person applies –
   (a) for an order under –
      (i) section 33 of the Supreme Court Act 1981[77]; or
      (ii) section 52 of the County Courts Act 1984[78], (which give the court powers exercisable before commencement of proceedings); or
   (b) for an order under –
      (i) section 34 of the Supreme Court Act 1981[79]; or
      (ii) section 53 of the County Courts Act 1984[80], (which give the court power to make an order against a non-party for disclosure of documents, inspection of property etc.).
(2) The general rule is that the court will award the person against whom the order is sought his costs –
   (a) of the application; and
   (b) of complying with any order made on the application.
(3) The court may however make a different order, having regard to all the circumstances, including –
   (a) the extent to which it was reasonable for the person against whom the order was sought to oppose the application; and
   (b) whether the parties to the application have complied with any relevant pre-action protocol.

Costs orders in favour of or against non-parties

48.2 (1) Where the court is considering whether to exercise its power under section 51 of the Supreme Court Act 1981[81] (costs are in the discretion of the court) to make a costs order in favour of or against a person who is not a party to proceedings –
   (a) that person must be added as a party to the proceedings for the purposes of costs only; and
   (b) he must be given a reasonable opportunity to attend a hearing at which the court will consider the matter further.
(2) This rule does not apply –
   (a) where the court is considering whether to –
      (i) make an order against the Legal Aid Board;
      (ii) make a wasted costs order (as defined in 48.7); and
   (b) in proceedings to which rule 48.1 applies (pre-commencement disclosure and orders for disclosure against a person who is not a party).

Amount of costs where costs are payable pursuant to a contract

48.3 (1) Where the court assesses (whether by the summary or detailed procedure)

[(75) and (76) *Authors' note: Footnotes 75 and 76 are missing because of the substitution of the new Section VIII Part 47, as printed above, by the Civil Procedure (Amendment No 2) Rules 2000, SI 2000/940 (L 9).*]

(77) 1981 c.54. Section 33 was amended by SI 1998/2940.

(78) 1984 c.28. Section 52 was amended by the Courts and Legal Services Act 1990 (c.41), Schedule 18, paragraph 43 and by SI 1998/ 2940.

(79) 1981 c.54. Section 34 was amended by SI 1998/2940.

(80) 1984 c.28. Section 53 was amended by the Courts and Legal Services Act 1990 (c.41), Schedule 18, paragraph 44 and by SI 1998/2940.

(81) 1981 c.54. Section 51 was substituted by section 4(1) of the Courts and Legal Services Act 1990 (c.41).

costs which are payable by the paying party to the receiving party under the terms of a contract, the costs payable under those terms are, unless the contract expressly provides otherwise, to be presumed to be costs which –

(a) have been reasonably incurred; and

(b) are reasonable in amount, and the court will assess them accordingly.

(The costs practice direction sets out circumstances where the court may order otherwise.)

(2) This rule does not apply where the contract is between a solicitor and his client.

Limitations on court's power to award costs in favour of trustee or personal representative

48.4(1) This rule applies where –

(a) a person is or has been a party to any proceedings in the capacity of trustee or personal representative; and

(b) rule 48.3 does not apply.

(2) The general rule is that where he is entitled to be paid his costs of the proceedings out of any fund held by him as trustee or personal representative, those costs shall be assessed on the indemnity basis.

(3) The court may order otherwise if a trustee or personal representative has acted for a benefit other than that of the fund.

Costs where money is payable by or to a child or patient

48.5(1) This rule applies to any proceedings where a party is a child or patient and –

(a) money is ordered or agreed to be paid to, or for the benefit of, that party; or

(b) money is ordered to be paid by him or on his behalf.

('Child' and 'patient' are defined in rule 2.3)

(2) The general rule is that –

(a) the court must order a detailed assessment of the costs payable by any party who is a child or patient to his solicitor; and

(b) on an assessment under paragraph (a), the court must also assess any costs payable to that party in the proceedings, unless the court has issued a default costs certificate in relation to those costs under rule 47.11.

(3) The court need not order detailed assessment of costs in the circumstances set out in the costs practice direction.

(4) Where –

(a) a claimant is a child or patient; and

(b) a detailed assessment has taken place under paragraph (2)(a),

the only amount payable by the child or patient to his solicitor is the amount which the court certifies as payable.

(This rule applies to a counterclaim by or on behalf of a child or patient by virtue of rule 20.3.)

Litigants in person

48.6(1) This rule applies where the court orders (whether by summary assessment or detailed assessment) that the costs of a litigant in person are to be paid by any other person.

(2) The costs allowed under this rule must not exceed, except in the case of a disbursement, two-thirds of the amount which would have been allowed if the litigant in person had been represented by a legal representative.

(3) Costs allowed to the litigant in person shall be –

    (a) such costs which would have been allowed if the work had been done or the disbursements made by a legal representative on the litigant in person's behalf;

    (b) the payments reasonably made by him for legal services relating to the conduct of the proceedings; and

    (c) the costs of obtaining expert assistance in connection with assessing the claim for costs.

(The costs practice direction deals with who may be an expert for the purpose of paragraph (2)(c).)

(4) Subject to paragraph (2), the amount of costs to be allowed to the litigant in person for any item of work to which the costs relate shall, if he fails to prove financial loss, be an amount in respect of the time spent reasonably doing the work at the rate specified in the costs practice direction.

(5) A litigant who is allowed costs for attending at court to conduct his case is not entitled to a witness allowance in respect of such attendance in addition to those costs.

(6) For the purposes of this rule, a litigant in person includes –

    (a) a company or other corporation which is acting without a legal representative; and

    (b) a barrister, solicitor, solicitor's employee or other authorised litigator (as defined in the Courts and Legal Services Act 1990[82]) who is acting for himself.

II Costs relating to solicitors and other legal representatives

Personal liability of legal representative for costs – wasted costs orders

48.7(1) This rule applies where the court is considering whether to make an order under section 51(6) of the Supreme Court Act 1981[83] (court's power to disallow or (as the case may be) order a legal representative to meet, 'wasted costs').

(2) The court must give the legal representative a reasonable opportunity to attend a hearing to give reasons why it should not make such an order.

(3) For the purposes of this rule, the court may direct that privileged[GL] documents are to be disclosed to the court and, if the court so directs, to the other party to the application for an order.

(4) When the court makes a wasted costs order, it must specify the amount to be disallowed or paid.

(5) The court may direct that notice must be given to the legal representative's client, in such manner as the court may direct –

    (a) of any proceedings under this rule; or

    (b) of any order made under it against his legal representative.

(6) Before making a wasted costs order, the court may direct a costs judge or a district judge to inquire into the matter and report to the court.

(7) The court may refer the question of wasted costs to a costs judge or a district judge, instead of making a wasted costs order.

(82) 1990 c.41.

(83) 1981 c.54. Section 51 was substituted by section 4(1) of the Courts and Legal Services Act 1990 (c.41).

Basis of detailed assessment of solicitor and client costs

48.8(1) This rule applies to every assessment of a solicitor's bill to his client except –

    (a) a bill which is to be paid out of the legal aid fund under the Legal Aid Act 1988[84]; or

    (b) where the solicitor and his client have entered into a conditional fee agreement as defined by section 58 of the Courts and Legal Services Act 1990[85].

  (1A) Section 74(3) of the Solicitors Act 1974(a) applies unless the solicitor and client have entered into a written agreement which expressly permits payment to the solicitor of an amount of costs greater than that which the client could have recovered from another party to the proceedings.

  (2) Subject to paragraph (1A), costs are to be assessed on the indemnity basis but are to be presumed –

    (a) to have been reasonably incurred if they were incurred with the express or implied approval of the client;

    (b) to be reasonable in amount if their amount was expressly or impliedly approved by the client;

    (c) to have been unreasonably incurred if –

      (i) they are of an unusual nature or amount; and

      (ii) the solicitor did not tell his client that as a result he might not recover all of them from the other party.

Conditional fees

48.9(1) This rule applies to every assessment (whether by the summary or detailed procedure) of a solicitor's bill to his client where the solicitor and the client have entered into a conditional fee agreement as defined in section 58 of the Courts and Legal Services Act 1990.

  (2) In this rule –

'the base costs' means the costs other than a percentage increase;

'percentage increase' means a percentage increase pursuant to a conditional fee agreement entered into between the solicitor and his client or between counsel and the solicitor, or counsel and the client; and

'costs' includes all fees, charges, disbursements and other expenses charged by the solicitor or counsel under the conditional fee agreement in question.

  (3) On an assessment to which this rule applies, the client may apply for assessment of the base costs or of a percentage increase or of both.

  (4) Where the client applies for assessment of the base costs, the base costs are to be assessed in accordance with rule 48.8(2) as if the solicitor and his client had not entered into a conditional fee agreement.

  (5) Where the client applies for assessment of a percentage increase, the court may reduce the percentage increase where it considers it to be disproportionate having regard to all relevant factors as they reasonably appeared to the solicitor or counsel when the conditional fee agreement was entered into.

  (6) The court will not vary a percentage increase where the client is a child or patient, except in accordance with paragraph (5).

(The costs practice direction specifies some of the relevant factors.)

---

(84) 1988 c.34.

(85) 1990 c.41. Section 58 was amended by the Family Law Act 1996 (c.27), Schedule 8, Part III, paragraph 61.

Assessment procedure

48.10(1) This rule sets out the procedure to be followed where the court has made an order under Part III of the Solicitors Act 1974[(86)] for the assessment of costs payable to a solicitor by his client.

(2) The solicitor must serve a breakdown of costs within 28 days of the order for costs to be assessed.

(3) The client must serve points of dispute within 14 days after service on him of the breakdown of costs.

(4) If the solicitor wishes to serve a reply, he must do so within 14 days of service on him of the points of dispute.

(5) Either party may file a request for a hearing date –

(a) after points of dispute have been served; but

(b) no later than 3 months after the date of the order for the costs to be assessed.

(6) This procedure applies subject to any contrary order made by the court.

(Other rules about costs payable in special cases can be found in Schedule 1, in the following RSC – O.30 (remuneration of receivers); O.49 (costs of garnishee).)

(For opening sections of the Costs Practice Direction, see after Part 43 above.)

[Authors' note: For the general Introduction to the Costs Practice Direction, see after Part 43 above.]

DIRECTIONS RELATING TO PART 48
COSTS – SPECIAL CASES

SECTION I COSTS PAYABLE BY OR TO PARTICULAR PERSONS

RULE 48.3 AMOUNT OF COSTS WHERE COSTS ARE PAYABLE PURSUANT TO CONTRACT

1.1 Where the court is assessing costs payable under a contract, the court may make an order that all or part of the costs payable under the contract shall be disallowed if the court is satisfied by the paying party that costs have been unreasonably incurred or are unreasonable in amount.

1.2 Rule 48.3 only applies if the court is assessing costs payable under a contract. It does not–

(1) require the court to make an assessment of such costs; or

(2) require a mortgagee to apply for an order for those costs that he has a contractual right to recover out of the mortgage funds.

1.3 The following principles apply to costs relating to a mortgage–

(1) An order for the payment of costs of proceedings by one party to another is always a discretionary order: section 51 of the Supreme Court Act 1981[1].

(2) Where there is a contractual right to the costs the discretion should ordinarily be exercised so as to reflect that contractual right.

(3) The power of the court to disallow a mortgagee's costs sought to be added to the mortgage security is a power that does not derive from section 51, but from the power of the courts of equity to fix the terms on which redemption will be allowed.

(4) A decision by a court to refuse costs in whole or in part to a mortgagee litigant may be–

(a) a decision in the exercise of the section 51 discretion;

(b) a decision in the exercise of the power to fix the terms on which redemption will be allowed;

---

(86) 1974 c.47.

---

1 [1983] Ch 171

    (c)   a decision as to the extent of a mortgagee's contractual right to add his costs to the security;

or

    (d)   a combination of two or more of these things.

The statements of case in the proceedings or the submissions made to the court may indicate which of the decisions has been made.

(5)   A mortgagee is not to be deprived of a contractual or equitable right to add costs to the security merely be reason of an order for payment of costs made without reference to the mortgagee's contractual or equitable rights, and without any adjudication as to whether or not the mortgagee should be deprived of those costs.

1.4 (1) Where the contract entitles a mortgagee to–

    (a)   add the costs of litigation relating to the mortgage to the sum secured by it;

    (b)   require a mortgagor to pay those costs, or

    (c)   both,

the mortgagor may make an application for the court to direct that an account of the mortgagee's costs be taken.

(Rule 25.(1)(n) provides that the court may direct that a party file an account)

(2)   The mortgagor may then dispute an amount in the mortgagee's account on the basis that is has been unreasonably incurred or is unreasonable in amount.

(3)   Where a mortgagor disputes an amount, the court may make an order that the disputed costs are assessed under rule 48.3

RULE 48.5 COSTS WHERE MONEY IS PAYABLE BY OR TO A CHILD OR PATIENT

1.5 The circumstances in which the court need not order the assessment of costs under rule 48.5(3) are as follows:

    (a)   where there is no need to do so to protect the interests of the child or patient or his estate;

    (b)   where another party has agreed to pay a specified sum in respect of the costs of the child or patient and the solicitor acting for the child or patient has waived the right to claim further costs;

    (c)   where the court has decided the costs payable to the child or patient by way of summary assessment and the solicitor acting for the child or patient has waived the right to claim further costs;

    (d)   where an insurer or other person is liable to discharge the costs which the child or patient would otherwise be liable to pay to his solicitor and the court is satisfied that the insurer or other person is financially able to discharge those costs.

RULE 48.6 LITIGANTS IN PERSON

1.6 In order to qualify as an expert for the purpose of rule 48.6(3)(c) (expert assistance in connection with assessing the claim for costs), the person in question must be a

    (1) barrister,

    (2) solicitor,

    (3) Fellow of the Institute of Legal Executives,

    (4) Fellow of the Association of Law Costs Draftsmen,

    (5) law costs draftsman who is a member of the Academy of Experts,

    (6) law costs draftsman who is a member of the Expert Witness Institute.

1.7 Where a litigant in person wishes to prove that he has suffered financial loss he should produce to the court any written evidence he relies on to support that claim, and serve a copy of that evidence on any party against whom he seeks costs at least 24 hours before the hearing at which the question may be decided.

1.8 Where a litigant in person commences detailed assessment proceedings under rule 47.6 he should serve copies of that written evidence with the notice of commencement.

1.9 The amount which may be allowed to a litigant in person under rule 46.3(5)(b) and rule 48.6(4) is £9.25 per hour.

1.10 Attention is drawn to rule 48.6(6)(b). A solicitor who, instead of acting for himself, is represented in the proceedings by his firm or by himself in his firm name, is not, for the purpose of the Civil Procedure Rules, a litigant in person.

SECTION II COSTS RELATING TO SOLICITORS AND OTHER LEGAL REPRESENTATIVES

RULE 48.7 PERSONAL LIABILITY OF LEGAL REPRESENTATIVE FOR COSTS – WASTED COSTS ORDERS

2.1 Rule 48.7 deals with wasted costs orders against legal representatives. Such orders can be made at any stage in the proceedings up to and including the proceedings relating to the detailed assessment of costs. In general, applications for wasted costs are best left until after the end of the trial.

2.2 The court may make a wasted costs order against a legal representative on its own initiative.

2.3 A party may apply for a wasted costs order–

(1) by filing an application notice in accordance with Part 23; or

(2) by making an application orally in the course of any hearing.

2.4 It is appropriate for the court to make a wasted costs order against a legal representative, only if–

(1) the legal representative has acted improperly, unreasonably or negligently;

(2) his conduct has caused a party to incur unnecessary costs, and

(3) it is just in all the circumstances to order him to compensate that party for the whole or part of those costs.

2.5 The court will give directions about the procedure that will be followed in each case in order to ensure that the issues are dealt with in a way which is fair and as simple and summary as the circumstances permit.

2.6 As a general rule the court will consider whether to make a wasted costs order in two stages–

(1) in the first stage, the court must be satisfied–

(a) that it has before it evidence or other material which, if unanswered, would be likely to lead to a wasted costs order being made; and

(b) the wasted costs proceedings are justified notwithstanding the likely costs involved.

(2) at the second stage (even if the court is satisfied under paragraph (1)) the court will consider, after giving the legal representative an opportunity to give reasons why the court should not make a wasted costs order, whether it is appropriate to make a wasted costs order in accordance with paragraph 2.4 above.

2.7 On an application for a wasted costs order under Part 23 the court may proceed to the second stage described in paragraph 2.5 without first adjourning the hearing if it is satisfied that the legal representative has already had a reasonable opportunity to give reasons why the court should not make a wasted costs order. In other cases the court will adjourn the hearing before proceeding to the second stage.

2.8 On an application for a wasted costs order under Part 23 the application notice and any evidence in support must identify–

(1) what the legal representative is alleged to have done or failed to do; and

(2) the costs that he may be ordered to pay or which are sought against him.

2.9 A wasted costs order is an order –

(1) that the legal representative pay a specified sum in respect of costs to a party; or

(2) for costs relating to a specified sum or items of work to be disallowed.

RULE 48.8 BASIS OF DETAILED ASSESSMENT OF SOLICITOR AND CLIENT COSTS

2.10 A client and his solicitor may agree whatever terms they consider appropriate about the payment of the solicitor's charges for his services. If however, the costs are of an unusual nature (either in amount or in the type of costs incurred) those costs will be presumed to have been unreasonably incurred unless the solicitor satisfies the court that he informed the client that they were unusual and, where the costs relate to litigation, that he informed the client they might not be allowed on an assessment of costs between the parties. That information must have been given to the client before the costs were incurred.

2.11(1) Costs as between a solicitor and client are assessed on the indemnity basis as defined by rule 44.4, proportionality is therefore not relevant.

(2) Attention is drawn to the presumptions set out in rule 48.8(2). These presumptions may be rebutted by evidence to the contrary.

2.12 Rule 48.10 and paragraphs 2.17 to 2.36 of this Practice Direction deal with the procedure to be followed for obtaining the assessment of a solicitor's bill pursuant to an order under Part III of The Solicitors Act 1974.

2.13 If a party fails to comply with the requirements of rule 48.10 concerning the service of a breakdown of costs or points of dispute, any other party may apply to the court in which the detailed assessment hearing should take place for an order requiring compliance with rule 48.10. If the court makes such an order, it may—

(a) make it subject to conditions including a condition to pay a sum of money into court; and

(b) specify the consequence of failure to comply with the order or a condition.

RULE 48.9 CONDITIONAL FEES

2.14(1) A client who has entered into a conditional fee agreement with a solicitor may apply for assessment of the base costs (which is carried out in accordance with rule 48.8(2) as if there were no conditional fee agreement) or for assessment of the percentage increase (success fee) or both.

(2) Where the court is to assess the percentage increase, proportionality is relevant and the court will have regard to all the relevant factors as they appeared to the solicitor or counsel when the conditional fee agreement was entered into.

2.15 Where the client applies to the court to reduce the percentage increase which the solicitor has charged the client under the conditional fee agreement, the client must set out in his application notice:

(a) the reasons why the percentage increase should be reduced; and

(b) what the percentage increase should be.

2.16 The factors relevant to assessing the percentage increase include—

(a) the risk that the circumstances in which the fees or expenses would be payable might not occur;

(b) the disadvantages relating to the absence of payment on account;

(c) whether the amount which might be payable under the conditional fee agreement is limited to a certain proportion of any damages recovered by the client;

(d) whether there is a conditional fee agreement between the solicitor and counsel;

(e) the solicitor's liability for any disbursements.

2.17 When the court is considering the factors to be taken into account, it will have regard to the circumstances as they reasonably appeared to the solicitor or counsel when the conditional fee agreement was entered into or at the time of any variation of the agreement.

RULE 48.10 ASSESSMENT PROCEDURE

2.18 Paragraphs 2.18 to 2.36 apply to orders made under Part III of the Solicitors Act 1974 for the assessment of costs. In these paragraphs "client" includes any person entitled to make an application under Part III of that Act.

2.19 The procedure for obtaining an order under Part III of the Solicitors Act 1974 is by the alternative procedure for claims under Part 8. The provisions of RSC Order 106 appear, appropriately amended, in Schedule 1 to the CPR.

2.20 Model forms of order which the court may make are set out in Forms 17, 18 and 19 of the Schedule of Costs Forms annexed to this Practice Direction.

2.21 Attention is drawn to the time limits within which the required steps must be taken: ie. the solicitor must serve a breakdown of costs within 28 days of the order for costs to be assessed, the client must serve points of dispute within 14 days after service on him of the breakdown, and any reply must be served within 14 days of service of the points of dispute.

2.22 The breakdown of costs referred to in rule 48.10 is a document which contains the following information:

    (a) details of the work done under each of the bills sent for assessment; and

    (b) in applications under Section 70 of the Solicitors Act 1974, an account showing money received by the solicitor to the credit of the client and sums paid out of that money on behalf of the client but not payments out which were made in satisfaction of the bill or of any items which are claimed in the bill.

2.23 Form 20 of the Schedule of Costs Forms annexed to this Practice Direction is a model form of breakdown of costs. A party who is required to serve a breakdown of costs must also serve–

    (1) copies of the fee notes of counsel and of any expert in respect of fees claimed in the breakdown, and

    (2) written evidence as to any other disbursement which is claimed in the breakdown and which exceeds £250.

2.24 The provisions relating to default costs certificates (rule 47.11) do not apply to cases to which rule 48.10 applies.

2.25 Points of dispute should, as far as practicable, be in the form complying with paragraphs 2.12 and 2.13 of the Directions Relating to Part 47.

2.26 The time for requesting a detailed assessment hearing is within 3 months after the date of the order for the costs to be assessed.

2.27 The form of request for a hearing date must be in Form 21 of the Schedule of Costs Forms annexed to this Practice Direction. The request must be accompanied by copies of–

    (a) the order sending the bill or bills for assessment;

    (b) the bill or bills sent for assessment;

    (c) the solicitor's breakdown of costs and any invoices or accounts served with that breakdown;

    (d) a copy of the points of dispute, annotated as necessary in order to show which items have been agreed and their value and to show which items remain in dispute;

    (e) as many copies of the points of dispute so annotated as there are other parties to the proceedings to whom the court should give details of the assessment hearing requested;

    (f) a copy of any replies served;

    (g) a statement signed by the party filing the request or his legal representative giving the names and addresses for service of all parties to the proceedings.

2.28 The request must include an estimate of the length of time the detailed assessment hearing will take.

2.29 On receipt of the request for a detailed assessment hearing the court will fix a date for the hearing or if the Costs Judge or District Judge so decides, will give directions or fix a date for a preliminary appointment.

2.30 (1) The court will give at least 14 days notice of the time and place of the detailed assessment hearing to every person named in the statement referred to in paragraph 2.26(g) above.

    (2) The court will when giving notice, give all parties other than the party who requested the hearing a copy of the points of dispute annotated by the party requesting the hearing in compliance with paragraph 2.26(e) above.

    (3) Attention is drawn to rule 47.14(6) and (7): apart from the solicitor whose bill it is, only those parties who have served points of dispute may be heard on the detailed assessment unless the court gives permission, and only items specified in the points of dispute may be raised unless the court gives permission.

2.31 (1) If a party wishes to vary his breakdown of costs, points of dispute or reply, an amended or supplementary document must be filed with the court and copies of it must be served on all other relevant parties.

(2) Permission is not required to vary a breakdown of costs, points of dispute or a reply but the court may disallow the variation or permit it only upon conditions, including conditions as to the payment of any costs caused or wasted by the variation.

2.32 Unless the court directs otherwise the solicitor must file with the court the papers in support of the bill not less than 7 days before the date for the detailed assessment hearing and not more than 14 days before that date.

2.33 Once the detailed assessment hearing has ended it is the responsibility of the legal representative appearing for the solicitor or, as the case may be, the solicitor in person to remove the papers filed in support of the bill.

2.34 (1) Attention is drawn to rule 47.15 (power to issue an interim certificate).

(2) If, in the course of a detailed assessment hearing of a solicitor's bill to his client, it appears to the costs judge or district judge that in any event the solicitor will be liable in connection with that bill to pay money to the client, he may issue an interim certificate specifying an amount which in his opinion is payable by the solicitor to his client. Such a certificate will include an order to pay the sum it certifies unless the court orders otherwise.

2.35 (1) Attention is drawn to rule 47.16 which requires the solicitor to file a completed bill within 14 days after the end of the detailed assessment hearing. The court may dispense with the requirement to file a completed bill. If it does so the time for a request by the solicitor for written reasons under rule 47.23 is 7 days after the date of the order dispensing with the requirement for a completed bill.

(2) After the detailed assessment hearing is concluded the court will–

(a) complete the court copy of the bill so as to show the amount allowed;

(b) determine the result of the cash account;

(c) award the costs of the detailed assessment hearing in accordance with Section 70(8) of the Solicitors Act 1974; and

(d) issue a final costs certificate showing the amount due following the detailed assessment hearing.

2.36 A final costs certificate will include an order to pay the sum it certifies unless the court orders otherwise.

2.37 Attention is drawn to Section VIII of Part 47 (appeal against decisions in detailed assessment proceedings).

SECTION III TRANSITIONAL ARRANGEMENTS

3.1 (1) This section deals with the application of the Civil Procedure Rules ("CPR") to taxation proceedings commenced before 26th April 1999.

(2) In this section "the previous rules" means the Rules of the Supreme Court 1965 ("RSC") or County Court Rules 1981 ("CCR"), as appropriate.

General Scheme of Transitional Arrangements concerning Costs Proceedings

3.2 (1) Paragraph 18 of the Practice Direction which supplements Part 51 (Transitional Arrangements) provides that the CPR govern any assessments of costs which take place on or after 26th April 1999 and states a presumption to be applied in respect of costs for work undertaken before 26th April 1999.

(2) The following paragraphs provide four further transitional arrangements:

(a) to provide an additional presumption to be applied when assessing costs which were awarded by an order made in a county court before 26th April 1999 which allowed costs "on Scale 1" to be determined in accordance with CCR Appendix A, or "on the lower scale" to be determined in accordance with CCR Appendix C.

(b) to preserve the effect of CCR Appendix B Part III, paragraph 2;

(c) to clarify the approach to be taken where a bill of costs was provisionally taxed before 26th April 1999 and the receiving party is unwilling to accept the result of the provisional taxation.

(d) to preserve the right to carry in objections or apply for a reconsideration in all taxation proceedings commenced before 26th April 1999.

Scale 1 or lower scale costs

3.3 Where an order was made in county court proceedings before 26th April 1999 under which the costs were allowed on Scale 1 or the lower scale, the general presumption is that no costs will be allowed under that order which would not have been allowed in a taxation before 26th April 1999.

Fixed costs on the lower scale

3.4 The amount to be allowed as fixed costs for making or opposing an application for a rehearing to set aside a judgment given before 26th April 1999 where the costs are on lower scale is £11.25.

Bills provisionally taxed before 26th April 1999

3.5 In respect of bills of costs provisionally taxed before 26th April 1999:
   (1) The previous rules apply on the question who can request a hearing and the time limits for doing so; and
   (2) The CPR govern any subsequent hearing in that case.

Bills taxed before 26th April 1999

3.6 Where a bill of costs was taxed before 26th April 1999, the previous rules govern the steps which can be taken to challenge that taxation.

Other taxation proceedings

3.7 (1) This paragraph applies to taxation proceedings which were commenced before 26th April 1999, were assigned for taxation to a Taxing Master or District Judge, and which were still pending on 26th April 1999.

   (2) Any assessment of costs that takes place in cases to which this paragraph applies which is conducted on or after 26th April 1999, will be conducted in accordance with the CPR.

   (3) In addition to the possibility of appeal under rules 47.20 to 47.26 any party to a detailed assessment who is dissatisfied with any decision on a detailed assessment made by a costs judge or district judge may apply to that costs judge or district judge for a review of the decision. The review shall, for procedural purposes, be treated as if it were an appeal from an authorised court officer.

   (4) The right of review provided by paragraph (3) above, will not apply in cases in which, at least 28 days before the date of the assessment hearing, all parties were served with notice that the rights of appeal in respect of that hearing would be governed only by Part 47 Section VIII (Appeal against Decisions in Detailed Assessment Proceedings).

   (5) An order for the service of notice under sub-paragraph (4) above may be made on the application of any party to the detailed assessment proceedings or may be made by the court of its own initiative.

PART 49

SPECIALIST PROCEEDINGS

49 (1) These Rules shall apply to the proceedings listed in paragraph (2) subject to the provisions of the relevant practice direction which applies to those proceedings.

(2) The proceedings referred to in paragraph (1) are –

(a) admiralty proceedings;

(b) arbitration proceedings;

(c) commercial and mercantile actions;

(d) Patents Court business (as defined by the relevant practice direction) and proceedings under –

(i) the Copyright, Designs and Patents Act 1988[(87)];

(ii) the Trade Marks Act 1994[(88)]; and

(iii) the Olympic Symbol etc Protection Act 1995[(89)] and Olympics Association Right (Infringement Proceedings) Regulations 1995[(90)];

(e) Technology and Construction Court Business (as defined by the relevant practice direction);

(f) proceedings under the Companies Act 1985[(91)] and the Companies Act 1989[(92)]; and

(g) contentious probate proceedings.

PRACTICE DIRECTION – CONTENTIOUS PROBATE PROCEEDINGS THIS PRACTICE DIRECTION SUPPLEMENTS PART 49 OF THE CPR AND REPLACES RSC ORDER 76 AND CCR ORDER 41.

General

1.1 This Practice Direction applies to contentious probate proceedings and to applications for the rectification of a will both in the High Court and in the county court.

(For the rules and procedure relating to non-contentious probate proceedings, see the Non-Contentious Probate Rules 1987 as amended. The Non-Contentious Probate Rules deal, among things, with the procedure for entering a caveat, for warning-off a caveat and for entering an appearance to a warning. If an application for the rectification of a will is not contentious, the application may be made to the Family Division: see Non-Contentious Probate Rules 1987, rule 55.)

(For the jurisdiction of a county court in respect of contentious probate proceedings and proceedings for the rectification of a will, see s.32 County Courts Act 1984.)

1.2 In this Practice Direction:–

(i) "probate claim" means a claim in respect of any contentious matter arising in connection with an application for the grant or revocation of probate or letters of administration and

---

(87) 1988 c.48.

(88) 1994 c.26.

(89) 1995 c.32.

(90) S.I. 1995/3325.

(91) 1985 c.6.

(92) 1989 c.40.

includes a claim for an order pronouncing for or against the validity of an alleged will, "claim form" means a claim form by which a probate claim is begun and "probate proceedings" means the proceedings in which a probate claim is brought.

(ii) "relevant office" means:-

    (a) in the case of High Court proceedings in a Chancery district registry, that registry,

    (b) in the case of any other High Court proceedings, Chancery Chambers at the Royal Courts of Justice, Strand, London, WC2A 2LL; and

    (c) in the case of county court proceedings, the office of the county court in question.

(iii) "testamentary script" means a will or draft thereof, written instructions for a will made by or at the request, or under the instructions, of the testator and any document purporting to be evidence of the contents, or to be a copy, of a will which is alleged to have been lost or destroyed.

Commencement of proceedings

2.1 If a probate claim is to be commenced in the High Court, the claim form must be issued out of Chancery Chambers or one of the Chancery district registries. (There are Chancery district registries at Birmingham, Bristol, Cardiff, Leeds, Liverpool, Manchester, Newcastle upon Tyne and Preston).

2.2 (i) If a claim form is wrongly issued out of a district registry other than a Chancery district registry, an application for the transfer of the claim to the Royal Courts of Justice or to a Chancery district registry should be made forthwith.

    (ii) The court may, in a case to which paragraph 2.2(i) applies, order the transfer on its own initiative.

2.3 On the issue of a claim form the relevant office will send a notice to Leeds District Probate Registry, Coronet House, Queen Street, Leeds, LS1 2BA, DX 26451 Leeds (Park Square), Telephone 0113 243 1505, requesting that all testamentary scripts and other relevant documents in any probate registry be sent to the relevant office.

2.4 A claim form must, before it is issued, contain a statement of the nature of the interest of the claimant and of the defendant in the estate of the deceased to which the claim relates.

2.5 Every person who may be affected by a probate claim, either as a beneficiary under a will in issue or on an intestacy, and who is not joined as a party to the probate claim, should be given notice of the proceedings. It may in some cases be appropriate for a representation order to be sought under RSC Order 15, rule 13 (Schedule 1 to the CPR) or CCR Order 5, rule 6 (Schedule 2 to the CPR).

2.6 The court may direct that notice of the probate claim be served on any such person as is mentioned in paragraph 2.5 and, for that purpose, rule 13A of RSC Order 15 (Schedule 1 to the CPR) applies to probate claims in the county court as well as to probate claims in the High Court.

2.7 Every person who is entitled, or claims to be entitled, to administer the estate of a deceased person under an unrevoked grant of probate or letters of administration must be made a party to any probate claim seeking revocation of a grant.

2.8 The commencement of a probate claim will, unless a court otherwise directs, prevent any grant of probate or letters of administration being made until the probate claim has been disposed of (see rule 45 of the Non-Contentious Probate Rules 1987: but see also s.117, Supreme Court Act, 1981 and paragraph 14 below).

Lodgment of grant in action for revocation

3.1 Where, on the issue of a claim form seeking revocation of a grant of probate or letters of administration, the probate or letters of administration, as the case may be, have not been lodged in court, then -

    (a) if a person to whom the grant was made is a claimant, he must lodge the probate or letters of administration in the relevant office within 7 days after the issue of the claim form;

    (b) if a defendant to the action has the probate or letters of administration in his possession or under his control, he must lodge it or them in the relevant office within 14 days after the service of the claim form on him.

In this paragraph "court" includes the principal registry of the Family Division or a district probate registry.

3.2 Any person who fails to comply with paragraph 3.1 may, on the application of any party to the probate claim, or by the court on its own initiative, be ordered to lodge the probate or letters of administration in the relevant office within a specified time.

3.3 Any person against whom an order is made under paragraph 3.2 shall not be entitled to take any step in the probate proceedings without the permission of the court until he has complied with the order.

Acknowledgment of service

4. A defendant on whom a claim form is served must, subject to CPR rule 10.3(2), file an acknowledgment of service within 14 days after service of the claim form on him.

Testamentary scripts

5.1 Unless the court otherwise directs, the claimant and every defendant who has acknowledged service of the claim form must by affidavit or witness statement:

    (a) describe any testamentary script of the deceased person, whose estate is the subject of the action, of which he has any knowledge or, if such be the case, state that he knows of no such script, and

    (b) if any such script of which he has knowledge is not in his possession or under his control, give the name and address of the person in whose possession or under whose control it is or, if such be the case, state that he does not know the name or address of that person.

5.2 Any affidavit or witness statement required by paragraph 5.1 must be filed, and any testamentary script referred to therein which is in the possession or under the control of the deponent must be lodged in the relevant office within 14 days after the acknowledgment of service by a defendant to the claim or, if no defendant acknowledges service and the court does not otherwise direct, before an order is made for the trial of the claim.

5.3 Where any testamentary script required by paragraph 5.2 to be lodged in the relevant office or any part thereof is written in pencil, then, unless the court otherwise directs, a facsimile copy of that script, or of the page or pages thereof containing the part written in pencil, must also be lodged in the relevant office and the words which appear in pencil in the original must be underlined in red ink in the copy.

5.4 Except with the permission of the court, a party to a probate claim shall not be allowed to inspect an affidavit or witness statement filed under paragraph 5.2 or any testamentary script lodged under paragraph 5.3 unless and until an affidavit or witness statement sworn or made by him containing the information referred to in paragraph 5.1 has been filed.

5.5 Copies of testamentary scripts lodged under paragraph 5.2 should be filed with the originals. The testamentary scripts will remain in the relevant office until the probate claim has been disposed of.

5.6 It is important that testamentary scripts should not be marked in any way; nor should they be stapled or folded.

5.7 (i) Any party desiring to have any testamentary script subjected to examination by an expert should make an application in accordance with CPR Part 23.

    (ii) The application notice or the written evidence in support should explain the nature and purpose of the examination and the points to which the examination should be directed.

    (iii) The court may order such an examination on its own initiative.

Failure to acknowledge service

6.1 A default judgment cannot be obtained on a probate claim and CPR rule 10.2 and Part 12 do not apply to probate claims.

6.2 Where any of several defendants to a probate claim fails to acknowledge service of the claim form, the claimant may, after the time for acknowledging service has expired and upon filing an affidavit or witness statement proving due service of the claim form on that defendant proceed with the probate claim as if that defendant had acknowledged service.

6.3 Where the defendant, or all the defendants, to a probate claim, fails or fail to acknowledge service of the claim form then, unless on the application of the claimant the Court orders the claim to be discontinued, the claimant may after the time for acknowledging service has expired apply to the court for an order for trial of the claim.

6.4 Before applying for an order under paragraph 6.3 the claimant must file an affidavit or witness statement proving due service of the claim form on the defendant or defendants and, if no particulars of claim were contained in or served with the claim form, he must file particulars of claim in the relevant office.

6.5 Where the court makes an order under paragraph 6.3, it may direct the claim to be tried on written evidence. (see also paragraph 10.3 below).

(For rules about written evidence, see Part 32 and the Practice Direction supplementing that Part).

Service of particulars of claim and defence

7.1 The claimant in a probate claim must, unless the court gives permission to the contrary or particulars of claim were contained in or served with the claim form, serve particulars of claim on every defendant who acknowledges service of the claim form and must do so before the expiration of 28 days after acknowledgment of service by that defendant or of 8 days after the filing by that defendant of an affidavit or witness statement under paragraph 5.1, whichever is the later.

7.2 If particulars of claim were contained in or served with the claim form or are served before the claimant has complied with paragraphs 5.1 and 5.2 above, the time for filing a defence shall, subject to CPR 15.4(2), be 28 days after the affidavit or witness statement required by paragraph 5.1 has been filed and the testamentary scripts have been lodged.

Defence and counterclaim

8.1 A defendant to a probate claim who alleges that he has any claim or is entitled to any remedy relating to the grant of probate of the will, or letters of administration of the estate, of the deceased person must add to his defence a counterclaim in respect of that matter.

8.2 If the claimant fails to serve particulars of claim, any such defendant may, with the permission of the Court, serve a counterclaim and the probate proceedings shall then continue as if the counterclaim were the particulars of claim and the counterclaiming defendant were the claimant.

8.3 A defendant may in his defence give notice that he will raise no positive case but will insist on the will being proved in solemn form of law and, for that purpose, will cross-examine the witnesses who attested the will.

(Attention is drawn to paragraph 2.2 of the Costs Practice Direction Relating to CPR Part 44 and supplementing CPR 44.3).

Contents of statements of case

9.1 Where the claimant in a probate claim disputes the interest of a defendant, he must state in his particulars of claim that he denies the interest of that defendant.

9.2 In a probate claim in which the interest by virtue of which a party claims to be entitled to a grant of letters of administration is disputed, the party disputing that interest must show in his statement of case that if the allegations he makes in it are proved he would be entitled to an interest in the estate.

9.3 Any party who wants to contend that at the time when a will, the subject of the probate claim, was alleged to have been executed the testator did not know and approve of its contents must specify in his statement of case the nature of the case on which he intends to rely, and no allegation in support of that contention which would be relevant in support of any of the following other contentions, that is to say:

(a) that the will was not duly executed,

(b) that at the time of the execution of the will the testator was not of sound mind, memory and understanding, and

(c) that the execution of the will was obtained by undue influence or fraud,

shall be made by that party unless that other contention also is made in his statement of case.

Default of pleadings

10.1 A default judgment cannot be obtained on a probate claim (see paragraph 6.1 above).

10.2 Where any party to a probate claim fails to serve on any other party a pleading which he is required by the CPR or this Practice Direction to serve on that other party, then, unless the court orders the claim to be discontinued or dismissed, that other party may, after the expiration of the period fixed by the CPR or this Practice Direction for service of the pleading in question, apply to the court for an order for trial of the probate claim; and if an order is made the court may direct the probate claim to be tried on written evidence.

10.3 If a trial is ordered under paragraph 10.2 (or under paragraph 6.2), the hearing may lead to an order pronouncing for the will in solemn form.

Summary judgment

11. Where an order pronouncing for a will in solemn form is sought on an application for summary judgment, the evidence in support of the application must include an affidavit or a witness statement proving due execution of the will. (CPR Part 24 and the practice direction supplementing Part 24 deal with summary judgment applications).

Discontinuance and dismissal

12.1 CPR Part 38 does not apply to a probate claim.

12.2 At any stage of probate proceedings the court may, on the application of the claimant, or of any party to the probate claim who has acknowledged service of the claim form, order the claim to be discontinued or dismissed on such terms as to costs or otherwise as it thinks just, and may further order that a grant of probate of the will, or letters of administration of the estate, of the deceased person, as the case may be, which is the subject of the claim, be made to the person entitled thereto.

12.3 An application for an order under this rule may be made by application notice in accordance with CPR Part 23.

12.4 An order for the discontinuance or dismissal of a probate claim under paragraph 11.2 will normally lead to a grant of probate or of letter of administration in common form.

Compromise of action

13.1 Where, whether before or after the service of the defence in a probate claim, the parties to the claim agree to a compromise, the Court may order the trial of the claim on written evidence.

(For a form of order which is also applicable to discontinuance and which may be adapted as appropriate, see Practice Form No. CH38).

13.2 Section 49 of the Administration of Justice Act 1985 permits a probate claim to be compromised without a trial if every "relevant beneficiary" has consented to the proposed order.

13.3 Applications under section 49 may be heard by a master or district judge and should be supported by affidavit or witness statement identifying the "relevant beneficiaries" and exhibiting their respective consents. Affidavits or witness statements of testamentary scripts (see paragraph 5 above) will still be necessary.

Application for order to bring in will, etc

14.1 Any application in a probate claim for an order under section 122 of the Supreme Court Act 1981 shall be for an order requiring a person to bring a will or other testamentary paper into the relevant office or to attend in court for examination.

14.2 An application under paragraph 13.1 shall be made by application notice in accordance with CPR Part 23. The application notice must be served on the person against whom the order is sought.

14.3 Any application in a probate claim for the issue of a witness summons under section 123 of the Act shall be for the issue of a witness summons requiring a person to bring into the relevant office a will or other testamentary paper.

14.4 An application under paragraph 13.3 may be made without notice and must be supported by an affidavit or witness statement setting out the grounds of the application.

14.5 An application under section 122 or 123 of the 1981 Act should be made to a master or district judge.

14.6 Any person against whom a witness summons is issued under section 123 of the 1981 Act and who denies that the will or other testamentary paper referred to in the witness summons is in his possession or under his control may file an affidavit or witness statement to that effect.

14.7 Section 32 of the County Courts Act 1984 enables orders under section 122 and 123 of the 1981 Act to be made in county court proceedings.

Administration pending the determination of a probate claim

15.1 An application under section 117 of the Supreme Court Act 1981 for an order for the grant of administration may be made by application notice in the probate proceedings in question.

15.2 Where an order for a grant of administration is made under the said section 117, RSC Order 30 (Receivers) rules 2, 4 and 6 and (subject to subsection (3) of the said section) rule 3 (Schedule 1 to the CPR), shall apply as if the administrator were a receiver appointed by the court; and every application relating to the conduct of the administration shall be made by application notice in the probate proceedings in question.

15.3 An order under section 117 may be made by a master or district judge.

15.4 If an order is made under section 117 an application for the grant of letters of administration should be made at the principal probate registry of the Family Division.

15.5 The appointment of an administrator to whom letters of administration are granted following an order under section 117 will cease automatically when a final order in the probate proceedings is made but will continue pending any appeal.

Probate counterclaim in other proceedings

16.1 In these paragraphs "probate counterclaim" means a counterclaim by which the defendant makes a probate claim in any proceedings other than probate proceedings.

16.2 Subject to the following paragraphs, this Practice Direction shall apply with the necessary modifications to a probate counterclaim as it applies to a probate claim begun by a probate claim form.

16.3 A probate counterclaim must contain a statement of the nature of the interest of the defendant and of the claimant in the estate of the deceased to which the counterclaim relates.

16.4 Unless within seven days after the service of a probate counterclaim in High Court proceedings an application is made for an order under CPR 3.2(e) or 3.4 for the probate counterclaim to be struck out or dealt with in separate proceedings and the application is granted, the court shall, if necessary on its own initiative, order the transfer of the proceedings to the Chancery Division (if it is not already assigned to that Division) and to either the Royal Courts of Justice or a Chancery district registry (if it is not already proceeding in one of those places).

16.5 If an order is made that a probate counterclaim be dealt with in separate proceedings, the order shall (if the proceedings are in the High Court) order the transfer of the probate counterclaim as required under paragraph 15.4.

Rectification of wills

17.1 Where an application is made for the rectification of a will and the grant has not been lodged in court, paragraph 5 of this Practice Direction shall apply, with the necessary modifications, as if the proceedings were probate proceedings.

17.2 A copy of every order made for the rectification of a will shall be sent to the principal registry of the Family Division for filing, and a memorandum of the order shall be endorsed on, or permanently annexed to, the grant under which the estate is administered

PRACTICE DIRECTION – APPLICATIONS UNDER THE COMPANIES ACT 1985 AND THE INSURANCE COMPANIES ACT 1982 THIS PRACTICE DIRECTION SUPPLEMENTS CPR PART 49 AND REPLACES, WITH MODIFICATIONS, RSC ORDER 102 AND CCR ORDER 49 RULE 3

General

1. (1) In this practice direction –

" the Act" means the Companies Act 1985.

"the companies court registrar" means any officer of the High Court who is a registrar within the meaning of any rules for the time being in force relating to the winding-up of companies;

"the court" includes the companies court registrar;

"the ICA" means the Insurance Companies Act 1982;

"the Rules" means the Civil Procedure Rules 1998.

(2) Applications under the Act may be made in the county court if the county court would have jurisdiction to wind up the company in question (see the definition of "the court" in section 744 of the Act). A company can be wound up in the county court if its paid-up capital is not more than £120,000 (s.117(2) Insolvency Act 1986).

(3) Every claim form or petition by which an application under the Act or the ICA is begun and all affidavits, witness statements, notices and other documents in those proceedings must be entitled in the matter of the company in question and in the matter of the Act, or the ICA as the case may be.

Commencement of proceedings

2. (1) Except in the case of the applications mentioned in sub-paragraph (4) below, every application under the Act, whether made in the High Court or in the county court, must be made by the issue of a claim form and the use of the procedure set out in CPR Part 8, subject to any modification of that procedure under this practice direction or any other practice direction relating to applications under the Act.

(2) Notice of an application under section 721 of the Act need not be given to the respondent and the claim form need not be served on him.

(3) A claim form issued under this paragraph must, in the High Court, be issued out of the office of the companies court registrar or a chancery district registry or, in the county court, out of a county court office.

(4) This paragraph does not apply to applications under sections 459 or 460 of the Act or to applications under the ICA or to any of the applications specified in paragraph 4(1) of this practice direction.

3. All High Court applications under the Act shall be assigned to the Chancery Division.

Applications made by petition

4. (1) The following applications under the Act in addition to applications under sections 459 and 460 of the Act and applications under the ICA must be made by petition, namely, applications:

(a) under section 5 to cancel the alteration of a company's objects,

(b) under section 17 to cancel the alteration of a condition contained in a company's memorandum,

(c) under section 130 to confirm a reduction of the share premium account of a company,

(d) under section 136 to confirm a reduction of the share capital of a company,

(e) under section 127 to cancel any variation or abrogation of the rights attached to any class of shares in a company,

(f) under section 425 to sanction a compromise or arrangement between a company and its creditors or any class of them or between a company and its members or any class of them,

(g)   under section 653 for an order restoring the name of a company to the register, where the application is made in conjunction with an application for the winding up of the company,

(h)   under section 690 to cancel the alteration of the form of a company's constitution,

(i)   under section 727 for relief from liability of an officer of a company or a person employed by a company as auditor,

(j)   under section 54(1) to cancel a special resolution to which that section applies,

(k)   under sections 157(2) or 176(1) to cancel a special resolution to which either of those sections applies, and

(l)   under section 170 in relation to the reduction of capital redemption reserve.

(2)   Paragraphs 5 to 14 of this practice direction apply to the applications specified in sub-paragraph (1).

5.   (1)   After the presentation of a petition by which any application mentioned in paragraph 4 is made, the petitioner, except where his application is one of those mentioned in sub-paragraph (2), must apply for directions by filing an application notice.

(2)   The exceptions referred to in sub-paragraph (1) are:

(a)   an application under section 425 of the Act to sanction a compromise or arrangement unless there is included in the petition for such sanction an application for an order under section 427 of the Act,

(b)   an application under section 653 of the Act for an order restoring the name of a company to the register,

(c)   an application under section 54(1) of the Act for an order cancelling a special resolution to which that section applies, and

(d)   an application under section 157(2) or 176(1) of the Act for an order cancelling a special resolution to which those sections apply.

(3)   At the directions hearing the court may by order give such directions for the hearing of the application as it thinks fit including, in particular, directions for the publication of notices and the making of any inquiry .

(4)   Where the application made by the petition is to confirm a reduction of the share capital, the share premium account, or the capital redemption reserve, of a company the Court may give directions:

(a)   for an inquiry to be made as to the debts of, and claims against, the company or as to any class or classes of such debts or claims,

(b)   as to the proceedings to be taken for settling the list of creditors entitled to object to the reduction and fixing the date by reference to which the list is to be made,

and the power of the court under section 136(6) of the Act to direct that section 136(3) to (5) thereof shall not apply as regards any class of creditors may be exercised at any directions hearing.

Reduction of capital and schemes of arrangement

6.   (1)   The consent of a creditor to such reduction as is mentioned in paragraph 5(4) may be proved in such manner as the Court thinks sufficient.

(2)   The evidence in support of a petition to confirm a reduction of capital need not show as regards any issue of shares made since 1900 for a consideration other than cash that the statutory requirements as to registration were complied with. It is sufficient to state in the petition the extent to which any issued shares (other than shares issued otherwise than for cash before 1901) are or are deemed to be paid up.

(3)   The existing practice will remain unaltered in respect of issues of shares otherwise than for cash made before 1901 whilst s.25 of the Companies Act 1867 remained in operation.

7.   (1)   This paragraph applies to:

(a)   schemes of arrangement under sections 425 to 427A of the Companies Act 1985, whether made with creditors or members,

(b)   schemes for the transfer of the whole or part of the long-term business of an insurance company to which schedule 2C to the ICA applies, and

(c)   reductions of capital, share premium account or capital redemption reserve.

References in this and subsequent paragraphs to "schemes" are to schemes falling within (a) or (b) above, and references to "reductions" are to reductions falling within (c) above.

(2) Petitions to sanction schemes will be heard by the Companies Court Judge.

(3) Petitions to confirm reductions will be heard by the Companies Court Registrar unless otherwise ordered. The Registrar will hear petitions to confirm reductions in open court on a Wednesday each week after completion of the list of winding up petitions.

Schemes and reductions in the long vacation

8. (1) The following requirements must be satisfied for a hearing to be fixed to sanction a scheme and/or confirm a reduction in the Long Vacation:

    (a) The application is one in which for financial, commercial or economic reasons a hearing before the end of the Long Vacation is desirable. This category will include cases of mergers and takeovers which arise in the summer and are likely to be affected by market fluctuations.

    (b) The application is one which could not with reasonable diligence have been made and prosecuted in time to be heard before the Long Vacation begins.

  (2) An informal application in chambers, to the Court Manager, accompanied by an advocate's certificate that requirements (a) and (b) are satisfied, must be made as soon as possible so that a suitable timetable may be settled, including a date for hearing.

  (3) In the case of reductions to be heard by the Registrar, certain applications which do not fall within the above categories will be heard provided (i) that there is an urgent need for a hearing or (ii) that there is sufficient time available after the Registrar has disposed of the urgent applications.

  (4) Applications to the Registrar in chambers for orders convening meetings to consider schemes and for directions on reduction applications will continue to be heard during the Long Vacation. Provided notice is given to the court before the Long Vacation begins, a timetable will be fixed which will enable any necessary documents to be settled in chambers and enable the Registrar to hear the application.

  (5) The Vacation Judge will be available to hear petitions to sanction schemes and any petitions to confirm reductions which require to be heard by a judge on one Wednesday in August and two Wednesdays in September on dates to be arranged and subsequently notified in the Long Vacation Notice which is printed in the Daily Cause List.

  (6) The Vacation Judge may also hear petitions to sanction schemes or confirm reductions on other days if he thinks fit.

9. (1) Attention is drawn to the undesirability of asking as a matter of course for a winding up order as an alternative to an order under s.459 Companies Act 1985. The petition should not ask for a winding up order unless that is the relief which the petitioner prefers or it is thought that it may be the only relief to which the petitioner is entitled.

  (2) Whenever a winding up order is asked for in a contributory's petition, the petition must state whether the petitioner consents or objects to an order under s.127 of the Act in the standard form. If he objects, the written evidence in support must contain a short statement of his reasons.

  (3) If the petitioner objects to a s.127 order in the standard form but consents to such an order in a modified form, the petition must set out the form of order to which he consents, and the written evidence in support must contain a short statement of his reasons for seeking the modification.

  (4) If the petition contains a statement that the petitioner consents to a s.127 order, whether in the standard or a modified form, but the petitioner changes his mind before the first hearing of the petition, he must notify the respondents and may apply on notice to a Judge for an order directing that no s.127 order or a modified order only (as the case may be) shall be made by the Registrar, but validating dispositions made without notice of the order made by the Judge.

  (5) If the petition contains a statement that the petitioner consents to a s.127 order, whether in the standard or a modified form, the Registrar shall without further enquiry make an order in such form at the first hearing unless an order to the contrary has been made by the Judge in the meantime.

(6) If the petition contains a statement that the petitioner objects to a s.127 order in the standard form, the company may apply (in the case of urgency, without notice) to the Judge for an order.

(7) Section 127 Order - Standard Form:

(Title etc.)

ORDER that notwithstanding the presentation of the said Petition

(1) payments made into or out of the bank accounts of the Company in the ordinary course of the business of the Company and

(2) dispositions of the property of the Company made in the ordinary course of its business for proper value between the date of presentation of the Petition and the date of judgment on the Petition or further order in the meantime

shall not be void by virtue of the provisions of section 127 of the Insolvency Act 1986 in the event of an Order for the winding up of the Company being made on the said Petition Provided that (the relevant bank) shall be under no obligation to verify for itself whether any transaction through the company's bank accounts is in the ordinary course of business, or that it represents full market value for the relevant transaction.

This form of Order may be departed from where the circumstances of the case require.

Case management

10. Every application under the Act shall be allocated to the multi-track and the CPR relating to allocation questionnaires and track allocation will not apply.

Service

11. Service of documents in proceedings in the High Court to which this practice direction applies will be the responsibility of the parties and will not be undertaken by the court. Subject to that CPR Part 6 applies.

Filing of documents

12. (1) Where an application to which this practice direction relates is proceeding in any Chancery district registry, all affidavits and witness statements made in connection with the application must be filed in that registry.

(2) Where an application to which this practice direction relates is proceeding in any county court, all affidavits and witness statements made in connection with the application must be filed in the office of that county court.

Drawing up of orders

13. The court will draw up all orders with the following exceptions:-

(a) orders by the Registrar on the application of the Official Receiver or for which the Treasury Solicitor is responsible under the existing practice,

(b) orders by the court in relation to reductions or schemes.

PRACTICE DIRECTION –
TECHNOLOGY AND CONSTRUCTION COURT
THIS PRACTICE DIRECTION SUPPLEMENTS CPR PART 49 AND
REPLACES, WITH MODIFICATIONS, ORDER 36 OF THE RULES
OF THE SUPREME COURT

General

1.1 This practice direction applies to cases allocated to the Technology and Construction Court ("the TCC").

1.2 A TCC claim is a claim which involves issues or questions which are technically complex or for which a trial by a judge of the TCC is for any other reason desirable.

1.3 TCC claims may be dealt with either in the High Court or, subject to paragraph 2.3 below, in a county court but cases allocated to the TCC will, unless and until a judge of the TCC otherwise directs, be dealt with by a judge of the TCC.

1.4 A judge will be appointed to be the judge in charge of the TCC (currently Mr Justice Dyson).

COMMENCEMENT OF PROCEEDINGS

2.1 Before the issue of a claim form relating to a TCC claim, the claim form, whether to be issued in the High Court or in a county court, should, if it is intended that the case be allocated to the TCC, be marked in the top right hand corner "Technology and Construction Court". The case will then be allocated to the TCC. The words "Technology and Construction Court" should follow the reference to "The ___ County Court" or "The High Court, Queen's Bench Division", as the case may be.

2.2 The TCC is a specialist list for the purposes of CPR Part 30 (Transfer) but no order for the transfer of proceedings from or to the TCC shall be made unless the parties have either:

    (1) had an opportunity of being heard on the issue, or

    (2) consented to the order.

2.3 A claim form marked as mentioned in paragraph 2.1 may not be issued in a county court office other than:

    (1) a County Court office where there is also a High Court District Registry; or

    (2) the office of the Central London County Court.

2.4 Where a claim form marked as mentioned in paragraph 2.1 is issued in the Royal Courts of Justice, the case will be assigned to a named TCC judge (the "assigned judge") who will have the primary responsibility for the case management of that case. All documents relating to that case should be marked, under the words "Technology and Construction Court" in the title, with the name of the assigned judge.

Applications

3.1 Where a claim form is to be marked as mentioned in paragraph 2.1, any application before issue of the claim form should be made to a judge of the TCC.

3.2 If an application is made before the issue of the claim form, the written evidence in support of the application must state, in addition to any other necessary matters, that the claimant intends to mark the claim form in accordance with paragraph 2.1.

3.3 Any application in a case which has been allocated to the TCC must be made to a judge of the TCC.

3.4 Where there is an assigned judge of a TCC case, any application in that case should be made to the assigned judge but, if the judge in charge of the TCC so authorises or if the assigned judge is not available, may be made to another judge of the TCC.

3.5 If an application is urgent and no TCC judge is available to deal with it, the application may be made to any judge who, if the case were not allocated to the TCC, would be authorised to deal with the application.

Case management

4.1 Every claim allocated to the TCC will be allocated to the multi-track and the CPR relating to track allocation will not apply.

4.2 Where a claim has been allocated to the TCC either on issue (i.e. in every case in which the claim form has been marked "Technology and Construction Court") or by transfer to the TCC, an application for directions (including an application for a fixed date of hearing) must be made by the claimant within 14 days of the filing by the defendant of an acknowledgment of service or of a defence (whichever is the earlier) or, as the case may be, within 14 days of the date of the order of transfer.

4.3 If the claimant does not make an application in accordance with paragraph 4.2-

    (1) any other party may do so or may apply for the claim of the claimant in default to be struck out or dismissed; or

    (2) a TCC judge may on his own initiative fix a directions hearing.

4.4 The provisions of CPR Part 29 and the practice direction supplementing that Part apply to the case management of TCC cases except where inconsistent with this or any other TCC practice direction. But reference in those provisions to a listing questionnaire shall be read as references to a pre-trial review questionnaire and paragraphs 8 and 9 of the practice direction do not apply. Attention is drawn, in particular, to the following provisions of CPR Part 29 and the supplementing practice direction:

CPR Part 29

rule 29.3(2)	(attendance of legal representatives)
rule 29.4	(agreed proposals)
rule 29.5	(variation of case management timetable)
rule 29.6	(pre-trial review (listing) questionnaire)

Practice Direction supplementing CPR Part 29

paragraphs 3.4 to 3.9	(general provisions)
paragraphs 5.1 to 5.8	(case management conferences)
paragraphs 6.1 to 6.5	(variation of directions)
paragraphs 7.1 to 7.4	(failure to comply with case management directions)
paragraphs 10.1 to 10.6	(the trial)

Case management conference

5.1 The first case management conference will take place at the directions hearing referred to in paragraphs 4.2 and 4.3 above.

5.2 When the court notifies the parties of the time and date of the hearing of the first case management conference it will also send them a case management questionnaire and a case management directions form. These documents will be in the forms annexed to this practice direction, and marked respectively Appendix 1 and 2.

5.3 The parties shall complete, exchange and return both forms by no later than 4pm two days before the date on which the case management conference is to take place. The parties are encouraged to try to agree directions by reference to the case management directions form.

5.4 If a party fails to exchange or return the forms by the date specified, the court may make an order which leads to the claim or defence being struck out, or impose such other sanction as it sees fit, or may hold a case management conference without the forms.

5.5 At the first case management conference, the court will usually fix the date for trial of the case and of any preliminary issue that it orders to be tried. It will also give case management directions. The directions will usually include the fixing of a date for a pre-trial review.

5.6 Whenever possible, the trial of a case will be heard by the assigned judge of that case.

Pre-trial review

6.1 When the court fixes the date for a pre-trial review it will also provide the parties with a pre-trial review questionnaire and a pre-trial review directions form. These documents will be in the forms annexed to this practice direction marked respectively as Appendix 3 and 4.

6.2 The parties shall complete, exchange and return both forms no later than 4pm two days before the date on which the pre-trial review is to take place. The parties are encouraged to try to agree directions by reference to the pre-trial review directions form.

6.3 If a party fails to exchange or return the pre-trial review questionnaire or pre-trial review directions form by the date specified, the court may make an order which leads to the claim or defence and any counterclaim being struck out, or it may impose such other sanction as it sees fit, or it may hold a pre-trial review without the forms.

6.4 At the pre-trial review, the court will give such directions for the conduct of the trial as it sees fit.

The Civil Procedure Rules

7.1 The Civil Procedure Rules and the practice directions supplementing them apply to TCC cases subject to the provisions of this practice direction and any other TCC practice direction.

APPENDIX 2
TECHNOLOGY AND CONSTRUCTION COURT

CASE MANAGEMENT CONFERENCE DIRECTIONS FORM

CLAIM 199 TCC No . ORDER ON CASE MANAGEMENT
CONFERENCE HELD   1999

( ) Trial: Week beginning   . Estimated length   days. [Directions, if appropriate, for separate trials of issues or for parties to serve and file proposals for such directions]

( ) This claim to be [consolidated] [managed and tried] with 19   TCC No   . [This] [19   TCC No   ] to be lead claim. [All directions in lead claim to apply to both claims unless otherwise directed.]

( ) Permission to amend [see below].

( ) Defence and any counterclaim to be served by   am/pm on   1999/20   .

( ) Reply to defence, if desired, and defence to any counterclaim, to be served by   am/pm on   1999/20   .

( ) Disclosure of documents by   am/pm on   1999/20   . [Standard disclosure dispensed with/limited/varied as follows:

].

( ) Claimant/defendant to serve a Scott Schedule [of defects and damages] [under paragraph   of the particulars of claim/defence] by   am/pm on   1999/20   . Column headings to be as follows: [see below].

( ) Defendant/claimant to respond to the Scott Schedule by   am/pm on   1999/20

( ) Signed statements of witnesses of fact to be served [and filed] by   am/pm on 1999/20   . [Directions, if appropriate, for control of evidence of fact under rule 32.1]

( ) [No expert evidence without further order] [Permission for expert evidence on the following terms: (see below)].

( ) [Inspections to be made/samples to be obtained/experiments to be conducted/calculations to be carried out as follows:

].

( ) Experts in like fields to hold discussions in accordance with rule 35.12 by   am/pm on   1999/20   on [all the issues arising in their common fields] [the following issues:

]

Statements under rule 35.12(3) to be prepared and filed by   am/pm on   1999/20   .

( ) The parties are to consult with each other and the court with a view to arranging service and (where required) filing of statements of case, witness statements, experts' reports, disclosure lists and other documents in computer readable form as well as in hard copy. Format for court disks:

( )[Time under paragraphs   above not to be extended without permission.]

()
()   Pre-trial Review: . Time allowed: . Parties to complete, file and serve
      pre-trial questionnaire, after consultation, by   am/pm on   1999/20   .
()   Liberty to restore. Costs in cause.

Permission to amend

The [Part 20] claimant/defendant to have permission to [re-]amend the [Part 20] particulars of claim/defence [and counterclaim]/reply to defence [and defence to counterclaim] in accordance with the draft initialled by the Judge. Re-service [to be effected by am/pm on 1999/20] [deemed to have been effected today]. The [Part 20] defendant/claimant to have permission to [re-]amend the defence/reply to defence [and defence to counterclaim] by am/pm on 1999/20 , limited to amendments consequential upon the amendment for which permission is first given above. The [Part 20] claimant/defendant to pay in any event the costs of and consequential upon that amendment, or thrown away thereby [and of this application].

Scott Schedule

Column headings:	1.	Serial number
	2.	
	3.	
	4.	
	5.	
	6.	
	7.	
	8.	
	9.	
	10.	
	11.	
	12.	

Expert Evidence

Party (or state "Joint")	Field	Name	Date for Exchange	Whether leave for oral evidence

Reports to be exchanged [and filed] by am/pm on the dates specified.

APPENDIX 4
TECHNOLOGY AND CONSTRUCTION COURT

PRE–TRIAL REVIEW DIRECTIONS FORM

( ) [Directions in relation to orders not yet complied with]

( ) Trial bundle to include [all admissible disclosed documents required by either party][documents in the following categories only:

.]

Claimant/defendant to serve proposed index of trial bundle by   am/pm   on 1999/20   .

Defendant/claimant to respond by   am/pm on   1999/20   . Trial bundle to be agreed by   am/pm on 1999/20 and filed by am/pm on   1999/20 with any witness statements and experts' reports not already filed.

( ) Claimant/defendant to open trial and to serve and file chronology, cast list and note of opening by   am/pm on   1999/20   . [Defendant/claimant to make an opening response and to serve and file a note of it by   am/pm on   1999/20 .]

( ) Disks (if obtainable) of statements of case, witness statements, experts' reports, trial bundle and opening notes, so far as not already filed, to be filed in   format by   am/pm on   1999/20   .

( ) [Adjourned hearing of pre-trial review, if required]

( ) Costs in cause.

PRACTICE DIRECTION – COMMERCIAL COURT
THIS PRACTICE DIRECTION SUPPLEMENTS CPR PART 49 AND
REPLACES, WITH MODIFICATIONS, ORDER 72 OF THE
RULES OF THE SUPREME COURT

General

1.1 This practice direction applies to commercial claims in the Commercial Court of the Queen's Bench Division.

1.2 (1) In this practice direction "commercial claim" includes any case arising out of trade and commerce in general, including any case relating to –

    (i)   a business document or contract,

    (ii) the export or import of goods,

    (iii) the carriage of goods by land, sea, air or pipeline,

    (iv) the exploitation of oil and gas reserves,

    (v) insurance and re-insurance,

    (vi) banking and financial services,

    (vii) the operation of markets and exchanges,

    (viii)business agency, and

    (ix) arbitration

and "commercial proceedings" has a corresponding meaning.

(2) "Judge" means Judge of the Commercial Court.

1.3 The rules relating to arbitration are set out in the Arbitration Practice Direction that supplements CPR Part 49.

1.4 The Civil Procedure Rules (the "CPR") apply to commercial proceedings in the Commercial Court subject to the provisions of this practice direction and any Commercial Court practice direction.

The commercial list

2.1 There shall be a list called "the commercial list" in which commercial claims in the Queen's Bench Division may be entered for trial in the Commercial Court, and one of the Commercial Court judges shall be in charge of that list.

2.2 All proceedings in the Commercial Court, including all pre-trial applications and any appeal from any judgment, order or decision of a master or district judge prior to the transfer of any case to the commercial list, shall be heard or otherwise dealt with by a Judge, except that:-

    (i) if an application is urgent and no Judge is available to deal with it, the application may be made to some other judge of the Queen Bench's Division authorised to hear applications in the Commercial Court; and

    (ii) unless a Judge otherwise orders, all proceedings for the enforcement of any judgment or order for the payment of money given or made in the Commercial Court shall be referred to a master of the Queen's Bench Division.

2.3 The commercial list is a specialist list for the purposes of the CPR (see e.g. Rules 16.3(5) and 30.5 of the CPR).

Entry of case in commercial list

3.1 The claim form by which a commercial claim intended to be entered in the commercial list is begun should be issued out of the Admiralty and Commercial Registry at the Royal Courts of Justice.

3.2 The claim form should, before it is issued, be marked with the words "Queen's Bench Division, Commercial Court" and on the issue of the claim form out of the said Registry the case will be entered in the commercial list.

3.3 Where a claim form is to be marked as mentioned in paragraph 3.2, any application before issue of the claim form should be made to a Judge.

3.4 If an application is made before issue of the claim form, the written evidence in support of the application must state, in addition to any other necessary matters, that the claimant intends to mark the claim form in accordance with paragraph 3.2.

3.5 If the Judge hearing an application made before the issue of the claim form is of the opinion that the case in question should not be entered in the commercial list, he may adjourn the application to be heard by a master or by a judge of the Queen's Bench Division who is not a judge of the Commercial Court.

Transfer to and removal from commercial list

4.1 At any stage of the proceedings of commercial proceedings not entered in the commercial list any party:-

   (1) may apply to a Judge for an order transferring the proceedings to the commercial list; or

   (2) may apply to the court where the proceedings are being dealt with for an order that they be transferred to the commercial list.

4.2 On an application under paragraph 4.1(2) the court may not itself make the order for transfer, but, if it considers the proceedings might be suitable to be entered in the commercial list, may adjourn the application for hearing by a Judge.

4.3 Where the Judge orders commercial proceedings to be transferred to the commercial list he may also order the proceedings to be transferred to the Royal Courts of Justice and at the same time may give directions for the management of the case.

4.4 A Judge may, on his own initiative, (but not unless the parties have had an opportunity of being heard or have consented) or on the application of any party, order proceedings in the commercial list to be removed from that list.

4.5 Where a commercial claim has been entered in the commercial list by virtue of paragraph 3.2, an application by a defendant, including a Part 20 defendant, to remove it from that list must be made within 7 days after the defendant has filed an acknowledgment of service or a defence, whichever is the later.

Dispensing with particulars of claim or defence

5. The Judge may at any time, before or after the issue of the claim form, order that proceedings in the commercial list be tried without the filing or service of particulars of claim or of a defence or of any other statement of case.

Directions and case management

6.1 All proceedings in the commercial list will be allocated to the multi-track and the CPR relating to allocation questionnaires and track allocation will not apply.

6.2 (1) If proceedings are transferred to the commercial list following an application under paragraph 4, then, unless the Judge who made the order for transfer gave directions for the management of the case, an application to a Judge for such directions shall be made within 14 days of the date of the order of transfer.

   (2) If the claimant does not make an application in accordance with paragraph 6.2(1), any other party may do so, or may apply for the claim of the claimant in default to be struck out or dismissed.

Ship's papers

7.1 Where in proceedings in the commercial list relating to a marine insurance policy an application for specific disclosure under Rule 31.12 of the CPR is made by the insurer, the Judge, if it appears to him to be necessary or expedient to do so, may make an order in such form as he thinks fit for the production of the documents specified in the order.

7.2 An order under this rule may be made at any stage of the proceedings and on such terms, if any, as to staying the proceedings or otherwise, as the Judge thinks fit.

Admiralty and Commercial Registry

8.1 All administrative acts which under the Civil Procedure Rules or any Practice Direction are to be carried out by the Court office shall in relation to cases in the commercial list be carried out by or through the Admiralty and Commercial Registry.

8.2 All documents which under the Civil Procedure Rules are to be filed with the Court office shall in cases in the commercial list be filed with the Admiralty and Commercial Registry.

8.3 All claim forms, arbitration forms (see the Arbitration practice direction supplementing CPR Part 49) issued in and other documents filed with the Admiralty and Commercial Registry are (if they need to be served) to be served by the parties, not by the Admiralty and Commercial Registry.

The Commercial Court Guide

9.1 The first edition of the Guide to Commercial Court Practice was published in 1986. The most recent edition has been the Fourth Edition published in 1997.

9.2 With the approval of the Judges of the Commercial Court a Fifth Edition has been prepared and adopted by the Commercial Court Committee. The Fifth Edition (now entitled "The Commercial Court Guide") is designed to be introduced at the same time as the new Civil Procedure Rules and the practice directions that supplement them.

9.3 The Fifth Edition incorporates and adapts into one text provisions of the Fourth Edition and of the many Practice Directions and Statements appended to it. The revision also incorporates a number of new provisions.

9.4 The combined result is intended to be a Guide that will, in the specialist context of commercial cases, serve the "overriding objective" defined in CPR Part 1. The Guide will be kept under review by the Judges of the Commercial Court and by the Commercial Court Committee.

9.5 The practice of the Commercial Court set out in this revised edition should be followed from 26 April 1999, subject to the provisions of this or any other Commercial Court practice direction and to any order that may be made in an individual case.

10. This practice direction supersedes all previous practice directions and Practice Statements in the Commercial Court.

PRACTICE DIRECTION – PATENTS, ETC
THIS PRACTICE DIRECTION SUPPLEMENTS CPR PART 49 AND REPLACES, WITH MODIFICATIONS, RSC ORDER 104, ORDER 100 AND ORDER 93, RULE 24 AND CCR ORDER 48A AND ORDER 49 RULE 4A

General

1.1 This practice direction applies to the business of the Patents Court and proceedings under the Copyright, Designs and Patents Act 1988, the Trade Marks Acts 1938 and 1994 and the Olympic Symbol etc Protection Act 1995 and Olympic Association Right (Infringement Proceedings) Regulations 1995.

1.2 The Civil Procedure Rules apply to Patents Court business and proceedings under the Copyright, Designs and Patents Act 1988, the Trade Marks Acts 1938 and 1994 and the Olympic Symbol etc Protection Act 1995 and Olympic Association Right (Infringement Proceedings) Regulations 1995 subject to the provisions of this and any other Patents Court practice direction.

1.3 Definitions In this Practice Direction –

"the 1949 Act" means the Patents Act 1949;

"the 1977 Act" means the Patents Act 1977;

"the Comptroller" means the Comptroller-General of Patents, Designs and Trade Marks;

"the Court," means the Patents Court;

"existing patent" means a patent mentioned in section 127(2)(a) or (c) of the 1977 Act;

"the journal" means the journal published pursuant to rules made under section 123 (6) of the 1977 Act;

"1977 Act patent" means a patent under the 1977 Act;

"patent" means an existing patent or a 1977 Act patent and includes any application for a patent, supplementary protection certificate granted pursuant to the Patents (Supplementary Protection Certificates) Rules 1997, the Patents (Supplementary

Protection Certificate for Medicinal Products) Regulations 1992 and the Patents (Supplementary Protection Certificate for Plant Protection Products) Regulations 1996.

"Patents Court" includes the Patents Court of the High Court and the Patents County Court.

"Patents Court business" includes:

(a) any claim under the Patents Acts 1949 to 1961 and 1977;

(b) any claim under the Registered Designs Acts 1949 to 1961;

(c) any claim under the Defence Contracts Act 1958, and

(d) all proceedings for the determination of a question or the making of a declaration relating to a patent (or an application for a patent) under the inherent jurisdiction of the High Court.

"the CPR" means the Civil Procedure Rules.

Allocation of Patents Court business

2.1 Patents Court business may be dealt with either in the High Court or the Patents county court.

2.2 Before the issue of a claim form relating to Patents Court business, the claim form, whether it is to be issued in the High Court or the county court, should be marked in the top right hand corner "Patents Court" and the claim will then be allocated to the Patents Court.

2.3 The Patents Court is a specialist list for the purposes of Part 30 of the CPR but no order for the transfer of proceedings to or from the Patents Court shall be made unless the parties have either:

(a) had an opportunity of being heard on the issue, or

(b) consented to the order.

2.4 Every claim in the Patents Court will be allocated to the Multi-track and the CPR relating to allocation questionnaires and track allocation will not apply.

2.5 (1) Where a claim has been allocated to the Patents Court either on issue (ie. in every case in which the claim form has been marked Patents Court) or by transfer to the Patents Court, an application for directions (including an application for a fixed date of hearing) shall be made by the claimant within 14 days of the filing by the defendant of an acknowledgment of service or of a defence (whichever is the earlier) or, as the case may be, within 14 days of the date of the order of transfer.

(2) If the claimant does not make an application in accordance with paragraph 2.5, any other party may do so or may apply for the claim of the claimant in default to be struck out or dismissed.

(3) Any application under this paragraph must be made to a judge of the Patents Court unless a judge of the Patents Court otherwise directs.

(4) On the hearing of the application for directions under paragraph 2.5(1) the judge shall give directions for any further directions hearing and direct the time by which the hearing of any further application for directions is to take place.

2.6 Except where inconsistent with the provisions of this Practice Direction, CPR Part 29 and the Multi-track Practice Direction apply to Patents Court business.

2.7 This practice direction shall apply with any necessary modifications to proceedings in respect of Registered Designs.

Service of documents

3.1 This rule applies to the service of any document on a party until such time as that party has provided an address for service in accordance with CPR rule 6.5.

3.2 Subject to sub-paragraph (3) below, for the purposes of any proceedings relating to a patent or a registered design (including proceedings for revocation, declaration as to non-infringement or groundless threats of infringement proceedings or any other proceedings of a kind mentioned in this Practice Direction) where any document is served in the manner authorised by CPR Part 6 at an address for service given in the register kept under section 32 of the 1977 Act or, as the case may be, section 17 of the Registered Designs Act 1949 –

(1) service shall be deemed to have been effected on the registered proprietor of the patent or registered design on the date on which the document was served at the said address;

(2) the party on whom service is deemed to have been effected under sub-paragraph (a) shall be treated, for the purposes of any provision of these rules which specifies a time-limit for responding to the document so served (whether by filing or serving an admission, filing a defence, acknowledging service, or otherwise), as having been served on the seventh day after the date on which the document was served at the said address.

3.3 Nothing in paragraph 3.2 shall prevent service being effected on the proprietor in accordance with the provisions of Part 6 of the CPR.

Application in proceedings before the court for permission to amend a patent specification under s.30 of the 1949 Act or s.75 of the 1977 Act

4.1 A patentee or the proprietor of a patent intending to apply in proceedings before the Court under section 30 of the 1949 Act or under section 75 of the 1977 Act for permission to amend his specification must give notice of his intention to the Comptroller accompanied by a copy of an advertisement –

(1) identifying the proceedings pending before the Court in which it is intended to apply for such permission;

(2) giving particulars of the amendment sought;

(3) stating the applicant's address for service within the United Kingdom;

(4) stating that a Statement of Reasons is available from that address; and

(5) stating that any person intending to oppose the amendment must within 28 days after the appearance of the advertisement give written notice of his intention to the applicant; such notice to be accompanied by a Statement of Opposition

and the Comptroller shall insert the advertisement once in the journal. A person who gives notice in accordance with the advertisement shall be entitled to be heard on the application subject to any direction of the Court as to costs.

4.2 The applicant must at the same time as giving notice to the Comptroller serve a copy of the Statement of Reasons together with a copy of the patent as proposed to be amended on all parties to the proceedings.

4.3 The Statement of Reasons referred to in paragraph 4.1(4) shall contain full particulars of the amendment sought, of the reasons therefor and of the reasons why the applicant contends that in the exercise of discretion the amendment should be allowed. In particular the Statement should contain

(1) A statement whether the amendment is by way of deletion of claims or re-writing of claims.

(2) Insofar as it involve re-writing claims, details as to why the proposed amendment is in accordance with the statutory requirements of an amendment.

(3) Insofar as the amendment is sought to distinguish (more clearly) over prior art, an indication of the prior art.

4.4 The Statement of Opposition shall contain full particulars of all grounds of opposition to the application to amend.

4.5 As soon as may be after the expiration of 35 days from the appearance of the advertisement the applicant must make his application under the said section 30 or 75, as the case may be, by an application notice in the proceedings before the Court; and the application notice, together with a copy of the specification certified by the Comptroller and showing in coloured ink the amendment sought, must be served on the Comptroller, the parties to the proceedings and any person who has given notice of his intention to oppose the amendment.

4.6 Not less than two days before the date fixed for the hearing of the application, the applicant, the Comptroller, the parties to the proceedings and any other opponent should serve on all other parties and on the Court a Statement of Directions being the directions which that party seeks for the further conduct of the proceedings. Any of the foregoing not serving a Statement of Directions shall take no further part in the proceedings without permission of the Court and shall not be liable for the costs thereof.

4.7 On the hearing of the amendment application the Court shall give such directions for its further conduct as it thinks necessary or expedient and, in particular, directions –

(1) determining whether the application shall be heard forthwith or with the other proceedings relating to the patent in question or separately and, if separately, fixing the date of hearing thereof;

(2) as to whether any evidence is necessary, and, if so, as to the manner in which the that evidence shall be given and, if written evidence is to be given, fixing the times within which the affidavits or witness statements must be filed;

(3) as to whether any disclosure is necessary, and, if so, as to the extent of disclosure and the manner and time within which the same is to be given.

4.8 Where the Court allows a specification to be amended, the applicant must forthwith file with the Comptroller an office copy of the order made in the Court and, if so required by the Court or Comptroller, leave at the Patent Office a new specification and drawings as amended, prepared in compliance with the 1949 or 1977 Act, whichever is applicable, and the rules made under those Acts respectively.

4.9 The Comptroller shall cause a copy of the order to be inserted at least once in the journal.

Application for revocation

5.1 An application under section 72 of the 1977 Act for the revocation of a patent shall be commenced by the issue of a claim form. This direction does not apply to an application made in existing proceedings. An application in existing proceedings shall be made by way of a counterclaim or other Part 20 claim (as defined in CPR rule 20.2(1)).

Claim for infringement

6.1 The claimant in a claim for infringement must serve with his claim form particulars of the infringement relied on, showing which of the claims in the specification of the patent are alleged to be infringed and giving at least one instance of each type of infringement alleged.

6.2 If a defendant in such a claim alleges, as a defence to the claim, that at the time of the infringement there was in force a contract or licence relating to the patent made by or with the consent of the claimant and containing a condition or term void by virtue of section 44 of the 1977 Act, he must serve on the claimant particulars of the date of, and parties to, each such contract or licence and particulars of each such condition or term.

Objections to validity

7.1 A person who presents a claim for the revocation of a patent must serve with his claim form particulars of the objections to the validity of the patent on which he relies.

7.2 A party to a claim concerning a patent who either challenges the validity of the patent or applies by counterclaim or other Part 20 claim for revocation of the patent must, serve his defence, counterclaim or other Part 20 claim (as the case may be), together with particulars of the objections to the validity of the patent on which he relies, within 42 days after service upon him of the claim form.

7.3 Particulars given pursuant to paragraph 7.1 or 7.2 must state every ground on which the validity of the patent is challenged and must include such particulars as will clearly define every issue (including any challenge to any claimed priority date) which it is intended to raise.

7.4 If the grounds stated in the particulars of objections include want of novelty or want of any inventive step, the particulars must state the manner, time and place of every prior publication or user relied upon and, if prior user is alleged, must:

(1) specify the name of every person alleged to have made such user,

(2) state whether such user is alleged to have continued until the priority date of the claim in question or of the invention, as may be appropriate, and, if not, the earliest and latest date on which such user is alleged to have taken place,

(3) contain a description accompanied by drawings, if necessary, sufficient to identify such user, and

(4) if such user relates to machinery or apparatus, state whether the machinery or apparatus is in existence and where it can be inspected.

7.5 If either (a) in the case of an existing patent one of the grounds stated in the particulars of objections is that the invention, so far as claimed in any claim of the complete specification, is not useful, or, (b) in the case of a patent one of the grounds stated in the particulars of objections is that the specification of the patent does not disclose the invention clearly enough and completely enough for the invention to be performed and it is intended, in connection with either of such grounds, to rely on the fact that an example of the invention which is the subject of any claim cannot be made to work, either at all or as described in the specification, the particulars must state that fact and identify each such claim and must include particulars of each such example, specifying the respects in which it is alleged that it does not work or does not work as described.

7.6 In any proceedings relating to a patent in which the validity of the patent has been put in issue on the ground of obviousness a party who wishes to rely on the commercial success of the patent must state in his pleadings the grounds upon which he so relies.

Admissions

8.1 Where a party desires any other party to admit any facts, he shall, within 21 days after service of a reply or after the expiration of the period fixed for the service thereof, serve on that other party a notice requiring him to admit for the purpose of the claim the facts specified in the notice.

8.2 A party upon whom a notice under paragraph 8.1 is served shall within 21 days after service thereof serve upon the party making the request a notice stating in respect of each fact specified in the notice whether or not he admits it.

Disclosure and inspection.

9.1 CPR Part 31 shall apply in a claim for infringement of a patent or a declaration of non-infringement of a patent or any proceedings where the validity of a patent is in issue.

9.2 Standard disclosure does not require the disclosure of documents in the following exempt classes :-

(1) documents relating to the infringement of a patent by a product or process if, before serving a list of documents, the party against whom the allegation of infringement is made has served on the other parties full particulars of the product or process alleged to infringe, including if necessary drawings or other illustrations;

(2) documents relating to any ground on which the validity of a patent is put in issue, except documents which came into existence within the period beginning two years before the earliest claimed priority date and ending two years after that date; and

(3) documents relating to the issue of commercial success.

9.3 Where the issue of commercial success arises in any proceedings specified in paragraph 9.1, the patentee shall, within such time limit as the Court may direct, serve a schedule containing the following details -

(1) where the commercial success relates to an article or product -

  (a) an identification of the article or product (for example by product code number) which the patentee asserts has been made in accordance with the claims of the patent;

  (b) a summary by convenient periods of sales of any such article or product;

  (c) a summary for the equivalent periods of sales, if any, of any equivalent prior article or product marketed before the article or product mentioned in sub-paragraph (a); and

  (d) a summary by convenient periods of any expenditure on advertising and promotion which supported the marketing of the articles or products mentioned in sub-paragraphs (a) and (c),

(2) where the commercial success relates to the use of a process -

  (a) an identification of the process the patentee asserts has been used in accordance with the claims of the patent;

  (b) a summary by convenient periods of the revenues received from the use of such process;

  (c) a summary for the equivalent periods of the revenues, if any, received from the use of any equivalent prior art process; and

  (d) a summary by convenient periods of any expenditure which supported the use of the process mentioned in sub-paragraphs (a) and (c).

Experiments

10.1 Where a party desires to establish any fact by experimental proof he must, at least 21 days before the service of the application notice for directions under paragraph 10.3 or within such other time as the Court may direct at a hearing for further directions pursuant to paragraph 2.5(4), serve on the other party a notice stating the facts which he desires to establish and giving full particulars of the experiments proposed to establish them.

10.2 A party upon whom a notice under paragraph 10.1 is served shall, within 21 days after service thereof, serve upon the other party a notice stating in respect of each fact whether or not he admits it.

10.3 Where any fact which a party desires to establish by experimental proof is not admitted he shall apply to the Court for directions in respect of such experiments.

Application for further directions

11.1 (1) The parties must comply with any directions given by the judge pursuant to paragraph 2.5(4) in respect of any hearing for further directions.

(2) If the claimant does not serve an application notice for further directions in accordance with this paragraph, the defendant may do so.

(3) The application notice must be accompanied by minutes of the order proposed, and such other documents as will be necessary for the hearing of the application.

11.2 At a further directions hearing under this paragraph the judge may give such directions relating to:

(1) the service of further pleadings or of further information pursuant to Part 18 of the CPR;

(2) disclosure and inspection of documents;

(3) requests for or the making of admissions pursuant to paragraphs 8.1 and 8.2 above and Part 14 of the CPR;

(4) the obtaining of written evidence relating to matters requiring expert knowledge, and for the filing of affidavits or witness statements and the service of copies thereof on the other parties,

(5) the holding of a meeting of such experts as the judge may specify, for the purpose of producing a joint report on the state of the relevant art;

(6) the exchanging of experts' reports, in respect of those matters on which they are not agreed;

(7) the making of experiments, tests, inspections or reports;

(8) the determination, as a preliminary issue, of any question that may arise (including any questions as to the construction of the specification or other documents)

and otherwise as the judge thinks necessary or expedient for the purpose of giving effect to the overriding objective. Where evidence is directed to be given by affidavit or witness statement, the witnesses must attend at the trial for cross-examination unless, with the concurrence of the Court, the parties otherwise agree.

11.3 On the hearing of an application under this paragraph the judge shall consider, if necessary of his own initiative, whether:

(a) the parties' advisers should be required to meet for the purpose of agreeing which documents will be required at the trial and of paginating such documents;

(b) an independent scientific adviser should be appointed to assist the Court, whether as an assessor under CPR rule 35.15 or otherwise.

Restrictions on admission of evidence

12.1 Except with the permission of the judge hearing any claim or other proceedings relating to a patent, no evidence shall be admissible in proof of any alleged infringement, or of any objection to the validity, of the patent, if the infringement or objection was not raised in the particulars of infringements or objections, as the case may be.

12.2 In any claim or other proceedings relating to a patent, evidence which is not in accordance with a statement contained in particulars of objections to the validity of the patent shall not be admissible in support of such an objection unless the judge hearing the proceeding allows the evidence to be admitted.

12.3 If any machinery or apparatus alleged to have been used before the priority date mentioned in paragraph 7.4(2) is in existence at the date of service of the particulars of objections, no evidence of its user before that date shall be admissible unless it is proved that the party relying on such user offered, where the machinery or apparatus is in his possession, inspection of it to the other parties to the proceedings or, where it is not, used all reasonable endeavours to obtain inspection of it for those parties.

Determination of question or application where comptroller declines to deal with it

13 Where the Comptroller –
  (1) declines to deal with a question under section 8 (7), 12 (2), 37 (8) or 61 (5) of the 1977 Act;
  (2) declines to deal with an application under section 40 (5) of that Act, or
  (3) certifies under section 72 (7)(b) of that Act that the question whether a patent should be revoked is one which would more properly be determined by the court,

any person entitled to do so may, within 28 days after the Comptroller's decision apply to the Court to determine the question or application.

Application by employee for compensation under section 40 of the 1977 Act

14.1 An application by an employee for compensation under section 40 (1) or (2) of the 1977 Act shall be begun by the issue of a claim form within the period which begins when the relevant patent is granted and which expires one year after it has ceased to have effect. Provided that, where a patent has ceased to have effect by reason of a failure to pay any renewal fee within the period prescribed for the payment thereof and an application for restoration is made to the Comptroller under section 28 of the said Act, the said period shall –
  (1) if restoration is ordered, continue as if the patent had remained continuously in effect, or
  (2) if restoration is refused, be treated as expiring one year after the patent ceased to have effect or six months after the refusal, whichever is the later.

14.2 Either at the hearing of an application for directions under paragraph 2.5(1) or at a hearing of an application for further directions under paragraphs 11.1– 11.3, the Court must give directions as to the manner in which the evidence (including any accounts of expenditure and receipts relating to the claim) shall be given at the hearing of the claim and, if written evidence is to be given, specify the period within which witness statements or affidavits must be filed.

14.3 The Court must also give directions as to the provision by the defendant to the claimant, or a person deputed by him for the purpose, of reasonable facilities for inspecting and taking extracts from the books of account by which the defendant proposes to verify the accounts mentioned in paragraph 14.2 or from which those accounts have been derived.

Procedure for the determination of certain disputes

15.1 The following proceedings must be begun by the issue of a claim form, that is to say-
  (1) proceedings for the determination of any dispute referred to the court under-
    (a) section 48 of the 1949 Act or section 58 of the 1977 Act;
    (b) paragraph 3 of Schedule 1 to the Registered Designs Act 1949;
    (c) section 4 of the Defence Contracts Act 1958; or
    (d) section 252 of the Copyright, Designs and Patent Act 1988;
  (2) any application under section 45(3) of the 1977 Act.

Appeals from the comptroller

16.1 In this paragraph "the Court" means the Patents Court of the High Court.

16.2 An appeal to the Court from a decision of the Comptroller in any case in which a right of appeal is given by the 1949 or 1977 Act must be brought by issuing a Notice of Appeal. The parties are, in this paragraph, referred to as "appellant" and "respondent" respectively.

16.3 The Notice of Appeal shall be issued:

(1) in the case of a decision on a matter of procedure, within 14 days after the date of the decision; and

(2) in any other case, within six weeks after the date of the decision.

16.4 The Comptroller may determine whether any decision is on a matter of procedure and any such determination shall itself be a decision on a matter of procedure.

16.5 Except with permission of the Court, no appeal shall be entertained unless the Notice of Appeal has been issued within the period specified in paragraph

16.3 or within such further time as the Comptroller may allow upon request made to him prior to the expiry of that period.

16.6 The Notice of Appeal may be given in respect of the whole or any specific part of the decision of the Comptroller and must specify the grounds of the appeal and the relief which the appellant seeks.

16.7 Except with the permission of the Court the appellant shall not be entitled on the hearing of the appeal to rely on any ground of appeal or to apply for any relief not specified in the Notice of Appeal.

16.8 The appellant shall, within 21 days of issuing the Notice of Appeal, serve a copy thereof on the Comptroller and any other party to the proceedings before the Comptroller.

16.9 After receiving the Notice of Appeal the Comptroller shall lodge with the Clerk or other person in charge of the Patents Court list all papers relating to the matter which is subject of the appeal.

16.10 A respondent who, not having appealed from the decision of the Comptroller, desires to contend on the appeal that the decision should be varied, either in any event or in the event of the appeal being allowed in whole or in part, must give notice to that effect, specifying the grounds of that contention and the relief which he seeks from the Court.

16.11 A respondent who desires to contend on the appeal that the decision of the Comptroller should be affirmed on grounds other than those set out in the decision must give notice to that effect, specifying the grounds of that contention.

16.12 A respondent's notice shall be served on the Comptroller and on the appellant and every other party to the proceedings before the Comptroller within 14 days after service of the Notice of Appeal by the respondent, or within such further time as the Court may direct.

16.13 A party by whom a respondent's notice is given must within 5 days after service of the notice on the appellant, furnish 2 copies of the notice to the Clerk or other person in charge of the Patents List

16.14 The Clerk or other person in charge of the Patents list shall give to the Comptroller and to the appellant and every other party to the proceedings before the Comptroller not less than seven days' notice of the date appointed for the hearing of the appeal, unless the Court directs shorter notice to be given.

16.15 An appeal shall be by way of rehearing and the evidence used on appeal shall be the same as that used before the Comptroller and, except with the permission of the Court, no further evidence shall be given.

16.16 Any notice given in proceedings under this rule may be signed by or served on any patent agent, or member of the Bar of England and Wales not in actual practice, who is acting for the person giving the notice or, as the case may be, the person on whom the notice is to be served, as if the patent agent or member of the Bar were a solicitor.

16.17 The Notice of Appeal shall be in the form annexed hereto or in such other form as may be approved by the Court.

Communication of information to the European Patent Office

17.1 The Court may authorise the communication to the European Patent Office or the competent authority of any country which is a party to the European Patent Convention of any such information in the files of the court as the Court thinks fit.

17.2 Before complying with a request for the disclosure of information under paragraph 17.1 the Court shall afford to any party appearing to be affected by the request the opportunity of making representations, in writing or otherwise, on the question whether the information should be disclosed.

Claim for rectification of register of patents or designs

18.1 Where a claim is made for the rectification of the register of patents, the claimant shall at the same time as serving the other party serve a copy of the claim form and the accompanying documents on the Comptroller, who shall be entitled to appear and to be heard on the application.

OTHER INTELLECTUAL PROPERTY MATTERS INCLUDED IN THIS PRACTICE DIRECTION

A. COPYRIGHT MATTERS

Additional damages under section 97(2) of the Copyright, Designs and Patents Act 1988

19.1 Where a claimant seeks to recover additional damages under section 97(2) of the Copyright, Designs and Patents Act 1988, he must so state in his claim form and the particulars of claim must set out the grounds relied upon in support.

Applications for delivery up and forfeiture under sections 99, 114, 195, 204, 230 or 231 of the Copyright, Designs and Patents Act 1988

20.1 An application under Sections 99, 114, 195, 204, 230 or 231 of the Copyright, Designs and Patents Act 1988 ("CDPA") shall be made by the issue of a claim form or, if made in existing proceedings, an application notice in those proceedings.

20.2 Where such an application is made the applicant shall serve the claim form or application notice on all persons having an interest in the goods, material or articles within the meaning of sections 114, 204 or 231 of the CDPA insofar as such persons are reasonably ascertainable.

B. TRADEMARK MATTERS

Definitions

21.1 In this section of this practice direction –

"the 1938 Act" means the Trade Marks Act 1938 as amended by the Trade Marks (Amendment) Act 1984 and the Patents, Designs and Marks Act 1986;

"the 1994 Act" means the Trade Marks Act 1994;

"the Olympic Symbol Act" means the Olympic Symbol etc. (Protection) Act 1995;

"the Olympic Symbol Regulations" means the Olympic Association Right (Infringement Proceedings) Regulations 1995;

"the Registrar" means the Comptroller-General of Patents, Designs and Trade Marks;

"the register" means the register of trade marks maintained by the Registrar pursuant to section 63 of the 1994 Act;

"appointed person" means a person appointed by the Lord Chancellor to hear and decide appeals under the 1994 Act.

Assignment to the Chancery Division

22.1 Proceedings in the High Court under the 1938 Act, the 1994 Act or the Olympic Symbol Act and Regulations shall be dealt with in the Chancery Division.

Appeals and applications under the 1938 Act, the 1994 Act and the Olympic Symbol Act and the Olympic Symbol Regulations

23.1 Every appeal to the High Court under the 1938 Act or the 1994 Act shall be heard and determined by a single judge.

23.2 Such appeals shall be brought by a Notice of Appeal in such form as may be approved by the court.

23.3 The Notice of Appeal must be issued within 28 days of the decision appealed from.

23.4 Within 21 days of issue the Notice of Appeal must be served on the Registrar and any Respondents and lodged with the Clerk or other person in charge of the Chancery List.

23.5 Every other application to the High Court under the said Acts and the Olympic Symbol Regulations must be begun by the issue of a claim form under CPR Part 8 or, if made in existing proceedings, an application notice in those proceedings.

23.6 Notices of Appeal, claim forms or application notices by which any such application is begun must be served on the Registrar.

23.7 Where –

(1) the Registrar refers to the High Court an application made to him under the 1938 Act or the 1994 Act;

(2) the Board of Trade under the 1938 Act or an appointed person under section 76 of the 1994 Act refers to that Court an appeal, then unless within one month after receiving notification of the decision to refer, the applicant or the appellant, as the case may be, makes to that Court the application or appeal referred, he shall be deemed to have abandoned it.

23.8 The period prescribed above in relation to an appeal to which paragraph 23.1 applies or the period prescribed by paragraph 23.7 in relation to an application or appeal to which that paragraph applies, may be extended by the Registrar on the application of any party interested and may be so extended although the application is not made until after the expiration of that period, but the foregoing provision shall not be taken to affect the power of the Court to extend that period.

23.9 Where under subsection (6) of section 17 or subsection (9) of section 18 of the 1938 Act an appellant becomes entitled and intends to withdraw the application which is the subject-matter of the appeal, he must give notice of his intention to the Registrar and to any other party to the appeal within one month after the Court has given permission under the said subsection (6) or the said subsection (9), as the case may be, for further grounds of objection to be taken.

23.10 Where an application is made under section 19 of the 1994 Act or under regulation 5 of the Olympic Symbol Regulations the applicant shall serve the claim form or application notice on all persons having an interest in the goods, material or articles within the meaning of section 19 of the 1994 Act or Regulation 5 of the Olympic Symbol Regulations as the case may be insofar as such persons are reasonably ascertainable.

Proceedings for infringement of registered trade mark; validity of registration disputed or revocation or rectification sought

24.1 Where in any proceedings a claim is made for relief for infringement of the rights conferred on the proprietor of a registered trade mark by section 9 of the 1994 Act, the party against whom the claim is made may in his defence put in issue the validity of the registration of that trade mark or may apply by counterclaim or other Part 20 claim for an order for revocation of the registration or for a declaration of invalidity of the registration or for rectification of the register, or may do any or all of those things.

24.2 A party to any such proceedings who in his pleading (whether a defence or counterclaim or other Part 20 claim) disputes the validity of the registration of a registered trade mark or seeks a declaration of invalidity or an order for revocation of the registration, or rectification of the register, must serve with his pleading particulars of the objections to the validity of the registration or of any grounds for revocation or rectification, on which he relies.

24.3 A party to any such proceedings who applies for an order for revocation of the registration or for a declaration of invalidity of the registration or for rectification of the register must serve on the Registrar a copy of his counterclaim or other Part 20 claim together with a copy of the particulars mentioned in paragraph 24.2 and the Registrar shall be entitled to take such part in the proceedings as he may think fit but need not serve a defence or other statement of case unless ordered to do so by the Court.

Service of documents

25.1 This rule applies to the service of any document on a party until such time as that party has provided an address for service in accordance CPR rule 6.5.

25.2 Subject to paragraph 25.3 for the purposes of any proceedings relating to a registered trade mark (including proceedings for revocation, declaration of invalidity or non-infringement or groundless threats of infringement proceedings or any other proceedings under the 1938 Act or the 1994 Act), where any document is served in the manner authorised by Part 6 of the CPR at an address for service given in the register kept under section 63 of the 1994 Act –

(1) service shall be deemed to have been effected on the registered proprietor of the trade mark on the date on which the document was served at the said address;

(2) the party on whom service is deemed to have been effected under sub-paragraph (1), shall be treated, for the purposes of any provision which specifies a time–limit for responding to the document so served (whether by acknowledging service, giving notice of intention to defend or otherwise), as having been served on the seventh day after the date on which the document was served at the said address.

25.3 Nothing in paragraph 25.2 shall prevent service being effected on the proprietor in accordance with the provisions of CPR Part 6.

Service of orders on the Registrar

Where an order is made by the Court in any case under the 1938 Act or the 1994 Act, the person in whose favour the order is made (if there is more than one, such one of them as the Court shall direct) shall serve an office copy of the order on the Registrar.

Notice of appeal

The Notice of Appeal is available in PDF format and can be viewed at: http://www.open.gov.uk/lcd/civil/procrules_fin/pdp-49e.pdf

PRACTICE DIRECTION – ADMIRALTY
THIS PRACTICE DIRECTION SUPPLEMENTS CPR PART 49
AND REPLACES, WITH MODIFICATIONS,
ORDER 75 OF THE RULES OF THE SUPREME COURT

General

1.1 This practice direction applies to all Admiralty proceedings.

1.2 The provisions of the Civil Procedure Rules and the Practice Directions that supplement them apply to Admiralty proceedings subject to the provisions of this practice direction, any other Admiralty practice direction and, where applicable, the Commercial Court Guide (see paragraph 16 below).

1.3 "Admiralty proceedings" means proceedings in the Admiralty Court of the Queen's Bench Division of the High Court of Justice and in any other court exercising Admiralty jurisdiction.

1.4 In this Practice Direction:-

(a) "the Admiralty Court" includes:-

(i) the Admiralty Court of the Queen's Bench Division of the High Court of Justice; and

(ii) any other court exercising Admiralty jurisdiction.

(b) "claim in rem" means an Admiralty claim in rem;

(c) "claim in personam" means an Admiralty claim in personam;

(d) a "collision claim" means a claim falling within section 20(3)(b) of the Supreme Court Act 1981, namely any action to enforce a claim for damage, loss of life or personal injury arising out of-

(i) a collision between ships; or

(ii) the carrying out or omission to carry out any manoeuvre in the case of one or more of two or more ships; or

(iii) non-compliance, on the part of one or more of two or more ships, with the collision regulations;

(e) a "salvage claim" includes any claim in the nature of salvage, any claim for special compensation under Article 14 of Schedule 11 to the Merchant Shipping Act 1995, any claim for the apportionment of salvage and any claim arising out of or connected with any contract for salvage services;

(f) "caveat against arrest" means a caveat entered in the caveat book under paragraph 6.3(1);

(g) "caveat against release" mean a caveat entered in the caveat book under paragraph 6.5(2);

(h) "caveat book" means the book kept in the Admiralty and Commercial Registry in which caveats under this practice direction are entered;

(i) "limitation claim" means a claim by shipowners of other persons under the Merchant Shipping Act 1995 for the limitation of the amount of their liability in connection with a ship or other property;

(j) "Marshal" means the Admiralty Marshal;

(k) "ship" includes any description of vessel used in navigation.

(l) "The Admiralty Registrar" means the Queen's Bench master with responsibility for Admiralty proceedings;

(m) " in rem claim form" means a claim form which an in rem claim is brought.

(n) Any references to the Merchant Shipping Act 1995 include any re-enactment thereof.

(o) "the CPR" means the Civil Procedure Rules.

1.5 The following claims must be commenced in the Admiralty Court.

(a) Any claim in rem;

(b) Any collision claim;

(c) Any limitation claim;

(d) Any application to the court under the Merchant Shipping Act 1995;

(e) Any salvage claim.

1.6 Any other claim within the admiralty jurisdiction of the High Court may be commenced either in the Admiralty Court or in the Commercial Court.

1.7 Any claim may be transferred to the Admiralty Court with the consent of the Admiralty Court.

1.8 A claim within paragraph 1.5 wrongly commenced in any other court will be transferred automatically to the Admiralty Court.

1.9 A claim form by which a claim within paragraphs 1.5 or 1.6 is begun may be issued out of the Admiralty and Commercial Court Registry or the registry of any Admiralty Court.

1.10 If a claim form referred to in paragraph 1.9 is issued out of a registry other than the Admiralty and Commercial Registry that other registry will immediately after issue send a copy of the claim by facsimile to the Admiralty and Commercial Registry, and will also send the original file to the Admiralty and Commercial Registry.

1.11 Subject to paragraph 1.13, the Admiralty Registrar shall, after the issue of a claim form referred to in paragraph 1.9 issue a direction in writing stating:

(a) whether the claim should remain in the Admiralty Court or should be transferred to another court; and

(b) if the claim is to remain in the Admiralty Court, whether it should be in the Admiralty Judge's list or should be placed in the Admiralty Registrar's list for trial in London or elsewhere.

In issuing these directions the Admiralty Registrar will have regard to the nature of the issues in dispute and the criteria set out in Rule CPR rule 26.8 insofar as they are applicable.

1.12 Where the Admiralty Registrar directs that the claim should be placed in the Judge's list, case management directions will be given and any case management conference or pre-trial review will be heard by the Admiralty Judge.

1.13 All matters concerning the arrest, detention, sale of property and the determination of priorities in a claim in rem, all proceedings concerning the ownership or the mortgage of a vessel registered under the Merchant Shipping Act 1995, all proceedings in a limitation claim and proceedings against the International Oil Pollution Compensation Fund under s.175 of the Merchant Shipping Act 1995 shall be dealt with only by the Admiralty Court of the High Court.

1.14 All Admiralty proceedings will be allocated to the multi-track and the CPR relating to allocation questionnaires and track allocation will not apply.

Claims *in rem*

2.1 (1) A claim in rem is begun by issuing an in rem claim form in Admiralty Form No. ADM1

2.1 (2) Subject to paragraph 4, the particulars of an in rem claim must

    (a) be contained in or served with the in rem claim form; or

    (b) be served on the Defendant by the Claimant within 75 days after service of the in rem claim form.

2.1 (3) The Claimant to a claim in rem may be named or may be described, but if not named in the in rem claim form shall upon the request of any other party, identify himself by name.

2.1 (4) The Defendant must be described in the claim form.

2.1 (5) An acknowledgment of service must be filed in every in rem claim. The period for filing the acknowledgment of service is 14 days after service of the claim form irrespective of whether the claim form contains particulars of claim. The acknowledgment must be in Admiralty Form No. ADM2. The person who acknowledges service must identify himself by name therein.

2.1 (6) The period within which an in rem claim form must be served is, subject to CPR rule 7.6, 12 months from the date of issue.

2.2 Service of an in rem claim form must be made in one of the following ways:

    (a) Upon the property against which the claim in rem is brought by fixing the in rem claim form, or a copy of it, on the outside of the property proceeded against in a position which may reasonably be expected to be seen. Where the property is freight, service may be made either on the cargo in respect of which the freight was earned or on the ship upon which that cargo was carried.

    (b) If the property to be served is in the custody of a person who will not permit access to it, by leaving a copy of the in rem claim form with that person.

    (c) Where the property has been sold by the Marshal, by filing the in rem claim form in the Admiralty and Commercial Registry.

    (d) Where there is a caveat against arrest, on the person named in the caveat as being authorised to accept service.

    (e) On any solicitor who has authority to accept service.

    (f) On such person and in such manner as is stated to constitute effective service in any agreement providing for service of the proceedings;

    (g) In any other manner directed under CPR rule 6.8 provided that the res or part thereof is within the jurisdiction of the Court; or

    (h) In such other manner as may be provided by rule or by practice directions .

2.3 In cases where the property is to be arrested, or in cases where the property is already under arrest in current proceedings, the Marshal will effect service of the in rem claim form if the Claimant requests the Court to do so. In all other cases Admiralty in rem claim forms are to be served by the claimant, not the Registry.

2.4 Where an in rem claim form has been issued, any person who wishes to defend the claim may file an acknowledgment of service notwithstanding that the in rem claim form has not been served.

2.5 Except as otherwise provided in this practice direction, after acknowledgment of service has been filed, the procedure relating to the claim shall be the procedure applicable to a claim in personam, but the claim also continues to be a claim in rem.

2.6 Where the defendants are described and not named on the claim form, for example as "The Owners of the Ship X", any acknowledgment of service in addition to stating the description appearing on the claim form shall also state the full names of the persons acknowledging service and the nature of their ownership. In the event of there being insufficient space on the acknowledgment of service form itself, such additional information shall appear on a separate document to accompany and be lodged with the acknowledgment of service form.

2.7 A Defendant who files an acknowledgment of service to an in rem claim form does not by doing so lose any right that he may have to dispute the Court's jurisdiction. (see CPR10.1(3)(b) and Part 11).

2.8 Any person who pays the prescribed fee may, during office hours, search for, inspect and take a copy of any claim form in rem whether or not it has been served.

Claims *in personam*

3.1 (1) A claim form by which a claim in personam is brought (an in personam claim form in Admiralty Form ADM1A) may be served within the jurisdiction as provided in CPR Part 6 and, except in the case of a collision claim, may be served out of the jurisdiction as provided Section III of Part 6.

3.1 (2) An in personam claim form may also be served out of the jurisdiction where:
   (a) the Defendant has agreed to submit the claim to the jurisdiction of the court; or
   (b) the claim is in the nature of salvage and any part of the services took place within the jurisdiction; or
   (c) the claim is to enforce a claim under sections 153 and/or 154 and/or 175 of the Merchant Shipping Act 1995,

   and the Court grants permission to serve the claim form out of the jurisdiction on an application in accordance with Section III of Part 6.

3.1 (3) In personam claim forms are to be served by the claimants, not by the Registry.

3.2 (1) An in personam claim form may seek judgment on liability alone and request that the amount of the claim be referred to the Admiralty Registrar, or be dealt with as the Admiralty Registrar may direct.

3.2 (2) The Claimant in a claim in personam may be named or may be described in the claim form, but if not named, shall, upon the request of any other party, identify himself by name.

3.2 (3) The Defendant in a claim in personam must be named in the claim form.

3.2 (4) Subject to paragraph 4, the particulars of an in personam claim must
   (a) be contained in or served with the claim form; or
   (b) be served on the Defendant by the Claimant within 75 days after service of the claim form.

3.2 (5) The person who files a defence must identify himself by name in the defence.

3.3 An acknowledgment of service must be filed in every in personam claim. Subject to paragraph B7.4 of the Commercial Court Guide, the period for filing the acknowledgment of service is 14 days after service of the claim form irrespective of whether the claim form contains particulars of claim.

Special provisions relating to collision claims

4.1 (1) A collision claim is begun by issuing a claim form. The claim form need not contain or be followed by particulars of claim and CPR rule 7.4 will not apply.

4.1 (2) An acknowledgment of service must be filed in every collision claim.

4.2 (1) In any collision claim each party shall, within 2 months after the filing by the Defendant of the acknowledgment of service or, in the event that the Defendant makes an application under CPR Part 11 (disputing the jurisdiction or the exercise by the court of its jurisdiction), within 2 months of the determination of the Defendant's application, file in the Registry a completed Admiralty Form No. ADM3 ("a Preliminary Act").

4.2 (2) A Preliminary Act shall contain–
   (a) in Part One of the Form, answers to the questions set out in that Part; and
   (b) in Part Two of the Form, a statement–
      (i) that the information in Part One is incorporated in Part Two;
      (ii) of any other facts and matters upon which the party filing the Preliminary Act relies;
      (iii) of all allegations of negligence or other fault which the party filing the Preliminary Act makes;
      (iv) of the relief or remedy which the party filing the Preliminary Act claims.

4.2 (3) A Preliminary Act is to be treated as a statement of case and must be verified by a statement of truth.

4.2 (4) Upon filing their Preliminary Act each party must give notice that he has done so to each other party. Within 14 days after the last Preliminary Act is filed each party must serve on every other party a copy of his Preliminary Act.

4.2 (5) After each party has filed his Preliminary Act, the claim shall proceed as any other Admiralty claim.

4.3. In any collision claim an application under CPR Part 11 disputing the Court's jurisdiction must be made within 2 months of the filing of the acknowledgment of service.

4.4 A claim form in a collision claim may not be served out of the jurisdiction unless-

(a) the case falls within section 22(a) to (c) of the Supreme Court Act 1981; or

(b) the defendant has submitted to or agreed to submit to the jurisdiction of the court,

and the Court grants permission in accordance with rule 6.21. If permission is granted the court will specify the period within which the defendant may file an acknowledgment of service and a Preliminary Act. Rule 6.21(4) does not apply.

4.5 Where, in a collision claim in rem, ("the original claim") -

(a) (i)   a Part 20 claim; or

(ii) a cross claim in rem

arising out of the same collision or occurrence is made; and

(b) (i)   the party bringing the original claim has caused the arrest of a ship or has obtained security in order to prevent such arrest; and

(ii) the party bringing the Part 20 claim or cross claim is unable to arrest a ship or otherwise to obtain security,

then the party bringing the Part 20 claim or cross claim may apply to the Admiralty Court to stay the original claim until sufficient security is given to satisfy any judgment that may be given in favour of that party.

4.6 In collision claims the skeleton argument of each party should be accompanied by a plot or plots of that party's case or alternative cases as to the navigation of vessels during and leading to the collision. All plots must contain a sufficient indication of the assumptions used in the preparation of the plot.

4.7 Where the authenticity of any document or entry in any document is challenged or where it will be suggested at trial that a document or entry in a document was not made at the time or by the person stated or is in any other way challenged in a manner which may require a witness to be produced at trial to support the document or entry in the document, such challenge must be raised in good time in advance of the trial to enable any such witness to be produced. In addition, the skeleton argument should make it plain what challenges to documents or entries in documents will be made.

4.8 (1) If a party to proceedings to establish liability for a collision claim (other than a claim for loss of life or personal injury)-

(a) makes an offer to settle the proceedings in the form set out in paragraph (2) not less than 21 days before the start of the trial;

(b) that offer is not accepted; and

(c) the maker of the offer obtains at trial an apportionment equal to or more favourable than his offer,

the maker of the offer shall, unless the court considers it unjust, be entitled to-

(i)   all his costs from 21 days after the date the offer was made; and

(ii) any costs incurred before the date from which the maker of the offer will be entitled to all his costs under paragraph (i) in the percentage to which he would have been entitled had the offer been accepted.

(2) The offer must be in writing and must contain-

(a) an offer to settle liability at stated percentages;

(b) an offer to pay costs in accordance with the same percentages;

(c) a term that the offer remains open for 21 days after the date it is made; and

(d) a term that on expiry of that period the offer remains open on the same terms except that the offeree should pay all the costs from that date until acceptance.

Proceeding against or concerning the International Oil Pollution Compensation Fund*

5.1 For the purposes of section 177 of the Merchant Shipping Act 1995 and the corresponding provision of Schedule 4 to the Act, any party to proceedings against an owner or guarantor in respect of liability under section 153 and/or section 154 of the said Act or the corresponding provisions of Schedule 4 to the Act may give the Fund notice of the proceedings by serving a notice in writing on the Fund together with a copy of the claim form and copies of the statements of case (if any) served in the proceedings.

5.2 The court will, on application by the Fund made without notice, grant permission to the Fund to intervene in any proceedings to which paragraph 5.1 applies, whether notice of the proceedings has been served on the Fund or not.

5.3 Where a judgment is given against the Fund in any proceedings under section 175 of the Merchant Shipping Act 1995 or the corresponding provision of Schedule 4 to the Act, the Admiralty Registrar will arrange for a stamped copy of the judgment to be sent to the Fund by post.

5.4 Notice by the Fund to the Admiralty Registrar of the matters set out in section 176(3)(b) of the Merchant Shipping Act 1995 and the corresponding section of Schedule 4 to the Act shall be in writing sent by post to, or delivered at, the Registry.

*See Chapter IV, Merchant Shipping Act 1995.

Arrest, release, interveners etc.

6.1 Except as provided in this Practice Direction, the Claimant in a claim in rem and a judgment creditor in a claim in rem is entitled to have the property proceeded against arrested by the Admiralty Court by filing an application to arrest in Admiralty Form No. ADM4 (which shall also contain an undertaking) accompanied by a declaration in Admiralty Form No. ADM5 upon which the Admiralty Court will issue an arrest warrant.

6.2 (1) An application for arrest may be made by filing the application notice in the Admiralty and Commercial Registry or the registry of any Admiralty Court.

6.2 (2) When the relevant registry is closed an application for arrest shall be dealt with in such manner (if any) as may be provided in Admiralty practice directions.

6.2 (3) Any party making an application for arrest must (i) request a search to be made in the caveat book before the warrant is issued in order to ascertain whether there is a caveat in force with respect to that property and (ii) file a declaration in Admiralty Form No. ADM5 containing the particulars required in paragraph 6.2(4). However the Admiralty Court may, if it thinks fit, give permission for the issue of the arrest warrant notwithstanding that the declaration does not contain all those particulars.

6.2 (4) The declaration required by paragraph 6.2(3) must state –

    (a) in every case:

        (i) the nature of the claim or counterclaim and that it has not been satisfied and if it arises in connection with a ship, the name of that ship; and

        (ii) the nature of the property to be arrested and, if the property is a ship, the name of the ship and her port of registry; and

        (iii) the amount of the security sought, if any.

    (b) in the case of a claim against a ship by virtue of section 21(4) of the Supreme Court Act 1981:

        (i) the name of the person who would be liable on the claim if it were commenced in personam ("the relevant person"); and

        (ii) that the relevant person was when the cause of action arose the owner or charterer of, or in possession or in control of, the ship in connection with which the claim arose, specifying which; and

        (iii) that at the time when the claim form was issued the relevant person was either the beneficial owner of all the shares in the ship in respect of which the warrant is required or (where appropriate) the charterer of it under a charter by demise, as the case may be; and

    (c) in the cases set out in paragraphs 6.2(7) and 6.2(8) that the relevant notice has been sent or served, as appropriate; and

    (d) in the case of a claim in respect of liability incurred under section 153 of the Merchant Shipping Act 1995, the facts relied on as establishing that the Court is not prevented from entertaining the claim by reason of section 166(2) of that Act.

    and must be sworn as an affidavit.

6.2 (5) No registry other than the Admiralty and Commercial Registry will issue an arrest warrant and where an application for arrest is made to any registry other than the Admiralty and Commercial Registry that registry will use its best endeavours to cause the application form and declaration and a copy of the form to be transmitted immediately to the Admiralty and Commercial Registry for consideration of the application and, if appropriate, the issue of the warrant. Thereafter the arrest shall be administered by the Marshal and all applications in respect thereof and in respect of the property under arrest other than an order for sale before judgment shall be made to and considered by the Admiralty Registrar himself or as he may direct.

6.2 (6) A warrant of arrest may not be issued as of right in the case of property in respect of which the beneficial ownership, as a result of a sale or disposal by any court exercising Admiralty jurisdiction, has changed since the claim form was issued.

6.2 (7) No warrant of arrest will be issued against a ship owned by a State where, by any convention or treaty, the United Kingdom has undertaken to minimise the possibility of arrest of ships of that State until notice in Admiralty Form No. ADM6 has been served on a consular officer at the consular office of that State in London or the port at which it is intended to cause the ship to be arrested and a copy of the notice is exhibited to the declaration filed under paragraph 6.2(3).

6.2 (8) Except with the permission of the court or when notice has been given under paragraph (7), a warrant of arrest shall not be issued in proceedings in rem against a foreign ship belonging to a port of a State in respect of which an order in council has been made under section 4 of the Consular Relations Act 1968, until the expiration of two weeks from appropriate notice to the consul.

6.2 (9) A warrant of arrest is valid for 12 months but may only be executed if the claim form has been served or remains valid for service at the date of execution.

6.3 (1) Any person may file in the Admiralty and Commercial Registry a notice requesting a caveat against arrest in Admiralty Form No. ADM7, undertaking to file an acknowledgment of service and to give sufficient security to satisfy the claim with interest and costs. Upon filing the notice of request a caveat shall be entered in the caveat book. The record of such caveats shall be open for inspection as provided in the Admiralty practice directions. Caveats shall be valid for a period of 12 months but may be renewed for a similar period or periods. The entry of a caveat against arrest shall not be treated as a submission to the jurisdiction of the English Court.

6.3 (2) Where a Claimant in a limitation claim has constituted a limitation fund in accordance with Article 11 of the Convention on Limitation of Liability for Maritime Claims 1976 and desires to prevent the arrest of property for a claim which may be or has been made against the fund, he must file in the Admiralty and Commercial Registry a notice requesting a caveat, in Admiralty Form No. ADM8, signed by him or his solicitor –

    (a) stating that a limitation fund in respect of the damage arising from the relevant incident has been constituted; and

    (b) undertaking to acknowledge service of the claim form by which any claim may be begun against the property described in the notice;

    and on the filing of the notice a caveat against the issue of a warrant to arrest the property described in the notice shall be entered in the caveat book.

6.3 (3) Property may be arrested notwithstanding that a caveat against arrest has been filed, but in such a case the Admiralty Court may if it considers that it is appropriate to do so, order that the arrest be discharged and that the party procuring the arrest do pay compensation to the owner of or other persons interested in the property arrested.

6.4 (1) The arrest of property may only be effected by the Marshal or his substitute.

6.4 (2) Arrest is effected by service on the property of an arrest warrant in Admiralty Form No. ADM9 in the manner set out in paragraph 2.2(a) or, where it is not reasonably practicable to serve the warrant, by service of a notice of the issue of the warrant in that manner upon the property or by giving notice to those in charge of the property.

6.4 (3) Property under arrest may not be moved without an order of the Admiralty Court and the property may be immobilised or otherwise prevented from sailing in such manner as the Marshal or his substitute may decide is appropriate.

6.4 (4) Upon arrest, standard directions will be issued by the Admiralty Registrar in Admiralty Form No. ADM10.

6.5 (1) Where property is under arrest an in rem claim form may be served upon it and, in addition, it may be arrested by any other person claiming to have an in rem claim against it.

6.5 (2) Any person claiming to have an in rem right against any property under arrest who wishes to be given notice of any application to the court in respect of that property or its proceeds of sale may file in the Admiralty and Commercial Registry a notice requesting a caveat against release in Admiralty Form No. ADM11. Upon the filing of the notice of request, a caveat shall be entered in the caveat book. The record of such caveats shall be open for inspection as provided in the Admiralty practice directions.

6.6 (1) Property will be released from arrest if:

    (a) it is sold by the Admiralty Court; or

    (b) the Admiralty Court orders release upon application made by any party; or

    (c) the arresting party and all caveators, if any, file in the Registry a request for release in Admiralty Form No. ADM12, or

    (d) any party files in the Registry a request for release in Admiralty Form No. ADM12(which shall also contain an undertaking) together with a consent to the release of the arresting party and all caveators, if any.

6.6 (2) Any application for release made when the Registry is closed shall be made in the manner provided by paragraph 17.5.

6.7 (1) Where the release of any property under arrest is delayed by the entry of a caveat under this rule, any person having an interest in the property may apply to the Admiralty Court for an order requiring the person who procured the entry of the caveat to pay damages to the applicant in respect of losses suffered by the applicant by reason of the delay and the Court may make such an order unless it is satisfied that the person procuring the entry of the caveat had a good and sufficient reason for doing so and for maintaining the caveat.

6.7 (2) Where an in rem claim form has been issued and security sought, any person who has filed an acknowledgment of service may apply to the Admiralty Court for an order specifying the amount and form of security to be provided.

6.7 (3) Where in relation to a claim in rem security has been provided to obtain the release of property under arrest or to prevent the arrest of property the Admiralty Court may at any stage:

    (a) order that the amount of security be reduced, and may stay the claim pending compliance with such order;

    (b) order that the Claimant be permitted to arrest or re-arrest the property proceeded against for the purposes of obtaining further security, provided that the total security provided shall not exceed the value of the property at the time of the original arrest or at the time security was first given if the property was not arrested.

6.8 Any person interested in property under arrest or in the proceeds of sale of property sold by the Admiralty Court or whose interests are affected by any order sought or made may be made a party to any claim in rem against the property or proceeds of sale where the Court considers it would be just and convenient and upon such terms as the Court may think fit.

6.9 Any application to the Admiralty Court concerning the sale of the property under arrest or the proceeds of sale of property sold by the Court shall be heard in public and the application notice served on all parties to the claim and caveators against the property or the proceeds of sale.

6.10(1) Where a ship is not under arrest but cargo on board her is, and those interested in the ship wish to discharge the cargo which is under arrest, they may, without intervening in the action, request the Marshal to take the appropriate steps. If the Marshal considers the request reasonable and if the applicant gives an undertaking in writing satisfactory to the Marshal to pay on demand the fees of the Marshal and all expenses to be incurred by him or on his behalf in taking the desired steps, the Marshal will apply to the court for the appropriate order.

6.10(2) Where those interested are unable or unwilling to arrange for such an undertaking to be given they may intervene in the action in which the cargo is under arrest and apply to the Admiralty Registrar for an order for discharge of the cargo and for directions as to the fees and expenses of the Marshal in and about the discharge and storage of the cargo pursuant to such order.

6.11 Where a ship is under arrest but cargo on board her is not, and those interested in the cargo wish to secure its discharge, one or other of the procedures outlined in paragraph 6.10(1) and 6.10(2) may be followed.

Default

7.1 If no acknowledgment of service and/or defence to a claim in rem (other than one to which paragraph 4 applies) is filed within the time required by this practice direction a Claimant may apply for judgment in default by filing an application in Admiralty Form No. ADM13, a certificate proving proper service of the claim form and evidence proving the claim to the satisfaction of the Admiralty Court . Where the claim form has been served by the Court it shall be presumed to have been properly served unless it is proved not to have been.

7.2 In the case of a claim to which paragraph 4 applies, where any party fails to file a Preliminary Act within the time specified any other party who has filed a Preliminary Act may apply for judgment in default:

(a) in a claim in rem, by filing an application in Admiralty Form No. ADM13, a certificate proving proper service of the claim form and evidence proving the claim to the satisfaction of the Admiralty Court. Where the claim form has been served by the Court it shall be presumed to have been properly served unless it is proved not to have been.

(b) in a claim in personam, in accordance with the rules in CPR Part 12 so far as applicable.

7.3 In the case of any other claim in personam, the rules as to judgment in default in CPR Part 12 will apply so far as applicable.

7.4 The Admiralty Court may, on such terms as it thinks just, set aside or vary any judgment entered in pursuance of paragraphs 7.1 or 7.2

7.5 Where a claim form has been served upon a party at whose instance a caveat against arrest was issued the Claimant may, after filing evidence to the satisfaction of the Admiralty Court verifying the facts on which the claim is based, apply to the Court for judgment in default provided that:-

(a) the sum claimed in the claim form does not exceed the amount specified in the undertaking given by that party or his solicitor to procure the entry of the caveat, and

(b) that party or his solicitor does not within 14 days after service of the claim form fulfil the undertaking given by him as aforesaid.

Sale by the court, priorities and payment out

8.1 (1) An order for the survey, appraisement, or sale of a ship may be made in a claim in rem at any stage of the proceedings on the application of any party.

8.1 (2) An order for sale before judgment may only be made by the Admiralty Judge.

8.1 (3) Unless the Admiralty Court otherwise orders, an order for sale will be in Admiralty Form No. ADM14.

8.1 (4) In giving directions for sale the Admiralty Court may fix a time within which notice of claims against the proceeds of sale must be filed, and the time and manner in which notice of that time must be advertised.

8.2 (1) Any party with a judgment against the property or proceeds of sale may at any time after the time referred to in paragraph 8.1(4) apply to the Admiralty Court for the determination of priorities. The application notice must be served on all persons who have filed a claim against the property.

8.2 (2) Unless otherwise ordered by the Admiralty Judge, a determination of priorities may only be made by the Admiralty Judge.

8.3 Payment out of the proceeds of sale will be made only to judgment creditors and in accordance with the determination of priorities or as the Admiralty Court may otherwise order.

8.4 (1) When proceeds of sale are paid into court by the Marshal and such payment is in a foreign currency, the funds will be placed on one day call interest bearing account unless otherwise ordered by the court.

8.4 (2) An application to place foreign currency on longer term deposit unless made at the same time as the application for sale, or other prior application, may be made to the Admiralty Registrar. Notice of the placement of foreign currency in an interest bearing account shall be given to all parties interested in the fund by the party at whose instance the foreign currency is invested.

8.4 (3) Any interested party who wishes to object to the mode of investment of foreign currency paid into court may apply to the Admiralty Registrar for directions.

Limitation claims

9.1 (1) Limitation may be relied upon by way of defence to any claim.

9.1 (2) A limitation claim may be brought by counterclaim with the permission of the Admiralty Court.

9.1 (3) A limitation claim is begun by the issue of a claim form in Admiralty Form No. ADM15 ("a limitation claim form"). The limitation claim form must be accompanied by a declaration :

    (a) proving the facts upon which the Claimant relies

    (b) stating the names and addresses (if known) of all persons who to the knowledge of the Claimant have claims against him in respect of the occurrence to which the claim relates, other than named defendants.

    and sworn as an affidavit.

9.1 (4) The Claimant and at least one of the Defendants must be named in the limitation claim form, but all other Defendants may be described.

9.1 (5) The limitation claim form must be served on all named Defendants.

9.1 (6) The limitation claim form may not be served out of the jurisdiction unless:

    (a) the case falls within section 22(2)(a) to (c) of the Supreme Court Act 1981;

    (b) the Defendant has submitted to or agreed to submit to the jurisdiction of the court; or

    (c) the Admiralty Court has jurisdiction over the claim under any applicable Convention, and the court grants permission on an application in accordance with Rule 6.21.

9.1 (7) Every Defendant upon whom a limitation claim form is served must either:

    (a) within 28 days of service file a defence to the limitation claim in Admiralty Form No. ADM16A or file a notice in Admiralty Form No. ADM16 that he admits the right of the claimant to limit liability; or

    (b) if he wishes to dispute the jurisdiction of the court or to argue that the court should not exercise its jurisdiction file within 14 days of service or, if the limitation claim form is served out of the jurisdiction, within the time specified in rule 6.22, an acknowledgment of service in Admiralty Form No. ADM16B.

9.1 (8) In the event that the Defendant files an acknowledgment of service pursuant to paragraph 9.1(7)(b) he will be treated as having accepted that the court has jurisdiction to hear the limitation claim unless he makes an application under CPR Part 11 within 14 days of filing his acknowledgment of service.

9.2 (1) Where one or more named Defendants admits the right to limit, the Claimant may file in the registry an application for a restricted limitation decree in Admiralty Form No. ADM17 and the Court will issue a decree in Admiralty Form No. ADM18 limiting liability only against such named Defendants as have admitted the Claimant's right to limit liability.

9.2 (2) A restricted limitation decree may be obtained against any named Defendant failing to file a defence within the time specified for doing so.

9.2 (3) A restricted decree need not be advertised, but a copy must be served on the Defendants to whom it applies.

9.2 (4) Where the right to limit is not admitted or the Claimant seeks a general limitation decree in Admiralty Form No. ADM19, he must within 7 days of the date of the filing of the defence of the named Defendant last served or the expiry of the time for doing so, apply for an appointment before the Admiralty Registrar for a case management conference at which directions will be given for the further conduct of the proceedings.

9.3 (1) When a limitation decree is granted the Admiralty Court:

    (a) may order that any proceedings relating to any claim arising out of the occurrence be stayed;

    (b) may order the Claimant to establish a limitation fund if one has not been established or make such other arrangements for payment of claims against which liability is limited as the Court considers appropriate;

    (c) may, if the decree is a restricted limitation decree, distribute the limitation fund;

    (d) shall, if the decree is a general limitation decree, give directions as to advertisement of the decree and fix a time within which notice of claims against the fund must be filed or an application made to set aside the decree.

9.3 (2) When the Admiralty Court grants a general limitation decree the Claimant must:

    (a) advertise it in such manner and within such time as the Court shall direct;

    (b) file in the registry a declaration that the decree has been advertised in accordance with (a) and copies of the advertisements.

9.4 Any person other than a named Defendant may apply to the Admiralty Registrar within the time fixed in the decree to have a general limitation decree set aside. Any such application must be supported by a declaration proving that the person has a good faith claim against the Claimant arising out of the occurrence and sufficient grounds for contending that the Claimant is not entitled to the decree obtained, either in the amount of limitation or at all.

9.5 (1) A limitation fund may be established before or after a limitation claim has been commenced.

9.5 (2) If a limitation claim is not commenced within 75 days of the date the fund was established, the fund will lapse and all monies in court, including any interest accrued therein, will be repaid to the person making the payment into court. The lapsing of a limitation fund shall not prevent the establishment of a new fund.

9.6 (1) The Claimant may constitute a limitation fund by paying into court the sterling equivalent of the number of special drawing rights to which he claims to be entitled to limit his liability under the Merchant Shipping Act 1995 together with interest thereon from the date of the occurrence giving rise to his liability to the date of payment into court.

9.6 (2) Where the Claimant does not know the sterling equivalent of the said number of special drawing rights on the date of payment into court he may calculate the same on the basis of the latest available published sterling equivalent of a special drawing right as fixed by the International Monetary Fund, and in the event of the sterling equivalent of a special drawing right on the date of payment into court under paragraph (1) being different from that used for calculating the amount of that payment into court the Claimant may–

    (a) make up any deficiency by making a further payment into court which, if made within 14 days after the payment into court under paragraph (1), shall be treated, except for the purposes of the rules relating to the accrual of interest on money paid into court, as if it has been made on the date of that payment into court, or

    (b) apply to the Admiralty Court for payment out of any excess amount (together with any interest accrued thereon) paid into court under paragraph (1).

9.6 (3) An application under paragraph 9.6(2) (b) may be made without notice to any party and must be supported by evidence to the satisfaction of the Court proving the sterling equivalent of the appropriate number of special drawing rights on the date of payment into court.

9.6 (4) On making any payment into court under this rule, the Claimant shall give notice thereof in writing to every named Defendant, specifying the date of payment in, the amount paid in, the amount of interest included therein, the rate of such interest, and the period to which it relates.

The Claimant shall also give notice in writing to every Defendant of any excess amount (and any interest thereon) paid out to him under paragraph 9.6(2)(b).

9.6 (5) Money paid into court under this paragraph shall not be paid out except under an order of the court.

9.7 (1) A claim against the fund must be in Admiralty Form No. ADM20.

9.7 (2) No later than the time fixed in the decree for filing claims, each of the Defendants must file and serve his statement of case on the limiting party and on all other Defendants. The statement of case must contain the particulars of the Defendant's claim. Any Defendant unable to do so must file a declaration in Admiralty Form No. ADM21 stating the reason for his inability. The declaration must be sworn as an affidavit.

9.7 (3) Within 7 days of the time for filing claims or declarations, the Admiralty Registrar will fix a date for a case management conference at which directions will be given for the further conduct of the proceedings.

References to the Admiralty Registrar

10 (1) The Admiralty Court may at any stage in the claim refer any question or issue for determination by the Admiralty Registrar (a "reference").

10 (2) Unless otherwise ordered, where a reference has been ordered:

(a) The Claimant must file and serve particulars of claim on all other parties within 14 days of the date of the order.

(b) Any party opposing the claim must file a defence to the claim within 14 days of service of the particulars of claim upon him.

10 (3) Within 7 days of the filing of the defence, the Claimant must apply for an appointment before the Admiralty Registrar for a case management conference at which directions will be given for the further conduct of the proceedings.

10 (4) Any decision of the Admiralty Registrar on the hearing of the reference may be appealed to the Admiralty Judge, by Notice in Admiralty Form No. ADM22 filed within 28 days of the decision on the reference appealed against.

Inspection of ship etc.

11 The Admiralty Court may, on the application of any interested persons or on its own initiative, make an order for the inspection by any person of any ship or other property, whether real or personal, the inspection of which may be necessary or desirable for the purpose of obtaining full information or evidence in connection with any issue in a claim or proposed claim whether in rem or in personam.

Agreement of solicitors to be made an order of the court

12 Subject to any restrictions contained in other Rules, any agreement in writing between the solicitors of the parties to any Admiralty claim dated and signed by those solicitors may, if the Admiralty Registrar thinks it reasonable, be filed in the Admiralty and Commercial Registry and the agreement shall then become an order of the Admiralty Court.

Undertakings

13 (1) Where in this practice direction any undertaking to the Marshal is required it shall be given in writing and to his satisfaction or in accordance with such other arrangements as he may require.

13 (2) Where any party is dissatisfied with a direction given by the Marshal in this respect he may apply to the Admiralty Registrar for a ruling.

Stay of proceedings

14　Where the Admiralty Court orders a stay of any claim in rem, any property under arrest in the action shall remain under arrest and any security representing the res shall remain in force unless the Court otherwise orders.

Provisions for the appointment of examiners in Admiralty etc.

15　(1)　The Admiralty Court may make an order with the consent of the parties for a deposition to be taken as if before an examiner but without the examiner actually being appointed or being present.

15　(2)　Where an order is made under paragraph 15(1) provision may be made for any consequential matters, but in the absence of such provision the following provisions shall apply:

　　(a)　the party whose witness is to be examined shall provide a shorthand writer to take down the evidence of the witness;

　　(b)　any representative, being counsel or solicitor, of either of the parties shall have authority to administer the oath to the witness;

　　(c)　the shorthand writer need not be sworn but shall certify in writing as correct a transcript of his notes of the evidence and deliver it to the solicitor for the party whose witness was examined, and that solicitor must file it in the Registry;

　　(d)　unless the parties otherwise agree or the court otherwise orders, the transcript or a copy of it, shall be made available to the persons who acted as advocates at the examination before it is filed, and if any of those persons is of the opinion that the transcript does not accurately record the evidence he shall make a certificate specifying the corrections which in his opinion should be made and that certificate must be filed with the transcript.

15　(3)　In a collision claim no order shall be made under CPR Part 34 authorising the examination of a witness before the Preliminary Acts have been filed, unless the Admiralty Court considers that there are special reasons for doing so.

15　(4)　The Lord Chief Justice may appoint such number of barristers or solicitors as he thinks fit to act as examiners of the Admiralty Court in connection with Admiralty claims, and may revoke any such appointment.

The Commercial Court Guide

16.1 The practice of the Commercial Court set out in the Commercial Court Guide should, except where inapplicable, be followed in Admiralty proceedings subject to the provisions of this or any other Admiralty practice direction and to any order that may be made in an individual case.

16.2 Part D of the Commercial Court Guide shall be modified as follows:

　　(a)　D3 shall not apply;

　　(b)　In the Admiralty Court the Case Management Information Sheet should be in the form of Appendix 6 to the Commercial Court Guide but also include the following additional question:

　　　　(20)a.　Do any of the issues contained in the List of Issues involve questions of navigation or other particular matters of an essentially Admiralty nature which require the trial to be before the Admiralty Judge or is there any other reason why you consider trial before the Admiralty Judge to be necessary?

　　　　b.　Are you prepared to have the case tried before a deputy nominated by the Admiralty Judge who has experience of such questions or matters?

　　　　c.　Do you consider that the court should sit with nautical or other Assessors? Are you intending to ask that the court sit with one or more Assessors who is not a Trinity Master? If so please state the reasons for such application.

16.3 One significant area of difference between practice in the Commercial Court and practice in the Admiralty Court is that in the Admiralty Court many interlocutory applications are normally heard by the Admiralty Registrar and this practice will continue, save as specifically mentioned elsewhere in this practice direction.

Use of fax when Registry is closed

17.1 When the Registry is closed (and only when it is closed) and Admiralty claim form may be issued on the following designated fax machine: 0171-936 6667 and only on that machine.

17.2 The procedure to be followed is set out in paragraph B3.11 and Appendix 3 of the Commercial Court Guide. 17.3(1) When the Registry is closed (and only when it is closed) a notice requesting a caveat against release may be filed on the following designated fax machine: 0171-936 6056 and only on that machine. This machine is manned 24 hours a day by court security staff (telephone 0171-936 6000). The notice requesting the caveat should be transmitted with a note in the following form for ease of identification by security staff:

> **"Caveat against release**
> Please find notice requesting caveat against release of the ... (name ship/ identify cargo) ... for filing in the Admiralty Court and Commercial Registry."

17.3(2) The notice must be in Admiralty Form No. ADM11 and signed by a solicitor acting on behalf of the intending caveator.

17.4(1) Subject to the provisions of paragraph 17.4(3) below, the filing of the notice takes place when the fax is recorded as having been received.

17.4(2) When the Registry is next open to the public, the filing solicitor or his agent shall attend and deliver to the Registry the document which was transmitted by fax together with the transmission report. Upon satisfying himself that the document delivered fully accords with the document received by the Registry, the court office shall stamp the document delivered with the time and date at which the notice was received, enter the same in the caveat book and retain the same with the faxed copy.

17.4(3) Unless otherwise ordered by the court, the stamped notice shall be conclusive proof that the notice was filed at the time and on the date stated.

17.4(4) If the filing solicitor does not comply with the foregoing procedure, or if the notice is not stamped, the notice shall be deemed never to have been filed.

Out of hours business (Admiralty Marshal)

17.5(1) This paragraph makes provision for release from arrest when the Registry is closed: see paragraph 6.6(2).

(2) An application for release under paragraph 6.6(1)(c) or (d) may when the Registry is closed be made in, and only in, the following manner:

    (a) The solicitor for the arrestor or other party applying must telephone the security staff at the Royal Courts of Justice (020 7936 6260) and ask to be contacted by the Admiralty Marshal, who will then respond as soon as practicably possible.

    (b) Upon being contacted by the Admiralty Marshal the solicitor must give oral instructions for the release and an oral undertaking to pay the fees and expenses of the Admiralty Marshal as required in Form No. ADM 12. The arrestor or other party applying must then send a written request and undertaking on Form No. ADM 12 by fax to a number given the Admiralty Marshal.

    (c) The solicitor must provide written consent to the release from all caveators (and from the arrestor if the arrestor is not the party applying) by sending such by fax to the number supplied by the Admiralty Marshal.

    (d) Upon the Admiralty Marshal being satisfied that no caveats against release are in force, or that all caveators, and if necessary the arrestor, have given their written consent to the release, the Admiralty Marshal shall effect the release as soon as practicable.

(3) Practitioners should note that the Admiralty Marshal is not formally on call and therefore at times may not be available to assist. Similarly the practicalities of releasing a ship in some localities may involve the services of others who may not be available outside normal working hours.

(4) This service is offered to practitioners for use during reasonable hours and on the basis that if the Admiralty Marshal is available and can be contacted he will use his best endeavours to effect instructions to release but without guarantee as to their success.

Use of postal facilities in the Registry

18.1 Applications together with the requisite documents may be posted to:

> The Admiralty and Commercial Registry
> Room E200
> Royal Courts of Justice
> Strand
> London
> WC2A 2LL

18.2 In addition to the classes of business for which the use of postal facilities is permitted by the CPR or the Commercial Court Guide, the filing of the following classes of documents shall also be permitted in Admiralty matters:

(1) Requests for notices of caveats

(2) Preliminary Acts

(3) Claims in References

(4) Agreements between solicitors under paragraph 12 of this practice direction.

18.3 Documents sent by post for filing must be accompanied by two copies of a list of the documents sent and an envelope properly addressed to the sender.

18.4 On receipt of the documents in the Registry, the court officer will, if the circumstances are such that had the documents been presented personally they would have been filed, cause them to be filed and will, by post, notify the sender that this has been done. If the documents would not have been accepted if presented personally the court officer will not file them but will retain them in the Registry for collection by the sender and will, by post, so inform the sender.

18.5 When documents received through the post are filed by the court officer they will be sealed and entered as filed on the date on which they were received in the Registry.

Drawing up of orders

19 All orders made in Admiralty proceedings will be drawn up by the parties unless otherwise ordered by the court.

Assessors

20.1 The usual practice in the Admiralty Court is to sit with Assessors when hearing collision claims or other cases involving issues of navigation or seamanship and the parties will not normally be permitted to call expert witnesses on matters of navigation or seamanship where the court sits with Assessors. The Assessors will usually be Trinity Masters. Parties should indicate at the Case Management Conference whether they consider that the case is suitable for Assessors and whether Assessors other than Trinity Masters would be appropriate.

20.2 Provision is made in CPR 35.15 for assessor's remuneration. The usual practice is for the court to seek an undertaking from the claimant (or appellant) to pay the remuneration on demand after the case has concluded.

PRACTICE DIRECTION – ARBITRATIONS
THIS PRACTICE DIRECTION SUPPLEMENTS CPR PART 49 AND REPLACES, WITH MODIFICATIONS, ORDER 73 OF THE RULES OF THE SUPREME COURT

PART I

The overriding objective

1. This Part of this practice direction is founded on the general principles in section 1 of the Arbitration Act and shall be construed accordingly.

Meaning of arbitration application

2.1 Subject to paragraph 22.2, "arbitration application" means the following

(1) an application to the court under the Arbitration Act;

(2) proceedings to determine –

    (a) whether there is a valid arbitration agreement;

    (b) whether an arbitration tribunal is properly constituted;

    (c) what matters have been submitted to arbitration in accordance with an arbitration agreement;

(3) proceedings to declare that an award made by an arbitral tribunal is not binding on a party;

(4) any other application affecting arbitration proceedings (whether instituted or anticipated) or to construe or affecting an arbitration agreement.

2.2 In this Part, an arbitration application does not include proceedings to enforce an award –

(1) to which Part III applies; or

(2) by a claim on the award.

Interpretation

3. In this Part –

" applicant" means the party making an arbitration application and references to respondent shall be construed accordingly;

"the Arbitration Act" means the Arbitration Act 1996 and any expressions used in this Part and in Part I of the Arbitration Act have the same meanings in this Part as they have in that Part of the Arbitration Act.

"arbitration claim form" means the arbitration claim form by the issue of which an arbitration application is begun.

Form and content of arbitration claim form

4.1 An arbitration claim form must be in the practice form No. 8A

4.2 Every arbitration claim form must –

(1) include a concise statement of

    (a) the remedy claimed, and

    (b) (where appropriate) the questions on which the applicant seeks the determination or direction of the Court;

(2) give details of any arbitration award that is challenged by the applicant, showing the grounds for any such challenge;

(3) where the applicant claims an order for costs, identify the respondent against whom the claim is made,

(4) (where appropriate) specify the section of the Arbitration Act under which the application is brought; and

(5) show that any statutory requirements have been satisfied including those set out, by way of example, in the Table Below.

Application made	Statutory requirements
section 9 (stay of legal proceedings)	see section 9 (3)
section 12 (extensions of time for beginning arbitral proceedings)	see section 12 (2)
section 18 (failure of appointment procedure)	see section 18 (2)
section 21 (umpires)	see section 21 (5)
section 24 (removal of arbitrators)	see section 24 (2)
section 32 (preliminary point of jurisdiction)	see section 32 (3)
section 42 (enforcement of peremptory orders)	see section 42 (3)
section 44 (powers in support of arbitral proceedings)	see section 44 (4), (5)
section 45 (preliminary point of law)	see section 45 (3)
section 50 (extension of time for making award)	see section 50 (2)
section 56 (power to withhold award)	see section 56 (4)
sections 67, 68 (challenging the award)	see section 70 (2), (3)
section 69 (appeal on point of law)	see sections 69 (2), (4), 70(2), (3)
section 77 (service of documents)	see section 77(3)

4.3 The arbitration claim form must also state

(1) whether it is made on notice or without notice and, if made on notice, must give the names and addresses of the persons on whom it is to be served, stating their role in the arbitration and whether they are made respondents to the application;

(2) whether (having regard to paragraph 15) the application will be heard by a judge sitting in public or in private; and

(3) the date and time when the application will be heard or that such date has not yet been fixed.

4.4 Every arbitration claim form shall be indorsed with the applicant's address for service in accordance with CPR Rule 6.5(2)

Issue of arbitration claim form

5.1 These paragraphs (5.1 to 5.7) are is to be read with the provisions of the High Court and County Courts (Allocation of Arbitration Proceedings) Order 1996 which allocates proceedings under the Arbitration Act to the High Court and the county courts and specifies proceedings which may be commenced or taken only in the High Court or in a county court.

5.2 These paragraphs (5.1 to 5.7) do not apply to applications under section 9 of the Arbitration Act to stay legal proceedings.

5.3 Subject to paragraphs 5.1 and 5.2 above, an arbitration claim form by which proceedings are commenced may be issued:

(1) out of the Admiralty and Commercial Registry in the Royal Courts of Justice, in which case the arbitration application will be entered into the commercial list;

(2) out of a district registry where a Mercantile Court has been established, in which case the arbitration application will be entered into the list of that Mercantile Court; or

(3) out of the office of the Central London County Court, in which case the arbitration application will be entered into the Business List of that court.

(Attention is drawn to the provisions relating to the commencement of proceedings contained in the Commercial Court Practice Direction and the Mercantile Court and Business Lists Practice Direction which supplement CPR Part 49).

5.4 Except where an arbitration claim form is issued out of the Admiralty and Commercial Registry, the Judge in charge of the list into which the arbitration application has been entered shall

(1) as soon as practicable after the issue of the arbitration claim form, and

(2) in consultation with the Judge in charge of the commercial list,

consider whether the application should be transferred to the Commercial Court or to any another list.

5.5 Where an arbitration claim form is issued out of the Admiralty and Commercial Registry, the Judge in charge of the commercial list may at any time after the issue of the arbitration claim form transfer the application to another list, court or Division of the High Court to which he has power to transfer proceedings.

5.6 In considering whether to transfer an arbitration application, the Judges referred to in paragraphs 5.4 and 5.5 shall have regard to the criteria specified in article 5 (4) of the High Court and County Courts (Allocation of Arbitration Proceedings) Order 1996 and the application shall be transferred if those Judges so decide.

5.7 In this practice direction "Judge in charge of the list" means:

(a) in relation to the commercial list, a judge of the Commercial Court;

(b) in relation to the list of a Mercantile Court, a Circuit mercantile judge of that court; and

(c) in relation to the Business List in the Central London County Court, a Circuit Judge authorised to deal with cases in that list,

but nothing in this paragraph shall be construed as preventing the powers of a judge of the Commercial Court from being exercised by any judge of the High Court.

Stay of legal proceedings

6.1 An application notice by which an application under section 9 of the Arbitration Act to stay legal proceedings is made shall be served –

(1) in accordance with CPR Rule 6.5 on the party bringing the relevant legal proceedings and on any other party to those proceedings who has given an address for service; and

(2) on any party to those legal proceedings who has not given an address for service, by sending to him (whether or not he is within the jurisdiction) at his last known address or at a place where it is likely to come to his attention, a copy of the application notice for his information.

6.2 Where a question arises as to whether an arbitration agreement has been concluded or as to whether the dispute which is the subject-matter of the proceedings falls within the terms of such an agreement, the Court may determine that question or give directions for its determination, in which case it may order the proceedings to be stayed pending the determination of that question.

Service of arbitration claim form

7.1 Subject to paragraphs 7.2 and 7.4 below and to paragraphs 6.1 and 8.1 to 8.4, an arbitration claim form shall be served in accordance with CPR Part 6.

7.2 Where the Court is satisfied on an application made without notice that

(1) arbitral proceedings are taking place, or an arbitration award has been made, within the jurisdiction; and

(2) an arbitration application is being made in connection with those arbitral proceedings or being brought to challenge the award or to appeal on a question of law arising out of the award; and

(3) the respondent to the arbitration application (not being an individual residing or carrying on business within the jurisdiction or a body corporate having a registered office or a place of business within the jurisdiction)

    (a) is or was represented in the arbitral proceedings by a solicitor or other agent within the jurisdiction who was authorised to receive service of any notice or other document served for the purposes of those proceedings; and

    (b) has not (at the time when the arbitration application is made) determined the authority of that solicitor or agent,

the Court may authorise service of the arbitration claim form to be effected on the solicitor or agent instead of the respondent.

7.3 An order made under paragraph 7.2 must limit a time within which the respondent must acknowledge service and a copy of the order and of the arbitration claim form must be sent by post to the respondent at his address out of the jurisdiction.

7.4 Where an applicant has made an arbitration application (the first arbitration application) and a subsequent arbitration application arising out of the same arbitration or arbitration agreement is made by a party to the first arbitration application (other than the applicant), that party's arbitration claim form may be served in accordance with CPR rule 6.5 or may be served on the applicant at his address for service given in his arbitration claim form, and on any other party to the first arbitration application at the address for service given in that party's acknowledgment of service in the first arbitration application, and on any further arbitration application the same provisions as to service will apply.

7.5 For the purposes of service, an arbitration claim form is valid in the first instance-

    (1) where service is to be effected out of the jurisdiction, for such period as the Court may fix;

    (2) in any other case, for one month, beginning with the date of its issue.

Service out of the jurisdiction

8.1 The Court may give permission to serve an arbitration claim form out of the jurisdiction if the arbitration application falls into one of the categories mentioned in the following table and satisfies the conditions specified.

Nature of application	Conditions to be satisfied
1. The applicant seeks to challenge, or to appeal to the Court on a question of law arising out of, an arbitration award.	Award must have been made in England & Wales. Section 53 of the Arbitration Act shall apply for determining the place where award is treated as made.
2. The application is for an order under section 44 of the Arbitration Act (Court powers exercisable in support of arbitral proceedings). Where the application is for an interim remedy in support of arbitral proceedings which are taking (or will take) place outside England and Wales, the Court may give permission for service out of the jurisdiction notwithstanding that no other remedy is sought.	None
3. The applicant seeks some other remedy or requires a question to be determined by the court, affecting an arbitration (whether pending or anticipated), an arbitration agreement or an arbitration award.	The seat of the arbitration is or will be in England & Wales or the conditions in Section 2(4) of the Arbitration Act are satisfied.

8.2 An application for the grant of permission under paragraph 8.1 must be supported by an affidavit or witness statement –

    (1) stating, or, if the grounds were set out in the application notice, confirming the grounds on which the application is made; and

(2) showing in what place or country the person to be served is, or probably may be found, and no such permission shall be granted unless it shall be made sufficiently to appear to the Court that the case is a proper one for service out of the jurisdiction under this paragraph.

8.3 Rules 6.24 to 6.27 shall apply to the service of an arbitration claim form under this paragraph as they apply to the service of other claim forms.

8.4 Any order made on an arbitration application may be served out of the jurisdiction with the permission of the court.

Evidence in support of arbitration application

9.1 The applicant shall file an affidavit or witness statement in support of the arbitration application which sets out the evidence on which he intends to rely and a copy of every affidavit or witness statement so filed must be served with the arbitration claim form.

9.2 Where an arbitration application is made with the written agreement of all the other parties to the arbitral proceedings or with the permission of the arbitral tribunal, the affidavit or witness statement in support must

(1) give details of the agreement or, as the case may be, permission; and

(2) exhibit copies of any document which evidences that agreement or permission.

Requirements as to notice

10.1 Where the Arbitration Act requires that an application to the Court is to be made upon notice to other parties notice shall be given by making those parties respondents to the application and serving on them the arbitration claim form and any affidavit or witness statement in support.

10.2 Where an arbitration application is made under section 24 , 28 or 56 of the Arbitration Act, the arbitrators or, in the case of an application under section 24, the arbitrator concerned shall be made respondents to the application and notice shall be given by serving on them the arbitration claim form and any affidavit or witness statement in support.

10.3 In cases where paragraph 10.2 does not apply, an applicant shall be taken as having complied with any requirement to give notice to the arbitrator if he sends a copy of the arbitration claim form to the arbitrator for his information at his last known address with a copy of any affidavit or witness statement in support.

10.4 This paragraph does not apply to applications under section 9 of the Arbitration Act to stay legal proceedings.

Acknowledgment of service

11.1 Service of an arbitration claim form may be acknowledged by completing an acknowledgment of service in Form No. 15A in accordance with CPR Rule 8.3.

11.2 A respondent who –

(1) fails to acknowledge service within the time limited for so doing; or

(2) having indicated on his acknowledgment of service that he does not intend to contest the arbitration application, then wishes to do so, shall not be entitled to contest the application without the permission of the Court.

11.3 The Court will not give notice of the date on which an arbitration application will be heard to a respondent who has failed to acknowledge service.

11.4 The failure of a respondent to give notice of intention to contest the arbitration application or to acknowledge service shall not affect the applicant's duty to satisfy the Court that the order applied for should be made.

11.5 This paragraph does not apply to –

(1) applications under section 9 of the Arbitration Act to stay legal proceedings; or

(2) subsequent arbitration applications.

Acknowledgment of service, etc, by arbitrator

12.1 An arbitrator who is sent a copy of an arbitration claim form for his information may make

(1) a request (without notice to any party) to be made a respondent; or

(2) representations to the Court under this rule,

and, where an arbitrator is ordered to be made a respondent, he shall acknowledge service within 14 days of the making of that order.

12.2 An arbitrator who wishes to make representations to the Court under this rule may file an affidavit or witness statement or make representations in writing to the Court.

12.3 The arbitrator shall as soon as is practicable send a copy of any document filed or made under paragraph 12.2 to all the parties to the arbitration application.

12.4 Nothing in this paragraph shall require the Court to admit a document filed or made under sub-paragraph (2) and the weight to be given to any such document shall be a matter for the Court.

Automatic directions

13.1 Unless the Court otherwise directs, the following directions shall take effect automatically.

13.2 A respondent who wishes to put evidence before the Court in response to any affidavit or witness statement filed in support of an arbitration application shall serve his affidavit or witness statement on the applicant before the expiration of 21 days after the time limited for acknowledging service or, in a case where a respondent is not required to file an acknowledgment of service, within 21 days after service of the arbitration claim form.

13.3 An applicant who wishes to put evidence before the court in response to an affidavit or witness statement filed under paragraph 13.2 shall serve his affidavit or witness statement on the respondent within 7 days after service of the respondent's evidence.

13.4 Where a date has not been fixed for the hearing of the arbitration application, the applicant shall, and the respondent may, not later than 14 days after the expiration of the time limit specified in paragraph 13.2, apply to the Court for such a date to be fixed.

13.5 Agreed indexed and paginated bundles of all the evidence and other documents to be used at the hearing shall be prepared by the applicant (with the co-operation of the respondent).

13.6 Not later than 5 clear days before the hearing date estimates for the length of the hearing shall be lodged with the Court together with a complete set of the documents to be used.

13.7 Not later than 2 days before the hearing date the applicant shall lodge with the Court –

(1) a chronology of the relevant events cross-referenced to the bundle of documents;

(2) (where necessary) a list of the persons involved;

(3) a skeleton argument which lists succinctly–

   (a) the issues which arise for decision,

   (b) the grounds of relief (or opposing relief) to be relied upon,

   (c) the submissions of fact to be made with the references to the evidence, and

   (d) the submissions of law with references to the relevant authorities,

and shall send copies to the respondent.

13.8 Not later than the day before the hearing date the respondent shall lodge with the Court a skeleton argument which lists succinctly–

(1) the issues which arise for decision,

(2) the grounds of relief (or opposing relief) to be relied upon,

(3) the submissions of fact to be made with the references to the evidence, and

(4) the submissions of law with references to the relevant authorities, and shall send a copy to the applicant.

Directions by the court

14.1 The rules of the CPR relating to allocation questionnaires and track allocation do not apply to arbitration applications, and the Court may give such directions as to the conduct of the arbitration application as it thinks best adapted to secure the just, expeditious and economical disposal thereof.

14.2 Where the Court considers that there is or may be a dispute as to fact and that the just, expeditious and economical disposal of the application can best be secured by hearing the application on oral evidence or mainly on oral evidence, it may, if it thinks fit, order that no further evidence shall be filed and that the application shall be heard on oral evidence or partly on oral evidence and partly on written evidence, with or without cross-examination of any of the witnesses, as it may direct.

14.3 The Court may give directions as to the filing of evidence and as to the attendance of witnesses for cross-examination and any other directions which it could give in proceedings begun by claim form.

14.4 If the applicant makes default in complying with these provisions or with any order or direction of the Court as to the conduct of the application, or if the Court is satisfied that the applicant is not prosecuting the application with due despatch, the Court may order the application to be dismissed or may make such other order as may be just.

14.5 If the respondent fails to comply with these provisions or with any order or direction given by the Court in relation to the evidence to be relied on, or the submission to be made by that respondent, the Court may, if it thinks fit, hear and determine the application without having regard to that evidence or those submissions.

14.6 Unless the Court orders otherwise, affidavits and witness statements may contain hearsay.

Hearing of applications: public or private

15.1 The Court may order that any arbitration application be heard either in public or in private.

15.2 Subject to any order made under paragraph 15.1 and paragraph 15.3, all arbitration applications shall be heard in private.

15.3 Subject to any order made under paragraph 15.1, the determination of a preliminary point of law under section 45 of the Arbitration Act, or an appeal under section 69 on a question of law arising out of an award shall be heard in public.

15.4 Paragraph 15.3 shall not apply to –

    (1)   the preliminary question whether the Court is satisfied of the matters set out in section 45 (2)(b); or

    (2)   an application for permission to appeal under section 69 (2)(b).

Securing the attendance of witnesses

16.1 A party to arbitral proceedings being conducted in England and Wales who wishes to rely on section 43 of the Arbitration Act to secure the attendance of a witness may apply for a witness summons in accordance with Part 34 of the CPR to the Admiralty and Commercial Registry or, if the attendance of the witness is required within the district of a district registry, at that registry at the option of the party.

16.2 A witness summons shall not be issued until the applicant files an affidavit or witness statement which shows that the application is made with the permission of the tribunal or the agreement of the other parties.

Securing for costs

17.1 Subject to section 70 (6) of the Arbitration Act, the Court may order any applicant (including an applicant who has been granted permission to appeal) to provide security for costs of any arbitration application.

Powers exercisable in support of arbitral proceedings

18.1 Where the case is one of urgency, an application for an order under section 44 of the Arbitration Act (Court powers exercisable in support of arbitral proceedings) may be made without notice on affidavit or witness statement (before the issue of an arbitration claim form) and the affidavit or witness statement shall (in addition to dealing with the matters required to be dealt with by paragraphs 9.1 & 9.2) state the reasons –

    (1)   why the application is made without notice; and

    (2)   (where the application is made without the permission of the arbitral tribunal or the agreement of the other parties to the arbitral proceedings) why it was not practicable to obtain that permission or agreement; and

    (3)   why the witness believes that the condition in section 44 (5) is satisfied.

18.2 Where the case is not one of urgency, an application for an order under section 44 of the Arbitration Act shall be made on notice and the affidavit or witness statement in support shall (in addition to dealing with the matters required to be dealt with by paragraph 9 and paragraph 18.1(3) above) state that the application is made with the permission of the tribunal or the written agreement of the other parties to the arbitral proceedings.

18.3 Where an application for an order under section 44 of the Arbitration Act is made before the issue of an arbitration claim form, any order made by the Court may be granted on terms providing for the issue of an arbitration claim form and such other terms, if any, as the court thinks fit.

Applications under sections 32 and 45 of the Arbitration Act

19.1 This paragraph applies to the following arbitration applications:

(1) applications for the determination of a question as to the substantive jurisdiction of the arbitral tribunal under section 32 of the Arbitration Act; and

(2) applications for the determination of a preliminary point of law under section 45 of the Arbitration Act.

19.2 Where an application is made without the agreement in writing of all the other parties to the arbitral proceedings but with the permission of the arbitral tribunal, the affidavits or witness statements filed by the parties shall set out any evidence relied on by the parties in support of their contention that the Court should, or should not, consider the application.

19.3 As soon as practicable after the written evidence is filed, the Court shall decide whether or not it should consider the application and, unless the Court otherwise directs, shall so decide without a hearing.

Applications for permission to appeal

20.1 Where the applicant seeks permission to appeal to the Court on a question of law arising out of an arbitration award, the arbitration claim form shall identify the question of law and state the grounds on which the applicant alleges that permission should be granted.

20.2 The affidavit or witness statement in support of the application shall set out any evidence relied on by the applicant for the purpose of satisfying the Court of the matters mentioned in section 69 (3) of the Arbitration Act and for satisfying the Court that permission should be granted.

20.3 The affidavit or witness statement filed by the respondent to the application shall –

(1) state the grounds on which the respondent opposes the grant of permission;

(2) set out any evidence relied on by him relating to the matters mentioned in section 69 (3) of the Arbitration Act, and

(3) specify whether the respondent wishes to contend that the award should be upheld for reasons not expressed (or not fully expressed) in the award and, if so, state those reasons.

20.4 As soon as practicable after the filing of the affidavits and witness statements, the Court shall determine the application for permission in accordance with section 69 (5) of the Arbitration Act.

20.5 Where permission is granted, a date shall be fixed for the hearing of the appeal.

Extension of time: applications under section 12

21.1 An application for an order under section 12 of the Arbitration Act may include as an alternative an application for a declaration that such an order is not needed.

Time limit for challenges to or appeals from awards

22.1 An applicant shall not be taken as having complied with the time limit of 28 days referred to in section 70 (3) of the Arbitration Act unless the arbitration claim form has been issued, and all the affidavits or witness statements in support have been filed, by the expiry of that time limit.

22.2 An applicant who wishes –

(1) to challenge an award under section 67 or 68 of the Arbitration Act; or

(2) to appeal under section 69 on a question of law arising out of an award, may, where the time limit of 28 days has not yet expired, apply without notice on affidavit or witness statement for an order extending that time limit.

22.3 In any case where an applicant seeks to challenge an award under section 67 or 68 of the Arbitration Act or to appeal under section 69 after the time limit of 28 days has already expired, the following provisions shall apply:

(1) the applicant must state in his arbitration claim form the grounds why an order extending time should be made and his affidavit or witness statement in support shall set out the evidence on which he relies;

(2) a respondent who wishes to oppose the making of an order extending time shall file an affidavit or witness statement within 7 days after service of the applicant's evidence, and

(3) the Court shall decide whether or not to extend time without a hearing unless it appears to the Court that a hearing is required, and, where the Court makes an order extending the time limit, the respondent shall file his affidavit or witness statement in response to the arbitration application 21 days after the making of the order.

PART II

Application of this Part

23.1 This Part of this practice direction applies to any application to the Court to which the old law applies and, in this rule, "the old law" means the enactments specified in section 107 of the Arbitration Act 1996 as they stood before their amendment or repeal by that Act.

23.2 This Part does not apply to proceedings to enforce an award –

(1) to which Part III of this practice direction applies; or

(2) by a claim based on the award.

23.3 Reference should be made to the other provisions of the CPR (except Parts I and III of this Part) for the procedure for any application not expressly provided for in this Part.

Matters for a judge in court

24.1 Every application to the Court –

(1) to remit an award under section 22 of the Arbitration Act 1950 ; or

(2) to remove an arbitrator or umpire under section 23 (1) of that Act; or

(3) to set aside an award under section 23 (2) of that Act, or

(4) to determine, under section 2 (1) of the Arbitration Act 1979, any question of law arising in the course of a reference,

must be made by the issue of an arbitration claim form under CPR rule 8.6 (a Part 8 claim form).

24.2 Any appeal to the High Court under section 1 (2) of the Arbitration Act 1979 shall be made by the issue of a Part 8 claim form.

24.3 An application for a declaration that an award made by an arbitrator or umpire is not binding on a party to the award on the ground that it was made without jurisdiction may be made by the issue of a Part 8 claim form, but the foregoing provision shall not be taken as affecting the judge's power to refuse to make such a declaration in proceedings begun otherwise.

Matters for judge in chambers or master

25.1 Subject to the foregoing provisions of this Order and the provisions of this rule, the jurisdiction of the High Court or a judge thereof under the Arbitration Act 1950 and the jurisdiction of the High Court under the Arbitration Act 1975 and the Arbitration Act 1979 may be exercised by a judge in chambers, a master or the Admiralty Registrar.

25.2 Any application

(1) for permission to appeal under section 1 (2) of the Arbitration Act 1979, or

(2) under section 1 (5) of that Act (including any application for permission), or

(3) under section 5 of that Act,

shall be made to a judge in chambers.

25.3 Any application to which this rule applies shall, where there are existing court proceedings be made by the issue of an application notice in those proceedings, and in any other case a Part 8 claim form.

25.4 Where an application is made under section 1 (5) of the Arbitration Act 1979 (including any application for permission), the Part 8 claim form or the application notice as the case may be, must be served on the arbitrator or umpire and on any other party to the reference.

Application in district registries

26.1 An application under section 12 (4) of the Arbitration Act 1950 for an order that a witness summons shall issue to compel the attendance before an arbitrator or umpire of a witness may, if the attendance of the witness is required within the district of a district registry, be made at that registry, instead of at the Admiralty and Commercial Registry, at the option of the applicant.

Time limits and other special provisions as to appeals and applications under the Arbitration Acts

27.1 An application to the Court –

   (1) to remit an award under section 22 of the Arbitration Act 1950; or

   (2) to set aside an award under section 23 (2) of that Act or otherwise, or

   (3) to direct an arbitrator or umpire to state the reasons for an award under section 1 (5) of the Arbitration Act 1979,

   must be made, and the Part 8 claim form or application notice, as the case may be, must be served, within 21 days after the award has been made and published to the parties.

27.2 In the case of an appeal to the Court under section 1 (2) of the Arbitration Act 1979, the application for permission to appeal, where permission is required, and the Part 8 claim form must be served and the appeal entered, within 21 days after the award has been made and published to the parties. Provided that, where reasons material to the appeal are given on a date subsequent to the publication of the award, the period of 21 days shall run from the date on which the reasons are given.

27.3 An application, under section 2 (1) of the Arbitration Act 1979, to determine any question of law arising in the course of a reference, must be made, and the Part 8 claim form served, within 14 days after the arbitrator or umpire has consented to the application being made, or the other parties have so consented.

27.4 For the purpose of paragraph 27.3 the consent must be given in writing.

27.5 In the case of every appeal or application to which this paragraph applies, the Part 8 claim form or the application notice, as the case may be, must state the grounds of the appeal or application and, where the appeal or application is founded on evidence by affidavit or witness statement, or is made with the consent of the arbitrator or umpire or of the other parties, a copy of every affidavit or witness statement intended to be used, or, as the case may be, of every consent given in writing, must be served with the Part 8 claim form or application notice.

27.6 Without prejudice to sub-paragraph (5), in an appeal under section 1 (2) of the Arbitration Act 1979 the statement of the grounds of the appeal shall specify the relevant parts of the award and reasons, or the relevant parts thereof, shall be lodged with the court and served with the Part 8 claim form.

27.7 In an application for permission to appeal under section 1 (2) of the Arbitration Act 1979, any affidavit or witness statement verifying the facts in support of a contention that the question of law concerns a term of a contract or an event which is not a one-off term or event must be filed with the court and served with the Part 8 claim form.

27.8 Any affidavit or witness statement in reply to written evidence under sub-paragraph (7) shall be filed with the court and served on the applicant not less than two clear days before the hearing of the application.

27.9 A respondent to an application for permission to appeal under section 1 (2) of the Arbitration Act 1979 who desires to contend that the award should be upheld on grounds not expressed or fully expressed in the award and reasons shall not less than two clear days before the hearing of the application file with the court and serve on the applicant a notice specifying the grounds of his contention.

Applications and appeals to be heard by commercial judges

28.1 Any matter which is required, by paragraph 24 or 25, to be heard by a judge, shall be heard by a judge of the Commercial Court unless any such judge otherwise directs.

28.2 Nothing in the foregoing sub-paragraph shall be construed as preventing the powers of a judge of the Commercial Court from being exercised by any judge of the High Court.

Service out of the jurisdiction

29.1 Subject to paragraph 29.2,

(1) any Part 8 claim form whereby an application under the Arbitration Act 1950 or the Arbitration Act 1979, is made, or

(2) any order made on such an application,

may be served out of the jurisdiction with the permission of the Court provided that the arbitration to which the application relates is governed by English law or has been, is being or is to be held within the jurisdiction.

29.2 A Part 8 claim form whereby permission to enforce an award is sought may be served out of the jurisdiction with the permission of the Court whether or not the arbitration is governed by English law.

29.3 An application for the grant of permission under this paragraph must be supported by an affidavit or witness statement stating the grounds on which the application is made and showing in what place or country the person to be served is, or probably may be found; and no such permission shall be granted unless it shall be made to appear to the Court that the case is a proper one for service out of the jurisdiction under this paragraph.

29.4 Rules 6.24 to 6.27 shall apply in relation to any such Part 8 claim form or order as is referred to in sub-paragraph (1) as they apply in relation to any other claim form.

PART III

Application of this Part

30.1 This Part of this practice direction applies to all enforcement proceedings (other than by an action or claim on the award) regardless of when they are commenced and when the arbitral proceedings took place.

Enforcement of awards

31.1 This rule applies to applications to enforce awards which are brought in the High Court and such an application may be made in the Royal Courts of Justice or in any district registry.

31.2 An application for permission under –

(1) section 66 of the Arbitration Act 1996;

(2) section 101 of the Arbitration Act 1996;

(3) section 26 of the Arbitration Act 1950; or

(4) section 3 (1)(a) of the Arbitration Act 1975;

to enforce an award in the same manner as a judgment or order may be made without notice by use of the practice form referred to in paragraph 4.1.

31.3 The Court hearing an application under paragraph 31.2 may direct that the form (in this Part of this practice direction called "the enforcement form") is to be served on such parties to the arbitration as it may specify and the enforcement form may with the permission of the court be served out of the jurisdiction irrespective of where the award is, or is treated as, made.

31.4 Where a direction is given under paragraph 31.3, paragraphs 11.1 to 11.5 and 13.1 to 17.1 shall apply with the necessary modifications as they apply to applications under Part 1 of this practice direction.

31.5 Where the applicant applies to enforce an agreed award within the meaning of section 51 (2) of the Arbitration Act 1996, the enforcement form must state that the award is an agreed award and any order made by the Court shall also contain such a statement.

31.6 An application for permission must be supported by affidavit or witness statement –

(1) exhibiting

   (a) where the application is made under section 66 of the Arbitration Act 1996 or under section 26 of the Arbitration Act 1950, the arbitration agreement and the original award or, in either case, a copy thereof;

   (b) where the application is under section 101 of the Arbitration Act 1996, the documents required to be produced by section 102 of that Act;

   (c) where the application is under section 3 (1)(a) of the Arbitration Act 1975, the documents required to be produced by section 4 of that Act;

(2) stating the name and the usual or last known place of residence or business of the applicant and of the person against whom it is sought to enforce the award respectively,

(3) stating, as the case may require, either that the award has not been complied with or the extent to which it has not been complied with at the date of the application.

31.7An order giving permission must be drawn up by or on behalf of the applicant and must be served on the respondent by delivering a copy to him personally or by sending a copy to him at his usual or last known place of residence or business or in such other manner as the Court may direct.

31.8The order may be served out of the jurisdiction without permission, and rules 6.24 to 6.27 shall apply in relation to such an order as they apply in relation to a claim form.

31.9Within 14 days after service of the order or, if the order is to be served out of the jurisdiction, within such other period as the Court may fix, the respondent may apply to set aside the order and the award shall not be enforced until after the expiration of that period or, if the respondent applies within that period to set aside the order, until after the application is finally disposed of.

31.10The copy of the order served on the respondent shall state the effect of paragraph 31.9.

31.11In relation to a body corporate paragraphs 31.1 – 31.10 shall have effect as if for any reference to the place of residence or business of the applicant or the respondent there were substituted a reference to the registered or principal address of the body corporate.

Nothing in paragraphs 31.1 – 31.10 shall affect any enactment which provides for the manner in which a document may be served on a body corporate.

Interest on awards

32.1Where an applicant seeks to enforce an award of interest, the whole or any part of which relates to a period after the date of the award, he shall file a certificate giving the following particulars

(1) whether simple or compound interest was awarded;

(2) the date from which interest was awarded;

(3) whether rests were provided for, specifying them;

(4) the rate of interest awarded, and

(5) a calculation showing the total amount claimed up to the date of the certificate and any sum which will become due thereafter on a per diem basis.

32.2The certificate under paragraph 32.1 must be filed whenever the amount of interest has to be quantified for the purpose of obtaining a judgment or order under section 66 of the Arbitration Act (enforcement of the award) or for the purpose of enforcing such a judgment or order by one of the means mentioned in RSC Order 45, rule 1 (Schedule 1 to the CPR).

Registration in High Court of foreign awards

33.1Where an award is made in proceedings on an arbitration in any part of Her Majesty's dominions or other territory to which Part I of the Foreign Judgments (Reciprocal Enforcement) Act 1933 extends, being a part to which Part II of the Administration of Justice Act 1920 extended immediately before the said Part I was extended thereto, then, if the award has, in pursuance of the law in force in the place where it was made, become enforceable in the same manner as a judgment given by a court in that place, RSC Order 71 (Schedule 1 to the CPR) shall apply in relation to the award as it applies in relation to a judgment given by that court, subject, however, to the following modifications:

(1) for references to the country of the original court there shall be substituted references to the place where the award was made; and

(2) the affidavit required by rule 3 of the said Order must state (in addition to the other matters required by that rule) that to the best of the information or belief of the deponent the award has, in pursuance of the law in force in the place where it was made, become enforceable in the same manner as a judgment given by a court in that place.

Registration of awards under the Arbitration (International Investment Disputes) Act 1966

34.1 In paragraphs 34.1 – 34.7 and in any provision of this practice direction as applied by this paragraph –

"the Act of 1966" means the Arbitration (International Investment Disputes) Act 1966;

"award" means an award rendered pursuant to the Convention;

"the Convention" means the Convention referred to in section 1 (1) of the Act of 1966;

"judgment creditor" and "judgment debtor" mean respectively the person seeking recognition or enforcement of an award and the other party to the award.

34.2 Subject to the provisions of paragraphs 34.1 – 34.7, the following provisions of RSC Order 71, namely, rules 1, 3 (1) (except sub-paragraphs (c)(iv) and (d) thereof) 7 (except paragraph (3)(c)and (d)) thereof), and 10 (3) shall apply with the necessary modifications in relation to an award as they apply in relation to a judgment to which Part II of the Foreign Judgments (Reciprocal Enforcement) act 1933 applies.

34.3 An application to have an award registered in the High Court under section 1 of the Act of 1966 shall be made by claim form under CPR rule 8.6.

34.4 The witness statement or affidavit required by Order 71, rule 3, in support of an application for registration shall –

(1) in lieu of exhibiting the judgment or a copy thereof, exhibit a copy of the award certified pursuant to the Convention; and

(2) in addition to stating the matters mentioned in paragraph 3 (1)(c)(i) and (ii) of the said rule 3, state whether at the date of the application the enforcement of the award has been stayed (provisionally or otherwise) pursuant to the Convention and whether any, and if so what, application has been made pursuant to the Convention, which, if granted, might result in a stay of the enforcement of the award.

34.5 There shall be kept in the Admiralty and Commercial Registry under the direction of the Senior Master a register of the awards ordered to be registered under the Act of 1966 and particulars shall be entered in the register of any execution issued on such an award.

34.6 Where it appears to the court on granting permission to register an award or an application made by the judgment debtor after an award has been registered –

(1) that the enforcement of the award has been stayed (whether provisionally or otherwise) pursuant to the Convention; or

(2) that an application has been made pursuant to the Convention, which, if granted, might result in a stay of the enforcement of the award,

the Court shall, or in the case referred to in sub-paragraph (2) may, stay execution of the award for such time as it considers appropriate in the circumstances.

34.7 An application by the judgment debtor under paragraph 34.6 shall be made by application notice and supported by affidavit.

**PRACTICE DIRECTION – MERCANTILE COURTS
AND BUSINESS LISTS
THIS PRACTICE DIRECTION SUPPLEMENTS PART 49 OF THE CPR
AND REPLACES, WITH MODIFICATIONS, ORDER 48C OF THE
COUNTY COURT RULES 1981 AND THE PRACTICE DIRECTIONS
ESTABLISHING MERCANTILE COURTS IN MANCHESTER, LIVERPOOL,
BIRMINGHAM, BRISTOL, LEEDS AND NEWCASTLE-UPON-TYNE. THE
LORD CHANCELLOR HAS GIVEN HIS APPROVAL TO A MERCANTILE
COURT FOR WALES AND CHESTER. THIS PRACTICE DIRECTION
COMPLEMENTS THE COMMERCIAL COURT PRACTICE DIRECTION,
ALSO SUPPLEMENTAL TO PART 49.**

General

1.1 In this practice direction:-

   (1) "mercantile claim" means a claim relating to a commercial or business transaction and includes (but is not limited to) any claim relating to -

     (i)   a business document or contract;

     (ii) the export or import of goods or the sale of goods;

     (iii) the carriage of goods by land, sea, air or pipeline;

     (iv) the exploitation of oil and gas reserves;

     (v)   insurance and re-insurance;

     (vi) banking and financial services;

     (vii) the operation of markets and exchanges;

     (viii)business agency;

     (ix) the customs and practices of particular trades, businesses or commercial organisations;

     (x)   commercial fraud;

     (xi) professional negligence in a commercial context;

     (xii) arbitration applications (paragraph 6 below)

    but does not include -

        (i) any claim concerning the sale of goods by or against an individual consumer; or

        (ii) any claim to which CPR Part 49 (other than rule 49(2)(c)) applies. and "mercantile proceedings" has a corresponding meaning.

   (2) "Mercantile Court" means one of the Mercantile Courts established to deal with mercantile claims in the High Court but does not include the Commercial Court of the Queen's Bench Division.

   (3) "Authorised county court" means the Central London County Court and any other county court authorised by the Lord Chancellor to operate a Business list for the purposes of dealing with mercantile proceedings.

   (4) "Mercantile judge" means, in relation to proceedings in the High Court, a judge, or a person authorised to sit as a judge, of a Mercantile Court and, in relation to proceedings in a county court, the judge or judges authorised to deal with cases in the Business list of an authorised county court.

1.2 Mercantile proceedings may be dealt with in the High Court subject to the restrictions on claims that can be commenced in the High Court (see CPR rule 16.3(5) and paragraph 2.1 to 2.4 of the Practice Direction that supplements CPR Part 7), or may be dealt with in an authorised county court.

1.3 The Civil Procedure Rules (the CPR) and the practice directions supplementing them apply to mercantile claims subject to the provisions of this practice direction.

1.4 For the purposes of the CPR the list of a Mercantile Court and the Business list of an authorised county court is a specialist list (see eg. CPR rules 2.3(2) and 16.3(5)(d)).

Commencement of proceedings:

High Court

2.1 A mercantile claim intended to be entered in the commercial list of the Commercial Court Queen's Bench Division should be begun by a claim form issued out of the Admiralty and Commercial Registry at the Royal Courts of Justice. (For further information reference should be made to the Commercial Court Practice Direction supplemental to CPR Part 49 and to the Commercial Court Guide).

2.2 (1) If a claimant wants a mercantile claim to be entered in the list of a Mercantile Court the claim should be begun by a claim form issued out of the district registry of the Mercantile Court in question and marked with the words "Queen's Bench Division, _____ District Registry, Mercantile Court".

(2) On the issue out of the said registry of a claim form so marked, the claim will be entered in the list of that Mercantile Court.

(3) Where a claim form is to be marked as mentioned in sub-paragraph (2), any application before the issue of the claim form should be made to a judge of that Mercantile Court.

(4) If an application is made before the issue of the claim form, the written evidence in support of the application must state, in addition to any other necessary matters, that the claimant intends to mark the claim form in accordance with sub-paragraph (1).

(5) If the mercantile judge hearing an application made before the issue of the claim form is of opinion that the claim should not be entered in the list of the Mercantile Court in question, he may adjourn the application to be heard by another judge or hear the application and direct that when the claim form is issued the claim should not be entered in that list.

County Court

2.3 (1) If a claimant wants a mercantile claim to be entered in the Business list of an authorised county court, the mercantile claim should be begun by a claim form issued out of the office of the county court in question and should be marked "_____ County Court, Business list".

(2) A claim form should not be issued and marked as mentioned in sub-paragraph (1) unless the mercantile claim has some connection with the Circuit in which the county court office is situated, for example, because:-

(i) the balance of convenience points to having the mercantile claim tried in that county court, or

(ii) the commercial or business transaction in question took place within the Circuit in which the county court is situated or one of the parties resides or carries on business within that Circuit.

(3) Where the value of a mercantile claim does not exceed £15,000, a mercantile claim may not be issued and marked as mentioned in sub-paragraph (1) except with the permission of a mercantile judge of the county court in question.

(4) A mercantile claim issued and marked as mentioned in sub-paragraph (1) will be entered in the Business list of the county court in question.

(5) Where a claim form is to be issued and marked as mentioned in sub-paragraph (1), any application before the issue of the claim form should be made to a mercantile judge of the county court in question.

(6) If an application is made before the issue of the claim form the written evidence in support of the application must state, in addition to any other necessary matters, that the claimant intends to issue and mark the claim form in accordance with sub-paragraph (1).

(7) If the mercantile judge hearing an application made before the issue of the claim form is of opinion that the claim should not be entered in the Business list of the county court in question, he may adjourn the application to be heard by another judge or hear the application and direct that when the claim form is issued the claim should not be entered in the Business list.

Transfer

3.1 Where mercantile proceedings are entered in the list of a Mercantile Court or in the Business list of an authorised county court, the provisions of CPR rule 26.2 (automatic transfer) do not apply.

3.2 At any stage in the course of mercantile proceedings not entered in the list of a Mercantile Court or the Business list of an authorised county court, any party may apply for an order transferring the case to a Mercantile Court or to the Business list of an authorised county court.

3.3 An application under paragraph 3.2 –

(1) may be made to a mercantile judge of the court to which it is proposed the case should be transferred; or

(2) may be made to the court where the mercantile proceedings are being dealt with.

3.4 The court where the mercantile proceedings are being dealt with may not itself make an order for transfer but, if it considers the case might be suitable to be dealt with by a Mercantile Court or in the Business list of an authorised county court, it may

(1) on an application under paragraph 3.3(2) adjourn the application for hearing by a mercantile judge of the court to which it is proposed the case should be transferred; or

(2) on its own initiative refer the case to a mercantile judge of that court for a decision as to whether an order for transfer should be made.

3.5 Where all parties consent to the transfer, an application for transfer should be made by letter addressed to the listing officer of the Mercantile Court or the authorised county court, as the case may be, enclosing the written consents of the other parties and the claim form and statements of case. The letter should state why the case is suitable for the Mercantile Court or, as the case may be, for the Business list of the authorised county court.

3.6 Where a mercantile judge orders mercantile proceedings to be transferred to the list of a Mercantile Court, or to the Business list of an authorised county court, he may at the same time give directions for the management of the case.

3.7 A mercantile judge may, on his own initiative (but not unless the parties have had an opportunity of making submissions), or on the application of any party, order a case in the list of a Mercantile Court or in the Business list of an authorised county court to be removed from that list and may at the same time give case management directions.

3.8 Where a case is in the list of a Mercantile Court by virtue of paragraph 2.2(2) or in a Business list by virtue of paragraph 2.3(4), an application by a defendant, including a Part 20 defendant, to remove it from that list must be made within 7 days after the defendant has filed an acknowledgment of service or a defence, whichever is the later.

3.9 Where proceedings in the Business list of an authorised county court are removed from that list, the mercantile judge may at the same time:-

(1) make an order allocating the proceedings to a track in accordance with CPR Part 26; or

(2) give directions for the purposes of allocation; and

(3) give case management directions.

Dispensing with Particulars of Claim or Defence

4. A mercantile judge may at any time, before or after the issue of the claim form, order that a case in the list of a Mercantile Court or in the Business list of an authorised county court be tried without the filing or service of particulars of claim or of a defence or of any other statement of case, but if such an order is made without any other party having had an opportunity to be heard that party may apply for it to be revoked.

Directions and Case Management

5.1 All cases in the list of a Mercantile Court or in the Business list of an authorised county court will be allocated to the multi-track. Subject to paragraph 3.9, the CPR rules relating to allocation questionnaires and to track allocation will not apply to them. They will be subject to case management by the court.

5.2 (1) If mercantile proceedings are transferred to a Mercantile Court or a Business list under paragraph 3 then, unless the mercantile judge who made the order for transfer gave directions for the management of the case, an application to a mercantile judge for such directions shall be made within 14 days of the date of the order of transfer.

(2) If the claimant does not make an application in accordance with sub-paragraph (1), any other party may do so or may apply for the claim of the claimant in default to be struck out.

5.3 (1) Subject to sub-paragraphs (2) and (3), interim applications in and trials of proceedings in a Mercantile Court or the Business list of an authorised county court shall be dealt with or heard, as the case may be, by a mercantile judge of the court in question;

(2) When an interim application needs to be dealt with urgently and a mercantile judge of the court in question is not available, the application may be dealt with by another judge, including a district judge.

(3) When the hearing of an application would involve the mercantile judge becoming aware of any matter which might embarrass him as the potential trial judge and there is no other mercantile judge of the court in question available to hear the application, the application may be heard by another judge, including a district judge.

(4) Matters concerning the enforcement of any judgment given in proceedings in a Mercantile Court or in the Business list of an authorised county court may be, and ordinarily will be, dealt with by a district judge.

(5) Subject to any express provision in a statute, rule or practice direction, sub-paragraphs (2), (3) and (4) above do not apply to applications for injunctions, freezing orders, search orders, committal or sequestration of assets.

(6) Nothing in this paragraph shall be construed as preventing the powers of a mercantile judge from being exercised by any judge of the High Court.

5.4 Paragraph 5 of the Practice Direction – The Multi-Track – supplementing CPR Part 29 applies to case management conferences in proceedings in a Mercantile Court or in the Business list of an authorised county court.

5.5 It is intended that a Mercantile Courts and Business Lists Guide will be prepared after consultation with the judges of the Mercantile Courts, the judges of the Central London County Court Business List and their respective Users Committees, and that the Guide will set out any special procedures to apply to the conduct of proceedings in Mercantile Courts and the Business lists of authorised county courts. In the meantime the practice set out in any "approved Guide" (see paragraph 5.6 below) should be followed subject to the provisions of this or any other Mercantile Courts and Business Lists practice direction and to any order that may be made in an individual case.

5.6 (1) In relation to mercantile proceedings in any Mercantile Court or in the Business List of the Central London County Court, an "approved Guide" is a Guide that has been approved by the Head of Civil Justice for the purpose of mercantile proceedings in that court or in that list.

(2) In relation to any Mercantile Court or Business list in respect of which there is for the time being no "approved Guide", Section D of the Commercial Court Guide, 5th Edition, relating to Case Management in the Commercial Court, shall be treated as the "approved Guide" for the purpose of mercantile proceedings in that court or in that list.

Arbitration Applications and Proceedings

6.1 An arbitration application (as defined in paragraph 2 of the Arbitration Practice Direction supplemental to CPR Part 49) and proceedings to enforce an award under section 26 of the Arbitration Act 1950 or under sections 66 or 101(2) of the Arbitration Act 1996, shall be treated as mercantile claims for the purposes of this practice direction and may be included in the mercantile list of a Mercantile Court or the Business list of an authorised county court.

6.2 A mercantile judge may also deal with any other application under the Arbitration Act 1979 which may be commenced in or transferred to the mercantile list of a Mercantile Court or the Business list of an authorised county court.

6.3 The provisions of the Arbitration Practice Direction supplemental to CPR Part 49 apply to such applications and proceedings.

Repeal of Previous Local Directions or Guides

7. This practice direction supersedes as from 26 April 1999 any local practice directions or Guides applicable to mercantile proceedings in any Mercantile Court or in the Business List of the Central London County Court.

PART 50

APPLICATION OF THE SCHEDULES

50 (1) The Schedules to these Rules set out, with modifications, certain provisions previously contained in the Rules of the Supreme Court 1965[93] and the County Court Rules 1981[94].

(2) These Rules apply in relation to the proceedings to which the Schedules apply subject to the provisions in the Schedules and the relevant practice directions.

(3) A provision previously contained in the Rules of the Supreme Court 1965 –

(a) is headed 'RSC';

(b) is numbered with the Order and rule numbers it bore as part of the RSC; and

(c) unless otherwise stated in the Schedules or the relevant practice direction, applies only to proceedings in the High Court.

(4) A provision previously contained in the County Court Rules 1981 –

(a) is headed 'CCR';

(b) is numbered with the Order and rule numbers it bore as part of the CCR; and

(c) unless otherwise stated in the Schedules or the relevant practice direction, applies only to proceedings in the county court.

(5) A reference in a Schedule to a rule by number alone is a reference to the rule so numbered in the Order in which the reference occurs.

(6) A reference in a Schedule to a rule by number prefixed by 'CPR' is a reference to the rule with that number in these Rules.

(7) In the Schedules, unless otherwise stated, 'the Act' means –

(a) in a provision headed 'RSC', the Supreme Court Act 1981; and

(b) in a provision headed 'CCR', the County Courts Act 1984.

PART 51

TRANSITIONAL ARRANGEMENTS

51 A practice direction shall make provision for the extent to which these Rules shall apply to proceedings issued before 26 April 1999.

---

(93) SI 1965/1776.
(94) SI 1981/1687.

PRACTICE DIRECTION – TRANSITIONAL ARRANGEMENTS
THIS PRACTICE DIRECTION SUPPLEMENTS CPR PART 51

Contents of this Practice Direction

1   (1) This Practice Direction deals with the application of the Civil Procedure Rules ('CPR') to proceedings issued before 26 April 1999 ('existing proceedings').

   (2) In this Practice Direction 'the previous rules' means, as appropriate the Rules of the Supreme Court 1965 ('RSC') or County Court Rules 1981 ('CCR') in force immediately before 26 April 1999.

General scheme of transitional arrangements

2   The general scheme is:

   (a) to apply the previous rules to undefended cases, allowing them to progress to their disposal, but

   (b) to apply the CPR to defended cases so far as is practicable.

Where the previous rules will normally apply

General principle

3   Where an initiating step has been taken in a case before 26 April 1999, in particular one that uses forms or other documentation required by the previous rules, the case will proceed in the first instance under the previous rules. Any step which a party must take in response to something done by another party in accordance with the previous rules must also be in accordance with those rules.

Responding to old process

4   A party who is served with an old type of originating process (writ, summons etc.) on or after 26 April 1999 is required to respond in accordance with the previous rules and the instructions on any forms received with the originating process.

Filing and service of pleadings where old process served

5   Where a case has been begun by an old type of originating process (whether served before or after 26 April 1999), filing and service of pleadings will continue according to the previous rules.

Automatic directions/discovery

High Court

6   (1) Where the timetable for automatic directions under RSC Order 25, rule 8 or automatic discovery under RSC Order 24 has begun to apply to proceedings before 26 April 1999, those directions will continue to have effect on or after 26 April 1999.

County Court

   (2) Where automatic directions under CCR Order 17, rule 11 have begun to apply to existing proceedings before 26 April 1999 or the court has sent out notice that automatic directions under CCR Order 17, rule 11 (Form N.450) will apply (even if the timetable will not begin until 26 April 1999 or after), those directions will continue to have effect on or after 26 April 1999.

   (3) However CCR Order 17, rule 11(9) will not apply and therefore proceedings will not be struck out where there has been no request for a hearing to be fixed within 15 months of the date when pleadings were deemed to close. (But see paragraph 19.)

High Court and County Court

   (4) However, if the case comes before the court on or after 26 April 1999, the new rules may apply. (See paragraph 15.)

Default judgment

7   (1) If a party wishes default judgment to be entered in existing proceedings, he must do so in accordance with the previous rules.

(2) Where default judgment has been entered and there are outstanding issues to be resolved (e.g. damages to be assessed), the court officer may refer the proceedings to the judge, so that case management decisions about the proceedings and the conduct of the hearing can be made in accordance with the practice set out in paragraph 15.

(3) If a party needs to apply for permission to enter default judgment, he must make that application under CPR Part 23 (general rules about applications for court orders).

(4) An application to set aside judgment entered in default must be made under CPR Part 23 (general rules about applications for court orders) and CPR Part 13 (setting aside or varying default judgment) will apply to the proceedings as it would apply to default judgment entered under the CPR.

(5) CPR rule 15.11 (claims stayed if it is not defended or admitted) applies to these proceedings.

Judgment on admission in the county court

8 (1) If a party to existing proceedings in the county court wishes to request judgment to be entered on an admission, he must do so in accordance with the previous rules.

(2) Where judgment has been entered and there are outstanding issues to be resolved (e.g. damages to be assessed), the court officer may refer the proceedings to the judge, so that case management decisions about the proceedings and the conduct of the hearing can be made in accordance with the practice set out in paragraph 15.

(3) If a party needs to apply for permission to enter judgment, he must make that application under CPR Part 23 (general rules about applications for court orders).

Order inconsistent with CPR

9 Where a court order has been made before 26 April 1999, that order must still be complied with on or after 26 April 1999.

Steps taken before 26 April 1999

10 (1) Where a party has taken any step in the proceedings in accordance with the previous rules that step will remain valid on or after 26 April 1999.

(2) A party will not normally be required to take any action that would amount to taking that step again under the CPR. For example if discovery has been given, a party will not normally be required to provide disclosure under CPR Part 31.

Where the CPR will normally apply

General principle

11 Where a new step is to be taken in any existing proceedings on or after 26 April 1999, it is to be taken under the CPR, Part 1 (overriding objective) to apply

Part 1 (overriding objective) to apply

12 Part 1 (overriding objective) will apply to all existing proceedings from 26 April 1999 onwards.

Originating process

13 (1) Only claim forms under the CPR will be issued by the court on or after 26 April 1999.

(2) If a request to issue an old type of originating process (writ, summons etc.) is received at the court on or after 26 April 1999 it will be returned unissued.

(3) An application made on or after 26 April 1999 to extend the validity of originating process issued before 26 April 1999 must be made in accordance with CPR Part 23 (general rules about applications for court orders), but the court will decide whether to allow the application in accordance with the previous law.

Application to the court

14 (1) Any application to the court made on or after 26 April 1999 must be made in accordance with CPR Part 23 (general rules about applications for court orders).

(2) Any other relevant CPR will apply to the substance of the application, unless this practice direction provides otherwise. (See paragraphs 13(3) (application to extend the validity of originating process) and 18(2) (costs)).

(3) For example, a party wishing to apply for summary judgment must do so having regard to the test in CPR Part 24. A party wishing to apply for an interim remedy must do so under CPR Part 25 etc.

(4) Any other CPR will apply as necessary. For example, CPR Part 4 will apply as to forms and CPR Part 6 will apply to service of documents.

(5) If the pleadings have not been filed at court, the applicant must file all pleadings served when he files his application notice.

First time before a judge on or after 26 April 1999

15 (1) When proceedings come before a judge (whether at a hearing or on paper) for the first time on or after 26 April 1999, he may direct how the CPR are to apply to the proceedings and may disapply certain provisions of the CPR. He may also give case management directions (which may include allocating the proceedings to a case management track).

(2) The general presumption will be that the CPR will apply to the proceedings from then on unless the judge directs or this practice direction provides otherwise. (See paragraphs 13(3) (application to extend the validity of originating process) and 18(2) (costs).)

(3) If an application has been issued before 26 April 1999 and the hearing of the application has been set for a date on or after 26 April 1999, the general presumption is that the application will be decided having regard to the CPR. (For example an application for summary judgment issued before 26 April 1999, with a hearing date set for 1 May 1999, will be decided having regard to the test in CPR Part 24 (summary Judgment).)

(4) When the first occasion on which existing proceedings are before a judge on or after 26 April 1999 is a trial or hearing of a substantive issue, the general presumption is that the trial or hearing will be conducted having regard to the CPR.

Where pleadings deemed to close on or after 26 April 1999

16 (1) This paragraph applies to existing proceedings where pleadings are deemed to close on or after 26 April 1999. However, this paragraph does not apply to those county court proceedings where notice that automatic directions apply (Form N.450) has been sent (in which case the automatic directions will apply – see paragraph 6).

(2) CPR Part 26 (case management – preliminary stage) applies to these proceedings.

(3) If a defence is filed at court on or after 26 April 1999, the court will serve an allocation questionnaire where CPR rule 26.3 would apply, unless it dispenses with the need for one.

(4) If pleadings have not been filed at court (this will normally be the case in the Queen's Bench Division) the claimant must file copies of all the pleadings served within 14 days of the date that pleadings are deemed to close.

(5) Unless it dispenses with the need for one, the court will then serve an allocation questionnaire.

(6) In the previous rules pleadings are deemed to close:
  (a) High court –
    (i) 14 days after service of any reply, or
    (ii) if there is no reply, 14 days after service of the defence to counterclaim, or
    (iii) if there is no reply or defence to counterclaim, 14 days after the service of the defence.
  (b) County court – 14 days after the delivery of a defence or, where a counterclaim is served with the defence, 28 days after the delivery of the defence.

(7) Where there are 2 or more defendants the court will normally wait until the claimant has filed copies of all the pleadings before serving an allocation questionnaire. However, the court may (in cases where there is a delay) serve allocation questionnaires despite the fact that pleadings have not closed in respect of any other defendant.

(8) The court will then allocate the proceedings in accordance with CPR rule 26.5.

(9) The CPR will then apply generally to the proceedings.

Agreement to apply the CPR

17 The parties may agree in writing that the CPR will apply to any proceedings from the date of the agreement. When they do so:

(a) all those who are parties at that time must agree,

(b) the CPR must apply in their entirety,

(c) the agreement is irrevocable,

(d) the claimant must file a copy of the agreement at court.

Costs

18 (1) Any assessment of costs that takes place on or after 26 April 1999 will be in accordance with CPR Parts 43 to 48.

(2) However, the general presumption is that no costs for work undertaken before 26 April 1999 will be disallowed if those costs would have been allowed in a costs taxation before 26 April 1999.

(3) The decision as to whether to allow costs for work undertaken on or after 26 April will generally be taken in accordance with CPR Parts 43 to 48.

(The costs practice direction contains more information on the operation of the transitional arrangements in relation to costs.)

Existing proceedings after one year

19 (1) If any existing proceedings have not come before a judge, at a hearing or on paper, between 26 April 1999 and 25 April 2000, those proceedings shall be stayed.

(2) Any party to those proceedings may apply for the stay to be lifted.

(3) Proceedings of the following types will not be stayed as a result of this provision:

(a) where the case has been given a fixed trial date which is after 25 April 2000,

(b) personal injury cases where there is no issue on liability but the proceedings have been adjourned by court order to determine the prognosis,

(c) where the court is dealing with the continuing administration of an estate or a trust or a receivership,

(d) applications relating to funds in court.

PART 52

APPEALS

Contents of this Part

I General rules about appeals

Scope and interpretation

52.1(1) The rules in this Part apply to appeals to –

    (a) the civil division of the Court of Appeal;

    (b) the High Court; and

    (c) a county court.

  (2) This Part does not apply to –

    (a) an appeal against an order under Part 27 (the small claims track); or

    (b) an appeal in detailed assessment proceedings against a decision of an authorised court officer.

(Rules 27.12 and 27.13 deal with appeals against orders under Part 27 (the small claims track).)

(Rules 47.21 to 47.26 deal with appeals against a decision of an authorised court officer in detailed assessment proceedings.)

  (3) In this Part –

    (a) "appeal" includes an appeal by way of case stated;

    (b) "appeal court" means the court to which an appeal is made;

    (c) "lower court" means the court, tribunal or other person or body from whose decision an appeal is brought;

    (d) "appellant" means a person who brings or seeks to bring an appeal;

    (e) "respondent" means –

      (i) a person other than the appellant who was a party to the proceedings in the lower court and who is affected by the appeal; and

      (ii) a person who is permitted by the appeal court to be a party to the appeal; and

    (f) "appeal notice" means an appellant's or respondent's notice.

  (4) This Part is subject to any rule, enactment or practice direction which sets out special provisions with regard to any particular category of appeal.

Parties to comply with the Practice Direction

52.2   All parties to an appeal must comply with the relevant practice direction.

Permission

52.3(1) An appellant or respondent requires permission to appeal –

    (a) where the appeal is from a decision of a judge in a county court or the High Court, except where the appeal is against –

      (i) a committal order;

      (ii) a refusal to grant habeas corpus; or

      (iii) a secure accommodation order made under section 25 of the Children Act 1989[95]; or

    (b) as provided by the relevant practice direction.

(Other enactments may provide that permission is required for particular appeals.)

  (2) An application for permission to appeal may be made –

    (a) to the lower court at the hearing at which the decision to be appealed was made; or

    (b) to the appeal court in an appeal notice.

---

(95) 1989 c.41.

(Rule 52.4 sets out the time limits for filing an appellant's notice at the appeal court. Rule 52.5 sets out the time limits for filing a respondent's notice at the appeal court. Any application for permission to appeal to the appeal court must be made in the appeal notice (see rules 52.4(1) and 52.5(3).)

(Rule 52.13(1) provides that permission is required from the Court of Appeal for all appeals to that court from a decision of a county court or the High Court which was itself made on appeal.)

    (3) Where the lower court refuses an application for permission to appeal, a further application for permission to appeal may be made to the appeal court.

    (4) Where the appeal court, without a hearing, refuses permission to appeal, the person seeking permission may request the decision to be reconsidered at a hearing.

    (5) A request under paragraph (4) must be filed within 7 days after service of the notice that permission has been refused.

    (6) Permission to appeal will only be given where –

        (a) the court considers that the appeal would have a real prospect of success; or

        (b) there is some other compelling reason why the appeal should be heard.

    (7) An order giving permission may –

        (a) limit the issues to be heard; and

        (b) be made subject to conditions.

(Rule 3.1(3) also provides that the court may make an order subject to conditions.)

(Rule 25.15 provides for the court to order security for costs of an appeal.)

Appellant's notice

52.4(1) Where the appellant seeks permission from the appeal court it must be requested in the appellant's notice.

    (2) The appellant must file the appellant's notice at the appeal court within –

        (a) such period as may be directed by the lower court; or

        (b) where the court makes no such direction, 14 days after the date of the decision of the lower court that the appellant wishes to appeal.

    (3) Unless the appeal court orders otherwise, an appeal notice must be served on each respondent –

        (a) as soon as practicable; and

        (b) in any event not later than 7 days,

    after it is filed.

Respondent's notice

52.5(1) A respondent may file and serve a respondent's notice.

    (2) A respondent who –

        (a) is seeking permission to appeal from the appeal court; or

        (b) wishes to ask the appeal court to uphold the order of the lower court for reasons different from or additional to those given by the lower court,

    must file a respondent's notice.

    (3) Where the respondent seeks permission from the appeal court it must be requested in the respondent's notice.

    (4) A respondent's notice must be filed within –

        (a) such period as may be directed by the lower court; or

    (b) where the court makes no such direction, 14 days after the date in paragraph (5).

(5) The date referred to in paragraph (4) is –

    (a) the date the respondent is served with the appellant's notice where –

        (i) permission to appeal was given by the lower court; or

        (ii) permission to appeal is not required;

    (b) the date the respondent is served with notification that the appeal court has given the appellant permission to appeal; or

    (c) the date the respondent is served with notification that the application for permission to appeal and the appeal itself are to be heard together.

(6) Unless the appeal court orders otherwise a respondent's notice must be served on the appellant and any other respondent –

    (a) as soon as practicable; and

    (b) in any event not later than 7 days,

    after it is filed.

Variation of time

52.6(1) An application to vary the time limit for filing an appeal notice must be made to the appeal court.

(2) The parties may not agree to extend any date or time limit set by –

    (a) these Rules;

    (b) the relevant practice direction; or

    (c) an order of the appeal court or the lower court.

(Rule 3.1(2)(a) provides that the court may extend or shorten the time for compliance with any rule, practice direction or court order (even if an application for extension is made after the time for compliance has expired).)

(Rule 3.1(2)(b) provides that the court may adjourn or bring forward a hearing.)

Stay(GL)

52.7   Unless –

    (a) the appeal court or the lower court orders otherwise; or

    (b) the appeal is from the Immigration Appeal Tribunal,

    an appeal shall not operate as a stay of any order or decision of the lower court.

Amendment of appeal notice

52.8   An appeal notice may not be amended without the permission of the appeal court.

Striking out(GL) appeal notices and setting aside or imposing conditions on permission to appeal

52.9(1) The appeal court may –

    (a) strike out the whole or part of an appeal notice;

    (b) set aside(GL) permission to appeal in whole or in part;

    (c) impose or vary conditions upon which an appeal may be brought.

(2) The court will only exercise its powers under paragraph (1) where there is a compelling reason for doing so.

(3) Where a party was present at the hearing at which permission was given he may not subsequently apply for an order that the court exercise its powers under sub-paragraphs (1)(b) or (1)(c).

Appeal court's powers

52.10(1) In relation to an appeal the appeal court has all the powers of the lower court.

(Rule 52.1(4) provides that this Part is subject to any enactment that sets out special provisions with regard to any particular category of appeal -where such an enactment gives a statutory power to a tribunal, person or other body it may be the case that the appeal court may not exercise that power on an appeal.)

(2) The appeal court has power to –

    (a) affirm, set aside or vary any order or judgment made or given by the lower court;

    (b) refer any claim or issue for determination by the lower court;

    (c) order a new trial or hearing;

    (d) make orders for the payment of interest;

    (e) make a costs order.

(3) In an appeal from a claim tried with a jury the Court of Appeal may, instead of ordering a new trial –

    (a) make an order for damages$^{(GL)}$; or

    (b) vary an award of damages made by the jury.

(4) The appeal court may exercise its powers in relation to the whole or part of an order of the lower court.

(Part 3 contains general rules about the court's case management powers.)

Hearing of appeals

52.11(1) Every appeal will be limited to a review of the decision of the lower court unless –

    (a) a practice direction makes different provision for a particular category of appeal; or

    (b) the court considers that in the circumstances of an individual appeal it would be in the interests of justice to hold a re-hearing.

(2) Unless it orders otherwise, the appeal court will not receive –

    (a) oral evidence; or

    (b) evidence which was not before the lower court.

(3) The appeal court will allow an appeal where the decision of the lower court was –

    (a) wrong; or

    (b) unjust because of a serious procedural or other irregularity in the proceedings in the lower court.

(4) The appeal court may draw any inference of fact which it considers justified on the evidence.

(5) At the hearing of the appeal a party may not rely on a matter not contained in his appeal notice unless the appeal court gives permission.

Non-disclosure of Part 36 offers and payments

52.12(1) The fact that a Part 36 offer or Part 36 payment has been made must not be disclosed to any judge of the appeal court who is to hear and finally determine an appeal until all questions (other than costs) have been determined.

(2) Paragraph (1) does not apply if the Part 36 offer or Part 36 payment is relevant to the substance of the appeal.

(3) Paragraph (1) does not prevent disclosure in any application in the appeal proceedings if disclosure of the fact that a Part 36 offer or Part 36 payment has been made is properly relevant to the matter to be decided.

II Special provisions applying to the Court of Appeal

Second appeals to the court

52.13(1) Permission is required from the Court of Appeal for any appeal to that court from a decision of a county court or the High Court which was itself made on appeal.

(2) The Court of Appeal will not give permission unless it considers that –

(a) the appeal would raise an important point of principle or practice; or

(b) there is some other compelling reason for the Court of Appeal to hear it.

Assignment of appeals to the Court of Appeal

52.14(1) Where the court from or to which an appeal is made or from which permission to appeal is sought ("the relevant court") considers that –

(a) an appeal which is to be heard by a county court or the High Court would raise an important point of principle or practice; or

(b) there is some other compelling reason for the Court of Appeal to hear it,

the relevant court may order the appeal to be transferred to the Court of Appeal.

(The Master of the Rolls has the power to direct that an appeal which would be heard by a county court or the High Court should be heard instead by the Court of Appeal - see section 57 of the Access to Justice Act 1999.)[96]

(2) The Master of the Rolls or the Court of Appeal may remit an appeal to the court in which the original appeal was or would have been brought.

Judicial review appeals

52.15(1) Where permission to apply for judicial review has been refused at a hearing in the High Court, the person seeking that permission may apply to the Court of Appeal for permission to appeal.

(2) An application in accordance with paragraph (1) must be made within 7 days of the decision of the High Court to refuse to give permission to apply for judicial review.

(3) On an application under paragraph (1), the Court of Appeal may, instead of giving permission to appeal, give permission to apply for judicial review.

(4) Where the Court of Appeal gives permission to apply for judicial review in accordance with paragraph (3), the case will proceed in the High Court unless the Court of Appeal orders otherwise.

Who may exercise the powers of the Court of Appeal

52.16(1) A court officer assigned to the Civil Appeals Office who is –

(a) a barrister; or

(b) a solicitor

may exercise the jurisdiction of the Court of Appeal with regard to the matters set out in paragraph (2) with the consent of the Master of the Rolls.

(2) The matters referred to in paragraph (1) are –

(a) any matter incidental to any proceedings in the Court of Appeal;

(b) any other matter where there is no substantial dispute between the parties; and

(c) the dismissal of an appeal or application where a party has failed to comply with any order, rule or practice direction.

---

(96) 1999 c.22.

(3) A court officer may not decide an application for –

    (a) permission to appeal;

    (b) bail pending an appeal;

    (c) an injunction$^{(GL)}$;

    (d) a stay$^{(GL)}$ of any proceedings, other than a temporary stay of any order or decision of the lower court over a period when the Court of Appeal is not sitting or cannot conveniently be convened.

(4) Decisions of a court officer may be made without a hearing.

(5) A party may request any decision of a court officer to be reviewed by the Court of Appeal.

(6) At the request of a party, a hearing will be held to reconsider a decision of –

    (a) a single judge; or

    (b) a court officer,

    made without a hearing.

(7) A single judge may refer any matter for a decision by a court consisting of two or more judges.

(Section 54(6) of the Supreme Court Act 1981[97] provides that there is no appeal from the decision of a single judge on an application for permission to appeal)

(Section 58(2) of the Supreme Court Act 1981[98] provides that there is no appeal to the House of Lords from decisions of the Court of Appeal that-

    (a) are taken by a single judge or any officer or member of staff of that court in proceedings incidental to any cause or matter pending before the civil division of that court; and

    (b) do not involve the determination of an appeal or of an application for permission to appeal,

and which may be called into question by rules of court. Rules 52.16(5) and (6) provide the procedure for the calling into question of such decisions)

PRACTICE DIRECTION – APPEALS
THIS PRACTICE DIRECTION SUPPLEMENTS PART 52

Contents of this Practice Direction

1.1 This practice direction is divided into three sections:

- Section I – General provisions about appeals
- Section II – General provisions about statutory appeals and appeals by way of case stated
- Section III – Provisions about specific appeals

SECTION I – GENERAL PROVISIONS ABOUT APPEALS

2.1 This practice direction applies to all appeals to which Part 52 applies except where specific provision is made for appeals to the Court of Appeal.

2.2 For the purpose only of appeals to the Court of Appeal from cases in family proceedings this Practice Direction will apply with such modifications as may be required.

Grounds for appeal

3.1 Rule 52.11(3) (a) and (b) sets out the circumstances in which the appeal court will allow an appeal.

---

(97) 1981 c.54; section 54 was amended by section 59 of the Access to Justice Act 1999 (c.22).

(98) 1981 c.54; section 58 was amended by section 60 of the Access to Justice Act 1999 (c.22).

3.2 The grounds of appeal should set out clearly the reasons why rule 52.11(3)(a) or (b) is said to apply.

Permission to appeal

4.1 Rule 52.3 sets out the circumstances when permission to appeal is required.

4.2 The permission of–

(a) the Court of Appeal; or

(b) where the lower court's rules allow, the lower court

is required for all appeals to the Court of Appeal except as provided for by statute or rule 52.3

(The requirement of permission to appeal may be imposed by a practice direction – see rule 52.3(b))

4.3 Where the lower court is not required to give permission to appeal, it may give an indication of its opinion as to whether permission should be given.

(Rule 52.1(3)(c) defines "lower court")

Appeals from case management decisions

4.4 Case management decisions include decisions made under rule 3.1(2) and decisions about:

(1) disclosure

(2) filing of witness statements or experts reports

(3) directions about the timetable of the claim

(4) adding a party to a claim

(5) security for costs

4.5 Where the application is for permission to appeal from a case management decision, the court dealing with the application may take into account whether:

(1) the issue is of sufficient significance to justify the costs of an appeal;

(2) the procedural consequences of an appeal (e.g. loss of trial date) outweigh the significance of the case management decision;

(3) it would be more convenient to determine the issue at or after trial

Court to which permission to appeal application should be made

4.6 An application for permission should be made orally at the hearing at which the decision to be appealed against is made.

4.7 Where:

(a) no application for permission to appeal is made at the hearing; or

(b) the lower court refuses permission to appeal,

an application for permission to appeal may be made to the appeal court in accordance with rules 52.3(2) and (3).

4.8 There is no appeal from a decision of the appeal court, made at an oral hearing, to allow or refuse permission to appeal to that court. See section 54(4) of the Access to Justice Act 1999 and rule 52.3(3) and (4).

Second appeals

4.9 An application for permission to appeal from a decision of the High Court or a county court which was itself made on appeal must be made to the Court of Appeal.

4.10 If permission to appeal is granted the appeal will be heard by the Court of Appeal.

Consideration of Permission without a hearing

4.11 Applications for permission to appeal may be considered by the appeal court without a hearing.

4.12 If permission is granted without a hearing the parties will be notified of that decision and the procedure in paragraphs 6.1 to 6.7 will then apply.

4.13 If permission is refused without a hearing the parties will be notified of that decision with the reasons for it. The decision is subject to the appellant's right to have it reconsidered at an oral hearing. This may be before the same judge.

4.14 A request for the decision to be reconsidered at an oral hearing must be filed at the appeal court within 7 days after service of the notice that permission has been refused. A copy of the request must be served by the appellant on the respondent at the same time. If no request is made for the decision to be reconsidered, it will become final after the time limit for making the request has expired.

Permission hearing

4.15 Notice of the hearing need not be given to the respondent unless the court so directs. The appeal court will usually so direct if the appellant is asking for a remedy against the respondent pending the appeal.

4.16 If notice of the hearing is to be given to the respondent, the appellant must supply the respondent with a copy of the bundle (see paragraph 5.6) within 7 days of being notified, or such other period as the court may direct. The costs of providing that bundle shall be borne by the appellant initially, but will form part of the costs of the permission application.

Appellants in receipt of services funded by the Legal Services Commission applying for permission to appeal

4.17 Where the appellant is in receipt of services funded by the Legal Services Commission (or legally aided) and permission to appeal has been refused by the appeal court without a hearing, the appellant must send a copy of the reasons the appeal court gave for refusing permission to the relevant office of the Legal Services Commission as soon as it has been received from the court. The court will require confirmation that this has been done if a hearing is requested to re-consider the question of permission.

Limited permission

4.18 Where a court, under rule 52.3(7) confines its permission to some issues only, it should expressly refuse permission on any remaining issues. Those other issues may only be raised at the hearing of the appeal with the appeal court's permission. The court and the respondent should be informed of any intention to raise such an issue as soon as practicable after notification of the court's order.

4.19 An application to raise a remaining issue will normally be dealt with at the outset of the appeal unless the court otherwise directs.

Appellant's notice

5.1 An appellant's notice (N161) must be filed and served in all cases. Where an application for permission to appeal is made to the appeal court it must be applied for in the appellant's notice.

Extension of time for filing appellant's notice

5.2 If an appellant requires an extension of time for filing his notice the application must be made in the appellant's notice. The notice should state the reason for the delay and the steps taken prior to the application being made.

5.3 Where the appellant's notice includes an application for an extension of time and permission to appeal has been given or is not required the respondent has the right to be heard on that application. He must be served with a copy of the appellant's bundle. However, a respondent who unreasonably opposes an extension of time runs the risk of being ordered to pay the appellant's costs of that application.

5.4 If an extension of time is given following such an application the procedure at paragraphs 6.1 to 6.6 applies.

Applications

5.5 Notice of an application to be made to the appeal court for a remedy incidental to the appeal (e.g. an interim remedy under rule 25.1 or an order for security for costs) may be included in the appeal notice or in a Part 23 application notice.

(Rule 25.15 deals with security for costs of an appeal)

(Paragraph 10 of this practice direction contains other provisions relating to applications)

Documents

5.6 The appellant must lodge the following documents with his appellant's notice in every case except where the appellant's notice relates to a refusal of permission to apply for judicial review (see paragraph 15.3 below):

(1) one additional copy of the appellant's notice for the appeal court; and

(2) one copy of the appellant's notice for each of the respondents ;

(3)   one copy of any skeleton argument (see paragraph 5.9)

(4)   a sealed copy of the order being appealed;

(5)   any order giving or refusing permission to appeal, together with a copy of the reasons for that decision;

(6)   any witness statements or affidavits in support of any application included in the appellant's notice; and

(7)   a bundle of documents in support of the appeal – this should include copies of the documents referred to in paragraphs (1) to (6) and any other documents which the appellant reasonably considers necessary to enable the appeal court to reach its decision on the hearing of the application or appeal. Documents which are extraneous to the issues to be considered should be excluded. The other documents will, subject to paragraph 5.7, include:

    (a)   any affidavit or witness statement filed in support of the application for permission to appeal or the appeal,

    (b)   a suitable record of the reasons for judgment of the lower court (see paragraph 5.12);

    (c)   where permission to appeal has been given or permission is not required; any relevant transcript or note of evidence (see paragraph 5.15 below)

    (d)   statements of case,

    (e)   any application notice (or case management documentation) relevant to the subject of the appeal,

    (f)   in cases where the decision appealed was itself made on appeal, the first order, the reasons given and the appellant's notice of appeal from that order,

    (g)   in cases where the appeal is from a Tribunal, a copy of the Tribunal's reasons for the decision, a copy of the decision reviewed by the Tribunal and the reasons for the original decision

    (h)   in the case of judicial review or a statutory appeal, the original decision which was the subject of the application to the lower court

    (i)   relevant affidavits, witness statements, summaries, experts' reports and exhibits;

    (j)   any skeleton arguments relied on in the lower court; and

    (k)   such other documents as the court may direct.

5.7   Where it is not possible to file all the above documents, the appellant must indicate which documents have not yet been filed and the reasons why they are not currently available.

5.8   Where bundles comprise more than 150 pages excluding transcripts of judgment and other transcripts of the proceedings in the lower court only those documents which the court may reasonably be expected to pre-read should be included. A full set of documents should then be brought to the hearing for reference.

Skeleton arguments

5.9   (1)   The appellant's notice must, subject to (2) and (3) below, be accompanied by a skeleton argument. Alternatively the skeleton argument may be included in the appellant's notice. Where the skeleton argument is so included it will not form part of the notice for the purposes of rule 52.8.

    (2)   Where it is impracticable for the appellant's skeleton argument to accompany the appellant's notice it must be lodged and served on all respondents within 14 days of filing the notice.

    (3)   An appellant who is not represented need not lodge a skeleton argument but is encouraged to do so since this will be helpful to the court.

Content of skeleton arguments

5.10 Skeleton arguments for the appeal court should contain a numbered list of points stated in no more than a few sentences which should both define and confine the areas of controversy. Each point should be followed by references to any documentation on which the appellant proposes to rely.

5.11 The appellant should consider what other information the appeal court will need. This may include a list of persons who feature in the case or glossaries of technical terms. A chronology of relevant events will be necessary in most appeals. In the case of points of law, authorities relied on should be cited with reference to the particular pages where the principle concerned is set out.

Suitable record of the judgment

5.12 Where the judgment to be appealed has been officially recorded by the court, an approved transcript of that record should accompany the appellant's notice. Photocopies will not be accepted for this purpose. However, where there is no officially recorded judgment, the following documents will be acceptable:

Written judgments

(1) Where the judgment was made in writing a copy of that judgment endorsed with the judge's signature.

Note of judgment

(2) When judgment was not officially recorded or made in writing a note of the judgment (agreed between the appellant's and respondent's advocates) should be submitted for approval to the judge whose decision is being appealed. If the parties cannot agree on a single note of the judgment, both versions should be provided to that judge with an explanatory letter. For the purpose of an application for permission to appeal the note need not be approved by the respondent or the lower court judge.

Advocates' notes of judgments where the appellant is unrepresented

(3) When the appellant was unrepresented in the lower court it is the duty of any advocate for the respondent to make his/her note of judgment promptly available, free of charge to the appellant where there is no officially recorded judgment or if the court so directs. Where the appellant was represented in the lower court it is the duty of his/her own former advocate to make his/her note available in these circumstances. The appellant should submit the note of judgment to the appeal court.

Reasons for Judgment in Tribunal cases

(4) A sealed copy of the Tribunal's reasons for the decision.

5.13 An appellant may not be able to obtain an official transcript or other suitable record of the lower court's decision within the time within which the appellant's notice must be filed. In such cases the appellant's notice must still be completed to the best of the appellant's ability on the basis of the documentation available. However it may be amended subsequently with the permission of the appeal court.

Advocates' notes of judgments

5.14 Advocates' brief (or, where appropriate, refresher) fee includes:

(1) remuneration for taking a note of the judgment of the court;

(2) having the note transcribed accurately;

(3) attempting to agree the note with the other side if represented;

(4) submitting the note to the judge for approval where appropriate;

(5) revising it if so requested by the judge,

(6) providing any copies required for the appeal court, instructing solicitors and lay client; and

(7) providing a copy of his note to an unrepresented appellant

Transcripts or Notes of Evidence

5.15 When the evidence is relevant to the appeal an official transcript of the relevant evidence must be obtained. Transcripts or notes of evidence are generally not needed for the purpose of determining an application for permission to appeal.

Notes of evidence

5.16 If evidence relevant to the appeal was not officially recorded, a typed version of the judge's notes of evidence must be obtained

Transcripts at public expense

5.17 Where the lower court or the appeal court is satisfied that an unrepresented appellant is in such poor financial circumstances that the cost of a transcript would be an excessive burden the court may certify that the cost of obtaining one official transcript should be borne at public expense.

5.18 In the case of a request for an official transcript of evidence or proceedings to be paid for at public expense, the court must also be satisfied that there are reasonable grounds for appeal. Whenever possible a request for a transcript at public expense should be made to the lower court when asking for permission to appeal.

Filing and service of appellant's notice

5.19 Rule 52.4 sets out the procedure and time limits for filing and serving an appellant's notice. The appellant must file the appellant's notice at the appeal court within such period as may be directed by the lower court which should not normally exceed 28 days or, where the lower court directs no such period, within 14 days of the date of the decision that the appellant wishes to appeal.

5.20 Where the lower court judge announces his decision and reserves the reasons for his judgment or order until a later date, he should, in the exercise of powers under rule 52.4(2)(a), fix a period for filing the appellant's notice at the appeal court that takes this into account.

5.21 Except where the appeal court orders otherwise a sealed copy of the appellant's notice, including any skeleton arguments must be served on all respondents to the appeal in accordance with the timetable prescribed by rule 52.4(3) except where this requirement is modified by paragraph 5.9(2) in which case the skeleton argument should be served as soon as it is lodged.

5.22 Unless the court otherwise directs a respondent need not take any action when served with an appellant's notice until such time as notification is given to him that permission to appeal has been given.

5.23 The court may dispense with the requirement for service of the notice on a respondent. Any application notice seeking an order under rule 6.9 to dispense with service should set out the reasons relied on and be verified by a statement of truth.

5.24 Where the appellant is applying for permission to appeal in his appellant's notice, there is no requirement at this stage for copies of the documents referred to at paragraph 5.6 to be served on the respondents. However, if permission has been given by the lower court or permission is not required, copies of all the documents must be served on the respondents with the appellant's notice.

(Paragraph 5.6 provides for certain documents to be filed with an appellant's notice)

Amendment of Appeal Notice

5.25 An appeal notice may be amended with permission. Such an application to amend and any application in opposition will normally be dealt with at the hearing unless that course would cause unnecessary expense or delay in which case a request should be made for the application to amend to be heard in advance.

Procedure after permission is obtained

6.1 This paragraph sets out the procedure where:

    (1) permission to appeal is given by the appeal court; or

    (2) the appellant's notice is filed in the appeal court and—

        (a) permission was given by the lower court; or

        (b) permission is not required.

6.2 If the appeal court gives permission to appeal, copies of all the documents referred to at paragraph 5.6 must be served on the respondents within 7 days of receiving the order giving permission to appeal.

(Part 6 (service of documents) provides rules on service) 6.3 The appeal court will send the parties—

    (1) notification of—

        (a) the date of the hearing or the period of time (the "listing window") during which the appeal is likely to be heard; and

        (b) in the Court of Appeal, the date by which the appeal will be heard (the "hear by date");

    (2) where permission is granted by the appeal court a copy of the order giving permission to appeal; and

(3) any other directions given by the court.

Appeal Questionnaire in the Court of Appeal

6.4 The Court of Appeal will send an Appeal Questionnaire to the appellant when it notifies him of the matters referred to in paragraph 6.3.

6.5 The appellant must complete and lodge the Appeal Questionnaire within 14 days of the date of the letter of notification of the matters in paragraph 6.3. The Appeal Questionnaire must contain:

(1) if the appellant is legally represented, the advocate's time estimate for the hearing of the appeal;

(2) where a transcript of evidence is relevant to the appeal; confirmation that a transcript of evidence has been ordered where this is not already in the bundle of documents.

(3) confirmation that copies of the appeal bundle are being prepared and will be held ready for the use of the Court of Appeal and an undertaking that they will be supplied to the court on request. For the purpose of these bundles photocopies of the transcripts will be accepted

(4) confirmation that copies of the Appeal Questionnaire and the appeal bundle have been served on the respondents and the date of that service;

Time estimates

6.6 The time estimate included in an Appeal Questionnaire must be that of the advocate who will argue the appeal. It should exclude the time required by the court to give judgment. If the respondent disagrees with the time estimate, the respondent must inform the court within 7 days of receipt of the Appeal Questionnaire. In the absence of such notification the respondent will be deemed to have accepted the estimate proposed on behalf of the appellant.

Respondent

7.1 A respondent who wishes to ask the appeal court to vary the order of the lower court in any way must appeal and permission will be required on the same basis as for an appellant.

7.2 A respondent who wishes only to request that the appeal court upholds the judgment or order of the lower court whether for the reasons given in the lower court or otherwise does not make an appeal and does not therefore require permission to appeal in accordance with rule 52.3(1).

7.3 A respondent who wishes to appeal or who wishes to ask the appeal court to uphold the order of the lower court for reasons different from or additional to those given by the lower court must file a respondent's notice.

Time limits

7.4 The time limits for filing a respondent's notice are set out in rule 52.5 (4) and (5).

7.5 Where an extension of time is required the extension must be requested in the respondent's notice and the reasons why the respondent failed to act within the specified time must be included.

Respondent's skeleton argument

7.6 The respondent must provide a skeleton argument for the court in all cases where he proposes to address arguments to the court. The respondent's skeleton argument may be included within a respondent's notice. Where a skeleton argument is included within a respondent's notice it will not form part of the notice for the purposes of rule 52.8.

7.7 Where the skeleton argument is not included within a respondent's notice it should be lodged and served no later than 21 days after the respondent receives the appellant's skeleton argument.

(Rule 52.5(4) sets out the period for filing and serving a respondent's notice)

Content of skeleton arguments

7.8 A respondent's skeleton argument must conform to the directions at paragraphs 5.10 and 5.11 above with any necessary modifications. It should, where appropriate, answer the arguments set out in the appellant's skeleton argument.

Applications within respondent's notices

7.9 A respondent may include an application within a respondent's notice in accordance with paragraph 5.5 above.

Filing respondent's notices and skeleton arguments

7.10The respondent must lodge the following documents with his respondent's notice in every case:

(1) two additional copies of the respondent's notice for the appeal court

(2) one copy each for the appellant and any other respondents; and

(3) two copies of any skeleton arguments

7.11If the respondent does not file a respondent's notice, he will not be entitled, except with the permission of the court, to rely on any ground not relied on in the lower court.

7.12If the respondent wishes to rely on any documents in addition to those filed by the appellant he must prepare a supplemental bundle and lodge it at the appeal court with his respondent's notice. He must serve a copy of the supplemental bundle at the same time as serving the respondent's notice on the persons required to be served in accordance with rule 52.5(6).

7.13The respondent's notice and any skeleton argument must be served in accordance with the time limits set out in rule 52.5(6) except this requirement is modified by paragraph 7.7.

Appeals to the High Court

8.1 This paragraph applies where the appeal court is the High Court and the lower court is a county court.

8.2 The following table sets out the following venues for each Circuit–

(a) Appeal centres – court centres where appeals to which this paragraph applies may be managed and heard.

(b) Hearing only centres – court centres where appeals to which this paragraph applies may be heard by order made at an appeal centre (see paragraph 8.5)

Circuit	Appeal Centres	Hearing Only Centres
Midland and Oxford Circuit	Birmingham Nottingham	Oxford Lincoln Leicester Northampton Stafford
North Eastern Circuit	Leeds Newcastle Sheffield	Teesside
Northern Circuit	Manchester Liverpool Preston	Carlisle
Wales and Chester Circuit	Cardiff Swansea Chester	
Western Circuit	Bristol Exeter Winchester	Truro Plymouth
South Eastern Circuit	*Central London*: Royal Courts of Justice *Provincial*: Lewes Luton Norwich Reading	Chelmsford St Albans Maidstone

8.3 The appellant's notice must be filed in the District Registry at an appeal centre on the Circuit in which the lower court is situated. Unless the appeal court otherwise orders the appeal will be managed and heard at that appeal centre.

8.4 The appeal court may transfer an appeal to another appeal centre (whether or not on the same circuit). In deciding whether to do so the court will have regard to the criteria in rule 30.3 (criteria for a transfer order). The appeal court may do so either on application by a party or of its own initiative. Where an appeal is transferred under this paragraph, notice of transfer must be served on every person on whom the appellant's notice has been served. An appeal may not be transferred to an appeal centre on another circuit, either for management or hearing, unless the consent of a Presiding Judge of that circuit has been obtained.

8.5 Directions may be given for—
   (a) an appeal to be heard at a hearing only centre; or
   (b) an application in an appeal to be heard at any other venue.
   instead of at the appeal centre managing the appeal.

8.6 Unless a direction has been made under 8.5, any application in the appeal must be made at the appeal centre where the appeal is being managed.

8.7 A respondent's notice must be filed at the appeal centre where the appellant's notice was filed unless the appeal has been transferred to another appeal centre, in which case it must be filed at that appeal centre.

8.8 The appeal court may adopt all or any part of the procedure set out in paragraphs 6.4 to 6.6.

8.9 (1) Appeals and applications for permission to appeal will be heard by a High Court Judge or by a person authorised under paragraphs (1), (2) or (4) of the Table in section 9(1) of the Supreme Court Act 1981 to act as a judge of the High Court;
   (2) Other applications in the appeal may be heard and directions in the appeal may be given either by a High Court Judge or by any person authorised under section 9(1) of the Supreme Court Act 1981 to act as a judge of the High Court.

Appeals to a judge of a county court from a district judge

8A1 The Designated Civil Judge in consultation with his Presiding Judges has responsibility for allocating appeals from decisions of district judges to circuit judges.

Re-hearings

9.1 The hearing of an appeal will not be a re-hearing (as opposed to a review of the decision of the lower court) unless it is required by any enactment or rule or the appeal is from the decision of a minister, person or other body and the minister, person or other body—
   (1) did not hold a hearing to come to that decision; or
   (2) held a hearing to come to that decision, but the procedure adopted did not provide for the consideration of evidence.

Appeals Transferred to the Court of Appeal

10.1 Where an appeal is transferred to the Court of Appeal under rule 52.14 the Court of Appeal may give such additional directions as are considered appropriate.

Applications

11.1 Where a party to an appeal makes an application whether in an appeal notice or by Part 23 application notice, the provisions of Part 23 will apply.

11.2 The applicant must file the following documents with the notice
   (1) one additional copy of the application notice for the appeal court and one copy for each of the respondents;
   (2) where applicable a sealed copy of the order which is the subject of the main appeal;
   (3) A bundle of documents in support which should include:
      (a) the Part 23 application notice
      (b) any witness statements and affidavits filed in support of the application notice
      (c) the documents specified in paragraph 5.6 (6) above in so far as they have not already been filed with the appellant's notice.

Disposing of applications or appeals by consent

Dismissal of applications or appeals by consent

12.1 These paragraphs do not apply where any party to the proceedings is a child or patient.

12.2 Where an appellant does not wish to pursue an application or an appeal, he may request the appeal court for an order that his application or appeal be dismissed. Such a request must contain a statement that the appellant is not a child or patient. If such a request is granted it will usually be on the basis that the appellant pays the costs of the application or appeal.

12.3 If the appellant wishes to have the application or appeal dismissed without costs, his request must be accompanied by a consent signed by the respondent or his legal representative stating that the respondent is not a child or patient and consents to the dismissal of the application or appeal without costs.

12.4 Where a settlement has been reached disposing of the application or appeal, the parties may make a joint request to the court stating that none of them is a child or patient, and asking that the application or appeal be dismissed by consent. If the request is granted the application or appeal will be dismissed.

Allowing unopposed appeals or applications on paper

13.1 The appeal court will not make an order allowing an appeal unless satisfied that the decision of the lower court was wrong. Where the appeal court is requested by all parties to allow an application or an appeal the court may consider the request on the papers. The request should state that none of the parties is a child or patient and set out the relevant history of the proceedings and the matters relied on as justifying the proposed order and be accompanied by a copy of the proposed order.

Procedure for Structured settlements and consent orders involving a child or patient

13.2 Settlements relating to appeals and applications where one of the parties is a child or a patient; and structured settlements which are agreed upon at the appeal stage require the court's approval.

Child

13.3 In cases involving a child a copy of the proposed order signed by the parties' solicitors should be sent to the appeal court, together with an opinion from the advocate acting on behalf of the child.

Patient

13.4 Where a party is a patient the same procedure will be adopted, but the documents filed should also include any relevant reports prepared for the Court of Protection and a document evidencing formal approval by that court where required.

Structured settlements

13.5 Where a structured settlement has been negotiated in a case which is under appeal the documents filed should include those which would be required in the case of a structured settlement dealt with at first instance. Details can be found in the Practice Direction which supplements CPR Part 40.

Summary assessment of costs

14.1 Costs are likely to be assessed by way of summary assessment at the following hearings:

    (1) contested directions hearings;

    (2) applications for permission to appeal at which the respondent is present;

    (3) dismissal list hearings in the Court of Appeal at which the respondent is present;

    (4) appeals from case management decisions; and

    (5) appeals listed for one day or less.

14.2 Parties attending any of the hearings referred to in paragraph 14.1 should be prepared to deal with the summary assessment.

Other special provisions regarding the Court of Appeal

Filing of Documents

15.1 (1) The documents relevant to proceedings in the Court of Appeal, Civil Division must be filed in the Civil Appeals Office Registry, Room E307, Royal Courts of Justice, Strand, London, WC2A 2LL.

(2) The Civil Appeals Office will not serve documents and where service is required by the CPR or this practice direction it must be effected by the parties.

Master in the Court of Appeal, Civil Division

15.2 When the Head of the Civil Appeals Office acts in a judicial capacity pursuant to rule 52.16, he shall be known as Master. Other eligible officers may also be designated by the Master of the Rolls to exercise judicial authority under rule 52.16 and shall then be known as Deputy Masters.

Judicial Review Appeals

15.3 Where the Court of appeal gives permission to apply for judicial review under rule 52.15(3) the court may, hear the application for judicial review. This will be rare, but may be appropriate where, for example, the High Court is bound by authority or for some other reason, an appeal to the Court of Appeal will be inevitable.

15.4 Paragraphs 5.6 and 5.19 above do not apply to cases where the appeal notice seeks permission to appeal a refusal to give permission to apply for judicial review. In such cases the following documents must be filed with the appellant's notice:

(1) one additional copy of the appellant's notice for the Court of Appeal

(2) one copy of the appellant's notice for each of the respondents to be sealed and returned

(3) the order refusing permission to apply for judicial review

(4) Form 86A;

(5) a copy of the original decision which is the subject of the application to the High Court

(6) any witness statements or affidavits in support of any application included in the appellant's notice;

(7) a copy of the bundle of documents used in the High Court

(8) the skeleton argument relied on in the High Court; and

(9) a transcript of the judgment.

15.5 The time for filing an appellant's notice in these circumstances is set out in rule 52.15(1). The arrangements for service on the respondent in paragraph 5.21 apply.

15.6 Where it is not possible to file all these documents, the appellant must indicate which documents have not yet been filed and the reasons why they are not currently available.

Listing and hear-by dates

15.7 The management of the list will be dealt with by the listing officer under the direction of the Master.

15.8 The Civil Appeals List of the Court of Appeal is divided as follows:

- The applications list – applications for permission to appeal and other applications.
- The appeals list – appeals where permission to appeal has been given or where an appeal lies without permission being required.
- The expedited list – appeals or applications where the Court of Appeal has directed an expedited hearing. The current practice of the Court of Appeal is summarised in Unilever plc. v. Chefaro Proprietaries Ltd. (Practice Note) [1995] 1 W.L.R. 24.
- The stand-out list – Appeals or application which, for good reason, are not at present ready to proceed and have been stood out by judicial direction.
- The fixtures list – where a hearing date for the appeal is fixed in advance.
- The second fixtures list – if an appeal is designated as a "second fixture" it means that a hearing date is arranged in advance on the express basis that the list is fully booked for the period in question and therefore the case will be heard only if a suitable gap occurs in the list.
- The short-warned list – appeals which the court considers may be prepared for the hearing by an advocate other than the one originally instructed with a half day's notice, or, if the court so directs, 48 hours notice.

15.9 Once an appeal is listed for hearing from the short warned list it becomes the immediate professional duty of the advocate instructed in the appeal, if he is unable to appear at the hearing, to take all practicable measures to ensure that his lay client is represented at the hearing by an advocate who is fully instructed and able to argue the appeal.

Requests for directions

15.10 To ensure that all requests for directions are centrally monitored and correctly allocated, all requests for directions or rulings (whether relating to listing or any other matters) should be made to the Civil Appeals Office. Those seeking directions or rulings must not approach the supervising Lord Justice either directly, or via his or her clerk.

Lists of authorities

15.11 Once the parties have been notified of the date fixed for hearing the appellant's advocate shall file, after consulting his opponent, for the purpose of pre-reading by the court, one bundle containing photocopies of the principal authorities upon which each side will rely at the hearing, with the relevant passages marked. There will in general be no need to include authorities for propositions not in dispute. This bundle should be made available 28 days before the hearing, unless the period of notice of the hearing is less than 28 days in which case the bundle should be filed immediately. Such bundles should not normally contain more than 10 authorities. If any party intends, during the hearing to refer to other authorities these may be included in a second agreed bundle to be filed by the parties at the hearing. Alternatively, and in place of the second bundle only, a list of authorities and text may be delivered to the office of the Head Usher of the Court of Appeal no later than 5.30pm on the last working day before the hearing is to commence.

Reserved judgments of the Court of Appeal

15.12 Unless the court orders otherwise, copies of a written judgment will be made available to the parties' legal advisers by 4 p.m. on the second working day before judgment is due to be pronounced on the condition that the contents are not communicated to the parties themselves until one hour before the listed time for pronouncement of judgment.

15.13 The judgment is made available to legal advisers primarily to enable them to consider the judgment and decide what consequential orders they should seek. The condition is imposed to prevent the outcome of the case being publicly reported before judgment is given, since the judgment is confidential until then. Every page of the judgment will be marked "Unapproved judgment: No permission is given to copy or use in court". These words carry the authority of the court.

15.14 Where a party is not legally represented a copy of the judgment will be made available to him at the same time as to legal advisers. It must be treated as confidential until pronouncement of judgment.

SECTION II – GENERAL PROVISIONS ABOUT STATUTORY APPEALS AND APPEALS BY WAY OF CASE STATED

16.1 This section of this practice direction contains general provisions about statutory appeals (paragraphs 17.1-17.6) and appeals by way of case stated (paragraphs 18.1-18.20).

16.2 Where any of the provisions in this section provide for documents to be filed at the appeal court, these documents are in addition to any documents required under Part 52 or section I of this practice direction.

Statutory appeals

17.1 This part of this section–

(1) applies where under any enactment an appeal (other than by way of case stated) lies to the court from a Minister of State, government department, tribunal or other person ("statutory appeals"); and

(2) is subject to any provision about a specific category of appeal in any enactment or Section III of this practice direction.

Part 52

17.2 Part 52 applies to statutory appeals with the following amendments:

Filing of appellant's notice

17.3 The appellant must file the appellant's notice at the appeal court within 28 days after the date of the decision of the lower court he wishes to appeal.

17.4 Where a statement of the reasons for a decision is given later than the notice of that decision, the period for filing the appellant's notice is calculated from the date on which the statement is received by the appellant.

Service of appellant's notice

17.5 In addition to the respondents to the appeal, the appellant must serve the appellant's notice in accordance with rule 52.4(3) on the chairman of the tribunal, Minister of State, government department or other person from whose decision the appeal is brought.

Right of Minister etc. to be heard on the appeal

17.6 Where the appeal is from an order or decision of a Minister of State or government department, the Minister or department, as the case may be, is entitled to attend the hearing and to make representations to the court.

Appeals by way of case stated

18.1 This part of this section—

    (1) applies where under any enactment—

        (a) an appeal lies to the court by way of case stated; or

        (b) a question of law may be referred to the court by way of case stated; and

    (2) is subject to any provision about to a specific category of appeal in any enactment or Section III of this practice direction.

Part 52

18.2 Part 52 applies to appeals by way of case stated subject to the following amendments.

Case stated by Crown Court or Magistrates' Court

Application to state a case

18.3 The procedure for applying to the Crown Court or a Magistrates' Court to have a case stated for the opinion of the High Court is set out in the Crown Court Rules 1982 and the Magistrates' Courts Rules 1981 respectively.

Filing of appellant's notice

18.4 The appellant must file the appellant's notice at the appeal court within 10 days after he receives the stated case.

Documents to be lodged

18.5 The appellant must lodge the following documents with his appellant's notice:

    (1) the stated case;

    (2) a copy of the judgment, order or decision in respect of which the case has been stated; and

    (3) where the judgment, order or decision in respect of which the case has been stated was itself given or made on appeal, a copy of the judgment, order or decision appealed from.

Service of appellant's notice

18.6 The appellant must serve the appellant's notice and accompanying documents on all respondents within 4 days after they are filed or lodged at the appeal court.

Case stated by Minister, government department, tribunal or other person

Application to state a case

18.7 The procedure for applying to a Minister, government department, tribunal or other person ("Minister or tribunal etc.") to have a case stated for the opinion of the court may be set out in—

    (1) the enactment which provides for the right of appeal; or

    (2) any rules of procedure relating to the Minister or tribunal etc.

Signing of stated case by Minister or tribunal etc.

18.8 A case stated by a tribunal must be signed by the chairman or president of the tribunal. A case stated by any other person must be signed by that person or by a person authorised to do so.

Service of stated case by Minister or tribunal etc.

18.9 The Minister or tribunal etc. must serve the stated case on—

    (1) the party who requests the case to be stated; or

    (2) the party as a result of whose application to the court, the case was stated.

18.10Where an enactment provides that a Minister or tribunal etc. may state a case or refer a question of law to the court by way of case stated without a request being made, the Minister or tribunal etc. must–

(1) serve the stated case on those parties that the Minister or tribunal etc. considers appropriate; and

(2) give notice to every other party to the proceedings that the stated case has been served on the party named and on the date specified in the notice.

Filing and service of appellant's notice

18.11The party on whom the stated case was served must file the appellant's notice and the stated case at the appeal court and serve copies of the notice and stated case on–

(1) the Minister or tribunal etc. who stated the case; and

(2) every party to the proceedings to which the stated case relates,

within 14 days after the stated case was served on him.

18.12Where paragraph 18.10 applies the Minister or tribunal etc. must–

(1) file an appellant's notice and the stated case at the appeal court; and

(2) serve copies of those documents on the persons served under paragraph 18.10

within 14 days after stating the case.

18.13Where–

(1) a stated case has been served by the Minister or tribunal etc. in accordance with paragraph 18.9; and

(2) the party on whom the stated case was served does not file an appellant's notice in accordance with paragraph 18.11, any other party may file an appellant's notice with the stated case at the appeal court and serve a copy of the notice and the case on the persons listed in paragraph 18.11 within the period of time set out in paragraph 18.14.

18.14The period of time referred to in paragraph 18.13 is 14 days from the last day on which the party on whom the stated case was served may file an appellant's notice in accordance with paragraph 18.11.

Amendment of stated case

18.15The court may amend the stated case or order it to be returned to the Minister or tribunal etc. for amendment and may draw inferences of fact from the facts stated in the case.

Right of Minister etc. to be heard on the appeal

18.16Where the case is stated by a Minister or government department, that Minister or department, as the case may be, is entitled to appear on the appeal and to make representations to the court.

Application for order to state a case

18.17An application to the court for an order requiring a minister or tribunal etc. to state a case for the decision of the court, or to refer a question of law to the court by way of case stated must be made to the court which would be the appeal court if the case were stated.

18.18An application to the court for an order directing a Minister or tribunal etc. to–

(1) state a case for determination by the court; or

(2) refer a question of law to the court by way of case stated, must be made in accordance with CPR Part 23

18.19The application notice must contain–

(1) the grounds of the application;

(2) the question of law on which it is sought to have the case stated; and

(3) any reasons given by the minister or tribunal etc. for his or its refusal to state a case.

18.20The application notice must be filed at the appeal court and served on–

(1) the minister, department, secretary of the tribunal or other person as the case may be; and

(2) every party to the proceedings to which the application relates,

within 14 days after the appellant receives notice of the refusal of his request to state a case.

Extradition

19.1Paragraphs 18.3 to 18.6 apply to appeals by case stated under–

(1) section 7 of the Criminal Justice Act 1988; and

(2) section 7A of the Fugitive Offenders Act 1967,

and references in those paragraphs to appellant and respondent shall be construed as references to the requesting state and the person whose surrender is sought respectively.

19.2 An application for an order under either of the sections mentioned in paragraph 19.1 or under section 2A of the Backing of Warrants (Republic of Ireland) Act 1965 requiring a court to state a case must be made in accordance with paragraphs 18.17 to 18.20 and the references in those paragraphs to a tribunal and the secretary of a tribunal shall be construed as references to the court and the clerk of the court respectively.

SECTION III – PROVISIONS ABOUT SPECIFIC APPEALS

20.1 This section of this Practice Direction provides special provisions about the appeals to which the following table refers. This Section is not exhaustive and does not create, amend or remove any right of appeal.

20.2 Part 52 applies to all appeals to which this section applies subject to any special provisions set out in this section.

20.3 Where any of the provisions in this section provide for documents to be filed at the appeal court, these documents are in addition to any documents required under Part 52 or sections I or II of this practice direction.

Appeals to the Court of Appeal	Paragraph
Competition Commission Appeal Tribunals	21.10
Contempt of Court	21.4
Decree nisi of divorce	21.1
Immigration Appeal Tribunal	21.7
Lands Tribunal	21.9
Nullity of marriage	21.1
Patents Court on appeal from Comptroller	21.3
Revocation of patent	21.2
Social Security Commissioners	21.5
Special Commissioner (where the appeal is direct to the Court of Appeal)	21.8
Value Added Tax and Duties Tribunals (where the appeal is direct to the Court of Appeal)	21.6

Appeals to the High Court	Paragraph
Agriculture Land Tribunal	22.7
Architects Act 1997, s. 22	22.3
Clergy Pensions Measure 1961, s. 38(3)	23.2
Commons Registration Act 1965	23.9
Consumer Credit Act 1974	22.4
Friendly Societies Act 1974	23.7
Friendly Societies Act 1992	23.7
Industrial and Provident Societies Act 1965	23.2, 23.7
Industrial Assurance Act 1923	23.2, 23.7

Industrial Assurance Act 1923, s. 17	23.6
Inheritance Tax Act 1984, s. 222	23.3
Inheritance Tax Act 1984, s. 225	23.5
Inheritance Tax Act 1984, ss. 249(3) and 251	23.4
Land Registration Act 1925	23.2
Law of Property Act 1922, para. 16 of Sched. 15	23.2
Medicines Act 1968, ss. 82(3) and 83(2)	22.3
Mental Health Review Tribunal	22.8
Merchant Shipping Act 1995	22.2
Nurses, Midwives and Health Visitors Act 1977, s. 12	22.3
Pension Act 1995, s. 97	23.2
Pension Schemes Act 1993, ss. 151 and 173	23.2
Pensions Appeal Tribunal Act 1943	22.5
Pharmacy Act 1954	22.3
Social Security Administration Act 1992	22.6
Stamp Duty Reserve Tax Regulations 1986, reg. 10	23.5
Taxes Management Act 1970, ss. 53 and 100C(4)	23.4
Taxes Management Act 1970, s. 56A	23.5
Value Added Tax and Duties Tribunal	23.8
Water Resources Act 1991, s. 205(4)	23.2

Appeals to the High Court	**Paragraph**
Local Government (Miscellaneous Provisions) Act 1976	24.1

Appeals to the Court of Appeal

Appeal against decree nisi of divorce or nullity of marriage

21.1(1)   The appellant must file the appellant's notice at the Court of Appeal within 28 days after the date on which the decree was pronounced.

(2)   The appellant must file the following documents with the appellant's notice–

(a)   the decree; and

(b)   a certificate of service of the appellant's notice.

(3)   The appellant's notice must be served on the appropriate district judge (see sub-paragraph (6)) in addition to the persons to be served under rule 52.4(3) and in accordance with that rule.

(4)   The lower court may not alter the time limits for filing of the appeal notices.

(5)   Where an appellant intends to apply to the Court of Appeal for an extension of time for serving or filing the appellant's notice he must give notice of that intention to the appropriate district judge (see sub-paragraph 6) before the application is made.

(6)   In this paragraph "the appropriate district judge" means, where the lower court is–

(a)   a county court, the district judge of that court;

(b)   a district registry, the district judge of that registry;

(c) the Principal Registry of the Family Division, the senior district judge of that division.

Appeal against order for revocation of patent

21.2(1) This paragraph applies where an appeal lies to the Court of Appeal from an order for the revocation of a patent.

(2) The appellant must serve the appellant's notice on the Comptroller-General of Patents, Designs and Trade Marks (the "Comptroller") in addition to the persons to be served under rule 52.4(3) and in accordance with that rule.

(3) Where, before the appeal hearing, the respondent decides not to oppose the appeal or not to attend the appeal hearing, he must immediately serve notice of that decision on—

(a) the Comptroller; and

(b) the appellant

(4) Where the respondent serves a notice in accordance with paragraph (2), he must also serve copies of the following documents on the Comptroller with that notice—

(a) the petition;

(b) any statements of claim;

(c) any written evidence filed in the claim.

(5) Within 14 days after receiving the notice in accordance with paragraph (2), the Comptroller must serve on the appellant a notice stating whether or not he intends to attend the appeal hearing.

(6) The Comptroller may attend the appeal hearing and oppose the appeal—

(a) in any case where he has given notice under paragraph (4) of his intention to attend; and

(b) in any other case (including, in particular, a case where the respondent withdraws his opposition to the appeal during the hearing) if the Court of Appeal so directs or permits.

Appeal from Patents Court on appeal from Comptroller

21.3 Where the appeal is from a decision of the Patents Court which was itself made on an appeal from a decision of the Comptroller-General of Patents, Designs and Trade Marks, the appellant must serve the appellant's notice on the Comptroller in addition to the persons to be served under rule 52.4(3) and in accordance with that rule.

Appeals in cases of contempt of court

21.4 In an appeal under section 13 of the Administration of Justice Act 1960 (appeals in cases of contempt of court), the appellant must serve the appellant's notice on the court from whose order or decision the appeal is brought in addition to the persons to be served under rule 52.4(3) and in accordance with that rule.

Appeals from Social Security Commissioners

21.5(1) This paragraph applies to appeals under section 24 of the Social Security Administration Act 1992 (appeal from the decision of a Commissioner on a question of law).

(2) The appellant must serve the appellant's notice—

(a) within 6 weeks after the date on which notice of the Commissioner's decision on permission to appeal to the Court of Appeal was given in writing to the appellant; and

(b) on—

(i) the Secretary of State; and

(ii) any person appointed by him to proceed with a claim,

in addition to the persons to be served under rule 52.4(3) and in accordance with that rule.

Appeals from Value Added Tax and Duties Tribunals

21.6(1) An application to the Court of Appeal for permission to appeal from a value added tax and duties tribunal direct to that court must be made within 28 days after the date on which the tribunal certifies that its decision involves a point of law relating wholly or mainly to the construction of –

(a) an enactment or of a statutory instrument; or

(b) any of the Community Treaties or any Community Instrument,

which has been fully argued before and fully considered by it.

(2) The application must be made by the parties jointly filing at the Court of Appeal an appellant's notice that–

(a) contains a statement of the grounds for the application; and

(b) is accompanied by a copy of the decision to be appealed, endorsed with the certificate of the tribunal.

(3) The court will notify the appellant of its decision and–

(a) where permission to appeal to the Court of Appeal is given, the appellant must serve the appellant's notice on the chairman of the tribunal in addition to the persons to be served under rule 52.4(3) within 14 days after that notification.

(b) where permission to appeal to the Court of Appeal is refused, the period for appealing to the High Court is to be calculated from the date of the notification of that refusal.

Appeals from Immigration Appeals Tribunal

21.7(1) This paragraph applies to appeals under section 9 of the Asylum and Immigration Appeals Act 1993 (appeal on a question of law from a final determination of an Immigration Appeals Tribunal).

(2) The period of time within which the appellant must file the appellant's notice at the Court of Appeal in accordance with rule 52.4(2) begins to run from the date of the tribunal's written decision to give or refuse permission to appeal.

(3) The appellant must serve the appellant's notice on the chairman of the tribunal in addition to the persons to be served under rule 52.4(3) and in accordance with that rule.

Appeal from Special Commissioners

21.8(1) An application to the Court of Appeal for permission to appeal from the Special Commissioners direct to that court under section 56A of the Taxes Management Act 1970 must be made within 28 days after the date on which the Special Commissioners certify that their decision involves a point of law relating wholly or mainly to the construction of an enactment which has been fully argued before and fully considered before them.

(2) The application must be made by the parties jointly filing at the Court of Appeal an appellant's notice that–

(a) contains a statement of the grounds for the application; and

(b) is accompanied by a copy of the decision to be appealed, endorsed with the certificate of the tribunal.

(3) The court will notify the appellant of its decision and–

(a) where permission to appeal to the Court of Appeal is given, the appellant must serve the appellant's notice on the Clerk to the Special Commissioners in addition to the persons to be served under rule 52.4(3) within 14 days after that notification.

(b) where permission to appeal to the Court of Appeal is refused, the period for appealing to the High Court is to be calculated from the date of the notification of that refusal.

Appeal from Lands Tribunal

21.9 The appellant must file the appellant's notice at the Court of Appeal within 28 days after the date of the decision of the tribunal.

Appeal from Competition Commission Appeal Tribunal

21.10(1) Where the appellant applies for permission to appeal at the hearing at which the decision is delivered by the tribunal and–

(a) permission is given; or

(b) permission is refused and the appellant wishes to make an application to the Court of Appeal for permission to appeal,

the appellant's notice must be filed at the Court of Appeal within 14 days after the date of that hearing.

(2) Where the appellant applies in writing to the Registrar of the tribunal for permission to appeal and–

(a) permission is given; or

(b) permission is refused and the appellant wishes to make an application to the Court of Appeal for permission to appeal,

the appellant's notice must be filed at the Court of Appeal within 14 days after the date of receipt of the tribunal's decision on permission.

(3) Where the appellant does not make an application to the tribunal for permission to appeal, but wishes to make an application to the Court of Appeal for permission, the appellant's notice must be filed at the Court of Appeal within 14 days after the end of the period within which he may make a written application to the Registrar of the tribunal.

Appeals to the High Court – Queen's Bench Division

22.1 The following appeals are to be heard in the Queen's Bench Division.

Statutory Appeals

Appeals under the Merchant Shipping Act 1995

22.2(1) This paragraph applies to appeals under the Merchant Shipping Act 1995 and for this purpose a re-hearing and an application under section 61 of the Merchant Shipping Act 1995 are treated as appeals.

(2) The appellant must file any report to the Secretary of State containing the decision from which the appeal is brought with the appellant's notice.

(3) Where a re-hearing by the High Court is ordered under sections 64 or 269 of the Merchant Shipping Act 1995, the Secretary of State must give reasonable notice to the parties whom he considers to be affected by the re-hearing.

Appeal where court's decision is final

22.3(1) This paragraph applies to an appeal to the High Court under–

(a) section 22 of the Architects Act 1997;

(b) section 82(3) and 83(2) of the Medicines Act 1968;

(c) section 12 of the Nurses, Midwives and Health Visitors Act 1997; and

(d) section 10 of the Pharmacy Act 1954.

(2) Every appeal to which this paragraph applies must be supported by written evidence and, if the court so orders, oral evidence.

(3) The appellant must file the appellant's notice within 28 days after the decision that the appellant wishes to appeal.

(4) In the case of an appeal under an enactment specified in column 1 of the following table, the persons to be made respondents are the persons specified in relation to that enactment in column 2 of the table and the person to be served with the appellant's notice is the person so specified in column 3.

1	2	3
Enactment	**Respondents**	**Person to be served**
Architects Act 1997, s. 22 Council of the United Kingdom	The Architects' Registration Council	The registrar of the
Medicines Act 1968, s. 82(3) and s. 83(2)	The Pharmaceutical Society of Great Britain	The registrar of the Society
Nurses, Midwives and Health Visitors Act 1997, s. 12	The United Kingdom Central Council for Nursing, Midwifery and Health Visiting	The registrar of the Council
Pharmacy Act 1954, s. 10	The Pharmaceutical Society of Great Britain	The registrar of the Society

Consumer Credit Act 1974: appeal from Secretary of State

22.4(1) A person dissatisfied in point of law with a decision of the Secretary of State on an appeal under section 41 of the Consumer Credit Act 1974 from a determination of the Director General of Fair Trading who had a right to appeal to the Secretary of State, whether or not he exercised that right, may appeal to the High Court.

(2) The appellant must serve the appellant's notice on—

(a) the Secretary of State;

(b) the original applicant, if any, where the appeal is by a licensee under a group licence against compulsory variation, suspension or revocation of that licence; and

(c) any other person as directed by the court.

(3) The appeal court may remit the matter to the Secretary of State to the extent necessary to enable him to provide the court with such further information as the court may direct.

(4) If the appeal court allows the appeal, it shall not set aside or vary the decision but shall remit the matter to the Secretary of State with the opinion of the court for hearing and determination by him.

The Pensions Appeal Tribunal Act 1943

22.5(1) In this paragraph "the judge" means the judge nominated by the Lord Chancellor under section 6(2) of the Pensions Appeal Tribunals Act 1943 ("the Act").

(2) An application to the judge for permission to appeal against a decision of a Pensions Appeal Tribunal—

(a) may not be made unless an application was made to the tribunal and was refused; and

(b) must be made within 28 days after the date of the tribunal's refusal.

(3) The appellant's notice seeking permission to appeal from the judge must contain—

(a) the point of law as respects which the appellant alleges that the tribunal's decision was wrong; and

(b) the date of the tribunal's decision refusing permission to appeal.

(4) The court officer shall request the chairman of the tribunal to give the judge a written statement of the reasons for the tribunal's decision to refuse permission to appeal, and within 7 days after receiving the request, the chairman must give the judge such a statement.

(5) Where permission to appeal was given by—

(a) the tribunal, the appellant must file and serve the appellant's notice;

(b) the judge, the appellant must serve the appellant's notice, within 28 days after permission to appeal was given.

(6) Within 28 days after service of the notice of appeal on him, the chairman of the tribunal must—

(a) state a case setting out the facts on which the decision appealed against was based;

(b) file the case stated at the court; and

(c) serve a copy of the case stated on the appellant and the respondent.

(7) A copy of the judge's order on the appeal must be sent by the court officer to the appellant, the respondent and the chairman of the tribunal.

The Social Security Administration Act 1992

22.6(1) Any person who by virtue of section 18 or 58(8) of the Social Security Administration Act 1992 ("the Act") is entitled and wishes to appeal against a decision of the Secretary of State on a question of law must, within the prescribed period, or within such further time as the Secretary of State may allow, serve on the Secretary of State a notice requiring him to state a case setting out—

(a) his decision; and

(b) the facts on which his decision was based.

(2) Unless paragraph (3) applies the prescribed period is 28 days after receipt of the notice of the decision.

(3) Where, within 28 days after receipt of notice of the decision, a request is made to the Secretary of State in accordance with regulations made under the Act to furnish a statement of the grounds of the decision, the prescribed period is 28 days after receipt of that statement.

(4) Where under section 18 or section 58(8) of the Act, the Secretary of State refers a question of law to the court, he must state that question together with the relevant facts in a case.

(5) The appellant's notice and the case stated must be filed at the appeal court and a copy of the notice and the case stated served on—

(a) the Secretary of State; and

(b) every person as between whom and the Secretary of State the question has arisen,

within 28 days after the case stated was served on the party at whose request, or as a result of whose application to the court, the case was stated.

(6) Unless the appeal court otherwise orders, the appeal or reference shall not be heard sooner than 28 days after service of the appellant's notice.

(7) The appeal court may order the case stated by the Secretary of State to be returned to the Secretary of State for him to hear further evidence.

Appeals by way of case stated

Reference of question of law by Agriculture Land Tribunal

22.7(1) A question of law referred to the High Court by an Agricultural Land Tribunal under section 6 of the Agriculture (Miscellaneous Provisions) Act 1954 shall be referred by way of case stated by the Tribunal.

(2) Where the proceedings before the tribunal arose on an application under section 11 of the Agricultural Holdings Act 1986, an—

(a) application notice for an order under section 6 that the tribunal refers a question of law to the court; and

(b) appellant's notice by which an appellant seeks the court's determination on a question of law,

must be served on the authority having power to enforce the statutory requirement specified in the notice in addition to every other party to those proceedings and on the secretary of the tribunal.

(3) Where, in accordance with paragraph (2), a notice is served on the authority mentioned in that paragraph, that authority may attend the appeal hearing and make representations to the court.

Case stated by Mental Health Review Tribunal

22.8(1) In this paragraph "the Act" means the Mental Health Act 1983 and "party to proceedings" means—

(a) the person who initiated the proceedings; and

    (b) any person to whom, in accordance with rules made under section 78 of the Act, the tribunal sent notice of the application or reference or a request instead notice of reference.

(2) A party to proceedings shall not be entitled to apply to the High Court for an order under section 78(8) of the Act directing the tribunal to state a case for determination by court unless–

    (a) within 21 days after the decision of the tribunal was communicated to him in accordance with rules made under section 78 of the Act he made a written request to the tribunal to state a case; and

    (b) either the tribunal

        (i) failed to comply with that request within 21 days after it was made; or

        (ii) refused to comply with it.

(3) The period for filing the application notice for an order under section 78(8) of the Act is–

    (a) where the tribunal failed to comply with the applicant's request to state a case within the period mentioned in paragraph (3)(b)(I), 14 days after the expiration of that period;

    (b) where the tribunal refused that request, 14 days after receipt by the applicant of notice of the refusal of his request.

(4) A Mental Health Review Tribunal by whom a case is stated shall be entitled to attend the proceedings for the determination of the case and make representations to the court.

(5) If the court allows the appeal, it may give any direction which the tribunal ought to have given under Part V of the Act.

Appeals to the High Court – Chancery Division

23.1 The following appeals are to be heard in the Chancery Division

Determination of appeal or case stated under various Acts

23.2 Any appeal to the High Court, and any case stated or question referred for the opinion of that court under any of the following enactments shall be heard in the Chancery Division–

  (1) paragraph 16 of Schedule 15 to the Law of Property Act 1922;

  (2) the Industrial Assurance Act 1923;

  (3) the Land Registration Act 1925;

  (4) section 205(4) of the Water Resources Act 1991;

  (5) section 38(3) of the Clergy Pensions Measure 1961;

  (6) the Industrial and Provident Societies Act 1965;

  (7) section 151 of the Pension Schemes Act 1993;

  (8) section 173 of the Pension Schemes Act 1993; and

  (9) section 97 of the Pensions Act 1995.

(This list is not exhaustive)

Statutory appeals

Appeal under section 222 of the Inheritance Tax Act 1984

23.3 (1) This paragraph applies to appeals to the High Court under section 222(3) of the Inheritance Tax Act 1984 (the "1984 Act") and regulation 8(3) of the Stamp Duty Reserve Tax Regulations 1986 (the "1986 Regulations").

(2) The appellant's notice must–

    (a) state the date on which the Commissioners of Inland Revenue (the "Board") gave notice to the appellant under section 221 of the 1984 Act or regulation 6 of the 1986 Regulations of the determination that is the subject of the appeal;

    (b) state the date on which the appellant gave to the Board notice of appeal under section 222(1) of the 1984 Act or regulation 8(1) of the 1986 Regulations and, if notice was not given within the time permitted, whether the Board or the Special Commissioners have given their consent to the appeal being brought out of time, and, if they have, the date they gave their consent; and

    (c) either state that the appellant and the Board have agreed that the appeal may be to the High Court or contain an application for permission to appeal to the High Court.

(3) The appellant must file the following documents with the appellant's notice—

    (a) 2 copies of the notice referred to in paragraph 2(a);

    (b) 2 copies of the notice of appeal (under section 222(1) of the 1984 Act or regulation 8(1) of the 1986 Regulations) referred to in paragraph 2(b); and

    (c) where the appellant's notice contains an application for permission to appeal, written evidence setting out the grounds on which it is alleged that the matters to be decided on the appeal are likely to be substantially confined to questions of law.

(4) The appellant must—

    (a) file the appellant's notice at the court; and

    (b) serve the appellant's notice on the Board,

within 30 days of the date on which the appellant gave to the Board notice of appeal under section 222(1) of the 1984 Act or regulation 8(1) of the 1986 Regulations or, if the Board or the Special Commissioners have given consent to the appeal being brought out of time, within 30 days of the date on which such consent was given.

(5) The court will set a date for the hearing of not less than 40 days from the date that the appellant's notice was filed.

(6) Where the appellant's notice contains an application for permission to appeal—

    (a) a copy of the written evidence filed in accordance with paragraph (3)(c) must be served on the Board with the appellant's notice; and

    (b) the Board—

        (i) may file written evidence; and

        (ii) if it does so, must serve a copy of that evidence on the appellant,

    within 30 days after service of the written evidence under paragraph (6)(a).

(7) The appellant may not rely on any grounds of appeal not specified in the notice referred to in paragraph (2)(b) on the hearing of the appeal without the permission of the court.

Appeals under section 53 and 100C(4) of the Taxes Management Act 1970 and section 249(3) or 251 of the Inheritance Tax Act 1984

23.4(1) The appellant must serve the appellant's notice on—

    (a) the General or Special Commissioners against whose decision, award or determination the appeal is brought; and

    (b) (i) in the case of an appeal brought under section 100C(4) of the Taxes Management Act 1970 or section 249(3) of the Inheritance Tax Act 1984 by any party other that the defendant in the proceedings before the Commissioners, that defendant; or

        (ii) in any other case, the Commissioners of Inland Revenue.

(2) The appellant must file the appellant's notice at the court within 30 days after the date of the decision, award or determination against which the appeal is brought.

(3) Within 30 days of the service on them of the appellant's notice brought, the General or Special Commissioners, as the case may be, must—

    (a) file 2 copies of a note of their findings and of the reasons for their decision, award or determination at the court; and

    (b) serve a copy of the note on every other party to the appeal.

(4) Any document to be served on the General or Special Commissioners may be served by delivering or sending it to their clerk.

(5) RSC Order 57 does not apply to appeals to which this paragraph applies.

Appeals under section 56A of the Taxes Management Act 1970, section 225 of the Inheritance Tax Act 1984 and regulation 10 of the Stamp Duty Reserve Tax Regulations 1986

23.5(1) The appellant must file the appellant's notice—

    (a) where the appeal is made following the refusal of the Special Commissioners to issue a certificate under section 56A(2)(b) of the Taxes Management Act 1970, within 28 days from the date of the release of the decision of the Special Commissioners containing the refusal;

(b) where the appeal is made following the refusal of permission to appeal to the Court of Appeal under section 56A(2)(c) of that Act, within 28 days from the date when permission is refused; or

(c) in all other cases within 56 days after the date of the decision or determination that the appellant wishes to appeal.

(2) RSC Order 57 does not apply to appeals to which this paragraph applies.

Appeal under section 17 of the Industrial Assurance Act 1923

23.6 The appellant must file the appellant's notice within 21 days after the date of the Commissioner's refusal or direction under section 17(3) of the Industrial Assurance Act 1923.

Appeals affecting industrial and provident societies etc.

23.7(1) This paragraph applies to all appeals under–

(a) the Friendly Societies Act 1974;

(b) the Friendly Societies Act 1992;

(c) the Industrial Assurance Act 1923; and

(d) the Industrial and Provident Societies Act 1965

(2) At any stage on an appeal, the court may–

(a) direct that the appellant's notice be served on any person;

(b) direct that notice be given by advertisement or otherwise of–

(i) the bringing of the appeal;

(ii) the nature of the appeal; and

(iii) the time when the appeal will or is likely to be heard; or

(c) give such other directions as it thinks proper to enable any person interested in–

(i) the society, trade union, alleged trade union or industrial assurance company; or

(ii) the subject matter of the appeal,

to appear and be heard at the appeal hearing.

Appeal from Value Added Tax and Duties Tribunal

23.8(1) A party to proceedings before a Value Added Tax and Duties Tribunal who is dissatisfied in point of law with a decision of the tribunal may appeal under section 11(1) of the Tribunals and Inquiries Act 1992 to the High Court.

(2) The appellant must file the appellant's notice–

(a) where the appeal is made following the refusal of the Value Added Tax and Duties Tribunal to grant a certificate under article 2(b) of the Value Added Tax and Duties Tribunal Appeals Order 1986, within 28 days from the date of the release of the decision containing the refusal;

(b) in all other cases within 56 days after the date of the decision or determination that the appellant wishes to appeal.

Appeals by way of case stated

Proceedings under the Commons Registration Act 1965

23.9 A person aggrieved by the decision of a Commons Commissioner who requires the Commissioner to state a case for the opinion of the High Court under section 18 of the Commons Registration Act 1965 must file the appellant's notice within 42 days from the date on which notice of the decision was sent to the aggrieved person.

Appeals to a county court

Local Government (Miscellaneous Provisions) Act 1976

24.1 Where one of the grounds upon which an appeal against a notice under sections 21, 23 or 35 of the Local Government (Miscellaneous Provisions) Act 1976 is brought is that–

(a) it would have been fairer to serve the notice on another person; or

(b) that it would be reasonable for the whole or part of the expenses to which the appeal relates to be paid by some other person,

that person must be made a respondent to the appeal, unless the court, on application of the appellant made without notice, otherwise directs.

PART 53

DEFAMATION CLAIMS

Contents of this Part

Scope of this Part

53.1 This Part contains rules about defamation claims.

Summary disposal under the Defamation Act 1996

53.2 (1) This rule provides for summary disposal in accordance with the Defamation Act 1996 ("the Act")[99].

(2) In proceedings for summary disposal under sections 8 and 9 of the Act, rules 24.4 (procedure), 24.5 (evidence) and 24.6 (directions) apply.

(3) An application for summary judgment under Part 24 may not be made if –

(a) an application has been made for summary disposal in accordance with the Act, and that application has not been disposed of; or

(b) summary relief has been granted on an application for summary disposal under the Act.

(4) The court may on any application for summary disposal direct the defendant to elect whether or not to make an offer to make amends under section 2 of the Act.

(5) When it makes a direction under paragraph (4), the court will specify the time by which and the manner in which –

(a) the election is to be made; and

(b) notification of it is to be given to the court and the other parties.

Sources of information

53.3 Unless the court orders otherwise, a party will not be required to provide further information about the identity of the defendant's sources of information.

(Part 18 provides for requests for further information.)

---

[99] 1996 c.31.

PRACTICE DIRECTION –DEFAMATION CLAIMS
THIS PRACTICE DIRECTION SUPPLEMENTS PART 53

General

1. This practice direction applies to defamation claims.

Statements of case

2.1 Statements of case should be confined to the information necessary to inform the other party of the nature of the case he has to meet. Such information should be set out concisely and in a manner proportionate to the subject matter of the claim.

2.2 (1) In a claim for libel the publication the subject of the claim must be identified in the claim form.

(2) In a claim for slander the claim form must so far as possible contain the words complained of, and identify the person to whom they were spoken and when.

2.3 (1) The claimant must specify in the particulars of claim the defamatory meaning which he alleges that the words or matters complained of conveyed, both

(a) as to their natural and ordinary meaning; and

(b) as to any innuendo meaning (that is a meaning alleged to be conveyed to some person by reason of knowing facts extraneous to the words complained of).

(2) In the case of an innuendo meaning, the claimant must also identify the relevant extraneous facts.

2.4 In a claim for slander the precise words used and the names of the persons to whom they were spoken and when must, so far as possible, be set out in the particulars of claim, if not already contained in the claim form.

2.5 Where a defendant alleges that the words complained of are true he must –

(1) specify the defamatory meanings he seeks to justify; and

(2) give details of the matters on which he relies in support of that allegation.

2.6 Where a defendant alleges that the words complained of are fair comment on a matter of public interest he must –

(1) specify the defamatory meaning he seeks to defend as fair comment on a matter of public interest; and

(2) give details of the matters on which he relies in support of that allegation.

2.7 Where a defendant alleges that the words complained of were published on a privileged occasion he must specify the circumstances he relies on in support of that contention.

2.8 Where a defendant alleges that the words complained of are true, or are fair comment on a matter of public interest, the claimant must serve a reply specifically admitting or denying the allegation and giving the facts on which he relies.

2.9 If the defendant contends that any of the words or matters are fair comment on a matter of public interest, or were published on a privileged occasion, and the claimant intends to allege that the defendant acted with malice, the claimant must serve a reply giving details of the facts or matters relied on.

2.10(1) A claimant must give full details of the facts and matters on which he relies in support of his claim for damages.

(2) Where a claimant seeks aggravated or exemplary damages he must provide the information specified in rule 16.4(1)(c).

2.11 A defendant who relies on an offer to make amends under section 2 of the Defamation Act 1996, as his defence must–

(1) state in his defence –

(a) that he is relying on the offer in accordance with section 4 (2) of the Defamation Act 1996; and

(b) that it has not been withdrawn by him or been accepted , and

(2) attach a copy of the offer he made with his defence.

Court's powers in connection with an offer of amends

3.1 Sections 2 to 4 of the Defamation Act 1996 make provision for a person who has made a statement which is alleged to be defamatory to make an offer to make amends. Section 3 provides for the court to assist in the process of making amends.

3.2 A claim under section 3 of the Defamation Act 1996 made other than in existing proceedings may be made under CPR Part 8 –

(1) where the parties agree on the steps to make amends, and the sole purpose of the claim is for the court to make an order under section 3(3) for an order that the offer be fulfilled ; or

(2) where the parties do not agree–

    (a) on the steps to be taken by way of correction, apology and publication (see section 3(4));

    (b) on the amount to be paid by way of compensation (see section 3(5)); or

    (c) on the amount to be paid by way of costs (see section 3(6)). (Applications in existing proceedings made under section 3 of the Defamation Act 1996 must be made in accordance with CPR Part 23)

3.3 (1) A claim or application under section 3 of the Defamation Act 1996 must be supported by written evidence.

(2) The evidence referred to in paragraph (1) must include–

    (a) a copy of the offer of amends;

    (b) details of the steps taken to fulfil the offer of amends;

    (c) a copy of the text of any correction and apology;

    (d) details of the publication of the correction and apology;

    (e) a statement of the amount of any sum paid as compensation;

    (f) a statement of the amount of any sum paid for costs;

    (g) why the offer is unsatisfactory.

(3) Where any step specified in section 2(4) of the Defamation Act 1996 has not been taken, then the evidence referred to in paragraph (2)(c) to (f) must state what steps are proposed by the party to fulfil the offer of amends and the date or dates on which each step will be fulfilled and, if none, that no proposal has been made to take that step.

Ruling on meaning

4.1 At any time the court may decide –

(1) whether a statement complained of is capable of having any meaning attributed to it in a statement of case;

(2) whether the statement is capable of being defamatory of the claimant;

(3) whether the statement is capable of bearing any other meaning defamatory of the claimant.

4.2 An application for a ruling on meaning may be made at any time after the service of particulars of claim. Such an application should be made promptly.

(This provision disapplies for these applications the usual time restriction on making applications in rule 24.4.1.)

4.3 Where an application is made for a ruling on meaning, the application notice must state that it is an application for a ruling on meaning made in accordance with this practice direction.

4.4 The application notice or the evidence contained or referred to in it, or served with it, must identify precisely the statement, and the meaning attributed to it, that the court is being asked to consider.

(Rule 3.3 applies where the court exercises its powers of its own initiative.)

(Following a ruling on meaning the court may exercise its power under rule 3.4.)

(Section 7 of the Defamation Act 1996 applies to rulings on meaning.)

Summary disposal

5.1 Where an application is made for summary disposal, the application notice must state –

(1) that it is an application for summary disposal made in accordance with section 8 of the Defamation Act 1996.

(2) the matters set out in paragraph 2(3) of the practice direction to Part 24; and

(3) whether or not the defendant has made an offer to make amends under section 2 of the Act and whether or not it has been withdrawn.

5.2 An application for summary disposal may be made at any time after the service of particulars of claim.

(This provision disapplies for these applications the usual time restriction on making applications in rule 24.4.1).

5.3 (1) This paragraph applies where –

(a) the court has ordered the defendant in defamation proceedings to agree and publish a correction and apology as summary relief under section 8(2) of the Defamation Act 1996; and

(b) the parties are unable to agree its content within the time specified in the order.

(2) Where the court grants this type of summary relief under the Act, the order will specify the date by which the parties should reach agreement about the content, time, manner, form and place of publication of the correction and apology.

(3) Where the parties cannot agree the content of the correction and apology by the date specified in the order, then the claimant must prepare a summary of the judgment given by the court and serve it on all the other parties within 3 days following the date specified in the order.

(4) Where the parties cannot agree the summary of the judgment prepared by the claimant they must within 3 days of receiving the summary –

(a) file with the court and serve on all the other parties a copy of the summary showing the revisions they wish to make to it; and

(b) apply to the court for the court to settle the summary.

(5) The court will then itself settle the summary and the judge who delivered the judgment being summarised will normally do this.

Statements in open court

6.1 This paragraph only applies where a party wishes to accept a Part 36 offer, Part 36 payment or other offer of settlement in relation to a claim for –

(1) libel;

(2) slander.

6.2 A party may apply for permission to make a statement in open court before or after he accepts the Part 36 offer or the Part 36 payment in accordance with rule 36.8 (5) or other offer to settle the claim.

6.3 The statement that the applicant wishes to make must be submitted for the approval of the court and must accompany the notice of application.

6.4 The court may postpone the time for making the statement if other claims relating to the subject matter of the statement are still proceeding.

(Applications must be made in accordance with Part 23)

Transitional provision relating to section 4 of the Defamation Act 1952

7. Paragraph 3 of this practice direction applies, with any necessary modifications to an application to the court to determine any question as to the steps to be taken to fulfil an offer made under section 4 of the Defamation Act 1952.

(Section 4 of the Defamation Act 1952 is repealed by the Defamation Act 1996. The commencement order bringing in the repeal makes transitional provision for offers which have been made at the date the repeal came into force).

PRACTICE DIRECTION

PROTOCOLS

GENERAL

1.1 This Practice Direction applies to the pre-action protocols which have been approved by the Head of Civil Justice.

1.2 The pre-action protocols which have been approved are specified in the Schedule to this Practice Direction. Other pre-action protocols may subsequently be added.

1.3 Pre-action protocols outline the steps parties should take to seek information from and to provide information to each other about a prospective legal claim.

1.4 The objectives of pre-action protocols are:

(1) to encourage the exchange of early and full information about the prospective legal claim,

(2) to enable parties to avoid litigation by agreeing a settlement of the claim before the commencement of proceedings,

(3) to support the efficient management of proceedings where litigation cannot be avoided.

COMPLIANCE WITH PROTOCOLS

2.1 The Civil Procedure Rules enable the court to take into account compliance or non-compliance with an applicable protocol when giving directions for the management of proceedings (see CPR rules 3.1(4) and (5) and 3.9(e)) and when making orders for costs (see CPR rule 44.3(5)(a)).

2.2 The court will expect all parties to have complied in substance with the terms of an approved protocol.

2.3 If, in the opinion of the court, non-compliance has led to the commencement of proceedings which might otherwise not have needed to be commenced, or has led to costs being incurred in the proceedings that might otherwise not have been incurred, the orders the court may make include:

(1) an order that the party at fault pay the costs of the proceedings, or part of those costs, of the other party or parties;

(2) an order that the party at fault pay those costs on an indemnity basis;

(3) if the party at fault is a claimant in whose favour an order for the payment of damages or some specified sum is subsequently made, an order depriving that party of interest on such sum and in respect of such period as may be specified, and/or awarding interest at a lower rate than that at which interest would otherwise have been awarded;

(4) if the party at fault is a defendant and an order for the payment of damages or some specified sum is subsequently made in favour of the claimant, an order awarding interest on such sum and in respect of such period as may be specified at a higher rate, not exceeding 10% above base rate (cf. CPR rule 36.21(2)), than the rate at which interest would otherwise have been awarded.

2.4 The court will exercise its powers under paragraphs 2.1 and 2.3 with the object of placing the innocent party in no worse a position than he would have been in if the protocol had been complied with.

3.1 A claimant may be found to have failed to comply with a protocol by, for example:

(a) not having provided sufficient information to the defendant, or

(b) not having followed the procedure required by the protocol to be followed (e.g. not having followed the medical expert instruction procedure set out in the Personal Injury Protocol).

3.2 A defendant may be found to have failed to comply with a protocol by, for example:

(a) not making a preliminary response to the letter of claim within the time fixed for that purpose by the relevant protocol (21 days under the Personal Injury Protocol, 14 days under the Clinical Negligence Protocol),

(b) not making a full response within the time fixed for that purpose by the relevant protocol (3 months of the letter of claim under the Clinical Negligence Protocol, 3 months from the date of acknowledgment of the letter of claim under the Personal Injury Protocol),

(c) not disclosing documents required to be disclosed by the relevant protocol.

PRE-ACTION BEHAVIOUR IN OTHER CASES

4 In cases not covered by any approved protocol, the court will expect the parties, in accordance with the overriding objective and the matters referred to in CPR 1.1(2)(a), (b) and (c), to act reasonably in exchanging information and documents relevant to the claim and generally in trying to avoid the necessity for the start of proceedings.

COMMENCEMENT

5.1 Compliance or non-compliance, as the case may be, with the protocols specified in the Schedule will be taken into account by the court in dealing with any proceedings commenced after 26 April 1999 but will not be taken into account by the court in dealing with proceedings started before that date.

5.2 Where, in respect of proceedings commenced after 26 April 1999, the parties have by work done before that date substantially achieved the object designed to be achieved by steps to be taken under a protocol, the parties need not take those steps and their failure to do so will not be treated, for the purposes of paragraphs 2 and 3, as non-compliance.

5.3 Where, in respect of proceedings commenced after 26 April 1999, the parties have not had time since the publication of the protocols in January 1999 to comply with the applicable provisions, their failure to have done so will not be treated, for the purposes of paragraphs 2 and 3, as non-compliance.

5.4 As and when an additional protocol is approved, a Practice Direction will specify the date after which compliance or non-compliance with that protocol will be taken into account by the court.

SCHEDULE

1. Personal Injury Protocol.

2. Clinical Negligence Protocol.

PRE-ACTION PROTOCOL

FOR PERSONAL INJURY CLAIMS

December 1996

CONTENTS

1 Introduction
2 Notes of guidance
3 The protocol

Annexes

A Letter of claim
B Standard disclosure lists
C Letter of instruction to medical expert

1 INTRODUCTION

1.1 Lord Woolf in his final Access to Justice Report of July 1996 recommended the development of pre-action protocols: 'To build on and increase the benefits of early but well informed settlement which genuinely satisfy both parties to dispute.'

1.2 The aims of pre-action protocols are:

- more pre-action contact between the parties
- better and earlier exchange of information
- better pre-action investigation by both sides
- to put the parties in a position where they may be able to settle cases fairly and early without litigation
- to enable proceedings to run to the court's timetable and efficiently, if litigation does become necessary.

1.3 The concept of protocols is relevant to a range of initiatives for good litigation and pre-litigation practice, especially:

- predictability in the time needed for steps pre-proceedings
- standardisation of relevant information, including documents to be disclosed.

1.4 The Courts will be able to treat the standards set in protocols as the normal reasonable approach to pre-action conduct. If proceedings are issued, it will be for the court to decide whether non-compliance with a protocol should merit adverse consequences. Guidance on the court's likely approach will be given from time to time in practice directions.

1.5 If the court has to consider the question of compliance after proceedings have begun, it will not be concerned with minor infringements, e.g. failure by a short period to provide relevant information. One minor breach will not exempt the 'innocent' party from following the protocol. The court will look at the effect of non-compliance on the other party when deciding whether to impose sanctions.

2 NOTES OF GUIDANCE

2.1 The protocol has been kept deliberately simple to promote ease of use and general acceptability. The notes of guidance which follow relate particularly to issues which arose during the piloting of the protocol.

SCOPE OF THE PROTOCOL

2.2 This protocol is intended to apply to all claims which include a claim for personal injury and to the entirety of those claims: not only to the personal injury element of a claim which also includes, for instance, property damage.

2.3 This protocol is primarily designed for those road traffic, tripping and slipping and accident at work cases which include an element of personal injury with a value of less than £15,000 which are likely to be allocated to the fast track. This is because time will be of the essence, after proceedings are issued, especially for the defendant, if a case is to be ready for trial within 30 weeks of allocation. Also, proportionality of work and costs to the value of what is in dispute is particularly important in lower value claims. For some claims within the value 'scope' of the fast track some flexibility in the timescale of the protocol may be necessary, see also paragraph 3.8.

2.4 However, the 'cards on the table' approach advocated by the protocol is equally appropriate to some higher value claims. The spirit, if not the letter of the protocol, should still be followed for multi-track type claims. In accordance with the sense of the civil justice reforms, the court will expect to see the spirit of reasonable pre-action behaviour applied in all cases, regardless of the existence of a specific protocol.

2.5 The timetable and the arrangements for disclosing documents and obtaining expert evidence may need to be varied to suit the circumstances of the case. Where one or both parties consider the detail of the protocol is not appropriate to the case, and proceedings are subsequently issued, the court will expect an explanation as to why the protocol has not been followed, or has been varied.

EARLY NOTIFICATION

2.6 The claimant's legal representative may wish to notify the defendant and/or his insurer as soon as they know a claim is likely to be made, but before they are able to send a detailed letter of claim, particularly for instance, when the defendant has no or limited knowledge of the incident giving rise to the claim or where the claimant is incurring significant expenditure as a result of the accident which he hopes the defendant might pay for, in whole or in part. If the claimant's representative chooses to do this, it will not start the timetable for responding.

THE LETTER OF CLAIM

2.7 The specimen letter of claim at Annex A will usually be sent to the individual defendant. In practice, he/she may have no personal financial interest in the financial outcome of the claim/dispute because he/she is insured. Court imposed sanctions for non-compliance with the protocol may be ineffective against an insured. This is why the protocol emphasises the importance of passing the letter of claim to the insurer and the possibility that the insurance cover might be affected. If an insurer receives the letter of claim only after some delay by the insured, it would not be unreasonable for the insurer to ask the claimant for additional time to respond.

REASONS FOR EARLY ISSUE

2.8 The protocol recommends that a defendant be given three months to investigate and respond to a claim before proceedings are issued. This may not always be possible, particularly where a claimant only consults a solicitor close to the end of any relevant limitation period. In these circumstances, the claimant's solicitor should give as much notice of the intention to issue proceedings as is practicable and the parties should consider whether the court might be invited to extend time for service of the claimant's supporting documents and for service of any defence, or alternatively, to stay the proceedings while the recommended steps in the protocol are followed.

STATUS OF LETTERS OF CLAIM AND RESPONSE

2.9 Letters of claim and response are not intended to have the same status as a statement of case in proceedings. Matters may come to light as a result of investigation after the letter of claim has been sent, or after the defendant has responded, particularly if disclosure of documents takes place outside the recommended three-month period. These circumstances could mean that the 'pleaded' case of one or both parties is presented slightly differently than in the letter of claim and response. It would not be consistent with the spirit of the protocol for a party to 'take a point' on this in the proceedings, provided that there was no obvious intention by the party who changed their position to mislead the other party.

DISCLOSURE OF DOCUMENTS

2.10 The aim of the early disclosure of documents by the defendant is not to encourage 'fishing expeditions' by the claimant, but to promote an early exchange of relevant information to help in clarifying or resolving issues in dispute. The claimant's solicitor can assist by identifying in the letter of claim or in a subsequent letter the particular categories of documents which they consider are relevant.

EXPERTS

2.11 The protocol encourages joint selection of, and access to, experts. Most frequently this will apply to the medical expert, but on occasions also to liability experts, e.g. engineers. The protocol promotes the practice of the claimant obtaining a medical report, disclosing it to the defendant who then asks questions and/or agrees it and does not obtain his own report. But it maintains the flexibility for each party to obtain their own expert's report, if necessary after proceedings have commenced, with the leave of the court. It would also be for the court to decide whether the costs of more than one expert's report should be recoverable.

2.12 Some solicitors choose to obtain medical reports through medical agencies, rather than directly from a specific doctor or hospital. The defendant's prior consent to the action should be sought and, if the defendant so requests, the agency should be asked to provide in advance the names of the doctor(s) whom they are considering instructing.

NEGOTIATIONS/SETTLEMENT

2.13 Parties and their legal representatives are encouraged to enter into discussions and/or negotiations prior to starting proceedings. The protocol does not specify when or how this might be done but parties should bear in mind that the courts increasingly take the view that litigation should be a last resort, and that claims should not be issued prematurely when a settlement is in reasonable prospect.

STOCKTAKE

2.14 Where a claim is not resolved when the protocol has been followed, the parties might wish to carry out a 'stocktake' of the issues in dispute, and the evidence that the court is likely to need to decide those issues, before proceedings are started. Where the defendant is insured and the pre-action steps have been conducted by the insurer, the insurer would normally be expected to nominate solicitors to act in the proceedings and the claimant's solicitor is recommended to invite the insurer to nominate solicitors to act in the proceedings and do so 7–14 days before the intended issue date.

3 THE PROTOCOL

LETTER OF CLAIM

3.1 The claimant shall send to the proposed defendant two copies of a letter of claim, immediately sufficient information is available to substantiate a realistic claim and before issues of quantum are addressed in detail. One copy of the letter is for the defendants, the second for passing on to his insurers.

3.2 The letter shall contain **a clear summary of the facts** on which the claim is based together with an indication of the **nature of any injuries** suffered and of **any financial loss incurred**. In cases of road traffic accidents, the letter should provide the name and address of the hospital where treatment has been obtained and the claimant's hospital reference number.

3.3 Solicitors are recommended to use a **standard format** for such a letter – an example is at Annex A: this can be amended to suit the particular case.

3.4 The letter should ask for **details of the insurer** and that a copy should be sent by the proposed defendant to the insurer where appropriate. If the insurer is known, a copy shall be sent directly to the insurer. Details of the claimant's National Insurance number and date of birth should be supplied to the defendant's insurer once the Defendant has responded to the letter of claim and confirmed the identity of the insurer. This information should not be supplied in the letter of claim.

3.5 **Sufficient information** should be given in order to enable the defendant's insurer/solicitor to commence investigations and at least put a broad valuation on the 'risk'.

3.6 The **defendant should reply within 21 calendar days** of the date of posting of the letter identifying the insurer (if any). If there has been no reply by the defendant or insurer within 21 days, the claimant will be entitled to issue proceedings.

3.7 The **defendant**('s insurers) will have a **maximum of three months** from the date of acknowledgment of the claim **to investigate**. No later than the end of that period the defendant (insurer) shall reply, stating whether liability is denied and, if so, giving reasons for their denial of liability.

3.8 Where the accident occurred outside England and Wales and/or where the defendant is outside the jurisdiction, the time periods of 21 days and three months may reasonably be extended up to 42 days and six months.

3.9 Where **liability is admitted**, the presumption is that the defendant will be bound by this admission for all claims with a total value of up to £15,000.

DOCUMENTS

3.10 If the **defendant denies liability**, he should enclose with the letter of reply, **documents** in his possession which are **material to the issues** between the parties, and which would be likely to be ordered to be disclosed by the court, either on an application for pre-action disclosure, or on disclosure during proceedings.

3.11 Attached at Annex B are **specimen**, but non-exhaustive, **lists** of documents likely to be material in different types of claim. Where the claimant's investigation of the case is well advanced, the letter of claim could indicate which classes of documents are considered relevant for early disclosure. Alternatively these could be identified at a later stage.

3.12 Where the defendant admits primary liability, but alleges contributory negligence by the claimant, the defendant should give reasons supporting those allegations and disclose those documents from Annex B which are relevant to the issues in dispute. The claimant should respond to the allegations of contributory negligence before proceedings are issued.

SPECIAL DAMAGES

3.13 The claimant will send to the defendant as soon as practicable a Schedule of Special Damages with supporting documents, particularly where the defendant has admitted liability.

EXPERTS

3.14 Before any party instructs an expert he should give the other party a list of the **name**(s) **of one or more experts** in the relevant speciality whom he considers are suitable to instruct.

3.15 Where a medical expert is to be instructed the claimant's solicitor will organise access to relevant medical records – see specimen letter of instruction at Annex C.

3.16 **Within 14 days** the other party may indicate **an objection** to one or more of the named experts. The first party should then instruct a mutually acceptable expert.

3.17 If the second party objects to all the listed experts, the parties may then instruct **experts of their own choice**. It would be for the court to decide subsequently, if proceedings are issued, whether either party had acted unreasonably.

3.18 If the **second party does not object to an expert nominated**, he shall not be entitled to rely on his own expert evidence within that particular speciality unless:

(a) the first party agrees,

(b) the court so directs, or

(c) the first party's expert report has been amended and the first party is not prepared to disclose the original report.

3.19 **Either party may send to an agreed expert written questions** on the report, relevant to the issues, via the first party's solicitors. The expert should send answers to the questions separately and directly to each party.

3.20 The cost of a report from an agreed expert will usually be paid by the instructing first party: the costs of the expert replying to questions will usually be borne by the party which asks the questions.

3.21 Where the defendant admits liability in whole or in part, before proceedings are issued, any medical report obtained by agreement under this protocol should be disclosed to the other party. The claimant should delay issuing proceedings for 21 days from disclosure of the report, to enable the parties to consider whether the claim is capable of settlement. The Civil Procedure Rules Part 36 permit claimants and defendants to make offers to settle pre-proceedings.

ANNEX A
LETTER OF CLAIM

To

Defendant

Dear Sirs

Re:

Claimant's full name

Claimant's full address

Claimant's Clock or Works Number

Claimant's Employer (name and address)

We are instructed by the above named to claim damages in connection with *an accident at work / road traffic accident / tripping accident* on   day of   (*year*) at (*place of accident which must be sufficiently detailed to establish location*)

Please confirm the identity of your insurers. Please note that the insurers will need to see this letter as soon as possible and it may affect your insurance cover and/or the conduct of any subsequent legal proceedings if you do not send this letter to them.

The circumstances of the accident are:–

(*brief outline*)

The reason why we are alleging fault is:

(*simple explanation e.g. defective machine, broken ground*)

A description of our clients' injuries is as follows:–

(*brief outline*)

(*In cases of road traffic accidents*)

Our client (state hospital reference number) received treatment for the injuries at name and address of hospital).

He is employed as (*occupation*) and has had the following time off work (*dates of absence*). His approximate weekly income is (*insert if known*).

If you are our client's employers, please provide us with the usual earnings details which will enable us to calculate his financial loss.

We are obtaining a police report and will let you have a copy of the same upon your undertaking to meet half the fee.

We have also sent a letter of claim to (*name and address*) and a copy of that letter is attached. We understand their insurers are (*name, address and claims number if known*).

At this stage of our enquiries we would expect the documents contained in parts (*insert appropriate parts of standard disclosure list*) to be relevant to this action.

A copy of this letter is attached for you to send to your insurers. Finally we expect an acknowledgment of this letter within 21 days by yourselves or your insurers.

Yours faithfully

ANNEX B

PRE-ACTION PERSONAL INJURY PROTOCOL

STANDARD DISCLOSURE LISTS

FAST TRACK DISCLOSURE

RTA CASES

SECTION A

In all cases where liability is at issue –

(i) Documents identifying nature, extent and location of damage to defendant's vehicle where there is any dispute about point of impact.
(ii) MOT certificate where relevant.
(iii) Maintenance records where vehicle defect is alleged or it is alleged by defendant that there was an unforeseen defect which caused or contributed to the accident.

SECTION B

Accident involving commercial vehicle as potential defendant –

(i) Tachograph charts or entry from individual control book.
(ii) Maintenance and repair records required for operators' licence where vehicle defect is alleged or it is alleged by defendants that there was an unforeseen defect which caused or contributed to the accident.

SECTION C

Cases against local authorities where highway design defect is alleged.

(i) Documents produced to comply with Section 39 of the Road Traffic Act 1988 in respect of the duty designed to promote road safety to include studies into road accidents in the relevant area and documents relating to measures recommended to prevent accidents in the relevant area.

HIGHWAY TRIPPING CLAIMS

Documents from Highway Authority for a period of 12 months prior to the accident –

(i) Records of inspection for the relevant stretch of highway.
(ii) Maintenance records including records of independent contractors working in relevant area.
(iii) Records of the minutes of Highway Authority meetings where maintenance or repair policy has been discussed or decided.
(iv) Records of complaints about the state of highways.
(v) Records of other accidents which have occurred on the relevant stretch of highway.

WORKPLACE CLAIMS

(i) Accident book entry.
(ii) First aider report.
(iii) Surgery record.
(iv) Foreman/supervisor accident report.
(v) Safety representatives accident report.
(vi) RIDDOR report to HSE.
(vii) Other communications between defendants and HSE.
(viii) Minutes of Health and Safety Committee meeting(s) where accident/matter considered.
(ix) Report to DSS.
(x) Documents listed above relative to any previous accident/matter identified by the claimant and relied upon as proof of negligence.
(xi) Earnings information where defendant is employer.

Documents produced to comply with requirements of the Management of Health and Safety at Work Regulations 1992 –

(i) Pre-accident Risk Assessment required by Regulation 3.

(ii) Post-accident Re-Assessment required by Regulation 3.

(iii) Accident Investigation Report prepared in implementing the requirements of Regulations 4, 6 and 9.

(iv) Health Surveillance Records in appropriate cases required by Regulation 5.

(v) Information provided to employees under Regulation 8.

(vi) Documents relating to the employees health and safety training required by Regulation 11.

WORKPLACE CLAIMS – DISCLOSURE
WHERE SPECIFIC REGULATIONS APPLY

SECTION A – WORKPLACE (HEALTH SAFETY AND WELFARE) REGULATIONS 1992

(i) Repair and maintenance records required by Regulation 5.

(ii) Housekeeping records to comply with the requirements of Regulation 9.

(iii) Hazard warning signs or notices to comply with Regulation 17 (Traffic Routes).

SECTION B – PROVISION AND USE OF WORK EQUIPMENT REGULATIONS 1992

(i) Manufacturers' specifications and instructions in respect of relevant work equipment establishing its suitability to comply with Regulation 5.

(ii) Maintenance log/maintenance records required to comply with Regulation 6.

(iii) Documents providing information and instructions to employees to comply with Regulation 8.

(iv) Documents provided to the employee in respect of training for use to comply with Regulation 9.

(v) Any notice, sign or document relied upon as a defence to alleged breaches of Regulations 14 to 18 dealing with controls and control systems.

(vi) Instruction/training documents issued to comply with the requirements of Regulation 22 insofar as it deals with maintenance operations where the machinery is not shut down.

(vii) Copies of markings required to comply with Regulation 23.

(viii) Copies of warnings required to comply with Regulation 24.

SECTION C – PERSONAL PROTECTIVE EQUIPMENT AT WORK REGULATIONS 1992

(i) Documents relating to the assessment of the Personal Protective Equipment to comply with Regulation 6.

(ii) Documents relating to the maintenance and replacement of Personal Protective Equipment to comply with Regulation 7.

(iii) Record of maintenance procedures for Personal Protective Equipment to comply with Regulation 7.

(iv) Records of tests and examinations of Personal Protective Equipment to comply with Regulation 7.

(v) Documents providing information, instruction and training in relation to the Personal Protective Equipment to comply with Regulation 9.

(vi) Instructions for use of Personal Protective Equipment to include the manufacturers' instructions to comply with Regulation 10.

SECTION D – MANUAL HANDLING OPERATIONS REGULATIONS 1992

(i) Manual Handling Risk Assessment carried out to comply with the requirements of Regulation 4(1)(b)(i).

(ii) Re-assessment carried out post-accident to comply with requirements of Regulation 4(1)(b)(i).

(iii) Documents showing the information provided to the employee to give general indications related to the load and precise indications on the weight of the load and the heaviest side of the load if the centre of gravity was not positioned centrally to comply with Regulation 4(1)(b)(iii).

(iv) Documents relating to training in respect of manual handling operations and training records.

SECTION E – HEALTH AND SAFETY
(DISPLAY SCREEN EQUIPMENT) REGULATIONS 1992

(i) Analysis of work stations to assess and reduce risks carried out to comply with the requirements of Regulation 2.

(ii) Re-assessment of analysis of work stations to assess and reduce risks following development of symptoms by the claimant.

(iii) Documents detailing the provision of training including training records to comply with the requirements of Regulation 6.

(iv) Documents providing information to employees to comply with the requirements of Regulation 7.

SECTION F – CONTROL OF SUBSTANCES
HAZARDOUS TO HEALTH REGULATIONS 1988

(i) Risk assessment carried out to comply with the requirements of Regulation 6.

(ii) Reviewed risk assessment carried out to comply with the requirements of Regulation 6.

(iii) Copy labels from containers used for storage handling and disposal of carcinogenics to comply with the requirements of Regulation 7(2A)(h).

(iv) Warning signs identifying designation of areas and installations which may be contaminated by carcinogenics to comply with the requirements of Regulation 7(2A)(h).

(v) Documents relating to the assessment of the Personal Protective Equipment to comply with Regulation 7(3A).

(vi) Documents relating to the maintenance and replacement of Personal Protective Equipment to comply with Regulation 7(3A).

(vii) Record of maintenance procedures for Personal Protective Equipment to comply with Regulation 7(3A).

(viii)Records of tests and examinations of Personal Protective Equipment to comply with Regulation 7(3A).

(ix) Documents providing information, instruction and training in relation to the Personal Protective Equipment to comply with Regulation 7(3A).

(x) Instructions for use of Personal Protective Equipment to include the manufacturers' instructions to comply with Regulation 7(3A).

(xi) Air monitoring records for substances assigned a maximum exposure limit or occupational exposure standard to comply with the requirements of Regulation 7.

(xii) Maintenance examination and test of control measures records to comply with Regulation 9.

(xiii)Monitoring records to comply with the requirements of Regulation 10.

(xiv)Health surveillance records to comply with the requirements of Regulation 11.

(xv) Documents detailing information, instruction and training including training records for employees to comply with the requirements of Regulation 12.

(xvi)Labels and Health and Safety data sheets supplied to the employers to comply with the CHIP Regulations.

SECTION G – CONSTRUCTION (DESIGN
AND MANAGEMENT) REGULATIONS 1994

(i) Notification of a project form (HSE F10) to comply with the requirements of Regulation 7.

(ii) Health and Safety Plan to comply with requirements of Regulation 15.

(iii) Health and Safety file to comply with the requirements of Regulations 12 and 14.

(iv) Information and training records provided to comply with the requirements of Regulation 17.

(v) Records of advice from and views of persons at work to comply with the requirements of Regulation 18.

SECTION H – PRESSURE SYSTEMS AND TRANSPORTABLE GAS CONTAINERS REGULATIONS 1989

(i) Information and specimen markings provided to comply with the requirements of Regulation 5.

(ii) Written statements specifying the safe operating limits of a system to comply with the requirements of Regulation 7.

(iii) Copy of the written scheme of examination required to comply with the requirements of Regulation 8.

(iv) Examination records required to comply with the requirements of Regulation 9.

(v) Instructions provided for the use of operator to comply with Regulation 11.

(vi) Records kept to comply with the requirements of Regulation 13.

(vii) Records kept to comply with the requirements of Regulation 22.

SECTION I – LIFTING PLANT AND EQUIPMENT (RECORDS OF TEST AND EXAMINATION ETC.) REGULATIONS 1992

(i) Record kept to comply with the requirements of Regulation 6.

SECTION J – THE NOISE AT WORK REGULATIONS 1989

(i) Any risk assessment records required to comply with the requirements of Regulations 4 and 5.

(ii) Manufacturers' literature in respect of all ear protection made available to claimant to comply with the requirements of Regulation 8.

(iii) All documents provided to the employee for the provision of information to comply with Regulation 11.

SECTION K – CONSTRUCTION (HEAD PROTECTION) REGULATIONS 1989

(i) Pre-accident assessment of head protection required to comply with Regulation 3(4).

(ii) Post-accident re-assessment required to comply with Regulation 3(5).

SECTION L – THE CONSTRUCTION (GENERAL PROVISIONS) REGULATIONS 1961

(i) Report prepared following inspections and examinations of excavations etc. to comply with the requirements of Regulation 9.

(ii) Report prepared following inspections and examinations of work in cofferdams and caissons to comply with the requirements of Regulations 17 and 18.

N.B. Further Standard Discovery lists will be required prior to full implementation.

ANNEX C

LETTER OF INSTRUCTION

TO MEDICAL EXPERT

Dear Sir,

Re: (Name and Address)

D.O.B. –

Telephone No. –

Date of Accident –

We are acting for the above named in connection with injuries received in an accident which occurred on the above date. The main injuries appear to have been (**main injuries**).

We should be obliged if you would examine our Client and let us have a full and detailed report dealing with any relevant pre-accident medical history, the injuries sustained, treatment received and present condition, dealing in particular with the capacity for work and giving a prognosis.

It is central to our assessment of the extent of our Client's injuries to establish the extent and duration of any continuing disability. Accordingly, in the prognosis section we would ask you to specifically comment on any areas of continuing complaint or disability or impact on daily living. If there is such continuing disability you should comment upon the level of suffering or inconvenience caused and, if you are able, give your view as to when or if the complaint or disability is likely to resolve.

Please send our Client an appointment direct for this purpose. Should you be able to offer a cancellation appointment please contact our Client direct. We confirm we will be responsible for your reasonable fees.

We are obtaining the notes and records from our Client's GP and Hospitals attended and will forward them to you when they are to hand/or please request the GP and Hospital records direct and advise that any invoice for the provision of these records should be forwarded to us.

In order to comply with Court Rules we would be grateful if you would insert above your signature a statement that the contents are true to the best of your knowledge and belief.

In order to avoid further correspondence we can confirm that on the evidence we have there is no reason to suspect we may be pursuing a claim against the hospital or its staff.

We look forward to receiving your report within _____ weeks. If you will not be able to prepare your report within this period please telephone us upon receipt of these instructions.

When acknowledging these instructions it would assist if you could give an estimate as to the likely time scale for the provision of your report and also an indication as to your fee.

Yours faithfully

PRE-ACTION PROTOCOL FOR THE RESOLUTION OF CLINICAL DISPUTES CLINICAL DISPUTES FORUM

December 1998

CONTENTS

EXECUTIVE SUMMARY

1. The Clinical Disputes Forum is a multi-disciplinary body which was formed in 1997, as a result of Lord Woolf's 'Access to Justice' inquiry. One of the aims of the Forum is to find less adversarial and more cost-effective ways of resolving disputes about healthcare and medical treatment. The names and addresses of the Chairman and Secretary of the Forum can be found at Annex E.

2. This protocol is the Forum's first major initiative. It has been drawn up care-fully, including extensive consultations with most of the key stakeholders in the medico-legal system.

3. The protocol –

   • encourages a climate of openness when something has 'gone wrong' with a patient's treatment or the patient is dissatisfied with that treat-ment and/or the outcome. This reflects the new and developing requirements for clinical governance within healthcare;

   • provides general guidance on how this more open culture might be achieved when disputes arise;

   • recommends a timed sequence of steps for patients and healthcare providers, and their advisers, to follow when a dispute arises. This should facilitate and speed up exchanging relevant information and increase the prospects that disputes can be resolved without resort to legal action.

4 This protocol has been prepared by a working party of the Clinical Disputes Forum. It has the support of the Lord Chancellor's Department, the Department of Health and NHS Executive, the Law Society, the Legal Aid Board and many other key organisations.

1 WHY THIS PROTOCOL?

MISTRUST IN HEALTHCARE DISPUTES

1.1 The number of complaints and claims against hospitals, GPs, dentists and private healthcare providers is growing as patients become more prepared to question the treatment they are given, to seek explanations of what happened, and to seek appropriate redress. Patients may require further treatment, an apology, assurances about future action, or compensation. These trends are unlikely to change. The Patients' Charter encourages patients to have high expectations, and a revised NHS Complaints Procedure was implemented in 1996. The civil justice reforms and new Rules of Court should make litigation quicker, more user friendly and less expensive.

1.2 It is clearly in the interests of patients, healthcare professionals and providers that patients' concerns, complaints and claims arising from their treatment are resolved as quickly, efficiently and professionally as possible. A climate of mistrust and lack of openness can seriously damage the patient/clinician relationship, unnecessarily prolong disputes (especially litigation), and reduce the resources available for treating patients. It may also cause additional work for, and lower the morale of, healthcare professionals.

1.3 At present there is often mistrust by both sides. This can mean that patients fail to raise their concerns with the healthcare provider as early as possible. Sometimes patients may pursue a complaint or claim which has little merit, due to a lack of sufficient information and understanding. It can also mean that patients become reluctant, once advice has been taken on a potential claim, to disclose sufficient information to enable the provider to investigate that claim efficiently and, where appropriate, resolve it.

1.4 On the side of the healthcare provider this mistrust can be shown in a reluctance to be honest with patients, a failure to provide prompt clear explanations, especially of adverse outcomes (whether or not there may have been negligence) and a tendency to 'close ranks' once a claim is made.

WHAT NEEDS TO CHANGE

1.5 If that mistrust is to be removed, and a more co-operative culture is to develop –

- healthcare professionals and providers need to adopt a constructive approach to complaints and claims. They should accept that concerned patients are entitled to an explanation and an apology, if warranted, and to appropriate redress in the event of negligence. An overly defensive approach is not in the long-term interest of their main goal: patient care;
- patients should recognise that unintended and/or unfortunate consequences of medical treatment can only be rectified if they are brought to the attention of the healthcare provider as soon as possible.

1.6 A protocol which sets out 'ground rules' for the handling of disputes at their early stages should, if it is to be subscribed to, and followed –

- encourage greater openness between the parties;
- encourage parties to find the most appropriate way of resolving the particular dispute;
- reduce delay and costs;
- reduce the need for litigation.

WHY THIS PROTOCOL NOW?

1.7 Lord Woolf in his Access to Justice Report in July 1996, concluded that major causes of costs and delay in medical negligence litigation occur at the pre-action stage. He recommended that patients and their advisers, and healthcare providers, should work more closely together to try to resolve disputes co-operatively, rather than proceed to litigation. He specifically recommended a pre-action protocol for medical negligence cases.

1.8 A fuller summary of Lord Woolf's recommendations is at Annex D.

WHERE THE PROTOCOL FITS IN

1.9 Protocols serve the needs of litigation and pre-litigation practice, especially –

- predictability in the time needed for steps pre-proceedings;
- standardisation of relevant information, including records and documents to be disclosed.

1.10 Building upon Lord Woolf's recommendations, the Lord Chancellor's Department is now promoting the adoption of protocols in specific areas, including medical negligence.

1.11 It is recognised that contexts differ significantly. For example: patients tend to have an ongoing relationship with a GP, more so than with a hospital; clinical staff in the National Health Service are often employees, while those in the private sector may be contractors; providing records quickly may be relatively easy for GPs and dentists, but can be a complicated procedure in a large multi-department hospital. The protocol which follows is intended to be sufficiently broadly based, and flexible, to apply to all aspects of the health service: primary and secondary; public and private sectors.

ENFORCEMENT OF THE PROTOCOL AND SANCTIONS

1.12 The civil justice reforms will be implemented in April 1999. One new set of Court Rules and procedures is replacing the existing rules for both the High Court and county courts. This and the personal injury protocol are being published with the Rules, practice directions and key court forms. The courts will be able to treat the standards set in protocols as the normal reasonable approach to pre-action conduct.

1.13 If proceedings are issued it will be for the court to decide whether non-compliance with a protocol should merit sanctions. Guidance on the court's likely approach will be given from time to time in practice directions.

1.14 If the court has to consider the question of compliance after proceedings have begun it will not be concerned with minor infringements, e.g. failure by a short period to provide relevant information. One minor breach will not entitle the 'innocent' party to abandon following the protocol. The court will look at the effect of non-compliance on the other party when deciding whether to impose sanctions.

2 THE AIMS OF THE PROTOCOL

2.1 The **general** aims of the protocol are –
- to maintain/restore the patient/healthcare provider relationship;
- to resolve as many disputes as possible without litigation.

2.2 The **specific** objectives are –

OPENNESS

- to encourage early communication of the perceived problem between patients and healthcare providers;
- to encourage patients to voice any concerns or dissatisfaction with their treatment as soon as practicable;
- to encourage healthcare providers to develop systems of early reporting and investigation for serious adverse treatment outcomes and to provide full and prompt explanations to dissatisfied patients;
- to ensure that sufficient information is disclosed by both parties to enable each to understand the other's perspective and case, and to encourage early resolution;

TIMELINESS

- to provide an early opportunity for healthcare providers to identify cases where an investigation is required and to carry out that investigation promptly;
- to encourage primary and private healthcare providers to involve their defence organisations or insurers at an early stage;
- to ensure that all relevant medical records are provided to patients or their appointed representatives on request, to a realistic timetable by any healthcare provider;
- to ensure that relevant records which are not in healthcare providers' possession are made available to them by patients and their advisers at an appropriate stage;
- where a resolution is not achievable to lay the ground to enable litigation to proceed on a reasonable timetable, at a reasonable and proportionate cost and to limit the matters in contention;
- to discourage the prolonged pursuit of unmeritorious claims and the prolonged defence of meritorious claims.

AWARENESS OF OPTIONS

- to ensure that patients and healthcare providers are made aware of the available options to pursue and resolve disputes and what each might involve.

2.3 This protocol does not attempt to be prescriptive about a number of related clinical governance issues which will have a bearing on healthcare providers' ability to meet the standards within the protocol. Good clinical governance requires the following to be considered –

(a) **Clinical risk management**: the protocol does not provide any detailed guidance to healthcare providers on clinical risk management or the adoption of risk management systems and procedures. This must be a matter for the NHS Executive, the National Health Service Litigation Authority, individual trusts and providers, including GPs, dentists and the private sector. However, effective co-ordinated, focused clinical risk management strategies and procedures can help in managing risk and in the early identification and investigation of adverse outcomes.

(b) **Adverse outcome reporting**: the protocol does not provide any detailed guidance on which adverse outcomes should trigger an investigation. However, healthcare providers should have in place procedures for such investigations, including recording of statements of key witnesses. These procedures should also cover when and how to inform patients that an adverse outcome has occurred.

(c) **The professional's duty to report**: the protocol does not recommend changes to the codes of conduct of professionals in healthcare, or attempt to impose a specific duty on those professionals to report known adverse outcomes or untoward incidents. Lord Woolf in his final report suggested that the professional bodies might consider this. The

General Medical Council is preparing guidance to doctors about their duty to report adverse incidents and to co-operate with inquiries.

3 THE PROTOCOL

3.1 This protocol is not a comprehensive code governing all the steps in clinical disputes. Rather it attempts to set out **a code of good practice** which parties should follow when litigation might be a possibility.

3.2 The **commitments** section of the protocol summarises the guiding principles which healthcare providers and patients and their advisers are invited to endorse when dealing with patient dissatisfaction with treatment and its outcome, and with potential complaints and claims.

3.3 The **steps** section sets out in a more prescriptive form, a recommended sequence of actions to be followed if litigation is a prospect.

GOOD PRACTICE COMMITMENTS

3.4 **Healthcare providers** should –

(i) ensure that **key staff**, including claims and litigation managers, are appropriately trained and have some knowledge of healthcare law, and of complaints procedures and civil litigation practice and procedure;

(ii) develop an approach to **clinical governance** that ensures that clinical practice is delivered to commonly accepted standards and that this is routinely monitored through a system of clinical audit and clinical risk management (particularly adverse outcome investigation);

(iii) set up **adverse outcome reporting systems** in all specialties to record and investigate unexpected serious adverse outcomes as soon as possible. Such systems can enable evidence to be gathered quickly, which makes it easier to provide an accurate explanation of what happened and to defend or settle any subsequent claims;

(iv) use the results of **adverse incidents and complaints positively** as a guide to how to improve services to patients in the future;

(v) ensure **that patients receive clear and comprehensible information** in an accessible form about how to raise their concerns or complaints;

(vi) establish **efficient and effective systems of recording and storing patient records**, notes, diagnostic reports and X-rays, and to retain these in accordance with Department of Health guidance (currently for a minimum of eight years in the case of adults, and all obstetric and paediatric notes for children until they reach the age of 25);

(vii) **advise patients** of a serious adverse outcome and provide on request to the patient or the patient's representative an oral or written explanation of what happened, information on further steps open to the patient, including where appropriate an offer of future treatment to rectify the problem, an apology, changes in procedure which will benefit patients and/or compensation.

3.5 **Patients and their advisers** should –

(i) **report any concerns and dissatisfaction** to the healthcare provider as soon as is reasonable to enable that provider to offer clinical advice where possible, to advise the patient if anything has gone wrong and take appropriate action;

(ii) consider the **full range of options** available following an adverse outcome with which a patient is dissatisfied, including a request for an explanation, a meeting, a complaint, and other appropriate dispute resolution methods (including mediation) and negotiation, not only litigation;

(iii) **inform the healthcare provider when the patient is satisfied** that the matter has been concluded: legal advisers should notify the provider when they are no longer acting for the patient, particularly if proceedings have not started.

PROTOCOL STEPS

3.6 The steps of this protocol which follow have been kept deliberately simple. An illustration of the likely sequence of events in a number of healthcare situations is at Annex A.

OBTAINING THE HEALTH RECORDS

3.7 Any request for records by the **patient** or their adviser should –

- **provide sufficient information** to alert the healthcare provider where an adverse outcome has been serious or had serious consequences;
- be **as specific as possible** about the records which are required.

3.8 Requests for copies of the patient's clinical records should be made using the Law Society and Department of Health approved **standard forms** (enclosed at Annex B), adapted as necessary.

3.9 The copy records should be provided **within 40 days** of the request and for a cost not exceeding the charges permissible under the Access to Health Records Act 1990 (currently a maximum of £10 plus photocopying and postage).

3.10 In the rare circumstances that the healthcare provider is in difficulty in complying with the request within 40 days, the **problem should be explained** quickly and details given of what is being done to resolve it.

3.11 It will not be practicable for healthcare providers to investigate in detail each case when records are requested. But healthcare providers should **adopt a policy on which cases will be investigated** (see paragraph 3.5 on clinical governance and adverse outcome reporting).

3.12 If the healthcare provider fails to provide the health records within 40 days, the patient or their adviser can then apply to the court for **an order for pre-action disclosure**. The new Civil Procedure Rules should make pre-action applications to the court easier. The court will also have the power to impose costs sanctions for unreasonable delay in providing records.

3.13 If either the patient or the healthcare provider considers **additional health records are required from a third party**, in the first instance these should be requested by or through the patient. Third party healthcare providers are expected to co-operate. The Civil Procedure Rules will enable patients and healthcare providers to apply to the court for pre-action disclosure by third parties.

LETTER OF CLAIM

3.14 Annex C1 to this protocol provides a **template for the recommended contents of a letter of claim**: the level of detail will need to be varied to suit the particular circumstances.

3.15 If, following the receipt and analysis of the records, and the receipt of any further advice (including from experts if necessary – see Section 4), the patient/adviser decides that there are grounds for a claim, they should then send, as soon as practicable, to the healthcare provider/potential defendant, a **letter of claim**.

3.16 This letter should contain a **clear summary of the facts** on which the claim is based, including the alleged adverse outcome, and the **main allegations of negligence**. It should also describe the **patient's injuries**, and present condition and prognosis. The **financial loss** incurred by the plaintiff should be outlined with an indication of the heads of damage to be claimed and the scale of the loss, unless this is impracticable.

3.17 In more complex cases a **chronology** of the relevant events should be provided, particularly if the patient has been treated by a number of different healthcare providers.

3.18 The letter of claim **should refer to any relevant documents**, including health records, and if possible enclose copies of any of those which will not already be in the potential defendant's possession, e.g. any relevant general practitioner records if the plaintiff's claim is against a hospital.

3.19 **Sufficient information** must be given to enable the healthcare provider defendant to **commence investigations** and to put an initial valuation on the claim.

3.20 Letters of claim are **not** intended to have the same formal status as a **pleading**, nor should any sanctions necessarily apply if the letter of claim and any subsequent statement of claim in the proceedings differ.

3.21 **Proceedings should not be issued until after three months from the letter of claim**, unless there is a limitation problem and/or the patient's position needs to be protected by early issue.

3.22 The patient or their adviser may want to make an **offer to settle** the claim at this early stage by putting forward an amount of compensation which would be satisfactory (possibly including any costs incurred to date). If an offer to settle is made, generally this should be supported by a medical report which deals with the injuries, condition and prognosis, and by a schedule of loss and supporting documentation. The level of detail necessary will depend on the value of the claim. Medical reports may not be necessary where there is no significant continuing injury, and a detailed schedule may not be necessary in a low value case. The Civil Procedure Rules are expected to set out the legal and procedural requirements for making offers to settle.

THE RESPONSE

3.23 Attached at Annex C2 is a template for the suggested contents of the **letter of response**.

3.24 The healthcare provider should **acknowledge** the letter of claim **within 14 days of receipt** and should identify who will be dealing with the matter.

3.25 The healthcare provider should, **within three months** of the letter of claim, provide a **reasoned answer** –

- if the **claim is admitted** the healthcare provider should say so in clear terms;
- if only **part of the claim is admitted** the healthcare provider should make clear which issues of breach of duty and/or causation are admitted and which are denied and why;
- if it is intended that any **admissions will be binding**;
- if the claim is denied, this should include specific comments on the allegations of negligence, and if a synopsis or chronology of relevant events has been provided and is disputed, the healthcare provider's version of those events;
- where additional documents are relied upon, e.g. an internal protocol, copies should be provided.

3.26 If the patient has made an offer to settle, the healthcare provider should **respond to that offer** in the response letter, preferably with reasons. The provider may make its own offer to settle at this stage, either as a counter-offer to the patient's, or of its own accord, but should accompany any offer by any supporting medical evidence, and/or by any other evidence in relation to the value of the claim which is in the healthcare provider's possession.

3.27 If the parties reach agreement on liability, but time is needed to resolve the value of the claim, they should aim to agree a reasonable period.

4 EXPERTS

4.1 In clinical negligence disputes expert opinions may be needed –

- on breach of duty and causation;
- on the patient's condition and prognosis;
- to assist in valuing aspects of the claim.

4.2 The civil justice reforms and the new Civil Procedure Rules will encourage economy in the use of experts and a less adversarial expert culture. It is recognised that in clinical negligence disputes, the parties and their advisers will require flexibility in their approach to expert evidence. Decisions on whether experts might be instructed jointly, and on whether reports might be disclosed sequentially or by exchange, should rest with the parties and their advisers. Sharing expert evidence may be appropriate on issues relating to the value of the claim. However, this protocol does not attempt to be prescriptive on issues in relation to expert evidence.

4.3 Obtaining expert evidence will often be an expensive step and may take time, especially in specialised areas of medicine where there are limited numbers of suitable experts. Patients and healthcare providers, and their advisers, will therefore need to consider carefully how best to obtain any necessary expert help quickly and cost-effectively. Assistance with locating a suitable expert is available from a number of sources.

5 ALTERNATIVE APPROACHES TO SETTLING DISPUTES

5.1 It would not be practicable for this protocol to address in any detail how a patient or their adviser, or healthcare provider, might decide which method to adopt to resolve the particular problem. But, the courts increasingly expect parties to try to settle their differences by agreement before issuing proceedings.

5.2 Most disputes are resolved by discussion and negotiation. Parties should bear in mind that carefully planned face-to-face meetings may be particularly helpful in exploring further treatment for the patient, in reaching understandings about what happened, and on both parties' positions, in narrowing the issues in dispute and, if the timing is right, in helping to settle the whole matter.

5.3 Summarised below are some other alternatives for resolving disputes –

- The revised NHS Complaints Procedure, which was implemented in April 1996, is designed to provide patients with an explanation of what happened and an apology if appropriate. It is not designed to provide compensation for cases of negligence. However, patients might choose to use the procedure if their only, or main, goal is to obtain an explanation, or to obtain more information to help them decide what other action might be appropriate.

- Mediation may be appropriate in some cases: this is a form of facilitated negotiation assisted by an independent neutral party. It is expected that the new Civil Procedure Rules will give the court the power to stay proceedings for one month for settlement discussions or mediation.

- Other methods of resolving disputes include arbitration, determination by an expert, and early neutral evaluation by a medical or legal expert. The Lord Chancellor's Department has produced a booklet on 'Resolving Disputes Without Going to Court', LCD 1995, which lists a number of organisations that provide alternative dispute resolution services.

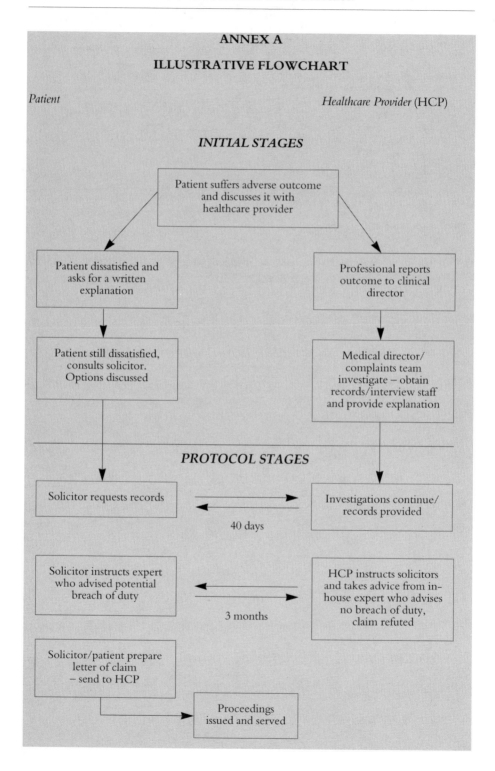

ANNEX A

ILLUSTRATIVE FLOWCHART

Patient   *Healthcare Provider* (HCP)

INITIAL STAGES

Patient suffers adverse outcome
and discusses it with
healthcare provider

Patient dissatisfied and
asks for a written
explanation

Professional reports
outcome to clinical
director

Patient still dissatisfied,
consults solicitor.
Options discussed

Medical director/
complaints team
investigate – obtain
records/interview staff
and provide explanation

PROTOCOL STAGES

Solicitor requests records

Investigations continue/
records provided

40 days

Solicitor instructs expert
who advised potential
breach of duty

HCP instructs solicitors
and takes advice from in-
house expert who advises
no breach of duty,
claim refuted

3 months

Solicitor/patient prepare
letter of claim
– send to HCP

Proceedings
issued and served

ANNEX B

MEDICAL NEGLIGENCE AND PERSONAL INJURY CLAIMS

A PROTOCOL FOR OBTAINING HOSPITAL MEDICAL RECORDS

CIVIL LITIGATION COMMITTEE

REVISED EDITION

JUNE 1998

THE LAW SOCIETY

APPLICATION ON BEHALF OF A PATIENT FOR HOSPITAL MEDICAL RECORDS FOR USE WHEN COURT PROCEEDINGS ARE CONTEMPLATED

PURPOSE OF THE FORMS

This application form and response forms have been prepared by a working party of the Law Society's Civil Litigation Committee and approved by the Department of Health for use in NHS and Trust hospitals.

The purpose of the forms is to standardise and streamline the disclosure of medical records to a patient's solicitors, who are investigating pursuing a personal injury claim against a third party, or a medical negligence claim against the hospital to which the application is addressed and/or other hospitals or general practitioners.

USE OF THE FORMS

Use of the forms is entirely voluntary and does not prejudice any party's right under the Access to Health Records Act 1990, the Data Protection Act 1984, or ss 33 and 34 of the Supreme Court Act 1981. However, it is Department of Health policy that patients be permitted to see what has been written about them, and that healthcare providers should make arrangements to allow patients to see all their records, not only those covered by the Access to Health Records Act 1990. The aim of the forms is to save time and costs for all concerned for the benefit of the patient and the hospital and in the interests of justice. Use of the forms should make it unnecessary in most cases for there to be exchanges of letters or other enquiries. If there is any unusual matter not covered by the form, the patient's solicitor may write a separate letter at the outset.

CHARGES FOR RECORDS

The Access to Health Records Act 1990 prescribes a maximum fee of £10. Photocopying and postage costs can be charged in addition. No other charges may be made.

The NHS Executive guidance makes it clear to healthcare providers that 'it is a perfectly proper use' of the 1990 Act to request records in that framework for the purpose of potential or actual litigation, whether against a third party or against the hospital or trust.

The 1990 Act does not permit differential rates of charges to be levied if the application is made by the patient, or by a solicitor on his or her behalf, or whether the response to the application is made by the healthcare provider directly (the medical records manager or a claims manager) or by a solicitor.

The NHS Executive guidance recommends that the same practice should be followed with regard to charges when the records are provided under a voluntary agreement as under the 1990 Act, except that in those circumstances the £10 access fee will not be appropriate.

The NHS Executive also advises –

- that the cost of photocopying may include 'the cost of staff time in making copies' and the costs of running the copier (but not costs of locating and sifting records);
- that the common practice of setting a standard rate for an application or charging an administration fee is not acceptable because there will be cases when this fails to comply with the 1990 Act.

RECORDS: WHAT MIGHT BE INCLUDED

X-rays and test results form part of the patient's records. Additional charges for copying X-rays are permissible. If there are large numbers of X-rays, the records officer should check with the patient/solicitor before arranging copying.

Reports on an 'adverse incident' and reports on the patient made for risk management and audit purposes may form part of the records and be disclosable: the exception will be any specific record or report made solely or mainly in connection with an actual or potential claim.

RECORDS: QUALITY STANDARDS

When copying records healthcare providers should ensure –

1. All documents are legible, and complete, if necessary by photocopying at less than 100% size.
2. Documents larger than A4 in the original, e.g. ITU charts, should be reproduced in A3, or reduced to A4 where this retains readability.
3. Documents are only copied on one side of paper, unless the original is two sided.
4. Documents should not be unnecessarily shuffled or bound and holes should not be made in the copied papers.

ENQUIRIES/FURTHER INFORMATION

Any enquiries about the forms should be made initially to the solicitors making the request. Comments on the use and content of the forms should be made to the Secretary, Civil Litigation Committee, The Law Society, 113 Chancery Lane, London WC2A 1PL, telephone 0171 320 5739, or to the NHS Management Executive, Quarry House, Quarry Hill, Leeds LS2 7UE.

The Law Society
May 1998

APPLICATION ON BEHALF OF A PATIENT FOR HOSPITAL MEDICAL RECORDS FOR USE WHEN COURT PROCEEDINGS ARE CONTEMPLATED

This should be completed as fully as possible

Insert   Hospital
          Name
          and
          Address

TO: Medical Records Officer   Hospital

1   a)   Full name of patient (including previous surnames)
     b)   Address now
     c)   Address at start of treatment
     d)   Date of birth (and death, if applicable)
     e)   Hospital ref. no if available
     f)   N.I. number, if available
2.   This application is made because the patient is considering
     a)   a claim against your hospital as detailed in para 7 overleaf   YES/NO
     b)   pursuing an action against someone else   YES/NO
3   Department(s) where treatment was received
4   Name(s) of consultant(s) at your hospital in charge of the treatment
5   Whether treatment at your hospital was private or NHS, wholly or in part
6   A description of the treatment received, with approximate dates
7   If the answer to Q2(a) is 'Yes' details of
     a)   the likely nature of the claim
     b)   grounds for the claim
     c)   approximate dates of the events involved
8   If the answer to Q2(b) is 'Yes' insert
     a)   the names of the proposed defendants
     b)   whether legal proceedings yet begun   YES/NO
     c)   if appropriate, details of the claim and action number
9   We confirm we will pay reasonable copying charges
10   We request prior details of
     a)   photocopying and administration charges for medical records YES/NO
     b)   number of and cost of copying x-ray and scan films YES/NO
11   Any other relevant information, particular requirements, or any particular documents not
     required (e.g. copies of computerised records)

Signature of Solicitor

Name   Address

Ref.   Telephone Number

Fax number

Please print name beneath each signature.

Signature by child over 12 but under 18 years also requires signature by parent

Signature of patient

Signature of parent or next friend if appropriate

Signature of personal representative where patient has died

FIRST RESPONSE TO APPLICATION FOR HOSPITAL RECORDS

NAME OF PATIENT

Our ref

Your ref

1   Date of receipt of patient's application

2   We intend that copy medical records will be dispatched within 6 weeks
     of that date   YES/NO

3   We require pre-payment of photocopying charges   YES/NO

4   If estimate of photocopying charges requested or pre-payment required the amount will be
     £   / notified to you

5   The cost of x-ray and scan films will be   £   / notified to you

6   If there is any problem, we shall write to you within those 6 weeks   YES/NO

7   Any other information

Please address further correspondence to

Signed

Direct telephone number

Direct fax number

Dated

**SECOND RESPONSE ENCLOSING PATIENT'S
HOSPITAL MEDICAL RECORDS**

Address   Our Ref.
                                                  Your Ref.

1   NAME OF PATIENT:
     We confirm that the enclosed copy medical records are all those within the control of the
     hospital, relevant to the application which you have made to the best of our knowledge and
     belief, subject to paras 2–5 below
                                                      YES/NO

2   Details of any other documents which have not yet been located

3   Date by when it is expected that these will be supplied

4   Details of any records which we are not producing

5   The reasons for not doing so

6   An invoice for copying and administration charges is attached   YES/NO

Signed

Date

ANNEX C

TEMPLATES FOR LETTERS OF CLAIM AND RESPONSE

C1 LETTER OF CLAIM

Essential Contents

1. Client's name, address, date of birth, etc.
2. Dates of allegedly negligent treatment
3. Events giving rise to the claim:
   - an outline of what happened, including details of other relevant treatments to the client by other healthcare providers.
4. Allegation of negligence and causal link with injuries:
   - an outline of the allegations or a more detailed list in a complex case;
   - an outline of the causal link between allegations and the injuries complained of.
5. The Client's injuries, condition and future prognosis
6. Request for clinical records (if not previously provided)
   - use the Law Society form if appropriate or adapt;
   - specify the records require;
   - if other records are held by other providers, and may be relevant, say so;
   - state what investigations have been carried out to date, e.g. information from client and witnesses, any complaint and the outcome, if any clinical records have been seen or experts advice obtained.
7. The likely value of the claim
   - an outline of the main heads of damage, or, in straightforward cases, the details of loss. Optional information

What investigations have been carried out

An offer to settle without supporting evidence

Suggestions for obtaining expert evidence

Suggestions for meetings, negotiations, discussion or mediation

Possible enclosures

Chronology

Clinical records request form and client's authorisation

Expert report(s)

Schedules of loss and supporting evidence

C2 LETTER OF RESPONSE

Essential Contents

1. Provide **requested records** and invoice for copying:
   - explain if records are incomplete or extensive records are held and ask for further instructions;
   - request additional records from third parties.
2. **Comments on events and/or chronology:**
   - if events are disputed or the healthcare provider has further information or documents on which they wish to rely, these should be provided, e.g. internal protocol;
   - details of any further information needed from the patient or a third party should be provided.
3. **If breach of duty and causation are accepted**:
   - suggestions might be made for resolving the claim and/or requests for further information;
   - a response should be made to any offer to settle.

4. **If breach of duty and/or causation are denied**:
   - a bare denial will not be sufficient. If the healthcare provider has other explanations for what happened, these should be given at least in outline;
   - suggestions might be made for the next steps, e.g. further investigations, obtaining expert evidence, meetings/ negotiations or mediation, or an invitation to issue proceedings.

Optional Matters

An offer to settle if the patient has not made one, or a counter offer to the patient's with supporting evidence

Possible enclosures:

Clinical records

Annotated chronology

Expert reports

ANNEX D

LORD WOOLF'S RECOMMENDATIONS

1. Lord Woolf in his Access to Justice Report in July 1996, following a detailed review of the problems of medical negligence claims, identified that one of the major sources of costs and delay is at the pre-litigation stage because –

    (a) Inadequate incident reporting and record keeping in hospitals, and mobility of staff, make it difficult to establish facts, often several years after the event.

    (b) Claimants must incur the cost of an expert in order to establish whether they have a viable claim.

    (c) There is often a long delay before a claim is made.

    (d) Defendants do not have sufficient resources to carry out a full investigation of every incident, and do not consider it worthwhile to start an investigation as soon as they receive a request for records, because many cases do not proceed beyond that stage.

    (e) Patients often give the defendant little or no notice of a firm intention to pursue a claim. Consequently, many incidents are not investigated by the defendants until after proceedings have started.

    (f) Doctors and other clinical staff are traditionally reluctant to admit negligence or apologise to, or negotiate with, claimants for fear of damage to their professional reputations or career prospects.

2. Lord Woolf acknowledged that under the present arrangements healthcare providers, faced with possible medical negligence claims, have a number of practical problems to contend with –

    (a) Difficulties of finding patients' records and tracing former staff, which can be exacerbated by late notification and by the health care provider's own failure to identify adverse incidents.

    (b) The healthcare provider may have only treated the patient for a limited time or for a specific complaint: the patient's previous history may be relevant but the records may be in the possession of one of several other healthcare providers.

    (c) The large number of potential claims which do not proceed beyond the stage of a request for medical records, or an explanation; and that it is difficult for healthcare providers to investigate fully every case whenever a patient asks to see the records.

ANNEX E

HOW TO CONTACT THE FORUM

The Clinical Disputes Forum

    Chairman

    Dr Alastair Scotland

    Director of Medical Education

    Chelsea and Westminster Hospital

    369 Fulham Road

    London

    SW1 9NH   Telephone: 020 8746 8000

    Secretary

    Sarah Leigh

    c/o Margaret Dangoor

    3 Clydesdale Gardens

    Richmond

    Surrey

    TW10 5EG   Telephone: 020 8408 1012

INDEX TO PARTS A AND B